Fifty Years of Forensic Science

Fifty Years of Forensic Science
A commentary

Edited by

Niamh Nic Daéid

*Centre for Forensic Science, University of Strathclyde,
Glasgow, UK*

A John Wiley & Sons, Ltd., Publication

This edition first published 2010,
© 2010 by John Wiley & Sons Ltd.

Wiley-Blackwell is an imprint of John Wiley & Sons, formed by the merger of Wiley's global Scientific, Technical and Medical business with Blackwell Publishing.

Registered office:
John Wiley & Sons Ltd, The Atrium, Southern Gate, Chichester, West Sussex, PO19 8SQ, UK

Other Editorial Offices:
9600 Garsington Road, Oxford, OX4 2DQ, UK
111 River Street, Hoboken, NJ 07030-5774, USA

For details of our global editorial offices, for customer services and for information about how to apply for permission to reuse the copyright material in this book please see our website at www.wiley.com/wiley-blackwell

The right of the author to be identified as the author of this work has been asserted in accordance with the Copyright, Designs and Patents Act 1988.

All rights reserved. No part of this publication may be reproduced, stored in a retrieval system, or transmitted, in any form or by any means, electronic, mechanical, photocopying, recording or otherwise, except as permitted by the UK Copyright, Designs and Patents Act 1988, without the prior permission of the publisher.

Wiley also publishes its books in a variety of electronic formats. Some content that appears in print may not be available in electronic books.

Designations used by companies to distinguish their products are often claimed as trademarks. All brand names and product names used in this book are trade names, service marks, trademarks or registered trademarks of their respective owners. The publisher is not associated with any product or vendor mentioned in this book. This publication is designed to provide accurate and authoritative information in regard to the subject matter covered. It is sold on the understanding that the publisher is not engaged in rendering professional services. If professional advice or other expert assistance is required, the services of a competent professional should be sought.

Library of Congress Cataloguing-in-Publication Data

Fifty years of forensic science: a commentary / edited by Niamh Nic Daéid.
    p. cm.
  Includes index.
  ISBN 978-0-470-68400-9
 1. Forensic sciences—Great Britain—History.   I. Nic Daéid, Niamh, 1967-
  HV8073.F45 2010
  363.250941—dc22
                                                2009026944

ISBN: 9780470684009

A catalogue record for this book is available from the British Library.

Typeset in 10/12pt Times by Laserwords Private Limited, Chennai, India.
Printed in Singapore by Fabulous Printers Pte Ltd.

1   2010

For Gill

Contents

Preface		xiii
Introduction		xv
SECTION I: THE PROFESSIONAL DEVELOPMENT OF FORENSIC SCIENCE		1
1 (1) - 1960	Criminal aspects of forensic science in Great Britain	2
4 (2) - 1964	Forensic science or sciences?	2
4 (4) - 1964	Shriving a science	3
5 (1) - 1965	A public image	4
5 (2) - 1965	Don't forget them in Swahililand	4
6 (2) - 1966	The vacant headquarters	5
9 (2a) - 1969	Six just men	6
9 (2b) - 1969	"A forensic scientist?"	7
13 (3) - 1973	I hold every man a debtor to his profession	9
14 (2) - 1974	Police perimeters – politics or planning	10
17 (4) - 1977	Theory and practice	12
20 (3) - 1980	Forensic Science – a broader basis	13
21 (1) - 1981	General practice in forensic science	15
24 (6) - 1984	Does forensic science have a future?	16
24 (6) - 1985	Does forensic science have a future?	21
25 (1) - 1985	But is it anything?	22
25 (1) - 1985	But is it anything?	24
25 (5) - 1985	Towards expert experts	25
26 (2) - 1986	Doctrine, Science, Belief, Evidence	26
26 (4) - 1986	The Forensic Science Society – a way forward?	32
26 (5) - 1986	All systems go?	34
27 (2) - 1987	Police productivity	35
29 (1) - 1989	Professional qualifications – a milestone	38
30 (5) - 1990	Brave New World	39
31 (2) - 1991	"Come forth into the light of things, let nature be your teacher"	41
31 (4) - 1991	Forensic science on the quality track	42
32 (2) - 1992	But is this being professional?	43
32 (4) - 1992	Can we help you, sir?	44
33 (3) - 1993	Is this where the buck stops?	45
34 (1) - 1994	An expert what?	46
34 (2) - 1994	Quo vadis?	47
35 (1) - 1995	Does forensic science give value for money?	48
35 (3) - 1995	Renascor	52
35 (4) - 1995	Lest we forget	53
36 (3) - 1996	Forensic futurology	53
36 (4) - 1996	Ambivalence – a problem for forensic science	54
37 (1) - 1997	Private or public	55
37 (3) - 1997	Jobs for the boys	56
38 (1) - 1998	Proactive forensic science	56
38 (4) - 1998	SOP or CPD, place your bets	58

39 (1) - 1999	Forensic apartheid?	60
39 (2) - 1999	Let me through, I'm a ummmm ...	60
39 (3) - 1999	Something nasty hiding ...	63
39 (4) - 1999	From Bach to Schoenberg	64
42 (2) - 2002	A professional body for forensic scientists	65
45 (1) - 2005	Professionalism – duties and privileges	67
45 (3) - 2005	Who guards the guards?	69
45 (4) - 2005	Everything changes and nothing is constant	70
47 (2) - 2007	Eight years on	71
47 (2) - 2007	Regulation of Forensic Physicians and the CRFP	73
47 (3) - 2007	CPD, an effective means of professional development...or is it?	74
48 (1) - 2008	President of the Forensic Science Society	76
48 (3) - 2008	The forensic science regulator	77

SECTION II: SCIENTIFIC DEVELOPMENTS AND RESEARCH — 81

2 (2) - 1961	The individuality of human bloodstaining	82
3 (1) - 1962	A breakthrough in forensic science	82
4 (1) - 1963	Driving over the level	83
4 (1) - 1963	Science before the fact	85
5 (4b) - 1964	The price of road safety	85
6 (1) - 1965	Progress in research	87
7 (4) - 1966	Demanding scientific evidence	88
9 (4) - 1968	Computer control	89
11 (2) - 1971	The defeat of the tail-gater	90
11 (3) - 1971	The New Zealand approach	91
14 (1) - 1974	Back to basics	92
16 (3b) - 1976	An independent witness required	93
19 (4) - 1979	Publish or perish	94
22 (2) - 1982	But is it science ...	94
22 (3) - 1982	Hair today ...	95
25 (2) - 1985	On body fluid frequencies	96
26 (1) - 1986	Publish or perish revisited	97
27 (1) - 1987	Through the looking glass	98
29 (6) - 1989	The highest order common sense	99
30 (1) - 1990	Profile of the Nineties	100
30 (6) - 1990	Official publications	100
33 (4) - 1993	DNA or Abracadabra	101
36 (1) - 1996	To research or capitulate?	102
36 (2) - 1996	Fireproof DNA?	104
37 (4) - 1997	Where will all the forensic scientists go?	104
40 (1) - 2000	Wizards and gatekeepers at the roadside?	105
40 (3) - 2000	The consent of the governed	107
41 (1) - 2001	The use of material from the dead in forensic science research: is it lawful and is it ethical?	108
43 (1) - 2003	Hunting truffles	109
44 (1) - 2004	Reiterative justice?	111
45 (2) - 2005	Science & Justice – DNA and the courts	113

47 (4) - 2007	DNA – what's next?	116
48 (4) - 2008	Do we value research?	117
49 (1) - 2009	Lessons from the past	118
49 (2) - 2009	IRMS	119

SECTION III: EVALUATION AND INTERPRETATION OF EVIDENCE   121

19 (3) - 1979	Away with the fuzz	124
23 (1) - 1983	Patience	125
23 (1a) - 1983	Statistics and forensic science – a fruitful partnership	126
23 (1b) - 1983	The probability of exclusion or likelihood of guilt of an accused: Paternity	128
23 (1c) - 1983	The probability of non-discrimination or likelihood of guilt of an accused: Criminal Identification	134
23 (1d) - 1983	What is the probability that this blood came from that person? A meaningful question?	140
23 (1e) - 1983	A frame of reference or Garbage in, Garbage out	145
23 (4) - 1983	On circumstantial evidence	147
26 (3) - 1986	Evaluation of associative physical evidence	148
23 (3a) - 1987	The use of statistics in forensic science	151
23 (3b) - 1987	The use of statistics in forensic science	153
28 (3) - 1988	Heads we win	154
37 (2) - 1997	Does justice require less precision than chemistry?	155
43 (2) - 2003	Sally Clark – a lesson for us all	158
44 (2) - 2004	Context-free forensic science	160
46 (1) - 2006	Lies, damn lies and statistics	161

SECTION IV: EDUCATION IN FORENSIC SCIENCES   165

2 (1) - 1961	Research and teaching in forensic science	168
2 (1) - 1961	A preliminary survey of education and research in the forensic sciences in the United Kingdom	168
9 (1&2) - 1968	Education in the forensic sciences	175
11 (1) - 1971	What is the future for the study and practice of the forensic sciences in Britain?	177
16 (2) - 1976	The Greeks had a word for it	178
44 (4) - 2004	Wither academic forensic science?	179
48 (2) - 2008	Educating the next generation	180
48 (4) - 2008	Letter to the Editor	183
48 (4) - 2008	Letter to the Editor	184
49 (1) - 2009	Letter to the Editor	187

SECTION V: FORENSIC SCIENCE AND THE LAW   191

1 (2) - 1960	An expert witness looks at the courts	192
3 (2) - 1962	The design of law courts	200
6 (4) - 1965	Bowlers, brollies and bi-focals	201
8 (1) - 1967	The expert witness	202
8 (2) - 1967	Two encouraging cases	203

10 (1) - 1970	Law and order	204
12 (2) - 1972	There is a time to speak	204
12 (3) - 1972	Not Pygmalion likely	207
12 (4) - 1972	Where have all the lawyers gone?	208
13 (2) - 1973	An honest opinion	214
15 (3) - 1975	Modern times	215
16 (3a) - 1976	A camel is a horse…	217
17 (2&3) - 1977	The four letter swear word	218
18 (3&4) - 1978	Not for the faint hearted	220
19 (2) - 1979	Preliminary hearings – just or unjust – justified or unjustified	221
20 (2) - 1980	The canons of expertise	222
24 (2) - 1984	Have you heard the one about …	224
24 (5) - 1984	Master or servant?	225
25 (4) - 1985	Don't Panic	226
27 (4) - 1987	Philosophy and obligations of a state-funded forensic science laboratory	227
27 (5) - 1987	Answers are easy	228
29 (2) - 1989	Science and law, a marriage of opposites	228
34 (3) - 1994	The image of the scientist and the lawyer	229
38 (2) - 1998	The role of the forensic scientist in an inquisitorial system of justice	233
40 (2) - 2000	And what of the evidence!	236
41 (3) - 2001	The boundaries of expert evidence	238
41 (4) - 2001	Reform of the criminal justice system in England and Wales	239
42 (3) - 2002	Justice in a goldfish bowl	240
42 (4) - 2002	Gristle in the sausage…	242
43 (3) - 2003	Coroners – what next for death investigation in England and Wales?	243
44 (3) - 2004	The Human Tissue Bill – an opportunity about to be missed?	245
46 (2) - 2006	All's fair in love and war	247

SECTION VI: FORENSIC MEDICINE — 249

5 (4a) - 1964	The smallest room but one	251
7 (3) - 1966	Decline and fall	253
10 (3) - 1970	How much specialisation in pathology can we afford?	254
12 (1) - 1972	"The six-and-a-half-year itch"	256
13 (4) - 1973	For action this day	258
14 (4) - 1974	Chair legs wanted	260
15 (2) - 1975	That muddy field	262
16 (1) - 1976	A national medico-legal service for Scotland	264
19 (1) - 1979	Sudden death of British nationals abroad – problem for pathologists, coroners and relatives	267
41 (2) - 2001	"Best value" in forensic pathology	269
42 (1) - 2002	Herding cats	270

SECTION VII: AN INTERNATIONAL COMMUNITY OF FORENSIC SCIENCE — 273

9 (3) - 1968	Another Academy	277
15 (4) - 1975	International co-operation in forensic science	277
17 (1) - 1977	Crime in the cornfields	279

23 (2) - 1983	Reaching out	280
24 (1) - 1984	1984 and all that	281
27 (3) - 1987	Forensic science and the justice system in the late Twentieth Century	282
29 (4) - 1989	Echoes of Empire	287
30 (2) - 1990	A matter of choice	288
30 (4) - 1990	They threatened its life with a railway share	289
38 (3) - 1998	International forensic science	289
40 (4) - 2000	Courts, politicians and constitutions	291
46 (3) - 2006	It's a big World out there	293

Index **295**

Preface

The Forensic Science Society held its inaugural meeting on the 31st October 1959 and the first volume of the *Journal of the Forensic Science Society*, later *Science and Justice*, was published the following year in 1960. The Journal, as it's known within the Society, has been published continuously ever since making it one of the longest established journals of its type in the World.

What makes the Society's journal truly different from its peers, is that each issue contains an editorial piece. This provides an invaluable and often fascinating commentary of the development of our profession, of our science and the articulation of our place within the judicial system. Over the past 50 years, forensic science has changed enormously, however it may be of interest for readers to note that many of the current perspectives and debates have been considered, sometimes at great length, by our predecessors many years ago. The influence of television programmes on forensic science education, for example, was first mentioned in an editorial in 1968, the development of a professional body for forensic scientists was first discussed in 1965 and the introduction of a forensic science watchdog examining professional standards was discussed as far back as 1973.

The existence of the editorials has provided the opportunity to produce this text. They have been divided into a number of broad categories and presented in chronological order within each section. The choice of how to categorise the editorials has been mine and hopefully I have done a good job which reflects the different topics well. In a few cases I have also chosen to include correspondence produced in response to the editorials to give a broader and developed perspective of the debate which was provoked. The authors of the editorials are sometimes anonymous (as was the policy of the Journal for many years), but were always respected members of the profession. Many of the pieces were penned by my learned and respected previous editors, Stuart Kind, Russell Stockdale, Roger Davis, Bill Tilstone, Brian Caddy and Robert Forrest. They have provided insightful and often very entertaining commentary in their writing and have made some marvellous choices for invited authors. It is a humbling experience to be considered within the same company.

This has been a fascinating and enjoyable project to work on. I'm delighted to be able to work with Wiley-Blackwell Publishers who listened to what began as one of my crazy ideas, and resulted in the production of this text to celebrate the Golden anniversary of the Forensic Science Society. Each section has a short commentary apart from the first two sections (the professional aspects of forensic science and the development of science and technology in the field) which are both introduced by Brian Caddy's initial comments.

I would like to thank my fellow contributors to the commentaries, Claude Roux, Max Houck, Brian Caddy as well as Sue Black, Robert Forrest, Jim Fraser, Katy Savage and Gillian Urquhart for useful and helpful discussions. I hope you, the reader, find the contents stimulating and enjoyable.

Niamh Nic Daéid,
Glasgow 2009

INTRODUCTION: WHAT IS THE FUTURE FOR FORENSIC SCIENCE?

Emeritus Professor Brian Caddy
University of Strathclyde, Glasgow

The question posed in the title above would suggest that there may be some reason to believe that the future of forensic science may be in doubt. But how can this be when everyone is aware of the relevance of this scientific discipline as portrayed by the media and the success of DNA databases in the identification of suspects involved in criminal acts? For a science to be successful it must be based upon sound scientific principles supported by continuing scientific research. Moreover, in order to attract appropriate funding for its development it must be seen as a financially viable discipline and one which can be professionally managed. Financially viable does not have to mean profitable although profitability should not be excluded but it does mean that it meets the needs of the society it serves. The problem with forensic science is that it is a discipline that is a collection of other disciplines one of which is not a science, namely law. So forensic science has two masters a scientific one and the legal and these two can sometimes be in conflict although some would argue that both are trying to "test" the truth, the one through experiment and the other by question and answer.

While the previous statements may be argued we must try and identify what we mean by forensic science. There have been many definitions proposed and few if any meet all aspects of the discipline but for our purposes we will mean "scientific investigations that support the legal process". The first questions therefore that must be asked is "within what arena must forensic science operate?" and to try and answer this question we must look at the governorship of forensic science and its management.

Governorship and Management of Forensic Science

There have been many debates as to where forensic science should be best placed in society if it is to be seen to demonstrate the impartiality it purports to apply to its function and no doubt this debate will continue in the future. Many countries see forensic science as residing within a Ministry of Justice or some other government department of state (or subunits of a country) and argue that this demonstrates an impartiality and commitment to justice. Funding for its activities comes directly from government sources and so is subject to the vagaries of government spending. This is a pattern common perhaps to most countries where central funding is common place. An alternative model is for the control of forensic science to be conducted through a police budget, that is, forensic science is under the control of police forces. Does such control impugn the integrity of forensic science and what happens when governments decide to cut police force budgets? Many would argue that forensic science works best when there is close contact between the investigating officer and the provider of forensic science services but should this mean under the control of police forces?

Could universities be encouraged and financed to establish forensic science services as a means to demonstrate not only impartiality but to provide bases for research into the discipline? A number of universities already fulfil such a role in some countries, usually those with a small population.

Finally, why should forensic science not become a purely commercial enterprise subject to the vagaries of the commercial world with its activities governed by its shareholders? Does such an arrangement not show impartiality and value for money? But can commercial forensic science be genuinely independent of government forces when governments have financial control over police forces and police forces are the paymasters of the commercial forensic science organisations? Moreover, do financial pressures on commercial organisations lead to "cutting corners" in the quality of forensic science and if so, what price justice then?

Clearly the positioning of forensic science in society is a debate that will continue but which ever model is adopted society needs to be assured that the practice of forensic science meets acceptable quality standards and this relates to professional management of forensic science laboratories and those delegated to recover items from, and to interpret, crime scenes.

What is quality forensic science and does the implementation of quality management systems mean that no mistakes will be made in the recovery, analysis, and interpretation of forensic science evidence? The answer must be no to this question because all such activities are carried out by humans all of whom possess human failings. All that such systems can achieve is to minimise the possibilities of such human errors. Unfortunately the media do not recognise this and often exploit those unfortunate to be at the centre of failures. The debate must therefore be, how can we best achieve quality in all we do in the forensic science arena? Such processes are not static in nature but represent a dynamic re-evaluation of best practices in quality management.

The concept of quality covers at least two aspects, one the accreditation of the individual to identify competence and the other the validation of systems. Most professional laboratories possess some form of accreditation for systems under ISO 17025 or ASCLD/Lab or some other national standards. These require operators to process samples according to written processes deviations from which can be tolerated providing the reasons for so doing and the different processes adopted can be rationalised and documented. The debates that will continue in this area surround the establishment of the standards and the processes that require validation. What is validation? There are various views expressed on what constitutes validation. Certainly it must include reproducibility studies; statistical evaluation of linearity (where appropriate), limits of detection, specificity etc. but should it also include publication in peer reviewed scientific journals, reproducibility by a different group of unrelated workers, acceptability by the wider scientific community (how does one assess this?) adoption by other laboratories in other countries and if the last, how many other countries and perhaps last, acceptability to the courts? Validation can become more of a problem when related to crime scene investigation because every crime scene is different but there are some international standards available that are helpful (ISO 17020 associated with the management of crime scenes, and the personnel framework under Skills for Justice) but whether these become universally accepted is open to debate.

What then of the accreditation of individual personnel, which is perhaps the most important area for controlling quality. Clearly persons involved in such work must meet the required ethical standard. But what is the ethical standard and how can one be assessed as meeting such a standard? This is a difficult area, and only when a person has failed to meet what may be considered an ethical approach to forensic work, does this arise. Should all forensic practitioners be examined psychologically for personality defects incompatible with forensic science practice, before being offered employment? If so, what would be, and who would describe, the psychological standards to be employed? Ethical status on its own does not ascribe competence to carry out forensic science testing. This begins through a training programme designed to see if the candidate can meet the standards of the proscribed testing procedure. The debate is what should be the length of training and at what point does a person become competent. Here it is important to distinguish between competence and experience. Experience on its own is not sufficient since a person could be incompetent and experienced e.g. "doing it wrong for 10 years." What, for example, would be a satisfactory training period for a person to search clothing, using a proscribed procedure, to recover samples for further examination? At the end of such a period would such a person be aware of the significance of the absence of any compromising material on garments given the circumstances of the case? Should such a person have a pre-knowledge of the circumstances surrounding the case, and if so, how much might this influence what might be sought for on the garments [1]. Should searching always be carried out "blind" so that casework details do not direct the search programme? These questions are still to be answered and the answers put into practice. Having completed the training programme, personnel will require monitoring/mentoring but at what point is competence to work on ones own identified – by random testing perhaps by an already competent experienced officer or regular double searching by different personnel as part of the quality control system with all the cost implications of such a process? All such training programmes are dynamic in nature as research leads to modifications to, and the introduction of, totally new processes and instrumentation. Are laboratories maintaining the currency of their training programmes and who, external to the organisation, monitors this?

This latter brings into focus the need for some body external to each forensic science organisation, and that includes crime scene workers usually attached to police forces? In the United Kingdom the organisation responsible for this is the United Kingdom Accreditation Service (UKAS) in collaboration with the Forensic Science Regulator. This latter is a Home Office appointment with powers to set standards and to monitor compliance with all standards [2]. Some, perhaps most, of these standards have been generated through UKAS but others have been developed under the auspices of the Regulator and Skills for Justice. The question that must be asked is "what is the mechanism by which compliance with these standards is to be monitored?" It would seem that many of the assessors using the proscribed standards are employed by the organisations whose personnel are to be tested. The correctness of assessment is to be monitored by UKAS through dip sampling the process. Will such monitoring demonstrate sufficient independence for the courts to recognise practitioners as being impartial and competent, or should the assessors be totally independent of all the forensic organisations and if so would this be a practical alternative option given that all the expertise resides within these organisations? Certainly any such alternative would be more expensive and in the present fiscal climate, unlikely to be financed.

Whether this, or alternative methods for assessing individual competences, is to be adopted by other countries, is yet to be seen but this arrangement will be looked upon with interest internationally.

Technology and Science

The rapid growth in the sciences especially in the area of molecular biology will undoubtedly have an impact upon the forensic sciences but perhaps an area which could benefit from further scientific appraisal starts at the beginning of the forensic process namely identification and recovery of material from the scene and in the laboratory, this latter often associated with clothing. Over recent times the use of different light sources on their own or in combination with chemical treatments have become routine and have successfully revealed material of forensic significance that was not obvious to the unaided human eye. But is there other technology developed by other scientific disciplines that can be used for this purpose? For example, one is amazed at the clarity and detail with which cameras employed by astronomers are used to explore the universe. Could these be adopted to scan garments for trace materials instead of employing chemical testing and the aided human eye with all the built in fallibility of the latter process? Forensic science needs to look to novel applications of methods and processes developed in other disciplines to enhance its repertoire of investigative tools.

The area the general public most associate with the forensic sciences is that of DNA. This technology has had an enormous impact upon the successful prosecution of felons but already decisions will have to be made to enhance the SGM plus system that is presently used by most counties, by the introduction of more loci. Different pre- amplification procedures have now been validated and implemented but more needs to be researched on the interpretation of mixtures and criteria for acceptability and rejection of given profiles obtained from mixtures [3]. It is important that any such criteria are accepted by the forensic DNA community at large. The use of very rapid DNA sequencers and the development of emulsion PCR could have an important part to play in forensic science applications. In respect of the former, this would need a complete change in the DNA data bases that have already been established which would be a costly exercise and unlikely to find favour with financing bodies.

An area already directed at DNA analysis (SNIPS) is that of Biochip technology. This has the potential for determining DNA profiles at the crime scene given that it can accommodate a contamination free environment [4, 5, 6, 7]. The advantages of this coupled with on line access to DNA databases could greatly increase the rapidity of person identification and would reduce the pressure on over- extended laboratories. The use of biochip technology for forensic purposes does not stop at DNA but can be used to detect drugs [8, 9] and explosives [10]. The former discoveries could have an impact not only upon the detection of users of illicit drugs, for example in prisons, and for post mortem toxicological investigations but also for monitoring road traffic infringements associated with drug taking especially if the system could accommodate both saliva and perspiration as test material.

The individualisation of chemicals associated with criminal activity has for many years been the aim of forensic scientists especially for the characterisation of illicit drug samples and explosives, with the aim of matching samples recovered from different sources and identifying the manufacturing source. Variations in the use of mass spectrometry coupled with separation techniques have been partially successful in meeting this objective but the introduction of stable isotope mass spectrometry [11] already has, and will continue to provide, improvements in the individualisation of such samples. This technique has found other applications within the forensic sciences.

The sensitivity of Raman spectroscopy was for many years an inhibitor of its widespread use as an analytical tool but with the advent of surface enhanced resonance Raman scattering (SERRS) its sensitivity has been greatly increased and its application to the individual characterisation of samples of forensic interest explored. Procedures are well advanced in using this technique for the characterisation of DNA samples, at present mainly restricted to diagnostic probes for medical purposes, but the advantages of using a multiplex system of DNA analysis that shows greater sensitivity than fluorescent systems and does not require the use of any separation analytical system must be addressed [12, 13].

From what has preceded and other techniques not referred to in this review, it is apparent that techniques are being developed that will enhance the identification and characterisation of materials of forensic interest. However, while such identifications and characterisations are essential, the results of such analyses need to be interpreted in the context of the case if the work is to be of any value to the legal process. Over recent years, following the work of Evett et al, [14], much effort has been invested on interpreting evidence from a sound rational scientific basis using Bayesian statistics, an area of statistics well suited to forensic science problems. Work is continuing in this area and in particular efforts are being made to put fingerprint identification on a sound scientific basis for the first time [15, 16].

One aspect of interpretation requires that there are in place appropriate databases that are, relevant, accurate, complete, and up to date. It is important that such data bases are monitored for their efficacy and documentation should be available to demonstrate that this is so. Data bases for DNA, footwear, paints, fibres, glass, and fingerprints etc. are expensive to run and maintain and the question arises as to whether those responsible for financing forensic science organisations are willing to provide the necessary capital to facilitate their continued availability?

The Legal-Science Interface

The interface between members of the legal profession and scientists can be a difficult one since few scientists have a good appreciation of the law and few lawyers have a full understanding of science especially where new and complex technology needs to be explored for acceptability to the legal process.

One question that has arisen since science was first admitted to the courtroom is that of expertise. How does the court know that the person giving the scientific evidence is an expert in his/her field? Many of the early experts were medically qualified and much emphasis was, and in some instances, still is, placed upon experience. While experience is important it must be associated with competence and the area of competence clearly defined. Failure to define the area of competence has lead to some serious miscarriages of justice because evidence has been presented to the courts, by an "expert witness", that was outside their area of competence. While this should not happen, even the most experienced scientific/medical witness can sometimes be coerced into making unsubstantiated comments when under pressure from skilled counsel. This type of problem may suggest that perhaps the adversarial legal process is not best suited to the delivery of scientific/medical evidence to the courts and that the inquisitorial process may be an advantage? This debate is one that will continue but which must also take into account the decision by the European Court of Human Rights that the accused must have "equality of arms" to the prosecuting authorities in relation to their own forensic analyses. This decision must surely lead to an adversarial process. But how do the courts operating in the adversarial systems of justice try to reassure the public that experts are delivering the correct science to the courts? It is usual for the courts to evaluate the professional qualifications of the witness to include degrees and laboratory experience although it has been known for the former to be forged. The rigor of the examination and cross examination is meant to illicit any shortcomings in the scientists ability but is this sufficient when it is recognised that lawyers don't have wide, if any, scientific knowledge? Larger laboratories will have quality management systems in place and lawyers could test compliance with such standards but do lawyers know what these standards are? An independent organisation, the Council for the Registration of Forensic Practitioners (CRFP), was able to provide a register of competent forensic practitioners through a rigorous assessment process but this has since ceased to operate mainly because of its cumbersomeness and high cost to the industry. It is suggested that the courts do need a register of competent practitioners open not only to the large companies but also to the small organisations who offer expert testimony.

Assuming that the expert is expert, the courts have another hurdle to surmount and that relates to the presentation of evidence arising from new technologies that have not previously been brought before the court. How does the court judge what is acceptable as evidence? The United States have tried to tackle this problem through the Frye hearings [17] and Daubert judgements [18] which identify the series of steps the court should look to before a technique becomes acceptable to any deliberations. A similar set of criteria have recently been proposed by the English Law Commission [19] who envisage the gatekeeper for such judgements to be the judges themselves. One must ask, for very complex scientific technologies, do the judges have the skills and knowledge to make such judgements even with the assistance of scientific advisors? The debate must continue?

Conclusions

From what has preceded it is clear that forensic science has a future. In practice it has become pivotal in its role in supporting criminal justice systems throughout the world. How forensic science is validated and integrated into criminal justice systems is still open to debate. As science develops newer methods will be added to the battery of tools available to support the justice systems but who will judge on the correctness and acceptability of such techniques has still to be decided by legal bodies. Much will depend upon financial support for the forensic science industry and this is either directly or indirectly controlled by governmental processes at the national or local level. Given that government spending in many countries has become very restricted it does not bode well for future developments in the forensic sciences. This view was recently vocalised by a government spokesman at a recent conference held by the Forensic Science Regulator in the United Kingdom when he said that the Home Office would not be supporting any research in the forensic sciences. Given that none of the government scientific research councils are either unwilling or unable to support research in the forensic sciences this does not auger well for future developments but it will survive because it is needed by the judicial process.

References

1. M J Saks, DM Risinger, R Rosenthal and W C Thomson, Context effects in forensic science: a review and application of the science of science to crime laboratory practice in the United States: *Science and Justice* **43**(2) (2003), 77–90.
2. The Forensic Science Regulator: *A Review of the Options for the Accreditation of Forensic Practitioners*, The Home Office, January 2009.
3. *The Caddy Report: A Review of the Science of Low Template DNA Analysis*, Home Office, April 2008.
4. Wan-Li Xing and Jing Cheng Eds., *Frontiers in Biochip Technology*, Springer, 2006.
5. E Verpoorte, Microfluidic chips for clinical and forensic analysis, *Electrophoresis*, **23**, 677–712, 2002.
6. L Peng, S H I Yeung, KA Crenshaw, CA Crouse et al, Real-time forensic DNA analysis at a crime scene using a portable microchip analyzer, Forensic Science International: Genetics, **2**, 301–309, 2008.

7. SHI Yeung, P Liu, N Del Bueno, SA Greenspoon and RA Mathies, Integrated sample cleanup-capillary electrophoresis microchip for high-performance short tandem repeat genetics, *Analytical Chemistry*, **81**, 210–217.
8. S C Bishop, M Lerch and BR McCord, Detection of nitrated benzodiazepines by laser-induced fluorescence detection on a microfluidic device, *Journal of Chromatography A*, **1154**, 481–484, 2007.
9. H Du, M Wu, W Yang, G Yuan, Y Sun, et al, Development of a miniturized competitive immunoassays on a protein chip as a screening tool for drugs, *Clinical Chemistry*, **51**:2, 368–375, 2005.
10. M Pumera, Analysis of explosives via microchip electrophoresis and conventional capillary electrophoresis: a review, *Electrophoresis*, **27**, 244–256, 2006.
11. *Science and Justice* **49**(2), 62–149.
12. D Graham and K Faulds, Surface-enhanced Raman scattering as a detector for molecular diagnostics, *Experimental Reviews of Molecular Diagnostics*, **9**(6) (2009), in press.
13. D Graham and K Faulds, Quantitative SERRS for DNA sequence analysis, *Chemical Society Reviews*, **37** (2008), 1042–1051.
14. G Jackson, S Jones, G Booth, C Champod and I W Evett, The nature of forensic science opinion – a possible framework to guide thinking and practice in investigations and in court proceedings, *Science and Justice*, **46**(1) (2006), 25–31.
15. C Champod and I W Evett, A probabilistic approach to fingerprint evidence, *Journal of Forensic Identification*, **51** (2001), 101–122.
16. D Meuwly, Forensic Individualisation from Biometric Data, *Science and Justice*, **46**(4) 2006, 205–213.
17. *Frye v United States, 54 App.D.C. 46, 293 F1013 (1923)*.
18. *Daubert v Merrell Dow Pharm., Inc., 509 U.S. 579, 586 & n.4 (1993)*.
19. Law Commission consultation, Consultation paper 190: Expert Evidence in Criminal Trials (2009): expert.evidence@lawcommission.gsi.gov.uk

SECTION I: THE PROFESSIONAL DEVELOPMENT OF FORENSIC SCIENCE

The very first editorial written by Stuart Kind in 1960 addressed the issue of criminal aspects of forensic science in Great Britain. There followed over 50 other commentaries on the changes and sometimes painful developments of our profession over the last half century. Forensic Science provision in the UK as well as elsewhere has, of course, changed enormously in this time. The editorials have demonstrated a maturing of the debate over time about what it means to be a professional forensic scientist. They address the development of practice and standards, the dramatic changes in service provision from the development of the home office laboratories through to the widening of the market place that we are experiencing today in 2009.

In 1973 an editorial discussed the introduction of a "forensic science watchdog to take thought of their interests...expecting the highest standards of behaviour...[and] perhaps enforcing those standards". Twenty years later in 1993 an editorial commenting on the Royal Commission on criminal justice for England and Wales discussed the establishment of a 'forensic science advisory council' and in 2008 the newly appointed forensic science regulator wrote for the journal.

N. Nic Daéid

1(1) - 1960: Criminal Aspects of Forensic Science in Great Britain

The security of the citizen is very largely determined by the detection and punishment of crimes directed against his person and his property.

Until comparatively recently the systematic application of science to investigations relating to crime was directed mainly to major offences such as murder or more generally to crimes against the person. The field of such investigations was known as Forensic Medicine and were carried out by medical men. Until comparatively recently the methods of diagnosis in poisoning cases were very limited, depending very largely on observation before and during illness prior to death together with post mortem appearance.

For many years little was done on the chemistry side. The work of Christison (1829) and Taylor (1844) laid the foundation of toxicology and to-day the detection and estimation of poisons and the ultimate presentation of this evidence in poisoning cases has passed from the medical man to the chemist.

In 1872 it became compulsory for local authorities to appoint a public analyst, but it was not until 1900 that proof of ability in analytical chemistry was required, to-day he must also be a competent microscopist.

Until fairly recently, the main source of scientific assistance available to the local police was from a local medical practitioner (usually the police surgeon) and the local public analyst.

In 1938 a system was devised by the Home Office to divide the country into regions, each served by a laboratory to be equipped with up-to-date apparatus, each laboratory to be staffed so as to make it as comprehensive as possible.

Although the scheme provides for most problems likely to arise it does not cover all; in some problems investigations (or information) of a very specialised nature may be required. Such contingencies are provided for by the utilization not only of other government laboratories, but also by the research and technical laboratories of many industries. Even the individual specialist can be pressed into service when required. Thus it becomes possible to bring to bear on a criminological problem the scientific resources of the country.

The development of Forensic Science has led to a considerable increase in the scientific evidence brought before the courts.

The normal training of solicitors and barristers includes very little science, thus with few exceptions, solicitors and barristers are poor scientists.

For those whose duty it is to "hearken" to scientific evidence some degree of "scientific appreciation" is essential in the administration of justice.

Scientists on the other hand, should present their evidence in a language understandable to a lay jury. The evidence of a brilliant scientist may be lost to a jury if presented in a highly technical or scientific language.

4(2) - 1964: Forensic Science or Sciences?

There are two opposing trends evident in thinking on forensic science. These can be roughly equated with the "lumpers" and "splitters" of classical taxonomy.

The first school of thought in its extreme form adheres to the view that a forensic scientist must be a general practitioner and be prepared to work in fields as far apart as document examination and traumatic pathology. That this view is absurd is accepted in most civilised countries and nowadays we seldom witness attempts by one specialist to transgress into the field of another.

The fact that this view is absurd is, however, often taken as a basis for quasi logical argument which seeks to show that for efficient working forensic science must be divided into what can best be described as academic specialities. Thus there is a growing tendency for all thinking on forensic science to be compartmentalised into "Chemistry", "Physics" and "Biology". Although physical evidence may be classified (with doubtful value) in this way for teaching purposes, in actual case work it can seldom be said to fall entirely into one of these divisions.

Sciences can be classified in two ways, either by *content* or by *purpose*. The first of these divisions includes the so called "natural" divisions of science such as Physics and Geology. The second division comprises the "technologies" such as Engineering and Medicine where the subject matter (which may be rather heterogeneous when viewed from the viewpoint of the academic scientist) is provided with a unifying cement of *purpose*.

The view that Forensic Science is a hotch potch of different specialities seems of late to have gained the upper hand and it is the purpose of this Editorial to suggest that this latter point of view is equally indefensible with the former. Leaving aside the established specialities such as Pathology, Psychiatry and Toxicology which pose special problems, the forensic scientist is concerned with the degree of individuality and identity of tangible objects. He is concerned with *"Information"* in the broadest sense whether it be information left by skin ridges in the form of fingerprints, information left by rifling marks on a bullet or tool marks on a safe, information left by blood, metal scrapings, paint chips, footprints, hairs, fibres, glass fragments and any other of the multitudinous materials likely to be transferred.

The fact that all these materials have other aspects than the purely informational ones is perfectly true and it would be an unwise forensic scientist who extrapolated his knowledge of the individuality of paint and glass to the extent of advising on the painting and glazing of a new building but this is saying no more than that the dermatologist does not necessarily know anything about the individual character of fingerprints and generally that one cannot classify phenomena but only *attitudes* towards phenomena.

It will probably not be long before Society wakens up to the fact that apprenticeship, although valuable, is probably not the most efficient way of training forensic scientists and it would be a tragedy if any courses which are then instituted were to be based on anything other than the concept of unity in forensic science despite what the academics may say.

4(4) - 1964: Shriving a Science

Was ever an area of human endeavour so cursed and so blessed as that of forensic science?

From its origins the beastly science proved of horrific yet riveting interest to devotee and observer alike. A background of cultured urbanity, of intelligent and vaguely scientific guesswork such as informed the creatures of Sir Arthur Conan Doyle's imagination set the trend for the great men of the age of forensic medicine now almost passed into obscurity. Were not Tidy and Willcox, Pepper and Roche Lynch, Littlejohn, Sydney Smith and the Glaisters just such combinations? And Spilsbury the greatest of all in public esteem, whose reputation made him a spellbinder of juries to the extent almost of embarrassing the outcome of his cases. The forerunners of the modern forensic scientist certainly were men of character, personality and renown. Merged in public imagination with the experts of fiction these clever, superior almost psychic figures descended as from Olympus to pronounce a doom acceptable to reader or juror.

But these days are almost gone. Today the tradition wavers and fails.

True the Crown pathologists still command a considerable following. Molly Lefebure could create an aura of hushed respect about the doings of one of the most eminent whose thoughtful, bowler-hatted figure is to be seen, sometimes even on television, perambulating the scene of some murder or the gruesome remains of a sudden tragedy. The endless spate of second class writing on crime and criminals still caters for such a market, and to a degree such is still the public image. But the complexity of the science, the sweep of its interests, the Babel of its languages seldom fully permeate public consciousness. It is easy to venerate the wisdom of a greybeard, but the anonymous toiler at his laboratory bench stirs little applause. And those faceless individuals among whom the great man's interests are fragmented seldom communicate with one another and may soon find it impossible to do so. What affinity does the lawyer whose concept of proof is a weighing of testimony adduced within rigid and archaic rules have for the scientist whose approach is to adopt whatever hypothesis for the moment fits all the known facts so long as it continues to contain them?

What communion is possible between the police officer whose concern is to fence his suspect with evidence sufficient to satisfy judge and jury and the serologist whose studies both confirm and disprove the Pauline assertion that God hath made of one blood all nations of men for to dwell on the face of the earth? And what feeling has the judge, reared probably in a literary/classical tradition for the most social and practical of all branches of science?

The shriving of forensic science demands first an improvement in intercommunication, and then a new public revelation. If reverence has given way to indifference, if the omnicompetent savant is yielding place to the pallid multitude of anonymous workers, the doubtful boon of public recognition may soon pass into the curse of blank rejection. To ensure its re-emergence forensic science must forego the empire-building of the celebrity of more spacious days in favour of informed public acceptance of the discipline rather than the man. Such a blessing well befits the modern age.

A.R.B.

5(1) - 1965: A Public Image

Over the past few years it has become very fashionable for organisations of all kinds to give attention to their "Public Image". Sometimes this has led to nothing more significant than a decision to present dried skim milk powder as the "heart of milk". However, when a Public Image is based on misinformation as to the facts themselves, the case for trying to correct it is raised to a quite different level.

What then is the Public Image of Forensic Science to-day? Nurtured by novels, radio, television and the newspapers, the forensic scientist is almost always an omniscient university pathologist, who pronounces with authority on all subjects. Partly this is a legacy of the past, as was pointed out in "Shriving a Science" (Editorial, this Journal, October, 1964). On the other hand, what is said now has an equal effect, and one can only envy the freedom of university pathologists to state their views and regretfully to contrast this freedom with the censorship which fetters the state-employed forensic scientist.

It is difficult to see how the Home Office could give their employees full freedom to pronounce on controversial subjects, but there is surely a compromise between this and acting as though it were necessary for every statement of every employee to have the status of Holy Writ. There is unquestionably a case for independent comment to be encouraged.

Despite the recent erosion of the forensic medicine departments in some British universities which is deplorable, the position of forensic science is infinitely worse, for there is not a single appointment in this subject other than in specialities ancillary to medicine.

The time is now opportune for the establishment, possibly in one or more of the newer universities, of a Department of Forensic Science for research and teaching in the subject. It would create a situation more in accord with present facts and needs than the outworn, but current, Public Image of forensic science, which in time it would also correct.

David Patterson

5(2) - 1965: Don't Forget Them In Swahililand

A recent reviewer of Glaister's new edition of *Medical Jurisprudence* objected to the inclusion by that author of simple laboratory tests on the grounds that such testing should be left entirely to specialists. While such a recommendation may be scientifically sound, it is hardly practical in these times for many parts of the world. Most of the newly-emerging nations are hardpressed to find even one forensic scientist, let alone a battery of specialists.

The older and larger nations are neither producing enough forensic scientists to take care of their own normal attrition nor providing for expansion. We may bewail the fact that general practitioners perform medico-legal autopsies or that routine chemists attempt toxicology, but until the universities and criminalistics laboratories can produce enough specialists to staff more than a hundred countries, a great deal of forensic science is going to be done by generalists.

As comedian Jimmy Durante once put it: "Those are the conditions what prevail".

Forensic science is at best a lonely trade, standing unique in the law enforcement field in that its practitioners cannot look for guidance and assistance from their police and lawyer associates. They can only get help from others of their kind, and their nearest colleague may be thousands of miles away in another country. Books and periodicals are the only ready source of forensic information to the man in Singaradja, Zihuatanejo, or the Seychelles. He has no other specialists with whom he can consult.

If we delete the simple tests from the textbooks or confine our periodical contributions to esoteric methodology and elaborate instrumentation, we are not being fair to our occasional colleague in the hinterland. We may deplore his dabbling in matters that we believe he's not qualified to do, but he's going to make the tests anyway because he has to. The simple microdiffusion tests of Feldstein, the paper chromatography of Clarke and Curry, or the fruit-jar techniques of Rieders are the lifelines of assistance to the district medical officer in Baluchistan with a murdered corpse on his hands.

Every publishing forensic scientist should pause now and then as he drafts another ponderous paper designed to impress his peers. Let him remember his less fortunate colleague in a remote place who has little equipment and a problem on his hands. However forensically untrained, these men need all the help they can get from us. Our books and periodical articles can give it to them.

Elliott B. Hensel

6(2) - 1966: The Vacant Headquarters

Forensic science is unique among the sciences in that it lacks a focus and a centre. Not only has it no one organised professional body, but it sports so many interests interlocking with other disciplines as almost to defy definition. Yet this stellate structure provides an unusual number of pressure points at which fruitful interaction takes place. Chemistry, police procedure, ballistics, pathology, criminal records... the list is almost as endless as you care to make it. And all have a part to play and an influence to exert.

Our last Editorial "Progress in Research" welcomed the opening of two new laboratories, the increased evidence of University activity, and the hopeful signs of growth which these manifest. This Editorial reviews several more scattered changes taking place on the wider scene embraced by forensic science, and the implications they present.

Eleven policemen will shortly commence to study law, economics and modern history at London and Manchester Universities and at the London School of Economics. They will do so under a scheme conceived and put into execution by the Bramshill Police College, ushering in a welcome new approach to police science and a foretaste of the type of candidate the police desire to attract to higher office in the future. The scholarship scheme is eventually to be expanded to cover sixty candidates.

Lawyers too are engaged in a period of self-analysis coupled with an unwonted urge to reform. Juries are to be permitted to decide by a majority, the necessity of police caution is under fire, the defence of alibi may have to be notified in advance of trial. A judge has expressed the hope, discussed in the Third Programme, that no obstacle will be put in the way of the use of scientific evidence in paternity cases. The possibilities of computerised fingerprint records on a national scale is receiving active consideration. The social conscience is being alerted to the misuse of drugs. Even the clergy are weighing in with the suggested abolition of the matrimonial offence in divorce law; and abortion may soon attain a new respectability.

Changes are in the air; reform is *de rigeur*. And all of this activity is excellent and greatly to be welcomed.

But as a recent Editorial "The Price of Road Safety" criticised the abolition of the individual's rights as proposed in an excessive enthusiasm for the imposition of breath, blood and urine testing by a recent White Paper (subsequently modified in the new Road Safety Bill) so there is need now for a degree of caution amongst the uncontrolled clamour of reform. The call is for sober reflection on a wide front, and for a planned approach to forensic science as a whole, taking account of its legal implications and its social impact.

Degree courses may produce more literate policemen; they will not themselves transform the police from an overworked body into a modern and effective force. Procedural amendments may facilitate the work of the Courts; they will not bring about significantly more efficient conviction of the guilty, nor abate the crime wave. Blood and urine alcohol tests carefully applied may serve in a proportion of cases to sharpen the ascertainment of impairment, but they will hardly put the drinking driver off the road.

Who in all this reform, apart from the Home Secretary with a responsibility (amongst so many others) for Government laboratories, is giving any thought to fostering the development of forensic science as an entity? Who is controlling the wise expenditure of funds to serve best the current and future needs of emerging knowledge? Who takes thought for the most fertile areas for research, for recruitment to the profession, for the co-ordination of scattered departments in different Universities with an interest in the subject once known as forensic medicine? And most of all, who will teach, expand, define and rationalise the subject of forensic science and ruthlessly expose to examination the philosophical foundations on which it is built and from which its fruits are offered in the service of justice?

The Forensic Science Society has made its mark especially amongst scientists. The British Academy of Forensic Sciences has played a useful role particularly amongst lawyers. But for the overall strategy needed to steer a steady and meaningful course no one person or body is responsible.

It is idle to deny that the past history of forensic science has had its factions and its recriminations. These must now be tolerated no longer. The elusive Institute of Forensic Science has remained a dream, and the British who have the ability and experience to lead the world in forensic science have seemed strangely averse to seize the opportunity to do so. There may never be a more opportune moment than the present. There is a turmoil in society, a mood of reform in our legislators, a willingness for change in our lawyers. Amongst scientists there is a keen stirring of interest and plenty of opportunities waiting to be exploited; and in the crime wave a problem of challenging magnitude to bite upon. This surely is the day for forensic science to assert its presence and to display its potentialities.

But this thing cannot be done in a corner, nor by a faction. It is a matter not only of science, not only of law, not only of practical politics. It is the harnessing of the whole spectrum of forensically implicated sciences in the service of the law and the community.

Clearly the first step is the integration of the splinter societies. The second is a massive and outward-looking reappraisal on something like the scale of a Royal Commission of the relation of science to the service of justice in a modern community.

The vacant headquarters is waiting to be possessed.

A.R.B.

9(2a) - 1969: Six Just Men

The post-war development in forensic science within the United Kingdom has occurred mainly in England. The Central Research Establishment, which is rapidly earning an international reputation, the eight Forensic Science laboratories and the Metropolitan Police laboratory are all situated in England.

While, of course, the bulk of the population live in the central and southern parts of these islands there are still upwards of five millions living in Scotland, mostly in the central belt between the major cities of

Glasgow and Edinburgh. For these five millions a separate system of Scots law operates with its own Courts and procedure, and all the necessary administrative scaffolding to support such a service to the community. It is true that crime is less prevalent in Scotland than in England and that the crime which occurs tends to be of a less sophisticated nature.

Making allowances for all these factors, however, it is still remarkable to discover that the provision of forensic science facilities for Scotland is so pitifully inadequate. One police force (Glasgow) has a small complement of half a dozen full-time qualified forensic scientists whose services are also made available when necessary to the whole of Scotland through the good offices of its Chief Constable. For the rest, various expert services such as photography, microscopy and fingerprinting may be provided either locally by trained police officers or from time to time by special references to one or other of the University departments of forensic medicine which co-operate with the police. Given the obvious limitations of the system this arrangement works well enough but inevitably, despite the occasional brilliant achievement, the overall standard of work cannot but fall short of what it ought to be. This is painfully obvious to those who are in a position to compare the standard and scope of the forensic science backing given to the average criminal case in England with that available for the average criminal case in Scotland. In consequence it follows that valuable evidence which could help towards either conviction or acquittal and which ought to be made available is often absent in Scotland. In present circumstances this constitutes an avoidable and quite inexcusable failure to attain to the highest standards.

Recently the Secretary of State has been meeting in Scotland with all who have a concern for improvement of the criminal law and bringing the offender rapidly to justice, and consideration has been given to what can be done to improve the means of detection and to strengthen the assistance given to the police. While this Society has never been disposed to disparage the excellent work done by both the uniformed and criminal investigation branches of the police or to suggest that scientific aids are any substitute for the arduous and painstaking work which underlie most of their successes, we feel obliged to point to the alarming neglect which is implied by the figure of six full-time forensic scientists to meet Scottish needs as against upwards of three hundred and fifty for England and Wales.

With such a slender staff there can be no possibility of research or teaching, virtually no self-contained career structure and, it would seem, little satisfaction in meeting the needs of the Courts for the sophisticated aids to justice which science can increasingly provide.

The current police publicity campaign features posters bearing the slogan "Don't leave it all to the police". If we were given to writing on bill-boards we would want to add "Nor to the six just men".

Surely Scotland deserves better than this.

A.R.B.

9(2b) - 1969: "A Forensic Scientist?"

The title of this editorial is given in quotes with a query because it is proposed to discuss the question – when can an individual be described with accuracy as a forensic scientist? If the dictionary is of any use as a guide, a forensic scientist is someone who applies his or her scientific knowledge to matters pertaining to the courts of law – a wide definition which could include some present-day criminals as well as investigators! The term could be appropriately applied on this basis, and with an equal measure of accuracy, to scientists working in a police forensic science laboratory, to someone who gives evidence occasionally on a specialised subject, such as car damage or the detection of the traces of metal by neutron activation methods. By the same reasoning a handwriting expert can be a forensic scientist, even though he has had no scientific training whatsoever of a fundamental basis; even a graphologist might claim the title if a truly scientific approach is used.

The term, therefore, makes no distinction as to occupation, branch of work or discipline; and equally it does not distinguish between the forensic scientist of many years' experience and the beginner. In the past this has not mattered so very much. Science was less ramified and scientists could be experts in a number of related fields. Many specialists were known personally to the Courts and accepted by them if of proved worth. Nowadays, however, forensic science is becoming increasingly specialised and new branches are continually forming, each creating a scientific circle of its own. Forensic odontology is a good recent example. More properly qualified forensic scientists are needed to cope with the increase in number and types of crimes, both by the police and because of this (and the legal aid system) by the defence.

The upshot of all this is that the time is rapidly approaching when a recognised qualification for the forensic scientist will become not just desirable, but essential. This type of qualification should be of such a status that it is accepted by the Courts, thereby eliminating, one hopes, an undignified feature of many cross examinations. Once properly established in fact, its acquisition could well be made compulsory for all who seek to describe themselves as forensic scientists and who give evidence in Court. A "grandfather clause" would, of course, have to be built into the regulations so that existing forensic scientists of long and high standing would be given the title on an emeritus basis. As they cease to work their number would decrease by wastage, until they become extinct; and future generations would have to comply with the official standard.

The organisation of such a qualification for the forensic scientist presents a number of problems. Thus, what should the standard be; who should administer the qualifications; how should the forensic scientist's knowledge and ability be tested; what weight should be given to experience as distinct from actual knowledge? Few will disagree that the standard adopted should be a high one – post-graduate it would seem, because this would guarantee a general basic scientific training followed by a period of specialisation. It might be argued that such a system could be unnecessary and even unfair in the case of the individual who finishes up as, say, a document examiner or a ballistics or car accident expert, since much of their scientific training would not be used. I would not agree with such a view. A scientific qualification is a hall-mark, not so much of actual knowledge acquired, as of the fact that the individual has had a scientific training. This training should have taught him how to think and reason in a scientific way and these qualities are as essential to the very special specialist as to the ordinary routine scientist.

Any such qualification should also be a guarantee that the bearer is a good court witness. One so often hears first class scientists who are appalling witnesses; and vice versa. In the former case many of the shortcomings could often have been cured or prevented by proper instruction. Perhaps in future the forensic scientist will do the actual scientific work and a professional evidence giver will put it before the Court. This would have many advantages, especially in saving the time of the scientist, but it might be difficult to incorporate into our present legal system.

A qualification without courses to train scientists to acquire it would be of very little use and here again an official lead is required. An analogy which could well be followed up exists already in the Fellowship of the Royal Institute of Chemistry in Food and Drugs which is the stipulated and official qualification for Public Analyst. The American Society of Questioned Document Examiners has for some years operated an excellent qualifying procedure for those who wish to become members. This consists of a written paper, a verbal examination and a minimum period of practical experience in the laboratory of a member or of someone of suitable equivalent qualification. There is also close scrutiny of ethical and other considerations connected with the candidate before he is admitted. Although the subject matter is highly specialised the overall scientific standard required is commendably high. In England the British Academy of Forensic Sciences is considering this qualification problem also.

The Forensic Science Society with its high proportion and number of scientific members should also be alive to the position. However, the last thing we should want are two "degrees" covering similar qualifications; there are many who deplore the fact that we have two societies covering similar subjects. There should certainly be comprehensive consultation between forensic science circles in this country, and probably also in some Commonwealth centres, so that a single adequate qualification acceptable to all is ultimately achieved.

Julius Grant

(Opinions expressed in Editorials do not necessarily reflect those of the Council of the Society).

13(3) - 1973: I Hold Every Man a Debtor to his Profession[1]

A recent writer[2], discussing the subject of professionalism, enumerated the factors likely to be present where an activity might be described as professional. The activity must have an intellectual basis. There will generally be a foundation though not necessarily perpetuation in private practice. An advisory function is often found coupled with the execution of the activity. There is likely to be a tradition of service marked by a degree of disinterested conduct. These traits may be discerned in the personal life and work of most members of the Forensic Science Society. Two further aspects of professionalism however seem meantime to be lacking from the existing structure and organization of forensic science. These aspects are (a) the existence of a representative institute concerned with safeguarding and developing the expertise and standards of its members, and (b) the existence and enforcement of a code of conduct.

These observations raise the question whether there is a need to provide some professional organization and to establish standards of professional practice amongst forensic scientists.

No doubt the principal difficulty in thinking of forensic scientists as professionals in the fullest sense is that they enjoy an embarrassment of professions.

The biologist, the chemist, and the consulting engineer would probably claim to be professional in their outlook and conduct. The pharmacist is already controlled by an apparatus of rules and etiquette which marks out his profession. The solicitor and barrister are subject to elaborate professional discipline, and the doctor belongs to one of the oldest professions which owes much to Hippocrates, that earliest propounder of professional ethics. The policeman and detective though still weakest perhaps on the score of academic grounding owe duties to their colleagues and to society which continually must take priority over their personal interests, and they are familiar with a code of conduct and discipline which is rigorously enforced and has recently been the subject of anxious study and improvement.

Presumably some notion of the desirability of establishing professional standards was present in the minds of the founders of the British Academy of Forensic Sciences for their original Constitution expressed a concern for acceptable modes of conduct and adumbrated some sort of status, though this aspect in practice could hardly become effective on a professional scale so long as admission continued to be virtually by invitation only. In the more open affairs of the Forensic Science Society it may be argued that professional considerations are beginning to assert themselves. It has been decided for instance that the Council do not approve of members mentioning the fact of membership in Court as though it were a guarantee of status. Nor is it regarded as acceptable for members to parade their membership on notepaper as if it inferred some merit in the member. The Constitution of the Society presently defines the objects of the Society as being "to advance the study, application and standing of forensic science and to facilitate co-operation among persons interested in forensic science throughout the world". It may fairly be claimed that the Society in the 14 years of its existence has promoted these objects with reasonable vigour and a measure of success. But are the objects pitched on a sufficiently high plane? They are silent upon the question of standards of conduct except perhaps for the cryptic power given to the Council in Paragraph 19 to recommend the removal of a member

---

[1] Francis Bacon: Preface to *The Elements of the Common Law*.
[2] F. A. R. Bennion: *Professional Ethics*.

if in the opinion of the Council the interests of the Society require it. Nor do they seek to impose duties upon members or to bring uniformity into their relationships.

Perhaps the most commendable aspect of the day-to-day behaviour of forensic scientists, and one which betrays the professional instinct as no other, is the extent to which such persons are accustomed to have their evidence on technical subjects challenged in Court by the evidence of another expert. It is sometimes said that in the professions "dog does not eat dog" – a slander which the professional man should resent more than almost any other. Such a charge has, for example, been levelled against the medical profession where perhaps it can be understood since the practice of medicine is more of an art than a science, and it is particularly difficult to label treatment as right or wrong. Yet it ought to be the province of a profession to see that no one is deprived of professional advice because the advice is difficult to obtain or because it involves criticism of another member of that profession. This is but a single example of one sphere in which help for the client may sometimes be required and under present arrangements may be lacking. A further matter which gives rise to some unease is the beginning of advertising of the services of forensic scientists. Without in any way implying that those who do advertise are lacking in professional skill or sensibility, the build-up of such a practice could he regarded as opening the way to less scrupulous persons of smaller or absent qualifications who might eventually bring forensic science itself into disrepute. Nor should it be forgotten that in writing in this Journal one is addressing a world audience. Surely there exists a unique opportunity for standards to be set which could have a coordinating influence upon experts throughout the world.

It is the purpose of this Editorial to suggest that forensic scientists require a watchdog to take thought for their interests; that nothing but good could come from expecting the highest standards of behaviour from members and where necessary expounding and even perhaps enforcing such standards. There is a need to make explicit the rules of professional conduct which ought to bind members to whom the most important and responsible tasks are committed on which the Courts rely in reaching decisions affecting the property and lives of other citizens. Certainly in the sphere of maintaining a high level of competence, a good standing and reputation with others, and a professional solidarity there seem to be strong arguments for providing a professional institute to lead the way, to secure the ground that has been won, and perhaps most of all to speak for the members whose interests are academically do different but professionally so similar. The Dentists' Code[3] refers to "the general cordial relationship which should exist between members of all professions". This attitude exists already amongst those whose interests lie in the field of forensic science.

The Forensic Science Society has an important role to play in taking the lead in asserting the need for standards of fairness, integrity, responsibility and impartiality and in short for the establishment of a professional basis for forensic science which would set levels of conduct and attainment as standards for Great Britain and models for the rest of the world.

Alistair R. Brownlie

14(2) - 1974: Police Perimeters – Politics or Planning

I write this in February 1974. The Police Forces of England and Wales are about to be reorganized and their boundaries altered to conform to the new pattern of Local Government that comes into existence on the April 1, 1974.

There is a continuing debate about the respective merits of a National Police Service and separate Police Forces controlled by Local Authorities, though this debate has not recently aroused much interest except amongst policemen themselves or their friends, and a limited number of social historians. Some people hold

---

[3] *Dentists' Code*, p. 10.

that central control is now so complete that it is no longer of the slightest importance to resist "nationalization". The Home Secretary makes regulations covering recruitment, equipment, housing, pay and other conditions of service. There are uniform standards throughout the country in methods of training of every kind. (In this Journal it is permissible to say that not enough time in police training at all levels is devoted to Forensic Science.)

Is, then, the debate about the merits of local or central control not only irrelevant but academic?

The debate has continued partly because the word "Police" has been used in so many different ways over the years. Radzinowicz has pointed out that the word entered the English language in the eighteenth century and was first used as Johnson defined it in his Dictionary, as "the regulation and government of a city or country, so far as regards the inhabitants".

At the other end of the scale it has been used to describe the activities of the municipal authorities responsible for street cleaning and sanitation. It has always amused the Scots to know that horse manure collected in the streets of Edinburgh was sold to pay for the police of the city.

Somewhere in between is the conception of "Police" maintaining law and order and detecting crime. It is in line with Johnson's definition of the word that the term "Police State" is most commonly used. The political scientist may use the term Police State without moral overtones, but to the man on the Clapham omnibus it is a term of abuse with alarming connotations.

In the eighteen-century discussions about the reform of internal order, Englishmen at any rate, "agreed that they were prepared to endure an unusual degree of violence in the streets and a consequential lack of personal security rather than to risk the incursions on their personal liberty which they considered was the price Europeans had to pay for their Police". To memories of the Star Chamber was added a resolute objection to the efficient police organization continued and improved by Napoleon in France after the Revolution. A Napoleonic Police was as objectionable to the Englishman of the nineteenth century as Himmler's Police would have been to an Englishman of the twentieth century.

When a professional Police Force was at last started in England it was confined to London, and ever since 1829 the London Metropolitan Police has remained the only National Police Force.

Provincial forces grew, at first haphazardly and afterwards with increasing regularity, from the Central Government. Politicians have continued to say that a centrally-organized Police Service would be obnoxious both to democracy and the liberty of the individual. The fact is that democracy is not mainly defended by unarmed and separate Police Forces but by the rule of law. A dictator can only assume power with the help of the Armed Forces and the suspension of the independent courts. In that situation policemen everywhere would be in the same position as ordinary citizens, however many different police forces might be in existence.

It is also said by those who dislike the idea of a "National Police Service" that local control ensures that local wishes and local idiosyncrasies are respected. The local policeman is not a faceless robot but a nice chap known to all by name. The concept of the "neighbourhood bobby" is an attractive one, but the ideal policeman is the product of temperament, training and tradition, not of the sort of local option that used to decide licensing hours. The police officer's discretion – whether exercised by the Commissioner of Police of the Metropolis or by the Police Constable on the beat – is based on a judgement about the current values of society. The discretion is exercised just as often in a division of the Metropolitan Police as in a village community in remotest Loamshire.

The argument that central control might result in greater police efficiency can be turned upside down. There is a common and widespread belief that the policeman should not be too efficient. The public prefer Dogberry to Barlow, but Dogberry is, or ought to be, out of date. The scientific approach is not now left to Holmes but also comes from Scotland Yard. There was a time when the ordinary policeman needed only to wear his uniform as if he meant it and to touch his forelock to his superiors. He needs now a professional training and gradually he is in the process of getting it.

It would be wrong, however, to dismiss as fantasy all that is said about the dangers of central control and the virtues of local control. There would be no point in trying to impose upon a reluctant public a police system they distrusted. There are many politicians who believe a government that attempted such a change would commit political suicide.

Objections to the latest plan for police reorganization should not be based upon a blind belief in the virtues of central government, however soundly based this belief may be. An alteration in police boundaries on this scale with all the attendant expense and disruption could only be justified by a pronounced increase in efficiency. The new arrangements are not expected to raise police standards in the preservation of life and property and the prevention and detection of crime. The public will not get a better service.

There is a case for leaving police boundaries as they are. There was a case for leaving them as they were in the sixties and the forties. There is no case for altering boundaries to conform to the currently fashionable view of local authority boundaries. The English (though not, I think, the Scots) pride themselves on being practical and having no use for theory or metaphysics. They might possibly be attracted by a scientific solution to police problems.

If police boundaries were drawn on scientific principles each police area would be centred round a control room sited according to the best advice from telecommunications experts. There would be about a dozen control rooms and a dozen police forces. Near the control room there would be sited the administrative headquarters, the Forensic Science Laboratory, Technical Services, Criminal Record Office and Training Schools. The Divisions of each force would be of different sizes, varying according to the differences in population and territory. The strength of Divisions might vary from 100 to 1,000 men. Local committees could advise Divisional Superintendents about local problems. The Chief Officer would report to a Police Authority appointed, as now, from local authorities and magistrates. Each Division would have an appropriate allocation of technical resources and trained Scenes of Crime Officers.

In the present and continuing need for strict economy, it would be necessary to make the fullest use of existing buildings. Operational control throughout the Region would be achieved by proper siting of transmitters without the need for each control room to be geographically exactly central.

Perhaps somewhere in the files of a Police Research and Planning Department some such scheme moulders away. More likely it has been shredded for waste paper.

A.A. Muir

17(4) - 1977: Theory and Practice

The Times on 13 May 1977 published a condensed version of *The Growth of Crime* by Sir Leon Radzinowitz and Joan King. In the book the authors discuss "Crimes we never hear about" and Sir Leon recalls,

> "In half a lifetime of watching and comparing, I have found myself inexorably drawn to the conclusion that we have been much too modest in our estimation of what is hidden. In the 1950's I was given a sharp twist in the direction by evidence brought to light by two of my colleagues at Cambridge in the course of a systematic study of sexual offences. That led me to express the doubt whether more than five in a hundred of such offences (leaving aside the serious crime of rape) were ever likely to come to light. Eventually I felt forced to the conclusion that the picture was almost as obscure for crime as a whole."
>
> "In a lecture to the Royal Society of Arts in 1964 I went so far as to suggest that crime fully brought into the open and punished represented no more than 15% of the great mass actually committed."
>
> "I admitted at the time that it was only a guess, but the evidence has lately been mounting and I stick to my estimate."

Any reader of this Journal could add to Sir Leon's "mounting evidence".

There still remain in this over-populated country communities who do not reckon to report crime to the Police. They may be remote villages, islands, (Lindisfarne) or high rise flats. Incest is an obvious example of a crime thought serious by some, and kept hidden by others.

A few years ago there was an investigation in County Durham into the murder of a young woman who worked in a large factory making television sets and components. The usual "routine enquiries" amongst fellow workers disclosed a number of unreported offences of stealing and dishonest handling in the factory. The management was not pleased and wanted no action taken in the interest of industrial harmony.

I see that a doctoral thesis has just been published on the subject of Fiddling of this kind.

Many crimes never get into Home Office statistics because some policeman either on the ground, or at the top, exercises his discretion not to prosecute. Not so long ago an Assistant Commissioner of the Metropolitan Police was criticised for circulating a memorandum directing that gaming clubs were not to be prosecuted unless there was evidence of cheating or that the club was frequented by criminals.

The man on the beat will often tell the disturbers of the peace to go home quietly; his motives may be avuncular or he may simply not have time to go to Court.

A wide discretion is exercised by the Police as to what offences shall or shall not be prosecuted. The day to day business of prosecuting offences up and down the country is shot through with discretion. It has never been the rule that suspected criminal offences must automatically be the subject of prosecution.

That might be described as the academic view. Where does this leave the criminologist, who must either work with the published statistics or philosophise about the limitless wickedness of his fellow-men?

In an address entitled "*Criminology – Its Search for an Identity*" given to the Criminology and Forensic Science Section of the 40th Australian and New Zealand Association for the Advancement of Science Congress at Canberra in January 1975, Dr. John Robson, the Director of the Institute of Criminology in the Victoria University of Wellington, discussed what distinguished criminologists over the years had seen as their function. Some criminologists have seen their discipline as a branch of psychiatry, others as a branch of sociology, others again as a part of social history. Dr. Robson believes that the criminologist (working admittedly with limited data) should be used to help in the formulation of a social programme.

"How much regulation will a community endure? What proportion of our economic resources should be set aside for crime prevention? What can the community afford? What is the community's correct sense of values for appraising the harm done by offences of various types? What quantity of offending will the community tolerate?"

Forensic scientists (and policemen too) have to get on with the crimes that are put on their plate; they are likely to regard philosophers with amused tolerance. It is no bad thing that they should lift their eyes occasionally from the bench and wonder whether their job and their existence is of any real importance.

Crime will not go away, Sir Leon might say, but if the subscribers to this Journal (and others like it) get better at their job, crime may possibly not get completely out of control.

A.A. Muir

20(3) - 1980: Forensic Science – A Broader Basis

Some years ago I shared the lecture platform at a seminar with a distinguished director of a Home Office Forensic Science Laboratory. He opened the proceedings with a talk on forensic science in the United Kingdom and never once mentioned any forensic science outside that of the Home Office and Metropolitan Police Laboratories. More recently, (Kind 1979), our president gave an address entitled "Forensic Science in the United Kingdom". In it he discussed the type of information produced by the forensic scientist. This was (1) information to help in the decision on whether a crime has been committed, (2) corroborative evidence of (1) and (3) evidence to incriminate or eliminate an individual.

These are but two examples of a tendency to equate forensic science with the application of science to aid the police in the apprehension and conviction of criminals. Surely this view of forensic science is too narrow and, because of its prevalence, so also is the basis of the Society. The adjective "forensic", which goes back to Roman times, means "related to, used in or connected with a court of law". Forensic science is, therefore, science used in connection with a court of law. The application of science to the apprehension and conviction of criminals is only part of the whole field of science applied in this way.

Once a person is charged with an offence in which scientific evidence is involved, his legal adviser is liable to need the services of a forensic scientist. He may need assurance that the prosecution evidence is sound and that it would be a waste of time and money to challenge the unchallengeable. He may be confronted with a client who denies the charge and offers another explanation of the facts put forward in evidence. In such a case the lawyer will want to know whether his client's story is, in fact, a possible interpretation of the facts and, if so, will require this opinion to be given in evidence.

Another field of forensic science arises from the development over the last century or so of a concern for health hazards. There is much legislation in the field of food adulteration, pollution and safety in toys. A large number of scientists are employed in works laboratories to prevent the commission of crimes under this legislation. Many other scientists work as public analysts to monitor the compliance with this legislation. All are just as much forensic scientists as those who work in what are sometimes referred to as "crime laboratories".

These examples all relate to forensic science used in connection with the criminal courts. There is, however, another great branch of the law, the civil law, with its own network of courts. There are many forensic scientists whose practices lie entirely in this field. There are at least 250 such practices which range from one man consultancies to ones with considerable numbers of professionally qualified staff. In this field actual court attendance is comparatively rare. In the criminal courts a person is either guilty or not guilty of the offence alleged. The civil courts, however, use the concept of partial blameworthiness and tend to set judgements which are not 100% in either direction. This is an inducement for parties to settle out of court, but the forensic scientists concerned have always to do their work in the expectation that it will be given in evidence and, hence, be subject to the scrutiny of cross-examination.

All forensic scientists have much in common and much to learn from each other. The scientist endeavouring to identify the origin of debris from the clothing of a murder victim has essentially the same problems as the one endeavouring to find out if dogfish has been used in the salmon spread. The investigator checking on a suspected arson is working in the same field as his counterpart who is trying to find the reason why Mrs Smith's chip pan went on fire. The work of the vehicle examiner lies in the same field as that of the consultant engineer giving evidence in a civil court on the failure of a steel structural member. Moreover the process of observation, deduction and explanation to laymen is common to all.

Should not the basis of the Society be broadened? We should all be gainers if the Society were truly a forum for all scientists whose work is related to the law. Should not the Society consider a recruitment drive in those areas of forensic science which lie outside those of the Home Office and Metropolitan Police Laboratories? Could we not, at an early date, have a major symposium in which no paper would be permitted which related to any topic concerned with assisting the police to apprehend and secure the conviction of criminals? In earnest of my plea I would be pleased to open the proceedings with a paper entitled "The Other Side of the Fence".

H.J. Yallop

Reference

Kind S. S., 1979, *J. Forens. Sci. Soc.*, **19**, 117.

21(1) - 1981: General Practice in Forensic Science

Is it reasonable to expect that a forensic scientist can develop or possess true scientific expertise in several diverse areas such as drug chemistry, arsons and explosives, serology, toxicology and trace evidence analysis well as being engaged in the training of new personnel, in addition to having supervisory duties?

With these words, Lappas (this Journal 1978, **18**, 171–180) dismisses as untenable the "generalist philosophy" in forensic science. His conclusions result from a survey of professional staffing in forensic science laboratories in the United States and they are convincing, particularly when applied to many of the smaller laboratories surveyed, which have staffs of just a handful of scientists.

In the United Kingdom, where the average number of scientists per laboratory is about 80 and where there is a well developed system of research, both in the operational laboratories and in the Central Research Establishment, the situation appears to suffer from none of the faults defined by Lappas. Is it then ideal? Is there no place for the "generalist philosophy" so firmly rejected by Lappas?

Before treading the path taken by their British colleagues, American forensic scientists should not only consider what they have to gain (which appears to be everything that Lappas recommends) but what they have to lose.

Is an ideal system one where important questions may be begged by giving the case to a forensic scientist who specialises in such a narrow field that he is blind to the crime detection implications of those aspects of his evidence materials which lie outside the field of his own expertise?

Are the police, the courts and through them, society, best served by well qualified and able specialists who lack the ability to work with police officers except through the medium of written specialist reports? Does it not appear that the distancing between the scientist and the investigator has gone too far when one director of a European laboratory proudly states that he tells all his new staff that he "doesn't care how long they take as long as they get it right"?

The realisation is growing within the community of forensic scientists that the disappearance of the generalist brings more problems than it solves. Yet this realisation finds little expression because few wish to return to the days of the self professed polymath who posed as an expert in everything.

The time has come for debate. This writer is quite convinced of the need for the generalist forensic scientist who, whilst he may not be skilled with the controls of an organic mass spectrometer, and may be somewhat at a loss with gel permeation chromatography, is as thoroughly familiar with the requirements of the courts and the investigating officer as he is with the scope and limitations of the scientific techniques which purport to fulfil them. If he is of a more philosophical turn of mind he may spend some of his time considering the fascinating field of theory and practice which modern scientific crime detection has revealed in conceptual and statistical matters. What are the criteria for the selection of background reference populations in evidence materials? Are the responsibilities of the forensic scientist to the courts and to the investigating officer the same? Is scientific evidence in court only interpretable in a Bayesian context?

Should lawyers be dragged, protesting, to consider the implications of science in their profession or would it be sufficient to make the writings of Alistair Brownlie, in the pages of this journal, required reading in legal education? Equally, should forensic scientists be compelled to take examinations in jurisprudence in addition to those in physical chemistry?

Most entrancingly of all, should we borrow a jury retiring room, during the law vacation, and closet six lawyers and six forensic scientists "without meat, drink or fire" to produce an agreed judgement on the notion of cause?

Unhappily, we could find that all twelve were too specialised to understand the question!

H.A.

24(6) - 1984: Does Forensic Science Have a Future?

(Guest Editorial)

WJ Rodger
Strathclyde Police Forensic Science Laboratory, 173 Pitt Street, Glasgow, United Kingdom G2 4JS

Society, in defence of an orderly existence, saw the necessity to take statutory action, hopefully to suppress such powerful human instincts as greed, lust and so on. It realised, correctly, that these instincts would not be expunged simply by immersion in legislative disinfectant and that laws, once made, had to be enforced; hence the establishment of policing systems. Although the first detective agency was set up at the beginning of the nineteenth century, it was the middle of the century before the telegraph proved its value in a murder case, the 1880s before Bertillon saw the immense potential of photography, and the early twentieth century before the first convictions were obtained with the aid of fingerprint identification. Each of these early technical developments in crime detection was highly significant, but collectively, and in terms of the times involved, they do not indicate a revolutionary cascade of events signifying the eagerness of the legal system to capitalise on the benefits of scientific and technological advance. The detective propensities of Sherlock Holmes, created in 1887 by Conan Doyle, remained in the category of science fiction for a period approaching half a century before forensic science institutions were established in this country. We might, therefore, identify a further indication of the reticence of the law, and society, to come to terms with science.

Clearly, there was what we might call an "incubation period" before scientific innovations found practical application in the field of criminal investigation.

It is, of course, cardinal that any technical advances be validated before introduction into the court of law, but we might wonder as to the justification for incubation periods measured in units of quarter- and half-centuries. The members of the criminal fraternity have never been slow to exploit new technology; their incubation period might aptly be described as an immaculate conception.

In its endeavours to maintain law and order, why should society give cognizance, and continue to give cognizance to forensic science? Sometimes the decision to use the forensic scientist does not rest with the investigating officer or the court of law, because it is necessary for a scientific examination to be carried out to establish whether or not an offence has been committed. It might be thought that without the scientist, firstly, certain laws could not be enforced, and secondly, that such laws could never have been drafted.

Taking the first point, in determining whether an offence has been committed, the extent of the demand for forensic science involvement will, in practice, depend on current legislation, public behaviour in response to that legislation and the police effort in supporting it. A simple example is cannabis, presently controlled in the United Kingdom, a fact that does not prevent its use by a significant percentage of the public. Not so long ago, enforcement varied from area to area, so that it might have seemed that some of these areas had no cannabis problem at all. Who could claim today that there is a part of the United Kingdom, for instance, where the number of cases requiring laboratory analysis would not be increased by the strategic attentions of an enlarged Drug Squad? But what would be the effect on the forensic science requirement if cannabis were legalised?

With drinking and driving, the introduction of substantive breathtesting devices has, to varying degrees throughout the world, reduced if not eliminated what was once a very significant caseload for forensic science laboratories. Who can say how much of today's hands-on laboratory technology will be similarly replaced by little red boxes?

On the second point, the active role of practising forensic scientists in the formulation of laws based on scientifically determined data should be fundamental, to ensure that Government produces a sound legislative framework. Forensic scientists can then provide statements which satisfy that framework without compromising their professional status and integrity. Certainly, "forensic" means "on behalf of the court of law", but it is not the role of the forensic scientist to accommodate the law by conceding scientific principles to political judgements, or by manipulating terminology to produce equivocal statements compatible with legal requirements.

For instance, because the law is based on precedent rather than present, it may enlist the services of forensic scientists to support legislation which substantially predates the very existence of forensic science laboratories. A classic example in the United Kingdom is the law relating to explosive substances. In the last few years, for varying reasons, there has been an intensification of law court deliberations on petrol bombs: are they pyrotechnic, are they explosive, and are they controlled by the Explosive Substances Act? This led to what one might consider to be an unseemly dichotomy of opinion as a result of endeavours by scientists on behalf of the prosecution and the defence to apply present day scientific knowledge and nomenclature to a law established one hundred years ago! If a particular law is incompatible with present day technology, then that should be clearly recognised as a problem for the court and not for the forensic scientist. New legislation is the answer, not scientific compromise.

In the changing years, it is incumbent upon the forensic scientist to develop and maintain a stronger and more effective interest, a stronger and more effective role and a stronger and more effective lobby in the framing of all relevant legislation.

Beyond this, surely, there is a guaranteed requirement for the services of the forensic scientist as a result of the "best" evidence rule, that fundamental principle which ensures that justice will be done. The rule states simply that "the best evidence must always be led" and forensic scientists know only too well that it is a principle wielded at times like a rod by the court to control the legal requirements and the legal acceptability of scientific evidence.

But just how inviolable is that rule? How, for instance, has it been affected in this country by the Health and Safety at Work Act? When this Act was introduced a few years ago, a committee was formed in Scotland to consider its effect in relation to the introduction and handling of hazardous materials in court. Two criteria were identified: the requirement under "best evidence" rules to preserve the evidential value of the materials; and the requirement to protect all persons handling them. The legal representatives in committee actually maintained that the first criterion, i.e., evidential value, must be achieved in its totality and what had to be ascertained was the best safety procedures consistent with that objective. Further deliberations were required before the priorities were reversed and it was finally conceded that "there may be instances where the interests of safety will override the need specified to preserve the evidential value of the articles concerned".

In June 1984, the Attorney General for England and Wales was quoted as saying "The criminal law has to balance society's need to convict and punish the genuinely guilty and society's interest in preventing the innocent from being wrongly convicted and punished" and he went on "We should not necessarily cling to rules of evidence which, while they might have carefully evolved over many years, in today's circumstances simply favour persons who are accused or suspected of crime" [1]. It is to be hoped that such an attitude provides sufficient mobility in the "best evidence" rule to come to terms with the fact that scientific evidence in many cases is becoming so complicated that it requires more and more individuals to conduct all the necessary examinations in any single case.

In the court's nonetheless justifiable desire to avoid hearsay evidence, a blind and rigid application of the rule could in some cases render forensic science impractical. Nor should it be left to the capriciousness of the individual court, or the whim of a particular prosecution or defence counsel as to how rigid that application should be. Is it naive to believe that its purpose is to enable the court of law to determine the truth, and that it is for the benefit of judge and jury as distinct from prosecution or defence? Is it wrong to ask if, in fact, our adversarial system in the United Kingdom is seeking the truth? It is imperative that the changing years produce a clearer and more uniform understanding by the courts of these potentially serious problems, so that they are not, in effect, denied the best evidence by the very rule designed to ensure it.

It is surely appropriate to consider these points in relation to the future of forensic science and, in particular, the much-debated independent role of the forensic scientist and the compatibility of that role in the adversarial system of law.

How is the forensic scientist to convince the public of his independence and refute the claim that his contribution is geared to the prosecution, when that prosecution effectively controls in what manner, and to what extent, his scientific evidence is presented in court? Since the forensic scientist can only answer questions put to him, a prosecutor needs to have sufficient knowledge of science and the skill to apply that knowledge in a line of questioning which is understandable, answerable, sensible and fair. It should permit the expert to present his evidence in an impersonal and neutral fashion, stating all relevant facts and making clear what inferences may or may not be drawn from these facts so that he is seen to be giving an independent, dispassionate evaluation.

Recently in a letter to a newspaper, unease was expressed at the use to which scientific evidence was put in one criminal proceedings, where a scientist intimated that a fibre found on the clothing of the victim could have come from the clothing of the accused. In summing up, the members of the jury were told by the Crown that "a single red fibre was *found* to have been transferred from the accused's jumper to the jumper worn by the victim", a statement clearly not conducive to promoting the image of the impartial forensic scientist.

The real significance of this example, however, is that it was published under the headlines "Forensic Science Fiction", presumably much more topical and attractive to readers than "Prosecuting Counsel Fiction", which, on the information printed, was clearly more appropriate to the facts. It would seem that no matter how impartial and independent the forensic scientist is, whether or not he is seen to be impartial and independent rests on a system which is at best unsatisfactory for the purpose and at times downright hostile to it.

As a result of deliberations by the High Court in Scotland, significant pronouncements were made on the standards which should be expected of the forensic scientist. A legal commentator highlighted them as follows: "The High Court is spelling out the supreme requirements for the expert, namely, that he shall not only give his evidence to the best of his ability but also supply a critique of that evidence drawing attention to its weaknesses as well as its strengths" [2]. Of particular significance was part of the criticism of a scientific witness because "he failed to mention in evidence" and "remained silent on this matter in the witness box". There was apparently no criticism of the fact that he was not asked by prosecuting counsel the question which would have elicited that information, nor was he asked by defence counsel that very same question which was so much, and so obviously, in the best interests of his client.

In a much earlier comment on the standards of expert scientific evidence [3] a renowned member of the English judiciary recommended the adoption of the following code of practice. "It should be a rigorous obligation on all experts to give the court, as clearly as they can, the limits of accuracy of their evidence, whether it is experimental or theoretical, and to disclose, if it be the fact, that other views exist in their profession. It should also be their duty to the court to indicate what inferences cannot properly be drawn from their evidence". All forensic scientists would surely consider this to be a desirable and, in fact, well-established basic principle. For it to be guaranteed to be so in practice, however, the oath the forensic scientist takes in the witness box might have to be changed to something like "I promise to tell the truth, the whole truth and nothing but the truth – if you promise to let me!"

In the pronouncements already mentioned, made by the High Court in Edinburgh, there was a clear indication of the very high standard required in written reports. The scientist has a duty in his statement to set down clearly the facts of each case and his opinion as to what inferences may be drawn from these facts. More importantly, from his own point of view, he has an opportunity to demonstrate autonomously his scientific integrity and impartiality. That, however, can only be realised if the system ensures that his statement in *toto* is brought to the full attention of the court. In this respect the forensic scientist in Scotland, for example, has a significant advantage, because he is normally available for precognition, i.e., pretrial interrogation by counsel for the prosecution or the defence. It still depends on the diligence and application of counsel to avail themselves of this facility and it has to be said that at times it seems to be pursued with varying levels of apathy, an unspoken acceptance, perhaps, of the impartiality of the forensic scientist. Whatever it is, the fact remains that precognition does add significantly to the independent status of the forensic scientist as working for the court rather than for either prosecution or defence.

Consideration is being given in England and Wales to the introduction of new legislation in this direction. In the Police and Criminal Evidence Bill, presently being debated in parliament, there is provision for requiring any party to proceedings before a Crown Court to disclose to the other party or parties any expert evidence which he proposes to adduce in the proceedings. All forensic scientists will surely welcome its introduction, but it is a symptom of the adversarial system that the proponents of such a provision are not short of challengers. While there may be sound reasoning in the statement that it is always right for the prosecution to provide evidence which may establish a man's innocence, but it can never be right that a defendant in advance has to provide evidence that may establish his guilt, it is difficult to reconcile it with impartiality insofar as it relates to scientific witnesses. If the Court is to know the truth of the scientific evidence, there can be no reasonable opposition to pretrial exchange of scientific statements.

It has been stated that "there should be a provision that all expert witnesses have the right to consult together regardless of the parties or their legal advisers", but what response might be expected for such arrangements from those independent forensic scientists who act on behalf of the defence? They are under no less pressure than any other forensic scientists since a defence expert who takes a view contrary to the best interests of his client is not likely to remain in employment, hence the criticism that they are suspect.

The law has pronounced on the standards required of the forensic scientist and, rightly, has not qualified this to indicate a special immunity for those scientists called on behalf of the defence. The court is entitled to expect from them no less a standard of professional qualification, integrity and expertise. If it is not seen to be vigilant in ensuring that it gets such a standard, the disservice it does to forensic science would be matched only by the disservice it does to itself and the cause of justice.

It is not inconceivable that the court's determination to prevent the conviction of the innocent could be foiled by an incompetent defence expert. It could be argued that the court is not the best qualified to judge such competence. The best judges are surely forensic scientists who should, therefore, be more involved in judging the competence of expert witnesses, just as, for instance, Law Societies judge and control the competence of solicitors.

Certainly, professional ethics and self-respect will normally operate to ensure that internecine exchanges do not occur between Crown and defence experts. There will always be differences of opinion but they do not have to be mutually destructive. Professional ethics, however, are not defined and controlled by law, and a system which deliberately sets scientist against scientist must depend very heavily on the scrupulous honesty and integrity of the competitors, manipulated as they are by their respective counsels, less for the common purpose of determining the truth of the matter, than for the diametrically-opposed purpose of securing a conviction or an acquittal.

It behoves forensic scientists to campaign actively to identify and highlight criteria for the accreditation of expert witnesses. The reputation and neutrality of forensic science should not be risked unnecessarily by exposure to hostilities in the court of law through the exploitation by both parties of self-styled experts.

The most obvious area for criticism of the independence of many forensic scientists is in their relationship with the police. Critics have pointed out that "their laboratories routinely work with the police and are staffed by police liaison officers; that there is no equivalent facility available to the accused; that police forces retain their own forensic laboratories and that they provide most of the material submitted for scientific examination". Associated with such criticism is the inference, and sometimes the statement, to the effect that forensic science laboratories are therefore not seen to be wholly independent.

If it is accepted that when a crime is committed, society should take steps to identify the offender and that the agency to carry out the investigation should be the police, they should make use of all legitimate means to pursue that end, including the best scientific assistance available. What, then, are the criteria required of a laboratory such that it can remain totally exempt from criticism from some quarters that it is not wholly independent?

The function of the forensic scientist is to assist in the investigation of crime which is carried out primarily by police officers. The forensic scientist, therefore, assists police officers. To state that is in no way to state that the integrity of the forensic scientist is suspect.

He must ensure, however, that his objectivity, that fundamental quality required of all forensic scientists, does not become suspect in his role in support of the investigating officers. Laboratories must be seen to be active in ensuring that this is so and is seen to be so, and in this direction, a system of quality assurance is paramount. The Strathclyde laboratory, for instance, while not formally a part of the Home Office Forensic Science Service, is privileged to be involved in their quality assurance programme.

It is appropriate to mention here another significant feature of the law in Scotland, which relates to corroboration. There must be corroboration of the evidence of any witness either by the testimony of another witness or by evidence of facts and circumstances. Effectively, this means that two scientists are involved in every case. Both sign the final report and both may be required to give evidence in that case, a further significant contribution to the assurance of objectivity.

Summing up so far, the future of forensic science will be better assured by positive action to maintain a mutually respectful relationship with the court of law and crime investigators. In assessing the value of his expertise to society as a whole, should not the forensic scientist feel confident that his contribution is indispensable, that in a situation where technology is used against the law, those responsible for law and order would wish to be seen to display a disposition and eagerness to utilise that same technology to the utmost?

How impeded would be the administration of justice in cases of murder, rape and serious assault without the ability to discriminate between individuals by grouping blood and semen?

In this world of high finance, how important is the document examiner in case of fraud, national and international?

As the density of traffic on the roads increases and the death toll goes on with sickening predictability, how essential is it to determine the causes of accidents, hopefully to reduce their recurrence?

How much more vital will become the role of the fire investigator in an increasingly commercialised society?

How efficient would be the process of bringing terrorists to justice without the explosives and firearms expertise now available?

How many drug pushers would be convicted and taken out of circulation without the benefit of qualitative and quantitative chemical analysis?

How much is all of that valued in the various countries throughout the world?

How much is it valued and appreciated in the United Kingdom?

How much is it valued in Scotland where, in 1983, the total cost for forensic science was significantly less than the expenditure in one police force for petrol?

When authorities make decisions to curtail forensic scientific services or to limit these services to a fixed resource irrespective of increasing crime statistics, are they not at least morally obliged to intimate that to the public and more significantly to those responsible for the administration of justice? In a system which does not provide for a total forensic science service, the court of law cannot and must not expect it nevertheless.

In commenting on suggestions that the laws should be changed to redress an existing imbalance which was in favour of the accused, an eminent Scottish judge said "If an increased risk of convicting the innocent is the price of the greater prospect of convicting the guilty, then as far as I am concerned, it is a price which no sound and just system of law can seriously afford to pay". No one can argue with that, but if there is any facility which can better ensure that the innocent remain free and the guilty are convicted, society has a right to demand that it is used unreservedly. I submit that forensic science is such a facility, and that in any society which proclaims the importance of law and order and wishes justice to be seen to be done, the future for forensic science must be secure.

Acknowledgement

This article is based on a presentation made at the Tenth Meeting of the International Association of Forensic Sciences, held at Oxford, September 1984.

References

1. *Glasgow Herald*, 20 June 1984.
2. *Criminal Law Review* (Scotland) 1981, p. 785.
3. *Criminal Law Review* 1968, p. 240.

24(6) - 1985: Does Forensic Science Have a Future?

From   **Tennyson Harris**
The Manchester Analytical Laboratories, 15 Aytoun St., Manchester, United Kingdom MI 3DT (March 1985)

Sir: I read Dr Rodger's guest editorial [1] with a great deal of interest and found myself agreeing with many of his sentiments.

However, only the insentient reader would fail to realise the author's ignorance of some of the facts. He simply cannot resist the temptation to join the cohorts who follow the banner bearing the insignia "Independents out! They're in it for the money!" "Aut prodesse volunt aut delectare", they proclaim.

Of course, as in all professions, there are a few whose ethics are questionable, but one would have thought that to-day's courts were sufficiently aware of this.

I cannot speak for others, but as an independent scientist I have long been a protagonist in the fight towards a frank exchange of views and opinions between 'opposing' scientists before any evidence is heard.

Surely Dr Rodger does not wish us to return to the days of the unchallenged evidence of apotheosised Crown experts.

Dr Rodger replies: I was pleased to read the commentary by Tennyson Harris re my editorial, not only because he took the trouble to read it.

Since I certainly cannot claim omniscience, I was disappointed that he did not enlighten me as to those facts of which he considers me ignorant, as I do not doubt his credentials for so doing.

In answer to his basic 'banner bearing' criticism, I humbly refer him to the following statement which was included in my paper, and I quote:

> *"Certainly professional ethics and self-respect will normally operate to ensure that internecine exchanges do not occur between Crown and defence experts."*

Reference

1. Does forensic science have a future? *Journal of the Forensic Science Society* 1984; **24**: 543–551.

25(1) - 1985: But is it Anything?

(Guest Editorial)

WJ Tilstone

Forensic Science Centre, Diveh Place, Adelaide, South Australia 5000

Journal policy promises anonymity to writers of Editorials, but, on this occasion, your Editor chooses not to conceal the obvious. Readers of the "Preliminaries", as the un-numbered pages of the Journal are termed, will see that I have moved from a University post in the United Kingdom to an operational post in Australia, and what follows draws on my experiences in these two roles to address the question of the development of forensic science – perhaps supplementing the excellent Guest Editorial by Dr Rodger in the previous issue of the Journal [1].

"But is it Science" asked if forensic science had the right to call itself a branch of science [2], and this question was waiting to haunt me on arrival in Australia. In brief, Edward Charles Splatt was convicted of murder in 1978; the means leading to his identification as a suspect, and the bulk of the evidence at trial, could be described as "forensic (science)". As a result of media pressure, a Royal Commission was established to review the circumstances of his conviction, and the Commissioner, Mr C Shannon QC, reported in August 1984 that Mr Splatt should be set free [3]. Some of the evidence presented by the defence during the Royal Commission, and discussed in detail by Mr Shannon, dealt with whether or not there is such a thing as forensic science. Thus Badger said "It is important to recognize that forensic science is not a branch of science like physics, chemistry or botany. It is the application of science to forensic problems *just* as 'industrial science' is the application of science to industrial problems" [4]. This theme was adopted by the Royal Commissioner; he believed "To describe (someone) as a forensic scientist is *merely* to describe the milieu in which his professional activities are carried out" [5] (my italics in both quotations).

The way in which the brief of Amicus Curiae in People v Brown [6] held serological tests not to meet the Kelly–Frye standard, likewise was to the effect that there is no such thing as forensic science, and unless the techniques used in forensic serology – or any other area of this non-existent science – have been validated in the broader scientific community, they are to be held not acceptable. In particular, the Amicus brief objected to techniques being handed on from forensic scientist to forensic scientist. In other words, the inference is that that part of Frye stating "... the thing from which the inference is made must be sufficiently established to have gained general acceptance in the particular field in which the technique belongs" [7] does not include forensic science as an appropriate field, and reference has to be made to Badger's physics, chemistry or botany.

The question of whether the genus *science* has a species *forensic* has become not a fine academic point, invented – almost – to fill the editorial pages of a journal, but rather a serious matter, central to our day-to-day work.

Let us, therefore, explore the duties of this work and match them to the assertions that they are *just* like industrial science or *merely* characterized by the milieu. The operational industrial scientist, or food scientist (another analogy of Badger [4]) certainly shares with us a foundation of analysis. But it could be argued (without overdue application of tongue to cheek) that analysis is one of the foundations of all physical sciences; organic chemists analyze the products of their syntheses: botanists analyze the results of their hybrids – or even test their hypothesis of genetics – by analysis.

Closer examination reveals significant differences. The food scientist, for example, is working in a known environment, analyzing known materials to known standards; even developmental work consists of testing deviations from knowns. In contrast – stark contrast – every time a forensic scientist takes up a case, he is dealing with an unknown: what happened is unknown; what evidential materials, and how many, were created is unknown; how uniquely they can be characterized is unknown. Each case approaches the status of fundamental scientific experiment, and the very existence and meaning of the scientific evidence is a theory to be tested, perhaps, by the principles of Popper – no amount of testing will *prove* it but only one properly-designed experiment may disprove it [8]. The hypothesis of presence at the scene, for example, may carry the day if not disproved, but with a degree of confidence which reflects the adequacy of the testing and the scientific foundation of the putative association. (Herein lies a clue to the source of conflict between science and law and between prosecution and defence scientists, but that is an issue requiring separate consideration; for now, what is important is the realization of how closely forensic science casework approaches fundamental science.)

Returning to the "milieu" concept, if ever anything justified recognition for forensic science, then surely it is the unique and demanding environment within which it is practised. It is real-world science; it is science directly serving society; it is science where every single experiment is subject to testing by those who wrote the rules and who are expert testers; but, most of all, it is science which is unique in its immediacy. The witness stand is a lonely place; the individual scientist is marooned without computer, without support staff, without the option of "Well, that didn't work, let's repeat the experiment with a few modifications, so ...". Forensic science is not a world of simulations, of multi-million dollar research groups. Justice and liberty depend as much on the translation of the science to its milieu as on the quality of the science itself.

It is important that this translation of science to the milieu is recognized as a fundamental characteristic of the entity that *is* forensic science, and that such recognition is made within forensic science – no challenges based on Frye which hinge on failure to recognize that forensic science both exists and is the "appropriate field".

It is important, too, that that recognition is made by our partners, the law. Another Antipodean experience is Chamberlain, where the (majority) assertion of the High Court that the very existence of a defence scientist who honestly held opposing views to the prosecution forensic scientist is *in itself* sufficient cause to *establish* reasonable doubt over scientific evidence – let's not bother about trying to determine where the truth may lie. This decision is a lamentable act of judicial cowardice, allowing the defence to escape its obligation of truly testing the prosecution science, and the court to escape its duty of weighing the merits of each and the credibility of the witnesses. All that is required, it seems, is for the defence to dust off some more or less obscure academic (preferably a Professor) and persuade him to disagree with part of the scientific evidence; (it is emphasized that the object of concern is the principle of the High Court decision, and no comment whatsoever is being made regarding the facts, evidence or witnesses in any of the court hearings in Chamberlain).

The third factor concerning recognition of the significance and weight to be attached to forensic, as opposed to some other type of science, is that other scientists must be educated as to what forensic science is, so that they may understand it to be a worthy field of scientific endeavour. Here is probably the major weakness. The world, it sometimes seems, overflows with "instant experts", for example university chemists, ready to speak up and speak out [8] on forensic science, to belittle its very existence, to highlight shortcomings (at least as they see them) in any case presented to them. Academic pathologists and surgeons are not unknown contributors here.

More than a century has passed since Thoreau wrote

"It takes two to speak the truth, – one to speak, and another to hear"

and that is so of forensic science today as much. as it ever was for anything. Resolution of these difficulties requires that forensic scientists speak and others hear, but because forensic science is almost exclusively provided from government or quasi-government departments, then the ability to speak is restricted, as will be the willingness of others to hear. Some efforts have been made to redress the balance; for example, research papers from forensic science laboratories are published in the more general scientific literature in addition to specialist journals.

The health of forensic science needs more than that to sustain it. If forensic science is to be granted respect and recognition by our scientific peers, if it is to speak openly – and, indeed, provocatively, if a climate of hearing is to be created, then it is vital that forensic science has a meaningful presence in the universities of the world. It must not be left to operational laboratories and academics from other specialisms, however good they may be, otherwise there will be nothing for scientists, lawyers and society at large to behold and say "Forensic Science *is*."

References

1. Rodger WJ. Does Forensic Science Have a Future? *Journal of the Forensic Science Society* 1984; **24**: 543–551.
2. Anon. But is it Science. *Journal of the Forensic Science Society* 1982; **22**: 101.
3. Shannon CR. *Royal Commission Report Concerning the Conviction of Edward Charles Splatt*. DJ Woolman, Government Printer, South Australia, 1984.
4. Badger, G. In: *Royal Commission Report Concerning the Conviction of Edward Charles Splatt*, p 50. DJ Woolman, Government Printer, South Australia, 1984.
5. Shannon CR. In: *Royal Commission Report Concerning the Conviction of Edward Charles Splatt*, p 50. DJ Woolman, Government Printer, South Australia, 1984.
6. People of State of California v. Albert Greenwood Brown, Crim. No. 22501, Riverside County No CR-18014.
7. Frye v. United States, 293 Fed. 1013, 1014 (Ct. App: DC 1923).
8. Selinger B. Science in the Witness Box. *Chemistry in Australia* 1984; **51**: 201–206.

25(1) - 1985: But is it Anything?

(Commentary – Correspondence © Forensic Science Society 1985)

From   **B Selinger**
Department of Chemistry, Faculty of Science, The Australian National University,, GPO Box 4, Canberra, ACT 2601, Australia (April 1985)

Sir: Your editorial But is it Anything? (*JFSS* 1985; **25**: 1–4) answers itself in that style would appear to be more important than content. Far from being an "instant expert", as you describe, I was acting (in my lecture "Science in the Witness Box") as a chemical critic. Criticism is the basis of scientific progress, or have you forgotten? Your refusal to comment on the forensic evidence of the Chamberlain case (your speciality) but comment on the High Court judgement (not, of course, on the report of the one member of the bench who is a chemist) is most disappointing.

With so many editorials and articles on how forensic science should operate, methinks the profession doth protest too much.

The Editor replies: I was going to print Ben's letter without comment, but then I realized that would have been unfair to him ("criticism is the basis of scientific progress").

The Editorial was quite firm that "Justice and liberty depend as much on the translation of the science to its milieu as on the quality of the science itself". I am at a loss how anyone could regard that as "style being more important than content", especially when earlier reference was made to forensic science having a foundation of analysis. I am especially at a loss how such an accusation could be made when "Science in the Witness Box" advocated the teaching of the *evidential skills* (my emphasis) of the courtroom.

With regard to Chamberlain, one of the principal rules for the expert witness is "Stay within the bounds of your expertise". I have had considerable direct involvement in Splatt: one of my staff from Scotland was a witness at the Royal Commission, as were two of my staff from Adelaide; I attended some of the hearing; I am responsible for changing the shape of forensic science in South Australia to meet the criticisms of the Royal Commission; I have discussed the Royal Commissioner's report with him, with lawyers and scientists. In the case of Brown, I have read the brief prepared by *Amicus*, and the response; I have a direct knowledge of the significance of the content of the brief, both in my court-going experience and executively as Director of a laboratory. In contrast, the only direct knowledge I have of Chamberlain is the High Court judgement – and a judgement is a judgement, whether unanimous or majority. Mind you, Dr Selinger and five of his academic chemist colleagues were happy to sit in judgement on the workbook of the forensic biologist who presented evidence for the Crown in Chamberlain, so, by those standards, his criticism of my restraint is probably fair.

Finally, with so much media publicity over forensic science, it would surely be remiss of us not to debate openly how forensic science should operate – after all, that is precisely what Ben did in "Science in the Witness Box". Seems we'll be damned if we do and be damned if we don't. As far as "so many editorials and articles" goes, a search of the principal international forensic literature covering a twelve-month period turned up 5. By coincidence, a casual search of the Australian general literature for the same period also turned up 5 articles on the same subject (or 4, if we count Dr Selinger's double publication of "Science in the Witness Box"). But then none of these was by a forensic scientist, and that would probably make it acceptable to those who would deny the existence of forensic science.

25(5) - 1985: Towards Expert Experts

(Guest Editorial © Forensic Science Society 1985)

RN Totty
Home Office Forensic Science Laboratory, Priory House, Gooch Street North, Birmingham, United Kingdom B5 6QQ

In 1973 an editorial appeared in this journal from the pen of Julius Grant [1] entitled "Towards a New Profession". Dr Grant's thesis was that there was no qualification, either national or international, for forensic scientists and he proposed that "the Fellowship of the Society could be awarded to those who comply satisfactorily with an acceptable standard of ability, expertise, integrity and knowledge". In 1985 the same writer, whilst noting the achievements of the Society in its first 25 years, regretted that his suggestions for a "professional body of scientists and all that this involves, notably the setting up of standards of qualifications in order to raise standards of expertise and exclude the back door expert" had not been taken further [2].

In the intervening years, other calls [3, 4] had been made for a change in the Society's role from that of a society for those interested in the "study, applications and standing" of forensic science (as laid down in the Society's constitution) to that of a "professional body capable of setting levels of conduct and attainment" for forensic scientists [3]. Another writer [5] saw the difficulty in establishing "criteria upon which a court may with some confidence accept a witness as competent to give the evidence he proposes to give" and advised forensic scientists to define carefully criteria of expertise.

These views were not unrepresentative of the opinions of forensic scientists and the need to establish formal professional standards has been accepted by many. Progress towards the achievement of this aim has been slow in the United Kingdom. Not so elsewhere! The certification scheme for forensic scientists in the United States of America and Canada is now well established and regulating boards oversee the certification of the integrity and ability of forensic scientists in several specialised fields, notably Questioned Document Examination, Toxicology and Odontology.

Your Society has not been idle; consultations and discussions have taken place during the past six years and have at last borne fruit. On pages 385–386 of this issue of the journal the general regulations for the award of the Diploma of the Forensic Science Society are published. This Diploma will be granted to scientists who achieve a high level of competence in their chosen forensic discipline and who can show satisfactory standards of integrity and conduct. The examination of questioned documents is one of the oldest branches of forensic science, although knowledge of the techniques and methods used is not widespread even today [6]. Courts do not always question the credentials of handwriting experts as closely as they might and indeed in the absence, until now, of any formal qualification in this discipline, it is difficult to see, from the practical viewpoint, what a court can do except enquire as to the length of the witnesses' experience and the number of times testimony has already been given. It is therefore particularly appropriate that it is in this discipline that the first Diplomas will be granted and the regulations for the Diploma in Document Examination appear on page 387 of this issue.

This development heralds a radical change in your Society, a change which will without doubt enhance the standing of forensic science and which is not, therefore, inconsistent with the aims of the Society's founders. After 25 successful years as a forum for discussion, the Society is about to take a true step to maturity as a Professional Body responsible for the establishment and maintenance of standards of expertise. The Society is now a leading international organization in the field of forensic science; the fostering of forensic science as a profession in its own right is now, rightly, a responsibility that the Society has assumed. I have no doubt that the Society, with your support, will acquit itself with distinction at this task.

References

1. Grant J. Towards a new profession. *Journal of the Forensic Science Society* 1973; **13**: 1–3.
2. Grant J. Twenty-five years on. *Journal of the Forensic Science Society* 1984; **24**: 539–541.
3. Anon. The canons of expertise. *Journal of the Forensic Science Society* 1980; **20**: 71–72.
4. Lawton, Lord Justice. The limitations of expert scientific evidence. *Journal of the Forensic Science Society* 1980; **20**: 237–242.
5. Brownlie AR. I hold every man a debtor to his profession. *Journal of the Forensic Science Society* 1973; **13**: 155–156.
6. Anon. Watching, doing and the black arts. *Journal of the Forensic Science Society* 1984; **24**: 155–156.

26(2) - 1986: Doctrine, Science, Belief, Evidence

(Guest Editorial © Forensic Science Society 1986)

SS Kind

Forensic Science Services Ltd, 7 Beckwith Road, Harrogate, North Yorkshire, United Kingdom HG2 OBG

Abstract

A recent editorial suggested that this part of the Journal should be a vehicle for provocative pieces. The Guest Editorial which follows fills that role, and is also deserving of a place in the Journal because it was the Presidential Address at the International Association of Forensic Sciences meeting in Oxford. [The Editor]

*Journal of the Forensic Science Society 1986; **26**: 85–94 Received 19 December 1985*

I must confess to a love affair. Not one of the type that, were I a well known film actor, might provide interest to newspaper readers for a day or so, but a much longer-lasting adventure which has caused me much joy and misery, elation and depression. It is a love affair with words. Now this is comparatively unusual in a scientist because as you know we deal with facts, with matters that we consider objective or, at the very least, with matters which, if uncertain, possess an uncertainty of a precisely and numerically describable kind.

By contrast, our police and legal colleagues are often distinguished by the very qualitative and imprecise nature of their statements. At least that is roughly how I believe many scientists would describe the situation. But before too many of you realise the awful and yawning nature of the deep linguistic and semantic pits which I have dug for myself by my use of such words as "fact", "objective", "qualitative" and the like, let me hasten back to comparatively firm ground and embark upon a much more restricted endeavour. My only excuse for such lack of prudence in the first place is that I've listened to so many lawyers pleading their cases in court that sometimes I'm not so sure that words mean anything. This is not a sneer at the lawyers but rather an acknowledgement that we scientists tend to be naively arrogant in our use of words and that we are, sometimes deservedly, taken down a peg or two in the witness box, an act which sometimes makes us think a little more deeply about what we say and write.

With the progressive intrusion of the scientist into the fields of the investigator and the lawyer, more and more people are becoming aware that science can perform some very useful functions in areas hitherto considered as far away from their orthodox territories. At any given moment, throughout the world, we can be sure there are many forensic scientists busy advising police investigators, lawyers, courts and legislators, in fields where the scientist has specialist knowledge and where the recipient of the advice has specialist needs. What efforts are being made by individuals and institutions to see that these scientists, and this advice, is best fitted to requirements? After all, many citizens may consider their freedom and reputation, not to say their fortunes, to be of equal importance with their health, and few believe that substantial amounts of public money should not be spent upon health problems. It is a wide field and here I only wish to consider one part, of which, through training and experience, I have special knowledge. However, although it is only part of the problem, it is of general interest throughout the whole field of scientific advice in judicial affairs.

I have tried to crystallize my subject in the four words of the title of this lecture, "Doctrine, Science, Belief, Evidence". "Doctrine" comes from the Latin where it means "teaching" or "learning". "Science" similarly has Latin roots where it means "knowledge". "Belief" is a Middle English word meaning "trust" or "acceptance". "Evidence" is again a Latin word where it means "distinctness". One can see how the individual meanings of the words have drifted over the centuries. Yet the general idea one gets from a consideration of the original four meanings, taken together, is remarkably similar to that which the four modern equivalents generate in the mind.

But first the backdrop – what qualifications have I to give my views and to advise on changes, if any, which I think should be made in our system of use of expert evidence? You may think perhaps that thirty-two years as a government scientist is hardly a good qualification to deal with the matter. Yet I would reply that fifteen years as an operational forensic scientist followed by over fifteen years as a director of both research and operational laboratories is a good start. If one adds to this service, for almost a quarter of a century, as an officer of our main professional society in the United Kingdom, the Forensic Science Society, one can see rather better, perhaps, the origins of my rather broadly based interests in forensic science.

Let me start with the origins of quality assurance in the Home Office Forensic Science Service. The first quality assurance procedures (although the name itself came much later) stemmed from the early days of the Home Office Central Research Establishment in the late nineteen sixties. CRE, set up so ably by its first director Alan Curry, was a ferment of ideas, and from this ferment sprang the first systematically applied performance monitoring tests (for that is what our quality assurance is, even if we fight shy of the name) in the Home Office Forensic Science Service.

Our enthusiasm for performance monitoring, however, was not universally shared by our colleagues. A large proportion believed that such tests were an insult to "professional integrity". The strength of this belief is best demonstrated by the story told by a colleague of what happened to him when he left CRE in those early days to take up a position in a large operational laboratory. Being an enthusiastic supporter of performance monitoring tests he advocated such a procedure to one of his new associates, who became so incensed at the suggestion that he invited my colleague outside to clarify the issue.

Things have developed since then and the issue has been clarified although not in the way envisaged in the story. There is a battery of tests and safeguards which have been incorporated into the Home Office scientist's working day. The system now is so well accepted and so highly regarded that, far from being an object of resistance, some non-Home Office laboratories have been accepted into the system at their own request.

I watched with interest the system develop during my period as Director of the Home Office Forensic Science Laboratory in Newcastle on Tyne, between 1969 and 1976. My interest was perhaps tinged with a little pride, since had I not been one of the pioneers at the Central Research Establishment who fought against stiff opposition to get the ideas introduced in the first place? Thus when I returned to the Central Research Establishment in 1976, this time as Director, it was to apply myself enthusiastically to performance monitoring matters which, in my absence, had become a major part of CRE's commitment.

Great care was applied in the designing of tests, both declared and undeclared. In the declared test the operational scientist knew he was being tested and was required to despatch his report to CRE for checking. In the undeclared test, however, which was very much more difficult to organise effectively, the test was submitted to the laboratory in the form of a normal case. This was done by seeking the co-operation of police forces to provide the accompanying documentation and the required environment to make the scientist believe he was working on a genuine case. It didn't always work. Experienced forensic scientists have an instinct for the slightly out-of-place and in this, and sometimes in other ways, the cover was occasionally blown. However, the system seemed to work rather well, although the competing demands for time by casework and test work sometimes caused problems.

The system developed and, in 1979, a special "Quality Assurance Section" was set up at CRE to cope with the work of test preparation. Parallel with this, cross-checking methods were produced in the operational laboratories, which sought to minimise error and omission and to maximise accuracy. The working case notes of the examining scientist began to be annotated with the records that such cross-checks had been carried out. These annotations frequently took the form of the initials of colleagues. In those cases where a specialist instrumental method had been used, and where the instrument operator was not the examining scientist himself, the name of the operator appeared on the case notes. All these procedures were facilitated by written guidelines produced by a "Quality Assurance Group" and also by a number of "Interlaboratory Advisory Committees", which were set up by the Forensic Science Service to advise the Controller and laboratory directors on specialist matters.

Such was the position when I returned to operational work as the director of the Wetherby Forensic Science Laboratory in 1982. Six years absence had caused changes but not sufficient, on the surface at any rate, to render the laboratory working day unrecognisable. The laboratory was much bigger than the Newcastle laboratory (of which it was the successor), and there was the higher degree of that specialism which is the normal consequence of larger staffs. There was certainly a higher degree of emphasis on what was known as "corporate responsibility", and the distinction between the reporting scientist and his technical assistant had in some measure become blurred.

My first feelings of disquiet arose about the time I recollect becoming irritated on reading a case report prepared by one of my younger reporting scientists. The report addressed itself to the bare question asked by the investigating officer without including other available information which, although not asked for, might have provided the investigator with an additional dimension upon which to base his enquiries. I commented on this to the scientist's departmental head, to receive the following reply. *"Things have changed since last you directed an operational laboratory. Nowadays people, particularly the younger ones, are so afraid that the case they are working on may be an undeclared trial that they address themselves to the minimum question. In that way they feel they are less likely to make mistakes"*.

The lawyers, too, became conscious of our concern for cross-checking, accuracy and corporate responsibility and this, in turn, transmitted itself to the ways in which they presented cases in court. In 1983 the prosecuting counsel in one case from my laboratory insisted I send to Court anyone who had been associated in the laboratory with that particular case. That included anyone whose name or initials were on the case papers. This meant a total of eleven scientific witnesses to go to Court on the one case. Fortunately three of them had the good sense to be on leave and unavailable, but the rest did go to Court. Had we, in seeking to identify the incompetent and the charlatan, unwittingly nurtured a monster?

The final story I wish to tell you concerns a question I put to a colleague, a very able examining and reporting scientist who is eminent in his own specialism. "What would you do" I asked, "if you examined a case, and after you formed a definite view of the matter you consulted colleagues as a check and they disagreed with you? Consider, further, that you went back to check your results and you remained firmly convinced that you were right. What would you say in your report to the Court"? Well, of course, first of all he said 'I can't imagine it happening'. But I insisted, "what will you tell the Court if you hold the minority opinion"? He replied "In that case I would tell the Court I couldn't help them, because it would be arrogant of me to do otherwise". I don't propose to comment on that ladies and gentlemen, but just to leave it with you to think about. On the one hand we have corporate responsibility, and on the other hand individual responsibility. The corporation does not give evidence, the individual does.

So what do we expect of an expert witness? I suspect we expect a highly trained and experienced individual, competent in his field, who is allowed to work in an environment where he has full control of his analytical processes and whose report is, after as much consultation as necessary, entirely his own, independent of all personal, institutional or governmental pressure. A witness who, once qualified individually by the Court, is allowed to give his evidence to be freely contested by the other side, and where the evidence may be impugned, freely, by the advocates for either side or by the judge.

For myself I've no particular objection to my personal reputation being impugned by lawyers, it sometimes can happen. Mainly I found Court lawyers to be pretty courteous people but, in some of my cases, it has been suggested that my performance and my personality have perhaps been a little less that adequate. But never have I been personally impugned in the judgement itself. Should it ever happen? I'm not speaking about any particular case – I've no doubt there are several cases that you can think of where the judgement itself has contained a judgement of the personal competence of the expert witness.

Now the point is this, ladies and gentlemen, with the ordinary witness the Court has no opportunity to choose him. Circumstances thrust him into Court. He may be a liar, he may be a cheat, and it is perfectly open as I see it for either side, or the judge himself, to condemn the individual as a liar or a cheat, or an incompetent or whatever. But the lawyers should get their minds clear. The Court has the choice, in the matter of expert witnesses, of qualifying the witness in the first place. I would suggest, at least as a point for consideration, that it is inexcusable for any Court to qualify a witness as an expert and then in the judgement itself to condemn him as incompetent or a liar.

I emphasise I am not talking about what barristers and solicitors and advocates say generally about us experts, or indeed what the judges say about the evidence. What I am referring to is what appears in the judgement itself about the individual expert witness whom the Court has, of its own free will, qualified as an expert. I suggest that the time is right for the lawyers to get together with the still immature forensic science institutions, such as the Forensic Science Society, to produce a list of principles to which the lawyer and the scientist should attempt to adhere. These should relate to what constitutes the qualification of a scientist to give evidence in Court, what should be the nature of formal monitoring tests, and who should administer them? Should employers do it at all?

If one works in a factory which produces tins of baked beans or motorcars, it is highly likely that quality assurance procedures will be employed, and it is perfectly proper for employers to use them because it is the employers who will be legally liable if something goes wrong. In the case of the expert witness, however, the individual liable is the expert in the witness box, not any institution. Now I'm not, ladies and gentlemen, shooting at any institution or any individuals and I am not referring to certain notorious cases. I am simply trying to identify what are the features which should occupy the attention of both lawyers and scientists over the next few years. Is it justified in the long run, for the government of a democratic state to provide the only substantial non-medical scientific input to the Courts? Now note I say "in the long run". Only a fool would imagine that the sophisticated and established network of laboratories within the United Kingdom could have been set up so effectively without the taxpayers' money but, once set up, should they continue exclusively to operate in this way? Again I must say I'm an ex-Home Office Scientist, I was proud to belong to the best forensic science service in the world, but nevertheless there are problems. It may be that the current system, under practical circumstances, cannot be bettered. If so, let us leave it as it is, but there are issues which I think must be considered.

Now let's turn to the Police. Currently, in Britain, the police pay for the Forensic Science Service in the sense that, through various accounts, the money comes out of that voted by Parliament for police services. Should it continue to do so? Have the police received, and do they continue to receive, an adequate service? How do they believe the programme of laboratory amalgamations and relocations over the past seven years has affected the service they receive? Should the laboratory be accessible to the defence and to the private citizen? If so, on what terms? Should nonlaboratory scientific advice be available on the spot to police forces in, perhaps, the form of a police scientific adviser? What sort of animal should he be? You will recollect, those of you who listened to Sir Lawrence Byford's Plenary Lecture, that he talked about the recommendation in the Byford Review of the Yorkshire Ripper Investigation, of a "laboratory on two feet", as he called it. This is the local adviser, a scientist on the spot. I know that at least one Chief Constable has pleaded for this scheme to be tried out without any success. Might not the local availability of scientific advice increase the effectiveness and reduce the cost of the laboratory service to the police?

Next question – why don't we go for the mixed economy in forensic science, with the government releasing certain senior scientists who wish to take up private practice, and make initial grants or loans to start them off? Over the years several people who have worked for me have left and "gone private" as they say. The last one told me that in the first year, and this is the only reference I shall make to payment, he earned twice as much as in his last year's official salary. So from that point of view, for the able scientist, it could be very attractive. It would also probably solve some of the problems which the police experience resulting from the current remoteness of the laboratory to some police forces. I should remind you that Chief Constables have no qualms about employing private medical practitioners, be they police surgeons, university professors or pathologists. Why should the scientist be any different?

We all know, of course that Chief Constables are not averse to employing private scientists anyway, sometimes instead of, and sometimes in addition to, government scientists. In some cases this properly attracts criticism on the basis of the inexperience of the private scientist involved. Might we not then satisfy the demand of the Chief Constable, the desires of the government scientist who wishes to branch out on his own, and reduce costs at the same time? Of course, one criticism of this suggestion is that small practices could not afford complex or costly scientific apparatus. This is perfectly true. But my reply would be that more than 90% of cases do not require such apparatus, and, furthermore, it is available for use in many universities on a fee paying basis. There is undoubtedly, ladies and gentlemen, a steadily increasing demand for the private practitioner in forensic science.

Returning to the topic of sophisticated instrumentation, I believe that concentration on highly sophisticated instruments is the cause of some of our present problems. Large central laboratories are the only ones which can afford expensive instruments, but large central laboratories tend to be a long way from the scene-of-crime and the detective conference. What happens then is that the active enquiring mind of the scientist turns away from the routine examination of parcel contents to the wide academic scientific vistas opened up by the X-ray fluorescence spectrometer, or the organic mass spectrometer and so on. Thus he turns from the problem and focuses his attention on the method. Sometimes he rationalises this by taking the name of this new specialism and putting the word "forensic" before it.

Please don't mistake my views. Again I reiterate the British Forensic Science Service is the best in the world and I say that to an international audience. I am proud to have been a part of it for over thirty years. I think I can also justly claim, together with many of my colleagues in the audience here today, the credit for having produced some of the developments which has made it a centre of scientific excellence. "Why then", you may say, "should we in any way change a winning team, a winning strategy"? My answer lies in the view that we should not assume that things will continue to go well and indeed, as I have demonstrated, there are disturbing indications that something is seriously wrong.

Doctrine, Science, Belief, Evidence. For "Doctrine" we must have the teaching that our universities and laboratories so richly yield, not an inflexible framework of rules, guidelines and performance tests. For "Science" we must have the questing spirit for organised knowledge even if this is at variance with received views. For "Belief" we must have that in which we, personally, have confidence, and for "Evidence" we must have that which is distinct and thus useful. These are not the words of some revolutionary but of someone who distrusts change so much that he still insists that he lives in the ancient county of the West Riding of Yorkshire despite modern name changes. Furthermore, I have little confidence in committees and even less in politicians. Yet despite all this I feel the matter requires looking at, not only by the user professions, the law and police, but also by the ordinary citizen who should pay substantial heed to the individual forensic scientist. Note I say "individual", not the consensus or what any authority says the consensus is, but the view of the individual forensic scientist, the man or woman who turns out at any time, day or night, to visit what Professor Bernard Knight once called 'That Muddy Field', the individual who, often nameless to the public (because he's a Civil Servant), picks up the telephone and tells the investigating officer in a case of triple murder followed by rape of the sole survivor, "I think out of all the hundreds of suspects you've got you should concentrate on X" and X it proves to be. These are the assets of civilised society and though I speak largely in the context of the United Kingdom because I feel we are pre-eminent in the field, my remarks must also be taken in the context of mankind as a whole.

So I've been posing the problems to you. Can I suggest any way out of them? I can't suggest individual solutions, ladies and gentlemen, but what I can do perhaps is to recapitulate quickly the issues which I feel should be debated and decided upon.

1. What criteria can we adopt in performance monitoring to detect the charlatan and the incompetent while at the same time not paralysing the opinion-forming process?
2. Are the separate, but related, requirements of the courts and the police best served by a large and progressively more remote government institution or can some other system, or modification of the present system, serve better?
3. What criteria should be adopted to define the qualifications of the expert, given that the final act of qualification is in the witness box in the individual case and what must we do to ensure that the witness arrives there best qualified?
4. What functions should government, the universities, the academic societies and the forensic science professional institutions such as the Forensic Science Society, discharge?
5. Is "laboratory accreditation" necessary or may it detract from the prime requirement, the accreditation of the individual?
6. Is the adversarial trial the best place for the first disclosure of scientific evidence, or will this lead to the increasing frequency of what has been called by one legal lecturer here 'trial by ambush'?
7. Should there be pre-trial consultation between the scientist and the advocate in the scientific context?

    I should say, digressing for a moment, ladies and gentlemen, that in all the cases in which I've given evidence I can count the times when I've been involved in a pre-trial consultation on the fingers of two hands.

8. Once accepted as an expert in a trial by the Court, is it ever justified to include in the judgement any ruling or observation on the character of the expert himself, as distinct from any judgement of the quality of his evidence?
9. Finally can we possibly accept with equanimity the situation in this country in forensic pathology, where we can anticipate a 50% loss of experts in forensic medicine over the next 5 years?

So we have all these substantial problems to solve and they are all related to each other. What can we do? I cannot possibly suggest in detail anything which would be applicable to each of the sixty-odd countries represented here at this meeting, but I can suggest one way in which the problems might be broached. When a governmental problem becomes of such a magnitude that it requires looking at fairly from all points of view, what we tend to do in the United Kingdom is to set up – well it's a committee I suppose, but it goes under a very very nice name, a "Royal Commission". I suggest ladies and gentlemen that the time has come to set up a Royal Commission on Expert Evidence – to examine the problem in all its features.

Thank you very much for listening to me.

Acknowledgements

This paper is an edited and slightly expanded version of the Presidential Plenary Address given at the Tenth Triennial Meeting of the International Association of Forensic Sciences, Oxford, England, Monday 24 September 1984.

26(4) - 1986: The Forensic Science Society – A Way Forward?

(Guest Editorial © Forensic Science Society 1986)

B Caddy
Forensic Science Unit, University of Strathclyde, 204 George Street, Glasgow, United Kingdom G1 1XW

Historical Perspective

The Forensic Science Society was founded 26 years ago by a group of enthusiastic scientists, medics, lawyers, police officers and academics with the aim of furthering the interests of all those involved in forensic work. The Constitution of the Society states that its role is "to advance the Study and Application of Forensic Science and to facilitate co-operation amongst persons interested in Forensic Science".

How have the aims of the Society been pursued? Until recent times the main emphasis has been placed in two areas, that of organising two conferences each year and that of producing a Journal. While distant planning may not have been all what it should, in general, the conferences have been well supported and the journal, after a period in the doldrums, now seems to be in good shape although there is still a mistaken belief amongst some that publication time is exceptionally long. In the area of publication there have also been single volumes produced which have shown reasonable success.

To what extent have members of the Society participated in these activities? In general, those participating in conferences tend to be of the upper echelons of their profession, and there is always a large core of the same people present at each conference. There are few who attend who have had only one or two year's contact with the forensic sciences. To some extent the same may be said of authors, particularly from the UK, who submit to the journal. Statistics to support this view would perhaps be more convincing but they are unavailable to the author; from these observations it would seem that the Society may be in danger of becoming a cosy select club which, from time to time, has contact with others in the public domain (e.g., the crime writers). The only new gem in the Society crown is the Diplomas of the Society (see later).

What has been the effect of our policies on the total membership of the Society and on the public image of Forensic Science and how do we compare with such bodies as the General Medical Council, The Law Societies, the Royal Society of Chemistry?

I would suggest that our policies have had little effect on the majority of ordinary members of the Society, especially the younger members, and virtually no impact upon non-members. The public at large is unaware of our existence except on those very few instances when a spokesman, associated with the Society, has been asked to express an opinion on a particularly contentious scientific-legal matter.

Although the forensic sciences have a superficially glamorous image in society, the public, as well as many lawyers, do not distinguish between Forensic Science and Medicine. In the light of recent cases the media have portrayed the Forensic Scientists as incompetents and that is now a belief held by some, perhaps many, sections of our society and this requires to be redressed. The inconsequential nature of our Society and its activities are perhaps best reflected in the general lack of consultation with the Society by our legislators and persons in positions of power and influence.

By comparison with the august bodies representing the medical and legal professions and the chemists, our Society fares badly. There are several reasons for this. These Societies are statutory bodies, membership of which is essential for the practice of that particular profession. The Royal Society of Chemistry is slightly different in that University degrees enable the practice of Chemistry. These Societies represent professions and offer advice to their members in terms of conditions of employment and their general welfare etc. Most such societies have a code of practice and are responsible for maintaining the standard of performance of their members to the extent that they can impose disciplinary measures. Such societies are routinely consulted by legislators and people in positions of power and authority. Why, for example, was the Royal Society of Chemistry in recent times (1980), asked to report to the Home Secretary on the Forensic Science Service in England and Wales when no approach was made to the Forensic Science Society? Why are there no members of the Forensic Science Society on the recent 5-member review panel of forensic science services? Who better to judge a forensic science service than forensic scientists?

What is the State of Forensic Science today? Whilst the rest of the world continues to expand its services and invest in personnel and equipment, the UK continues to contract. The service is underfinanced especially in terms of salaries, witnesses are attacked in Court and the turnover in staff has begun to accelerate especially for the more able scientists. What role has the Forensic Science Society played in counteracting this decline – none! From what was, perhaps the best forensic science service in the world, the UK system is rapidly becoming second best. These are some of the problems. What are the solutions?

The Way Forward?

A good public image must be sustained. One way to achieve this is for a small group of the Society, perhaps a lawyer, a scientist, a medic, and an investigating officer, to be made responsible for surveying media reports of cases in which contentious decisions have been taken and any proposed new legislation. Such surveys should then be assessed professionally and pronouncements made via the media – for example, some decisions under the RTA.

Another important means of promoting the Society is to build up a Parliamentary Lobby. How often has this Society invited MPs or Ministers to address its members? I would suggest that this should be a regular commitment. How often has the Society expressed its views on proposed legislation to MPs and Ministers without being directly approached? Rarely, if at all!

The Society should become the Watchdog of the Forensic Sciences especially in terms of the professionalism of witness. It must not be afraid to speak out against incompetence and should maintain a record of such problems.

The new venture of the Society into means of accreditation is the beginning of this process and we should strive to become the statutory body for ratifying forensic scientists by a rapid expansion in this area.

The Society must also speak for its members in terms of their conditions of employment, and should act as a channel through which dissatisfaction in the forensic sciences, in all its forms, can be conveyed to appropriate authorities from employers through to ministers and Members of Parliament.

Since most of the above proposals refer to forensic scientists as compared with the other sections of our society, most of whom are represented by a statutory body (GMC, Law Society etc.), then a liaison committee of the Society should be established to coordinate our relationship with these organisations.

Promotion of the professional image must be associated with scholarship and it is suggested that two ways of promoting this would be to offer scholarships in Forensic Science (cf, Canadian Forensic Science Society). The Society should also become the fulcrum of Forensic Science literature and the establishment of a Forensic Library is one way of assuring this.

Finally, the international image of the Society must be enhanced. For this reason it is important that overseas members and non-members are encouraged to participate in our accreditation schemes. This would be further stimulated by a much more regular participation/representation, in the name of the Society, at international conferences. Furthermore the Society should organise conferences in other countries through its local representatives.

The implementation of what has preceded would require, initially, the employment of a young scientifically qualified Society Manager possessing all the drive that such a course(s) of action will require.

Many will disagree with these views but if this editorial brings about some discussion and action then it will have served its purpose.

The Editor adds: This Editorial, written by Dr Brian Caddy, was presented as a paper to the Council of the Society. Council are keen that Society members have the earliest opportunity to read it, digest it, react to it, and maybe even write letters about it. The whole question it addresses is obviously very controversial and the paper fits well into the concept of Editorials which was recently espoused in these columns (*Journal of the Forensic Science Society* 1985; **25**: 405).

26(5) - 1986: All Systems Go?

(Editorial © Forensic Science Society 1986)

On Editorials [1] suggested one reason for having an editorial in a learned journal might be to stimulate discussion on controversial subjects. That bold exhortation had hardly been put to bed when Stuart Kind's IAFS Presidential address found its way into the Journal office. Such a manuscript probably warranted publishing in its own right, because of the fact of its status. However, it proved to be so full of controversy, on and between the lines, that it was published as a Guest Editorial [2].

Almost everyone will find something objectionable in it; many will see it as a breath of fresh air, and a welcome re-assertion of the significance of the individual Expert Witness. Whatever one's own stance, it undoubtedly challenges the direction in which forensic science is going today, and it is up to the proponents of modern practices to reply. That is precisely the purpose of the present Editorial, which wishes to address one of the many areas which attracted Presidential displeasure, that of laboratory, and individual, accreditation.

Webster defines accredit and accredited: "to put trust in" and "accepted as valid or credible", a theme developed in the Introduction of The American Society of Crime Laboratory Directors Laboratory Accreditation Manual, wherein the proposals are described as "... a ... program which a crime laboratory may elect in order to demonstrate that its management, operations, personnel, procedures and instruments, physical plant and security, and personnel safety procedures meet certain standards. The accreditation process is one form of quality assurance program, which may be combined with proficiency testing, continuing education, and other programs to help the laboratory strive to give better overall service to the criminal justice system". We now have a concept of laboratory accreditation being a concern that the system has regard for its people – their safety, their training, their performance – so that the users of forensic science may have confidence in the service delivered.

There are many issues buried in this simple, reassuring, view of the system. It explains almost all that has gone wrong with forensic science in recent times. Too many of us have forgotten (if we ever were aware) that forensic science is a service, and that modern concepts of excellence based on a genuine customer-orientation [3] apply just as much here as in any other service or industry. The "In Search of Excellence" philosophy also emphasises that people are an organisation's most important asset, and that leads to consideration of the argument implicit in "Doctrine, Science, Belief, Evidence" that there is some conflict between the organisation, exercising its corporate responsibility, and the individual, who has a personal responsibility for the scientific examination and the testimony based upon it.

Preposterous! Certainly the Courts must and will retain the right to qualify individuals as Experts, but forensic science services are provided from organisations, whether they be a conglomerate like the English Home Office Forensic Science Service, or a single-handed operation of the type recently described by Joy Kuhl [4]. It is the inescapable duty of these organisations to develop systems which will provide the best service, taking account of their particular circumstances. If the systems so developed espouse the principles of accreditation outlined above, then the individual forensic scientist is aided and protected. It is adoption of the principles that is important; after all, wouldn't all of us prefer to work in laboratories with stated objectives of "To improve the quality of laboratory services provided to the criminal justice system" and "To develop and maintain criteria which can be used by a laboratory to assess its level of performance and strengthen its operation"? Society certainly would regard these and other accreditation objectives [5] favourably.

References

1. Anonymous. On editorials. *Journal of the Forensic Science Society* 1985; **25**: 405.
2. Kind SS. Doctrine, science, belief, evidence. *Journal of the Forensic Science Society* 1986; **26**: 85–93.
3. Peters TJ and Waterman RH. *In Search of Excellence*. Sydney: Harper and Row, 1984.
4. Kuhl J. *The forensic scientist in isolation*. Proceedings of the Ninth Australian International Symposium on the Forensic Sciences, Melbourne, February 1986.
5. American Society of Crime Laboratory Directors, Laboratory Accreditation Board, Accreditation Manual, February 1985.

27(2) - 1987: Police Productivity

(Editorial © Forensic Science Society 1987)

The paper by Kemp and Fischer, which appears on page 89 of this issue, makes comment on the changes seen within police forces in America, due to financial constraints. In many ways, these same changes and the measures being adopted to cater for them are now a feature of policing in Britain.

"Creative and innovative management practices" are essential for the police to function effectively against this background, but often measures taken are, of necessity, compromise measures which limit the damage caused by cutbacks rather than improve the service provided to the public.

Back to basics. British police forces have long been aware of the need for economy. This has been emphasised by central government in recent years in police circulars on Manpower, Effectiveness and Efficiency, and has accelerated a trend back to the "basics" of policing. This trend has been evident in the movement of police officers back to operational roles and also in the attempt to increase their availability for operational duties at a time when increased expectations are made of police.

Vehicle replacement programmes and the development of computers and other new technology have suffered from financial constraints with growing implications on the effectiveness of forces.

Shared resources. In the development of technology, forces in Britain share a pooled experience through the offices of the Police Requirements Support Unit and Scientific Research and Development Branch. Although there are practical difficulties in ensuring that information is up-to-date and comprehensive, these agencies allow much early ground work in areas of development to be carried out more efficiently. Major crime is a useful example of an area in which computer equipment has been made available by one force to another to the greater benefit of the Service. Also, regional technical support units exist in some areas, providing a pool of technical equipment.

Patrol scheduling. This aspect has been looked at by a number of forces and is still the subject of research in others. The freedom to alter shift patterns has been restricted with recent changes in regulations but efforts continue to be made to obtain greater flexibility. This has been achieved in some areas, notably Devon and Cornwall, where 63 different shift patterns exist to cater for local needs and seasonal fluctuations.

Job-related training. Training is given at various stages to Constable, Sergeant and Inspector ranks both centrally and in-force. Beyond this level, training is focussed on Superintendent level with Command Courses at the Scottish Police College and the Police Staff College at Bramshill. Training in specialist areas such as Communications, Crime Prevention, Major Enquiries and Female and Child Care is also provided, and the use of videos and new technology in many forces has made more use of limited manpower and increased the flexibility of training.

Participative management. This form of management has been used for some time in many forces. The formation of Project Teams and Working Parties allows senior officers to make decisions on major areas of development based on a clear presentation of facts. At a time when resources are concentrated more and more in operational areas, however, it can be difficult to find the staffing commitment required of such efforts.

Use of micro computers. Micros bring the benefits of computers to users without the large costs incorporated in minis or mainframes. However, there will continue to be a range of solutions to computing needs and not all will be met by micros. Micros, because of their comparatively limited power, tend to be less "user-friendly" than machines with greater processing capabilities, but, more and more, they can be seen as a means of providing the advantages of computers at limited cost.

Managing calls for service. Prioritisation or graded response to calls for service has been undertaken either informally at busy periods or formally in forces for a number of years. While clearly the police attend calls for assistance from members of the public which in a strict sense are not their responsibility, and while at times, such as severe winters, for example, police officers become auxiliary plumbers, it could not be envisaged that such requests would ever be flatly refused. The opportunities for the police to be seen in a helpful and caring role are sometimes in certain areas regrettably few but can give the police the chance to be seen as a caring service and not always as a reactive force. Any supposed benefits in the diversion of such requests to other agencies can be outweighed by the loss of the contact enjoyed at present in non-enforcement situations and which assists the continued co-operation of the public.

Alternative methods of reporting incidents. Much research is currently being carried out into ways in which the police officer's time can be more effectively spent. The Home Office-backed consortium of police officers assisting West Midlands Police in increasing the operational availability of police officers, the development of administrative support units in West Mercia and the widespread drive towards civilianisation are all attempts at achieving this.

Criminal case investigation. This system already operates in most forces with enquiries being delegated back to uniform officers to continue any enquiry not requiring CID involvement. The immediate filing of reports in circumstances where the complainer has been seen, where local enquiry has been made by the officer attending initially, and where nothing further is to be gained by another visit to the complainer, is obviously to be desired, but less clear-cut are the advantages of "screening" of crimes to any greater degree. This depends largely on the ability of the officer to take the initial report to the full satisfaction of the complainer or aggrieved person.

Peace Officer standards and training services. In some forces there has been a reluctance to allow "outside" bodies to examine force structures too closely. Recently, consultants were used in the Scottish Criminal Record Office computerisation project, and the area of computerisation, particularly in England, has seen other examples of the use of consultants. This is an area where there can be some cost-justification of such an approach although the Service remains guarded in its view of such agencies, particularly in this time of financial constraint.

The idea put forward in the paper by Kemp and Fischer suggests agencies within State Authorities with the expertise available to assist police forces. Such a scheme is not available in the United Kingdom other than, perhaps local authority computer expertise, and it is difficult to envisage how this could be achieved other than through the offices of the Police Requirements Support Unit, Scientific Research and Development Branch, or the National Training Institutions.

Commercial crime watch. Such an approach has been utilised in a number of British forces for a number of years under Early Warning systems whereby information regarding shoplifters, suspicious persons, counterfeit currency and missing children can quickly be passed to commercial premises within mainly town centres. An Association for the Prevention of Thefts from Shops is particularly active in England to assist in such schemes.

Crisis assistance teams. All supervisors within the Service are actively encouraged to take an interest in officers under their control and give help if required. If further assistance is required, reference is often made to a force Welfare Officer and, if necessary, the force Medical Officer, who provide professional assistance. Some work has been done in relation to counselling for officers with alcohol-related problems and Welfare Officers are daily involved in bereavement, financial and marital counselling.

Police chaplain programme. Force chaplains exist and will give help if asked. Organisations such as the Christian Police Association are also active within forces.

Spousal information programme. Problems are usually dealt with by Welfare Officers as they arise. It is difficult to imagine some of the suggestions made and doubtful if they would have any value. Further involvement of spouses is more likely to cause problems.

Management ride-along programme. The opportunity already exists for operational management to be seen "at the line level" on a regular basis. For police administrative personnel, a healthy policy of "job rotation" should ensure that awareness can be kept at a high level and that they are not too remote from operational developments. Perhaps, with greater civilianisation of senior administrative duties, a need might emerge for a greater understanding by them of operational duties.

Conclusion

Kemp and Fischer have provided an interesting insight, albeit in a rather simplistic form, into strategies adopted by the American law enforcement services to achieve greater cost effectiveness in a period of severe financial restraint. The issues they describe have parallels within the British Police Service and may be common to policing world-wide.

Reference

1. Kemp RL and Fischer HA. More on police productivity: beyond cutback to creativity. *Journal of the Forensic Science Society* 1987; **27**: 89–92.

29(1) - 1989: Professional Qualifications – a Milestone

(Editorial)

In many of the well-established disciplines such as chemistry, physics, biochemistry and the various branches of biology, e.g., botany and zoology, there are indicators of professional knowledge and competence in the form of academic qualifications, such as degrees granted by universities or diplomas issued as the result of examination by professional societies, of which the Institute of Biology and the Royal Society of Chemistry are two well-known examples. These qualifications can be put forward in court as strong factors in establishing the status of the holder as that of an expert.

The Council of the Forensic Science Society became concerned some years ago about training and related matters in forensic science and set up in 1975 an Educational Committee to examine the situation. Progress was slow until 1981 when Dr Brian Caddy submitted a report to the Council entitled "Professional awards in forensic science – reasons for the establishment of professional awards". This was accepted and the Educational Committee was reconstituted as the Professional Awards Committee (PAC) with the remit of implementing whatever was appropriate in the Caddy Report. The PAC at the outset decided to concentrate on those areas of forensic expertise not covered by educational qualifications. For example, there are no formal courses leading to a degree in document examination. The objective would be for the Society to remedy this by setting up its own professional qualifications in these subjects. Thus we did not intend to follow the example of some of our North American colleagues who apparently aimed at establishing a more general type of "forensic scientist" qualification. This we felt covered too many areas of expertise to make an examination process at all possible. Moreover, departures from professional standards where qualifications already existed, e.g., chemistry or biology, could be dealt with by the Ethics Committee of the society concerned.

Document examination seemed to be an obvious starting area but it was first necessary to draw up general conditions for the award of any Diploma offered by the Society. These were approved by the Council and were published in the Journal in 1985 [1] together with requirements for the Diploma in Document Examination [2], the latter having been reached by consultation with leading document examiners. A panel of examiners was set up and since then several examinations have taken place, with the names of successful candidates being published in the Journal.

During this period it became evident from correspondence with some potential candidates that an addition to Section 5 of the Diploma regulations was necessary to take account of research contributions in the field.

This was published in 1987 [3], but did not affect the status of previous examinees. The PAC has since been dealing with other areas of expertise with the result that regulations for a Diploma in Firearms Examination have been approved by the Council and published in the Journal [4] and satisfactory progress is being made towards a similar Diploma for the Examination of Scenes of Crime.

The Kelly–Frye case in the United States [5] aroused considerable controversy on the grounds that the techniques used by the forensic scientists had been validated only by other forensic scientists and not by independent academic experts. Similar considerations obviously apply to the Diplomas which the Society is offering, though in this instance we are dealing with the standard of the examinations. Fortunately in the United Kingdom there is an organisation which is concerned with academic standards, the Council for National Academic Awards (CNAA).

The CNAA was set up by Royal Charter in 1964 with its objective being "the advancement of education, learning, knowledge and the arts by means of the grant of academic awards and distinctions". It is autonomous and is the largest single degree-awarding body in the United Kingdom. The PAC has carried out discussions with the CNAA with the outcome that the CNAA would recognise the Society's diplomas as they came into being and scrutinize the examination results from the candidates. This is a major step forward and the text of the agreement appears elsewhere in this issue of the Journal.

In the first instance it applies to the Diploma in Document Examination. The Board of Examiners mentioned in Section 6 of the Agreement with the CNAA has been set up with the following members:

> B Caddy   R Radley
> DM Ellen   RN Totty
> J Grant   RL Williams

It is important to note that Diploma candidates from the UK can also register with the CNAA for their Postgraduate Diploma and the award of this will depend upon the scrutiny by the CNAA of the examination results mentioned above. The CNAA Diploma will list *those areas in which the diplomate has satisfied the examiners*. There are also good prospects that the grant of the CNAA Diploma will eventually be available to persons from overseas. The CNAA Diploma is applicable to those who have a degree *or its equivalent* and the importance in forensic work of a sound basic scientific training cannot be overemphasized. However, the CNAA are prepared to interpret the term "equivalent" sympathetically and would consider each application on its merits, e.g., a satisfactory length of experience in the expertise could be a valid "equivalent". This view will obviously have a considerable bearing on the Firearms and Scenes of Crime Diplomas.

Candidates interested in being considered for the CNAA Diploma have to register 12 months before sitting the examination, but this is less onerous than it might seem since it takes the Society about this time to set up the examinations.

It would be remiss in ending this editorial not to record the debt which is owed to the many members of the sub-committees who have contributed to the setting up of the Diplomas and especially to Dr Brian Caddy who as secretary of the PAC has carried the burden of the major part of the work.

RL Williams, Chairman PAC

References

1. Diplomas in professional subjects. *Journal of the Forensic Science Society* 1985; **25**: 385–386.
2. Diploma in document examination. *Journal of the Forensic Science Society* 1985; **25**: 387.
3. Amendment to Diploma Regulations. *Journal of the Forensic Science Society* 1987; **27**: 372.
4. Regulations for the Diploma in Firearms Examination. *Journal of the Forensic Science Society* 1988; **28**: 71.
5. *People v Kelly* (1976) 17 Cal 3d 24; and *Frye v United States* (DC Cir 1923) 54 US App DC 46, [293 Fed 1013].

30(5) - 1990: Brave New World

(Editorial)

The Home Office Forensic Science Service (HOFSS) with its six operational laboratories and a Central Research and Support Establishment (CRSE) has for many years since the second world war provided a sophisticated and comprehensive forensic science service to police forces and the courts of law outside the London Metropolitan area in England and Wales. The Service is funded through the Police Support Services vote; police forces pay on a per capita basis (ie, based on the number of police officers in the force), so that the cost is shared between the Home Office and local police authorities through the Common Police Services arrangements. However, following the recommendations of a Home Affairs Committee Report on the Forensic Science Service published in 1989 [1, 2], all the funding as described will change. The HOFSS is moving towards executive agency status in April 1991 when each police force will face direct charging on items when they submit them to the laboratory for scientific examination.

However, as a study of the Report reveals, not everyone was enthusiastic about the idea. The dissenters included some members of the Committee itself and the Association of Chief Police Officers (ACPO).

An amendment tabled by Mr Tony Worthington MP urged the Committee to reject the whole concept of direct charging to the police on a piece-work basis and amongst the reasons cited he thought (it) "would discourage police forces from using forensic science services on a speculative basis at the start of an investigation". Mr Worthington rejected "the unexamined assertion that an effective mechanism for regulating the demand and supply of a service is for the customer to pay the supplier for the amount of the service used". He went on "This is not a fact but a value judgement" [1, p XXXVII]. The amendment was defeated by two votes to one (the Committee had a quorum of three). The memorandum to the Committee from the ACPO said it was their view that a change in funding would be counterproductive. Further they added "There are enough problems in the minds of investigating officers without adding the question 'Can I afford to send this to the laboratory?'" [2, p 227]. The ACPO's concerns have been more publicly reported in a Sunday newspaper [3].

Executive agency status means, in effect, that the HOFSS will have to compete in "the market place" to provide a forensic science service to the police and in due course become financially independent of the Home Office. In a leader article in the September 1990 issue of the Forensic Science Service's magazine "The Lab", the author candidly acknowledges that the "new" FSS faces an uphill task; "Moving to a financial position where the Service is recovering its full costs means that, overall, police authorities will be paying more than at present for forensic science. It is therefore vital that the FSS convinces the police that the charge for services is good value for money". Behind such views there lies also the recognition that the winds of competition may be keen. Police forces, who in turn are trying to cut costs, may decide to use the services of other analytical laboratories in the commercial sector, or even the nearest hospital laboratory, should they prove cheaper. The dangers of insufficient income generation from the police to maintain the present levels of staff and equipment are obvious.

As befits the leader of any group in which a radical change in philosophy is necessary, the Director General of the HOFSS, Dr Janet Thompson, is maintaining an "up-beat" and optimistic attitude as she briskly introduces changes which will turn senior scientists into salesmen and businessmen, with an eye directed as keenly towards the financial balance sheet as the mass spectrophotometer or electron microscope.

The new FSS comes into being with an impressive dowry from the old HOFSS. Apart from highly skilled staff with long experience and modern sophisticated equipment, it has a high reputation both at home and abroad. The change-over to executive agency status next April will, in the first place, of necessity be directed towards ensuring that the police forces of England and Wales are given priority and are well served. Nevertheless, even now, potential new customers should be sought. The skills of the staff could, for example, be directed towards undertaking work on a contract basis for industry. In particular, however, the international market should be considered.

The FSS should not only step up its training of overseas staff at its training centre in Birmingham, but also consider marketing study packs on particular topics as is done so successfully by the Open University. Overseas access to the data banks held by CRSE should be encouraged. Quality Assurance (QA) kits, method manuals, specialised reagents and even the offer of analytical services to customers abroad, should not be overlooked. The sale of British expertise abroad has a long history as a buttress to the home economy.

For some Home Office forensic scientists, however, brought up in the best traditions and ideals of the British Civil Service (yes – there are still some civil servants who view it as a privilege to be part of a long tradition of public service), the change to a "market economy" will not be easy.

We wish the new FSS well.

PH Whitehead

References

1. Home Affairs Committee First Report, The Forensic Science Service, Volume I. London: Her Majesty's Stationery Office, 1989.
2. Home Affairs Committee First Report, The Forensic Science Service, Volume 11. London: Her Majesty's Stationery Office, 1989.
3. *The Independent on Sunday*, 21 October 1990.

31(2) - 1991: "Come forth into the light of things, Let Nature be your teacher" [1]

(Editorial)

Starrs has asserted that there are dangers in forensic scientists being in possession of circumstantial information when they begin work on a case, the basis of his concern being that it will introduce an unconscious bias [2]. This view has been supported by Neufeld (see discussion reported in reference [3]). There can be few things more difficult to deal with than unconscious bias. By definition, we don't know when it arises in ourselves, and it could be very hard to spot in others. It must surely be prevalent in an adversarial justice system. Witnesses are all called on the instructions of one side or the other. Some may be visibly partisan. Lawyers handling the most serious criminal matters are regularly exposed to the hidden pressures of the circumstances of the offence and the people involved – victim and accused.

They are also subjected to the hidden pressure of winning – they are the only overtly partisan players and have to deal with the emotional and career pressures of success in the gladiatorial conflict. The system recognises many of the potential pitfalls, and has developed many procedural checks and balances. Rules on leading questions and on Identity Parade conduct are two of the more obvious examples. The legal profession exercises strict ethical codes, the transgression of which can lead to withdrawal of recognition.

The forensic sciences should be outside of most of these pressures. The overwhelming bulk of cases which withstand the regular testing of scientific evidence by examination and cross-examination would support that contention. We would all like to be as good as possible, and should not hide behind that bulk when challenged by the unconscious bias assertion. Let us therefore examine it in more detail. The issue as presented is that knowledge of the circumstances surrounding the offence, and especially the kind of information which often comes with the police request, will induce an unconscious bias which will lead to erroneous results or conclusions. There has also been a suggestion that laboratories working from within a police department will be more likely to experience these problems.

An understanding of the philosophy and methods of science reveals something quite different. The planning and design of scientific experiments demands awareness of all previous knowledge that may impact on the experiment and the formulation of the precise hypothesis to be tested (the null-hypothesis). Without that knowledge, the experimental design may be deficient – some aspect may be missed or defective – it may be quite simply wrong. Unconscious bias has been known to scientists for centuries.

It comes into play not in the design but in the conduct of the experiment. Many processes have been developed to help, but most are variations on the theme of "blind" reading of results. That is, the person who reads the results is not aware of the experimental source of the sample giving rise to those results. There are techniques to help us when the code is broken and the significance of the results is assessed. Our experimentalist colleagues have an array of statistical techniques to test their results against those predicted from the experimental null-hypothesis. All of us are bound by the convention that any conclusion presented on the basis of scientific experiment must provide the data along with the conclusion so that our peers can judge for themselves.

How do the forensic sciences measure up to these standards? There is no good reason to limit the background information presented. At worst the forensic scientist should be regarded as no different from any of the other people involved. At best, the information will assist in making sure the right tests are done in the right way and on the right materials.

The issue of unconscious bias in reading the test results and their interpretation is covered by good laboratory practices, such as those laid down by the American Society of Crime Laboratory Directors (ASCLD) in their laboratory accreditation program. The widespread use of automation, the independent reading of results by two observers, and case file audits all safeguard against that unwitting subjectivity which we all wish to avoid. Ironically, so does the almost overwhelming burden of the workload that nearly all laboratories face. The acceptance by laboratories that it is part of the humdrum process of the justice system (in those places which have an adversarial system) to test minutely the strength of the evidence, is also a strong safeguard. This is the forensic expression of that part of the scientific method which requires presentation of the data on which conclusions are drawn. Viewed in this light, matters such as Castro [4] are illustrations of the strength of the forensic science system.

Concerns about the placement of forensic science laboratories within police departments are also questionable in this context. Cases can indeed be mounted for not placing laboratories in police departments, but they are not based on unconscious bias. The author would argue that the values which must hold in a forensic science laboratory must be scientific values; these values can be achieved in a police laboratory, but they are different from police values and how readily they are achieved will depend on many things. In some circumstances it may be easier outside of the police, but there are many exemplary laboratories which are police laboratories. I would also argue that the main reason for locating forensic science laboratories outside of police departments is the simple one that policing is only one part of the justice system, and it is better to have one laboratory serving the whole system, providing the same standards and access to all parties.

I have tried to set out a refutation of the "unconscious bias" concern by considering the way that science works and by referring to best laboratory practice, such as is needed by the ASCLD accreditation process. I would like to end the article with an expression of quite conscious bias. I have worked in academic and operational posts in the forensic sciences, and have worked on the instructions of police, public prosecutor, civilian agencies, and defence. I have seldom felt pressured by overt or covert "guidance".

There have been few extreme instances – perhaps three. All were from the defence.

WJ Tilstone

References

1. Wordsworth W. *The tables turned*.
2. Starrs JE. The forensic scientist and the open mind. *Journal of the Forensic Science Society* 1991; **31**: 111–149.
3. Henderson Garcia C. Plenary discussion, 12th Meeting of the International Association of Forensic Sciences. *Journal of the Forensic Science Society* 1991; **31**: 163–166.
4. Lander ES. DNA fingerprinting on trial. *Nature* 1991; **339**: 501.

31(4) - 1991: Forensic Science on the Quality Track

(Editorial)

During my four years as Editor, forensic science has been forced on the public consciousness through more newspaper stories, magazine features and radio and television programmes than ever before. In my early days as a forensic scientist, I used to explain to enquirers that my job involved "looking at clues with microscopes and things to help find out what happened in a crime". Nowadays, such an explanation is not required; the response to the "I'm a forensic scientist" prompt is usually "What about the forensic evidence in the so-and-so case?" Sadly, this change in awareness had been brought about by the previously-unthinkable association of official forensic science with miscarriage of justice. Lawyers, police officers, parliamentarians and scientists are now all too aware that criminal proceedings can go badly wrong if sensible questions are not asked, and careful answers given, at the right time.

Calls for greater accountability, for a detachment from police interests and even for training to include a social science perspective [1], have been made. With the Royal Commission on Criminal Justice looming, managers, in an official forensic science service already committed to financial change and a broader "customer base", have turned their attention to quality management. Accreditation is likely to play a key role in the new strategy, seeking to assure minimum levels of competence among practitioners and introduce documented, minimum standards for procedures.

Scientists need to be concerned with quality, no more so than in that peculiar hotch-potch of analytical sciences that has come to be known as forensic science. Few would dispute that our citizens have the right to expect uniformly high quality from a public service. Fine, but an individual will generate true quality from within [2], not as a result of external pressure to conform to "quality" standards. A conscious fostering of professional pride, commitment, experience and enquiring minds must go hand-in-hand with formal accreditation. Otherwise, quality in forensic science will be like a veneer, having more to do with keeping up appearances than the pursuit of excellence.

Roger J Davis

References

1. Price, Christopher. Forensic science needs open minds. *New Scientist*, 20 July 1991.
2. Pirsig, Robert M. *Zen and the art of motorcycle maintenance*. London: Corgi Books, 1976.

32(2) - 1992: But is this Being Professional?

(Editorial)

In many countries throughout the world, especially those possessing sophisticated laboratory resources, and particularly those which operate under an adversarial legal system, the role of the forensic scientist, medical practitioner, policeman and lawyer working in the legal process is being questioned. Why has this apparently growing disbelief in the legal process occurred? Why is the public perception of the courts, the judges and professional witnesses, one of cynicism, with a chariness towards accepting their decisions which would remove many antisocial members of our society to a "safe place"? Undoubtedly, in the United Kingdom this has been brought about through a number of recent criminal cases which have been reviewed, on more than one occasion, by the Appeal Courts. These have demonstrated clear weaknesses in the processing of criminal cases, from the scenes of the crimes to the courts of law, and the decisions made by these courts and their associated appeal systems. The cornerstone of any legal system of criminal justice must be the professionalism of its professionals, and society needs to be reassured that the professionals are up to the standards it has grown to expect, and that such standards will be maintained once they are reached. The answer to such questions lies in accreditation, a process which, external to any particular organization, tests that organization and the people who work within it.

Over many years, forensic science laboratories have subjected their activities to quality assurance programs using both declared tests, in which individual scientists know that they are being assessed for their experimental expertise, and undeclared tests, in which "exhibits" submitted as a case are processed through the laboratory. This latter is a much more searching exercise since it tests the laboratory system as well as individual expertise. Should the results of such tests be in the public domain? If the public are to be reassured as to the expertise of forensic science laboratories, perhaps they should. Undoubtedly such proposals would alienate some scientists who believe that such a decision would lead the legal profession to misrepresent any quality assurance figures to the courts. But is this being professional?

There are at least two schemes of laboratory accreditation being implemented in operational forensic science laboratories, those of the American Society of Crime Laboratory Directors, and the National Measurement and Accreditation Service (NAMAS). These systems have the merit of being independent of the organizations being accredited, and independent inspectors are appointed. Such schemes require full details of the analytical processes being employed by the practising forensic scientists to be written down, and adhered to.

What of personal accreditation? How good are the forensic scientists who work in these laboratories? Recruitment to most forensic science laboratories requires a good university degree in an appropriate discipline. Many forensic science organizations also run internal training programmes, some more than others, until the scientist is considered of a standard to present evidence to the courts, a de facto self-accreditation. But how are the courts to judge? Those forensic scientists who are in private practice are unlikely to have a programme of training and will probably not work in an accredited laboratory. Is the defence being supported by second-best science and are the courts aware of this?

If the answer to any of these questions is in the affirmative, one solution could be the establishment of a statutory body with whom all forensic scientists must be registered. Such a body should be independent of governments and official laboratories and should function as a disciplinary board, guided by rules established through an ethics committee. Perhaps it should monitor the performance of its members on a 5-year cycle. Could the Forensic Science Society be such a body for the United Kingdom?

Forensic scientists are well on the way to putting their house in order but what of others involved in the legal process? It should be remembered that it was the professionalism of forensic scientists which highlighted those criminal cases which had led to miscarriages of justice. Where are the accreditation schemes for the medical profession, for policemen, for lawyers, not forgetting judges? Are their working practices being continually monitored by an external organization? What steps are being taken on a 5-yearly basis to determine if their standards as practitioners are being maintained?

32(4) - 1992: Can We Help You, Sir?

(Editorial)

"Service – work done to meet some general need; ready to obey orders or be used; what employee or subordinate or vassal is bound to; work done on behalf of employer; provision of what is necessary for due maintenance of thing or operation."

These are just some of the ways in which the Oxford English Dictionary chooses to define "service". To all those involved in the forensic sciences, the word "service" is central to their existence; it is their *raison d'être*. They provide a forensic science service – or do they? The central feature of any good service is that it meets the need of the employer of that service – in their case, the judicial system. This does not mean police forces, or government departments, or legal representatives, or judges, or victims, or defendants, but all these interdependent groups as one integrated body.

How far does any service meet the needs of its judicial system? Is it true that financial restraints imposed upon police forces mean that only a selection of exhibits out of a much larger number, in a case, are presented to a forensic science laboratory for examination? The implications of this may not be fully understood by the judicial system in terms of the interpretation of any analytical results for the courts. Are forensic science laboratories overburdened with work to the extent that policemen are discouraged from submitting exhibits because of the time required for processing? Such delays can result in long periods of remand for prisoners or even the release of dangerous criminals on bail. What reasons are there for any delay in processing cases? Do they arise from insufficient staffing levels or the wrong use of staff already employed? Are these staff inadequately provided for in terms of equipment, training and state of morale to "provide what is necessary for due maintenance of [the] operation?" Is the recipient able to exploit the service to the maximum benefit of the judicial process? Why do the legal profession, policemen and forensic scientists find it so difficult to communicate in terms that each can understand, to maximize the impact of the services they each give to the legal process?

Can a service only be provided through a business-structured organization driven by the profit motive, or are there some services which a society must have, irrespective of cost, because they form an essential part of the foundations of that structured and complex society? I would maintain that any judicial system is the rock upon which its society will develop or founder. It is a measure of our state of civilization. Do we wish to leave it in the hands of businessmen? May those who are responsible for those services, especially the forensic sciences, have the courage to face up to, and the vision to overcome, those who would emasculate the legal process for an unsustainable creed.

33(3) - 1993: Is this Where the Buck Stops?

(Editorial)

The question as to who is ultimately responsible for the quality of forensic science offered by the public and private sector laboratories to the courts is one that has been the subject of much thought throughout the profession. This particular question has been brought into focus in the United Kingdom by the report of the recent Royal Commission on Criminal Justice for England and Wales, under Lord Runciman [1]. One of the major recommendations of this committee was the establishment of a new Forensic Science Advisory Council, whose role would be to monitor "the performance and standards of police in-house laboratories, large public sector laboratories and firms and experts in the private sector". By so doing, it is presumed that the public will become assured of the excellence of forensic science, and the service which it offers to the criminal justice system. But will this be the case?

The report gives no guidance as to the membership of such a body, and its ability to carry out its function. There is no cognizance of the fact that more than 90% of forensic scientists belong to aligned public sector laboratories. Is it from these that the 'few' will be chosen, or is forensic science to be submitted to a panel of faceless bureaucrats whose views change with the wind of political expediency and Treasury pressure? If the former, is this not a case of self-accreditation? If the latter, who understands the science? An alternative would be to make use of the independence of academics, or 'industrial' scientists, these latter much beloved by free marketeers as having to accommodate and withstand the rigours of the market place. Are there sufficient academics with enough knowledge of forensic science, who can be tempted from their esoteric researches? Is knowledge of the cut and thrust of the industrial market place sufficient reason for the appointment of industrial scientists? Are we perhaps to expect that some of their number will be made up by parliamentarians.

Very few of these have the slightest knowledge of scientific matters, although it is certainly true that many have the legal knowledge. What are the criteria for such appointments to be? Perhaps a new type of person, a "regulatory scientist" is required, with a knowledge of the sciences and how they interact with legal systems?

If such an Advisory Council comes into existence, what will be its powers of enforcement? Is there a danger that such a council will usurp the roles of the courts in dictating whom they will, and will not, accept as expert witnesses? What happens if a private forensic science company refuses to agree to the requirements of the Advisory Council, maybe for perfectly sound commercial reasons. Will that company be prevented, directly or indirectly, from giving evidence as an expert witness on behalf of a defendant? Clearly the powers of such a committee should be those of its title-advisory. Any "enforcement" of whatever it proposes or suggests should be by dint of sound scientifically-based argument. No one could quarrel with the idea of developing forensic science qualifications and training programmes for expert witnesses. Still less could arguments be made against accredited laboratory procedures. It is not what is to be done, but the means by which it is to be done and the finances available to do it, which may give cause for concern. One has little confidence in a report which polarizes forensic scientists, as evidenced by the statement "experts who give evidence must do so on behalf of either the prosecution or the defence and not on behalf of the court". Can such a body give the correct guidelines to the establishment of a ruling body for forensic science?

Reference

1. The Royal Commission on Criminal Justice. Cm2263. London: HMSO, 1993.

34(1) - 1994: An Expert What?

(Editorial)

"Someone trained by practice, skilful, a person having special skill or knowledge" – so the Oxford Dictionary defines an expert. What is interesting about this definition is the emphasis placed upon skill, almost to also the exclusion of knowledge. Moreover, there is an implication that such skills are attained by practice. What has such a definition to say about the forensic scientist as an expert?

Traditionally, forensic scientists have been recruited with an academic qualification, thought suited to the particular post. Such qualifications were, and perhaps still are, considered a measure of the potential of a candidate and an indication of the level of the knowledge base. Few would accept that such recruits, at this stage of their career, show the necessary skills to practise as a forensic scientist and expert. How then does this transition occur? The commonest way has been for a candidate to work alongside an experienced practitioner, a kind of apprenticeship scheme. This continues until the employee's organisation is satisfied, usually on the recommendation of the experienced practitioner, that the individual has obtained the required skills and, perhaps, the knowledge base. The problem with such a system is that the practices inherited by the recruit will be bad as well as good. Moreover, organisations by their very nature tend to develop within their structure a particular ethos. This in turn generates a mind set which can sometimes lead to a reduction in lateral thinking, always considered essential for the good practice of forensic science. What is required is a national, if not an international, set of criteria against which all forensic experts can be judged. Such criteria must be established independently of any single organisation.

For the United Kingdom, such criteria are being identified under the auspices of the National Council for Vocational Qualifications and the Scottish Vocational and Educational Council. These are national bodies independent of any forensic science organisations, although the initiative for this development was orchestrated by the Forensic Science Service (FSS), a government agency operating under the Home Office. The FSS is to be congratulated on such an initiative. Although the scheme is in its infancy and restricted to a small number of defined areas, this must be seen as an important way forward. The scheme places emphasis not only on the identification of skills in the work place, but also on the presence of a suitable knowledge base. Such a scheme will require reaccreditation after a given period of practice, and no longer will accreditation for life be accepted. It is interesting that such a scheme has much in common with the Diplomas of the Forensic Science Society. It is good to think that the Society has again been leading the way for the profession.

For those requiring further details, Keith Hadley's article on National Vocational Qualifications, on page 5 of this issue, should be informative.

34(2) - 1994: Quo Vadis?

There can be nobody working within the forensic science sector who does not have some view on the role of a forensic scientist. The word "forensic" comes forensic from the same source as the word "forum", one of whose meanings is a public place of debate where the protagonists of different views surrounding a particular philosophical point might argue their respective stances without let or hindrance. This would suggest that the forensic scientist is at the centre of debate.

This debate has traditionally been in the law courts (another meaning of the word forum) where, in the adversarial legal system, the forensic scientist's evidence is tested, using question and answer, by the side representing that aspect of the argument for which he/she has not been called.

However, in recent times the forensic scientist has been at the centre of another debate, connected, quite by chance, with other translations of the word "forum", ie, the market and business. Part of this debate has been directed at the quality of the work of the forensic scientist, referred to in an earlier editorial [1], but in these times of economic stringencies a much wider debate has ensued, centred around the question of who should pay for forensic science. The forensic scientist is now truly entering the market place. The role of forensic science is to provide an impartial and comprehensive scientific support for the courts to reach a decision, beyond reasonable doubt, as to the guilt or innocence of a person charged with an offence. It is important, therefore, for the forensic science community and the public to ask whether the market place is the best environment in which forensic science should operate.

There is little doubt that, in the main, business thrives on competition. To be able to produce a better article or service and at lower cost than its competitors is the driving force behind a company's success. But how do firms achieve this? There are a number of factors which make for success and efficiency in business, including the use of automated procedures which reduce labour costs and human error; the refusal to take on work which cannot produce a profit; the setting of quality standards which will mean that customers will wish to buy; a rapid sales response time; a happy and contented workforce able to find satisfaction in the work they do and proud of the product they produce; a commitment to research and development which will keep the company ahead of its competitors. It is pertinent to ask how the sciences fit into this pattern and especially how the services provided for the defence conform.

Certainly only the larger "public sector" laboratories have sufficient flexibility to invest heavily in automation but this investment can only occur if the customer is prepared to pay for services at the appropriate level. Can this part of the criminal justice system refuse to take on analyses because they are not cost effective? Is this what society wishes, that someone may be convicted because some analyses are not performed?

Quality standards are central to the successful pursuit of forensic science and a great deal of effort is being made to look at standard procedures and the accreditation of personnel. The small independent workers are unlikely to be able to conform to these standards because of cost, and these people are usually the ones on whom the defence is most dependent. Does this mean that the "independents" will be "squeezed out" as would happen in industry, or should some mechanism be sought to bring them up to standard?

A rapid response time may mean that a forensic science laboratory is performing all the necessary work in a highly efficient manner or it can mean that only a very minimum number of tests are being performed. Is this what justice demands?

Are the work forces in forensic science laboratories inspired and working to their maximum capacity or are they disillusioned? Research and development during times of stringency are usually the areas industry has traditionally cut back. Does this apply to the forensic sciences? Because DNA presently has centre stage, does this mean that other areas are neglected?

Could it be that there are some things, in society, for which we must pay, whatever the cost, if we are to be identified as democratic and civilized?

Reference

1. Editorial. An expert what? *Journal of the Forensic Science Society* 1994; **34** (1): 3.

35(1) - 1995: Does Forensic Science Give Value for Money?

(Editorial)

(This editorial is based on a paper presented by the Chief Constable of the West Mercia Constabulary to the joint meeting of the California Association of Criminalists and the Forensic Science Society at Pasadena, California, USA, 19–22 October 1994).

About ten years ago, I interviewed a very senior police officer for a project I was doing on a Police Staff College course. He had not the slightest idea of the size of the budget of the area for which he was responsible. He was a police officer, not an accountant, and budgets were things for other people to worry about.

Those days have long gone. The concept of effectiveness, efficiency and economy – "the three 'Es'" in the Home Office Circular 114183 – was the first gust of the wind of change sweeping through the public sector to be felt in the corridors of police management. The wind has grown much stronger since, with assistance from the Audit Commission and with encouragement from examples in the National Health Service and in education, and, indeed, wherever one looks in the public and private sector.

The main ingredients of the changes are to do with value for money, with slimmed-down management and with proper devolvement of responsibility and of finance to operational units. My own force of 2000 police officers and 1000 civilians has lost nearly half of its 40 superintendent ranks in the last two years. Those remaining have more responsibility and much more understanding of, and say in, their budgets?

I monitor their performance by setting standards of operation for the force and then collecting and comparing their results. This is a loose/tight arrangement; most matters are loose – I allow them to get on and respond to local conditions, but the standards set for the force are tight and I watch the performance indicators relating to those standards very carefully.

This follows on up to Government level. The Home Secretary has set key objectives for all Chief Constables and Police Authorities for 1994/1995:

to maintain, and if possible, increase the number of detections for violent crimes: to increase the number of detections for burglaries of people's homes; to target and prevent crimes which are a particular local problem in partnership with the public and other local agencies; to provide high visibility policing so as to reassure the public; to respond promptly to emergency calls from the public.

I am to be measured, set in league tables and publicly assessed by my performance against those objectives. I am developing a Policing Plan to be agreed with my new Police Authority which will set out those objectives, local objectives and priorities and give costs of police activities. How much does patrolling cost? How much do the dog section, or traffic, or school visits cost? And, what choices have to be made given increasing demands and, at best, static budgets.

Chief Officers have to set priorities and in policing that is hard because we have always seen ourselves as a service, not a business. We like to have time for the old lady or small child, even if time is scarce and other demands are pressing, and even if it does not improve our position in the league table.

The requirement to be aware of key objectives, to produce policing plans and to cost police activities and functions is intended to do two things. First, it should ensure that everything we do in a force should be integrated and directed towards our stated objectives. Secondly, it should produce the evidence for choices between activities and functions if resources do not allow everything to be done.

None of this is revolutionary and I have made it sound more simple than it is. We have always prioritized and made choices, but increasingly it is much more on the basis of hard information and out in the open. Thus policing will become even more political and controversial. Resource allocation decisions are now made openly rather than secretly, by senior rather than junior officers, and resources are becoming tighter. Another dimension is that Chief Constables now have more control over their budgets and decision making is administratively easier.

You will not have failed to appreciate where this leaves forensic science. To continue to be one of the items in the Policing Plan, rather that one of those taken out, forensic science must contribute to its key objectives and give value for money in competition with other functions which might also contribute to the Policing Plan.

Quite simply, I have to be sure that forensic science is a better use of the £2.4m of my £96m budget than spending it on informants, computers, more police officers, horses, dogs or helicopters. Is it?

Of the £2.4m of my budget spent on forensic science, £1.1m goes to fingerprints and photography and £1.3m to forensic science; of the £1.3m going to forensic science, half of that is my Forensic Science Service (FSS) budget and the other half is staff time on non-fingerprint work.

Now, £1.3m per annum would buy me a very big helicopter every year, or 70 extra police constables for the beat, and that is what the public demands. I have never yet had a politician or member of the public say to me, "Chief, what we need is a bigger forensic science budget". Let us assume that fingerprints and photography do give value for money – and I do assume that, not wishing to make any more enemies. That is not to say that there could not be efficiencies and savings. I remain ashamed that it took the Audit Commission, a set of accountants, to point out to Chief Constables some years ago that it was time to sort themselves out in the management of fingerprints. There are new fingerprint technologies and equipment coming along to improve efficiency which we must adopt.

Does forensic science, excluding fingerprints, give value for money? We need to look at the recent history of the FSS, the biggest provider by far of forensic science to UK forces outside the Metropolitan Police. The Service rightly enjoys a high reputation for integrity, quality of work and for its research and development programme. As a government department it stood more exposed than any police force, and the same winds of political and management change which affected the police service have been at work on the FSS.

In the Rayner Report of the early 1980s – the first breath of the wind of change – it was recommended that although there could and should be efficiencies and economies, there should be no change in the status of the FSS as a common police services-funded government department. Seven years later, the management consultants Touche Ross, and then the Home Office Affairs Select Committee, took the opposite view and considered that the only way to deal with rising crime and therefore submissions to the FSS – given a static FSS staff – was to introduce market forces. The potential problems of this flavour of the decade approach were recognized, viz., fragmentation and loss of research capabilities through cherry picking, operational decisions being made on financial grounds and so on, but the market concept swept over any such objections.

In 1991 the FSS became an agency. It must now recover its costs by direct charging – it has to show value for money. In the words of Janet Thompson, Director of the FSS, "The first three years as an Agency with a hard charging regime has resulted in changes in customer behaviour, which have required the adoption of new management procedures and disciplines in the Forensic Science Service". (Annual Report of

FSS, 1993). That is precisely why the change to agency status was advocated. The aim was to change customer behaviour and also to sharpen up, where needed, the practices of the FSS. Those aims have progressed and have produced the debate we are now engaged upon. Having focused the mind of customers on cost and continuing to improve internal practices, value for money considerations automatically appear. I have much respect for the FSS; it has come through a baptism of fire in the first three years as an agency and is the better for it. The quality is high and turn-round times are improved. There may be alternative providers of forensic science presently and in the future. The market forces concept expects that to happen and welcomes it, but however the market develops, Chief Constables are still left with the decisions to make on the allocation of resources, and they will make them on the basis of key objectives and policy plans.

In 1993, in my force, I spent £707,968 to help solve 90 burglaries through useful physical trace evidence. Every burglary/dwelling case cost nearly £10,000 and every burglary/other case something over £6,000 for forensic science. Those costs included Scenes of Crime Officers' time and FSS charges. By contrast, the total cost to identify 510 burglars by fingerprint was £541,706; every burglary/dwelling fingerprint identification cost £1,151 and burglary/other £983. So, fingerprints give much better value for money than physical trace evidence and they are a sole identifier, not just something "useful", the definition of which varies from person to person and between groups of people.

To be fair, it is true that there is a high return of usefulness on those cases of physical evidence which are submitted. In a Kent/FSS project in 1993, 23,000 burglary scenes were visited, which resulted in a total of 791 fingerprint identifications (3.5%) and 119 submissions of physical evidence to the FSS (0.5%). Of these submissions, 76% were subjectively assessed as being useful or very useful in the content of the case. However, I am at a loss to know whether these figures (and there are similar ones from Crownhill in Devon and elsewhere), are good or not in terms of value for money. A 76% return of usefulness is impressive, but 76% of a little is even less than a little. Could it be 76% of something by better awareness and training of police officers and Scenes of Crime Officers (SOCOs)? And if it were 76% of something, could I afford to submit enough to make an impact on volume crime?

With regard to violent crime, physical trace evidence resulted in conclusive or strong evidence to link suspect to offence in 30 assault cases and 14 sexual offences in West Mercia in 1993, again a very small proportion of the total number of such cases. Only 5% of recorded crime is violent, although, of course, the more serious the violent crime, the greater the import of forensic science, partly because of the likely incidence of bodily fluids and also because of the amount of time which can be spent at the scene and in the laboratory. I do not dismiss the major contribution of forensic science to those high profile cases which concern the police and horrify the public.

Earlier I posed two tests for forensic science, namely that it should contribute to key objectives and likely policing plans, and that it should compare, in terms of value for money, with other policing functions in the realization of the policing plan. My contention is that in burglary and in car crime – the volume crime which plagues the police and infuriates the public-forensic science plays no significant part. In this important, publicly-identified prominent area, forensic science is not presently giving value for money. It contributes little to the policing plans against volume crime now being produced.

The second question is more difficult. Of course, more police officers would help in visible policing, in response times and possibly in crime reduction and detection. I say possibly, but I think that 25 police constables in a burglary squad would solve me more than 90 burglaries a year. The £707,968 I spent on burglaries and forensic science last year would buy me 38 extra police constables, and the Head of my Criminal Investigation Department would drool at the thought of £700,000 more in his informants' fund and promise me more than 90 burglaries cleared up on the strength of it.

So, do I pull the plug on forensic science, at least for burglaries and car crime, as some forces apparently have done and others might be contemplating? I hope not.

I recognize that forensic science work is interdependent; we must think hard before cutting the budget so drastically and expecting our laboratories to continue to do the excellent work on serious crime and in research that the FSS does. Also, the whole thrust of investigations as expressed by the Royal Commission and by the Audit Commission in 'Tackling Crime Effectively' is to more, not less, reliance on intelligence work, surveillance and forensic science work, all suitably integrated. I readily admit that my somewhat simplistic presentations of figures and costs is not yet nearly as sophisticated as it should be. I am not setting out to prove conclusively that spending money on more "coppers, cars or computers", and not on forensic science for burglary, would give better value for money. The evidence is still being gathered and in this respect the work of the joint FSS/Association of Chief Police Officers study now being conducted is very important. This work is looking at the forensic science environment, the way costs should be set and also how best forensic science can be used by the police, particularly in volume crimes. Much of the likely emphasis is going to be on improvements which the police themselves can make. We do need to be more forensic science aware, better at screening and selecting, ever more professional in scene examining and preserving, and much better at integrating forensic intelligence with crime patterns and other information. The proposed cost structure will, in my view, help us to make value for money choices – how many fibre examinations will be called for if the full amount is charged to a force in the future?

Previous work on value for money questions in forensic science is now inconclusive. The Ramsay Report of 1987 was pre-agency and pre-policing plans, and needs to be reassessed. Work on a comprehensive assessment of cost effectiveness across the whole criminal justice system was not available to the Home Affairs Select Committee on Forensic Science in 1989 and has still not been conducted.

We need a process for Investigating Officers to assess costs and needs and probabilities supported by central submissions offices. It has been suggested that a Bayesian approach would help to assess the probabilities. As I had some difficulty in understanding that theory at university myself, I hesitate to pronounce too strongly, but we need something to help police officers operate on rather more than just experience and hunch.

The current theme in policing is partnership and that needs to be continued and progressed during and after the joint study to find better applications of forensic science. More and more forces are considering or conducting Bumblebee type operations, which are intelligence-led police initiatives to target burglars rather than the crime and bring about an increase in the detection of dwelling house burglaries. These initiatives are likely to progress into permanent operations. My force is examining, with the FSS, what can be done to mark uniquely suspects or vulnerable property. We are looking at how central indices for crime scene shoemarks and prisoner shoemarks can best be established. We are also examining the potential for searching all burglary suspect's clothing for trace evidence – treating him as a crime scene.

This is a re-evaluation of the relationship between FSS and a police force. Suspect clothing could be submitted. The FSS would identify what trace evidence was present, e.g., glass or paint; the police would then submit those possible matches taken from thorough scene examination and gatherings of control samples.

All of these initiatives, and I am sure you will have more and that more will develop, will require new awareness, effort and training by both the police and the forensic science provider. But I believe that with assistance to investigating officers to judge probabilities and likely value for money they show us the way forward.

And then there is DNA. Any thoughts about moving away from forensic science are quickly removed by the potential of DNA to solve many crimes, including burglary. The pioneering work done by the FSS enables a database to be created; the law will soon allow samples to be taken and within a few years, given good will and proper financing, we will have another sole identifier to sit beside fingerprints. The prospect is exciting and will re-emphasize the importance of forensic science as an investigative tool. We lead the world in this and need to ensure that we continue to do so.

The police and the FSS and other providers have changed over the last decade. We all keep books and look at the figures in ways which would not have occurred to us then. Some people bemoan the need to do so, but it is inevitable and with scarce public money it is right. We can see the writing on the wall and are seeking to change awareness and methods towards finding more cost-effectiveness. The future is exciting and forensic science is firmly a part of it; it has the real capacity to provide the police with an unequivocal value for money service.

DC Blakey QPM MBA
West Mercia Constabulary
Hindlip Hall, Hindlip
Worcester WR3 8SP

35(3) - 1995: Renascor

(Editorial)

Few would disagree with the premise that forensic science is at its most effective when there is close co-operation between the forensic science laboratory, its scientists and the investigator – the police officer.

For many years there has been a debate as to whether the forensic science laboratory should be an integral part of police forces. Some have argued that such an arrangement prejudices the role of the forensic scientist, but this view was countered by Lord Cameron of Lochbroom in his Firth Memorial Lecture when he said "Independence comes from professional integrity and not from financial independence". This fact was reflected in the international standing of the largest police forensic science laboratory in the United Kingdom – the Metropolitan Police Forensic Science Laboratory, usually affectionately referred to as the Met Lab. This was an organization developed, tested and honed by men of scientific vision and insight such as LC Nickolls (Nick), Hamish Walls and Ray Williams, and maintained by the present director, Brian Sheard. It became a world focus for all that was excellent in forensic science. Its research and development teams were of the best and its insight into the handling of casework second to none.

Because of this reputation the Met Lab is consulted far and wide by the agencies of foreign governments and its international voice is listened to with respect by many from overseas laboratories and organizations. As a result of this standing, morale has been high, research teams active, and its staff well respected in the courts by all branches of the legal profession. Few would have predicted ten years ago the change in status this outstanding forensic science laboratory is now undergoing, even when it became apparent that government dogma was determined to expose forensic science to market forces. The Metropolitan Police Forensic Science Laboratory was the only competition for the Government's forensic leviathan, the Forensic Science Service, in terms of equipment, scientific personnel and breadth of service. But where is competition now? Like all commercial companies who face opposition, the alternatives for the Forensic Science Service were to capitulate, to offer fierce competition, or to buy out the opposition. As the much larger of the two organizations, the latter was its chosen course of action. Although it is clearly politically inexpedient to say so, and it will always be publicly denied and presented as a merger, this is nevertheless a take-over, the full consequences of which have yet to be realised. One does wonder if this was always the Government's hidden agenda! It is interesting to speculate that if a similar development had occurred in the manufacturing industries, whether such a merger would have been referred to the Monopolies Commission. This is as may be, but what of the future of this outstanding laboratory? Clearly its organization will change; it will become more commercially orientated and it will have to look to new horizons. Science, no matter how excellent, is no longer enough. Shall we, within the months ahead, be hearing the jubilant cry – "we are reborn" – renascor?

Or will some other cry be more apposite?

35(4) - 1995: Lest We Forget

(Editorial)

Much has been said about Forensic Science entering the market place. Its pros and cons have been hotly debated. but this recent development only applies to the criminal law. Forensic practitioners who operate within the civil law have long been in the market place. where the outcome of any legal decision may have enormous implications for the survival of companies, or the loss of employment for many hundreds and sometimes thousands of people. In fact, the repercussions for society of civil litigation centred on analytical work probably far exceeds the impact of any criminal forensic investigation.

Those involved in civil work must maintain the same rules as do those in criminal law in terms of preservation of items, exposure to contamination and the establishment of the continuity of evidence, etc. Moreover. those involved in civil litigation must offer a far wider spectrum of specialities, from medical misdemeanours to aeronautical engineers looking for design faults, and analytical chemists analysing illicit perfumes and adulterated cosmetics. Such lists of experts are inexhaustible.

Forensic scientists operating within the criminal law may be able to learn much from those in the civil law. Whilst the burden of proof is not the same, "beyond reasonable doubt" compared with "the balance of responsibilities", the civil position on disclosure has much to be recommended. Here the analytical work carried out by both sides is disclosed in detail to the opposing parties. This means that the fundamental areas of disagreement can be identified, discussed and, where necessary, brought before the courts. Many forensic scientists working within the criminal law would see the advantage in such an arrangement. A variation of this idea was amongst the proposals of the last Royal Commission on Criminal Justice, so why are the lawyers so "agin it"! Is there no justice in truth?

36(3) - 1996: Forensic Futurology

(Editorial)

Life can only be understood backwards; but it must be lived forwards said the Danish philosopher Kierkegaard. He was right, of course, but his aphorism is just another way of saying that from our experience of life we must choose our own paradigm to assist us in understanding and surviving future events.

The crime investigator, the research scientist and those who stake their money on horses all follow the same broad pattern of (1) reflecting upon past events, (2) distilling some sort of pattern from them and then (3) considering the logical consequences. From these outcomes there may follow a new line of criminal inquiry, a scientific experiment, or the wagering of the housekeeping money on a racing certainty.

As the experience of life of each of us grows we tend to look back more often and refine our paradigms still further. "Why didn't we see at the time...?" becomes a larger, and component in our thoughts. This comprehensive *esprit d'escalier* permeates all life, including that of scientists.

One of the most telling examples of how the obvious can be missed in science lies in the example given by the statistician RA Fisher. He said: *It is a remarkable fact that had any thinker in the middle of the nineteenth century undertaken, as a piece of abstract and theoretical analysis, the task of constructing a particulate theory of inheritance, he would have been led, on the basis of a few very simple assumptions, to produce a system identical with the modern scheme of Mendelian or factorial inheritance* [1].

Well, Fisher's thinker never got around to it, which is rather a pity because it seems at least likely that we forensic scientists would have got our DNA characterisation methods somewhat earlier had he done so.

On the same line of thinking might we not have predicted something like the present techniques in DNA analysis many years ago merely by reflecting about it? After all the powers of the cell in the specific reproduction (or "amplification") of genes have been known for a long time. Was it a matter waiting for to catch up, thus allowing us to do what we already knew the cell could do? Did we all miss the idea until the technology stimulated it? Did even the science fiction writers miss the idea?

Can forensic thinkers come up with predictions of future major developments in forensic science? If so might the publication of these ideas accelerate progress, or would it be just as effective simply to wait until a suitable and unforeseen new technology arrives and goes in search of a problem?

Arthur C Clarke's predicted uses of the artificial satellite is a good example of a successful prophecy, although later technology would doubtless have found the problem anyway. Wasn't it also Clarke who was responsible for the wry division of the history of ideas into:

stage one – "it's impossible"
stage two – "it's possible but not worth doing"
stage three – "I said it was a good idea all along"

As Clarke implies there is no kudos in being a scientific prophet. Those of us who are old enough to have opposed a subsequently successful idea seldom wish to publicise our opposition, and the young accept the idea as an established fact, and condemn all the rest as history.

But in the field of forensic futurology the old have two great advantages. We have a wealth of experience in forensic science and we have nothing to lose. Our careers are going nowhere so we can take the risk of making fools of ourselves without repercussions. So, keeping Samuel Johnson's dictum in mind that "the purpose of experience is to limit the imagination" let us use our experience and, if we've any imagination left, speculate reasonably on where forensic science is going. Of course there is no reason why the young cannot produce their predictions too, if they wish. However, please keep in mind the fact that the younger you are, the longer you will have to live with your mistakes.

Stuart Kind

Reference

1. Fisher RA. *The Genetical Theory of Natural Selection*. New York: Dover Publications, 1958; p7.

36(4) - 1996: Ambivalence – A Problem for Forensic Science

(Editorial)

Public perception of forensic science usually coincides with media activity. Where forensic science has been involved in bringing to justice perpetrators of particularly vicious crimes then the public sees this as science in the service of the legal process, as scientific sleuthing. The popularity of detective fiction means that the market for forensic science as an entertainment and as a demonstration of the application of good science to the solution of crimes is assured. A contrary view arises when mistakes or, more likely, apparent mistakes are made by the forensic scientist, especially if these mistakes coincide with high profile cases. The OJ Simpson trial is a prime example of a situation where crime scene officers are portrayed as not fulfiling their role correctly and the forensic scientists seemed to be unaware of the problem of contamination. The stigma which arises from such cases must be removed if public confidence is to be restored to any forensic science service.

It remains to be asked what are the mechanisms by which public confidence can be restored? The first must be a demonstration that the processes and analyses carried out meet independently devised national and international standards. In the west much has been achieved in this direction by, for example, ASCLD in the United States and elsewhere, and NAMAS in the United Kingdom.

Additionally, the competence of personnel in implementing these standards must be demonstrated. Already developments in this area are beginning to see accreditation through, for example, vocational qualifications in the United Kingdom and schemes devised by the American Board of Criminalists. Are these two approaches sufficient in themselves to restore public confidence? With these schemes most organisations also operate quality assurance systems which may often include declared and undeclared quality assurance testing. It has to be recognised, however, that human frailty being what it is even all such schemes cannot guarantee a 100% freedom from error or perceived error. Do we then as forensic scientists have to live with this dilemma or is there something additional to these control measures we can implement? It is true that when problems are brought to public attention the media normally overemphasises its relevance or, more problematically, distorts the facts surrounding the problem. Surely some kind of independent intermediary body is required which is able to identify the problem and propose and implement solutions before they meet the full gaze of the media. Care must be taken to demonstrate that this independent body is truly so and that it cannot be accused of a 'cover up'. It must produce reports to be placed in the public domain at a time and place conducive with a rational appraisal of the problem.

Who or what will fulfil this role?

37(1) - 1997: Private or Public

(Editorial)

For those forensic scientists who work in the adversarial system the use of private commercially oriented forensic practitioners has long been an accepted fact of life. The expertise of some of these private practitioners has been looked upon, especially by those in public sector forensic science, as being less than satisfactory in the expertise they claim to demonstrate and some especially in the United States have been identified as complete charlatans. Unfortunately in most countries where such "experts" practice there is no mechanism to prevent their continued use by the legal professions. One reason for this is that such "scientists" may present themselves well in court, that is to say, they are expert as witnesses but not expert witnesses. Such a minority of private inexpert witnesses do little for the reputation of the majority of good independent forensic scientists. Reputable private practitioners have been encouraged to demonstrate their provenance by external validation under, for example, ISO 9002, but how can the behaviour of the unethical be controlled? The last and ultimate controlling mechanism for expressing and rejecting such practitioners has always been considered to be the courts of law. How are the courts to determine expertise? The usual guide has been academic qualifications and experience but there are records of some "forensic scientists" falsifying academic qualifications and experience.

Does this same problem exist in the inquisitorial system of justice which claims to be a seeker after the truth unlike the adversarial system which is often portrayed as a contest between rival views neither of whom is concerned with the truth. There appears no reason, in most inquisitorial systems, why the accused, given the necessary financial resources, should not consult with an independent forensic scientist although any such reports may not be acceptable to the courts who appoint their own expert; usually from a state supported laboratory. And who is to validate the independent scientific advice offered to the accused to enable his/her legal representative to ask the pertinent questions of the state scientist in court? The problem is then no different from that of experts in the adversarial system of justice.

Perhaps it is for the forensic science profession to regulate itself unless statutory requirements are in place, as may be true for some countries. It is clearly easier for public sector laboratories to self-regulate their activities because of the greater resources available for training and external validation but it is not so easy for the small private practitioner. This may be an argument for establishing an independent organisation for the small private practitioners which would enable a collective view of independent forensic science practice to be expressed to the courts. But is this what forensic science needs or is a professional organisation which validates all practicing forensic scientists to be preferred?

37(3) - 1997: Jobs for the Boys
(Editorial)

As a result of the past activities and practices of some forensic scientists in various countries of the world there has arisen a need to raise standards of practice and the quality of work performed in forensic science laboratories. This struggle for perfection has meant many laboratories adopting accreditation through various organisations including UKAS in the United Kingdom, ISO 9000 in Europe and ASCLD and NATA in the United States and Australia respectively. Additionally, because of the growing international nature of criminal activities there is also a perceived requirement for laboratories in the different countries to standardise their procedures to facilitate an exchange of information. Such standardisation is greatly assisted by the development of the standard operational procedures (SOPs) developed as a requirement of the accrediting bodies. Further, SOPs and methods are also an essential requirement in the establishment of meaningful databases. Perhaps the ultimate example of the latter being the SOPs required for the establishment of DNA databases. Some standard operational procedures, depending upon the forensic discipline, are complex and challenging while others are pedestrian and routine but even the former can lose their attraction over time. To have highly qualified, enthusiastic young forensic scientists involved in such procedures can present a managerial problem since boredom can lead to mistakes as the production line of the motor industry, has proved in the past. Like the motor industry some of the answers may lie in the development of robotic systems but not all answers to the problem reside here. It is essential if those working in forensic science laboratories are to develop as professionals that they must achieve job satisfaction because it is only by this means that morale remains high and mistakes are avoided. Does small team working remove the drudgery from operational routines or is there some other solution to this problem?

38(1) - 1998: Proactive Forensic Science
(Editorial)

Three years ago there appeared in the April–June issue of The Journal of the Forensic Science Society 1994, an account of some of the presentations at the 34th Annual General Meeting of the Society. The situation prompting the theme "Forensic Science in the Market Place" is somewhat indigenous to the United Kingdom. The presentations dealt with this theme, but a number of equally important more general issues were raised.

In fairness, before getting into the discussion of the more general points, this author's position on the so-called "agency status" issue should be made explicit. It would seem that this was imposed from "on high" by individuals in government who do not appreciate the nature of the forensic science enterprise. It appears to be misguided, but it may not be proper for an outsider to inject his opinions into the debate on a national issue in another country without being invited to do so. For this reason, and because there is a danger of oversimplification, this editorial focuses instead on those issues that were raised which have applicability to the more general situation. These would apply equally well to the situation with respect to most laboratory systems in the United States. Forensic science is under-appreciated and widely misunderstood around the world.

In his presentation Dr. William Rodger pointed out that there is nothing inherently wrong with forensic scientists having close ties to the police as long as they remain scientists in outlook and approach. The potential for corrupting pressures on scientists in this role are not trivial. The situation is further complicated in that many of these pressures and influences are subtle and difficult to recognise by inexperienced scientists. These difficulties can and *must* be overcome, because close ties to the investigation are essential if a forensic scientist is to be maximally effective. The alternative is to have a situation where the forensic scientist is little more than a technician operating in a reactive mode, allowing non-scientists to define and circumscribe the scope of the scientific investigation. If meaningful scientific questions are not framed with respect to possible physical evidence, the potential value of this evidence will not be realised, and little or misleading information will be developed. This same point was made by Dr. Angela Gallop in her presentation. The approach to a forensic investigation must be scientific and holistic. This is only possible where forensic scientists are involved from the outset.

The seemingly simple task of collecting evidence from a crime scene, when properly appreciated, requires a scientific approach and scientific knowledge. In order for evidence to be collected, it must first be recognised. Recognition of evidence is far more demanding than many realise. Some evidence is obvious. Other crucially important evidence may never be recognised unless a scientific approach involving rigorous application of the scientific method is used at the scene early in the investigation. The use of experienced forensic scientists at crime scenes is not the norm in most parts of the world. This underutilisation is not exclusively a problem caused by shortages of resources, although such shortages are nearly universal in this field. The underutilisation is most likely explained by a widespread lack of awareness of the advantages to be gained by having scientists at crime scenes. Certainly the advent of agency status didn't create this problem. However, unless steps are taken to offset some of the inhibiting aspects of charging for services that aren't fully appreciated, there is a danger that it could exacerbate it.

Historically, many forensic science laboratories in the US were patterned after clinical laboratories because these resented a familiar model. Others were patterned after existing government analytical laboratories. The clinical model was especially common for those laboratories which were set up in medical examiners' offices but was used in others as well. Despite this, a forensic science laboratory is not the same as a clinical chemistry (or other strictly analytical) laboratory. The fundamental difference goes deeper than differences in the nature of the samples and the analytical schemes applied. Rather, it goes to the question of scientific assessment of the problems to be addressed. In the case of the clinical laboratory example the physician makes the assessment and then requests laboratory tests selected from among a finite number of possible tests, each of which has a pre-defined protocol. The samples are of limited variety. Each sample within a given class has been prepared and handled in the same fashion. Little science is necessary once the sample enters the sample stream in the laboratory. The work can be carried out by technicians and automated methods. The results from the laboratory are then sent to the physician who interprets them. The laboratory itself in this case is very unlike a forensic science laboratory. Although, the overall process involved, not the laboratory operation itself, is somewhat analogous to what should happen in a system for the delivery of forensic science services.

However, it can be argued that the forensic science situation can be significantly more complex. Thus, there needs to be scientific assessment and sample selection at the beginning of the case and scientific interpretation and integration of the results at the conclusion of the analyses. Serious problems exist especially at the front end.

A related issue needs some attention. Worldwide, there is also a problem in appreciating that forensic science (or criminalistics) is a discipline in its own right. If the assertion that forensic science is not a discipline in its own right, but is instead a loose collection of established disciplines (e.g., physics, chemistry, biology, biochemistry, molecular biology, etc.), is to be accepted, this implies that the work in a forensic science laboratory or service can be neatly partitioned into activities falling within these established disciplines. By analogous reasoning medicine could be carried out by biochemists, anatomists, physiologists, pharmacologists, etc. working together. We would find this ludicrous. Why? Is this because of historical factors or our familiarity with medicine? By what mechanism does a new discipline in science come to be recognised? Is forensic science less distinct from the disciplines which contribute to it than molecular biology is to biochemistry, for example? Most experienced forensic scientists would answer this rhetorical question in the negative. Forensic science uses the scientific knowledge developed in other disciplines, but uses it in different ways to solve the complex and varied problems encountered. The problems and the thought processes necessary to deal with them are distinctly different. No other science is concerned with the process of individualisation, for example. The approach to problem solving is also different.

Scientific questions need to be framed early during the crime scene investigation. Without the right questions being thoughtfully framed, there is little hope of getting all of the relevant answers. Worse, a wrong or misleading answer may result! It is difficult to understand why so many people, including some forensic scientists, fail to recognise this. Clearly, most people seem to understand that evidence which is destroyed, compromised, or left at the crime scene cannot contribute to the solution of the crime. What seems to be more subtle and not appreciated is that much of the critical physical evidence may not be obvious, and that it is necessary to use the scientific method to select the significant items from among a myriad of unrelated material.

Every crime scene is different, and thus, each demands its own unique approach.

In what other scientific arena do non-scientists define anything other than the general problem to be explored? The approaches to the problem solution are left to those best qualified to design them, viz., scientists. Some might counter that non-scientist administrators in funding agencies dictate to research scientists what they are to do. This is only true with respect to the general problem (e.g., find a cure for cancer). Here it is recognised that the research design is left to those best qualified to formulate the scientific questions to be addressed by the research.

In short, the point needs to be made that forensic science and the need for scientific expertise and assessment does *not* begin at the laboratory door. We need to break with the confining legacy left by the early developmental history of many forensic science laboratories. Although the *status* quo is not acceptable, a continuing lack of appreciation of the situation and a failure to act may even result in a slow retrograde slide.

Peter R De Forest

38(4) - 1998: SOP or CPD, Place Your Bets

(Editorial)

When you buy a pen, and it doesn't work, would you feel better knowing that it comes from a company that is ISO9000 registered? Thought not. What if I tell you that they subscribe to three different external accreditation schemes? Any better? No? I suspect that you may think you'd paid rather too much for the pen and the additional cost has been a waste of resource.

On the other hand, if you bought a hi-fi that worked perfectly and sounded superb, then I was to tell you that it had been built by an enthusiast in his kitchen, would you immediately return the hi-fi? Unless you are a label person, presumably not.

From a client perspective the only requirements of any product is that it meets their specification. This simple lesson seems to have become lost, or hopefully temporarily mislaid, in the organisational rush toward accreditation.

Since the mid-80s we have been creating the so-called customer-oriented environment by processes such as TQM, and third-party accreditation schemes exemplified by BS5750 and ISO9000. What makes this so surprising is that almost all of the output of these is the creation of internal documents detailing processes that already existed and have met customer requirements previously. Where these have not met the need, the simple selective pressures of the market eliminate, or force change on, poor performers.

Even the creation of a mountain of documented processes can never guarantee that the staff tasked with implementing the documents actually do so.

Registration means conformity to documented practices. However, this conformity was not designed to assess, and therefore does not necessarily lead to:

- good product quality
- product that satisfies client needs
- comparable levels of product quality among accredited companies
- better quality than non-accredited companies
- good or improving productivity, responsiveness, competitiveness, or workforce development.

Ongoing audits are a tool for assessing continuing compliance, and foster improvements only to the extent necessary for maintaining compliance.

I am in favour of TQM as the creation of customer-driven specifications and efficient, continually improving, effective internal processes to create outputs that meet those specifications. I am enthusiastic about Quality Assurance.

What I am against is the creation of an entire customer-independent industry that consumes large amounts of resources in the creation of documents that enables the dubious benefit of third-party accreditation.

There *are* many benefits to an organisation in documenting processes. But this should be restricted to those processes where the documentation yields a benefit. Consistency is a major benefit.

So accreditation does little to ensure customer requirements are met. But surely we must do *something* to ensure that the courts receive reliable, valid scientific results and opinion. Of course we should.

All processes, accredited or not, depend on people to ensure they work. Reliability is as much a function of the operational staff as the documentation.

It is reaching the status of dogma in management cultures that 'staff are our most important asset'. Unfortunately, this is not matched by supportive action, probably because it is fundamentally untrue. The most important asset in any scientific process is scientific knowledge. The scientist is the supplier and validator of this knowledge and as such it is the *skill* of the scientist that is the most important asset. It is for this reason that we must focus investment on scientific training.

The skilled, ethical, trained, continuously improving scientist will simply not report results that emanate from an unsatisfactory process. It is the scientist's competence that 'validate' the process through knowledge of the requirements and the process.

The current discussion in the UK of a Professional Register and the associated development of individual competence assessments could yield greater benefits, and at less cost if done in the right way, than the current obsession with organisational accreditation. It is far easier to document a process than ascertain the knowledge required to do it and interpret the output, but this should not deter us from setting competence standards. These must include knowledge requirements as well as mechanical competence, and a means of ensuring continuing maintenance of these skills, for those who would wish to be 'forensic practitioners'.

Of course, this does not imply that I favour any of the current methods of competence assessment; that is a discussion for another day!

Laboratories should document appropriate, but rarely all, procedures where there is readily identifiable benefit in doing so. They should invest heavily in staff training and motivation to continually improve reliability, knowledge, and validity of what they do. Managers have finite resources. More of these resources should be used to develop individual competence, rather than accreditation schemes, on the basis that a collection of competent, ethical scientists will deliver better science than a perfectly organised collection of Standard Operating Procedures delivered by bored, poorly trained, and unmotivated scientists.

Dr Allan Jamieson

39(1) - 1999: Forensic Apartheid?

(Editorial)

Few of us would disagree with Dr Thompson [1] that forensic science is indeed international in its concepts and through the many personal and organisational contacts but is it truly democratic in its implementation? Certainly the developed world has seen and implemented working practices in the forensic sciences which have enabled science to actively support the legal processes operating in the individual countries. Nowhere better is this seen than in the use of DNA data bases which are beginning to revolutionise the detection of volume crime to the same level, or even better, than that of fingerprints. In addition DNA evidence continues to be used as supportive evidence in all types of crime, including serious crime. DNA has become the ultimate technique for personal identification.

Let us now take a wider view of the forensic sciences and especially DNA. Developed countries have used the technology in support of their criminal legal systems but we must not forget that such powerful technology could be used in other ways that may not be consistent with democratic processes. For example, it could be used to monitor the movement of personnel between counties by requiring a DNA profile to form part of a passport or it might be a requirement to register your DNA profile with the authorities before you are given the right to vote or even to become a member of a political party. On another level it might become a requirement to provide a DNA profile to be checked against a data base before you are allowed to take possession of a firearm. All these represent alternative uses to which DNA can be put and some of them would be considered by some countries as an infringement of their citizen's civil liberties.

Other countries may take the view that it might become a useful means of controlling the undesirable elements where undesirable may mean 'those with whom the governing body do not agree'. Can forensic science be used as a repressive agent of government is what we are really asking?

There are a number of countries throughout the world where the repression of civil liberties is practised and by no means are all of these in the developing countries but for those developing countries which do practice repression in one form or another is it correct for the developed nations to be supporting such regimes through the training and provision of forensic science services? Many parallels could be drawn with South Africa during the apartheid era where many considered the imposition of sanctions promoted the struggle and ultimate success of the democratic processes. But is this a fair and relevant comparison? While the training and implementation of a forensic science service could be used repressively could it not also be an opportunity to demonstrate the democratic process and to show how it might be used to eliminate corruption and to support the development of civil rights. Does not the beginnings of practical democracy reside within the judicial process and is not forensic science part of that process? It is suggested that not only should we support the use of forensic science in such countries but that it is our duty to promote such relationships because only by communicating can we hope to influence the growth of democracy. But there may be some who hold a different view?

39(2) - 1999: Let Me Through, I'm a ummmm...

(Editorial)

One of the hallmarks of a profession, as opposed to a skilled trade, is the degree to which the professional routinely makes decisions on the basis of expertise and ability in complex situations where there may be no, or little, previous history. For example, although a lawyer dealing with a particular case may have dealt with similar cases before, the circumstances will not be identical to those previously encountered and he will have to make decisions on how best to handle the case in hand, based on expertise, experience and applied intelligence.

The degree to which these decisions require the bringing together of rules, knowledge and intelligence, determine the separation of the skilled manual worker from the professional worker.

Professional work then, by its nature, requires a degree of knowledge and latitude on the part of the practitioner that, to a great extent, defies strict definition. The professional is identified by a basic level of knowledge, normally a degree followed by a term in service, that equips the professional to practise.

Some, if not most, professions endorse the practitioner after the initial in-service period with some form of license to practise. This may be a statutory endorsement, such as State Registration for Medical Laboratory Scientific Officers, or a peer system such as is used by the Royal College of Pathologists. This endorsement is very like a driving license; a basic level of skill is acknowledged but the drivers must then use their own critical judgement on the appropriate speed for bends under the conditions prevailing at the time.

And so to forensic science. A discipline, or rather many disciplines, in which the practitioners would wish to see themselves regarded as professionals. How does forensic science set about promoting itself as such?

There are two strands to this, the attempt to introduce a Professional Register, and the, initially separate but increasingly entwined, introduction of competency assessments – the most ubiquitous of which are the NVQ/SVQ qualifications.

Judging by the hostility to N/SVQs in other professional 'sectors', you will probably be the first, and perhaps the only, profession to use N/SVQs. If this is the case then forensic science as a profession is no more. There will be trades using N/SVQs, and professions, such as law and medicine, that do not.

Why has forensic science been favoured for this pioneering role among the professions? Because the other, established, professions are vigorously resisting this perceived diminution of professional status by 'competency testing'. Forensic science has yet to achieve an identity. In the UK it is a small number (less than 3,000) of mostly government employed or controlled scientists. But, by including Scenes of Crime Officers, Fingerprint Officers and similar (most employed by the Police) that have few widely recognised professional measures and can be encompassed in the term 'forensic practitioner', a lever is found to engage similar competence tests in the professional scientific areas.

Let us not forget some employers' agenda: one large forensic science organisation has a need to have scientists trained to report in "weeks rather than months". Is this the hallmark of a profession? To be specific, does this list, quoted from NVQ documents, have an equivalent in medicine or law?

(a) You select a work area that is appropriate for the effective and efficient recovery of potential evidential material.
(b) You check the work area is free of contamination.
(c) You cheek the availability of an adequate supply of consumables, tools and protective clothing.
(d) You check that equipment and reagents required are available.
(e) You report identified equipment faults outside of your area of responsibility to the relevant person without delay.

Would the public be reassured that their lawyer had to be told to make sure his desk was tidy, and that he had the right books to hand; that their doctor had to be told or assessed for his ability to check that his stethoscope was working, and that he zipped down the corridor immediately to report that the couch was sticking? No. The professional is marked by the ability to work under and with licence, but with accountability.

But to whom should you be accountable? There is much talk of the need to serve the customer (the Court), indeed a recent conversation has included the need to satisfy the 'customer's customer' (i.e. the public). But how do these customers judge your decisions? Would you ask a jury to survey your house or diagnose the pain in your side? If the profession is to be independent and impartial, as science must be, accountability must first be to the profession. Otherwise, if the customer is partial (and are not both sides in a court partial) or the concepts of social justice change (e.g. in an autocracy), then impartial science is compromised.

The next level of accountability must be to the broader scientific community. Forensic science is a branch, or several branches, of science that depends on these for its validity. Only when professional accountability is in order need the 'external' customer be considered. Better science will assist better justice – in the sense of impartial justice. To depart from this principle of the primacy of scientific accountability is to prioritise legal, above scientific, considerations.

Any monitoring body, such as the Register of Forensic Practitioners currently under discussion, must recognise these priorities in the structures created to arbitrate standards in the profession.

What makes the scientist an expert is not their mechanical skill, but the ability to use scientific method and knowledge to deliver an opinion on the support that particular physical evidence gives to a hypothesis. We must remain clear that it is the delivery of opinion that separates the expert from other witnesses, not the ability to clear a bench. Employers would do better to consider where the skills of their staff are best deployed. The principle of the job being done by the lowest grade of staff capable of performing it (i.e. cost efficient) would necessitate a major rethink in most laboratories. Do you really need a degree to load a gas chromatograph or search clothes? Given the requirement of the scientist as an expert in assessing and delivering opinion on evidence, is it then necessary that they should know how to do these manual things?

Consider an experienced scientist assessing a case for the appropriate examinations. He requests several others, each skilled in a particular task, for example search or DNA profiling, to perform examinations and analysis and return the results to him. Having assessed the responses and having completed all the necessary work, through others, he compiles a report. The scientist has never left the office. Is the opinion invalid? How do we assess the competence of such an individual?

The General Medical Council (GMC) says of General Practitioner competence assessment that "although doctors must be able to prove they are competent, they should not be required to sit examinations again". A record of work reviewed by peers is the Doctors' order.

Is it now time to open the debate on what activities within forensic science constitute professional practice and those that are skilled manual work? The latter are amenable to competency testing by what, for the sake of conciseness, I will term traditional methods. Professional practice has been performed in many other disciplines for years; the GMC, the GTC and Council for Professions Supplementary to Medicine have all had responsibilities in maintaining professional standards. Licensing followed by peer review Within professional practice for forensic scientists one of the paramount skills, or competencies, must be the ability to assist the court by providing honest, informed, comprehensible, impartial opinion. It is this that should be the focus of professional competency assessment. One way of doing so is by peer review.

I have, in a previous article [2], urged an organisational focus on output, not process. This principle is valid as much for individual as for organisational performance. The report and testimony are the outputs of the forensic scientist. Is it beyond the scope of the 'sector' to assess reports and testimony retrospectively for each scientist? Not by the scientist deliberately compiling (and choosing) 'evidence' to satisfy a planned visit, but by unannounced visits and examination of random cases by trained assessors. The assessor training and organisation becomes the mechanism for the maintenance of standards within the profession.

It is a view frequently espoused that many of the alleged foul-ups in forensic science will be avoided by competency testing. Unfortunately the majority of these were organisational, not individual, failures. Of the individual failures to meet standards, most of the complaints seem to be based on the behaviour, rather than competence, of the perpetrators. It is for this reason that a Professional Code of Practice is essential for anyone wishing to be a professional forensic scientist.

To continue the car license analogy: when you career into a bend and create an 'accident' a court reviews your display of skill, or lack of it. It decides whether you have been reckless, careless, or innocent. In the same way professional bodies generally operate by review of performance.

What I am advocating is that we determine the key features that make forensic science a profession and not a trade. That forensic scientists (you know who you are, even if managers struggle with the definition) stand up and identify themselves as professionals; distance themselves from those who are not: think; behave; look; and organise as professionals. Study those that are clearly regarded as professional and learn from them. A basic licensing procedure followed by regular peer review of a random selection of casework linked to conformance within an ethical code will begin the process. But it is up to individuals, by their commitment to science, their behaviour, their 'professionalism', to make this a profession.

So what about NVQs, SVQs, and their like. My advice is, Run! Run from this while you still can (i.e. before someone writes an SOP or NVQ for running. 1: First, check that you are facing in the right direction and will not run into a wall . . .).

Dr Allan Jamieson

References

1. *The Times*, 2nd February 1999.
2. Editorial. SOP or CPD, place your bets. *Science & Justice* 1998; **219**.

39(3) - 1999: Something Nasty Hiding . . .

(Editorial)

I remember reading a story about Charles Babbage, the Victorian computer pioneer and mathematician who, amongst his many other distinctions, was Lucasian Professor of Mathematics at Cambridge University, and a Fellow of the Royal Society. So from this I think we can agree that Charles was a very accomplished man. The trouble was, according to the story, that he couldn't write comprehensible English and he was dependent upon the efforts of others to convert his writings into a graspable text. I suppose he was so used to working at the level of logical languages that the use of higher level languages (he might have considered them to be 'lower level') that he developed no faculty in the field. One can't be good at everything.

In those cases where Charles was talking to his specialist contemporaries it probably didn't matter. They would understand what he was saying anyway. But in those examples where he was speaking to non-scientists and non-mathematicians (fund-holding politicians for example) it mattered a great deal to Charles. So the mechanical development of his ideas was held up by financial barriers. Perhaps in the long run even that didn't matter. As I type this editorial on the modern electronic version of the Babbage 'Analytical Engine' I can't help but think that, in this technology driven world, the development of the transistor might have generated a dozen modern day Babbages even if Charles had never been born.

So what's all that got to do with forensic science? Well, isn't it a question of 'output' in both cases? Doesn't the forensic specialist write his report for a crime investigator or for a court sitting as a tribunal of fact? Has not the police investigator, the magistrate or the jury member the right to expect that the expert witness enunciates his results in something more akin to BASIC than to machine code? But not everyone believes that the forensicist (I think I just invented the word) must aim for full comprehensibility to the non-specialist. There is a small but voluble section of forensic scientists, and their adherents, that seeks to solve the problem by changing the structure of the judicial process to one where the specialist himself makes the decisions simply because he believes it is too difficult for Joe or Jill Citizen to decide for themselves. The days of the priesthoods will never pass. If you are bewildered by the complexities of life then all you need do is produce a formula that will interpret complexity for yourself, even if not for others. Then, if others resist, you might even seek to impose the formula upon them. After all it is for their own good.

But apart from the dedicated system-monger, scientific or otherwise, we should all make the effort to speak to Joe and Jill. We must admit that we live and work in a world which is more a product of experience than of logic, more of contingency than of design. Furthermore we are stuck with it.

Anyone who reaches a mature age without realising this is indeed an intellectual pachyderm. Let us attempt to communicate this knowledge to the young. Any budding forensic specialist should profit by a period of bag carrying for the investigator, or paper shuffling for the criminal lawyer, before he starts to learn about quantum mechanics, gene frequencies or Bayesian statistics.

In other words, have a jolly good look at the forest before you dive into a particular thicket. There might be something nasty hiding there.

Stuart Kind

39(4) - 1999: From Bach to Schoenberg

(Editorial)

Most would agree that Bach was the master of counterpoint, the art of adding melodies as accompaniment according to strict rules of composition. No better is this illustrated than in his Brandenburg Concerti, familiar to many of us and to be recommended to those who don't often listen to 'classical' music. It is the way that one tune not only compliments another but enhances both the enjoyment and excitement of the listener.

I would challenge any rock enthusiast to refrain from tapping his/her foot when listening to such music – you are not the only ones to discover 'the beat'. The excitement generated from listening to such music and the interplay of the various tunes reminds some of us 'older generation' forensic scientists of the way we felt about our discipline and the way we saw it interacting with the legal process. The tunes were our developments in the new technologies which, in earlier years, were very crude and unsophisticated, and the counterpoint was the exciting way in which we interacted with the police forces, wrote our reports and went to Court to present our evidence. There was a buzz of excitement.

But this parallel was not as perfect as some of us may have believed because some of us forgot an important part of counterpoint – that of complying with the strict rules of composition. It is this latter which prompted many countries into a rethink of what forensic science was about and where and how it should fit into the legal process. This became a time when we sought to provide an 'agreeable effect of apt arrangement of parts' or, as the musicologists would describe it, 'a combination of simultaneous notes to form chords'. These represent the Oxford English definitions of harmony.

There is a drive towards harmonisation in the forensic sciences which arises partly from a requirement to meet financial targets but also to provide the best and fastest service to police forces and the courts of law. Such processes are to be commended but they have brought to forensic science a need for rigorously implemented quality assurance programmes and a breaking down of the different operations into discrete entities, much the same as a mass production line often seen in manufacturing industries. There is nothing wrong with such concepts and activities providing harmony is maintained within the laboratory system and all are using the same tone scale. Problems can arise and apparent disharmony ensue if some are using a different tone scale.

The music of Schoenberg does not always appeal to those who listen to Mozart or Beethoven. This doesn't mean that the music of Schoenberg shouldn't be listened to but it does perhaps require more understanding and thought and a retuning of our aural senses. Forensic scientists must not be afraid of new organisational systems and methods and must be prepared to adapt – isn't that the way science progresses?

Those of you who have taken the trouble to read some of my editorials will shortly have the opportunity to read those of my successor as Editor. I hope I have been able to make some small contribution to our discipline through the pages of this journal which has seen some important changes, including the provision of translations of our abstracts to support our international remit and improvements in our layout by moving to an A4 format. Sorry to those of you who had to adjust your book shelves. All of this was only possible with the help of our loyal staff at the Society's headquarters and particularly Jill Armitage, Jane Cross and our proof reader Rosita Whittall. I would like to offer my thanks to all of these and the many others who have given freely of their time. I would finally like to pass on my best wishes to my successor.

Brian Cadd

42(2) - 2002: A Professional Body for Forensic Scientists
(Editorial)

MJ Allen
Document Evidence Limited, Gatsby Court, 172 Holliday Street, Birmingham B1 ITJ, United Kingdom

It is perhaps the greatest indictment of our profession that for some reason forensic scientists have not seen fit to organise themselves in a professional and regulated way that encourages all that should be encouraged, such as best practice, ethical behaviour, awareness of and an ability to apply up-to-date methods, and that discourages all the things that should be discouraged, such as sloppy practice, bias and unprofessional conduct.

These are categories that surely are recognised across all manner of professions that are fit to call themselves professions. So why have forensic scientists been so reluctant to address these issues, to organise themselves into the kind of collective grouping from which individuals can obtain support from colleagues and which can provide a structure of qualifications and accreditations that certify the competence of the scientist in the witness box?

Is it because we are all far too busy? That doesn't help but it's a pretty feeble reason. Is it that we don't consider it important enough to bother with? The results of a survey of document examiners carried out before the meeting of the Questioned Documents Group of the Forensic Science Society held in Birmingham on 17 October 2001 showed firstly that out of about 100 people who received the survey, 30 replied and, secondly, of those 30 all thought a professional body was desirable. (You can be forgiven for thinking that a return rate of 30% is nothing to write home about, but if you ask those in the know it is very good indeed.) So this would suggest, at the very least, a commitment to the principle. Is it that there is no obvious model of what a professional body should be which could be used and adapted to our needs? That is true up to a point although undoubtedly much could be learned from how other professional groups organise themselves. So what is needed is a focal point for discussing and promoting the idea of a professional body for forensic scientists, and to take it from the idea stage to a practical reality in a sensible period of time. And the benefits to the individual scientist, irrespective of whether they are employed by a large organisation or whether they are self-employed, should be such that they would want to be part of it, rather than just feel that they ought to be part of it.

So, the question arises what should a professional body look like, what should it do, what benefits will accrue to those who are part of it, and what sacrifices need to be made? And where do the existing organisations such as the Forensic Science Society, the Council for the Registration of Forensic Practitioners (CRFP), and the Academy of Experts fit into the picture? (And if you are thinking what about the other organisations not listed, the point has been made.)

Before addressing those questions, it would be useful to ask the question what is it that makes a competent forensic scientist? A simple and innocent question, but one that is likely to attract a multiplicity of answers, much heated discussion and not always much illumination. However, there are perhaps four key areas that can be defined that cover a good deal of the ground.

Firstly, knowledge. It goes without saying that this is an absolute requirement and yet how many qualifications can be pointed to that are forensically relevant? The Forensic Science Society has played a part with the introduction of a series of Diplomas, there are Masters courses at universities, for example Strathclyde and Kings, London, and in the last couple of years a considerable number of undergraduate courses in forensic science have appeared (these latter courses using the attractiveness of the f-word to entice youngsters, who would otherwise become accountants, into a career in science, and not creating a cohort of unemployed forensic scientists). Whilst conventional academic qualifications obviously have a part to play, they are a measure of achievement at a point in time; how much better to have in place a qualification that allows the person holding it to demonstrate not just a high level of knowledge at a particular moment, but a continuing career-long progress keeping up with current technologies and methods. This should not just be by the obtaining of brownie points from conference attendances but should be from occasional relevant courses which meet agreed standards and which fulfil real and relevant needs. Suitably accredited university courses could probably best deliver this, possibly via the internet. Further, a professional body should supply to its members details of relevant published papers, perhaps recommending particularly meritorious papers as required reading, together with advance details of conferences.

Perhaps a series of web-based multiple-choice questions every few years could test an appropriate level of understanding of such updating material.

In other words, a sensible level of occasional distance learning.

A second component is a requirement to show an ability to do a case correctly. This should most definitely not be confused with the ability to obtain a scientifically justifiable conclusion. Use of appropriate methods, acceptable ways of recording the results of observations, and accepted scientific criteria for interpretation, all form part of this process. It is the process which, in essence, has been chosen by CRFP to test the suitability of potential registrants.

In other words, assessing procedures.

Thirdly, and most importantly, is the ability to obtain the correct answer. Correct here is defined as a conclusion which most accurately reflects making correct observations and attributing to them appropriate significance in accordance with established scientific criteria. Organisations may well have their own procedures for testing this aspect of the job, but there needs to be a system of testing to agreed standards, which the scientist can rightly point to as being a demonstration of their ability. One mechanism with a long track record is the use of controlled trials with known material and "known" results.

In other words, proficiency testing.

Lastly, there is a requirement that those who go to court should be able to present their evidence to a reasonable standard. Whilst there are certain standards below which it would be unacceptable to go, this is a subjective area with personal preferences of style playing a part. And there are very real practical difficulties of assessment – how many wasted trips to court before you finally get to see the candidate give evidence? At the very least, the reporting to a professional body of unprofessional behaviour by an individual should be investigated and may give grounds for removal from it.

In other words, an assessment of presentational ability.

Out of all this comes the outline of a qualification which does not yet exist but one which needs to exist. It should be able to demonstrate current, relevant knowledge, acceptable, monitored casework practice, appropriate interpretative skills employing accepted scientific criteria in mock cases, and a sound ability to present oral evidence.

Some such processes should be monitored on a reasonably regular basis and, providing standards are maintained, individuals should be certified. That is, the court should be satisfied that the attaining of certification is grounds for an initial presumption of competence at the very least. Some countries seem to want to publish statistical evidence as to current competence of the "I get 87.2% of my cases right" variety. This is, in my view, flawed, not least because it would encourage endless meaningless arguments about how this general statistic applies to this particular case. Much more satisfactory is for the courts to accept the simple, if mind-bogglingly obvious, fact that forensic scientists are human and therefore just might make a mistake. (Any individual or organisation that asserts otherwise is, frankly, talking tosh.) So, it should be perfectly reasonable for a court to infer from the aforementioned that a scientist has done his or her best to get the right answer. If there is any suggestion to the contrary, the seriousness of such allegations can hardly be understated.

To return to the questions posed about how all of this could happen. It requires a new organisation to be created. An organisation that can work with the existing organisations but one that over-arches them, and an organisation that is run for the benefit of those who form it, that is the forensic scientists themselves. CRFP exists to regulate the profession. It does not exist to set standards or to see that scientists measure up to those standards. Currently, the Forensic Science Society fulfils a role as a focus for discussion within the profession and for those allied to it and has helped to promote qualifications with its various diplomas, but again this does not meet the needs described above. And other organisations speak with similarly representative voices.

A professional body should be created to set the standards in our profession, to create and oversee the implementation of occupationally relevant qualifications that are meaningful and can rightfully be said to demonstrate those very elements which are considered the most important. And now for the really tricky question – who can be bothered to do all of this. The answer to this should be a resounding all of us if we really are the profession we say we are. Sure, there are going to be those who make it happen, hold endless tedious meetings trying to find ways to make the idea a practical reality, battering their heads against walls of intransigence, but there is not one iota of point in people putting themselves out if there is no mandate from those in the profession. Which leaves the last question: is this a worthwhile exercise or is it a (well-intentioned) waste of time?

I lied. There is a myriad of other questions from who to how to when to how much. But they are not yet worth contemplating...

© The Forensic Science Society 2002

Keywords Forensic science, editorial, document examination, professions, management.

45(1) - 2005: Professionalism – Duties and Privileges

(Editorial)

Robert Forrest

We all know that being a professional carries both duties and responsibilities. Traditionally, belonging to a profession has also carried certain privileges. Ultimately, the purpose of any professional privilege must be to facilitate the work of the professional in the interests of the public as a whole and, just possibly, to facilitate recruitment and retention to what are difficult and demanding, what's the word? – professions. Some privileges are inherent in the functions that the members of a particular profession carry out. Examples include the right of audience of barristers and the right to prescribe of physicians. Others are granted to make the work of professionals easier in the public interest. In the forensic arena there is currently the right, shared with public analysts, of some forensic scientists to give documentary evidence by certificate rather than by statement. There are few, if any, other privileges that forensic scientists have in their workplace at present.

The end point of the delivery of professional services by many, but not all, forensic professionals is the provision of factual and opinion evidence in court. Life for the court-going forensic professional is not always a bed of roses. One or two privileges would certainly make the work easier. A start would be acceptance by listing officers that a statement of unavailable dates by a professional or expert witness would normally mean just that, that one is unavailable for a good reason. Whilst, when assisting the court at the request of the prosecution, the expert is usually, but not always, asked for a list of unavailable dates, and other, often intimate, information these often appear to be ignored when the dates of trials are fixed. Worse, even when copies of summons from other courts, blocking out dates, are provided these may also be ignored. As for the supposedly over arching supremacy of the coroner's subpoena, I have had to point out to Crown Prosecution Service (CPS) case managers and lawyers that it is I, and not they, who would have to sit in the cells if I do not comply with the summons of the coroner. The coroner's subpoena, properly drafted, is such a potent tool that it should be used sparingly. To be asked to block out two weeks so that one can attend at an inquest for an hour or so on one unspecified day during that two weeks is not reasonable, except in the most exceptional case. This is particularly so if the 'summons' is signed by the coroner's officer rather than by the coroner herself, is thus invalid, and a bright CPS lawyer spots this, with the result that one becomes piggy in the middle in an undignified and unprofessional fight for one's body (and brains) between different courts.

When the forensic professional actually gets to court there can still be problems. One such problem is that the different courts apply different standards at their security checkpoints. There can be no certainty that the innocent contents of one's briefcase that are acceptable at the entrance to one court building will be acceptable elsewhere. The default mode for court security officers is always courtesy. The exceptions can be particularly unpleasant by comparison. My worst court experience was to have all electronic gadgets in my briefcase and in my pockets confiscated on entry to the court building. When I remonstrated, pointing out that I needed them to assist the court, I was rewarded with a put down in public by a security guard of, I think, the opposite sex. The court did not react with sympathy when I was asked to do some complex 'what if' calculations whilst in the witness box and I had to point out that I had had my calculator, programmed in anticipation of just such questions, confiscated at the court building entrance despite my reasonable explanation as to why I needed to retain it in my possession. The gall of that episode was spiced by having seen a police officer, also a witness for the prosecution, enter the court building festooned with radio, baton, mobile phone and CS spray. There are other examples of the courts not treating all who enter their doors, to assist the court as professionals, as equal security risks. Some security officers, on finding a mobile phone in my briefcase, ask, 'Are you a doctor or lawyer?' as if those two professions had any especial charisma of virtue. Two crown courts I regularly assist as an expert will routinely impound my Dictaphone and camera, leaving my laptop, with the facility to make sound recordings for several hours, and my mobile phone, with built in camera, in my possession. Of course, I know, as does every forensic professional, that one should not take photographs within the court building or attempt to record court proceedings. I consider it to be treating me as less than a professional that I am not treated with the elementary degree of trust that assumes I know, and will follow, the proper rules for behaviour in court.

One of the advantages of professional registration ought to be that the court leaves the tools of one's profession in one's possession on entry to the court building, in the knowledge that any impropriety in their use can be dealt with not only by the court but by one's professional organisation. Even in the present climate of paranoia about security, it is difficult to see how such a privilege would constitute any sort of a security risk.

It is also not particularly 'professional' to find oneself sitting next to the accused and/or his family whilst waiting to give evidence or when eating one's lunch.

My case, in asking that recognition of the professional status of members of the Forensic Science Society should bring with it some of the privileges of other 'servants of the court' is simply that this would make our demanding work less stressful and enable us to carry it out with greater efficiency in the interests of justice.

45(3) - 2005: Who Guards the Guards?

(Editorial)

Professor Jim Fraser, President

As England and Wales appears set to embark on the unique experiment of entirely private provision of forensic science to the criminal justice system, a number of searching questions need to be posed. The proposed changes[1] to the Forensic Science Service could place the largest provider and the only remaining public sector provider in private hands. The rationale and processes for the possible privatisation of the Forensic Science Service were rightly challenged by the recent Select Committee on Forensic Science but this is not the fundamental issue. There are currently two other private strategic suppliers of forensic science in an already existing market place. The real question is how do we ensure that the rapidly expanding private market in England and Wales meets the needs of the criminal justice system? Furthermore, can it be in the interests of justice for the supply of forensic science services to be exclusively governed by the demands or standards of the private sector? Given the views of the Select Committee on Forensic science[2] and the response of the Government to their report[3], the answer to this question appears to be: no.

The perceived benefits of a competitive market as distinct from the benefits of privatising the FSS need to be clearly distinguished. In a private market companies have flexibility in terms of their structure, financing, products and services but fundamentally, they are in business to make money. They are also in business to compete with their rivals. There are two primary means by which competitive advantage can be achieved[4]; differentiation – having products or services more desirable than those of your competitors, or cost – supplying the same things more efficiently than your competitors. Both of these approaches bring benefits to customers but they also present them with new risks. The ultimate in differentiation is to be the sole supplier of a unique product (ideally patented) for your exclusive use. But if this is a product that the criminal justice system overall would benefit from, how can this be right? A further difficulty is how one balances the intellectual property rights of an individual company with a competitive market place and the overall needs of criminal justice.

Cost advantage allows businesses to supply the same products while gaining a better surplus than their competitors. Often this is translated into lower prices. Since the largest user of forensic science in England and Wales is the police service, savings in public money are to be welcomed. But these are not widgets being bought by the police service. In addition to the normal requirements of good public sector procurement (value for money, fairness, transparency etc), detailed knowledge of many aspects of forensic science is also needed. However, with the exception of some specialist roles (e.g. Senior Investigating Officer and Senior Crime Scene Investigator) ignorance of forensic science in the police service is well known and documented[5]. Consequently, there is a danger that procurement in some instances may be made exclusively on the basis of price as opposed to value for money and quality. We can agree that two examples above are worst case scenarios but given these risks and others that are readily identified, what are the expected benefits of a private forensic science market? It appears that the main drivers for a private market are freedom from public sector constraint for the FSS and equality of arms for their strategic competitors, Forensic Alliance and LGC. Tangible benefits to customers are harder to identify.

Nevertheless, there is one key area that distinguishes forensic science provision in England and Wales: speed of delivery. In many instances drugs analysis and DNA profiling are carried out within a few days of

---

[1] Francis Bacon: Preface to *The Elements of the Common Law*.
[2] F. A. R. Bennion: *Professional Ethics*.
[3] *Dentists' Code*, p. 10.
[4] House of Commons Select Committee on Science & Technology (2005). *Forensic Science On Trial*. London, HMSO.
[5] ibid.

submission and in a significant proportion of cases, on the same day. This contrasts strongly with the public sector provision of forensic science around the world which is almost universally characterised by backlogs. In some countries this is also compounded by lack of resources and poor infrastructure. A recent American report[6] estimated the backlog of cases in US publicly funded laboratories at just over 500,000 – an increase of 70% on their backlogs at the beginning of the same year (2002). The report also estimated the need for an additional 1900 staff at a cost of $70 million to achieve a 30 day turnaround time. If justice delayed is justice denied, then with the correct safeguards, perhaps there are benefits from a competitive market that are in the interests of justice.

Despite this the public is likely to be sceptical of the full scale privatisation of something so close to the criminal justice system. Recent high profile miscarriages involving expert witnesses and tragedies on the railways, whatever the objective evidence, are likely to act as a stimulant to the public imagination of what may go wrong.

There is therefore, on the face of it, an unassailable case for regulation of forensic science in England and Wales in order to manage the risks and issues likely to be encountered in a new and developing market. These are likely to include: anti-competitive behaviour and predatory pricing, cartels, ensuring continuity and scope of service provision, equality for providers, maintenance and development of standards and prevention market distortion or collapse. The regulation of such a complex enterprise is no trivial matter and will require the cooperation of a large number of stakeholders with often divergent interests. The prize to be won is the continued development of what is widely recognised as world class forensic science. The cost of failing to deal with these issues does not bear contemplation.

45(4) - 2005: Everything Changes and Nothing is Constant[1]

(Editorial)

Robert Forrest

I am writing this editorial on 21st December, the shortest day of the year in the northern hemisphere, the winter solstice, Winterset or Yule. Call it what you will, it is a time when change is in the air and is also a time to look forward, even though the worst of the winter is to come. This year that is particularly true of at least two of the major forensic science Journals. The *Journal of Forensic Science* is changing its publisher and *Science and Justice* will have a new editor with effect from the next issue. It is a useful time to take stock and ask some questions about what the purpose of a journal aimed at forensic science practitioners is and, more to the point, what that purpose should be.

Jones, in the first paper of this edition of the Journal, analyses the citation record of papers published in the *Journal of Forensic Science*. It is hardly surprising that he identifies papers dealing with the forensic uses of DNA technology as being those which are most highly cited. One might argue that this implies that a forensic science journal editor who wishes to enhance the impact factor of her journal should aim to publish as many (high quality) papers on DNA technology as possible. This argument is only valid if the sole function of the journal is the self referential one of enhancing its impact factor. For an editor to take the decision to publish a paper, after peer review, by looking only at the effect that that paper may have on his journal's impact factor is inappropriate. One might argue that it is as inappropriate as a decision by a university to divest itself of its department of forensic pathology, academic forensic pathologists in the UK having to spend more time in

---

[6] *Forensic Science on Trial: Government response to the Committee's Seventh report of Session 2004–05*, The Stationery Office Ltd, London 2005.
[1] Francis Bacon: Preface to *The Elements of the Common Law*.

practice than they do in writing grant applications, in order to enhance the Faculty of Medicine's Research Assessment Exercise Rating. Just as the function of a university in the UK is, or ought to be, wider than chasing a Research Assessment Exercise rating, so the function of a forensic science journal ought to be more than to simply chase a high impact factor. The publications of relevant papers that influence practice will be positively reflected in the impact factor, but it is the publication of papers that influence and help practitioners in a particular discipline and inform practitioners in other disciplines, and those who commission forensic science services, of cutting edge developments that the editor should be aiming to attract and publish. Any consequential enhancement of the impact factor is merely an epiphenomenon.

General review papers also have a vital function; they are used as sources by students, who should, of course, always be encouraged to look beyond the review to the primary source material. They can also help managers, lawyers and perhaps even legislators to reach a better understanding of difficult issues. A good, recent, example of such a review is one by Jones describing the Swedish experience of a zero tolerance regimen for the presence of illicit drugs in drivers' blood. [1] One can predict that this review will be read by many practitioners, hopefully read by policy makers, probably in abstract, and will certainly be widely cited.

The publication of book reviews remains an important journal function even in the age of the World Wide Web. As budgets and even personal incomes shrink the question as to whether or not a particular book is worth buying for oneself or one's department becomes more focused. The on-line blurb on the booksellers' website may not be helpful and the opportunity to thumb through a dead tree copy of a highly specialised tome at a real bookshop, even in a university city, so as to be able to make an informed buying decision, may simply not be there. A crisp, critical and well informed book review in a specialist journal is invaluable in informing the decision to purchase or not to purchase an expensive book.

One of the properties that a journal needs to fulfil its functions is accessibility. Today that means accessibility over the Internet. Simply having abstracts selected by National Library of Medicine reviewers available through a medline search is no longer good enough. If a scientist wants to refer to a key paper then there is no substitute for having the paper itself downloaded to her desktop in the same format as it was published in the journal. At present, this is an area in which *Science and Justice* is sadly deficient. It is a facility that the Journal must offer to its subscribers if it is to remain competitive and it is not something that the Forensic Science Society can offer within its own resources. This means that one of the most important jobs of the next editor will be to navigate through the shoals inherent in developing a partnership with one of the major publishers for the publication of the journal, with all the added value for members of the Society and journal subscribers that this will bring. I wish her luck; it will probably be the most important change in the Journal's history. It is something that will certainly enhance the utility of the journal to its readers and will make it more attractive to potential authors. A time of change indeed. Onward and upward... I hand over the reins to Dr Niamh Nic Daéid with all best wishes for the fascinating task ahead.

Reference

1. Jones A. Driving Under the Influence of Drugs In Sweden with Zero Concentration Limits In Blood For Controlled Substances. *Traffic Injury Prevention*. 2005 December 2005;**8**:317–22.

47(2) - 2007: Eight Years On

Being interviewed for the post of first Chief Executive of CRFP, eight years ago, I was asked how long I would intend to stay if appointed. Straight off the top of my head I said "Five years minimum, ten years maximum". I'm a man of my word. The organisation has developed and the job with it: time for someone new to take things on, and I wish Peter Ablett nothing but the best.

To a specialist in professional regulation there is no challenge as exciting as establishing a new organisation. Sound preliminary work had been done but policies, structures, procedures and rules were all largely virgin territory. Opening up a blank book and starting to write was the right kind of thrill. This is the best job I have ever had.

We have held fast to the central principles we set down at the outset: independent assessment of competence, focusing squarely on real life casework; robust external quality assurance; transparent documentation and open references; equal treatment for all parts of the sector; universal, free access to the register; time-limited registration and no automatic right to it.

We lived through all the questions that arise whenever a new professional register starts:

- "I've been doing this job for 30 years – what do I have to prove?"
- "My daily work is my proof of competence"
- "My clients have never complained"
- "Filling in forms means time away from work"
- "Who is fit to assess me?"
- "My work can't be measured by generic standards"
- "A register doesn't guarantee nothing will go wrong" and our old friend:
- "Who will assess the assessors?"

I'd heard them all before but the simple fact is that professionals of all kinds face the same challenge in the modern world: no one takes their abilities or their credentials for granted anymore; they must expect their advice to be questioned, even by inarticulate critics; and they must demonstrate, throughout their careers, that they have achieved, and are maintaining, the proper attitudes, knowledge and skills.

No one has singled out forensic practice, despite its high profile. It is a general trend for professionals and it is not going to change, despite the undisputed fact that UK forensic practice remains in many ways the envy of the world. Creating a register is the simplest way to define that thoroughly competent practice, put a boundary around it, protect it and celebrate it.

Have we achieved our objectives? In the main, I believe we have – simply because the register exists, is solidly established and is starting to be used. Those who commission forensic practice – lawyers, the police, the Legal Services Commission and Scottish Legal Aid Board – have a vested interest in quality assurance and risk management. Cases such as those of Barian Baruchi and Gene Morrison, fraudsters who managed to convince their astonishingly unwary paymasters that they had some form of expertise, demonstrate the power of the 'cult of the expert' and the danger of asking too few questions.

This year the case of Damilola Taylor has demonstrated not the register's inadequacy but the need for it to go further – taking in scientists who participate in the forensic process but would not normally report to court. The enquiry by Brian Caddy, a man who caught the vision for CRFP at the outset, made a coherent case for this and I hope my successors will take it forward without delay.

In truth I would like to have gone faster but the register's slow pace of growth was inevitable in an environment where people don't usually do anything unless they absolutely have to. CRFP has yet to make much headway with forensic medical practitioners – a group, difficult to regulate, who are seeing their forensic work steadily eroded with the development of advanced practice by nurses, radiographers and others. And there are still too few users consulting the register before committing their cash to an 'expert'. But that will come.

I have nothing but admiration for our enthusiastic group of professional assessors – now about 240 in number, all forensic practitioners – whose liberal gifts of time represent a real investment in the future of their professions. We have evolved a sound governance structure with a strong focus on the user. And we have a solid platform from which to extend the register to new groups: we are in serious discussion with forensic psychologists and accountants. Even the pathologists will come in eventually.

Eight years on the challenges have changed but the issue remains: how can the courts be assured that the forensic work of which they take delivery – painstaking, methodical, no stone unturned – is reliable and grounded in sound professional ethics? Many things are needed to secure that assurance.

Give the definitive register a chance and all the rest will flow from it.

Alan Kershaw
CRFP, UK

47(2) - 2007: Regulation of Forensic Physicians and the CRFP

(Correspondence)

Dear Madam,
We read with disappointment the article 'Eight years on' by Mr Kershaw, former Chief Executive of the Council for the Registration of Forensic Practitioners (CRFP) [1]. He stated: *CRFP has yet to make much headway with forensic medical practitioners – a group, difficult to regulate, who are seeing their forensic work steadily eroded by the development of advanced practice by nurses, radiographers and others*. In the August 2007 newsletter of the CRFP he wrote: *We have failed to penetrate far into the world of forensic medicine – the pathologists preferring to remain apart and the physicians succumbing to the magnetic pull of gold plating their systems, inducing paralysis*.

Some years ago, the Education and Research Committee of the former Association of Forensic Physicians (AFP) piloted the CRFP's proposed assessment process for forensic physicians. Our research indicated that the process was fundamentally flawed and failed to meet its objective of identifying forensic competence. As such, it could not be recommended to Association members.

Instead, the AFP proposed a modified appraisal based assessment to the CRFP. The CRFP chose not to take the matter further, preferring to open registration to forensic physicians without the support of the only professional body representing this group of doctors. We understood at the time that this decision was based on an overwhelming demand from practitioners, something that has clearly not been borne out through experience.

One of the AFP's concerns with the proposed registration of forensic physicians was the CRFP's stated desire to register all those practising the craft, rather than just those who provide expert evidence to the courts. The Association was concerned that this might lead to misunderstandings about the extent of a registered doctor's skills and knowledge. These were clearly well founded concerns given Kershaw's comment that there are still too few users consulting the register before committing their cash to an 'expert'. Registration with the CRFP does not confer expert status on a forensic physician and was never intended to. In the interests of justice, it is essential that those responsible for the register are clear on this point and do not add to any confusion.

The AFP's primary aims were to promote the (officially unrecognised) medical specialty of clinical forensic medicine and to raise standards through education and research. However, over the last 10–15 years it became increasingly clear that there was a need to separate the representative and educational functions of the Association by establishing an appropriately recognised professional and academic institution. Thus, in 2004, an approach was made to the Royal College of Physicians in London to investigate the possibility of forming a faculty of the College. Simultaneously, and serendipitously, other medical practitioners within the UK medical system with predominantly medico-legal workloads (medico-legal advisers of the three UK medical defence organisations and medically qualified coroners) also approached the College with a similar request. The Faculty of Forensic and Legal Medicine of the Royal College of Physicians was established in April 2006 to incorporate these three disciplines and was the first new Faculty within the RCP for over two decades.

The Faculty has been founded to achieve the following objectives:

- to promote for the public benefit the advancement of education and knowledge in the field of Forensic and Legal Medicine.
- to develop and maintain for the public benefit the good practice of Forensic and Legal Medicine by ensuring the highest professional standards of competence and ethical integrity.

The Faculty intends to exercise its powers to establish a training pathway in forensic and legal medicine and achieve specialist recognition of the specialty. It will also work with the General Medical Council to ensure that there are processes for the relicensing and recertification of forensic physicians that are fit for purpose.

Far from inducing paralysis, we view the work of the Faculty, and of the AFP before that, as the best way of moving forward and achieving a professionally-led medical specialty that serves the best interests of the criminal justice system and the wider public.

Yours faithfully
Ian F. Wall
Association of Forensic Physicians, United Kingdom

Guy A. Norfolk
Faculty of Forensic and Legal Medicine, United Kingdom
24 October 2007

Reference

1. Kershaw A., Eight years on, *Science and Justice* **47** (2007) 49.

47(3) - 2007: CPD, An Effective Means of Professional Development... or Is It?

(Editorial)

Continual professional development (or CPD) is often a useful phrase to produce whenever the development of staff is mentioned, or when you need to tick a box on your professional development plan at appraisal time. But what does it really mean? How, and in what way, can 'CPD' help professionals become more effective at their work? What are professional development courses supposed to achieve? Are they the same as a training course? The answer to the last question is "no" not if they are run correctly.

Those involved in the running of CPD courses may be aware of some of the underlying educational theories relating to its provision but no one has really explored this in the context of the criminal justice system as a whole, which, by its very nature is a complex, multi-layered environment with many underlying rules and codes. Surely if we're going to go on such professional development courses we want to be reassured that the underlying methodology is educationally sound in terms of understanding the fundamental issues relating to the sector. Unfortunately in many cases this is either not considered or worse still, simply ignored.

Within criminal (and in some cases civil) investigations, collaboration raises issues in relation to the interaction between the professional groups involved in a particular case. In such settings, individual practitioners (e.g. police, crime scene examiners, scientists, pathologists, legal professionals, the judiciary) while drawing on their own expertise, also need to recognise, respect and coordinate their work with the expertise of other professionals and wider reference groups. Such expertise might include scientific, investigative and legal theory and procedure, critical thinking and problem solving, evaluative methodology, use of intelligence and link analysis, knowledge acquisition, transfer and management. These practices can be implemented at an individual and organisational level to produce data with real intelligence value.

Obviously not all investigations will involve all of these aspects, however, efficient and productive criminal investigation also requires effective inter-professional understanding as well as collaborative and communication skills. Core dimensions involved are the understanding, integration and communication of the different spheres of knowledge, concepts and experience that individuals involved bring to the process. This involves for example:

(i) contextualised evaluation, problem solving and critical interpretation of the crime scene during the investigative phase;
(ii) interpretation of the analytical results derived from seized items within the case context involving scientific methodology and hypothesis testing;
(iii) effective communication of this evaluation and interpretation for intelligence and crime linkage purposes to other professional groups and to lay persons in the court room.

All of these processes are contained within a legal framework which often imposes rules and values upon professionals. Research suggests that the interfaces between different areas of expertise are likely to produce an environment of what has been called 'troublesome knowledge' [1]. Within a criminal investigation such troublesome knowledge can introduce barriers to the transference of information between phases of an inquiry. The individuals involved interact in complex stratified environments and establishing the knowledge base and understanding of the roles involved and developing the skills required and applied within these environments are key aspects of successful outcomes. Within all domains of professional practice there seem to be particular concepts that can be considered as gateways, opening up new and previously inaccessible ways of thinking about something. A so-called 'threshold concept' [2] enables access to a transformed way of understanding, or interpreting something without which the practitioner cannot progress. Threshold concepts are transformative, irreversible and integrative, entail a shift in practitioner subjectivity and an extended use of professional or scientific discourse. Such concepts are inherently problematic because new ways of thinking demand a new integration of ideas and this requires the practitioner to accept a transformation of their own understanding and as we all know, change is difficult!

Sometimes the troublesome nature of knowledge stems from its being tacit – that which remains mainly personal and implicit at a level of 'practical consciousness' [3] though its emergent but unexamined understandings which are shared within a specific community of practice. Specific 'ways of thinking and practising' have developed within disciplines and professional practices to represent particular understandings and ways of seeing and thinking. In certain cases, practitioners may grasp concepts but the barrier to their learning appears to lie at a deeper level of understanding. This is particularly so within a complex learning community [4] such as that collectively constituted by the various professional groupings involved in the criminal justice sector.

A crucial component of developing truly effective CPD will be to gain an insight into the ways that inter-professional understandings and misunderstandings of the practices and roles of colleagues in multi-professional investigation teams might hinder or enhance processes of problem formulation or solution. The task for designers of professional development programmes is to identify the source of these barriers and devise strategies which help the course recipients overcome the areas where troublesome knowledge presents itself. This is a challenge laid squarely at the door of CPD course providers.

So, next time you think of doing a CPD course remember that it's not just about being a passive recipient of information. The key to success is, as always, finding the most meaningful way of working and communicating with others involved not just in your field of expertise, but also with colleagues who are the providers of the samples and the users of your reports in the courts. Choose your course wisely!

Acknowledgements

The Editor wishes to thank Ray Land and Diane McDonald for useful discussions on the topic.

N. Nic Daéid
Editor Science and Justice

References

1. D. Perkins, Constructivism and troublesome knowledge, in: J.H.F. Meyer, R. Land (Eds.), *Overcoming Barriers to Student Understanding: Threshold concepts and troublesome knowledge*, Routledge, London, 2006.
2. J.H.F. Meyer, R. Land (Eds.), Overcoming *Barriers to Student Understanding: Threshold concepts and troublesome knowledge*, Routledge, London, 2006.
3. A. Giddens, *The Constitution of Society*, Polity Press, Cambridge, 1984.
4. D.M. McDonald, *Complex learning communities*, Proceedings of the Society 2005 Conference, Qawra, Malta, 2005.

48(1) - 2008: President of the Forensic Science Society

(Editorial)

This is my first editorial ever! What should I say or pontificate on? There are many issues that could be raised; ethics in forensic science, the utility or evidential significance of a single particle of contact trace material, digital technology as the next hot topic, or questions about the commercialisation of forensic science in England and Wales. I could contribute to the debate of any of these but think, for this editorial, I will stick to what I feel passionate about and know many of you reading this will as well – The Forensic Science Society. There will be many further opportunities for debate!

I am delighted and honoured to be elected President and would like to share some thoughts on what I believe the Society should be doing over the next few years. Top of my list would be enhancing our professional status by rising to the challenge of being the Professional Body for Forensic Science. This is closely followed by the opportunities to increase our sphere of influence with stakeholders and the criminal justice system.

I feel very humbled to be elected to the position of President. As a member of the Society for over 30 years I have had the opportunity to work with many of the past presidents – preeminent individuals in their field of science, law enforcement or the judiciary. Past presidents have had core performance themes; the membership base being key, along with publication of the journal containing original papers of scientific importance and influence, and high quality scientific conferences convened to meet the interests of membership and delegates.

For the last 15 years the performance themes have included the development of diplomas, recognised and acknowledged as a high standard. More recently the core performance measures have also included the Accreditation Scheme for Universities who teach forensic science. The Science and Technology Select Committee report on 'Forensic Science on Trial' (2004) commented positively on the work of the Society in relation to accreditation. We now have a rigorous and continually developing accreditation scheme for those universities involved in delivering forensic science qualifications. There are three standard components within the accreditation scheme and universities are required to undertake the interpretation component and choose either or both the crime scene or laboratory components. Only those who achieve the high standard will receive accreditation.

In 2004, under the leadership of then President Professor Jim Fraser, the Society underwent a significant change of status from learned society to professional body. As a result, expectations have risen and a spotlight has been on the Society – will we really be the professional body, can we step up to the mark? I am confident that the Society is moving in the right direction. Over the last years key organisations are actively seeking our views on consultation documents and the Society is a member of the stakeholder forum for the Forensic Science Regulator. We are also involved in the work of the Forensic Science Advisory Council and have good links with other bodies in the criminal justice system including CRFP and Skills for Justice. I believe it is important that the Society maintains and strengthens these links and actively seeks to network with other potential partners both in the UK and internationally.

I envisage a number of key challenges for the Council in the next few years. Firstly, improving and strengthening links with the members, seeking their views and involving them much more in activities. An enabling opportunity will be provided by our new website with the benefits of 'member only' areas. The Membership and Ethics Committee will also be using the website to consult with members using an online questionnaire.

Secondly, the Council plans to implement a Continuing Professional Development (CPD) process which I believe will be a positive initiative for the Society. Thirdly, we need to ensure the office systems at our Harrogate headquarters are operating efficiently and effectively – this administrative support is so critical because the majority of our Council members and those involved with the diplomas, accreditation scheme and editorial boards are contributing on a voluntary basis. We are very grateful for their continued endeavours on behalf of the Society. In concluding this editorial, can I leave you with a thought. As we continue along the path of professional status it is not too early to start thinking who you might wish to be part of the 2008–09 Council and lead the Professional body for the future? We will need a new President Elect, Vice President, Honorary Secretary and Council members. Please consider if you would like to play an active part in the work of your professional body? There is one particularly special event to look forward to in 2009 when we celebrate the 50th Anniversary of the Society, originally launched in Nottingham in 1959. How exciting is that! I look forward to serving the Society and all our members in my presidential year.

Brian W.J. Rankin

48(3) - 2008: The Forensic Science Regulator

(Editorial)

I am grateful for this opportunity to write an editorial for *Science and Justice* to introduce myself, the work I am asked to undertake, and to explain how I plan to achieve the tasks I have been set.

The supply of forensic science services in England and Wales is changing to become an open competitive market. Quality standards have been high, but as the supplier model changes my primary role is to maintain and enhance those standards across the entire market place so that the courts and the public can have confidence in the reliability of scientific evidence. I will also have oversight of quality standards applying to the national forensic science databases, starting with the National DNA Database® and moving on to the new National Ballistics Intelligence System. I have to be in a position to offer objective and authoritative advice to Ministers and others on forensic science issues and to manage complaints about the quality of forensic science provision. My work plans for the next year are set out in my business plan that is published on my website. How I intend to achieve all this is to be laid out in the Manual of Regulation that I propose to publish for consultation in July or August.

I am also grateful for the support I receive from the Forensic Science Society whose President, Brian Rankin, sits on my advisory council and was the first person to send me a welcoming message with offers of support after I had accepted the job as the Forensic Science Regulator.

Regulators have to reach out to their stakeholder community. Good communication, and through that consultation, is essential and accepted good practice. In the field of forensic science, with all its facets and different disciplines, it would be arrogant in the extreme to assume for one moment that I could attempt to fathom the complexities of the important and valuable work done by practitioners in all aspects of forensic science. I deliberately use the term 'practitioner' so as to include all those who work at the collection and analysis of forensic material, and the presentation of evidence resulting from that. I will rely on stakeholders and practitioners to provide the insight and assistance I need to achieve my task of setting and monitoring standards.

One of my early strategies is to meet as many of the stakeholder groups and individuals as I possibly can. I have met a broad range of people covering all aspects of forensic science in the UK. Please note the reference to the UK. Although I am a public appointee, recruited and paid by the Home Office, I plan to continue the arrangement reached by my predecessor with the Scotland and Northern Ireland authorities to work with them to deliver a single set of UK-wide standards for forensic science.

I have met with people from all corners of the forensic community covering practitioners, business leaders, academics, civil servants, police and so on. It has been a pleasurable and extremely informative process that will continue. One thing is absolutely certain; everyone wants to deliver the very best possible standards, a natural extension of that is to commit to working with me and my team to deliver those standards. This is crucial and central to my whole work plan. I have small and committed team of eight people with large expectations placed upon us. The only possible way we can expect to achieve our goals is to draw extensively on the teams of 'professional volunteers' that I am forming who will take on the bulk of the work that has to be done. My team will provide all the support that is needed.

My vision is to create a solid framework of standards founded on some basic principles: providers of forensic services should be accredited by a recognised independent accreditation body to accepted standards, practitioners should be able to demonstrate their ongoing competence and professional development, methods (products and services) should be based on sound science supported by sufficient data and validated according to acceptable scientific procedures. Records of accreditation, competence and validation must be accurate, retained and available for disclosure through the court process.

The standards framework must be accessible and will come with good guidance. I want to develop effective methods for monitoring compliance with standards and in achieving all this will rely heavily on delivery partners who have established processes, for example the UK Accreditation Service which provides independent accreditation against international standards. The benefits of this to the Criminal Justice System and the reputation of forensic science are obvious, as is the continuing confidence of the public whose interests are central to our work.

The engine room of our work will be the specialist groups of professional volunteers that I call together to tackle specific standards issue. The first groups that are in the process of being formed will cover: generic quality standards, DNA analysis, digital forensics, the end-user (courts) perspective, risk model and practitioner quality standards. The practitioner group is an additional one agreed recently to review the available options for the accreditation of practitioners involved in forensic science.

Details can be found on my website at: http://police.homeoffice.gov.uk/operational-policing/forensic-scienceregulator/. You can also find copies of the regular newsletters we send out. You can, if you wish, apply to receive the newsletters, free of charge, via email as they are issued.

I am supported in my work by the Forensic Science Advisory Council whose role is to advise me on forensic issues. The Council is well established and has already met four times. I am grateful for the valuable support the members give me and have absolute confidence in their advice. My confidence, and I hope theirs, was reinforced in the work we did to respond to the recent review led by Professor Brian Caddy of the science used in the analysis of low template DNA. I am not a biologist or chemist and have had to run fast to catch up with the science behind the analysis of trace amounts of DNA. It is very encouraging to know that I have people on my team, the Council, and among other stakeholder groups, who are ready and available to support me in the way they do.

We are all moving through a period of change as the forensic market opens up to be more competitive, as the police procurement process moves into the final stages and as the regulation of standards steps up a gear or two. I am pleased that this period of change coincides with the Forensics21 programme led by Chief Constable Chris Sims and delivered by the National Policing Improvement Agency. Forensics21 aims to challenge, enable and improve the use of forensic science services; quality standards are an integral part of this programme.

Forensic Science in the UK already delivers services of a high standard but can be improved with a coherent framework of quality standards built on some clear and basic principles. There will be an opportunity in the near future to comment on the details of this when I publish my Manual of Regulation for consultation. I look forward to receiving your contributions.

Andrew Rennison
1st Floor, SE Quarter, Seacole Building 2 Marsham Street
London SW1P 4DF, UK

SECTION II: SCIENTIFIC DEVELOPMENTS AND RESEARCH

35 editorials have discussed the development and the problems associated with the development of a research base in forensic science. The debate surrounding the provision of a contextualized research base in the forensic sciences is currently in focus. Again our debate has begun to mature, with more recent editorials beginning to discuss what are arguably the more important issues relating to forensic science research. Having a common and shared understanding of the nature of research, the evaluation of the effectiveness and value of such research and the development of a mature research partnership including investment in a funding base are all essential topics of discussion to move us forward. The fundamental understanding by criminal justice practitioners of what serious scientific research actually is, what it can deliver and what are realistic timescales for delivery are being explored. The challenges to be faced by all of us within the sector as a result of the findings of the US National Academy of Sciences report (2009) need to be debated in a mature, reflective and collaborative manner in order to develop our science.

The past 50 years have seen enormous developments in science and in scientific instrumentation applied to forensic analysis. The dominance of DNA since the late 1980s is obvious and we often forget that the last half century also saw fundamental developments in chemical analysis within forensic practice. The development of forensic applications for GCFID, GCMS, FTIR, Raman and more latterly IRMS have had huge impact in what is now achievable. The introduction of AFIS has changed the face of fingerprint interpretation across the globe forever and developments in biometrics, computers, digital and audio technology continue and will continue to have significant impact.

N. Nic Daéid

2(2) - 1961: The Individuality of Human Bloodstaining

The determination of the degree of individuality of a human bloodstain rests almost entirely on the application of serological methods designed to detect the characteristic antigens and antibodies of the various blood group systems. In practice this means the antigens of the ABO system although limited success has been enjoyed with other systems such as MN, Rhesus and Kell.

It seems unlikely that techniques in use at present, or in the foreseeable future, in blood group serology will be able to provide a statistically highly significant association between a bloodstain and a particular individual even though this can be done on liquid blood samples. If we are ever to be able positively to associate a bloodstain with a particular individual then there is much to be said for the view that forensic biologists must begin to look outside the field of blood group serology.

The answer to this problem may, in principle at any rate, be a rather simple one. Since we are frequently concerned with the comparison of two bloodstains, one from a scene-of-crime and the other from a suspect (as distinct from the case where a comparison of a bloodstain with a sample of liquid blood is required) then should we not begin to consider those quantitative characters, both hereditary and environmental in origin, which vary from moment to moment in the blood of an individual.

By restricting our search to those stable and genetically determined characters such as the blood group antigens are we not ignoring those features in the blood of an individual which may enable us to say "these two blood stains were shed by the same person at the same moment of time"?

There is probably sufficient data in published form at the present time on the blood levels of various substances to enable us to decide in principle if this is possible. If it is, then there will arise the practical problems of deterioration, contamination and of analytical techniques but these should not be insurmountable. By selecting those factors not subject to deterioration (for example metallic constituents) and by doing multiple analyses on different parts of the same stain and surrounding fabric then it may be possible to determine the levels of various constituents at the moment the blood was shed. The methods of carrying out large numbers of analyses on extremely small amounts of material must be given attention but modern physical aids including automatic analytical procedures may be the solution here. We may in this way gain results of a higher probative value than fingerprints.

A hundred years ago it would have been dismissed as fanciful nonsense had anyone suggested that a single fingerprint impression contained enough information to associate it positively with a single individual. The work of Herschel, Faulds, Galton and Henry changed this to such a degree that the use of fingerprints in identification is now commonplace.

In a progressive scientific organisation such as ours 'fanciful' concepts such as that outlined above should be the subject of everyday discussion and investigation. We may yet see forensic examinations of bloodstains pass into the hands of the inorganic chemist who, albeit with the aid of highly sophisticated instrumentation, may show that the problem is in essence a very simple one.

3(1) - 1962: A Breakthrough in Forensic Science

Perkons and Jervis, of the University of Toronto, have produced some experimental results which may herald the start of a new chapter in the history of forensic identification methods.

Using the delicate analytical tool of neutron activation combined with gamma ray spectrometry they claim to show, to use their own words, "that hair from any one individual has a unique micro-composition as compared with other individuals."

Much more work will be required before this claim can be finally substantiated but the analytical results produced are such as to suggest that their claim may well be correct.

Using the content of Germanium, Copper, Sodium, Arsenic, Bromine, Gold, Zinc and Mercury as the basis for their investigation they have produced weighty evidence for the following points:-

1. The micro-composition of human head hair varies widely among individuals.
2. The micro-composition of the head hair of a single individual varies only to a small degree with position on the scalp, time, and change of diet.
3. The numbers of factors and the degrees of difference between individuals in these factors suggest that results of as high a probative value as finger-prints may be obtained.

One of the great advantages of the analytical method used by Perkons and Jervis is that the sample can be produced for Court in a substantially unchanged condition so that further analyses may be performed if desired.

In seeking to show that the changes in composition along the length of an individual's hair are minor in comparison with inter-personal differences, Perkons and Jervis have made an interesting omission in that they failed to compare the linear variation in composition of several hair samples from the same individual.

If, as seems to be probable, the linear variations in composition are similar for all the hairs on an individual's head, then it holds the promise that sometime in the future we shall not only be able to say that the hair found at the scene belonged to X but that it left his head on a certain date! With this dizzy prospect, I leave you until the next issue.

S.S. Kind.

4(1) - 1963: Driving Over the Level

The appearance of *Alcohol and Road Traffic*, the report of the Third International Conference is a tribute to those persons who are deeply concerned with the daily toll of deaths caused on the highways of the world by the drinking driver. It is not the purpose of this editorial to criticise this particular publication (it is, indeed, ably reviewed elsewhere in the pages of this issue) but to question the lack of clarity of purpose of those participating in most present day discussions on alcohol and driving.

The reports of such discussions often leave one with the impression that the statistics, technical methods and clinical anecdotes are those which have been produced *ad nauseum* over the past twenty years.

The basis of legislation relating to the drunken motorist is the known facts that

(a) the ability of an individual to control a motor vehicle decreases with increased alcohol intake.
(b) individuals vary in their reactions to a given amount of alcohol as a result of a number of factors including health, genetic makeup and personal history.

With these facts in mind several countries have produced legislation laying down various levels of body alcohol concentration at which an individual may be presumed to be influenced or uninfluenced (these words are used as a convenient shorthand for the various legislative formulae used). Biological variability is sometimes allowed for in these statutes by a penumbral zone of body alcohol concentration which may be taken as *prima facie* evidence of influence.

Many analysts, clinicians and lawyers seem to feel intuitively that the uncertainty of these levels is a reflection of our imperfect knowledge of the subject and that further research will allow the absolute correlation of concentration and effect and the production of the scatter-free graph so beloved of the physical scientist. Thus they await eagerly the results of more accurate chemical analyses, of more elegant clinical diagnoses and of larger statistical samples in their asymptotic approach to a non-existent dynamic relationship between consumption and effect.

Much time, paper and money could be saved if all people concerned would keep before them the facts that

(a) the relationship between body concentration of alcohol and its effect is a probabilistic one and
(b) that society legislates (with few exceptions) for populations and not for individuals.

Any legislation which relates concentration and effect in an individual can do so only by introducing legal presumption. Presumptions, legal or otherwise, are unsatisfactory things and while society must legislate for the population it must do so in as adequate a manner as possible so that personal injustice, or indeed feelings of injustice, are as few as possible.

The two most simple minded solutions to the problem are

(a) to ignore the clinical findings and rely entirely on the chemical ones to prove degree of influence in an individual
(b) to ignore the chemical findings and rely entirely on the clinical ones to prove degree of influence in an individual.

A third solution which is more logical would be to argue by analogy as follows

(a) I know that in certain areas of Great Britain it is an offence to drive at over 30 miles per hour
(b) I am convinced that I am a safer driver at 40 mph than are some of my contemporaries at 30 mph
(c) If I were charged with exceeding the speed limit I would not produce, nor would the court listen to, argument (b) as a defence because
(d) the offence I am charged with is the *act* and not any *result* of the act.

Now translate this type of reasoning into alcohol and road traffic terms and let us imagine that some enlightened legislature, having regard to the known probabilistic relationship between body alcohol concentration and its influence on the production of road accidents (in exact analogy with speed limits and road accidents) promulgates a statute which says

> *any person found driving, or to be in charge of a motor vehicle whilst having a blood (urine) alcohol concentration greater than X per cent shall be deemed to be guilty of an offence.*

Note here there is no reference to effect nor indeed is any effect presumed. The offence is the act itself and not any real or presumed effect of the act.

The virtues of such legislation are manifold.

(a) the defendant is not convicted of being under the influence of alcohol when he knew he was not, i.e., there is no sense of personal injustice.
(b) no clinical examination is necessary nor is the court appearance of any expert medical witness required.
(c) no "presumptions" need be built into the legislation
(d) the offence is a simple yes/no decision the value of which can be determined simply by equipment at present available or likely to be in the near future.

The reluctance of Parliament to introduce statutory alcohol levels might be reduced if the legislation were on the lines of that proposed above.

A good argument could be produced for a fairly low statutory level (say 50 mg/100 ml in the blood) and penalties somewhat lower than those in force at present. To the howl that will inevitably arise at the suggestion of reduced penalties there is the answer that there can still be the graver "dangerous" and "due care" statutes, and there is no reason to exclude alcohol evidence from these cases in exactly the same way that evidence of speed is not excluded. Indeed in much the same way that a jury may be influenced by knowledge of exceeding the speed limit in a charge of dangerous driving they may be also influenced by evidence of exceeding the alcohol concentration limit.

In any event any further thought on the subject should be qualified by the recognition of the superfluity of further dosage effect studies of either statistical or anecdotal nature, by the need to produce simple instruments for body alcohol concentration determination and by a drive to educate legislatures in the necessity to introduce laws of the simple type outlined above.

4(1) - 1963: Science Before the Fact

It is in offences against property that the forensic scientist most regularly produces valuable examples of physical evidence. This is sometimes in the transfer of impressions (e.g., of jemmies) but more usually in the form of transferred materials such as paint, glass, metal and safe ballast from the scene to the person of the criminal.

These materials, the prime purpose of which is structural, protective or decorative are used by the forensic scientist to connect a criminal with a scene of crime.

A unique connection may be established if a distinctively shaped paint flake recovered from a suspect's clothing is found to fit into a damaged area of paint at a scene of crime. However, if no such fit is present the scientist may be restricted to saying that the paint flake is of the same colour and chemical constitution as that at the scene and that it could have come from there. These qualified decisions are a result of the fact that the paint in question may have been used for painting at more than one place and, indeed, may be of a type which has enjoyed very wide sales.

It is obvious that in situations of high security such as safes, strongrooms, jewellers shops and the like that more evidence towards convicting the guilty would be gained if the materials used were satisfactory not only from a structural, protective and decorative standpoint but also had concealed in them a means of direct identification.

Restricting our view for the moment to paints, it would be possible for "Security Paints" to be manufactured in restricted batches and sold under strictly controlled conditions with a sample from each batch to be lodged at some central repository for record and comparison purposes.

Just how much "individuality" can be built into a paint or other transferrable material without affecting its primary properties is a matter for research, as are the analytical techniques to be used in their subsequent detection and identification, but these are problems which can be overcome.

5(4b) - 1964: The Price of Road Safety

The law is intended to avoid disputes and to afford means of settling these where they arise. Its purpose is to provide a framework in which to live rather than to prescribe conditions of living. It does not settle what a man must believe or how he must behave except so far as necessary to establish a peaceful community in which all men may safely live out their lives. In our country there still exists a measure of freedom of thought, expression, opinion and action which far outstrips that of most of the civilised world. Although we do not always realise it, this forms a large part of our national heritage. It is well worth preserving.

Most of our road traffic laws accord well enough with these principles. That there must be rules, even sometimes arbitrary rules, is obvious. That these rules may have to be progressively modified to meet particular developing situations is understandable. But modifications of this kind which restrict liberty rarely take place unless they fit in with the general spirit and ethos of our laws, and they seldom introduce entirely new principles except where the need for departure from existing principles is fully and amply proved and supported by public opinion. To venture upon such innovations without the backing of substantial public opinion is dangerous as it leads to large-scale non-observance of the law bringing the whole system into disrepute.

Recent and impending developments in legislation regarding alcohol and road safety bear the marks of hastily and ill-devised measures to combat a desperate situation[1].

There is no doubt that the problem of road traffic accidents is grave and that the role played in these by drink is increasingly being realised. There is no question but that stern measures against the driver who drives while affected by drink are justified. But while proof that abolition of drink from the roads would save more than a proportion of accidents is lacking, the most revolutionary methods are not yet called for. The attempt to bring scientific evidence to support the campaign to eliminate drinking drivers, though highly commendable in itself, leaves something to be desired in practice.

The 1962 Road Traffic Act required the court to have regard to evidence as to the quantity of alcohol in the driver's circulation but gave no guidance on the amount considered to impair driving ability, and beyond giving sanction to the use of evidence of blood, breath and urine alcohol levels, the 1962 Act failed to take the matter much further forward. But the projected road safety legislation outlined in a recent White Paper[2] shows how the Government intend to move.

A screening breath test is proposed which may be applied by the police at random, subject to power of arrest should the driver refuse the test without good cause and the police have reason to suspect that he has alcohol in his body. Breath tests would not be given in evidence which would be restricted to capillary blood (now to be analysed by micro-methods), and where this is refused to two urine tests. Failure by a driver to provide one or other without good cause would result in similar penalties to those which would have been imposed had the driver been convicted. Coupled with this the Government propose an arbitrary level of blood alcohol of 80 mg/100 ml. above which driving ability would be deemed to be impaired.

These proposals, which the White Paper admits are drastic, in fact infringe at least three important principles hitherto regarded as basic to our law. The first is that the *onus* of proving a crime lies upon the Crown and they can expect and compel no assistance from the accused. The second is that hitherto our Courts have refused to compel submission to the needle in any circumstances. And the third is that penalties should be related to the offender and his offence and not pitched enormously high for purely policy reasons.

Although it is proposed that prosecutions against persons with a lower blood alcohol level than 80 mg/100 ml. will still be competent, it is likely that convictions in these cases will become almost impossible to obtain since demonstration of a "permitted" level of blood alcohol is bound to be taken as a favourable factor. The fixing of a prescribed limit will be taken as a tacit admission that drinking up to that limit is not per se objectionable, if it is not actually sanctioned. Individual drinkers will be able to measure fairly exactly the quantity of alcohol which they can safely drink to keep within the limit, and amateur analysts may even make their appearance in the larger public houses for the convenience of patrons. A "do it yourself" test kit is already on the market.

The most serious and unacceptable features of the proposals however are the power to screen at random all drivers whether or not suspected of having taken drink to excess, with a view to fishing for and compelling the disclosure of evidence to ensure conviction, and the swingeing penalties upon the driver who refuses to supply blood or urine samples and is thereafter treated virtually as though he were guilty. This is indeed a legislative example of "Heads I win, tails you lose". Can such powers and penalties possibly secure public approval, even when set against the grave national menace of the drinking driver.

Would it not be better for the law to restrict the taking of screening breath tests to cases where there is other evidence to suggest that a driver has consumed too much drink, and to permit drivers who refuse blood

---

[1] *Road Safety Legislation 1965–6; Cmnd. 2859, H.M.S.O., 116*.
[2] *Road Safety Bill: first reading 27th January, 1966*.

or urine tests to endeavour to justify their refusal in evidence to the Courts with whom the decision and disposal of their cases will rest.

If the Government proceed on the lines of the White Paper, as they seem to be doing, they should first make clear to the public that what they are proposing is a nation-wide inquisition coupled with a reversal of the presumption of innocence in the case of any who do not fall in with their methods.

A.R.B.

6(1) - 1965: Progress in Research

The need for additional provision in Great Britain of facilities for Forensic Science and in particular for the need of a research laboratory has been a recurring topic in Editorials in this Journal over the years. It is therefore pleasant to record that the Government has decided to open two new laboratories. Both are to be situated at Aldermaston in premises previously occupied by the Atomic Energy Authority. One is to be an additional regional laboratory with a responsibility for providing service to the police for an area West of London, and the areas covered by the existing laboratories will be rearranged to suit.

The second laboratory is a complete innovation and is to be concerned with research. Details are as yet scarce, but the close proximity of atomic reactors should allow the possibilities of neutron activation analysis in the field of forensic science to be fully explored.

All this is very encouraging and a big improvement on the present situation in this country, where reliance has been placed on enthusiasm of individuals in the various laboratories to carry out their research between their other tasks. This is not to imply that anything whatsoever should be done to discourage innovations from the scientists in the existing laboratories since the mere provision of buildings of itself has never produced a single new idea. What can be done in the new research laboratory is to provide the facilities and the time for the tackling of longer range problems than is possible at present. One of these which is of great importance, and has led to spectacular failures in Scientific Evidence from time to time, is to build up an accurate picture of the "normal environment" examples of which are the distribution of trace materials or particular physiological conditions. This is necessary because in Forensic Science it is frequently impossible to carry out control experiments.

In my opening address at the Inaugural meeting of the Forensic Science Society I said that it was my view that Forensic Science should not become isolated from the main body of science. This still remains a danger to be guarded against, despite the provision of the new research laboratory. A continuous cross-fertilisation of ideas is necessary and one way of ensuring this (apart from the inevitable recruitment of new graduates into the profession) is the formation of University departments devoted to its study. This is not a plea for the rather unrealistic idea at present current, that the administration of the Forensic Science laboratories should be taken out of the hands of the Home Office and should be based on University departments, but rather that education, research and specialised assistance in non-routine cases should clearly be recognised by the Home Office as a function of the Universities. This recognition should take the form of immediate and positive action in the setting up of research units in British Universities to work in close conjunction with existing departments of Law, Science, and Medicine.

A beginning has been made by the University of Strathclyde which has instituted a one year course to be given in the Department of Pharmacy, leading to the degree of M.Sc. in Forensic Science. A suitable immediate response from the Government would be to finance a number of Research Fellowships tenable in various Universities, pending further action on the lines suggested above.

For the present, however, let us wish the new research laboratory at Aldermaston well, and look forward to the publication of its first research paper in these pages.

D.P.

7(4) - 1966: Demanding Scientific Evidence

Though not all forensic scientists know or care whether the proof of paternity in bastardy suits is eased or rendered more difficult by the use of blood tests, there is a sense in which serological evidence today plays the kind of pioneering role which fingerprint evidence was playing in the 1900's when British Courts were first being introduced to their significance[1]. More than that, the process is now under the scrutiny of the Law Commission[2], and in due course a report on its feasibility and the wisdom of giving the Courts power to demand serological evidence will doubtless be issued. For the handful of blood group serologists the event will be of great interest; for the wrongly accused men who under present arrangements may be adjudged to paternity on the evidence of a malicious or muddled girl with minimal corroboration such news will be good. Rut it may not be realised by the general band of forensic scientists that their speciality is here under close examination, and that scientific proof itself may receive either commendation or discredit according to how the Law Commission advises.

Among the matters in issue at the present time are the following. The first fundamental question is the reliability of the scientific reports of blood examination, of the classification and description of blood group systems and of the enormously widespread testing which has taken place in every country over many years. There is world-wide acceptance of the basic propositions of blood grouping and the accepted theory is amenable to cross-checking by practical, statistical and other methods. Will the Courts be urged to rely and depend upon this vast accumulation of scientific experience? If it fails to merit approval how far must scientific proof go to become credible to the law.

The second question at stake is what happens when scientific evidence conflicts with legal presumption? This arises sharply when the presumption of paternity is challenged. To put it simply the law presumes that the husband of a woman who bears a child during the marriage is father of that child. Such an event, of course, is not invariably the responsibility of the husband. Where it is necessary to counter the presumption what weight of evidence is required? Some Courts have held the presumption to be almost irrebuttable. To do so is to fly in the face of facts, and has led one commentator to liken the judges to men who in modern conditions persist in declaring that the earth is flat[3]. How long will this perversity persist.

The third question under review is whether if scientific evidence is valid and can throw light on matters otherwise incapable of illumination (as, for example, in segregating father from non-father in cases where even the mother can not be sure) it should be used. Is it not time to give the Courts power to require the best evidence possible?

And a final point. Blood group evidence involves the notion of mathematical probability. It is open to the theoretical possibility of mutation which can be estimated in terms of probability. In a few rare cases blood group evidence may offer probability evidence tending to establish a positive finding of paternity in terms which have hitherto been deemed too hot to handle, or too open to misinterpretation for untutored judges. Only now are some Courts in Great Britain coming for the first time to hear evidence of statistical probability in everyday affairs. Whether the Courts are equipped to understand this kind of evidence and where it may lead are open questions.

It is sufficient to say that scientific evidence is under the microscope in a significant but restricted field. This concerns all who support this Society, one of whose declared aims is to encourage the application of scientific evidence. Its outcome may have a wider significance than even the Law Commission realise.

A.R.R

---

[1] *Cf. R. v. Castleton (1909)* **3** *Cr. App. R. 74 C.C.A.; Hanzilton v. H.M. Adv. 1934 J.C.I.*
[2] *Working Paper of the Law Commission: Family Law – Proof of Paternity in Civil Proceedings. Briefly noted in New Law Journal of 27th July, 1967.*
[3] *Eurtholomew: 1961 Modern Law Review, Vol. 24, 313ff.*

9(4) - 1968: Computer Control

The scientist of sixty years ago who found himself miraculously translated to a laboratory of thirty years later would not have found his surroundings vastly changed. The equipment would be a little more sophisticated, varnished brass was giving way to enamel and chrome plate but the change in design was minimal and he would have had little difficulty in resuming work in his new surroundings.

The last generation of laboratory development has changed all that. Instruments previously confined to the research laboratory started to appear in the routine lab. and once the flow had started it rapidly gained momentum. The main attraction of the newer instruments was the non-destructive nature of the examination so that the sample could be recovered for further tests. Even if sample was consumed, the sensitivity of these techniques meant that only minute amounts of material were required and the loss could be tolerated. The ability of the new instruments to determine smaller and smaller amounts meant that the chemists who thought in terms of milligrams rapidly became conditioned to thinking in micrograms, then in nanograms and now in picograms; each step representing a thousandfold increase in sensitivity.

With their special problems the forensic science laboratories were not slow to utilise the newer techniques and the labour-saving facilities which recording instruments possessed meant that many more samples could be examined and more parameters determined aiding identification or comparison. With the increase in the amount of information generated, not only in the laboratory but in the scientific community at large, the problem of handling the data began to become acute. It is all very well amassing a collection of say, infrared data but not very helpful if the information contained is not readily accessible. A simple, very efficient method of dealing with infrared curves has been developed by A. S. Curry, at Aldermaston, but although this is a great improvement, it will become limited when a very large number of curves are to be searched. When it is also necessary to relate one set of data to others to produce the final result the difficulties multiply.

Apart from the logistics of data handling there is also the problem of increasing work load. Often the investigation is simple and repetitive, and perhaps the best example in this category is the determination of alcohol in blood and urine. The basic technique is very simple but requires a gas chromatograph. A human operator has then to dilute the sample, inject into the instrument, check for proper operation and that only ethanol is present and, finally, calculate the result. Much of the analyst's time is, therefore, spent in elementary chemical procedures or calculations. It is possible to arrange to inject the sample automatically but some adjustment of the instrument and the final calculation are still time consuming operations.

One answer which springs to mind is the computer control of the instruments followed by the collection of data and any calculation. Much of the laboratory data is already in numerical terms or can be easily coded in this way so that the same system could serve to control both the instruments and the handling of data.

Unfortunately, when the word "computer" is mentioned, a vision of acres of equipment in air conditioned rooms and a bill looking like the National Debt of a minor South American republic springs to life and the concept becomes only a passing thought. This was true ten years ago but with the advent of small computers taking up less room than a desk and costing under £5,000 complete with all the input and print-out accessories, we should think again. The small size of this equipment means very fast working and such an instrument could collect information from over thirty instruments and calculate a result in less time than it takes to read this line.

True, its capacity for storing information is limited, but this is capable of expansion and with the introduction of a large computer holding a large central data store, the ability of a small computer at a peripheral laboratory to transfer information to or from a large data complex at very high speeds offers great flexibility.

During the day the peripheral instrument could serve the needs of the laboratory and store information which was later to be used to retrieve data from the main computer. This latter operation could take place at night and the returned information temporarily stored so that it could be printed out on an ordinary teletype ready for use the following day.

The Home Office are to introduce an elaborate central data handling system using a very large computer. Inevitably, this is still in the future and there will be many problems before all the forensic science laboratories have access to it. With a closely integrated scientific community like the Forensic Science Service and a comparatively small number of laboratories there is a good case for a study of the small computer under actual working conditions. If it did no more than handle the laboratory instrumentation and calculations together with the existing infrared data retrieval (and it could also easily include UV, GLC and TLC data), it would make sound economic sense to-day. With its potential for the future it should be an investment as significant as the introduction of the first spectrophotometer.

H.L.

11(2) - 1971: The Defeat of the Tail-Gater

A recent report in a British national newspaper *(Daily Telegraph*, August 28th, 1970) highlights the prevalence of shunting accidents, that is accidents resulting from one car colliding with the back of another. These accidents occur because drivers keep too close to the vehicle in front and fail to concentrate.

Common recommendations about minimum distances usually relate the spacing distance to vehicle speed. These distances are sometimes defined in terms of vehicle lengths and sometimes in terms of absolute distance. One such recommendation, in the British *Highway Code*, is that a yard clearance should be allowed for every mile per hour of car speed.

There is, however, no specific British legislation in existence dealing with people who drive too close, or as they are picturesquely known in some North American states, *tail-gaters*. However, prosecutions can be brought under Section 3 of the Road Traffic Act, 1960 (Careless Driving).

It appears that the question of minimum distance between vehicles is receiving active consideration in official quarters in the United Kingdom in relation to heavy vehicles but there appears to be no indication that the same attention is being given to the predominant vehicle on our roads, the private car. An example of the type of legislation which might be enacted is found in Section 78 of the Ontario Traffic Act, which states:

Section 78(1) The driver or operator of a motor vehicle shall not follow another vehicle more closely than is reasonable and prudent having due regard for the speed of such vehicle and the traffic and the conditions of the highway
Section 78(2) The driver or operator of a commercial motor vehicle, when driving on a highway outside of a city, town or village, shall not follow within two hundred feet of another commercial vehicle but this shall not be construed to prevent one commercial motor vehicle overtaking and passing another such vehicle

Thus Section 78(1) although specifying the offence of following too closely does not define this, leaving it to the test of "reasonableness". In relation to heavy vehicles, however, an absolute minimum distance is defined in Section 78(2) irrespective of speed.

Whilst it is no function of the scientist (except in his capacity as a member of society) to suggest what legislation should be made, it is at least reasonable for him to point out that any minimum distance legislation, if enacted, can only logically, in the present crowded state of our roads, be related to speed. He may also point out how such legislation might be enforced.

The radar speed meter is now a common feature of our roads. These instruments give an indication of the closing speed of the vehicle on to the stationary radar apparatus at the road side. They can only give a minimum indication of the speed since the quantity measured is that vector component of the car's velocity which is directed towards the radar speed meter. For absolute accuracy the meter itself would have to be directly in front of the vehicle. This may possibly be a desirable feature in the eyes of some drivers but can hardly be so in relation to the enforcement of the speed limit laws.

Let us now consider the situation where Parliament has laid down a minimum tailing distance related to the speed of the following vehicle, and that legislation has to be enacted on the basis that the onus is upon the following vehicle to keep his distance and that this distance should be a minimum of one yard for every mile per hour. It would be pointless for authority to expect this law to be enforced on the basis of the subjective evidence of stationary or moving observers and we must now search for an easily made and interpreted measurement which relates distance and speed. In essence the problem should prove a simple one and indeed a low priced system which may prove suitable is already on the open market*.

Imagine the situation where an instrument analogous to the radar speed meter is mounted upon the back of a police car. This instrument could measure the absolute distance of the following car and its closing speed. An input would be provided to add the police car's own speed to the closing speed of the following vehicle and the result expressed in terms of yards distance divided by miles per hour. Anything less than one would constitute an offence. It is obvious that the same meter, capable as it would be of measuring the comparatively complex quantity of distance/speed of a following car would also be capable of being used as an ordinary radar speed meter.

The social aspects of such a procedure are quite another thing from the technical and whilst it is not the function of this Journal to comment upon the desirability of introducing such procedures as these at least we may make the legitimate comment, as scientists, that such procedures are *possible* and the legitimate comment, as members of society, that *something* must be done to reduce the dreadfully high incidence of shunting accidents.

It is commonplace nowadays in the world of industry to relate pay awards to productivity agreements. Should such legislation as this be enacted, might not the forensic scientist expect an increment – after all he detects two offences for the price of one.

J.O.

11(3) - 1971: The New Zealand Approach

The job of the forensic scientist is to analyse the physical residue of complex events. Not for him the carefully controlled laboratory experiments where all variables save one are held constant. Neither does he (unlike the research scientist) choose the events he studies and his methods must be leavened with a good deal of common sense and flexibility. His approach must be multidisciplinary up to the point where he either solves the problem or identifies it as one for the academic specialist. In practice the latter alternative seldom occurs.

Real events do not conform to the boundaries of academic disciplines and indeed the classification of phenomena into such groups as Biology, Chemistry and Physics owes more to the attitude of the classifier than to the nature of the phenomena. This has led to a divergence between the forensic scientist and his academic colleagues. The experienced forensic scientist is a searcher for physical information without regard to the boundaries of academic disciplines, an approach which, like every other, contains some hazards but probably not as many on balance as the academic attitude.

Despite the welcome appearance of institutions such as the Home Office Central Research Establishment, research in the field of forensic science still tends to follow restricted laboratory lines probably owing to the academic background of most researchers and the huge complexity of real situations.

There has of late, however, occurred a refreshingly new and practical approach to the experimental study of complex phenomena in forensic science. Examples of this are the work of Nelson & Revell in New Zealand

---

*HP35200A Doppler Radar Module.
Hewlett Packard 1217 Meyrin – Geneva, Switzerland.

who experimentally demonstrated the backward fragmentation of window glass when broken by impact. Not for them the mere laboratory demonstration of the phenomenon using automatic devices but also the final heroic confirmation by high speed photography of what happens when an individual strikes a sheet of window glass with a hammer (this Journal, 1967, **7**, 2).

This pragmatic attitude was again displayed by Nelson in his investigation of petrol fires in enclosed rooms (ibid., 1970, **10**, 1). Here again theory was finally confirmed by the ultimate test, an experimental petrol fire in an enclosed room.

The same practical approach has been shown by Mitchell and his co-workers at the Cardiff Forensic Science Laboratory in Wales in their experimental investigations of injuries to the head caused by the explosion of detonators in the mouth (using the heads of dead sheep) (ibid., 1969, **9**, 26), and of a puzzling motor vehicle accident (ibid., 1970, **10**, 149).

This approach where the experimenter is not inhibited by the complexity of the situation is happily becoming more common and is to be encouraged. Doubtless in certain types of case, particularly of the offences-against-the-person variety, such experiment might be inconvenient but there are many fields in which this approach can be used. It is far easier to reconstruct the probable sequence of events from the examination of the physical residues when the examiner has carried out, or has first-hand knowledge of, experiments dealing with the same or similar circumstances.

Put another way, all forensic scientists who are called upon to examine the scenes of safe-blowing should be accomplished blowers of safes. It is as simple as that.

N.A.

14(1) - 1974: Back to Basics

Perusal of recent forensic science books and journals reveals few, if any, procedures that can be done without elaborate instrumentation. The present generation of up-and-coming forensic workers cannot seem to function without gas chromatographs, magnetic spin resonators, or computers. When these machines break down – and they frequently do – the helpless scientist has nothing to fall back upon except a hastily summoned mechanic. He is not likely to have been trained how to do his work manually with the most elementary apparatus.

Lest I be accused of advocating a return to horse and buggy in the jet age, I hasten to point out that what I think is needed is a more thorough apprenticeship in basic craft skills. Naval cadets still learn seamanship on square-rigged sailing vessels, and any qualified physician remembers how to deliver a baby even after years of practice in an unrelated speciality. But, our science faculties seem to be turning out splendid instrument jockeys who wouldn't know a Marme crystal if they stumbled over it, can't do simple glassblowing, or make first echelon repairs to their microscopes. In short, people who are unable to fabricate a bullet trap from an empty oil drum or grow bacteria in a discarded whisky bottle. They may never have to do it, but they ought to know how just in case.

Lord Peter Wimsey once complained that we never learn how to do anything really useful in school, like how to pick a lock. Forensic science is full of little problems like that, and we can't ever hope to have a sufficient number of specialists on tap to cover every contingency. Technical versatility to handle a variety of assignments implies training and experience with a variety of tools and techniques. I submit that our schools are skimping on that. Perhaps the educators have been frightened away by strident student demand for relevancy-relevant, that is, to the problems and issues of immediate concern to the student.

What are these craft skills? First of all, I think, would be a better grounding in "relevant" mathematics, with emphasis on probability plus drill with the slide rule in case the electronic calculator breaks down. Next is microscopy, for every forensic discipline uses this instrument although few users can correctly adjust the illumination. How many of us can produce Kohler or critical illumination without thinking about it or looking it up in a book? Photography, of course, with the skill to produce a picture acceptable to the courts – and in the kitchen sink if necessary.

Mechanical skills should be stressed, from sawing a board to using a soldering iron. Every scientific worker should be qualified to clean, calibrate, and adjust each and every piece of apparatus he uses, just as the carpenter hones his own plane and sharpens his own saw. Blueprints and electrical wiring diagrams should be as instantly comprehensible as the racing form is to a handicapper. Proper use of screwdrivers, wrenches, and pliers ought to be demonstrated to the satisfaction of Ph.D. examiners.

But more fundamental is that the forensic scientist should be familiar with the most simple way of doing any analytical procedure. He should always know another alternative way of doing anything. He should know how to titrate if the colorimeter lamp burns out. He should know how to mix his own photo developer if the packaged soup runs out during a long weekend. His ingenuity should encompass the ability to substitute one chemical for another, to splice a wire, plug a leak, improvise a microdiffusion unit from bottles, dust a latent fingerprint with manganese dioxide and a chicken feather, produce precipitin sera by injection of goats, know that paraldehyde will work just as well as acetaldehyde in the Duquenois–Negm reagent, extract codeine from cough syrup to get a standard for his colour tests, and – how to pick a lock.

Elliott B. Hensel

16(3b) - 1976: An Independent Witness Required

The division of people into either "secretors" or "non-secretors" of the groups A, B and 0 on the basis of an examination of semen and saliva is well established. Altogether five groups are recognized ("non-secretor", A, B, 0 and AB secretors), and the grouping of secretions, especially in cases of sexual assault, may be very useful.

However, in recent years, Fiori and his colleagues (Fiori et al., 1971, 1973; Panari et al., 1976) have been fractionating saliva and semen by column chromatography and have produced results which suggest that the true picture is much more complicated. Instead of just five groups these workers present evidence that there may be up to twenty different types. Obviously the ability to break down a population to this extent would be very valuable, especially as the grouping of semen and saliva stains is relatively poorly advanced compared with the range of groups into which a bloodstain can be typed.

Although the work of Fiori and his colleagues would seem to be of much potential significance to forensic scientists it appears to have received relatively little attention.

A recent report by Rutter and Whitehead (1975) however, has cast some doubt on Fiori's findings and a further paper (in this issue of the Journal) has confirmed the failure of the British authors to fractionate saliva into the number of groups, or types, reported by Fiori et al. The Italian group have, in turn, produced a spirited reply to the British work (Fiori, 1976).

Is there not another worker in the field prepared to act as referee?

References

Fiori, A., 1976, *Forensic Science* **7**, 91.
Fiori, A., Giusti, G. V., Panari, G., and Porcelli, G., 1971, *J. Chromatogr.*, **55**, 337.
Fiori, A., Giusti, G. V. and Panari, G., 1971, *J. Chromatogr.*, **55**, 351.
Fiori, A., Giusti, G. V. and Panari, G., 1971, *J. Chromatogr.*, **55**, 365.
Fiori, A., Panari, G., Giusti, G. V. and Brandi, G., 1973, *J. Chromatogr.*, **84**, 335.
Panari, G. Rossi, G. and Fiori, A., 1976, *Forensic Science*, **7**, 55.
Rutter, E. R. and Whitehead, P. H., 1975, *Forensic Science*, **5**, 163.
Rutter, E. R. and Whitehead, P. H., 1976, this Journal.

19(4) - 1979: Publish or Perish

The experienced forensic scientist realises that, like engineering and medicine, his own speciality is a technology. He takes a well established framework of scientific fact and procedure and he applies it in real day-to-day circumstances which are, in detail, irreproducible. This "one-off" nature of forensic science case-work easily leads to an attitude of mind verging on contempt for published scientific work. This attitude may concede that a few good snippets can be hidden in a mass of published verbiage but that, usually, these are not worth seeking. If a published scientific article is not treated as trivial then it is often charged with being obscure.

Presumably the critics belonging to the anti-publishing school must communicate and this can only mean that they use the shifting sands of the spoken word. Unfortunately many scientists believe that they can maintain a consistent logical position without writing, although a view may shift gradually to a contrary attitude even when the holder himself does not notice the change.

A more rigid conceptual framework is required in forensic science. Verbal discussions should be used for the fine tuning of concepts, for rational assessment, and as an aid to the intuitive leaps which so often lead to real scientific progress. The pure oral tradition should be kept for folk-songs and Irish jokes.

Having said all this, it must be conceded that publication is a very imperfect medium for informing the forensic scientist. It is fraught with seemingly insuperable difficulties particularly in the decision whether or not to publish a submitted article. The editor's decision is, and must remain, a subjective one. He must decide whether the article is comprehensible or if it can practically be made so by a reasonable amount of sub-editing. He must face the fact that the more specialised an article is then the more he must rely upon his specialist referees. He must then have the commonsense to realise that the more specialised a field the greater the probability that personal and esoteric considerations will obtrude. There is no complete solution to this problem but it can be ameliorated by courageous and responsible editing.

Unless concepts and methods are published, and so subjected to the assessment and the criticism of peers, then at best (should they be correct), they will be a long time taking their rightful place in the framework of scientific knowledge. At worst (should they be incorrect), they will live a longer harmful life – a sort of oral alchemy conditioning our attitude of mind.

Forensic science requires a flexible enquiring mind, a wide knowledge, a profound expertise, great energy, some intuition and, as far as it is given to human beings, complete honesty. It requires neither the repetitive pot-boiling author nor the pen-tied verbal critic but, if we are to have one of these two evils, let us have the lesser one.

Forensic scientists must publish or forensic science will perish.

J.O.N.

22(2) - 1982: But Is It Science . . .

This is a materialistic age when progress is becoming synonymous with acquisition of worldly goods, from personal effects to Third World Countries' National Airlines. Forensic Science is not immune and its literature often gives an air of the method supplanting the problem. Case reports are out-numbered by papers of the type "A new method to measure...", and laboratories are all too often judged by their hardware content. Advances in methods are certainly important – specificity is vital, increasing sensitivity means evidence can be detected where it would previously have been missed and that preservation of sample is facilitated, and behind a plethora of possessive acronyms (GC-MS, SEM-MPA, XRF) lies an ability to detect trace evidence that would have astounded the pioneers of Forensic Science.

Orfila would have been delighted to have today's technology at his command but one wonders what Locard would have made of it all. Locard had the wisdom and the ability to stand above technology, to ask what Forensic Science was about, and to formulate his exchange principle. Paul Kirk, too, had the ability to divorce himself from the technology and to ask what makes Forensic Science different from other quantitative and qualitative sciences, and indeed whether criminalistics (the synonym is deliberately chosen to avoid begging the question) could properly be described as a science.

There are many obstacles preventing a confident assertion that criminalistics is a science. Some of the obstacles are fundamental and some are mere distractions. One of the principal distractions is the uncomfortable feeling that the laboratory-based criminalist performing endless comparisons does not deserve the epithet scientist. Has he allowed himself to become a mere technician and technology to supplant science? He derives satisfaction, and justly so, from his knowledge that he has used the best tests for the local laboratory circumstances, has offered an excellent amalgam of speed, sensitivity and specificity, has performed commendably in all the quality assurance checks, and has produced a report which says nothing which is any way misleading or prejudicial. He will also take great satisfaction in pointing to the large number of cases he has handled which have successfully shown positive trace contacts or positive identification of controlled drug substances.

The successes brought about by the marriage of technology with the effective organisation of criminalistic services only highlight the lack of progress in other areas. Perhaps the first feature of criminalistics to catch the public eye was the implementation of fingerprinting, but little other than the technology has changed since Dr. Henry Faulds wrote to Nature in 1880. Give the criminalist an accused and materials to compare with each other or give him fingerprints and he will give you results but in the absence of these he is disappointingly ineffective.

Men such as Locard and Kirk were broad-shouldered giants, and if criminalistics is to be forensic science and not forensic technology and its proponents forensic scientists not forensic technicians, then there is a great need for more of today's practitioners to use these vantage points to see far and guide the development of the subject as a science.

22(3) - 1982: Hair Today . . .

Human head hairs are much beloved of fictional forensic scientists and detectives who are able to identify single hairs aided only by a magnifying glass and their own rare talent. Were this so in fact as well as in fiction then the assistance the forensic scientist could give the investigating officer or the Court would be enormously increased.

Hairs are characterised by their possessing features which are used to type any body tissue – the genetically determined polymorphisms used for blood grouping, or by their possessing unique features associated with extraneous dyestuffs, the protein structure of hair, or the acquisition of trace metals. It is 20 years since an Editorial in the Journal hailed "A breakthrough in Forensic Science" and said of results from Toronto applying neutron activation analysis that "This may herald the start of a new chapter in the history of forensic identification methods". The qualifier was well chosen; hair characterisation by NAA has not been a success and indeed the value of the technique in other fields of forensic science suffered somewhat because of this false start.

Work on hair characterisation has continued and amongst the most fruitful results to date, some of which were reported in the April issue of the Journal, have been those on grouping of sheath cell tissues by enzyme polymorphisms. As well as affording characterisation of individual hairs this seemed an attractive prospect in that it was generally held that sheath cell material was of evidential value in its own right, being consistent with forcible removal of the hair rather than its shedding at the end of the natural cycle of growth. The paper by King and colleagues in this issue strikes at the very root of this ancient premise and shows that the presence of sheath cells is not a reliable indicator of forcible removal. Most plucked hairs were found to have no sheath cells but sheath cells were found on some naturally shed hairs. Indeed, association with forcible removal cannot be reliably made on single hairs, but requires measurement of the anagen/telogen ratio in bulk samples.

Thus although sheath cell typing has been an advance in characterisation, particularly when multiple enzyme grouping is used, its application is hampered by the requirement for relatively fresh cells to be present, by the minority of shed hairs possessing the tissue, and its further interpretation is limited by the most important results reported by King and colleagues. Interest and progress in other areas of hair characterisation, including microscopy and biochemical analysis of the substance of hair, continue to attract attention and some significant papers will be published in the forthcoming issues of the Journal. This research should now receive an added impetus but the ready, unique, characterisation of single shed human hairs remains, in the words of the most famous fictional Forensic Scientist and Detective, Mr. Sherlock Holmes, "Quite a three pipe problem".

25(2) - 1985: On Body Fluid Frequencies

(Guest Editorial)

JW Thorpe

Forensic Science Unit, University of Strathclyde, 204 George Street, Glasgow, United Kingdom GI1 XW

It is common practice when reporting blood grouping results to include a figure representing the frequency of occurrence of the particular group combination in a population. The data for these calculations can be obtained from a number of sources, for example, blood transfusion records, studies involving population genetics or individual forensic science laboratory records. Such sources do not necessarily include information on the particular genetic markers used by forensic scientists, do not necessarily involve large samples of the population and do not necessarily cover all areas of the United Kingdom. The collection of data in this issue overcomes these problems and has the additional advantage that the results have been obtained using the technology currently employed in forensic science laboratories.

As a data collection, the information in this issue is to be commended for including allele frequencies, which are of value to those engaged in the investigation of parentage disputes. This also is a part of forensic science and reliable estimates of allele frequencies are essential for the calculations being employed [1].

The possession of this type of database for body fluid examination contrasts markedly with the lack of them in other fields, such as hair examination. The use of the data can provide objective assessments of the grouping systems to be desired in a laboratory, and the system or systems which could be most usefully employed upon a particular stain, and guidance to the courts when assessing the results. This objective assessment is not only useful but also imparts an air of "science" which may be lacking when subjective judgements must be used.

This database is, however, only one of the many that will be necessary if subjective judgement is to be eliminated. Decisions made on the basis of population frequencies have to be modified subjectively. One example would be when choosing a system to examine a particular stain. Population data may indicate one system but the stain size may suggest another.

There are deficiencies when attempting to provide guidance to the Courts for assessing the significance of grouping results. At present, all that can be done is to indicate the coincidence that has occurred if the blood has not come from the suspect source. Even in this, the numerical assessment has to be supplemented by a verbal statement to the effect that "the blood could not have come from ... but could have come ...". Current numerical assessment refers only to stains and general populations. They do not take into account the parties more intimately involved. These defects are well-known and statistical techniques to overcome them are being developed [2, 3, 4]. The techniques have at least one more feature in common. They are independent upon databases which supplement population phenotype frequencies.

To implement these techniques fully, there is a need to know more about blood transfer and stain occurrence within the general population, to mention but two areas. This need has been emphasised by the above authors and, indeed, some work has been done [5, 6]. This collection of phenotype data should act as an incentive to greater efforts to rectify the paucity of information in these vital and related areas.

References

1. Lee, Chang Lin. Numerical Expression of Paternity Test Results Using Pre-determined Indexes. *American Journal of Clinical Pathology* 1980; **73**: 522.
2. Selvin S, Greenbaum BW and Myhre BA. Probability of Non-discrimination or Likelihood of Guilt of an Accused: Criminal Identification. *Journal of the Forensic Science Society* 1983; **23**: 27–33.
3. Evett IW. What is the Probability that This Blood Came from This Person? A Meaningful Question? *Journal of the Forensic Science Society* 1983; **23**: 35–39.
4. Gettinby G. An Empirical Approach to Estimating the Probability of Innocently Acquiring Bloodstains of Different ABO Groups on Clothing. *Journal of the Forensic Science Society* 1984, **24**: 221–227.
5. MacDonnell HL and Bialousz LF. *Flight Characteristics and Stain Patterns of Human Blood*. Washington DC: National Institute of Law Enforcement and Criminal Justice, 1971.
6. Briggs TJ. The Probative Value of Bloodstains on Clothing. *Medicine, Science and the Law* 1978; **18**: 79–83.

26(1) - 1986: Publish or Perish Revisited

(Editorial © Forensic Science Society 1986)

Recent years have brought with them ample evidence of good health in the forensic science publication arena. This journal has changed to six issues per annum, Forensic Science International to 12; the Journal of Forensic Sciences continues with unabated strength and variety; and many previously captive authors have enriched other journals, such as the Journal of Chromatography and the New England Journal of Medicine, with their writings. It thus seems that the Editorial exhortation of 1979 that "Forensic Scientists must publish or forensic science will perish" has been heeded [1].

That splendid Editorial raised, and answered, many questions, including Editorial licence and the problems which result from the "one-off" nature of forensic science case-work. However, the aspect of publishing which is firmly occupying centre stage (or should it be centre-fold?) is that of the value of work published in the open literature because of the opportunity that it provides for objective peer appraisal. Across the world, oral "hand-me-downs" are being deemed inappropriate to the correct practice of forensic science. Some critics have even suggested that using unpublished modifications to methods, or techniques devised "in-house", is unacceptable [2]. That extreme position conveniently ignores the fact that quantitative and objective evaluations can be made to justify introducing new or revised techniques to case-work.

Nonetheless, the general thrust is clear and should not be resisted – forensic scientists must indeed publish or forensic science will indeed perish, not from atrophy of the intellect, but by frontal assault from an affronted judiciary.

References

1. J.O.N. Publish or Perish. *Journal of the Forensic Science Society* 1979; **19**: 235.
2. Grunbaum BW. Genetic typing of physiological stain evidence: a proposal for quality assurance guidelines. *California Attorneys for Criminal Justice Forum* 1984; **11**: 11–18.

27(1) - 1987: Through the Looking Glass

(Editorial © Forensic Science Society 1987)

Nineteen-eighty-six should have been a good year for forensic science. Signs of a new and determined professionalism were widespread. University activities showed a healthy growth – Berkeley was again producing graduate students and AFTE was making encouraging noises about degree courses. The Forensic Science Society at last introduced its Diploma scheme, starting with Questioned Documents. The ASCLD initiatives in proficiency testing and accreditation were gaining considerable support. The first real individualising technique in biology was reported from Britain. There was a steady undercurrent of excitement about the Vancouver meeting of a rejuvenated IAFS.

Yet one was left with a feeling of disquiet, disquiet that the year may just have seen the most fundamental challenges to forensic science, challenges the more potent because of their source – from within forensic science from the judiciary.

The findings in Albert Greenwood Brown and in Young are the cause for concern. These two cases, one in California, one in Michigan, shared the common theme of admissibility of forensic serology methods (although there were other issues, especially in Brown).

The place that methods should hold in forensic science has been a fruitful subject for debate at the bar for some time. Many beers have been shared as the likes of Alan Curry and Stuart Kind have tried to persuade colleagues that forensic science must become consciously orientated to problem solving and not become dominated by a methods orientation. However, the problem-solving ability of the scientist is often constrained by the methods available to give valid analytical results. Sound methodology is therefore the bedrock of forensic science. The legal bar understands this too.

The focus of judicial concern in Brown and Young was the Frye standard (or its modification as a result of relevant State decisions). At its simplest, electrophoretic analysis of biological fluids, for enzyme phenotyping, using the Multi Enzyme System was challenged on the grounds that it did not meet the required standard of scientific acceptability. The challenges asserted that the technique was essentially an 'in-house' development, and although based on starch gel electrophoresis (undeniably an accepted and acceptable general procedure) it was a version which compromised optimal separation conditions to permit the simultaneous analysis of three enzyme systems from a single sample. Because it is a compromise, and because it is used only in the forensic science community, the argument ran, it fails to meet the standards required by Frye.

The Californian Court ducked the issue, finding that other evidence was more than sufficient to uphold the verdict of the trial court, but implying that the court should have conducted a preliminary hearing to determine whether the MES evidence would be admitted, that is, should have had a Frye hearing. This at least 14 years after starch gel electrophoresis of PGM was published, and 6 years after introduction of MES.

The Michigan court evaluation was even more appalling. Not only did it reject the evidence, it managed to introduce a new legal paradox. The version of Frye which pertains in Michigan restricts evidence in a Frye hearing to that from disinterested parties, being in effect a prohibition on testimony from anyone who earns their living by practising in the area of concern. Not content with the logic gap of how to determine that a technique has achieved acceptability in the relevant scientific community when you refuse to admit the testimony of members of that community, the Michigan court ventures further into absurdity by refusing testimony from a respected serologist in the field of paternity testing on the grounds that his expertise was too far removed from the area of concern.

Let us consider where this leaves forensic science. It means that the intraprofessional concern about standards, which led to the Forensic Science Society Diploma scheme, will be questioned on the basis that the training and evaluation is by interested parties. It means that academic initiatives such as that from AFTE will be disregarded, the teachers being deemed too close or too far from the relevant area of science. It means that DNA typing will either never be admitted or will need such an inordinate period of stage-managed evaluation and tuition that the courts will lose years of its potential benefit. It means that the gigantic steps to produce objective improvement and evaluation which have been taken by ASCLD initiatives such as the CTS proficiency program will be wiped out. Or it could.

Consider the ASCLDICTS proficiency testing program. It contains a wealth of data testifying to the reliability of techniques and practitioners in all areas of forensic science including enzyme typing. It matters not a jot that some other real or hypothetical system is 'better'. What does matter is that the system used is giving the correct answer. That is known at the time of testing, from the results of simultaneously processed controls, and is confirmed by the results of internal and external quality assurance programs. This total assurance of the reliability of the method is international.

If Michigan, or any other court for that matter, cannot distinguish between fact and fantasy at such a simple level, then the gulf between science and law looks to be widening to proportions which can only mean that the law is denying itself the advantages of evidence which is objective, factually correct, in many instances not available from any other source, and, at its least, provides truly independent corroboration of other evidence. Perhaps Lewis Carroll got it right in 'through the looking glass'.

'Contrariwise,' continued Tweedledee, 'if it was so, it might be; and if it were so, it would be: but, as it isn't it ain't. That's logic.'

29(6) - 1989: The Highest Order Common Sense

Nothing gladdens the heart of an ex-editor so much as the news that one of his elderly writings has stirred the soul of a contemporary editor. A recent issue of the Journal of Forensic Identification (1989; 39: 331) reproduces an editorial from the Journal on the subject of why forensic scientists should publish [1].

The message is the same today as it was then. Re-reading that old editorial makes me realise how things have scarcely changed and how, with the possible exception of research papers, we still write so little. I say "possible" because I know of a good deal of first-rate research, immaculately performed and recorded, which will languish forever in laboratory note-books simply because of the inexplicable reluctance of the researchers finally to convert it to a form suitable for publication.

Scientific research, it seems, will always attract its share of excellent mid-field players who, when they face the goal, suffer a loss of nerve. Presumably they get such intellectual satisfaction from playing the ball that they believe it sufficient justification for being in the game. We must reluctantly face the fact that unawarded Nobel Prizes languish in laboratory filing cabinets as often as they do in editorial reject piles.

But is there a deeper reason for not publishing our findings for a wider audience of colleagues to appraise? Is some of our best laboratory work unpublished because of a basic unease regarding the flimsiness of our conceptual foundations? Few forensic scientists are as comfortable discussing concept as they are when discussing technique. There are not many successors to California's Paul Kirk.

Sengupta [2] seems to crystallize this need for intensive conceptual analysis when he pleads for forensic scientists to attempt to enunciate the "fundamental theories" of forensic science and to "bring ... hidden sense to the surface". His was not a call for expensive resources but simply a demand upon intellect, logic and reflective thought. It is here that forensic scientists need to develop most as writers; not in place of, but in addition to, the publication of laboratory findings.

Of course, Sengupta said it much more elegantly. He called it simply the "highest order common sense". I doubt if anyone could put it better than that.

References

1. JON (Kind SS). Publish or perish. *Journal of the Forensic Science Society* 1979; **19**: 235.
2. Sengupta D. Forensic scientists and common sense. *Journal of the Forensic Science Society* 1988; **28**: 259.

Stuart S Kind

30(1) - 1990: Profile of the Nineties

Scientists have always been great creators of abbreviations of one form or another. Most scientific acronyms are used as shorthand exclusively by biochemists or whomever, but occasionally one breaks out into the great lay consciousness. A prime example must be DNA (deoxyribonucleic acid), which was in common enough usage by the early nineteen seventies to warrant a dictionary entry of its own [1]. Discoveries concerning DNA, the "thread of life", included the unravelling of the genetic code and establishing the principles of gene replication, the elegant process that forms the basis of reproduction. In this issue of the Journal, with two original DNA papers from John Smith of ICI Diagnostics and his colleagues, we see part of the process of translating these basic principles of molecular biology into forensic science.

At the Forensic Science Society's Autumn Meeting last year, the Firth Memorial Lecturer, Sir Peter Imbert, talked about the ways in which the partnership between police officers and forensic scientists is going forward. It is clear that while the Police recognise the importance of DNA profiling, new legislation may be needed for them to be able to utilise, on our behalf, the full potential of the technique in criminal investigations. If the promise of polymerase chain reaction technology is fulfilled, the coming decade may see forensic scientists able to deduce identity from a single cell. The ground must surely be prepared properly for exploiting this, the ultimate contact trace.

Reference

1. Macdonald AM (ed). *Chambers 20th Century Dictionary*. Edinburgh: W&R Chambers 1972: 380.

JFSS 1990; **30**(1): 1

30(6) - 1990: Official Publications

(Editorial)

By the time this issue of the Journal is read, the buzz of the 12th meeting of the International Association of Forensic Sciences will have long subsided. The immediate Past-President of the IAFS and ex-editor of the Journal will be back in his office listening, according to his recent editorial [1], to his customers whoever they may be. *Customer* is one of the words that characterize the new thinking in British forensic science Pat Whitehead talked about in our last issue [2]. *Management, resources, accreditation, marketing* and *performance* are others, and changes in the way 'official' forensic science is organized and carried out are of more than just academic interest to the Forensic Science Society. The Scientific Civil Service was prominent in the formation of the Society and has always been the Journal's most reliable source of good papers.

I thought it might be interesting to see how forensically-inclined civil servants have 'performed' in recent years by carrying out a mini-survey of the forensic science literature over the last decade. A reasonable *Performance Indicator* (PI) would be the annual total (t) of papers in the Journal of the Forensic Science Society and Forensic Science International emanating from the Home Office Forensic Science Laboratories and Central Research and Support Establishment, the Metropolitan and Strathclyde Police Laboratories and the Northern Ireland Forensic Science Laboratory. Papers from these laboratories have appeared in other 'forensic' journals and specialist serial publications concerned with spectroscopy, pharmacology, haematogenetics, chromatography and so on, but the numbers were relatively small.

The results of this short study were revealing. Year on year t went up and down, ranging from a high of 37 papers published in 1982 down to just 15 in 1988. The five year annual means and $(n - 1)$ weighted standard deviations were much more consistent: 25 ± 7 for 1980–1984 and 24 ± 7 for 1985–1989. Surprisingly, perhaps, fewer papers were published during the five years up to 1979 – the mean annual total was 22 ± 4.

JFSS, editors past and present are familiar with the problem of persuading forensic scientists to become authors. Will we continue to attract part of their valuable time if the competition for it becomes fiercer in the coming years? In five year's time, when I will have calculated the next PI, I'll let you know.

References

1. Tilstone WJ. They threatened its life with a railway share. *Journal of the Forensic Science Society* 1990; **30**: 191–192.
2. Whitehead PH. Brave new world. *Journal of the Forensic Science Society* 1990; **30**: 269–271.

33(4) - 1993: DNA or Abracadabra

(Editorial)

DNA
When the tree of life
was just a shoot
in some
primeval swamp
and man was
still a gleam
in the eye
of early storms,
a thread
of continuity
was steadily
condensing
from pre-historic soup
to eukaryotic forms.
Adenine and cytosine,
guanine and thymine,
an alphabet translated
to identify, defined
by an inheritance
of coded instructions;
remembered in great detail,
selection so designed.
Encouraged by polymerase
to duplicate the recipe,
this huge encyclopaedia
of long repeated reigns,
held for generations,
long configurations,

> linear sequences
> conformity sustains.
> This sinuous helix,
> molecular
> contortion, twisted round
> and super-coiled
> elegance sublime,
> resisting mutation,
> except in adversity,
> bequeathed by
> our forebears,
> a catalogue of time.
>
> **GM Willott**
>
> Can Mendel ever have imagined what was to come as he tended his monastery garden? Or Watson and Crick in their 'ivory tower' (now a bicycle shed) have imagined the consequences? Yet their works were direct ancestors of discoveries which were to have, and are having, a massive impact on such diverse fields as agriculture, medicine, and anthropology. Within our own field, forensic science, biology is now providing evidence of previously unobtainable weight through the introduction of DNA analyses.
>
> This advance, however, has had its price. In the legal process, lawyers face the task of having to present or challenge the new scientific evidence. This means re-education in an alien discipline, rather than using the comfortable and slightly familiar topics from their law school years. In the laboratory, the advent of DNA technology provides managers with the problems of supplying satisfactory accommodation, the necessary equipment and reagents, of validating results both before and during use, and above all, of staff training. In all these aspects, requirements and costs are far higher than anything previously encountered in forensic biology, providing a veritable 'black hole' for resources.
>
> Yet the technology is changing rapidly; what is in use today is already about to be replaced by the new, and the whole cycle from research through to the courts repeats itself.
>
> Daunting though the above may be, perhaps the worst aspect is the mesmeric effect. No conference is complete without it and one sometimes wonders about cases. Is DNA the ingredient without which no investigation is complete and its presence a hallmark, a magic wand suited to all circumstances? Perhaps there is a need for perspective. DNA is a tool in the forensic scientists' box, no more and no less. Admittedly, it is a powerful tool and when it is needed it is indispensable. But it should not blind us to the value of, nor detract from, well established techniques in other disciplines.
>
> **JW Thorpe**
> *Forensic Science Unit*
> *University of Strathclyde*
> *204 George Street*
> *Glasgow G11XW*

36(1) - 1996: To Research or Capitulate?

(Editorial)

In times of economic hardship industrial companies, especially in the United Kingdom, always appear to make the most savage cuts in their research and development budgets. Why this should be is difficult to understand, but usually research and development teams are small in comparison with the rest of the company, are easily identifiable and, in the short term, their productivity has little direct effect upon the company. Additionally, the company decision makers are not usually scientists but accountants and lawyers with little understanding of research and development.

The problem with this type of knee-jerk response to economic pressures is that research teams are then dispersed and may be difficult, if not impossible, to rebuild over a short time span and in a high tech industry a company will lose a competitive edge to its rivals. Alternatively, no direct competition makes companies complacent, thus justifying a return to research and development. Rarely is research and development seen as a vehicle for raising morale within a company by rotating suitable personnel from the "work face" to the research and development department and vice versa.

When assessing the value of research and development it is also important that the direction of development must be in accord with the mission of the company. If not, then either the company requires to change its mission, and for some high tech industries this may become necessary, or more likely the research direction must be changed.

But what, you may justifiably ask, has all this to do with forensic science? The public perception of research and development in the forensic science community is almost completely directed towards the implementation of DNA technology, and this perception is emphasised through national and international conferences, most of which are dominated by reports of developments in DNA analysis. No-one denies the importance of DNA research and the impact it has had on solving serious crimes. Research into DNA technology will continue but systems centred on STRs are now in place, or being put into place, in most technologically advanced countries. Does this mean that apart from fine tuning of the systems further advances will not be sought? If so, will opportunities be taken to reduce the input into forensic science research? Are the commercial pressures on the forensic science community forcing research to become more restrictive as prophesied by Lord Dainton.

Other questions also need to be addressed concerning the emphasis of the research effort and how the research relates to customer demand. Surely the biggest demand for forensic support lies in other areas, especially drugs, house breaking, motor vehicle crime and fraud. These are the areas which affect the general public, your next door neighbour and even you. Where is the research and development which supports the investigators in these areas of crime? Take one example. The biggest workload for most laboratories throughout the world is in the area of drug analysis. If drug casework entering the forensic science laboratories were halved then this would remove much of the pressures being experienced by workers in this field. One way to achieve this would be to provide a hand held device to the police and customs which would specifically identify any drug and, where necessary, quantify the sample. Where is the fundamental research being carried out which would enable such devices to be developed? Perhaps there is a commercial aspect to this question since the production of such devices would remove an income generating capacity from forensic science laboratories. Is this the way to conduct research and development for forensic science? Would it not be better for governments to provide targeted money, perhaps through research councils, to those expert groups capable of completing the necessary research programmes? But what are the necessary research programmes? To determine this it may make sense to form joint consultative committees between the forensic science community and the universities – after all, was not DNA typing first used in a university department? Such committees would be in a position to identify front line research which could have an application to the forensic sciences. For those having a wider perspective, perhaps forensic science could act as a springboard to researches which would have a worldwide effect on the general community.

Science & Justice 1996; **36**(1): 1

36(2) - 1996: Fireproof DNA?

(Editorial)

The success of any organism or organisation depends on many factors of which the prime one is the persistence of a stable pattern. This is not to say that such a pattern must be incapable of evolutionary change. Such rigidity of structure and function is just as sure a way to extinction as change for the sake of change. The problem is to get the balance right.

With organisms the job is done by the action of natural selection working upon countless individuals but with organisations we are permitted no such luxury. Nevertheless in an uncompetitive world an organisation, like a species, may survive for a very long time, cocooned by monopoly against a changing habitat until disaster strikes.

There is a growing feeling that such a state of affairs applies to the International Association of Forensic Sciences. Including the foundation meeting in 1957 this body has held thirteen triennial meetings in countries all over the world and the general opinion of participants appears to be that it has performed remarkably well. After each meeting the Association renews itself with the appointment of a new president who names an entirely new local organising committee and the whole cycle starts anew. There is no way of profiting by previous experience.

The whole structure reminds one of the *phoenix*, the mythical bird that was condemned to live for a while and then to immolate itself whereupon a new *phoenix* arose from the ashes of the old. One can only assume, in the light of modem genetic research, that the *phoenix* possessed something in the nature of fireproof DNA.

The IAFS likewise needs fireproof DNA in the form of a permanent location where the lessons learned together with the records and financial accounts of the previous meetings can be located and it would be the place to which enquiries about past and future meetings could be addressed. Furthermore it would provide a focus to which participants in the triennial meetings could address their comments and complaints for the benefit of the presidents of future meetings. The increasing use of E-mail would both facilitate communication and ease the storage of the input. Thus future presidents would have a solid database upon which to establish decisions.

Where to establish such a record centre? It should be in a small but scientifically advanced country without the political and trading clout of the larger countries and it should already possess a multidisciplinary forensic science institute of international reputation. In such an institute should the fireproof DNA of the IAFS be located. Do you know of any such place?

Stuart Kind

37(4) - 1997: Where Will all the Forensic Scientists Go?

(Editorial)

Utopia – that perfect society in which everything is optimised to make life agreeable to its citizens, where there are no failures and no deviance from accepted behaviours, where life is forever pleasant and all are satisfied. Is this what we all strive for, a life with no changes or repercussions from decision making? Is this the future for mankind? If it is, there is unlikely to be a place for forensic scientists or forensic science, but one only has to read, look or listen to the media to become more aware that our society is far from meeting its Utopia. It is interesting, however, for us as forensic scientists to speculate on what the future holds.

It probably was always so but recent international conversations with many involved in the forensic sciences always identify the major problem as one of resourcing forensic science. As the science develops so equipment becomes more expensive, but even more expensive is that of staffing costs. Additionally, there is a growing realisation amongst others in the legal process that forensic science can dramatically influence the role of the investigator as well as that of the lawyer and this realisation can exhaust even the most well provided for and economically managed forensic science organisation. Investigators and lawyers are also experiencing budgetary restriction, so how is the use of forensic science to be increased and its implementation maximised.

What are the developments in the sciences which lead us to believe that forensic science has a future? One of the most important developments in recent years have been in personal identification through fingermarks and DNA. Already, for fingermarks we have seen the introduction of automated fingerprint recognition (AFR) systems and recently the at-scene identification of a fingermark through on-site computer linkage with the centralised database has occurred. It can be expected that at-scene identification will become routine and with satellite linkage even extend to countries and subjects in distant lands.

But what of DNA? Many countries are generating their own databases for DNA and it is to be hoped that such databases will become compatible between countries for it is only by this means that we will maximise our use of DNA technology. However, a major step forward will undoubtedly arise when we are in a position to abandon gel-based DNA profiling in favour of silica chip technology. Already we see progress in looking for single point mutations in DNA by the use of DNA strands immobilised onto the microchip. From these small beginnings we shall see hand held microchip-based devices placed in the hands of the crime scene officer which will have the capability of relaying the scene DNA profile to the data bank for comparison purposes. The data bank then becomes a primary function of the forensic science laboratory but as robotization advances this role will be managed by a small number of technicians.

Footwear marks examination is likely to undergo a similar evolution. These have now been recognised as of prime evidential value and a number of computer based systems have been developed which will match a print with a shoe type. As yet such systems will not directly compare a mark with a specific shoe but the knowledge of the footwear comparison expert must be capable of being rationalised in expert systems to permit such computer comparisons to be made.

With the advent of microcolumns being etched onto microchips the miniaturisation of gas chromatographic and capillary electrophoretic systems seems to be assured as crime scene instruments, especially when new detector systems for drugs, fire accelerants and explosives have been developed. This means that few forensic scientists will be required in the laboratories – only technicians. One can predict that the future role of the forensic scientist will be as a crime scene officer, or is there some other way our profession will develop?

Science & Justice 1997; **37**(4): 223

40(1) - 2000: Wizards and Gatekeepers at the Roadside?

(Editorial)

Doctors in the UK have been usefully divided into Wizards and Gatekeepers [1]. The Gatekeepers are general practitioners whose diagnostic strategy has to be optimised so as to detect the relatively uncommon examples of genuine pathology from the mass of triviatrics that passes through their doors every day. The Gatekeepers expect normality. The Wizards are the hospital-based doctors who deal with the abnormal cases already identified for them by the Gatekeepers. The Wizards expect abnormality.

At present at the roadside we have Gatekeepers. In England and Wales about 860,000 people a year are asked to provide a sample of breath for roadside screening for alcohol. About 12% either provide samples that give positive results or refuse to provide a sample. Thus the vast majority, nearly 90% of persons asked to provide samples, can be expected to be normal. That is they will provide a negative breath sample at the current cut off level of 35 micrograms per 100 ml of breath. So the average traffic officer in this context is a Gatekeeper.

What about drugs and driving? We know from the preliminary report of a study of the incidence of drugs and alcohol in road traffic fatalities that about 22% of drivers who die in road traffic accidents have a potentially impairing drug in their blood or urine at the time of their death [2]. Such drivers are no more likely to have a blood alcohol concentration above the permitted limit than drug free drivers. About 22% of dead drivers have blood alcohol concentrations above the permitted limit. So in round terms, using that somewhat blunt test of impairment, dying in a road traffic accident, less than 20% of drivers might be impaired by drugs alone.

Since the commonest drug to be detected is cannabis, evidence of its use being found in about 10% of the dead drivers, and since the presence of cannabinoids in blood by no means implies impairment, about half of those drivers with a potentially impairing drug in their blood and no alcohol present, might actually have been impaired at the time of their death. For argument's sake, take it as 10%. This may, in fact, be a gross overestimate when the effects of tolerance to prescribed drugs is taken into account. Dead drivers are roughly twice as likely to have an alcohol concentration above the permitted limit than living drivers tested at the roadside. If the same is true for drug associated impairment about 5% of those tested at the roadside might be drug impaired.

Enter the Wizards ... road traffic police officers who have undergone additional training to enable them to identify drivers impaired by drugs by an appropriate neurological examination at the roadside, including testing of pupillary reactions, balance, fine movement and co-ordination. In the United States, officers who have graduated from Drug Recognition Expert (DRE) courses appear to have a high sensitivity for detecting drug impaired drivers, but have false positive rates of about 5% [3]. So if the Wizards use their tests, which are fine when the prevalence of impaired subjects is high, on the 757,000 potentially impaired drivers annually who provide negative breath tests, they might well pick up the 5% of drivers who are actually impaired by drugs. They will, however, also pick up an equal number of drivers who are not drug impaired. If the incidence of drug impaired drivers subject to roadside testing is only 1% then the Wizards will arrest an additional 45,420 drivers a year of whom only a sixth, 7,570, will actually have drug associated impairment. That would give the police more than 100 highly irritated customers each day. If the abbreviated training that the British Road Traffic Officers will go through, compared to the American DRE officers, means that their specificity for detecting impairment falls to below 5% then there will be even more false positives, i.e. even more irritated customers.

Roadside drug use testing using sweat wipes or saliva has its own problems. How many drivers with a headache who have swallowed a couple of Co-codamol tablets (Co-codamol tablets containing 5 mg of codeine and 500 mg of paracetamol (acetaminophen) are available without prescription in the UK) is it worth arresting and subjecting to a blood or urine test to catch one heroin user rolling stoned? I'll happily leave that question to the politicians.

Most persons who persistently misuse drugs will seek medical advice for their problem, if only to obtain legal supplies of methadone and/or benzodiazepines. Since drug misuse and dependence are medical conditions that are in general incompatible with holding a driving licence, a doctor caring for a patient with a drug misuse problem should advise that patient to report their condition to the Driver and Vehicle Licensing Agency (DVLA) [4]. If a patient with a medical condition incompatible with holding a driving licence declines to report their condition to the DVLA as is required by law, and still continues to drive after counselling, then the advice from the General Medical Council is that the doctor should report the clinical details of the case to the DVLA medical branch. A cost effective way of reducing the numbers of drug misusing drivers might be to remind doctors caring for them of their ethical obligations as set out by the General Medical Council.

So where do we go from here? There is no easy answer. It's undeniably fun to train as a Wizard. But Wizards make bad Gatekeepers. However, the trickle down of their knowledge and skills through the police service can only increase the awareness of police officers about drug associated impairment and improve the care given to intoxicated persons taken into custody. One thing is very clear. We need research, research and more research to inform policy and debate.

ARWF

References

1. Mathers NJ, Hodgkin P. The Gatekeeper and the Wizard – a fairytale. *British Medical Journal* 1989; **298**:172–174.
2. *ICADTS Reporter*. Vol. 8, No. 3 Summer 1997.
3. Bigelow GE et al. Identifying Types of Drug Intoxication: Laboratory Evaluation of a Subject Examination Procedure. National Highway Traffic Safety Administration, *Pub. No. DOT HS 806 753* (1985).
4. *At a glance guide to the current medical standards of fitness to drive.* July 1999. Drivers Medical Unit, DVLA, Swansea.

40(3) - 2000: The Consent of the Governed

(Editorial)

'Law is that which is consented to by the king and people' [1]

The need for government to govern with the consent and agreement of the governed is as real now as it was in the 15th Century. Laws, to be enforceable, have to seem to be just and reasonable to at least a sizeable minority of the population. When they are not then they fail, sometimes with disastrous results. Prohibition in the United States is only one such example. Something of the same can be seen in the United Kingdom at present where, as petrol prices rise faster than inflation, so old crimes, once dormant, raise their ugly heads. Once again there is the diversion of agricultural fuel to road use, and the systematic theft of petrol from filling stations. Similarly, the mass smuggling of tobacco and alcohol through the Channel Tunnel could be construed as a failure of a sizable minority of the governed to consent to a high indirect tax regimen on these products.

Consent to being governed has to be informed consent and in a society that purports to be an educated society the degree of information available to the governed should be of the highest quality. There is no place for paternalism in restricting the availability of information on the grounds of political expediency. Free publication of information and research in learned scientific journals should not be restricted other than on the requirements of national security, as very tightly defined, and on the likelihood of prejudice of the legal process in a particular case. An exception is that personal information about a particular individual should not be disclosed without their agreement save in the most exceptional circumstances.

Science, including science as applied to the judicial process, only flourishes when conducted openly, with the free communication of information between researchers and practitioners.

The incorporation of the European Convention on Human Rights into English and Scots law has, as one of its many effects, imposed the need for the courts to recognise that there should be an equality of arms as between the prosecution and defence in criminal trials. This should go beyond the discovery process and extend to the exclusion of evidence based on data, procedures or instrumental readouts where the processes involved have not been placed in the public domain either by publication in the peer reviewed literature, as patent applications or in some other way equally accessible to both sides. Just as there is no place for the 'personal series of one', so there should be no place for the use of restricted databases, or the use of analyses based on technology not wholly open to independent scrutiny.

Thus the role that journals such as *Science & Justice* play in the judicial process is vital. Without free access to crucial information about the technology of the scientific investigation of crime the governed cannot give informed consent through their elected representatives to the enactment of laws which may be enforced by application of technology. The most appropriate source of such information is high quality learned journals. If good scientific evidence that any part of the technology on which the investigation of crime depends is flawed becomes apparent to practitioners, an early response should be to prepare and submit their data for publication in the peer reviewed scientific literature.

In short, publish or society may perish.

Robert Forrest, Editor

Reference

1. Fortescue, John. *De Natura Legis Nature* (c. *1463*)

41(1) - 2001: The Use of Material from the Dead in Forensic Science Research: Is It Lawful and Is It Ethical?

(Editorial)

The medical profession in the United Kingdom has recently suffered from a spate of highly publicised incidents that have shaken public confidence. In particular, the scandal over the retention of children's body parts collected at post mortem examination at Bristol Royal Infirmary and in Children's Hospitals in Birmingham, Liverpool and Glasgow has had a major adverse effect on the public's perception of the medical profession. Arguably these hospitals have been unlucky; virtually any pathology department will have one or two items (I resist the temptation to say skeletons, reserving that nightmare for the archaeologists and anthropologists) in their cupboard that they might prefer to remain there.

Can forensic scientists regard what happened to some nonforensic pathologists with any degree of complacency? I would say, no, we can not. More to the point, we should not. The Bristol Royal Infirmary Inquiry Interim Report should be required reading for everyone who works with post mortem material. The report lumps together organs, biopsy material and fluids under the single term "material" which at least has the advantage of being an inclusive and non emotive term [1].

In the past, forensic scientists have enjoyed a limited access to post mortem material. Identification Officers may have been able to use some human material in their training, at least in some cities, and toxicologists may have had tissue made available for research. During one recent investigation a coroner's officer arranged for the collection of urine samples from deceased persons undergoing coroner's post mortem examinations to establish a "normal range" for insulin and C-peptide in post mortem urine. It has not been unheard of for the pathologist to be asked to collect a blood sample for DNA profiling as part of a major investigation from every young male dying in a particular coroner's jurisdictions. Samples have been obtained from bodies at coroners' post mortems for the confirmation or exclusion of paternity. Two major research studies into the toxicology of road traffic crash victims have been carried out in the UK using blood samples obtained at post mortem examination.

Are such studies lawful or ethical without or even with the consent of the deceased's next of kin? That is a very moot point.

In England and Wales, post mortem examinations are carried out lawfully under two separate acts, The Coroners Act 1988 and the Human Tissue Act 1961. When a post mortem is carried out under the Coroners Act, the pathologist is only to retain tissue if it is the cause of death and only for as long as the coroner thinks fit [2]. Clearly, there is no mandate here for the collection of material for teaching or research and method development. Similar rules apply in other jurisdictions, for example, in Florida [3].

The Human Tissue Act 1961 authorises post mortem examination and the removal of any part of the body by a medical practitioner if and only if the spouse and surviving relatives have not objected, if the deceased expressed no objection in life and, in a coroner's or Procurator Fiscal's case, with her consent. There is a catch; the Act clearly says in Section 1 that the removal of body parts is only for therapeutic purposes or for **medical** education or research. (My emphasis.) A recent European Court judgement may well narrow the definition "medical"; it can no longer mean "anything that a doctor might care to do", but should be restricted to activities in relation to the diagnosis and treatment of disease [4]. Medical education and research clearly does not include the removal of material, even with the consent of the relatives, for teaching identification officers their skills or for establishing reference ranges for abused drugs in hair or muscle, for a speculative search of DNA databases, or to establish paternity. Of course, a court may decide to treat a body as any other sort of evidence and order part of it to be seized for evidential purposes.

Parenthetically, there is an interesting dichotomy between the views of pressure groups who demand that no material should be retained after post mortem without absolutely explicit permission from the relatives, and other pressure groups who would like to see an opt out system so that anyone dying may have their organs harvested for transplantation unless an objection has been positively registered by the deceased in life.

Clearly, the law needs to be amended. After the final report of the Bristol Inquiry Parliament may enact some alterations to the Human Tissue Act. It is to be hoped that the drafters of the new legislation will do so with care, not in haste, and that the needs of those who investigate crime will be taken into account. The gifts of life and knowledge that the dead can make to the living are just that, gifts. A dead body is not a piece of state property to be harvested without regard to the views of the deceased in life or her relatives after death.

Robert Forrest

References

1. The Inquiry into the management of care of children receiving heart surgery at the Bristol Royal Infirmary: Interim Report – Removal and Retention of Human Material. Bristol Royal Infirmary Inquiry, May 2000. (www.bristol-inquiry.org.uk)
2. Coroners Rules 1984 r.9 & r.12
3. Medical Examiners Act (Fl. Stats. 2000, Title XXIV, Ch. 406.11)
4. Non-therapeutic medical acts attract value-added tax. Court of Justice of the European Communities D v W. Case C-384198. Times Law Report 24 October 2000.

43(1) - 2003: Hunting Truffles

(Editorial)

ARW Forrest
Editor, Science & Justice

In any knowledge-based profession, one of the most difficult tasks faced by the practitioner is keeping up with the literature. How can one sieve and sift the enormous and exponentially increasing mass of paper and electronic data available to ensure that one responds competently to the demands of one's professional body for continuing professional development and to the, sometimes different, need to have the intellectual tools to hand to deal with casework and still have time for a life? Each of us will have a different approach to the problem, but there are some general strategies available. I am going to describe mine; it works for me, as a medically qualified toxicologist, but many people may prefer a more focused approach.

The first task is to make sure that one is aware of what is going on elsewhere in one's discipline and to avoid getting locked into an inflexible and insular personal and/or corporate view of the way one should approach a particular problem. Reading professional journals, attending conferences (not forgetting the bar meetings) and membership of mailing lists are all tools fit for this purpose. There are others. Nothing is more refreshing than a professional challenge. When a case goes to trial and one's evidence is challenged, if there is a degree of trust present, which isn't always the case, lunch with the expert from the other side, with counsel's permission, can be stimulating and educational.

Journals are an important resource. But not all journals are equal. For example, there is a view that Thursday is the best day of the week, not just because it's the day before Friday, but because it is the day that the *New England Journal of Medicine* arrives. Any serious medic avidly devours its mixture of high impact original research, case presentations, authoritative reviews and commentary. *The Lancet* is similar if a little more orientated towards the presentation of fundamental research. Some other journals provide an illustration of the validity of Sturgeon's Law[1]. Browsing them can be a task more akin to hunting for the excellent parts of the curate's egg than truffle hunting.

All of these journals have a web presence. The *New England Journal of Medicine* and *The Lancet* only allow access to the full text of papers in. DOC or. PDF format if you are a subscriber or your employer has a corporate subscription. This access only continues as long as you have a subscription, a most effective tool for locking in subscribers. *(New England Journal of Medicine* does operate a scheme allowing free access to full text papers from developing countries.) The *British Medical Journal* allows free electronic access to its full text to the world at large.

Then there are the other general, non-forensic, journals; *Science, Nature, New Scientist, Scientific American* and *The Economist* amongst others. They all need reading, but not from cover to cover. Even with the high speed web access and electronic subscriptions to these journals provided by my employer, there is still no substitute for sitting in a library scanning one's way through a pile of journals looking for gold. The fastest web access can't substitute for having the real thing in one's hands when one is browsing, a necessary luxury for professionals, rather than when one is simply looking for task orientated information, for which the web is incomparable. When searching the web for task orientated papers one does have to choose one's search engines and databases with care and a regard to fitness for purpose.

Next there are the specialist forensic and non-forensic journals. Some, like the *Journal of Forensic Sciences* and the *Journal of Analytical Toxicology*, get read from cover to cover. Some, like the *Journal of Clinical and Forensic Medicine, Science, Medicine and the Law* or *Clinical Chemistry* get browsed and some, like *Journal of Chromatography* or *The Analyst* only get read as part of task orientated searches, particularly as I have to walk half a mile up a hill to the library where I can see them in hard copy. Life and humanity being the way it is, a library where the workers aren't won't get used appropriately.

General browsing is an essential part of keeping up to date. This can be guided with the help of the lists of interesting abstracts that appear in some journals, such as *Microgram Bulletin*. These are useful, but they do rely on the validity of other practitioners' judgements about what is relevant to one's own practice. Again there is no substitute for being able to work one's way through a pile of back numbers of, for example, the *British Journal of Clinical Pharmacology* or even *Criminal Law Review* in a warm, quiet and uncrowded library. If only...! The reality is that after getting to the library and finding a seat and a pile of relevant journals, one eventually finds oneself standing at the back of a long queue of student members of one of the caring professions all copying what appears to be the total contents of the *Journal of Alternative Dietetics* for 1986 whilst one waits for access to the only working copier in order to copy a short abstract on paracetamol (acetaminophen) pharmacokinetics in infants.

---

[1] Usually cited in polite society as '90% of everything is crud'. Derived from a quotation by the Science Fiction writer Theodore Sturgeon: "Sure, 90% of science fiction is crud. That's because 90% of everything is crud."

When browsing, one can find truffles in the most surprising of places. Something relevant to drink driving cases in *Canon Law Abstracts?* Surely not! How about a paper on the practical and theological issues raised by alcohol dependent priests who have to drink the remains of sanctified wine, which by canon law must contain alcohol, at the end of Mass or Holy Communion? Fortune may well favour the prepared mind, and accepting what serendipity sometimes offers when reading in the literature is accepting a gift of fortune.

Where does *Science & Justice* fit into this? Of course, it aims to publish high quality peer reviewed papers from the cutting edge of forensic science. Where possible these papers have to have something for the general readership as well as the specialist. That isn't always possible, but I do try to make sure that each subscriber to the journal can find something interesting and relevant to his or her practice in every issue. Often, the conference reports contain material that is highly relevant to practice. Overall, I am trying to position *Science & Justice* as being something more akin to the style of the *New England Journal of Medicine* for forensic science than to being the equivalent of the *British Medical Journal* for forensic science. That is to say, I would rather publish good science and good reviews than a disproportionate number of soul searching papers on topics such as professional registration or whether forensic science is or is not a profession.

One problem is that not everything published in *Science & Justice* currently gets indexed in the electronic databases such as MEDLINE or EMBASE. This means that the electronic browser may miss something critical to their search if they restrict themselves to those databases. One way of addressing this will be to have an electronic full text version of the journal online with abstracts available to all but full text restricted, at least initially, to subscribers. The browser who searches with *Google* or a similar search engine will then, hopefully, gets hits to all papers in *Science & Justice* rather than just on those indexed by MEDLINE. A yearly updated CD-ROM edition of the journal, with a searchable index. would be a useful bonus for subscribers.

All of these developments may require the Society to develop an association with a commercial publisher. Whilst the expertise undoubtedly exists to execute these developments within the Society, the time to do it does not. All professionals seem, despite working time directives, to have to work harder and harder. Voluntary work for learned societies is now perceived by employers, particularly in the public sector, as being something that they are less willing to support than in the past. Consequently, many of those who would have devoted time and effort to their learned societies, arguably producing significant benefits overall to their employer and to the community, now find their desire to promote their profession through their learned society squeezed between the increasing demands of work and the desire to spend quality time with their family. This inevitably means that learned societies have to look for different ways of carrying out their traditional functions. The reluctance of some employers to support any activity by the professionals they employ which is not seen to be immediately task orientated also has an adverse effect on the production of scientific papers. "Publish or perish" is not something that is applicable to the career development of most British forensic scientists. Getting papers out of forensic scientists with something to say that other practitioners need to hear is one of the hardest tasks I face as editor.

What I hope this editorial achieves is not only to encourage forensic science practitioners to browse widely through the scientific literature in search of truffles to support their practice but also to plant truffles in the literature for others to find.

44(1) - 2004: Reiterative Justice?

(Editorial)

One minor but sometimes lucrative (for "experts" and lawyers) quirk of the English and Scottish legal systems is the provision in Drink Driving Law of certain defences requiring the "back calculation" of blood or breath alcohol concentrations under more or less hypothetical circumstances. There is the statutory "hip flask" defence where the defendant claims that his breath, blood or urine alcohol concentration would not have been over the permitted limit but for alcohol consumed after the time of the alleged offence [1]. There is the statutory defence to the charge that arises when a person is found intoxicated, in charge of her vehicle, and she claims that she would not have driven whilst her alcohol concentration was still above the permitted limit [2, 3]. Finally, there is the case law allowing a defendant who has plead guilty to a drink driving charge to argue special reasons, including "laced drinks" in mitigation of sentence [4].

Basically none of the techniques used in the calculations in such cases are rocket science, and practitioners from a variety of disciplines, from public analysts through generic forensic scientists to clinical biochemists have been accepted by the courts as having the relevant expertise. For the literate and numerate defendant, two minutes with Google will provide him with a wealth of information from the Internet [5].

With such a wide spectrum of practitioners having been accepted by the Courts in such cases, it has inevitably been the case that not all of those giving expert evidence have necessarily been aware of the standards normally expected of an expert witness. Indeed, the Council for the Registration of Forensic Practitioners has felt it necessary to set out quite explicitly in the case of experts assisting in alcohol technical defence cases that: "the term 'technical defence' does not mean that such practitioners prepare reports only for the defence in a court case. In all cases the duty of registered practitioners is to the court, not to those instructing them" [6].

One example of the way in which expert evidence can be used by some defendants, with or without the knowledge of those giving them legal advice, in such cases is by the reiterative recalculation of the amount of alcohol it was necessary to consume after the offence, in the case of a "hip flask defence", or the amount of alcohol it would have been necessary to lace a drink with to produce a result implying that, but for that added alcohol, their blood, breath or urine alcohol concentration would have been below the permitted limit at the relevant time. The scenario is that the defendant gets the first expert report and uses it to recalculate the post-incident alcohol consumed or the amount of alcohol used to lace his beer and then submits a revised account of events, sometimes via another solicitor to another expert or even the same expert and then obtains a report more favourable to his case. Obviously, such conduct by the defendant and his witnesses may be unlawful. The ethical position of the solicitor and the expert is, at best, moot.

We suggest that experts who do not wish to participate in such questionable practices should register with the Council for the Registration of Forensic Practitioners and adhere to their ethical code. Further we would suggest that there are some basic rules they should apply when accepting instructions to prepare a report in alcohol technical defence cases.

- Decline to proceed to prepare a report without a written proof of evidence from the defendant and his relevant witnesses including specific information about exactly what was drunk and when and the defendant's physique;
- Decline to proceed without an assurance from the instructing solicitor that any and all previous expert witness statements have been included in the bundle along with the instructions;
- Refer to all such reports as have been disclosed to the expert in the report;
- In preparing a report do not be specific about the amount of alcohol that may be missing from a particular account. If the Solicitor specifically asks you to do that, state that you have been requested to provide this information;
- When preparing a report use a specific calculated Widmark factor, taking into account the imprecision of the calculation and consider a range of alcohol elimination rates, specifying a most probable result of the calculations and giving a realistic estimate of the imprecision.

If a report is prepared taking these recommendations into account, it will be much handier for the unscrupulous defendant to use it as the basis for a spurious or perjured defence by expert and advocate shopping after he and his witness have prepared a revised account.

When the Criminal Justice Bill 2003 is finally enacted, it will become easier for the prosecution to spot this reprehensible practice. Section 33 includes a provision as follows: "If the accused instructs a person with a view to his providing any expert opinion for possible use as evidence at the trial of the accused, he must give to the court and the prosecutor a notice specifying the person's name and address". At the very least this provision should flag up to the alert prosecutor the possibility of a reiterative use of experts in such cases. Unfortunately, this does not get round the problem of the inexperienced prosecutor being handed the file on the morning of the trial.

Finally, we very much hope that Lord Auld's recommendation that expert statements in criminal trials should include a declaration that the expert understands that his duty is to the Court, not to those who instruct him, will be implemented just as soon as parliamentary time allows [7]. Any competent and ethical expert understands this. Nonetheless, making such a declaration in an expert statement a statutory obligation will usefully remind both those preparing the statement and those instructing them of the expert's obligations.

Robert Forrest
Paul Williams

References

1. Road Traffic Offenders Act 1988, s. 15(3)
2. Road Traffic Act 1988m s. 5(2)
3. *DPP v Frost [1989] RTR 411*
4. *Pugsley v Hunter [1973] 1 WLR 578*
5. e.g. http://www.desperateground.org/widmark.htm or http://www.drunkdrivingdefense.com/publications-articles/101-ways-avoid-dui.htm
6. http://www.crfp.org.uk/contents/specialip
7. http://www.criminal-courts-review.org.uk/11.htm#p76 at para 132.

45(2) - 2005: Science & Justice – DNA and the Courts[1]

(Editorial)

Stephen Sedley

In principle, DNA analysis has made it possible to establish to a very high degree of probability the human source of even a minute quantity of biological matter – most notably blood, semen or saliva. The science is complex, and the degree of certainty not absolute, especially when it is necessary to differentiate between twins or siblings. But it has begun to revolutionise the process not only of detection by police but of proof in court. What is particularly welcome is that it is as potent in eliminating those who are wrongly suspected or accused as it is in tracking down the guilty.

The availability of DNA analysis has already had a marked effect on mendacious defences advanced in rape cases – the not very beneficial effect of shifting the fib from identity ('It wasn't me') to consent. But it illustrates the potency of this means of identification, stumbled on exactly 20 years ago at Leicester University by Alec Jeffreys.

Although the science itself is still being debated – for example, in relation to the number of features that need to be shared by the sample and the suspect in order to reduce the risk of error to an acceptably minute

---

[1] *This article first appeared in the London Review of Books and is reprinted by permission. It formed part of a lecture given by Lord Justice Sedley at Leicester Law School under the title 'Rarely Pure and Never Simple: the law and the truth'. The author is a Lord Justice of Appeal and has sat as the UK judge in the European Court of Human Rights*

level, and in relation to the true margin of error – what I am concerned with here are the human rights and civil liberties implications of the procedures. My argument is that the case is growing for a national database holding the DNA profile of everyone living in or entering the country.

The present system, sanctioned by legislation, is that the police may take and keep a DNA sample from everyone they arrest, whether or not the person is charged or convicted. This has the unfortunate effect of putting the innocent on a par with the guilty. It draws a not very logical line between innocent people who have and have not passed through the hands of the police. But it does not follow that the law should be moved back to what it once was, so as to require the police to destroy their DNA records of everyone not eventually convicted. What follows no less logically is that the taking and retention of an individual's DNA profile should not depend at all on whether he or she happens to have come into the hands of the police.

A routine sample of the blood of newly born children is already kept. Hospitals need it in order to be able to rapidly treat a number of serious conditions, and – although it will readily yield a DNA profile – the sample is held only for medical purposes.

To obtain a DNA record, nothing more than a speck of saliva is needed: the taking of a sample, in other words, does not amount in any significant sense to an invasion of bodily integrity. What matters far more is the need for coercion. In relation to people under arrest, the power of coercion is ready-made. But for the rest of us, a good case has to be made for compulsory submission even to such a non-invasive process.

When the question of the police retention of samples was before the appellate committee of the House of Lords last July, evidence was given that, of some 130,000 retained DNA profiles of people who had not been convicted, around 6000 had been subsequently linked to samples found at scenes of crimes, which included 86 murders or attempted murders and 94 rapes. This is not, of course, to say that the match solved the crime: there could have been many innocent explanations. But in each case it was a start. We now know that the burglary detection rate almost quadruples when DNA is recovered from the scene of the crime.

The House of Lords decided that the retention of DNA samples of people who had not been convicted was probably not a violation, even in principle, of their right to respect for private life under Article 8(1) of the ECHR, but that if it was, it was proportionate and amply justified under Article 8(2) and did not constitute discrimination contrary to Article 14. The situation the courts were and still are facing under the present legislation, however, is an illogical halfway house between the retention of only the profiles of those convicted – a manifestly inadequate measure – and the sampling of the whole population, a measure which Parliament has so far not addressed.

There are without doubt things which need tidying up first. The present police practice, sanctioned by law, is to retain the sample as well as the digitised DNA profile obtained from it. It should be enough to keep the profile on record. If it appears to match a scene-of-crime sample, the suspect will in any event have to give a fresh sample for comparison with the evidential sample. But there exists a good possibility that sooner or later more will be able to be deduced than is now possible from individuals' genetic material. If one day it becomes possible to anticipate and treat disease by more sophisticated DNA profiling, a universal national register will need to hold samples, not just profiles. Therefore the possibility of segregating a universal database from the police database needs to be regarded.

It needs to be a strong premise of the discussion that the DNA data on the police national computer is to be used solely – as it is now by law – for the purposes of preventing, detecting, investigating and prosecuting crime. Cross-referral for medical purposes raises other issues – for example, discriminatory insurance practices – which do not have to cloud the present question. There is a parallel case to be made for a separate national register maintained for benign purposes, such as identifying disaster victims without the distressing procedure of taking samples from their close relatives, or tracing lost or abducted children, and perhaps one day for making medical prognoses. If this were to be the sole authorised national database – and it is much harder to find civil liberties objections to it than to a police database – provision would have to be made for a restricted, and perhaps judicially authorised, linkage to the police national computer where a need could be proved.

What is the rationale of objection to a comprehensive national DNA database? Although, in a cogent partial dissent in the House of Lords case, Baroness Hale argued that the collection of data about something as intimate as a person's genetic make-up is an invasion of their private life requiring justification under Article 8(2), she agreed with the rest of the appellate committee that a complete justification by demonstrated proportionality was made out. That is my view too; but – as I think the whole of the House recognised – the justification would have been plainer and more logical still if the logging of people's DNA profiles did not depend on the fortuity of their having passed through the hands of the police.

It can be, in fact, something rather worse than a fortuity. We know that there is an ethnic imbalance in arrests for certain types of offence, as well as in the use of stop and search powers. This is a serious issue which has to be separately addressed; but it has the unacceptable consequence that members of some ethnic minorities face a disproportionately high chance of getting on to the police DNA database without being convicted of anything. A universal and uniform database will at least resolve this problem.

There remains the concern about possible abuse, that the police might in future use the data not merely for detection but for personality profiling – especially since one of the purposes already sanctioned by law is crime prevention. I think this concern is real. A number of states – and there are indications that England and Wales may join them – have begun to allow the indefinite detention of sexual offenders on the basis of predicted behaviour. Apart from possession of the Y chromosome, which appears to be connected to aggression but which is a characteristic of all males, there is no hard evidence that heredity is a predictor of criminality. But the endeavour to establish genetically determined propensities is unlikely to stop, and we need to decide sooner rather than later whether we are prepared to let a police database be used for this purpose. If we are not, the surest way of preventing it is to store the digitised profile but to destroy the sample. Perhaps we also ought to have something larger in mind: that the perennial risk of future abuse is a sound argument against needed present reform only if it is a risk which cannot be adequately guarded against.

The need for independent corroborative evidence does not diminish but grows with an increased use of DNA profiling. Each of us must have innocently left our DNA – perhaps a hair or a fingerprint – in places which will one day be the scene of a crime. Suspicion – proof even more so – has to be based on more than such coincidences. But where at present the only identifiable DNA will belong to people who have been arrested, with the associated risk that only the usual suspects will fall under suspicion, a universal database will ensure that the process of elimination starts from the full range of potential suspects.

Even then, no one can rule out the risk of a corrupt police officer planting DNA evidence at the scene of a crime – a hair from the suspect's comb would suffice. But this is not a new problem, and it is not confined to genetic material: dust from a safeblowing will do just as well. Even fingerprints can be planted. And the risk of DNA planting is already there in the present system. You deal with such risks by discipline and training; not, unless there is genuinely no alternative, by abandoning the system.

What is more troubling is that everyone whose DNA is identified at the scene of a crime comes under a degree of pressure to establish their innocence. This is already true for both convicted and unconvicted people on the existing police database. But if it is a price that society is ready to pay, it should arguably be paid by all its members equally. This is the big issue that Parliament needs to debate and decide. The principal task of the courts will continue to be to ensure that, whatever the range of admissible evidence, coincidence is not confused with proof.

I readily accept that a national police DNA database will not be the end of the road. Not only will the growing range of information obtainable from DNA profiles put pressure on Parliament in future years to enlarge the uses to which the database may be put; there will also be calls for separate and parallel databases dedicated to other purposes. Few if any will be able to achieve legislative backing, but a number may start to operate in a form of take-it-or leave- it coercion: in other words, the price of securing a benefit – insurance, for example – may be that you provide a DNA sample and consent to any analytical use the holder wishes to make of it. To the extent that the adoption of a universal statutory police register of DNA profiles may help to make such moves seem acceptable, I accept that it is undesirable. But the answer for a modem society has to be in tight control of the sort that the data protection legislation is already accustoming us to, on the misuse of information.

There is, in other words, no gain without risk; but in a society disturbed not only by serious crime but also by the possibility of people being mistakenly acquitted or convicted of it, the potential gain represented by a comprehensive national DNA register is considerable; and the risks, so long as they are confronted, are controllable. I make no case for or against the introduction of compulsory identity cards; but a society which feels able, as ours does, to give serious consideration to such a step ought not to turn its face away from the case for a universal DNA register as part of a modem criminal justice system.

47(4) - 2007: DNA – What's Next?

(Editorial)

We've come a long way in just over 20 years. The developments in DNA technology as applied to forensic science since the mid 1980s, and the first successful use of DNA in a criminal case in the UK, have been remarkable. The development of better and more sensitive technological advances in DNA profiling techniques and analytical methods fills the research and forensic science literature like no other topic related to our field.

DNA, perhaps used in the past as a last attempt to uncover trace evidence or only in high profile cases, is now arguably a routine analysis and has certainly proved its worth in volume crime as well as in sexual assaults and murder cases. The potential of the technique is also well recognised by the police, courts and general public, thanks to CSI and other television programmes of that ilk.

Significant developments in DNA techniques and analysis have been brought about by some of the most serious challenges of our times, particularly those involving mass fatalities. The occurrence of large scale terrorist incidents such as the World Trade Centre attack in New York and mass disasters like the Asian Tsunami have resulted in the development of the science in an effort to identify victims under extreme circumstances. Developments in mitochondrial DNA, Y-STR and SNP analysis have allowed the determination of unprecedented amounts of information from a wide variety of samples including those which may be highly degraded or years old and related to so called 'cold cases'. At the same time low copy number DNA techniques, can facilitate the recovery of genetic information from minute amounts of cellular material.

The use of DNA profiles as evidential material has not been without its difficulties. This is nowhere more evident than in the various aspects of evaluating the evidential value of results obtained in the context of the particular case in question. The introduction of the Bayesian mechanism of evaluation has been a huge challenge to both the practitioner and the recipient of the information alike. The choice of terminology used to explain likelihood ratios and match probabilities of DNA evidence has proven to present significant difficulties within the judicial system and it is still the case that both prosecutor and defence fallacies occur from time to time.

So what of the future? The technological advances seem very promising. Developments in nanotechnology providing probes for minute quantities of DNA and lab-on-a-chip technology bringing the laboratory to the crime scene are on the horizon. The UK National DNA Database now holds over four million DNA profiles and is one of the biggest of its kind in the world. In Europe approximately five and a half million DNA profiles are maintained on police, judicial or forensic science related databases. The retention of genetic information and its use is, however, not without controversy, not least in the UK. There are growing concerns and ethical debate relating to issues such as the indefinite retention of DNA profiles on the database, the holding of juvenile genetic information and the use of familial searching for criminal justice purposes. These debates are gaining momentum in England and Wales and similar debates are being conducted in other jurisdictions.

The legal position in the UK with the advent of the Human Tissue Act also clouds the issue somewhat. This is particularly evident when one is attempting to engage in research within the forensic, or any other, field involving cellular materials which may be external to the criminal justice system.

Perhaps a more sinister development, certainly in the UK, is the rampant commercialisation of forensic science provision and the 'pay for services' culture that seems endemic within the sector. Cash strapped police forces tender for forensic services, including DNA services, and go with the provider that fits with their needs and budget. Decisions as to what type of samples to send for DNA and other analysis are no longer made by scientists but by managers and budget holders, with the certain knowledge that one or two large resource intensive cases may wipe out the budget for future cases. New technologies and developments are impressive in their range of applications, but if they are unnecessary or so expensive that other samples of (potential) evidential importance or of non-DNA type are being neglected as a consequence, one has to ask whether justice is being served. Perhaps something to think about.

N. Nic Daéid

48(4) - 2008: Do We Value Research?

In most areas of science there is an acceptance of the value of research if not a continual chorus of why there is a need more. For applied research the general argument goes like this: research generates knowledge and knowledge leads to better understanding of the world, helping us to improve our lot; cures for disease, more efficient trains, and the iPod. This is of course something of an over simplification because the connection between the new knowledge and the outcome, especially if it is a social outcome such as 'justice', is complex and tenuous. To achieve such desirable outcomes requires knowledge to flow from the 'laboratory' through a complex series of conduits into the field, and to make a difference in the hands of practitioners and users. This requires a systematic approach, understanding of knowledge exchange and careful application of resources. Even if this approach is taken, research into evidence based medicine over the past decade or so suggests that the knowledge exchange frequently falters before the outcome.

Bring together the main stakeholders from a forensic environment and it will be quickly obvious that knowledge exchange is equally problematic. In 2006 I was invited to explore the issues of research and development for the European Network of Forensic Science Institutes (ENFSI) [2]. A series of meetings led to a one day seminar which included academics, researchers, forensic practitioners, managers and police representatives from throughout Europe. The seminar reached a number of important conclusions for forensic research. Firstly, the research environment is complex consisting of a number of independent professions: police, academia, scientists, and lawyers. Secondly, the relationship between practitioners and researchers was poor and requires active support to be productive. Finally crime is a complex issue and research in this area requires effective interdisciplinary cooperation. Given this, a successful research program will not occur without the active and focused participation of relevant stakeholders. It is the last of these conclusions which is the most significant and which was accepted by the ENFSI membership with the implementation of a committee (the European Academy of Forensic Science) to provide leadership and focus on research. Key activities of the committee include the development and implementation of a research strategy to meet the priorities of the ENFSI membership, improvement of knowledge transfer and facilitation of collaboration between researchers and practitioners. Early successes of the committee include influencing the research agenda of the EU (see FP7 [3]) and improved understanding of the research capacity and capability of European forensic institutes.

Yet it is still my perception that research is undervalued by the forensic community. Is this the case with all practitioner communities: engineers, architects, etc? Or does it tell us something about the nature of forensic practice? Forensic science works at the interface between science and law and invariably involves the police. The knowledge engine which drives policing is 'common sense'. There is comparatively little research into policing and the vast majority of it is ignored by the police. The consequence of this common sense approach is that you don't need rigorous evidence to back up any argument or decision, just personal experience. The limitations of this approach are evident in the variation in police tactics to address the same problems in different law enforcement agencies around the world. How the police use (or fail to use) forensic science is a particularly good example.

The law also values common sense above almost any other commodity, leading to the curious irony of a system which makes decisions about the significance of 'evidence' but has no evidence that one of the main decision making mechanisms – juries – is effective. For a fuller explanation of this issue see Dawkins [1].

Forensic practitioners are continually required to interact with lawyers and the police officers usually to provide a common sense interpretation of scientific findings. Is it possible that many gradually lose sight of their scientific training? I encounter evidence of this almost daily, in opinions made in statements and reports, in discussions, flawed research methodologies and indifference in the practitioner community where there are very few forensic scientists actively engaged in research. So do we value research? Why of course we do – its only common sense isn't it?

References

1. Dawkins R., *A Devil's Chaplain*, Weidenfield & Nicolson, London, 2003.
2. Fraser J., Research and development in the European Network of Forensic Science Institutes, *Problems of Forensic Sciences* **LXXI** (2007) 334–336.
3. FP7, Cooperation Work Program: Security, http://cordis.europa.eu/fp7/dc/index.cfm?fuseaction=UserSite.FP7DetailsCallPage&call_id=137#infopack.

Jim Fraser

Science and Justice **48** (2008) 163

49(1) - 2009: Lessons from the Past

The Forensic Science Society is fifty years old this year. It was founded in 1959 when conducting police investigations and the role of the scientist in such investigations were very different to how they are today. Having said that, reading some of the earliest editorials in 'The Journal of the Forensic Science Society' as it was then, illustrates that some of the areas of difficulty within the crime scene to court process really haven't changed all that much over the years. The interaction between science and the law was as difficult then as it can sometimes be now, with the closing comments of the very first editorial stating that "the evidence of a brilliant scientist may be lost to a jury if presented in a highly technical or scientific language". The issues of forensic science education and research base were much debated as far back as 1960! The external public perception of forensic scientists was a topic of considerable discussion and in particular the integrity, competence and professionalism of forensic scientists. So what has changed? What have we learnt? Where are we going?

Now we live in different, and perhaps, more uncertain times, with increased treats on our national and personal safety as well as rapid changes and challenges in how we conduct our business. How forensic scientists and practitioners integrate and work within the criminal justice sector has changed immeasurably since 1959, and is going through another rapid period of change at the moment, certainly in the UK. Communication, collaborative effort and above all the spirit of friendship at a Global level are stronger and more progressive than ever in the history of our profession. Organisations such as ENFSI[1], SMANZFSL[2], ASCLD[3] and many more, reach across national and intercontinental boundaries to join forces in the global development of our work.

There have been enormous technological changes in the last 50 years, including the introduction of the AFIS system (1977), the use of SEM for gunshot residue analysis (1974), the introduction of GCMS (1976) and FTIR (1977) as analytical tools in forensic chemistry, the development and introduction of EMIT (1988) in forensic toxicology and of course the dominance of DNA analysis in forensic biology. We have refined the technology to be better, faster, more mobile and easier to use and work in quality controlled accredited laboratories. In more recent years we have stretched and matured our views and methods in the interpretation of the evidential value of the results obtained from analysis, engaging (sometimes with difficulty) with some complex mathematical concepts to move us forward.

Fundamental to our role is the service of justice, an admirable objective, and we owe it to those She serves to strive to produce the best quality of work that is within our capabilities. There is no room for complacency, no matter how large or small the case or circumstances may be. The work and recommendations of organisations such as Skills for Justice, the office of the Forensic Science Regulator, NPIA[4] and CRFP[5] are all fundamentally endeavouring to further the development of our professionalism in the UK, (as do similar organisations for our overseas colleagues), but it's not always a palatable or easy journey. The discussions of the past (interaction with the legal system, education, research, professionalism etc.) are still the discussions of today. So, let's bring on the debates and rise to the challenges they will bring to all of us in whatever capacities we work, but also embrace and learn from the lessons of the past and reflect on what our predecessors have shown us.

N. Nic Daéid

Science and Justice **49** (2009) 1

49(2) - 2009: IRMS

(Editorial)

It gives me great pleasure and satisfaction to be able to write the editorial for this special edition of Science and Justice which focuses on the forensic application of isotope ratio mass spectrometry (IRMS) and related disciplines.

Since 2001, I have been at the heart of a network created to develop the forensic application of IRMS, the FIRMS (Forensic Isotope Ratio Mass Spectrometry) Network. FIRMS was established in 2002 with funding obtained from the United Kingdom Environmental and Physical Sciences Research Council (EPSRC). Once the EPSRC funding period ended FIRMS was supported by the UK Home Office. FIRMS has now agreed a funding structure which will provide financial independence and allow the Network to continue to deliver its objectives.

FIRMS was born out of recognising two things: the potential of IRMS to address questions posed by investigators which might otherwise remain unanswered regarding the source and history of illicit and other forensic materials; and the need to assemble an appropriate community to direct development and forensic provision. The initial Network was drawn from academia, service providers, instrument manufacturers, forensic practitioners and investigators.

---

[1] European Network of Forensic Science Institutes.
[2] Senior Managers Australia and New Zealand Forensic Science Laboratories.
[3] American Society of Crime Lab Directors.
[4] National Police Improvement Agency.
[5] Council for the Registration of Forensic Practitioners.

FIRMS exists to promote the forensic application of IRMS and allied disciplines, collectively termed 'Isotope Forensics', and to promote good forensic practice. Isotope Forensics is well on the way to becoming a common approach where profiling of illicit materials or human provenancing is required. IRMS has already been used successfully in two major terrorist trials in the UK and in a variety of investigations and trials in the UK, Europe and the USA.

FIRMS encourages all members that provide a forensic service to obtain accreditation to ISO 17025 and FIRMS facilitates the process. Several members are already accredited to that standard. However, they are among the larger providers, the main business of which is forensic science. Small specialist providers in academia, particularly single academics, are unlikely to seek or obtain accreditation to ISO 17025. Without any regulatory cover they put at risk justice systems. FIRMS provides a means of accrediting practice using a number of mechanisms including peer review and inter-laboratory comparisons. These ensure that evidence placed before the courts in the field of Isotope Forensics is of sufficient quality. Until systems are in place which include such niche providers, FIRMS will continue to develop its regulatory function and provide accreditation to those providers.

Appropriate databases and a Bayesian or Likelihood Ratio approach to evaluation are fundamental to Isotope Forensics. The development of such databases is a key task for FIRMS and in the UK the Steering Group is liaising with the Forensic Regulator and the UK Accreditation Service (UKAS) to ensure that FIRMS databases and associated enquiry tools meet the needs of investigators and justice systems.

Both in terms of accrediting practice and database development, FIRMS will work with the Regulator and UKAS to ensure that Isotope Forensics continues to be of benefit to investigators and justice systems.

As with most other bodies in the UK, the loss of the Council for the Registration of Forensic Practitioners (CRFP) and the advent of the Forensic Regulator have already had a direct impact on FIRMS, particularly in the regulation of small specialist providers. In appointing a Regulator, the UK again leads the way and it is hoped that this Government initiative in the regulation of forensic practice will be more successful than the last one, the CRFP. Perhaps the most important point to bear in mind, both for FIRMS and the wider forensic science community, is that, with the inclusion of the Prüm treaty into the legal framework of the European Union (EU), a cooperative future lies ahead. It follows that the development, practice and regulation of forensic science need to be coherent across the EU. Common standards will be essential if forensic science is going to play an effective role in combating crime, particularly terrorism, and delivering justice throughout the EU and in the wider global community. FIRMS recognises these needs.

Finally, special mention should be made of Max Coleman, former Professor of Sedimentology at the University of Reading and currently with NASA Jet Propulsion Laboratory, for his support for FIRMS without which the Network would not have been established.

I commend this special issue to you and ask that any one interested in membership of FIRMS or further information should, in the first instance, email FIRMS@dstl.gov.uk and consult the website www.forensic-isotopes.org.

Sean Doyle
Chair of the FIRMS Steering Group

SECTION III: EVALUATION AND INTERPRETATION OF EVIDENCE

Methods of interpreting data derived from items presented for both evidential and intelligence purposes have developed significantly over recent decades. This has predominantly focused on the development and introduction of a likelihood ratio approach with many developments originating from Europe (Evett, Jackson, Aitken, Lucy, Champod, Taroni, etc) and New Zealand (Buckleton, Curran, Triggs, Walsh etc). Over these years, forensic practitioners have wrestled with the concepts and the means by which to articulate their findings to both investigators and the triers of fact.

In February 2009, the latest of a series of reports relating to forensic science emerged from the National Academy of Science in the United States. The report, "Strengthening Forensic Science in the United States: A Path Forward (2009)", made a variety of recommendations relating specifically to the presentation and interpretation of evidence.

"Recommendation 3 of the NAS report: (a) Studies establishing the scientific bases demonstrating the validity of forensic methods. (b) The development and establishment of quantifiable measures of the reliability and accuracy of forensic analyses. Studies of the reliability and accuracy of forensic techniques should reflect actual practice on realistic case scenarios, averaged across a representative sample of forensic scientists and laboratories. Studies also should establish the limits of reliability and accuracy that analytic methods can be expected to achieve as the conditions of forensic evidence vary. The research by which measures of reliability and accuracy are determined should be peer reviewed and published in respected scientific journals. (c) The development of quantifiable measures of uncertainty in the conclusions of forensic analyses."

The NAS report discussed, in particular, one of the fundamental issues relating to the interpretation of forensic evidence, the concept of Individualisation.

"Often ... forensic evidence is offered to support conclusions about 'Individualisation' .... With the exception of nuclear DNA analysis, however, no forensic method has been rigorously shown to have the capacity to consistently, and with a high degree of certainty, demonstrate a connection between evidence and a specific individual or source."

In Europe, these concepts come as no surprise within the forensic science community and the specific recommendations of the report have been topics of discussion and debate for many years. European laboratories have, for a number of years, implemented strategies, particularly in the determination of errors and measurement uncertainty relating to the generation of measured data.

The first editorial within the *Journal of the Forensic Science Society* (as it was then called) specifically discussing statistics appeared in 1979 (*Away with the fuzz*), and suggested a future where statistics, if presented in court, would bamboozle the jury

"... no longer would the qualified expert state the scientific facts and give his opinion on their worth under the alleged circumstances. He would be reduced to stating his findings in probabilistic terms surrounded by a haze of statistical fuzz".

Fifty Years of Forensic Science: A commentary   Edited by Niamh Nic Daéid
© 2010, John Wiley & Sons, Ltd.

The point was made that the presentation of rigid and numerate scientific thought to the Court would inevitably cause discomfort to the jury, who probably would "*not understand...such attempts to explain the significance of the evidence*". Further it was suggested that legal professionals would feel that an essential function of the Court (to make informed decisions relating to innocence or guilt) was being usurped. Indeed, it could be argued that these very fears were to be realised as various appeal cases were heard in the UK due to the much maligned "prosecutor's fallacy".

The specific lexicon used by scientists to communicate their interpretation of evidence can be problematic at best, though more from genuine confusion than design. This was recognised and discussed in some of the early editorials relating to interpretation. In 1983 a series of editorials and commentaries were presented which examined how to make use of statistics in court. Interestingly the NAS report (26 years later) reiterates this point;

"*...Many terms are used by forensic scientists in scientific reports and in court testimony that describe findings, conclusions, and degrees of association between evidentiary material (e.g., hairs, fingerprints, fibers) and particular people or objects. Such terms include, but are not limited to "match," "consistent with," "identical," "similar in all respects tested," and "cannot be excluded as the source of." The use of such terms can and does have a profound effect on how the trier of fact in a criminal or civil matter perceives and evaluates scientific evidence.*"

The continuing work and the developing paradigm put forward (much of it in *Science and Justice*) by champions in evidence interpretation has brought us closer to having a genuine understanding of the nature of the problem. The ability to determine the value of evidence within the framework of circumstances of a specific case and whether that evidence can be individually and unambiguously attributed to a particular source or individual becomes the matter of paramount importance. This is an issue that we struggle with in almost every evidence type.

DNA has often been referred to as the 'gold standard' of evidence. The last 20 years has seen over 5,000 research papers published relating to DNA and its use in forensic science, more than for any other evidence type. In the same time frame, nearly 1,200 research papers on the interpretation of evidence have been published, a quarter of which related to DNA evidence alone, and 67% of which were produced since the year 2000. Only with DNA evidence may we say that we have a robust statistical basis for the assessment of individualisation and discussions on how this relates to source or whether such a relationship can be established are currently discussed. With low template DNA, source determination becomes far more difficult.

Individualisation relating to other evidence types and in particular those relating to subjective interpretation (such as tool marks, shoeprints, handwriting etc) are far more problematic. Background databases of sufficient quality and size for much of these evidence types simply do not exist in many cases. Samples with more conventional numerical measurements (such as glass, fibres, paint, drugs) are better placed but again background databases are sporadic and not well defined. There are complex issues surrounding the development of robust and fit for purpose databases for both well defined and ill defined points of comparison within data sets, not least understanding measurement uncertainty for subjective measurements. The type of data, how large the databases require to be and what mathematical tools would best serve the interpretation of such data are areas which need further debate and development.

The influence of different types of bias in data collection have yet to be addressed or resolved. Confirmation bias, observation bias, bounded rationality (where choices are made based on the information available, the time available and the cognitive abilities of the decision maker) are all areas which need research and exploration as their effect on the data produced is largely unscripted. This is again documented in the NAS report *"Recommendation 5 ... encourage research programs on human observer bias and sources of human error in forensic examinations. ... In addition, research ... should ... quantify and characterize the amount of error."* This is an area where we really have only begun to scratch the surface.

N. Nic Daéid

19(3) - 1979: Away with the Fuzz

The introduction of numerical evidence in court proceedings has been with us for a long time. Statutory rules on the amount of meat in sausages and fat in ice cream co-exist with rules on the distance of car headlamps from the road surface and the time you can leave your car parked in certain places. Similarly, evidence on the level of alcohol in the blood is now commonplace and there are few judges or practised advocates in the criminal courts who have not heard the forensic biologist testify to the bloodgroups present in bloodstains and their relative commonness in the population at large.

This trend towards more numerical assistance for the courts is one in which this journal has been amongst the pioneers. An early editorial probably represents the first published argument for a statutory blood alcohol level being used as an offence per se as distinct from the analytical figure being considered as evidence that an accused person is "under the influence of alcohol", whatever that may mean (Kind, 1963). Similarly our pages have carried enormous amounts of data on blood group frequencies in selected populations, mercury levels in fingerprint officers and iron and calcium levels in the glass that showers the housebreaker as he smashes a window to gain entry.

Inevitably the growth of this useful (and intellectually fascinating) trend has attracted the attention of that guardian of numerical significance, the statistician. Whilst many of his contributions have been useful some of his more extreme pronouncements have been less so. An example of the latter variety is one where it is proposed that the presumption of innocence should be abolished and, thereafter, a probability of guilt, calculated from a statistical assessment of the worth of all the evidence, should be combined with a factor which assesses the harm done to Society by convicting the innocent, relative to that caused by absolving the guilty. The final numerical result would then be used to determine the sentence of the courts (Lindley, 1977). Such a suggestion stimulates the imagination. One can imagine certain politicians attracting such adverse social utility factors that the merest whiff of a suspicion of kicking the neighbour's cat would be sufficient to warrant life imprisonment (not altogether a bad thing in some cases).

But apart from these bizarre diversions there remains a hard kernel of opinion which seeks not only to quantify evidence at the scientific stage, but also to assess it at the legal stage, in the absence of statutorily defined figures. Thus no longer would the qualified expert state the scientific facts and give his opinion on their worth under the alleged circumstances. He would be reduced to stating his findings in probabilistic terms surrounded by a haze of statistical fuzz. Human nature and professional groups being what they are, we would soon see statisticians add the job of legal assessors to that of scientific assessors. Thus one more function of commonsense will be superseded.

The monitoring of discrete scientific procedures, by numerical criteria in the laboratory, is invaluable. In this way not only do we identify the specific and accurate method, the able experimentalist and the unsuspected phenomenon but we have a strong weapon to expose the charlatan. But to take these methods out of the laboratory and into the court of law with the hope that they will be of equal effectiveness in assessing the evidence of lay and expert witnesses alike ignores the fact that procedures in a court of law are several orders of magnitude more complex than in the laboratory.

Perhaps one day it will come to pass that sociological phenomena will be sufficiently well understood to apply these procedures in the legal process (although many may believe that such an exposure of human beings may be more than human beings can stand). Then shall we see the expert witness as part of a chimera with his own instruments, stripped of all integrity (for who requires integrity now?) and the whole assessed by the statistician on the bench, ephemerally assisted by a judge.

Indeed it may come to pass but, until that day arrives – away with the statistical fuzz!

References

Kind, S. S., 1963, Driving over the Level, *J. Forens. Sci. Soc.*, **4**, 1.
Lindley, D. V., 1977, Probability and the Law, *The Statistician*, **26**, 203.

23(1) - 1983: Patience

"The meaning doesn't matter if it's only idle chatter of a transcendental kind"

One of the major developments in forensic science in the last five years or so has been the increasing attention paid to non-methodological aspects. Certainly, accurate and unimpeachable observations in the laboratory or at the scene are essential, but the value of forensic science to the Court of Law lies in interpretation of these facts and translation of the science and technology into an opinion of their worth in the case being tried. Such is no easy task, and the limits of the problem may be represented by the ability of the expert witness to answer two questions: are the observations consistent with the alleged events, and, how likely are alternative explanations? The apparent simplicity of these questions is deceiving. In a burglary case, glass fragments may not be transferred to or retained by clothing, or their presence may be missed by an inexpert analyst. Given this uncertainty in the absence of glass traces, how difficult does interpretation become when fragments are detected?

Some years ago, the question of somehow bringing the rigid evaluation of the quality of evidence at the scientific stage to bear upon the quality of the evidence at the court stage was posed in the Editorial "Away with the Fuzz" [1]. This made the fairly reasonable point that the carry-over of rigid, numerate, scientific thought from the laboratory to the Court would inevitably cause discomfort to the other partners in the trial process; to the jury, who probably would not understand the significance of such attempts to explain the significance of the evidence, and to the legal men, who would feel that an essential function of the Court was being usurped. Response to the editorial heightened suspicions that the concept of statistical evaluation of evidence brings out the worst in forensic scientists, and perhaps for reasons that are not well understood.

"If this young man expresses himself in term too deep for me, why, what a very singularly deep young man this deep young man must be!"

So it seems is the attitude of many whenever attempts are made to remove statistics from the laboratory to the court side. This reflects the conflict between art and science, because undoubtedly some of the best (and worst!) forensic scientists are those with the personality to bring conviction and understanding to their evidence, communicating in Court with a flamboyance which is out of place in the dry and exacting laboratory environment. Perhaps it is also a reflection of the discomfort that many non-mathematical scientists experience when having to deal with statistics. It surely however should not be thus in forensic science, since statistics is a very young branch of the mathematical sciences and its principles were pre-dated by several centuries in Courts of Law. Each and every court begins by formulating a null hypothesis (such as presumption of innocence in criminal trials in the U.K.), tests it (presentation of evidence for and against) and accepts or rejects the null hypothesis at a predetermined probability level (beyond reasonable doubt or on balance of probability). This is what the statistician does, and the parallel must not be lost by senseless mechanistic dispute over translating "beyond reasonable doubt" into an exact probability, the necessary distribution function for which could not be determined.

"Prithee, pretty maiden – prithee, tell me true"

Perhaps some of the difficulty in assessing scientific evidence as rigidly as scientific experiment lies in the paucity of experimental and observational papers in forensic statistics. We attempt to redress the balance somewhat in this issue of the journal. The approach of the professional statistician entranced by forensic science is given in the guest editorial by Aitken. This is followed by three papers which look at three different aspects of statistics in one field of forensic science – blood grouping. Selvin, Grunbaum and Myhre present an up-to-date but traditional review of the application of statistics in paternity testing, where the Civil Courts have shown themselves much more adaptable than the Criminal Courts to receiving helpful statistical advice from their expert witnesses. The same authors have also presented a fairly straightforward development of these arguments, used in paternity testing, to the interpretation of blood grouping in crime cases. Evett gives us a rather different view of the application of statistics in crime cases, showing so clearly how the correct solution can only be obtained after we have been able to pose the correct question. All three papers deal to some extent with Bayesian statistics, which are both part of, and contrary to, mainstream thinking in forensic science. Information is used as it comes in to enhance current awareness and to lead the investigator to form conclusions with greater and greater degrees of confidence, but yet the confident and exact assertion of conventional applications of statistics, as for example in t-testing or estimation of probabilities of occurrence of an event given background population data, is absent. It is hoped that these articles will be of some help to forensic scientists, even those practising outwith the blood field, because undoubtedly some patience is required before the full benefits of statistics to the forensic scientist will be known and accepted; patience for the forensic scientists to understand and formulate the questions to which they seek answers; patience for the statisticians to understand the questions and formulate their replies.

W. S. Gilbert, in one small part of his libretto for "Patience" managed, as the excerpts quoted in this Editorial show, to encompass most forensic scientists' attitudes to statistics – idle chatter, terms too deep for me, but yet all we seek is understanding and perhaps for statistics to don the mantle of the pretty maiden and help the scientist in Court "tell me true".

Reference

1. LD. Away with the Fuzz. *Journal of the Forensic Science Society* 1979; **19**: 159–160.

23(1a) - 1983: Statistics and Forensic Science – A Fruitful Partnership

(Editorial)

C.G.G. Aitken

Department of Statistics, University of Edinburgh, Mayfield Road, Edinburgh, United Kingdom EH9 3JZ

Statisticians come in for continual criticism when they try to apply their methods in other fields of study. "Statistics can prove anything" and "lies, damned lies and statistics" are two comments which spring readily to mind and with which I am often accosted when I inform someone that I am a statistician. Forensic science is a fairly recent arrival in the field of statistical applications. Most of the statistical analyses are carried out by forensic scientists with only a smattering of statistical knowledge while very few statisticians as yet carry out analyses on forensic science data.

One related aspect, though not directly concerned with forensic science, is the controversy surrounding statistics and the law. Lawyers are afraid that statisticians will usurp the role of the judge and jury, sitting as assessors in the courts, weighing up the probabilities and pronouncing a verdict on the basis of their findings. There is much evidence which is not amenable to statistical analysis and never will be. However, there is also much evidence which is suitable and it would be a pity if a lawyer's fear of statistics meant that such evidence was not produced in court.

Returning to the main theme, too often statisticians are seen as enemies of the scientist, ready to do battle and attack all those who dare meddle in their subject and misuse it in so doing. This is far from the truth. Statisticians should be seen, and would like to be seen, as partners of scientists in general and forensic scientists in particular, advising the scientist at each stage of his investigation: in the design of a survey, in the analysis and interpretation of a matching problem, for example, and in the presentation of results for publication or as evidence in a court of law.

In this context, a little learning is a dangerous thing. Too often forensic scientists, in common with other scientists, have been exposed to a small dose of statistics in the form of a self-contained service course. This course is probably a neatly packaged collection of statistical techniques, mostly dealt with superficially, and the forensic scientist may well leave the course believing he is ready to tackle anything which the numerical world may throw at him. However, the real numerical world is not like the ideal world of a service course and, the caveats given in the course having been all too soon forgotten, there will often be hidden traps of which the forensic scientist will not be aware. With no statistical knowledge he would automatically have sought statistical advice, with a little knowledge he will try to do it himself and all too often he will come to grief. This is not a plea for the abolition of service courses but rather the opposite, the elevation of statistics to a more important place in the curriculum of a scientist's training. Unfortunately, in the current financial crisis facing university education this ideal is still a long way from realisation.

One of the main concerns of statistics is the measurement of variation. In forensic science this will occur naturally, for example in the size distribution of particles within the silt fraction of soils or in the refractive indices of particles of glass. An ability to assess this variation correctly may be vital in the administration of justice. Too often have I seen, for example, confidence intervals wrongly constructed or wrongly interpreted. It is only right that this task of assessing variation should be left to those best equipped to do it, namely the statisticians. I would not expect to be permitted to carry out a forensic analysis; why should forensic scientists object when a statistician asks to do the statistical analysis?

Another of my fears concerns the reporting of the applications of statistics to forensic science. Most of these applications are reported in forensic science journals and the analyses have been done by forensic scientists. In my experience these analyses are of a low level or on an "ad-hoc" basis. There are few forensic science problems discussed in the statistical literature. Those which are discussed are, for the greater part, highly theoretical and not intelligible to most forensic scientists. It seems to me that there should be more liaison between the two disciplines, not only in the investigation but in the publication of the results. This could take the form of joint publications; the statistical aspects could be emphasized in a statistical journal, the forensic aspects in a forensic journal. Certainly every paper with a statistical component which is submitted to a forensic science journal should be subject to refereeing by a statistician.

There is an unjustified fear of statistics among non-numerate people. Their lack of numeracy is reflected in a distrust of conclusions drawn from tables of figures which, to them, are incomprehensible. It is here that one aspect of a statistical training which is not perhaps fully appreciated is useful, namely the ability to consider data objectively and to present results clearly. Of course this aspect applies to any subject involving figures, not only forensic science. However, to further this end of objective data consideration, there are many statistical techniques, for example in the branches of discrimination, classification, similarity measures and sample surveys, which have proved useful in forensic science with its emphasis on identification and matching. The subject, I feel therefore, provides more scope for rigorous statistical analysis than is perhaps realized.

This editorial began by quoting the phrase "Statistics can prove anything". This is, of course, nonsense. A properly conducted statistical argument, with its strengths and weaknesses explained and with a full understanding of the underlying assumptions, can contribute much towards a greater understanding of a set of data, forensic or otherwise. There may be lies, there may be damned lies but please, do not think of statistics, or statisticians, as being similarly dishonest. Statisticians are as concerned as everyone else in the legal profession with an honest, objective appraisal of numerical evidence and wish to help, in partnership with forensic scientists, in distinguishing knowledge, inference, opinion and emotional reaction. Please help us so to do.

23(1b) - 1983: The Probability of Exclusion or Likelihood of Guilt of an Accused: Paternity

S. Selvin
Department of Biomedical and Environmental Health Sciences, University of California, Berkeley, CA 94720, U.S.A.

B. W. Grunbaum
Environmental Physiology Laboratory, University of California, Berkeley, CA 94720, U.S.A.

B. A. Myhre
School of Medicine, University of California, Los Angeles, Harbor General Hospital, Torrance, CA 90509, U.S.A.

Abstract

The relative efficiency of genetic blood group systems to exclude individuals is discussed. The potential for exclusion based on the combination of genetic systems is calculated showing the utility of genetically controlled polymorphic enzyme/protein and immunologic systems. The key to assessing the guilt or innocence in a paternity dispute using genetic evidence is the estimation of the probability of not being excluded by chance alone. This probability is computed under two sets of conditions: a random male supplied the genes in question, or a male with a phenotype identical to the accused supplied the genes in question. Contrasting these two probabilities leads to an estimate of the likelihood of guilt or innocence associated with the evidence from blood group genetic systems. The presentation gives two tables for the calculation of these non-exclusion probabilities in paternity disputes for currently used biochemical and immunological systems. The role of Bayes' theorem is discussed in conjunction with these non-exclusion probabilities.

Introduction

Evidence based on genetic analysis often clearly shows that in paternity disputes an accused male could not have contributed the genes to a child. The matter of adjudication is simple – the excluded person is thus not guilty. When genetic evidence fails to exclude a person, then neither guilt nor innocence is proven. However, this genetic circumstantial evidence can be assessed in terms of statistical probabilities. Two basic issues surrounding the use of genetic evidence in paternity proceedings are the efficacy of each system employed and the probability of non-exclusion. Both of these topics are addressed in this presentation.

One measure of usefulness of a genetic system is called the average probability of exclusion [1] which indicates the likelihood that a genetic system will eliminate an innocent individual from consideration. This probability is briefly described and calculated for twenty blood group systems, thus providing a measure of efficacy which will aid in the choice of optimal systems for genetic testing.

The probability that a genetically non-excluded man is the biologic father directly relates to the weight of circumstantial evidence in a paternity dispute. To provide a numeric expression reflecting the significance of this circumstantial evidence, two probabilities are necessary: the probability that the paternal gene observed in the child comes from a randomly selected male, and the probability that the paternal gene observed in the child comes from a randomly selected male with the same phenotype as the putative father. The contrast of these two probabilities yields numeric assessments of the genetic circumstantial evidence. This presentation provides a number of algebraic expressions and a method to calculate these two conditional probabilities. The method is illustrated using data collected from up to 5000 blood donors analyzed as part of a project entitled "Admissibility of Technical Physical Evidence" [2].

Average Probability of Exclusion

A common method for quantifying the usefulness of a system is to calculate the average probability of exclusion. The average probability of exclusion is defined as the likelihood that a specific genetic system will provide evidence which excludes an innocent man. A general expression for the average probability of exclusion for codominant genetic systems where all genotypes are detectable is available [3]. This rather complex expression reduces in the two-allele codominant system to average $P(exclusion) = pq(1 - pq)$ where p and q represent the gene frequencies of the alleles under consideration. That is, if the gene frequency of a particular allele such as $p = PGM^1 = 0.771$, then the average $P(exclusion) = (0.771)(0.229)(1 - (0.771)(0.229)) = 0.145$ for that system. This probability indicates that it is expected that 14.5% of innocent men will be excluded by employing the PGM-system. Clearly, if the frequency of any allele is 0.0 or 1.0, then the average probability of exclusion is 0.0 since population is homogeneous for that allele. When a gene frequency differs from 0.0 and 1.0, the average probability of exclusion increases from a minimum of 0.0 to a maximum value. The maximum occurs when all alleles involved in the genetic system are equally frequent (i.e., if k alleles exist, then the gene frequencies are each $1/k$) and the maximum probability of exclusion is $(k - 1)(k^3 - k^2 - 2k + 3)/k^4$ for a k-allele system [3]. When $k = 2$, the maximum probability of exclusion occurs when the allele frequencies associated with a specific system $= 0.5$ giving the maximum average $P(exclusion) = 0.188$. Other maximum values are easily computed (e.g., $k = 3$, $P(exclusion) = 0.370$ or $k = 4$, $P(exclusion) = 0.504$). Contrasting the average probability of exclusion based on observed gene frequencies with the theoretical maximum is one measure of the the relative efficacy of a genetic system.

Table 1 shows the observed average probabilities of exclusion for 20 systems divided into seven red cell antigens and thirteen protein/enzyme systems where the gene frequencies come from a white population [2]. Also included are the maximum probabilities attainable based on a specific number of alleles associated with each system (k). The efficacy for a specific system with a given number of alleles is easily assessed by comparing these two probabilities. For example, Kidd, Haptoglobin and Glutamic Pyruvic Transaminase systems are close to the maximum possible value and, therefore, nearly optimally effective systems. Other genetic systems are essentially useless from an efficacy point of view (e.g., Kell, Hemoglobin, and Peptidase).

The efficacy of several systems to exclude an innocent individual when used jointly can be quantified by calculating the probability an accused person is eliminated by one or more of a series of genetic systems. That is, if the average probabilities of exclusion for a series of genetic systems are represented as $e_1, e_2, e_3, \ldots, e_m$, then the overall average probability of exclusion is:

$$P(\text{one or more exclusions}) = 1 - (1 - e_1)(1 - e_2) \ldots (1 - e_m)$$

where m represents the number of systems involved. For example, if interest is focussed on the five most effective immunologic systems (Table 1), then the overall average probability of exclusion $= 1 - (1 - 0.152)(1 - 0.404)(1 - 0.312)(1 - 0.183)(1 - 0.187) = 1 - 0.231 = 0.769$. The five most effective enzyme/protein systems (Table 1) similarly give an overall average probability of exclusion of 0.612. The combined average probability exclusion for both groups is $1 - (0.231)(0.388) = 0.910$. As before, this probability indicates that 91.0% of innocent men tested using these 10 systems are expected to be eliminated from consideration by genetic evidence.

The product of a series of probabilities to calculate the probability of the joint occurrence of a set of phenotypes entails the assumption of statistical independence. Statistical independence among genetic systems is an expected property since the sources of association among human genotypes such as mutation, selection, assortative mating and inbreeding will generally not act at detectable levels. Furthermore, the major blood group systems have been shown empirically [2] to lack any measurable association which is consistent with theoretical population genetic models [4] which predict independence of Mendelian inherited traits for random mating populations.

Table 1 The Average and Maximum Probabilities of Exclusion*

	Number of alleles	Average P (exclusion)	Maximum P (exclusion)
Red Cell Systems			
ABO	4	0.152	0.504
Rh	8	0.404**	0.743
MNSs	4	0.312	0.504
Kell	2	0.034	0.188
Duffy	3	0.183	0.370
Kidd	2	0.187	0.188
P-system	2	0.039	0.188
Enzyme/Protein Systems			
Haptoglobin	2	0.184	0.188
Group Specific Component	2	0.163	0.188
Hemoglobin	2	0.000	0.188
Adenylate Kinase	2	0.035	0.188
Adenosine Deaminase	2	0.044	0.188
Erythrocyte Acid Phosphatase	3	0.243	0.370
Esterase D	2	0.092	0.188
G-6PD (female)***	2	0.008	0.188
Phosphoglucomutase	2	0.145	0.188
6-Phosphogluconate dehydrogenase	2	0.016	0.188
Glyoxalase	2	0.185	0.188
Peptidase	2	0.000	0.188
Glutamic Pyruvate Transaminase	2	0.185	0.188

*all gene frequencies come from white California sample [2]
**approximate – overestimates the average probability of exclusion
***males add no information since the genotype is completely determined by the mother

Probability of Non-Exclusion

The probability that a specific phenotype is observed in an offspring can be viewed as a function of the information available from the parental phenotypes. The simplest case occurs when information is not available from the parents of a specific individual and, therefore, the probability of observing a specific phenotype is strictly a function of the gene frequencies. Notationally, the frequency of a specific phenotype is represented as:

$$P(c = A_m | \text{mother}) \, P(c = A_f | \text{father})$$

which is a product of the probability that the child receives a maternal allele represented by A_m and the probability that the child receives a paternal allele A_f. If the frequency of allele A_m is represented as p and the frequency of allele A_f is q and both parents are randomly selected individuals, then the frequency of $A_m A_f$ offspring is $P(c = A_m | m = \text{random}) P(c = A_f | f = \text{random}) = pq$. This calculation is based on the assumption that all individuals involved come from a large random mating population at Hardy-Weinberg equilibrium with respect to the human blood groups being considered and are unrelated. This assumption is also made in all subsequent calculations and is generally considered valid for calculations concerning human blood groups. (Note: the maternal gene is listed first and this convention will be followed throughout this presentation).

Table 2 Six Expressions for the Calculation that a Child's Phenotype Arises by Chance (i.e. P(Non-Exclusion)) Employing Different Types of Parental Information

1. $P(c = A|m = \text{random}) = P(c = A|f = \text{random}) = p$
2. $P(c = a|m = \text{random}) = P(c = a|f = \text{random}) = q$
3. $P(c = A|m = AA) = P(c = A|f = AA) = 1.0$
4. $P(c = a|m = Aa) = P(c = a|f = Aa) = 0.5$
   $P(c = A|m = Aa) = P(c = A|f = Aa) = 0.5$
5. $P(c = A|m = A^+) = P(c = A|f = A^+) = (p^2 + pq)/D$
6. $P(c = a|m = A^+) = P(c = a|f = A^+) = pq/D$

The quantity $D = p^2 + 2pq$ is the frequency of the dominant phenotype A^+ where p and q represent gene frequencies of the dominant and recessive alleles, respectively.

In the case of paternity testing, information is available on the parental phenotypes and can be incorporated into the probability that specific genes are observed in the child. Typically, the parental phenotypes will be either AA (homozygous), Aa (heterozygous) or A^+ (homozygous or heterozygous with dominance present). The conditional probabilities associated with the occurrence of these three specific parental situations are given by expressions 3–6 in Table 2. For example, if it is known that the mother is heterozygous and the father is assumed to be randomly chosen, then the probability of exclusion associated with Aa children with a maternal A-allele and a paternal a-allele is $P(c = A|m = Aa)P(c = a|f = \text{random}) = (0.5)q$ where, as before, q represents the frequency of the a-allele (expressions 2 and 4; Table 2).

The genotype of the putative father is another relevant piece of information and can be incorporated into the calculation of the probability that a specific child's phenotype arose by chance. Again, using the expressions in Table 2 the probability of non-exclusion is relatively easy to calculate. For example, if the mother is again heterozygotic Aa and the putative father is aa, then the probability of non-exclusion associated with an Aa child is $P(c = A|m = Aa)P(c = a|f = aa) = (0.5)(1.0) = 0.5$ (expressions 4 and 3, Table 2).

The case where the genotype cannot be completely identified (i.e. dominance) presents a slightly more complex picture. However, the expressions given in Table 2 remain useful. The probability of non-exclusion is the sum of the probabilities associated with all the possible genotypes that could produce the phenotype of the child in question. The conditional probabilities for each parental gene are found using Table 2, multiplied together and summed, giving the probability of non-exclusion. The results are presented in Table 3 for all 12 possible mother-child-"father" combinations when dominance is present. Consider for example, the case where the child has phenotype B^+ (ABO-system, B^+ meaning BB, BO or OB phenotypes), the mother B^+ and the father is assumed to be randomly selected. Here, three possible genotypes exist for an offspring with a B^+ phenotype (BB, BO, and OB, where as before, the maternal gene is listed first). The probability of non-exclusion is the sum of the probabilities of non-exclusion associated with the three genotypes. That is, if the frequency of the B-allele is p and the O-allele is q, then

$$P(\text{child} = B^+|m = B^+, f = \text{random}) = P(c = B|m = B^+)P(c = B|f = \text{random})$$
$$+ P(c = B|m = B^+)P(c = O|f = \text{random}) + P(c = O|m = B^+)P(c = B|f = \text{random})$$
$$= [(p^2 + pq)/D]p + [(p^2 + pq)/D]q + [pq/D]p = p[(p+q)^2 + pq]/D$$

where $D = p^2 + 2pq$ is the frequency of the B^+ phenotype (the above expressions come from Table 2) The other 11 expressions also in Table 3 are derived from similar considerations.

Table 3 The Probability of Non-Exclusion for Genetic Systems with Dominance*

"Father" = random
$P(\text{child} = A^+ | m = A^+, f = \text{random}) = p[(p+q)^2 + pq]/D$
$P(\text{child} = aa | m = A^+, f = \text{random}) = q$
$P(\text{child} = A^+ | m = aa, f = \text{random}) = p$
$P(\text{child} = aa | m = aa, f = \text{random}) = q$

"Father" = A^+
$P(\text{child} = A^+ | m = A^+, f = A^+) = p^2(p+q)(p+3q)/D$
$P(\text{child} = aa | m = A^+, f = A^+) = pq/D$
$P(\text{child} = A^+ | m = aa, f = A^+) = p(p+q)/D$
$P(\text{child} = aa | m = aa, f = A^+) = pq/D$

"Father" = aa
$P(\text{child} = A^+ | m = A^+, f = aa) = p(p+q)/D$
$P(\text{child} = aa | m = A^+, f = aa) = 1.0$
$P(\text{child} = A^+ | m = aa, f = aa) = 0.0$
$P(\text{child} = aa | m = aa, f = aa) = 1.0$

*Again, $D = p^2 + 2pq$ is the frequency of A^+, where A^+ is AA or AO genotype

Table 4 illustrates the calculation of the probability of non-exclusion for a case employing the probabilities given in Tables 2 and 3 for five typical genetic systems. This hypothetical case is as follows:

	ABO	MNSs	P-system	Rh-system	Haptoglobin
Child	B^+	MSs	P_2P_2	CcDee	1–2
Mother	B^+	MSs	P_2P_2	CCDee	2–2
Putative Father	B^+	MSs	P^+_1	CcDee	1–2

Two summaries are employed to give an overall assessment of the likelihood the putative father is indeed the biologic father. The first of these summaries is called the paternity ratio. The paternity ratio is the probability of non-exclusion associated with the assumption that the child's phenotype arose from a man whose genetic make-up was the same as the putative father divided by the probability that the child's phenotype arose from a randomly selected male. These two probabilities are simply the product of the similar probabilities of non-exclusion calculated for each genetic system derived from Table 2. These values (derived in Table 4) for the hypothetical example are: $(0.424)(0.281)(0.539)(0.442)(0.422) = 0.0120$ ("father" = random), and $(0.766)(0.500)(0.350)(0.489)(0.500) = 0.033$ ("father" = given). The paternity ratio is therefore $r = 0.033/0.012 = 2.75$.

A related but more complex summary of the genetic evidence involves the use of Bayes' theorem. Bayes' theorem applied to paternity calculations (sometimes called the Essen-Möller formula) yields a measure of the likelihood of guilt. Bayes' theorem states that the probability of paternity is

$$P(\text{father} | \text{not excluded}) = \frac{P(\text{not excluded} | \text{father}) P(\text{father})}{P(\text{not excluded})}$$

$$= \frac{1}{1 + \frac{1 - P(\text{father})}{P(\text{father})} \cdot \frac{1}{r}}$$

Table 4 An Illustrative Example Using 5 Genetic Systems to Assess the Likelihood of Guilt of a Putative Father* Using Tables 2 and 3

ABO System   Child = B$^+$ Mother = B$^+$
"Father" = random:
P(child = B$^+$|m = B$^+$, f = random) = $(0.074)[(0.738)^2 + (0.074)(0.664)]/(0.104) = 0.424$
if "Father" = B$^+$:
P(child = B$^+$|m = B$^+$, f = B$^+$) = $(0.074)^2(0.074 + 0.0664)[(0.074) + 3(0.664))/(0.104)^2 = 0.776$

MNSs system   Child = MSs   Mother = MSs
"Father" = random: 199
P(c = MSs|m = MSs)P(c = MS|f = random) × P(c = Ms|m = MSs)P(c = MS|f = random)
  = $(0.5)(0.317) + (0.5)(0.245) = 0.281$
if "Father" = MSs:
P(c = MS|m = MSs)P(c = Ms|f = MSs) + P(c = Ms|m = MS)P(c = MSs|f = MSs)
  = $(0.5)(0.5) + (0.5)(0.5) = 0.500$

P System   Child = P$_2$P$_2$ Mother = P$_2$P$_2$
"Father" = random:
P(child = P$_2$P$_2$|m = P$_2$P$_2$, father = random) = 0.539
if "Father" = P$^+_1$:
P(child = P$_2$P$_2$|m = P$_2$P$_2$, father = P$^+_2$) = 0.350

Rhesus System   Child = CcDee   Mother = CCDee   "Father" = random:
P(c = CDe|m = CCDee)P(c = cDe|f = random) + P(c = CDe|m = CCDee)P(c = cde|f = random)
  + P(c = Cde|m = CCDee)P(c = cDe|f = random)
  = $\{[(0.382)^2 + (0.382)(0.010)]/(0.154)\}(0.044) + \{[(0.382)^2 + (0.382)(0.010)]/(0.154)\}(0.408)$
    $+\{(0.382)(0.010)/(0.154)\}(0.044) = 0.442$
if "Father" = CcDee:
  P(c = CDe|m = CCDee)P(c = cDe|f = CcDee)
  + P(c = CDe|m = CCDee)P(c = cde|f = CcDee)
  + P(c = Cde|m = CCDee)P(c = cDe|f = CcDee)
  = $(0.975)\{[(0.044)(0.382) + (0.044)(0.010)]/(0.346)\}$
    $+ (0.975)\{(0.382)(0.408)/(0.346)\}$
    $+ (0.025)\{[(0.044)(0.382) + (0.044)(0.010)]/(0.346)\} = 0.489$

Haptoglobin System   Child = Hp^{1}Hp^1 Mother = Hp^{2}Hp^2 "Father" = random:
P(c = Hp^2|m = Hp^{2}Hp^2)P(c = Hp^1|f = random) = $(1.0)(0.422) = 0.422$
if "Father" = Hp^{1}Hp^2:
P(c = Hp^2|m = Hp^{2}Hp^2)P(c = Hp^1|f = Hp^{1}Hp^2) = $(1.0)(0.5) = 0.500$

Gene frequencies employed [2]
B: 0.074 O: 0.664 A: 0.262; Ms: 0.317 MS: 0.245 Ns: 0.379 NS: 0.059; P$_1$: 0.461 P$_2$: 0.539; CDe: 0.382 Cde: 0.010 cDe: 0.044 cde: 0.408 CDE: 0.008 CdE: 0.000 cDE: 0.136 cdE: 0.012; Hp^1: 0.422 Hp^2: 0.578.

where r is the paternity ratio and P(father) is the a priori probability that the accused is the biologic father. Often the value for P (father) is set at 0.5 yielding P(father|not excluded) = $1/(1 + 1/r)$ as an assessment of an accused man's guilt or innocence. For the above example, this transformation gives $1/(1 + (1/2.75)) = 0.733$. This value is often interpreted as the probability that a man whose phenotype does not exclude him on the grounds of genetic evidence supplied the set of paternal genes observed in the child. However, the probabilitistic interpretation of this expression involves several complicated and subtle issues. For example, the probability 0.733 contains the implicit assumption that half the men charged in a paternity action without regard to the genetic evidence are guilty (certainly an equivocal assumption).

Other complications, beyond the scope of this presentation, exist when values like 0.733 are interpreted as a probability. However, this transformation does convert r to a number between 0.0 and 1.0 where values observed near the extremes reflect on the likelihood of innocence or guilt. The genetic literature contains a number of papers discussing the role of Bayes' theorem and its use to calculate the probability of guilt in paternity testing situations [5-7].

References

1. Fisher RA. Standard calculation for evaluating a blood-group system. *Heredity* 1951; **5**: 51-102.
2. Grunbaum BW. Distribution of gene frequencies and discrimination probabilities for 22 human blood systems in four racial groups. *Journal of Forensic Sciences* 1980; **25**: 428-444.
3. Selvin S. Probability of nonpaternity determined by multiple allele codominant systems. *American Journal of Human Genetics* 1980; **32**: 276-278.
4. Li CC. *Population Genetics*. Chicago, Illinois: The University of Chicago Press, 1968.
5. Langency A and Piston G. Probability of paternity: Useless. *American Journal of Human Genetics* 1975; **27**: 558-561.
6. Valentine J. Statistical evidence in paternity cases: Imperative. *American Journal of Human Genetics* 1976; **28**: 620-621.
7. Salmon D and Brocteur J. Probability of paternity. *American Journal of Human Genetics* 1976; **28**: 622-625.

23(1c) - 1983: The Probability of Non-discrimination or Likelihood of Guilt of an Accused: Criminal Identification

S. Selvin
Department of Biomedical and Environmental Health Sciences, University of California, Berkeley, CA 94720, U.S.A.
B. W. Grunbaum
Environmental Physiology Laboratory, University of California, Berkeley, CA 94720, U.S.A.
B. A. Myhre
School of Medicine, University of California, Los Angeles, Harbor General Hospital, Torrance, CA 90509, U.S.A.

Abstract

The relative efficacy of genetic blood group systems is explored in terms of the probability of non-discrimination. This probability is used to assess the value of anti-sera and blood group systems to exclude falsely accused individuals. In criminal identification situations, it is often useful to assess the likelihood that a non-excluded defendant's blood was found at the scene of a crime. The probability that an accused individual who matches a specific set of blood phenotypes was present at a crime scene is derived and discussed. These calculations are illustrated with examples using blood group data from up to 5000 samples from blood donors.

Introduction

This presentation of the issues surrounding the application of blood group genetics to criminal identification is a continuation of our previous paper which concerns the use of genetic evidence in paternity disputes [1]. The valid assessment of genetic circumstantial evidence is the goal in both but the logic and statistical/probabilistic methods differ. This difference arises primarily from the fact that paternity investigations involve evidence derived from the phenotypes of three people (mother, child and putative father) whereas in criminal identification a defendant's blood is compared to a given set of phenotypes.

The use of mathematically derived probabilities in criminal identification is certainly not a new phenomenon. The case of the People versus Collins has been widely discussed in lay as well as professional publications. The case was described in Newsweek magazine and has been considered in two elementary statistics textbooks [2, 3]. Briefly, Malcolm Collins was arrested because he matched six characteristics described by witnesses, and accused of robbery. He was black, owned a yellow car, had a moustache and beard. His girlfriend was white with blond hair worn in a ponytail style. Assuming the elementary probabilities are: yellow car (0.1), moustache (0.25), ponytail (0.1), blond hair (0.33), black man with a beard (0.1), and interracial couple (0.001); then multiplying them together yields a probability of about 1 in 12 million that a randomly selected person will match all six characteristics by chance. The jury seemed persuaded that the correspondence between Mr. Collins and the six characteristics was not coincidental ("beyond a reasonable doubt") and returned a verdict of guilty.

Almost everyone who has reviewed the case points out two fundamental problems with the probability of 1 in 12 million. The elementary probabilities are of dubious origin since the frequencies of the six characteristics are not accurately tabulated for any relevant population and, furthermore, these characteristics are not statistically independent. The opinion of the California Supreme Court which overturned the original conviction, cited these two errors. The court's decision contained considerable insight into the statistical issues and stated "... mathematics, a veritable sorcerer in our computerized society, while assisting the trier of fact in the search of truth, must not cast a spell over him" [4]. It should also be noted that a probability such as 1 in 12 million presented in the Collins case, when derived from well-defined and independent frequencies, could reflect the guilt or innocence of a defendant. However, this value is not the probability a person who matches the characteristics in question is falsely accused.

A reviewer of this paper suggested that another view of the probability that the accused person (Mr. Collins) possesses all six characteristics is provided by an application of the truncated binomial distribution. Let p be the probability a person possesses all six characteristics; then the probability P that all six occur in more than one person given they occurred for a specific case is

$$P = 1 - [Np(1-p)^{N-1}]/(1 - (1-p)^N)$$

where N is the size of the population of interest. For example, if $N = 12 \times 10^6$ then $P = 0.42$ or if $N = 250{,}000$ then $P = 0.01$ when $p = 1/(12 \times 10^6)$.

The same issues debated in the case of the People versus Collins arise when blood found at the scene of a crime matches the blood of a defendant. However, evidence from the analysis of blood group systems provides an opportunity to employ valid probabilistic arguments in criminal identification. Blood group genetic variants often have well-defined frequencies and are distributed in a statistically independent manner [5]. These two properties, lacking in the Collins case, make it possible to calculate useful quantitative measures of the strength of genetically derived circumstantial evidence.

The following presentation addresses two questions critical to the courtroom application of genetic data in criminal investigation and identification: the efficacy of specific systems or combinations of systems to exclude innocent individuals is discussed then the assessment of the likelihood of a given defendant being present at the scene of a crime is investigated. The evaluation of genetic systems and the calculation of probabilities related to guilt are illustrated with the data collected from up to 5000 blood donors described in detail elsewhere [5, 6].

Table 1 Illustrative Example of the Calculation of the Non-Discrimination Probability for the ABO-System and A_1A_2BO-System

	Phenotypic frequency*		Phenotypic frequency*
A-type	$P_1 = 0.417$	A_1-type	$P_1 = 0.325$
B-type	$P_2 = 0.104$	A_2-type	$P_2 = 0.092$
AB-type	$P_3 = 0.039$	B-type	$P_3 = 0.104$
O-type	$P_4 = 0.441$	A_1B-type	$P_4 = 0.029$
		A_2B-type	$P_5 = 0.010$
		O-type	$P_6 = 0.441$
$Q_{ABO} = P_1^2 + P_2^2 + P_3^2 + P_4^2$		$Q_{A_1A_2BO} = P_1^2 + P_2^2 + P_3^2 + P_4^2 + P_5^2 + P_6^2$	
$= 0.381$		$= 0.320$	

*based on gene frequencies from Grunbaum, [6]; $A_1 = 0.196$, $A_2 = 0.066$, B $= 0.074$ and O $= 0.664$

Probability of Discrimination

A measure of the efficacy of a specific blood group system to individualize a defendant's blood is the probability of non-discrimination. This probability is defined as the probability that two individuals selected at random from the same population match with respect to one or more phenotypes. This concept was first applied to problems concerning ecologic diversity [7] and later to blood group genetics [8]. Symbolically, the probability of non-discrimination associated with the i-th blood group system is:

$$Q_i = P_1^2 + P_2^2 + \cdots + P_n^2$$

where P_j represents the phenotypic frequency of the j-th phenotype and n represents the number of distinct phenotypes within the i-th blood group system. For example, the ABO-system is made up of four phenotypes (n = 4) and, using gene frequencies from Grunbaum [6], the value of $Q_{ABO} = 0.381$ (see Table 1). Therefore, the probability that two randomly selected individuals have the same ABO-phenotype is 0.381 and the probability of discrimination $(1 - Q_1)$ is 0.619. These calculations are based on the assumption that a defendant comes from a large random mating population at Hardy-Weinberg equilibrium with respect to the human blood groups being considered. This assumption is also made in all subsequent calculations and is generally considered valid for calculations concerning human blood groups.

The concept of non-discrimination can be extended to a series of genetic systems. The probability of non-discrimination when m systems are employed in the comparison of two samples of blood is the product $Q_1Q_2Q_3 \ldots Q_m$ where Q_1 is the non-discrimination probability of a specific system. Therefore, the probability that two randomly chosen individuals do not match for at least one phenotype for a series of m comparisons is $1 - Q_1Q_2Q_3 \ldots Q_m$ which is the general expression for the probability of discrimination. The probability of discrimination applied to criminal identification measures the likelihood a blood group system or series of systems will exclude an innocent individual from consideration.

The non-discrimination probability is effectively used to judge the gains associated with employing more complex analyses within a blood group system. That is, for several systems, a choice exists of specific anti-sera which yield more precise determinations of an individual's phenotype. For example, an A_1-phenotype could be detected within an A-type blood from the ABO-system. If A-type blood is analyzed for the A_1- and A_2-subgroups producing a total of six ABO-phenotypes, then the probability of non-discrimination is $Q_{A_1A_2BO} = 0.320$ (see Table 1) showing a 19% gain over $Q_{ABO} = 0.381$ (previous example) where the analysis involved four phenotypes. This type of calculation is important in laboratory settings where accuracy and costs are important whenever additional anti-sera are considered.

Probabilities of non-discrimination are similarly useful to quantify and compare the efficacy of specific blood group systems to exclude accused individuals. The efficacy of a genetic system is maximum when the probability of non-discrimination is minimum. In other words, a defendant is most likely to be excluded when a given system or combination of systems used in the genetic analysis produce the smallest possible probability that the phenotypes compared will match by chance alone. The minimum value for the probability of non-discrimination occurs when all alleles involved in the system are equally frequent. When k alleles are present (i.e., frequency = 1/k), then the minimum probability of non-discrimination is $(2k-1)/k^3$. This value continues to be the minimum probability of non-discrimination for systems with dominance. Since the inability to detect all genotypes within a system only increases the probability of non-discrimination, the minimum probability of non-discrimination for systems with dominance remains $(2k-1)/k^3$. Thus, when k = 2 the minimum probability of non-discrimination is 0.375 for all two-allele systems. The minimum non-discrimination probability for a series of systems is simply the product of the individual minimum values associated with each specific system. Some examples of these minimum probabilities are given in Table 2 and serve as a reference point for assessing the utility of a blood group system.

Some blood group systems are substantially less useful in terms of excluding innocent individuals (e.g., Kell system where Q = 0.825 and the minimum = 0.375) and other systems are very useful as they almost reach the minimum possible value (e.g., Kidd system where Q = 0.3753 and the minimum = 0.375). Comparison of the efficacy of a series of systems involves the product of the single Q_1-values. For example, the probability of non-discrimination associated with the red cell systems (Table 2; systems 1–7) is $(0.320)(0.205)\ldots(0.587) = 0.000619$. The same value for the protein/enzyme systems (Table 2; system 8–20) is $(0.381)(0.435)\ldots(0.380) = 0.00158$. The overall likelihood of excluding an innocent individual obviously increases with each additional system employed. Not surprisingly, using a large number of systems make it possible, at least theoretically, to discriminate between two samples of blood so that innocent individuals are almost certainly excluded. Using all 20 systems in Table 2 produces a probability of non-discrimination that is extremely small (9.65×10^{-7}, or almost one person in a million).

Table 2 The Non-Discrimination Probabilities* for a White Population and the Minimum Possible Value for 20 Blood Group Systems

	Q_i	Minimum		Q_i	Minimum
1. ABO-system	0.320	0.185	11. Adenylate Kinase	0.862	0.375
2. Rh-system	0.205	0.029	12. Adenosine Deaminase	0.828	0.375
3. MNSs-system	0.152	0.109	13. Erythrocyte Acid Phosphatase	0.308	0.185
4. Kell	0.825	0.375	14. Esterase D.	0.654	0.375
5. Duffy	0.342	0.185	15. Glucose-6-Phosphate Dehydrogenase	0.994	0.375
6. Kidd	0.375	0.375	16. Phosphoglucomutase	0.480	0.375
7. P-system	0.587	0.375	17. 6-Phosphogluconate Dehydrogenase	0.933	0.375
8. Haptoglobin	0.381	0.375	18. Glyoxalase-1	0.379	0.375
9. Group Specific Component	0.435	0.375	19. Peptidase-A	1.000	0.375
10. Hemoglobin	1.000	0.375	20. Glutamic Pyruvic Transaminase	0.380	0.375

*from Grunbaum, [6] for a white population

Probability of Presence at a Crime Scene

An important use of evidence derived from genetic analysis is the application to courtroom arguments. If no question arises as to whether the defendant was present at a crime scene, then circumstantial evidence provided by a genetic analysis is not useful. However, if the question of presence or absence arises, then assessment of the genetic evidence in terms of a probability is indeed helpful.

The calculation of the probability that a person was present at the scene of a crime based on genetic evidence is a function of two other probabilities: the probability of coincidence derived from the genetic analysis and the probability that a defendant was present at the crime scene derived without reference to the genetic data (prior probability). These two probabilities are combined to provide an estimate of the likelihood a defendant's blood was found at a crime scene when the accused was not excluded by genetic phenotyping.

The probability that a randomly selected person matches a given set of phenotypes is called the probability of coincidence. This probability is occasionally confused with the probability of non-discrimination (previous section). However, the probability of coincidence refers to the likelihood that a specific set of given phenotypes is observed in a randomly selected individual by chance alone. For example, the probability that a randomly selected person matches an A-type (ABO-system) is the frequency of A-individuals in the population from which the person was chosen (about 0.4 for most white populations). Furthermore, the probability of coincidence refers to one individual and a single phenotype within the genetic system whereas the probability of non-discrimination is a measure of the likelihood of matching between two individuals for any of a series of phenotypes within the blood genetic system.

The probability of coincidence associated with a series of systems is simply the product of the given phenotype frequencies. If C represents the probability of coincidence, then

$$C = P_1 P_2 P_3 \ldots P_m$$

where, as before, P_i represents the phenotypic frequency associated with the i-th system and m represents the number of systems analyzed. For example, consider the set of phenotypes: A (ABO-system), ccddee (Rh-system), MSs (MNSs-system) and kk (Kell system). The probability of coincidence for these four phenotypes is $(0.417)(0.166)(0.155)(0.904) = 0.00970$, based on gene frequencies given in Grunbaum [6]. A slight increase in statistical precision is achieved by estimating the phenotypic frequencies from gene frequencies rather than directly from the empirically derived phenotype frequencies. For example, the frequency of the A-phenotype [6] is estimated as $((0.262)^2 + 2(0.262)(0.664)) = 0.417$ (see [9] for details on this type of calculation) compared to a calculation based on the number of A-phenotypes divided by the total number of samples analyzed which is $371/914 = 0.406$.

In criminal identification the probability of coincidence is calculated under two assumptions: the defendant was present and the defendant was not present at the scene of the crime. If the accused person's blood was found at the crime scene then the probability of coincidence is 1.0 (denoted: P(coincidence|present = 1.0)). Of course, this calculation can be more complicated if more than one person's blood is involved. Alternatively, the assumption is made that the accused was not present at the scene of the crime and the probability of coincidence is computed based on the hypothesis that the blood represents a random selection from some relevant population (denoted: C = P(coincidence|not present)). This value is the probability of coincidence described in the previous paragraphs. The circumstantial evidence against an accused increases as the ratio 1.0/C increases. This value is often (e.g., People versus Collins [4]) interpreted as the likelihood a defendant has been falsely accused. However, interest should be focused on a related but different probability. In fact, the probability of critical importance is the probability a person whose blood matches that found at a crime scene was present (denoted: P(present|coincidence)).

To further assess the genetic circumstantial evidence surrounding a person whose blood matches that found at a crime scene, an application of Bayes' theorem can be used to compute an estimate of

P(present|coincidence). This quantitative measure related to a defendant's guilt can be calculated by combining the prior probability of presence (denoted: P(present)) and the evidence derived from the genetic data to produce the probability the defendant's blood was found at the crime scene. Symbolically, this probability is

$$P(\text{present}|\text{coincidence}) = \frac{P(\text{coincidence}|\text{present})P(\text{present})}{P(\text{coincidence})}$$

The value P(present|coincidence) is called the posterior probability of presence. The term P(coincidence) is the weighted average of two probabilities: the probability that an accused person's blood was found at the crime scene and the probability that the defendant's blood matches by chance. Symbolically, P(coincidence) = P(coincidence|present)P(present) + P(coincidence|not present)P(not present). Therefore,

$$P(\text{present}|\text{coincidence}) = \frac{1.0}{1.0 + C[P(\text{not present})|P(\text{present})]}$$

This expression shows that when the value C decreases, the P(present/coincidence) approaches 1.0 for realistic values of P(present). That is, when the probability is small that a person who was assumed not present at the crime scene matches the given blood phenotypes, then it can be inferred that the defendant was, in fact, at the crime scene (i.e., not falsely accused). For the sake of an example, say it is known that P(present) = P(not present) = 0.5; then the P(present|coincidence) is based on a person who matches for blood group systems A, ccddee, MSs and kk (previous example) is $1.0/(1.0 + 0.0097) = 0.990$. However, an exact determination of the likelihood that an accused was present at a crime depends on an accurate value of P(present).

Discussion

The application of the probability of non-discrimination is relatively straight-forward. On the other hand, the probability an accused individual who matches a specific set of phenotypes was at the scene of a crime (i.e., P(present|coincidence)) is a much more subtle concept. Occasionally confusion exists between this probability and the probability a person selected at random matches a given set of phenotypes (i.e., P(coincidence|not present)). Clearly, the probability of greatest interest is the probability that a defendant was present at the crime scene when the accused was not excluded by genetic evidence since, presumably, a person who does not match does not come to trial. The probability of matching a set of phenotypes when the accused is assumed not to have been present is related but in fact is a different measure of guilt. The practical difference in interpretation between these two probabilities can be extremely small since small values of C usually imply that the P(present|coincidence) is close to 1.0. That is, if P(coincidence|not present) = 1 in 12 million, then P(present|coincidence) is essentially 1.0. However, it is important to make a clear distinction between these two probabilities since P(present|coincidence) rests on an accurate estimation of the prior probability (i.e., without regard to the genetic evidence) that the accused was present at the scene of the crime. In most cases a realistic estimate of the P(present) does not exist and, therefore, the P(present|coincidence) cannot be accurately established. Typically, all that can be said is that if C is small then P(present|coincidence) will be close to 1.0 for all but very small values of P(present).

It is also important to note that the muliplicative nature of the value C makes it rather liable to influences from sampling variation and bias in the gene frequencies. The effect of sampling variation can be reduced by employing gene frequencies estimated from large amounts of data. The most probable source of bias in gene frequencies is the racial classification of the defendant. Small differences in phenotypic frequencies arising from the racial misclassification of an accused person multiply in the computation of C which can potentially introduce rather severe bias.

It has been suggested that non-genetic characteristics can be used in criminal identification, e.g., paint [10]. The probabilities discussed here apply equally to these situations. However, like the human blood group systems, the frequencies of the characteristics involved must be well defined and demonstrated to be independently distributed.

References

1. Selvin S, Grunbaum BW and Myhre BA. The Probability of Exclusion or Likelihood of Guilt of an Accused: Paternity. *Journal of the Forensic Science Society* 1983; **23**: 19–25.
2. Freeman D, Pisani R and Purves R. *Statistics.* New York: WW Norton & Co, 1979.
3. Huber A and Runyon RP. *General Statistics*. Reading, Mass: Addison-Wesley Co., 1973.
4. *People v. Collins, 1968, 68CAL. 2d 319, 320, 438P. 2nd 33, 66CAL. RPTR. 497.*
5. Grunbaum BW, Selvin S, Pace N and Black DM. Frequency Distribution and Discrimination Probability of Twelve Protein Genetic Variants in Human Blood as a Function of Race, Sex and Age. *Journal of Forensic Sciences* 1978; **3**: 577–587.
6. Grunbaum BW, Selvin S, Myhre BA and Pace N. Distribution of Gene Frequencies and Discrimination Probabilities for 22 Human Blood Genetic Systems in Four Racial Groups. *Journal of Forensic Sciences* 1980; **2**: 428–444.
7. Simpson EH. Measures of Diversity. *Nature* 1949; **23**: 688.
8. Fisher RA. Standard Calculations for Evaluating a Blood-group System. *Heredity* 1951; **5**: 51–102.
9. Li CC. *Population Genetics*. Chicago, Illinois,: The University of Chicago Press, 1968.
10. Tippett CF, Emerson VJ, Fereday MJ, Lawton F, Richardson A, Jones LT and Lampert SM. The Evidence Value of the Comparison of Paint from Sources Other Than Vehicles. *Journal of the Forensic Science Society* 1968; **8**: 61–65.

23(1d) - 1983: What is the Probability that This Blood Came from That Person? A Meaningful Question?

I. W. Evett

Home Office Central Research Establishment, Aldermaston, Reading, Berkshire, United Kingdom RG7 4P N

Abstract

The paper discusses, on the basis of Bayesian inference, the type of question which the forensic scientist should attempt to answer in the context of the investigation of a crime. By means of simple examples it is argued that, as far as the scientist is concerned, the first question in the title is not, in general, meaningful.

Introduction

The first question in the title is of a type which the forensic scientist is asked from time to time in relation to many kinds of physical evidence. It is convenient to talk about the blood example because the data involved are simpler than in other cases such as glass and paint, but the basic philosophy must be the same, whatever the evidence type. The discussion is confined to a case example in which the blood in the question is a stain which has been left at a crime scene by the person who committed the crime. It is assumed that the investigator has found a suspect and he is concerned with establishing the strength of the link between the suspect and the crime. The scientist carries out a comparison between the bloodgroup of the stain and the bloodgroup of a sample given by the suspect.

There can be little argument that the question is meaningful in the sense that an answer to it will be of enormous help to the investigator. However, from the scientist's point of view the question is only meaningful if he can give a meaningful answer. In certain circumstances the answer is simple: for example, if the bloodgroups of the stain and suspect are different, then the answer must be zero. If the suspect is one of two people who must have committed the crime and his bloodgroup is the same as that of the bloodstain while that of the other suspect differs then the answer must be one. However, in general when the groups match, the circumstances are not so simple. The discussion considers the separate roles of the investigator and the scientist and it is argued that the question in the above form is not, in general, the one which the scientist should attempt to answer. Attention is directed to the class of questions with which the scientist can and should concern himself.

The underlying philosophy of this approach has been presented before by Finkelstein and Fairley [1] and by Lindley [2].

Example

It will be assumed that the scientist's results, to be summarised by the letter F, are as follows:

F

Bloodstain is of group *

Suspect's blood is of group *

In addition, the scientist knows from data previously collected that:

Blood of group * occurs in 5% of the general population.

If the suspect is one of a total population of potential suspects of, for example, one million, then in the population there will be about 50,000 individuals with blood of the particular group. So, on the scientific evidence alone, and completely divorced from all other information, the answer to the question in the title is 1/50,000 or 0.00002! This would not appear to be particularly helpful to the investigator.

Probability and Odds

Simply speaking, probability is a means of describing uncertainty. If a man is asked, for example, "Is it going to rain tomorrow?" he might answer "It is probable" or "It is very probable" or "It is improbable" and so on, according to his degree of conviction which will be based on the information which is available to him such as: it is autumn; it is raining today; the television forecast promises rain; his rheumatism is playing up.

Such measures of uncertainty can be handled mathematically if they are allowed to take values on a scale zero (the event certainly *will not* occur) to one (the event certainly *will* occur). There are certain other necessary requirements.

To give an estimate of a probability it is always necessary to have some background information. To take a very simple example, one would be unwise to answer the question "What is the probability that this coin will, when tossed, land showing a head?" without finding out whether the coin has a head on one side and a tail on the other, whether it is balanced, whether it will be tossed onto a smooth surface and so on. Given the normal conditions most people would not consider it unreasonable to say that the probability is 0.5: the coin is just as probable to land heads as tails.

It is conventional to denote probabilities in the following way:

$$p(A|I)$$

This is merely a convenient shorthand way of denoting the rather cumbersome phase "The probability of the event A given the information I". For the coin tossing example:

$$p(H|\text{Coin is balanced, etc}) = 0.5$$

where H denotes the event that the coin lands showing a head.

The weather forecasting example is much more complex and different people will have different degrees of belief in the proposition that it will rain tomorrow. From one individual we might have:

$$p(R|\text{Rheumatism is playing up etc}) = 0.9$$

where R denotes the event that it rains tomorrow. The fact that this probability is very subjective, varying from individual to individual, will not detract from the force of the argument which follows.

It will be necessary to refer to the event that A does not happen, which is denoted by $\overline{A}$. It is necessary, and very sensible, for the probability of A occurring and the probability of A not occurring to sum to 1, thus:

$$p(A|I) + p(\overline{A}|I) = 1$$

So, for the coin tossing example:

$$p(\overline{H}|\text{coin is balanced, etc}) = 1 - 0.5 = 0.5$$

where $\overline{H}$ denotes the event that the coin lands showing tails. For the weather forecasting example:

$$p(\overline{R}|\text{Rheumatism is playing up, etc}) = 1 - 0.9 = 0.1$$

where $\overline{R}$ denotes the event that it will not rain tomorrow.

In many contexts it is simpler to talk in terms of *odds* rather than probabilities. The odds on an event A are the probability of A occurring divided by the probability of A not occurring, i.e.:

$$\text{Odds on } A = p(A|I)/p(\overline{A}|I)$$

For the coin tossing example:

$$\text{Odds on } H = 0.5/0.5 = 1 \text{ (or "evens")}$$

For the weather forecasting example:

$$\text{Odds on } R = 0.9/0.1 = 9 \text{ (or 9 to 1 on)}$$

If the odds on an event are less than one then it is common practice to invert them and call them "odds against". If, for example, the odds on some event A were 0.01, it could be said that the odds against A were 100 (or 100 to 1 against).

The Investigator's Problem

The investigator has found a suspect and he has acquired some information. He has the scientific information (which in the example under consideration is very simple) and all the other information, some contradictory and some unreliable, which his enquiry has unearthed. He must consider whether to charge the suspect, whether the case will stand up in court, and whether the true culprit is still at large. In the terms of the model being considered here, he is concerned with the odds in favour of the suspect having committed the crime. This can be denoted in shorthand as:

$$\frac{p(C|F, I)}{p(\overline{C}|F, I)}$$

where C denotes the event that the suspect committed the crime and left the blood at the scene, (for this discussion it is assumed that there is no doubt that the blood was left by the person who committed the crime); F denotes the forensic scientist's result; and I denotes all the other information. The last might consist of an eye witness report, a tip-off from an informant, the investigator's own local knowledge and it might also contain apparently contradictory information, such as an alibi from the suspect's wife. Processing complex information such as this defies scientific techniques because there are far too many imponderables. This paper is not concerned with how the investigator forms his view and takes his decision but, rather, considers the way in which the scientific evidence can best be presented to fit into the context of the investigation.

In terms of the model, the problem is to progress from:

$$\frac{p(C|I)}{p(\overline{C}|I)}$$

the investigator's odds *before* he has heard the scientist's results, to:

$$\frac{p(C|F, I)}{p(\overline{C}|F, I)}$$

the investigator's odds *after* he has heard the scientist's results.

Bayes' Theorem

The mathematical result which enables this transition is called Bayes' Theorem, which in this example, gives the result:

$$\frac{p(C|F, I)}{p(\overline{C}|F, I)} = \frac{p(F|C, I)}{p(F|\overline{C}, I)} \frac{p(C|I)}{p(\overline{C}|I)}$$

The odds after the scientific result (the posterior odds) therefore equal the odds before the scientific result (the prior odds) multiplied by the term $p(F|C, I)/p(F|\overline{C}, I)$. It is this middle term in the expression which dictates the way in which the scientist's results should be presented.

The theorem tells us that, while the investigator concerns himself with questions of the type "What is the probability that the blood at the scene came from this suspect?", the scientist is concerned with two questions of a completely different type: "What is the probability of this blood grouping result if the suspect *has* committed the crime?" ($p(F|C, I)$) and "What is the probability of this blood grouping result if the suspect *has not* committed the crime?" ($p(F|\overline{C}, I)$). There is a profound difference. The investigator is concerned with the probability (or odds) of an *uncertain* event C given known information: the scientist is concerned with the probability of a *known* event (his scientific observations) under alternative hypotheses.

In the example under consideration, assume that the information I consists solely of an eyewitness report that the suspect was seen running from the scene of the crime. The scientific evidence is evaluated as follows:

The scientist's results contain two observations, which could be called: F_1, the group of the bloodstain at the scene; and F_2, the bloodgroup of the suspect. It can be very simply shown that in this example the relevant term in the theorem reduces to $p(F_1|C, I)/p(F_1|\overline{C}, I)$. If the suspect had indeed committed the crime and left the blood then it could have no bloodgroup other than the observed bloodgroup $*$. So $p(F_1|C, I) = 1$. On the other hand, if the suspect had not committed the crime then clearly some other person must have been responsible. The information I gives us no reason to confine our attention to any particular group of the community so, *as far as his bloodgroup is concerned*, this other person would be just someone at random: $p(F_1|\overline{C}, I)$ then is the probability that some person at random in the population would have blood of group $*$: this is known to be 5% or 0.05. The scientist's evidence in this case is therefore summarised as a multiplying factor of $1/0.05 = 20$, incorporated as:

$$\text{Posterior odds} = 20 \times \text{Prior odds}$$

The magnitude of the prior odds will, of course, depend on the investigator's assessment of the eyewitness report and it is also clear that different investigators would form different assessments. No doubt, many investigators would be reluctant to attempt to express their assessment in numerical terms, but that is not the issue here. The important points have been made: the class of questions with which the scientist should concern himself has been identified and the relevance of his results to the investigation has been demonstrated. Whatever the odds before the scientist does his work, in this particular case they are increased 20 fold by his results.

Table 1 shows some very tentative numerical examples corresponding to various qualities of the eyewitness evidence in the hypothetical case described above.

Circumstances

Few would dispute that the scientist must have a knowledge of the circumstances of the crime if he is to give the most help to the investigator. The Bayesian approach demonstrates the way in which the circumstances (i.e. the information I) can dictate the sort of scientific questions which are relevant to the enquiry. A simple illustration can be given by modifying the case example.

Assume that the blood grouping results were as before. Now the information I consists of a tip-off from an informant and an account from an eyewitness who cannot give a detailed description but can say that the person who committed the crime was a negro. This example is of value because the frequency of blood groups can vary between ethnic groups.

Table 1 Numerical Examples Corresponding to Various Qualities of Eyewitness Evidence in the Hypothetical Case

Information I	Prior odds on C	Posterior odds on C
No eyewitness	1/1,000,000	1/50,000
Suspect selected at random	Million to 1 against	50,000 to 1 against
Eyewitness – short sighted	1/5	4
	5 to 1 against	4 to 1 on
Eyewitness – rather vague	1	20
	Evens	20 to 1 on
Good eyewitness	5	100
	5 to 1 on	100 to 1 on

Let it be assumed the suspect is a negro. As before, if the suspect had committed the crime and left the blood then the stain must be the observed bloodgroup $*$. So $p(F_1|C, I) = 1$. However, in this case if the suspect did not commit the crime then some other negro did. To evaluate $p(F_1|\overline{C}, I)$ requires a knowledge of the distribution of bloodgroup $*$ among the population of negroes. Assume that, among negroes, $*$ has a frequency of 50%, then $p(F_1|\overline{C}, I) = 0.5$, and in this case the scientist's evidence only multiplies the odds on guilt by a factor of 2.

Therefore, given that considerations are restricted to negroes only, the evidential weight of the blood grouping result is considerably less because of the racial variation in blood of group $*$. The investigator, on the other hand, in forming his prior odds will have used the information that the suspect and the person who committed the crime are both of the same race.

Discussion

The above examples are very simple, but as circumstances become more complex the mathematics become more difficult. When blood is transferred from the crime scene to the criminal, the Bayesian approach provides an elegant means of combining bloodgroup results with considerations of transference and persistence and also the chance of finding bloodstains on the clothing of the average man in the street. This will be the subject of a future report, and the present paper has been concerned with philosophy rather than detail.

In answer to the question. "What is the probability that this blood came from that person (the suspect)?" the scientist has to recognise that the suggestion that the suspect was out of the country at the time of the offence is relevant. The investigator is best placed to assess the value of this information and the scientist should confine himself to answering questions of the type "What is the probability of the blood evidence if the suspect did commit the crime?" and "What is the probability of the blood evidence if the suspect did not commit the crime?" The ratio of the two answers is crucial.

(*This paper was presented at the Autumn Symposium of the Society in London, November 1981*).

References

1. Finkelstein MO and Fairley WB. *Harvard Law Review* 1970; **84**: 1801.
2. Lindley DV. *The Statistician* 1977; **26**: 203.

23(1e) - 1983: A Frame of Reference or Garbage In, Garbage Out

A clear definition of a problem is often identical with the solution of the problem itself. The progress of modern science is a history of the development from the intuitive grasp of problems to their explicit definitions. In many fields, however, the explicit definition still evades us and this is probably most so in branches of the biological and medical sciences. A doctor may make his diagnosis on the basis of certain subjectively identified features which he then compares, intuitively, with his mental store of subjectively similar patterns in the past. The advent of computer diagnosis techniques is interesting but these only present us with the beginning of the process which perhaps will some day allow us to diagnose and define on an objective basis. However, this imperfection in our diagnostic procedures does not prevent judgements being made and actions being taken, although there is little value in doing anything when the likelihood of harm by doing something is more than the likelihood of harm resulting from doing nothing at all.

Forensic scientists have long made subjective decisions on the relative commonness of transferred materials. Possibly some of these procedures have been naive at best and dogmatic at worst but few would doubt the competence of the experienced forensic scientist in such matters, even were they hard put to define objectively the scale against which competence should be judged.

There is, however, an increasing tendency to attempt to formalise and quantify these procedures [1]. This in itself is not a bad thing unless the attempt itself to quantify something automatically leads to the belief that such quantification is possible in the present state of knowledge.

The provision of background reference populations of data against which to judge the data in a particular case [2] is the only meaningful basis upon which information can be judged. However, many of these attempts to provide backgrounds seem to show a lack of appreciation of the complex of features which condition the nature and extent of transferred materials. The problem is usefully elaborated by reference to the situation as it might be were there no experimental limitations to the gathering of the supposedly relevant data. Consider transferred glass particles. Would we have all the information needed if it were possible, by some scientific method as yet uninvented, to divide conceptually all glass in the United Kingdom (wherever it may occur in windows, containers, or motor vehicles) into one milligram, or whatever, size samples and from these to determine instantly all physical parameters? Would this then represent the background upon which to consider transferred glass particles in criminal cases? Is it proper and relevant to point out that transferred glass particles tend to occur preferentially from sub-sets of the population data and to say that any selection of a sub-set of data partly begs the question to be proved?

Is it not a measure of the confusion that surrounds this subject when two experienced forensic scientists of many years professional association and friendship can dispute hotly on the validity of statistical decisions applied to grouped data which result from the pooling of data from several glass particles where one proponent holds that, subject to certain well-defined assumptions and statistical safeguards, it is a perfectly proper procedure whereas the other equally firmly insists that any grouping of data in this manner begs the very questioned which is to be proved?

Is it relevant to gather large amounts of statistical data on the chemical constitution and colour of fibres from figures which are either provided by manufacturers or which result from experimental determinations on a *selected* population? Must not all such populations be arbitrarily selected? Is it proper for a forensic scientist to state that a particular fibre is *in his experience* very uncommon whereas enquiries show that it is a constituent of a popular type of mass-produced garment which has been on the market, via the multiple stores, for at least a year? Is a forensic scientist justified in arguing that the only proper population against which to assess the worth of his transfer material evidence is the background of those transferred materials which he has *himself* examined in case work throughout the years of his career? Is it valid to argue that the crude percentage occurrence of a fibre in a "total" fibre population is irrelevant because of the normal fractionating effect of fibre properties, market distribution and so on which render such information valueless at best and dangerous at worst.

Are we not trying to run before we can walk by attempting to quantify the unquantifiable and perhaps even the undefinable? Might not our approach be better that of the medical practitioner who subjectively diagnoses a physical state in his patient and treats it according to the hopefully valid assumption that such a procedure is more likely to lead to a beneficial result than pure inaction? Finally, might not this attitude restore to the forensic scientist some of the professional esteem (and self-esteem) which has been progressively disappearing over the years in proportion to the size of the largely worthless data banks upon which he is increasingly prone to base his judgements?

Perhaps the computers should be left to rust and the time, hitherto used to program them and feed them with data, devoted to intra-and inter-professional discussions on conceptual matters largest amongst which should figure "What is the nature of the problem which we, as forensic scientists, are attempting to solve?"

References

1. LD. Away with the Fuzz. *Journal of the Forensic Science Society* 1979; **19**: 157–158.
2. Kind SS, Wigmore Rosemary, Whitehead PH and Loxley DS. Terminology in Forensic Science. *Journal of The Forensic Science Society* 1979; **19**: 189–191.

23(4) - 1983: On Circumstantial Evidence

(Editorial)

On pleasant summer afternoons, one may regard the uncertainty of next week's Court more from the viewpoint of its possible impact on holiday plans rather than that of the impact of the forensic science evidence on the outcome of the case. Indeed, if we consider the latter at all, it may be to question the purpose of forensic science and then return to daydreams of holidays yet to come. What would happen if we resisted this temptation and pondered instead on the significance of forensic science to the Court? We might pursue the daydream analogy and postulate that if it has any true significance then it is to tell a story: by examination of a crime scene (or its civil law analogues) or of exhibits collected from places or people, the forensic scientist should try and piece together what exactly it was took place.

This contrasts somewhat with the conventional classification in which forensic science evidence would be reduced to two types – contact evidence and characteristic evidence; the former to link people, objects and places, the latter to identify what or who the objects or persons are. Thus bloodstains on clothing or at a scene would be grouped and the results used both as contact and characteristic evidence to place a person at a scene. For the purposes of the present illustration we shall not consider the various statistical approaches to the example used [1, 2, 3], but shall simply ask if this examination adds much to the story we may tell, and the answer is that unless it excludes someone, it probably adds very little. Furthermore, if it fails to exclude, then the strength of the evidence is outwith the control of the investigator, depending as it does on the "groupability" of the stain (size, condition, age) and the genotype of the person who shed the blood.

Grouping of the bloodstain in this example has not helped us to piece together the circumstances of the crime, but a different sort of examination could do just that, as, for example, MacDonell showed many years ago [4]. Put at its simplest, a smeared stain of the deceased's blood on the front of the shirt of a man accused of beating his wife to death tells no story, but spatters up the arm of his shirt speak volumes, and yet this type of evidence has not so far been considered sufficiently important by forensic scientists to warrant independent recognition. How then can we classify it?

One immediately thinks of evidence indicating the circumstance of a crime as being circumstantial, but "circumstantial evidence" already has a well-established and quite different meaning. Your Editor's dictionary gives circumstanced as the adjective for circumstance, but "circumstanced evidence" sounds clumsy. Finding a suitable adjective may prove as difficult as changing the accepted meaning of "circumstantial evidence", but, to paraphrase Kelvin, if we knew what to call it, then, perhaps, we could begin to make more use of it.

We must also consider the extent to which any of our evidence is circumstantial in the generally accepted sense. This was touched upon in an earlier Editorial [5] when it was suggested two questions be asked to assess the scientist's findings, the second of these being "How likely are alternative explanations?" Forensic Science must not shy from this challenge, but should meet it fairly and squarely, which means by experiment and communication in the open scientific press. Apart from the demands of fairness, which probably lie more heavily on the Forensic Scientist than on our peers in other sciences, it is only thus that our findings can be tested and truly become accepted or be found inadequate. It is also the best way to improve the quality of our evidence – an open challenge to our peers to find solutions to questions raised. The paper by John Lloyd in 265 this issue of the Journal is an excellent example, addressing itself as it does to all of these issues in what is a rather emotive area.

References

1. Selvin S, Grunbaum BW and Myhre BA. The Probability of Exclusion or Likelihood of Guilt of an Accused: Paternity. *Journal of the Forensic Science Society* 1983; **23**: 19–25.

2. Selvin S. Grunbaum BW and Myhre BA. The Probability of Non-discrimination or Likelihood of Guilt of an Accused: criminal Identification. *Journal of the Forensic Science Society* 1983; **23**: 27–33.
3. Evett IW. What is the Probability that This Blood Came from That Person? A Meaningful Question? *Journal of the Forensic Science Society* 1983; **23**: 35–39.
4. MacDonell HL and Bialousz LF. *Flight characteristics and stain patterns of human blood*. Washington: US Department of Justice, Law Enforcement Administration, National Institute of Law Enforcement and Criminal Justice. 1971.
5. Anon. Patience. *Journal of the Forensic Science Society* 1983; **23**: 1–2.

26(3) - 1986: Evaluation of Associative Physical Evidence

(Guest Editorial)

BD Gaudette
Central Forensic Laboratory,, Royal Canadian Mounted Police, Ottawa, Canada

Forensic scientists deal with complex scientific evidence, the significance of which the layman has little or no understanding. It is therefore natural and legitimate for us to attempt to evaluate the significance of our evidence through use of statistics. It can also be dangerous. Does this then mean that presentation of statistics should be avoided? I think not. Many things in life which are dangerous if abused are of great value when used properly. The use of statistics in evaluating associative physical evidence falls into this category. Indeed, the benefits and necessity of applying statistical reasoning to evidential value determinations have been well documented [1]. The existence of certain statistical pitfalls does, however, mean that forensic scientists must be extremely careful in their use of statistics. Without using mathematical symbols or equations, this editorial will discuss four steps and enumerate some factors that can lead to proper statistical evaluation of associative physical evidence. (Elsewhere [2], I have attempted to relate the various factors in a value equation.) Much of the basic philosophy of forensic science that follows should be applicable whether or not statistics are involved.

The first step is *developing a conceptual framework* for the role of associative physical evidence, and its components, in the judicial process. The purposes of the courts are, first, to determine guilt or innocence and, second, to take appropriate action such as sentencing. The determination of guilt depends on many factors; among these are proof that a crime was committed, intent, mental condition, rules of law and evidence, witness credibility, establishment of prerequisite associations, alternative explanations for associations, and alibis. Forensic scientists from different disciplines may have evidence relevant to any of these factors. Trace evidence, however, is usually related to just one factor – establishment of associations.

Associative evidence is defined as that evidence which attempts to establish associations between any combination of the following: accused, victim, crime scene or weapon. Associative evidence can take many forms. In addition to the physical evidence forensic scientists are concerned with, associative evidence can be provided through eyewitness testimony as well as statements of suspects and victims. Accordingly, associative physical evidence is usually only one component of associative evidence which, in turn, is but one of many factors used in determining guilt or innocence.

Let us now examine some of the components of associative physical evidence. The first component, identification, involves classification of the questioned evidence material (e.g. blood – human blood – type A, PGM-1 etc., or fibre – wool – light blue wool, etc.). The second component is comparison of the questioned evidence material to a known sample. In the third component, interpretation, the forensic scientist evaluates the significance of the evidence.

Another way of looking at these three components is to examine the thought processes a forensic scientist follows. On the basis of the results of an examination, a forensic scientist draws a conclusion which he or she then interprets in giving an expert opinion. Identification yields results; comparison leads to the conclusion; and interpretation produces the expert opinion.

An understanding of the preceding conceptual framework can assist us in the second step towards proper statistical evaluation of associative physical evidence – defining the fundamental question. Let us examine three general types of questions that, at first glance, may appear equivalent:

What proportion of the suspect population would have characteristics the same as those possessed by the questioned physical evidence?
What is the probability of a coincidental match between the questioned physical evidence and the known sample?
What is the value of the evidence in establishing a particular association?

These three questions can be related to the components of associative physical evidence as follows. Question one evaluates the significance of an identification and may be answered by population studies and data bases which provide frequency of occurrence data. Question two evaluates comparisons. However, if we wish to evaluate the significance of associative physical evidence, we must ask questions of the third type. Accordingly, question three is the fundamental question.

Let us now examine the reasons why question three is better than questions of the first two types. Since identification is only a component of comparison which is in turn only a component of interpretation, it can be readily seen that questions of the first type are inadequate to assess the value of the evidence. As Stoney [3] states "the rarity of a Crime Object is itself irrelevant; it is relevant only in that it makes corresponding Suspect Objects rarer".

The second question deals with assessing the significance of comparisons. It is concerned not only with the relative frequency of blood, fibre, glass etc. types in the suspect population, but also with probability of coincidental occurrences of other prerequisite events such as: one particular hair type (out of approximately nine types on the scalp) being the one found in evidence [4]; a person having a blood stain on his or her clothing; a particular textile material shedding fibres; an object having damage (e.g. pieces, paint chips or buttons missing). Accordingly, the second question is more relevant than the first. However, it still only deals with a component of association.

Probability of a coincidental match is an important component of the answer to the third question. However, we must also consider two others. One is the probability of an incorrect association being made as a result of examiner error(s). These can occur at either the identification or comparison stage and can be due to such factors as inadequate training, improper methodology, malfunctioning equipment, outdated or improperly prepared reagents, low natural ability, carelessness or corruption.

The final component to the answer to the third question is alternative explanations for the evidence. Even where no examiner errors and no coincidental matches occur, it is still possible that in spite of the evidence there was no association. One such explanation is secondary transfer – the perpetrator of a crime might transfer to a crime scene evidence picked up as a result of previous associations. Assume, for example, that while individuals A and B are drinking together in a bar, A loses a hair which is deposited on B's shirt. If B then commits a crime, a secondary transfer of A's hair to the crime scene could occur and result in evidence indicating that A was at the crime scene, when in fact he had been nowhere near it. Other alternative explanations for the evidence include contamination and deliberate planting of evidence.

Since it is amenable to consideration of many important factors, question three is superior to the other two questions. A further advantage is that, in addition to applying to individual pieces of evidence, question three can also be used to evaluate the collective evidential value of physical evidence (e.g., all the fibre evidence in a case, or even all the physical evidence related to a particular association).

We have seen that there are important differences in these three questions (and their answers). If the forensic scientist is not extremely careful, statistics presented in relation to identification will become generalized in the mind of a juror as being directly applicable to association or even guilt [5].

This demonstrates the importance of the third step leading to proper statistical evaluation of associative physical evidence – placing the statistical answers in the proper context. As a result of the many factors involved in determining evidential value, it is unlikely that the forensic scientist will have statistical data that is sufficient of itself to answer question three.

Statistics relating to questions one or two can still be used, provided the forensic scientist is careful to point out their place and limitations. Another alternative is to use what I have termed the "touchpoint approach" [2, 6]. In this approach, a qualitative assessment of the net effect, on a particular case, of the various evidential value factors is used to modify quantitative average probability statistics which serve as a point of reference. Average probabilities have the advantage of being less variable, less population dependent and easier to estimate than specific conditional probabilities.

Obtaining a proper statistical evaluation of associative physical evidence requires one final step – clearly stating all assumptions and substantiating their reasonableness. A common approach to the use of statistics in court testimony is to present frequency of occurrence data simply with no additional explanations. As the preceding analysis has demonstrated, frequency tells only part of the story. In presenting frequency of occurrence data without any other information, the following assumptions are implicit: the probability of incorrect association due to examiner error is negligible; the probability of incorrect association due to coincidental occurrence of other prerequisite events is not important; no explanations other than association exist for the evidence; and the population for which frequency data are quoted is representative of the suspect population.

Some or all of these assumptions can be reasonable or self-cancelling. However, in many cases, at least one will fail. Presentation of frequency data on its own will then lead to a distorted picture of the value of the evidence, along with a false sense of exactness.

Presenting scientific results as opinion evidence is only possible if a criminal court allows it. For various reasons, there may be instances where statistical evaluation of associative evidence is deemed inadmissible. Although the court's receptiveness to statistical evaluation of evidence will obviously have a bearing on decision making, most of the concepts presented in this editorial should apply whether or not statistics are actually used in court.

An understanding of the conceptual framework for the role of associative physical evidence, and its components, in the judicial process can lead to formulation of the fundamental question: "What is the value of the evidence in establishing a particular association?" If the forensic scientist then ensures that statistical answers are used in accordance with the basic philosophy of forensic science and that they are placed in the proper context with all assumptions spelled out and substantiated, a proper statistical evaluation of associative physical evidence will be obtained. Such evaluations can then help forensic scientists make many important decisions. Examples include whether and how to use statistics in court testimony, decisions as to design and use of data bases, research priorities and design, as well as managerial decisions about resource allocation. It is hoped that the concepts presented in this editorial will stimulate the thinking of other forensic scientists and be of assistance in decision making.

References

1. Eggleston R. *Evidence, Proof and Probability (second edition)*. London: Weidenfeld and Nicholson Ltd., 1983.
2. Gaudette BD. Assessing the value of associative evidence. *Journal of the Forensic Science Society* 1984; **24**: 404–405.
3. Stoney, DA. Evaluation of associative evidence: choosing the relevant question. *Journal of the Forensic Science Society* 1984; **24**: 473–482.
4. Gaudette BD. A supplementary discussion of probabilities and human hair comparisons. *Journal of Forensic Sciences* 1982; **27**: 279–289.

5. Tribe LH. Trial by mathematics: precision and ritual in the legal process. *Harvard Law Review* 1971; **84**: 1329–1393.
6. Gaudette BD. Some further thoughts on probabilities and human hair comparisons. *Journal of Forensic Sciences* 1978; **23**: 758–763.

23(3a) - 1987: The Use of Statistics in Forensic Science

(Commentary – Correspondence)

From   CGG Aitken

Sir: It was with dismay that I read the guest editorial "Evaluation of associative physical evidence" by Gaudette [1] in a recent issue of the Journal. While it is good to see such strong support for the general idea of the use of statistics in forensic science, it is a great pity that most of the advances made in the applications of statistics to forensic science in this country over the last few years have been totally ignored. I refer to the increasing emphasis on Bayesian ideas. Gaudette indeed uses Bayes' Theorem in his approach but only as an exercise in probability theory and he does not use Bayesian ideas to their full capacity.

In 1983 Evett [2] first pointed out in this Journal the importance of Bayes' Theorem to the forensic scientist, though there had been some discussion elsewhere earlier (Finkelstein and Fairley [3] and Lindley [4, 5]), see also Good [6] and references therein for a brief survey of the weight of evidence. Evett [2] discussed the roles of the scientist and the investigator in a forensic investigation and explained how Bayes' Theorem provided a link between the two roles. These ideas were reiterated at the International Association of Forensic Sciences conference at Oxford in 1984 [7] and a general theory has been described [8]. I, myself, referred to the Bayesian approach as "the best measure we have" for assessing the value of evidence in the Kelvin Lecture to the British Association for the Advancement of Science and reported in *The Guardian* (29 August, 1985).

Gaudette discusses four steps which he claims can lead to a proper statistical evaluation of associative physical evidence. The first step refers to the development of a conceptual framework. This is precisely what was done by Evett [2] and yet no mention is made of this work in the Editorial. The second step concerns the definition of the fundamental question. The first two questions are merely secondary to the third question. However, the third question is not even the fundamental question. Gaudette's procedure is a two-stage procedure: first establish an association, according to some pre-defined criterion, then assess the similarity through an average probability. This work has been superseded in the United Kingdom through the work of Lindley [4] and Evett [7, 8]. In their work two likelihoods are compared, one assumes the control and recovered items to come from the same source and the other assumes the recovered items to come from some source other than the control. There is no requirement to define an "association" and the procedure is more sensitive than the "average" probability which assigns the same value to all associations. Also Gaudette's approach concentrates on discrete data. The Bayesian approach of Lindley and Evett may be used for continuous data also. The third and fourth steps concern the placement of statistical answers in the proper context and the statement of all assumptions. Both these steps are considered automatically by a Bayesian analysis where the context and assumptions are considered when the prior distribution is chosen.

Gaudette prefers what he calls average probabilities to the use of frequency data. However, average probabilities can be very misleading and give results which bear little relationship to the true state of affairs. One analogy, mentioned by I. W. Evett in a personal communication, is that of a person who keeps a broken clock because it is right twice a day. He does not know when it will be right but at least it will be right twice a day. Similarly an average probability will be right sometime but we will not know when it is right. A forensic example will further illustrate numerically the misleading nature of average probabilities.

Consider the ABO system of bloodgrouping. The four phenotypes and their frequencies for a white California population (Berry and Geisser, [9]) are as follows.

Phenotype	0	A	B	AB
Phenotypic frequency	0.479	0.360	0.123	0.038

Suppose a crime is committed and a blood stain is left at the scene of the crime. The measurement of the blood group would be the recovered measurement. A suspect who would be the control is found with the same blood group as the stain. Gaudette's average probability would be

$$0.479^2 + 0.360^2 + 0.123^2 + 0.038^2 = 0.376$$

This figure is used as a measure of the probability of the evidence of association, conditional on there being no association, in fact. Suppose, however that the suspect is of phenotype AB. Then the probability of a match, given the suspect is of phenotype AB, is the probability that the blood stain is of phenotype AB, conditional on the suspect being of phenotype AB. If, in fact, there was no association then this probability is just the probability that a person, the person who left the blood stain, chosen now at random from some population is of phenotype AB. This is just 0.038. This probability bears very little resemblance to the average probability 0.376.

Of course, great care has to be taken in the presentation of these figures, as Gaudette explains in detail. We have to assume that the population for which frequency data are quoted is representative of the suspect population. This assumption, however, applies no less to the calculation of average probabilities than to the calculation of conditional probabilities. Gaudette argues that presentation of frequency data makes several other implicit assumptions. The two assumptions concerning probability of incorrect association could be accommodated by appropriate weighting functions when evaluating the required probabilities. Other explanations for the evidence could be considered in any verbal or written report presented with the statistical analysis.

I wrote in another guest editorial [10] in this Journal: "A properly conducted statistical argument, *with its strengths and weaknesses explained* (italics new) and with a full understanding of the underlying assumptions, can contribute much towards a greater understanding of a set of data forensic or otherwise."

I stand by these words still. Any statistical argument, be it a Bayesian argument based on frequency data or an argument based on average probabilities, has to be prepared to stand close scrutiny. If the Bayesian argument and an argument based on average probabilities were placed under such scrutiny, it is the Bayesian argument which would stand the longer.

I firmly believe that the Bayesian approach to the "Evaluation of Associative Physical Evidence" is the best approach currently that there is. The publication of an editorial under that title which ignores the Bayesian approach sets the cause of statistics in forensic science back many years.

References

1. Gaudette BD. Evaluation of associative physical evidence. *Journal of the Forensic Science Society* 1986; **26**: 163.
2. Evett IW. What is the probability that this blood came from that person? A meaningful question? *Journal of the Forensic Science Society* 1983; **23**: 35.
3. Finkelstein MO and Fairley WB. A Bayesian approach to identification evidence. *Harvard Law Review* 1970; **83**: 489.
4. Lindley DV. Probability and the law. *The Statistician* 1977; **26**: 203.
5. Lindley DV. A problem in forensic science. *Biometrika* 1977; **64**: 207.
6. Good IJ. Weight of Evidence: A Brief Survey. In *Bayesian Statistics 2*, Bernardo JM, De Groot MH, Lindley DV and Smith AFM (Eds.), Elsevier Science Publishers, 1985, 249.
7. Evett IW. *A Discussion of the Deficiencies of the Coincidence Method for Evaluating Evidential Value: and a Look towards the Future*. Presented at the Tenth Triennial Meeting of the International Association of Forensic Sciences, 1984, Oxford, U.K.

8. Evett IW. A quantitative theory for interpreting transfer evidence in criminal cases. *Applied Statistics* 1984; **33**: 25.
9. Berry DA and Geisser S. *Inference in cases of disputed paternity*. University of Minnesota, Technical Report no. 404, 1982.
10. Aitken CGG. Statistics and forensic science – a fruitful partnership. *Journal of the Forensic Science Society* 1983; **23**: 3.

August 1986

Department of Statistics
University of Edinburgh
Edinburgh

23(3b) - 1987: The Use of Statistics in Forensic Science

(Commentary – Correspondence)

From **BD Gaudette**

Sir: A 1983 editorial in this journal stated that "Undoubtedly some patience is required before the full benefits of statistics to the forensic scientist will be known and accepted; patience for the forensic scientists to understand and formulate the questions to which they seek answers; patience for the statisticians to understand the questions and formulate their replies." [1]. Perhaps Dr. Aitken's letter [2] is evidence that there is still a lack of understanding between statisticians and forensic scientists.

My overall purpose in the editorial was not to review recent developments in statistical theory pertaining to forensic science, but rather to offer guidance to forensic scientists on the practical use of statistics in evaluating associative evidence. In the editorial I stated "Much of the basic philosophy of forensic science [I presented] should be applicable whether or not statistics are involved." Similarly, the basic philosophy is applicable regardless of the type of statistical theory used – Bayesian or otherwise.

It is my view that any form of statistical analysis employed should fit the conceptual framework and complement the thought process of the forensic scientist. Accordingly, I was dismayed that Dr. Aitken took exception with what he calls my "two stage procedure: first, establish an association, according to some pre-defined criterion, then assess the similarity". My point is that since this is exactly the thought process a forensic scientist uses, the same process should be used in the statistical analysis.

There is, undeniably, a place for statistical theory in forensic science. However, forensic scientists, who must present, explain and defend their opinions in court and who have to live with the imperfections of real world data, must temper theory with practicability. It is illustrative to modify slightly Dr. Aitken's analogy of the broken clock. Assume a man crossing a desert notes that his watch has stopped. A while later he encounters another man who, having no watch, asks him the time. The first man could give one of three possible answers:

(a) "I don't know. My watch is broken".
(b) "My watch says 2 o'clock".
(c) "When my watch stopped it was 2 o'clock. I can't give you the exact time now, but based on the position of the sun in relation to what it was when my watch stopped, I would estimate that it is a few hours after 2".

The objectives of my editorial were four-fold. The first was to attempt to convince forensic scientists who give answers that are equivalent to (a) of the advantages and necessity of employing some sort of statistics in evaluating associative physical evidence. The second purpose was to suggest that, as exemplified by answer (b), although statistics (such as blood group frequencies) can be based on "objective" measurements and can in isolation represent true statements, if they are not used properly, they are not good aids to decision making. Accordingly, it is necessary to understand the conceptual framework in which the statistics are to be used, define the fundamental question that they are to answer, place them in the proper context by pointing out their limitations and clearly state and substantiate the reasonableness of all assumptions made. My third purpose was to show how complex the evaluation of associative physical evidence is and discuss some of the factors involved. The fourth point was that although we don't presently have data available to calculate all the factors and complexities, we can still use what data we do have as benchmarks or touch-points. As exemplified by answer (c), this represents a distinct improvement in information content over (a) and (b).

I did not suggest that where specific conditional probabilities are available, (as in the particular ABO blood grouping example Dr. Aitken gives) average probabilities are superior; nor did I suggest that an argument based on average probabilities is superior to a Bayesian argument. (First, they are not necessarily mutually exclusive. Secondly, this would be akin to arguing that answer (c) in my desert analogy would be superior to a time check from Greenwich. Average probabilities and the touchpoint approach are advocated not because they are theoretically superior but because, in most instances, the many factors and variables involved in evaluating the associative evidence in any particular case make average probabilities the best practical alternative available.)

Despite the apparent lack of understanding, it was encouraging to see that there are some points with which Dr. Aitken is in agreement with me. Perhaps this is an indication that although patience is still needed, the day when there is general agreement on the subject of evaluation of associative evidence amongst forensic scientists, statisticians, and the courts, is drawing nearer.

References

1. Editorial. Patience. *Journal of the Forensic Science Society* 1983; **23**: 1–2.
2. Aitken. CGG. The use of statistics in forensic science. *Journal of the Forensic Science Society* 1987; **27**: 113–116.

November 1986

Royal Canadian Mounted Police Central Forensic Laboratory
Box 8885, Ottawa
Canada, K1G 3M8

28(3) - 1988: Heads We Win

(Editorial)

Forensic scientists learn early on in their careers about conforming to the legal system. Assuming that one or other side doesn't always call them along to court just to admire the architecture, they soon experience, at first hand, basic differences between the workings of scientific and legal establishments. Weeks of work in the laboratory may be undermined irretrievably by one ill-considered reply from the witness box, irrespective of how carefully the report of findings has been written. In science there is no fixed point where fact stops and opinion begins; in the Crown Court, objectivity is achieved by learned guidance from the judge, followed by the statistical smoothing of individual subjectivity in the jury room.

One of the standing achievements of the Forensic Science Society is the climate which it creates for exchanges that contribute to interdisciplinary understanding. Even so, getting to know the realities of one's own profession and the ins and outs of another is hard. Professor David Gee points out [1] that doctors and scientists do need better training in order to perform adequately as expert witnesses. Both should, he argues, acquire a thorough grasp of the techniques of questioning used by counsel in court.

A reciprocal understanding is also desirable, but still a long way off. The remark that "more and more allegations of wrongful conviction rest on whether the forensic science evidence given to the jury was *wholly accurate*" (my italics) was made in a recent article [2]. It seems reasonable enough at first sight; expert witnesses should strive for accuracy in court through truthfulness and professionalism. In reality, though, how many achieve complete accuracy in their court testimony? Indeed, how many scientists, irrespective of discipline, can look back at their conclusions and make such a claim? The 1980s will probably turn out to be one of the most eventful decades for forensic science. Among other things, it may be remembered as a time when a certain fact should have been grasped by everyone involved – simply, that the exploitation of science in our adversarial system is not conducive to statements from the witness box always being "wholly accurate".

Experienced forensic scientists are usually able to advise on the *potential* strengths and weaknesses (evidential value) of scientific matters. Currently, for example, a senior forensic scientist in a busy laboratory, possibly with a substantial backlog of cases, may advise that the scientific examination requested in one unstarted case is very likely to assist in establishing the issue, whereas that requested in another stands little chance of establishing anything meaningful. Nobody can claim that such an approach is "wholly accurate"; from the scientist's point of view it is a practical approach to resource management. Whether it is seen as such by others – lawyers, for example – is another matter.

References

1. Gee DJ. Training the expert witness. *Medicine, Science and the Law* 1988; **28**: 93–97.
2. McConnell B. Science and science fiction in court. *The Law Society's Gazette*, 16 December 1987: 3640–3641.

37(2) - 1997: Does Justice Require Less Precision than Chemistry?

(Editorial)

The philosopher Jeremy Bentham's question posed so long ago in his treatise on "Judicial Evidence" [1] seems to me to raise the issue whether justice (by which he means the law operating as it should to produce a just result) can or should be measured as a chemist measures the ingredients in the medicine he is dispensing, i.e. whether justice is capable of exact definition down to the smallest observable, countable quantity. If so this means mathematics: the precision of the method being determined by the smallest difference in quantity of that which is measured. If that is the burden of Bentham's question then I think the answer is in the affirmative. It is true that lawyers are familiar with the concept of *weighing* evidence – but that usually means putting everything in favour on one side of the scales of justice and everything against on the other – essentially a matter of balance or comparison which does not require separate measurements of weight nor the attribution of numerate values to the items of evidence. In truth I think that mathematics beyond the simplest enumeration and the schoolboy multiplication tables at present has little place in the law. I know that it has been said that lawyers know how many beans make five, but I doubt if legal arithmetic extends much further. So perhaps this is what Bentham implied: that mathematics are alien to the law.

These thoughts are prompted by a consideration of "Interpreting Evidence" [2] – one of the most challenging books ever to have been written for lawyers, though one which has not escaped all criticism [3].

It is true that there have been recurrent attempts to introduce mathematics to the law. One writer [4] almost 50 years ago proposed to attach a statistical weight to specific items of evidence in an attempt to provide a consistent theory of probability to assist legal fact-finding, but his scheme failed to prosper. More recently scientific writers have drawn attention to the benefits which would accrue from some such scheme and the difficulties involved [5] but so far law and science have failed to engage in this way except perhaps in a few cases of paternity exclusions based on blood group serology.

Robertson and Vignaux argue persuasively in their book "Interpreting Evidence" for a reassessment in the area where law and science meet of the fundamentals of logical reasoning about evidence. This demands, they assert, the application of Bayes theorem – a logical rule the truth of which cannot be doubted – concerns the updating of knowledge when new evidence is considered. The probability of the evidence supposing the assertion is true is compared with the probability of the evidence supposing the assertion is not true, giving a ratio known as the likelihood ratio. This comparison performed for each new piece of evidence makes explicit the logical reasoning process naturally applied by the layman in the business of daily living. The difficulty is that though all of this is commonplace to scientists and is continually used by them, it is strange and unfamiliar territory to lawyers who are intimidated by the expression of the likelihood ratio in figures, rather than in vague verbal assessments.

Recently in several cases involving the assessment of DNA evidence the English courts have been drawn into a consideration of how or whether mathematical probability evidence can be justifiably used in court. In the first case of *Michael Gordon* [6] the question considered by the Court of Appeal was whether the evidence of a visual match between the DNA profiles of crime stains from each of two rapes and the accused's sample could be supported by a statistical evaluation of the match. This latter aspect of the case was challenged with expert evidence for the defence critical of the Crown's measurements which were claimed to be insufficiently precise to support the use of the statistical database to calculate the probability of the match. Since probabilities running into millions had been put before the jury, having a dramatic quality which must have influenced them, the conviction was quashed and the case sent for retrial. So far as Gordon's appeal was concerned the court were not satisfied that a match had been established, and statistical evaluations based on a false premise would have been wildly misleading. In the earlier case of *Deen* [7] where the statistical evaluation of a DNA match in a triple rape case was strongly challenged, the court found that there were two distinct questions:

1. What was the probability that an individual would match the DNA profile from the crime sample given that he was innocent?
2. What was the probability that an individual was innocent given that he matched the DNA profile from the crime sample?

The "prosecutor's fallacy" revealed in Deen's case consisted in giving the answer to the first question as the answer to the second. The continuation of this error, with the trial judge having spoken of probability approximating "pretty well to certainty", rendered the verdicts unsafe. However, in a further and different appeal of *Stephen Cooke* [8] where it was alleged that the trial judge had confused the "match probability" with the "likelihood ratio" the Appeal Court disagreed, holding that the trial judge had simply explained the two concepts without suggesting that the mathematical ratios were the same.

The courts' obvious difficulties in handling probability evidence of this kind surfaced again in the twin rape and buggery cases of *R. v. Docherty* and *R. v. Adams* [9] when the Court of Appeal, Criminal Division set out the procedure which should henceforth be adopted. First, the scientists should adduce the evidence of the DNA comparisons with a calculation of the random occurrence ratio; second, they should provide the defence with details of how the calculations had been carried out sufficient for the defence to scrutinise the basis of the calculations; and third, the forensic science service should make available to the defence expert, if requested, the databases on which the calculations were founded. The question for the jury would then be "whether you are sure it was the defendant who left that stain, or whether it is possible that it was one of that small group of men who share the same DNA characteristics".

Had this judgment been delivered a few months earlier it would have prevented the procedures which in the appeal of *Denis Adams* [10] revealed an extraordinary experiment where a jury were encouraged themselves to apply statistical probabilities to their consideration of the evidence. The Adams case concerned a rape trial where the prosecution case rested entirely on expert evidence describing the DNA profiling of a sample taken from the complainant which was compared with the sample taken from the accused. The Crown expert obtained a visual match and calculated that the chance of a randomly chosen unrelated man matching the DNA profile was 1 in 297 million rounded down for convenience to 1 in 200 million. As well as denying that he was the perpetrator of the rape, the accused claimed alibi as to which he and his girl-friend gave evidence before the jury. At an earlier identification parade the complainant had failed to pick out the accused or anyone else.

In an attempt to challenge the prosecution case a defence statistician was allowed to explain to the jury, without objection by the Crown, that it was logical and consistent for the jury to consider the rest of the evidence in the case in statistical terms using Bayes theorem. Indeed he said this was "the only logically sound and consistent approach" to such situations. The defence expert made certain criticisms of the methodology of the Crown experts (including the "rounding down") and then proceeded to explain Bayes theorem to the jury and to guide them how they might apply this to four aspects of the evidence, namely (1) the probability that the offence was committed by a local man (which the accused was) (2) the non-identification evidence, (3) the accused's own evidence and (4) the alibi evidence. In charging the jury the judge said that they had heard the defence statistician explaining Bayes theorem and it was entirely for them to decide whether to apply it to their consideration of the evidence. They need not do so, but if they did they must have regard to all of what the statistician had said. After a period of some five hours (which perhaps suggests a good deal of discussion and pencilled calculation) the jury convicted unanimously.

Not surprisingly the matter was taken to appeal and criticism was there made of the way the judge dealt with the defence expert's exposition of Bayes theorem and of the fact that he allowed the jury to indulge in the statistical exercise. The Appeal Court took the view – provisionally because they had not had the benefit of argument both in favour and against – that the use of statistics trespassed on an area peculiarly and exclusively within the province of the jury (namely the way they evaluate the relationship between one piece of evidence and another); and that the use of a mathematical formula applied to evidence was inappropriate and might be impractical should different jurors apply different values to particular items of evidence. Jurors evaluate evidence, it was said, by the joint application of their individual common sense and knowledge of the world to the material before them. The conviction was quashed being regarded as unsafe, but the court ordered a retrial.

This appears to signal a fairly comprehensive rejection of the use of probability calculations in English criminal law and a dashing of the hope expressed by Robertson and Vignaux that logic, probability and inference would provide the language in which lawyers and scientists would communicate with each other. What is not plain is whether the decision in *Denis Adams* precludes the presenting to a jury of expert evidence explaining the calculations of the statistician as to the effect of his application of Bayes theorem to the evidence. That would seem to be a matter of expert evidence which a jury could consider and accept or reject.

Such is the situation in Scots criminal law as the case of Welsh [11] demonstrates. All of which seems to confirm that justice in the United Kingdom does not require or welcome the precision of the chemist. Or at least at present it does not encourage the amateur to dabble.

Alistair R. Brownlie

References

1. Jeremy Bentham. *Treatise on Judicial Evidence*. Dunmont, 1825, 43.
2. Robertson B and Vignaux GA. *Interpreting Evidence: Evaluating Forensic Evidence in the Courtroom*. Chichester: John Wiley & Sons, 1995.

3. Redmayne M. Science Evidence and Logic. *The Modem Law Review* 1996; **59**: 747–760. See also Correspondence "Hamlet without the Prince" *Science & Justice* 1996; **36**: 65. "Interpreting Evidence" *Science and Justice* 1996; **36**: 129.
4. Good. *Probability and the Weighing of Evidence*, 1950.
5. Walls HJ. "What is Reasonable Doubt?" [1971] *Crim L.R.*, 458; R. Coleman & Walls "The Evaluation of Scientific Evidence" [1974] *Crim L.R.*, 276.
6. Michael Gordon [1995] 1 Cr. App. R. 290.
7. R.v. Deen 1994 Times L.R. 11 (10th January 1994).
8. Stephen Cooke [1995] 1 Cr. App. R. 318.
9. R. v. Docherty R. v. Adams 1996 Times L.R. 504 (16th August 1996).
10. Denis Adams [1996] 2 Cr. App. R. 467.
11. Welsh v. H.M. Advocate 1992 S.L.T. 193.

Science & Justice 1997; *37(2): 73–74*

43(2) - 2003: Sally Clark – A Lesson for us All

(Editorial)

ARW Forrest
Editor, *Science & Justice*

Readers in the UK will need no reminding of the saga of Sally Clark; for those outside the UK a brief précis is in order [1]. Her first son, Christopher, died in December 1966 at the age of 11 weeks. After a post mortem examination by Dr Alan Williams, a consultant pathologist to the Home Office, the death was determined to be due to natural causes (Sudden Infant Death Syndrome or SIDS). Signs of recent injury were attributed to resuscitation attempts. There things rested until her second son, Harry, died at eight weeks of age in 1998. Again Dr Williams carried out a post mortem examination. As is usual in an unexpected death in infancy case multiple samples, including cerebro-spinal fluid, were collected and submitted for microbiological examination. All of those samples grew out a pure growth of *Staphlococcus aureus*. Whilst Dr Williams received the microbiology results these were apparently not passed on to the other experts in the case, whether they were assisting court at the request of the prosecution or the defence. Other, later contested, evidence of injury was apparent and Dr Williams, and others, considered that Harry's death was due to shaking. This led to a re-examination of the evidence in Christopher's case. Ultimately, Mrs Clark was tried and convicted of the murder of both Christopher and Harry following a trial at Chester Crown Court in 1999. At the trial, Professor Roy Meadow, a distinguished paediatrician who has been the target, with several other paediatricians, of campaigns directed against those diagnosing Munchausen's syndrome by proxy [2], assisted the Court at the request of the prosecution. When he was examined in chief, he estimated that the probability of two SIDS deaths in a family with middle class characteristics was 1:73,000,000 or one case every 100 years in England, Scotland and Wales by chance. This figure was obtained as the product of 1:8543*1:8543. 1:8543 being the probability of a SIDS death in a family with no risk factors. This analysis was roundly criticised in the medical literature and firmly defended by Professor Meadow [3, 4].

In the event Sally Clark was convicted on both charges. Her husband and her many supporters did not accept the convictions and there was a vigorous campaign, both through legal and extra curial channels, to secure her release.

The Court of Appeal was not impressed with the arguments presented on her behalf at her first appeal saying, in part: "... we consider that there was an overwhelming case against the appellant at trial. If there had been no error in relation to statistics at the trial, we are satisfied that the jury would still have convicted on each count. In the context of the trial as a whole, the point on statistics was of minimal significance and there is no possibility of the jury having been misled so as to reach verdicts that they might not otherwise have reached. Had the trial been free from legal error, the only reasonable and proper verdict would have been one of guilty" [5].

Matters did not rest there and Sally Clark's supporters continued their investigations. These included a review of all of the medical records of the two children. Their case notes included the microbiology reports showing the pure growth of Staphylococcus from multiple sites in Harry's body. These data were passed on the Criminal Cases Review Commission (CCRC). The CCRC considered Sally Clark's case and passed it back to the Court of Appeal. The judgement of a differently constituted Court was handed down earlier this year; they concluded that Sally Clark's original conviction was unsafe [1].

The Crown elected not to take up their option to try her again and she was released. The court heard evidence on the significance of the microbiological findings from both the Crown and the appellant. The evidence for the appellant emphasised the possibility of sudden death as a result of staphylococcal toxins – a variant of Toxic Shock Syndrome. The Crown presented evidence indicating that this did not fit the known facts of Harry's death. The Court of Appeal considered that this was evidence which should have been put before the jury at the first trial. They also considered that the statistical evidence given by Professor Meadow would have had a non-trivial effect on the jury saying "... it may have had a major effect on their thinking notwithstanding the attempts by the trial judge to down play it".

One of the most interesting parts of the 2003 judgement is a long section on the approach of the pathologist to the suspicious death. The Court's analysis is equally relevant to any investigator or scientist involved in the investigation of a suspicious death. In short; get as much information about the case as possible; do the examination keeping meticulous notes and consider all the possibilities and all the evidence, both positive and negative, normal and abnormal. The report should set out the conclusions and why they have been reached showing that relevant alternative hypotheses have been considered and why they are not as well supported by the evidence as the formulation favoured by the pathologist. The recording of the finding and results of the special investigations for review by others is vitally important. The Court quotes from a statement made by Dr Williams before the second appeal in which he said "It is not my practice to refer to additional results in my post mortem unless they are relevant to the cause of death, as the specimens were referred to another consultant". The Court did not consider this approach acceptable; clearly it cannot be in an adversarial criminal justice system. It is, in effect, the expert trying the case and deciding what is relevant evidence, not the Court. To state the obvious, it is Courts, not experts, who should try cases.

There are lessons in the case of Sally Clark for all of us who assist the courts as investigators, experts or advocates. Justice requires meticulous preparation, comprehensive note taking, opinions soundly based in recorded and/or reproducible fact, sharing of data between experts, valid scientific deductions and a willingness to think again as data emerges, or re-emerges. Also scientific and opinion evidence should be presented in court objectively and not emotively. Opinion evidence should be testable, not *ex cathedra*. That requires the information on which the opinion is based to be shared.

References

1. *R v Sally Clark. [2003] EWCA Crim 1020*.
2. http://www.msbp.com
3. Watkins SJ. Conviction by mathematical error? *British Medical Journal* 2000; **320**: 2–3.
4. Meadow R. A case of murder and the BMJ. *British Medical Journal* 2002; **324**: 41–3.
5. *R v Sally Clark (2000) CA (Henry LJ, Bracewell J, Richards J) 2/10/2000*.

44(2) - 2004: Context-free Forensic Science

(Editorial)

Can forensic science ever be context-free so far as the reporting officer is concerned? This question lies at the heart of all expert and opinion evidence. The suggestion, implicit and explicit, that when the forensic scientist is asked to examine trace evidence to see whether or not it is likely that it can be matched to crime scene evidence this should be done in a context-free manner with her knowing nothing of the context in which the evidence has been recovered is one which theoretically has some merit. At least it may have merit where there is an almost pure separation between the testable and falsifiable conclusions of the scientist, and the inferences to be drawn from the scientist's conclusion by the trier of fact in the case. Or is even that so?

Even in the purest of such technologies, DNA 'fingerprinting', context is important for the scientific interpretation of the data. The 'brother' defence is a clear example. To produce a truly context-free question may require the person who is asking the question to formulate it in a manner that is convoluted to the point where the answer will only be of very limited value to the trier of fact. This is not to deny that there are circumstances where knowledge of what appear to be the facts of the case as the giver of opinion evidence understands them to be may result in (unconsciously) biased and misleading evidence being given to the court. In a common law jurisdiction where the judge cannot assist the jury by summing up the evidence as well as instructing them on the relevant law this may become a major problem. Possibly the US courts might learn something from the way in which English judges are able to assist juries in their fact finding exercise, albeit recent cases have reminded us that this may not perfectly remedy inappropriate opinion evidence.

Much forensic science cannot be interpreted in a context-free manner in any case. Post-mortem toxicology is a good example. Giving a simple number, say a blood methadone concentration, to a jury is useless in isolation. Comparing that number with concentrations of the drug found in plasma during therapeutic use of the drug in life is likely to be positively misleading. In toxicology interpretation, context is everything. The trier of fact needs to be educated by the expert witness as to a variety of phenomena, such as post-mortem redistribution, concentration site dependency, the effects of putrefaction and many other matters in order for them to be able to put a drug concentration into its appropriate context with all the other information they have provided to them. The problem with post-mortem toxicology is that objective data from which conclusions in relation to post-mortem drug concentrations may be drawn are often simply not available. The difficulties in carrying out the necessary scientific work to produce such data will be compounded in the United Kingdom if the Human Tissue Bill currently before Parliament is enacted into law in its present form. How many toxicologists will wish to do the appropriate research if a technical infraction of the proposed Human Tissue Act might earn them three years in jail? At present the toxicologist may be able to help the court by drawing inferences from evidence which the jury can then combine with other evidence. For example, in a drug facilitated sexual assault case involving gamma hydroxybutyrate (GHB), it would be relevant for the toxicologist to explain to the court that the complainant's urine might contain no GHB even if she had been administered it for it is ephemeral and may have been metabolised between the time of the alleged offence and the time the urine sample was donated. It would be for the jury and not the toxicologist to draw inferences from the fact that the defendant's hard disk was full of data relating to the effects, manufacture and purchase of GHB.

True context-free forensic science is a Platonic ideal. In my view it is undesirable in many cases where the opinion of an expert can assist the trier of fact. The expect opinion has to be opinion based on sound science and has to be expressed in as neutral a way as possible. The judge has to be capable of assessing the expert evidence so as to be able to assist the jury when summing up. This is a clear problem for US judges who cannot assist the jury in the way that English judges can. Good expert evidence is a stool with three legs; Competent, validated and regularly appraised expert witnesses giving evidence based on sound scientific research and methods before judges able to help juries, where appropriate, with the use of that evidence in the context of the case as a whole. Professional registration of those giving expert evidence helps to support the first leg. In the US the federal rules of evidence, albeit by no means perfect help with the second leg. In the UK registration of those giving opinion evidence should help to exclude those providing junk science based evidence to the courts. A scientifically literate judiciary would address the third leg.

Two judges were present at the Autumn 2003 meeting of the Forensic Science Society. How can we persuade more to attend next year?

Robert Forrest

46(1) - 2006: Lies, Damn Lies and Statistics

(Editorial)

Dr N Nic Daéid

The problems associated with the presentation of scientific evidence in court have always been challenging. Indeed, all one has to do is look back an uncomfortably few number of years for illustrations of gross misinterpretations of scientific evidence either by scientists themselves from the witness box, by the legal experts during examination or in summation of such evidence to the jury. The difficulties in presenting and communicating often complex scientific information to a lay audience are not new. Neither are the rules by which we must operate within a legal or judicial framework, after all legal systems of one form or another were in existence long before forensic science was applied to criminal or civil investigations. Yet, even with rules, laws of evidence and hard lessons of the past learned through the appeal courts, there are persistent and recurring difficulties in communication between the scientific expert and the court.

Science can be investigative, corroborative or exclusionary and we as scientists require to make sense of the results of our tests and experiments within the case context in order best to serve the court. Most will agree that scientists can provide information that can be used as intelligence in the development of a particular investigative or evaluative strategy and in some cases that information may be directly adduced as evidence in a court proceeding. Science is often an iterative process involving the evaluation of results in the context of background and known data and expressing this evaluation of factual findings qualified by statistically informed opinions. While most forensic scientists will agree on matters of clearly established fact, the difficulties begin to arise in the areas of evaluation of the support or otherwise these facts can give to the various hypotheses presented. The assessment of evidential value has been the subject of much detailed and healthy debate for many years within the forensic science community, but the question remains as to whether these complex debates act to produce a coherent method of reporting the value of factual evidence and whether the consequent phraseology ultimately clarifies or confuses the jury.

In some jurisdictions, the admissibility of expert evidence requires that the process and analysis from which such evidence has been derived should meet specific criteria, such as the Daubert criteria (Appendix), and there is considerable merit to this approach. The introduction of inferences derived from the analyses of data has in the past led to considerable confusion in the court room because they have been presented to the jury in a manner which might be misunderstood. This has occurred in some notable cases in the recent past. After the *R v. Deen* 1993, *R v. Doheny/Adams* 1997 cases the Royal Statistical Society (RSS) commented that:

> the Court of Appeal has recognised these dangers [..of the misinterpretation of likelihood ratios in relation to DNA evidence..] in connection with probabilities used for DNA profile evidence, and has put in place clear guidelines for the presentation of such evidence. The dangers extend more widely, and there is a real possibility that without proper guidance, and well-informed presentation, frequency estimates presented in court could be misinterpreted by the jury in ways that are very prejudicial to defendants.

In the current system in England and Wales the convention is that an expert expresses an opinion of identity of source for certain types of evidence such as fingerprints, handwriting, footwear marks and toolmarks. However, if the situation arises where the expert can make a statistical assessment of the weight of the evidence (for example in relation to DNA evidence) then the court will not allow them to express an opinion as to the identity of the source and the statistic is put to the jury for them to decide. This implies that the emerging methods for statistical assessments of fingerprint comparisons may inevitably lead to a major cultural change.

As a consequence, the scientist should not be asked in legal examination to overstep their role to express an opinion on the identity of the individual who left, for example, a crime scene stain. Similarly, the scientist must be cautious as to not unwittingly express such an opinion through the use of terminology while giving evidence. This clearly places a burden on both the legal and scientific parties to provide unambiguous information to the jury to allow them to reach their conclusions.

However, the use of statistical opinion is not a problem associated only with DNA evidence as recent appeal cases have illustrated. The RSS have again expressed in their comments following the Sally Clarke case, grave concerns that matters of scientific evidence and the use of statistics in expressing that evidence are being misunderstood:

> Aside from its invalidity, figures such as the 1 in 73 million are very easily misinterpreted.... Some press reports at the time stated that this was the chance that the deaths of Sally Clark's two children were accidental... This (mis-) interpretation is a serious error of logic known as the Prosecutor's Fallacy

Furthermore, comments reported in the *Guardian* newspaper (March 2005) relating to similar cases have again brought into sharp focus the difficulties facing the scientist and legal profession alike in the presentation of scientific evidence involving the use and interpretation of statistics.

> One judge admitted that most senior judges were "innumerate" when it came to DNA evidence. The committee says it is "entirely unsatisfactory" that there is no agreed test or protocol for validating scientific evidence before it is presented in court. It calls for a new Forensic Science Advisory Council, one of whose first tasks would be to develop a "gatekeeping" test for expert evidence. This would be based on the US system, which bans the use of any new scientific technique in court until it has been reviewed and accepted by the scientific community.

Today, expert evidence of all types and disciplines is under higher scrutiny than ever before. It is important for the scientist to impart the message that, while we may use statistical evaluation, statistics alone cannot prove the identity of a person or an item and we must be cautious in selecting and validating the statistical or probabilistic model used for a particular question to ensure that it is both reliable and correctly applicable. In some cases this can be a particular challenge.

Appendix; Daubert Criteria

1. Whether the expert's technique or theory can be or has been tested — that is, whether the expert's theory can be challenged in some objective sense, or whether it is instead simply a subjective, conclusory approach that cannot reasonably be assessed for reliability.
2. Whether the technique or theory has been subject to peer review publication.
3. The known or potential rate of error of the technique or theory when applied.
4. The existence and maintenance of standards and controls.
5. Whether the technique or theory has been generally accepted in the scientific community.

SECTION IV: EDUCATION IN FORENSIC SCIENCES

Much has been written in relation to the development of education in forensic science, particularly in recent years. The proliferation of academic courses, in particular, in the UK since 1990 has been dramatic, often provoking alarm amongst practitioners and employers alike. In 2009 there were over 500 listed combinations of undergraduate courses with 'forensic' in the title being offered by over 70 UK universities. Questions over the 'value' of many of these courses have been hotly debated at many levels including at a UK government Select Committee and recently in the 2009 Skills for Justice report – "Fit for purpose: Research into the provision of Forensic Science degree programmes in UK HEI's".

The development of postgraduate courses in the UK has not been so dramatic until comparatively recently. Early editorials discuss the establishment of the Masters degree in Forensic Science at the University of Strathclyde which was first established in 1967. Since 2004 the number of postgraduate courses in the UK have also increased to over 100 being offered in 2009. Of course, the increase in forensic science courses is not exclusive to the UK, although this has been without doubt the most dramatic. Increased numbers of undergraduate courses with 'forensic' in the title have also occurred in the United States, Canada and Australia as well as other countries. Academic accreditation schemes have been introduced in the UK by the Forensic Science Society and in the US by FEPAC (Forensic Science Education Programs Accreditation Commission), in order to provide some means of establishing (for both applicants and employers) a measure of the nature and levels of forensic content in these courses. Universities who achieve accreditation are certified and published on the relevant web sites.

Many attribute the rapid increase in popularity of forensic science courses to a so called, and widely referred to, 'CSI effect' and its assumed influence with young people to apply to forensic science courses. It might surprise many readers (and educators) that in fact the influence of television on the popularity of forensic science was recognised as far back as 1968 (!) so this is perhaps not as new a phenomena as many would think. Indeed the interest in specialised training and education in forensic science for police and legal practitioners was referred to by Professor Reiss as early as 1906, which led to the creation of the first School of its kind in the world in 1909 (currently known as *Ecole des Sciences Criminelles* at the University of Lausanne). The television and Internet have perhaps brought forensic science to a wider audience and meant that some higher education establishments took opportunistic advantage of the increase in popularity in filling their courses.

The debates that have ensued over the years in relation to education follow a range of topics that we, rather depressingly, have not significantly advanced since the 1960's. For example, the issue of identity of source was discussed in the very first editorial in 1961 and provides some sense that this is an issue, perhaps, at the crux of forensic science, and one of the features that identifies forensic science as a discipline. The sorting and evaluation of the closeness of a 'match' in a way that is useful to the criminal justice system is the point that is of real importance. The lack of research and development into fundamental questions such as identity of source is a major point in the recent National Academy of Science – "Strengthening Forensic Science in the United States: A Path Forward" published in 2009. Notwithstanding the extraordinary contributions of Evett, Jackson and colleagues in the UK, Champod and Taroni in Switzerland and Buckleton and colleagues in New Zealand, this has to beg the question as to whether, globally, we have really shifted our position in half a century.

The interactions between Academic establishments and practitioners has also been discussed and in particular the development of quality research which is core to the development of a robust scientific discipline. In the 1960–70's, only three specialised university programmes existed (Strathclyde, Lausanne and Berkley) all of whom were research active in an academic sense. The tension today, in 2009, between what counts as 'research' within an academic context or a practitioner context is still current, and the basic deficiency in research into 'forensic science' is still evident with much peripheral/opportunistic interest, but few core research projects of ongoing depth and breadth. Most obvious is perhaps the lack of integration of legal research into forensic science and vice versa. It was recently stated in correspondence provoked by the editorial "Educating the next generation" (page 180 of this text) that *"the publication rate of the largest UK producer of peer reviewed papers in forensic science roughly equates to one year's publication output for a single department in one university. [This] clearly illustrates the immense gulf between forensic research and other disciplines"* (page 188). Moreover the rate of publication by universities offering courses in Forensic Science is dominated by three or four institutions globally with many failing to publish even a single research paper in the field within the past ten years. This may be an appalling reflection on the state of education and research within the field, especially its difficulty, if not inability, to generate and sustain a global critical body of research. Why is this the case?

The second editorial relating to research (1961) perhaps lays out the fundamental problem.... *"the present inability of scientists in Home Office and other Government Forensic Science Laboratories to make a large contribution to fundamental research in their own field. This.... is the inevitable result of the pressure of routine work"* (page 170).

In the same editorial the following observations were made; *"Very few workers are devoting most of their time to [research] investigations based on a long-term programme.... A relatively large number of workers are engaged in short-term ad hoc investigations. These investigations are sporadic and uncoordinated and are therefore, in general, unlikely to be productive.... There is a widespread appreciation of the problems which require attention in the field of forensic science; canalization of this enthusiasm and interest into effectual action is a matter for immediate and urgent attention."*

Well, it can be argued that nothing really has changed in over forty years, and it can also be argued that the focus in forensic science has been on technological developments without significantly and systematically researching into the fundamental questions which include those relating to inference, identity, uncertainty and integration of forensic science case data with other dimensions of policing and justice. Part of the problem, in our view, is related to the way forensic science research is funded and regarded within traditional academic circles in most countries. To some extent, to 'stay alive' forensic researchers based in academia have to tweak their work to fit with an existing academic model, and by doing so, they rarely achieve investigations into the fundamental forensic questions. This is why it is necessary to establish research partnerships between academia/research institutions and operational Organisations. The main question of course is: why can't forensic science attract large research grants? If it could, then it would become more attractive to 'elite universities'. It's interesting to note that in Australia, none of the reputable forensic programs are delivered by a Go8 (elite) university. A similar situation exists in the United Kingdom with the Russell group universities. These institutions often criticise forensic science for being too applied as a research domain; however, because of the attractiveness of the topic to students, they still try to capitalise upon the interest by providing forensic short courses or other courses through traditional science curricula. This emphasizes that many university funding formulae may act as the source of many problems, especially the tension between teaching and research experienced by such institutions.

Perhaps the educational future for forensic science is to stop taking the traditional and all too commonly held narrow view of criminal law-driven forensic science. It may be unpalatable to many, but the traditional view that the only educational sequence for a successful forensic scientist is science first and forensic science second is not necessarily correct. The key is the development of a strong scientific/problem-solving mind. Perhaps we should re-think the whole topic and, reverberating similar calls by Margot in 1994 (*Forensic Science Education...or How Do We Foster Quality*. Proceedings of the 3rd meeting of the European Network of Forensic Science Institutes; Linköping, 31–37), produce a generalised holistic approach, focusing around what forensic science actually is, that being the study of traces very broadly defined as remnants of human activities. The enabling sciences are therefore considered tools and not the quest for fundamental questions. The traditional view which sees forensic science as a 'lump' from chemistry or biology, etc., does not help, and the perspective that forensic science can be used as a tool to "teach science through forensic science" is naive at best. A traditional chemist or biologist would be disinterested in the questions that become key issues for a forensic scientist. Thus, the question of what is forensic science remains; ironically, criminologists, lawyers and even economists seem to be more interested in this question than forensic scientists themselves. This is not only sad but arguably dangerous, and we should rightly retake leadership of our field!

Included in this section is some correspondence (2008) which epitomises one worrying perspective of how forensic science education is viewed, and highlights both the naivety and potential motivation with which some higher education institutions view the opportunities provided by the increase in popularity of our profession. Such university business models perhaps explain why forensic science often seems to be used as a cash cow to recycle existing pet areas.

"HEIs have their own drivers and that is educating people on courses they want to attend. Science education has to adapt to currently decreasing numbers and if forensic science can attract new students to train as scientists then this means survival for many university departments."..... *"Having survived dwindling numbers, the department has now managed to start offering pure chemistry again. So one could argue that forensic science kept science provision alive and whether UCLAN were FSSoc accredited or not, this was good for science and for UCLAN"*.

Given these statements, what is the real interest in forensic science by some of the universities that deliver forensic related courses? It is not with this paradigm that fundamental forensic science knowledge will advance. Perhaps a good expression for this situation is: forensic science is like a mistress: good enough to have fun with, but not good enough to raise the family.....

N. Nic Daéid and C. Roux

2(1) - 1961: Research and Teaching in Forensic Science

The report on Education and Research in the Forensic Sciences in the United Kingdom (reproduced in full on pages 2 to 7) is a further sign of the reawakening of interest in a field which has been in eclipse in Great Britain since the onset of the Second World War. That time saw the cessation of those excellent Forensic Science Circulars published by the Stationery Office and the suspension of such limited research facilities as then existed in the Home Office Laboratories.

Just how far the suggestions for future research in the Education and Research report reflect what is really desirable as distinct from the specialist interests of the individuals replying to the questionnaire is a matter still to be determined, but this can be an objection to most surveys of this kind. It also may be that the various suggestions for research are coloured by the existing cheeseparing facilities and that most people will have suggested topics possible within the existing research framework.

What is less a matter of opinion is however the obvious omission of those less esoteric fields where there is a chronic need for methods which has existed for so long that people assume the problems are insoluble. To take but two examples; the presentation of evidence on the individuality of human head hair is commonplace in the courts of law in many countries and has been so for many years; but the usefulness of such evidence is far more limited than the authors of detective novels will allow. We are still limited to "could have a common origin" when comparing two samples of head hair and yet much biological evidence strongly suggests that human head hair is as peculiar to the individual as fingerprints.

The second omission is the necessity for research into the automatic sorting of single fingerprints collections. It is still popularly supposed that if a criminal leaves a single good print at a scene of crime and his fingerprints are on record then it is merely a matter of time before his prints are located in the collection and his identity established. That this is so often the case is a tribute to the efficiency of fingerprint officers in the tedious business of classification and searching but these same officers must admit that the unmatched crime-collection fingerprint pairs on record must be substantial indeed. Punched card techniques are never likely to be more than a partial solution to the matter and this field would seem to offer great promise for a research team comprising biologists, electronic experts and fingerprint specialists.

What are the solutions to these problems? Would the establishment of a chair or chairs in forensic science in British Universities help or is the subject too heterogeneous to allow any logical focal point for the setting up of separate departments? Would forensic appointments in existing University science departments be the solution, or even the grafting of forensic science appointments on to existing departments of forensic medicine? On the other hand, has progress in the past been impeded by the view that all forensic science is forensic medicine?

The answers to all these problems are still to come and it is important that before decisions are made all relevant views are carefully weighed. "Relevant" in this context should include evidence not only from the United Kingdom but from all countries advanced enough to provide for scientific evidence in courts of law and not only from professional expert witnesses but from those University scientists whose own special fields are used (and sometimes abused) in the witness box.

The overseas readership of this journal could help by pointing out the virtues and faults of the provisions for scientific evidence in their own countries and in this way we in the United Kingdom together with our own substantial experience could build a logical and useful system and avoid past errors.

2(1) - 1961: A Preliminary Survey of Education and Research in the Forensic Sciences in the United Kingdom

Since the beginning of 1960 the Education and Research Committee of the British Academy of Forensic Sciences in collaboration with the Forensic Science Society has been engaged in a survey of research and education in forensic science in the United Kingdom.

So far, the enquiry has been a fact-finding one and, because of the wide connotations of "forensic," attention has been directed to projects which appeared to be consciously designed to further forensic ends.

The main tool of the enquiry has been a questionnaire which was circulated to all members of the Academy and The Forensic Science Society and to some University Departments and all Home Office Forensic Laboratories.

Up to date 312 questionnaires have been issued and 161 returned. The present report is based on the information in these returns.

The questionnaire attempted to elicit information in two broad fields, namely, Research and Education. The object was to determine what was going on at the moment in each of these fields and also to obtain suggestions for desirable activities in the future.

The results of the survey may be summarised under four headings.

1. *Education.* The information showed that Education in its broadest sense in the Forensic Sciences is almost completely confined to three sorts of activity;
   (a) Police and Detective Training Courses.
   (b) Courses for Medical and Law Students in some Universities.
   (c) Sporadic lectures and short courses for specialised groups of people (e.g. Magistrates, Young Solicitors, G.P1s., Postgraduate Students of Psychiatry, Junior Members of the Law Society, Army Pathologists, Probation Officers and Social Workers). These lectures and courses are organised by such bodies as the Magistrates Association, Law Society, Association of Police Surgeons, College of General Practitioners, Association of Clinical Pathologists, British Medical Association, Medico Legal Society and the Royal Institute of Public Health. There are also short intensive courses such as a blood grouping course at Sheffield.

   Many persons supplying information about these courses stated that they played some part in them and there is clearly no shortage of enthusiasm or talent. In general, however, Universities and Technical Colleges play only a small part in the provision of instruction in the forensic sciences. There is nowhere any formal course aimed at producing forensic scientists and their training appears to be based on the apprentice system. At the moment it seems fair to conclude that of those vitally concerned in forensic matters, only the Police have adequate educational facilities.

   It is clear that lectures and short courses for specialised groups of people are considered to be most valuable. 92% of the replies said so, usually emphatically, and only 8% expressed doubts or reservations. The principal criticism of the existing courses is that they are not given regularly. A further recurring plaint was the omission of forensic medicine from some medical curricula and final examinations. Apart from this, although the replies revealed considerable disquiet at the general position of education in forensic science, there were practically no suggestions as to how it could be improved.

2. *Research: The Present Position.* Of the 161 persons replying, 76 took part in research of some kind. But it is significant that only 13 spend the major part of their time on such work. A synopsis of research problems currently under active investigation and also of suggestions for topics meriting early investigation is presented in Appendix B.

   The break-down of the replies giving information on current research is into major and minor projects. The projects were divided into major and minor depending on whether they appeared to be full-time or part-time activities respectively. This classification, of course, carries no implication of evaluation of the relative importance of these projects but is based solely on an estimate of the time devoted to them during the normal working week of the investigator.

   Many of the minor investigations are largely concerned with chemical and physical techniques in connexion with forensic analytical problems. The brunt of this work is borne by the Home Office Laboratories and arises naturally from the day-to-day problems they encounter. However, a limited number of University scientists also tackle such problems from time to time. The variety is astonishing, ranging from the analysis of motor oils through lipstick, writing inks and seminal stains, to the determination of age, stature, and race from ancient bones. It is clear that the necessity for such investigations coupled with the pressure of routine work inevitably precludes the pursuit of fundamental or long-term researches in the laboratories concerned. Furthermore, although the total number of minor projects may, at first glance, appear to be impressive the comments which accompanied the data leave little doubt that in the majority of instances the time devoted to the individual problems is so limited that useful results are unlikely to be obtained in the near future if at all.

If the problems are considered in three categories, Medical, Legal (coupled with Sociology, Psychiatry and Statistics), and Scientific the first and third groups are well represented, whereas the second group, especially on a major basis is relatively poorly represented.

In Appendix C an attempt is made to give some idea of the distribution of research activities among Institutions. The data shown in the table emphasize the present inability of scientists in Home Office and other Government Forensic Science Laboratories to make a large contribution to fundamental research in their own field. This as observed above is the inevitable result of the pressure of routine work.

3. *Research: The Future.* Included in Appendix B are suggested problems meriting immediate and intensive investigation. The suggestions cover a wide field but the most generally supported ones were, in order of popularity: haematology, toxicology, pathology and anatomy, trace substances, and time of death. Within these fields the suggestions might be formulated as:

   (a) Development of objective methods for determination of the time of death and postmortem changes.
   (b) Development of micromethods for the identification and determination of the origin of modern polymeric substances, ceramics and glasses, fibres, paints and oils.
   (c) Development of methods for the detection of blood and for the determination of age, sex and grouping in blood stains.
   (d) Development of methods for the extraction, identification and microanalysis of drugs, toxic substances and their metabolites.

   It will be seen from sections 4 & 6 of Appendix B that a large number of suggestions was received in the fields of law, psychology, psychiatry, and sociology for problems worthy of investigation. The suggestions were so diverse that it is difficult to formulate any particular problems as being more pressing than others. This difficulty does not detract, of course, from the value of the individual suggestions.

4. *Research: General Conclusions.* A consideration of the overall results of the survey in respect of research activities in forensic science leads to the following general conclusions:

   (a) Very few workers are devoting most of their time to investigations based on a long-term programme.
   (b) A relatively large number of workers are engaged in short-term ad hoc investigations. These investigations are sporadic and uncoordinated and are therefore, in general, unlikely to be productive.
   (c) It is disquieting to find that the Home Office and other Government Laboratories are unable to make the contributions to fundamental research in forensic science which might be expected from their great practical experience in this field. This presumably reflects a lack of appreciation by the authorities concerned of the value and necessity of fundamental research in the field administered by them.
   (d) There is a widespread appreciation of the problems which require attention in the field of forensic science; canalization of this enthusiasm and interest into effectual action is a matter for immediate and urgent attention.

Appendix "A"

The Format of the Questionnaire

The questionnaire was designed to be as simple and informal as possible conducive with obtaining the desired information. It would have been a simple matter to design a far more comprehensive document, but in view of the plethora of such forms in recent years and the length of time required to complete them, a simple format was considered to be likely to be most effective.

The questionnaire is shown below-

A – Research

1. *Are you personally involved in research on problems of forensic importance?*
2. *If so, please give a brief description of the project together with the number and status of any other workers taking part and the address at which the research is carried out.*
3. *Whether you are personally engaged in such research or not, would you please give a brief description of any problems which, from your own experience, merit investigation.*

B – Education

1. *Do you take part in or have knowledge of any courses designed specifically for the tuition of special groups in some aspect of forensic science? (e.g., for such special groups as postgraduates, technicians, police, etc.). If the answer is yes, please give details – (e.g., duration of course, full or part time, outline of topics covered).*
2. *Do you consider that special lectures and/or demonstrations for groups of people such as magistrates, judges and counsel would be useful for better appreciation of the value and limitations of scientific evidence? Do you know of any such lectures or demonstrations which are at present offered regularly?*

C – Comments

Please add any comments or suggestions you care to make on matters not covered in (A) or (B).

Appendix "B"

Research Projects

The following table is a synopsis of research problems currently under active investigation and of suggestions for those topics which merit early investigation for forensic purposes. The arrangement is according to subject matter, the subdivisions being somewhat arbitrary. Research topics listed are receiving minor attention (as defined in the main part of this report) unless otherwise noted. The number in parenthesis following each topic is the number of persons who returned a questionnaire which indicated activity or suggested activity on the particular topic. In general, it was not possible to estimate the number of other people (e.g. research assistants, technicians) also involved in the work although the questionnaire attempted to elicit this information.

Some replies in Sections A2 and A3 did not represent specific topics for research or were too obscurely worded to allow a clear interpretation. Liberal editing of the replies was essential for economy of space as well as for the reasonable formulation of problems and projects.

Current Research	Suggestions
1. ALCOHOL (a) General effects of alcohol on driving and other human activities (1 major, 3 minor) (b) Reabsorption of alcohol from the bladder (1) (c) Evaluation of the accuracy of the Breathalyzer (1) (d) Estimation and metabolism of ethylalcohol (1)	7 suggestions, all covered by topics in left hand column, 4 concerning 1 (a), 2 concerning 1 (d), 1 concerning 1 (e).

Current Research	Suggestions
(e) Assessment of value of vapour phase chromatography for determination of alcohol in urine (1) (f) Comparison of enzymic and chemical methods for determination of alcohol in blood and urine (1)	
2. BALLISTICS (a) Methods for graphical examination of striation marks (1) (b) Historical aspects of the use of small arms (1)	Comparison of the lethal potentialities of all firearms (1).
3. HAEMATOLOGY (a) Blood group genetics (1 major, 1 minor) (b) Stability of carbon monoxide in dried blood (1) (c) Age of blood stains by use of reflected light methods (1) (d) Serology of hair and of adipocere (1)	21 suggestions, all concerned with age, sex, group and detection of blood.
4. LEGAL (a) Review of Law concerned with blood and blood groups (1) (b) Factors involved in recidivism, attempted suicide and remanding in custody (1) (c) Collection of evidence illustrating the necessity for bringing substantive law into line with modern medical knowledge (1) (d) Review of the application of the Homicide Act, 1957 (1) (e) History of legal medicine (1)	(i) Methods for the most effective presentation of expert evidence (2). (ii) Collection of evidence indicating the necessity for further control of industrial products (e.g. descriptions and information concerning drugs, gas, and new pharmaceutical products) (3). (iii) Reviews of the functions of Coroners (2), of the Firearms Act (1), of deficiencies in cremation certification (1), of dogmas current in divorce courts (1).
5. PATHOLOGY AND ANATOMY (a) Occurrence and nature of lipids in serum and arteries in coronary thrombosis (2) (b) Drowning and resuscitation – diatom studies and lung pathology (1 major, 3 minor) (c) Studies concerned with causes, pathology and enzymology of sudden death of young human beings (6) (d) The distribution of elements in teeth (1) (e) Assessment of age from teeth (2) (f) Establishment of sex, age, stature and ethnic group from bodily remains (3) (g) Study of decompression sickness (1) (h) Pathology of cerebral anoxia (1 major) (i) Histological changes in isolated myocarditis (1) (j) Significance of pulmonary embolism in traumatic pathology (1 major) (k) Pathology of ante-mortem fear, and diagnosis of ante-mortem anoxia (1 major) (l) Histochemistry of gunshot wounds, and forensic exfoliate cytology (1)	5 suggestions concerning 5 (e) & (f) 2 concerning 5 (c) 2 concerning 5 (0) (i) Postmortem features of anoxia (2) (ii) Development of reliable methods for the establishment of virginity (1) (iii) Establishment of the sequence of occurrence of multiple injuries sustained in a very short time (1). (iv) Clarification of factors influencing the rate of growth of hair (1). (v) Applicability of Royal Air Force methods of investigating accident pathology to cases involved in other modes of transport (1).

Current Research	Suggestions
(m) Coal gas poisoning – resuscitation (1), kidney failure in (1) (n) Decomposition of the body-formation of adipocere (1 major, 1 minor) and changes in hair (1 major). (o) Pathology of trauma (1) (p) Industrial pulmonary disease (1 major)	
6. PSYCHOLOGY, PSYCHIATRY AND SOCIOLOGY (a) Psychological and social aspects of homicide (1) and suicide (1) (b) Psychology and somatotype photography of Borstal boys (1 major) (c) Comparative system of medico-legal investigation of unexpected and unexplained death (1) (d) Effect of personal susceptibility to injury in actions brought under negligence, trespass and nuisance (1) (e) Re-education of subnormal delinquents with multiple convictions (1)	(i) Problems connected with the term "psychopath" in psychiatry and in law (3). (ii) Relation of mental abnormality to criminal career, and responses to penal treatment (1). (iii) Value of personality tests in assessment and prediction of behaviour (1). (iv) Review of extent and nature of psychiatric treatment given to prisoners (1). (v) Patterns of (1) and social and psychological factors effecting delinquency (2). (vi) Age of puberty and mind–sex relationships in developing adolescents (1). (vii) Nature and causes of anxiety states in Police Officers (1).
7. QUESTIONED DOCUMENTS (a) Detection of erasures (1) (b) Determination of age of documents, typescript and ink writing (1 major, 2 minor) (c) Restoration of obliterated writing and typescript (1 major)	3 suggestions concerning 7 (a), (b) and (c). The use of soft x-rays in detection of chemically bleached ink and in detection of writing on coloured backgrounds (1)
8. TECHNIQUES (MISCELLANEOUS) (a) Development of methods for the photomicrography of skin (1) (b) Applications of colour photography (1). gas chromatography (3) and low angle x-ray diffraction (1) to forensic problems (c) Assessment of the usefulness of differential thermal analysis of soil in forensic work (1) (d) Use of electrophoretic and chromatographic techniques on extracts of seminal stains (1)	1 suggestion concerning 8 (c) (i) Potentialities of square-wave polarography in analysis of pigments and small paint samples (1). (ii) Correlation of surface appearance of skin with underlying histology (1).
9. TIME OF DEATH (a) Rates of cooling of bodies after death (2) (b) Rates of decrease in enzyme activities in post-mortem tissues (1 major) (c) Post-mortem changes in soft tissues with special reference to spermatology (1)	12 suggestions, all concerned with development of reliable methods for establishing time of death. No lines of investigation suggested which are not covered in 9 (a), (b) or (c).

Current Research	Suggestions
10. TOXICOLOGY (a) Development of methods for extraction of toxic substances from biological materials (2 major, 1 minor) (b) Investigations concerning agricultural hazards (1) (c) Barbiturates – absorption and excretion in children (1), paper chromatography (1) and nature of barbiturate blisters (1) (d) Chemistry and pharmacognosy of khat (1) (e) use of activation analysis as a means for detecting and estimating poisons (1 major) (f) Effects and detection of doping in racehorses (1 major) (g) Microtechniques in alkaloid chemistry (1 major, 1 minor) (h) Toxicology of oil products (1 major) (i) Development of colour test for fluorides (1) (j) Dose/tissue relationship and symptomatology (1)	2 suggestions concerning 10 (a) 1 suggestion concerning 10 (c) 1 suggestion concerning 10 (f) 1 suggestion concerning 10 (g) 3 suggestions concerning 10 (j) (i) Development of infra-red spectrophotometric methods for use in toxicology (2). (ii) Isolation and estimation of fluoroacetamide and fluoroacetic acid in tissue (1). (iii) Systematic investigation of the metabolism and toxicology of tranquillizers and other new drugs (3). (iv) Investigation of the effects of drugs on driving (1). (v) Systematic investigation of the excretion products of common labile poisons (1). (vi) Development of methods for determination of arsenic other than by electrolytic techniques (1).
11. TRACE SUBSTANCES (a) Identification of paper and plant fibres, with particular reference to the use of the polarizing microscope (1) (b) Development of micromethods for comparative analysis of soil (1)	2 suggestions concerning 11 (b) (i) Development of methods for the identification of natural and man-made fibres (6). (ii) Development of methods for the identification and analysis of glass, paints, oils and synthetic polymers (5).
12. UNCLASSIFIED (a) Survey of Clinical Forensic Medicine (6) (b) Medical and design factors causing air craft accidents (1) (c) Nature of accident cases in the aged (1)	(i) Development of reliable methods for detecting, distinguishing and ageing stains – semen, saliva, perspiration and urine (7). (ii) Investigation into entomological aspects of various types of crime (1). (iii) Classification of anaesthetic deaths in terms of safety techniques (1). (iv) Effects on occupants of forces encountered in aircraft accidents (1). (v) Investigation of the physical fitness of licence holders involved in accidents (1).

Appendix "C"

Distribution of Research Activities among Institutions

The following table shows the number of persons who returned questionnaires and are actively engaged in research in forensic science in relation to the type of institution in which they do their research work. In general, those persons engaged on research on a major time basis have one or more assistants whereas those engaged on a minor time basis tend to work alone.

Institutions	Major	Minor
Home Office and other government Forensic Science Laboratories	3	18
Hospitals and other NHS Institutions	2	11
University Departments	9	18
Industrial and other Institutions	2	16

9(1&2) - 1968: Education in the Forensic Sciences

Acting on the suggestion of Prof. Francis Camps, the CIBA Foundation convened a small informal Working Party representing science, medicine, therapeutics, physics, chemistry, and the law, to discuss education in forensic medicine and science. This was held on the 2nd May, 1969, under the Chairmanships of Sir Charles Cunningham and Sir Frederick Lawton, Q.C., and I was invited to participate – partly as Secretary of the Society and partly to present the viewpoint of the non-official forensic scientists

That a problem exists in this field is beyond question. As Secretary of the Society I receive about 100 letters a year asking "How can I become a forensic scientist?" Most of them, it is true, come from youthful aspirants who have probably been inspired by television, but many are serious enquiries from people of undergraduate or graduate standing. They all receive replies rather inadequately I fear, because it is difficult to know what to advise except perhaps in the case of graduates, who can at least be referred to the courses run by the University of Strathclyde.

The problem as I see it is two-fold, firstly to supply trained men for the future, and secondly, to establish a standard of qualification which the Courts will recognise as indicative of a person fit in every respect to give evidence on forensic science matters (see Grant, The Problems of the Defence Expert, Edinburgh Symposium, 1969). The first is of course, the greater and more urgent necessity. In the past, the sound grounding of general science provided by a good Honours university degree has enabled the scientist or medical man to adapt his knowledge to forensic problems with little difficulty, and experience has filled in the gaps. However, with the increasing sophistication of scientific methods and the greater measure of specialisation continually being imposed on the scientist, this method cannot be regarded as a real solution to the problem of training experts to assume the considerable responsibility of providing and presenting evidence in Courts of Law. The obvious and only answer would appear to be a specialised training course at graduate level for those who wish to take up forensic science as a career; the problem then arises – how is such a course to be realised.

As always, the question of cost looms large. Actually the annual intake of forensic scientists of what may be described as the elite category is not large, and in times of financial stringency as at present, the provision of a special course by direct Government grant might have to be balanced against other causes which might be regarded in official quarters as more deserving or more urgent. There does however, appear to be a simpler answer to this problem, namely the provision of special part-time courses by Colleges of Science in the more important centres. I have in mind something analogous to the excellent Branch E course in food and drugs for the Fellowship of the Royal Institute of Chemistry, and which I took myself many years ago, at the then

Chelsea Polytechnic. This Fellowship has come to be recognised for many years as an essential qualification for the post of Public Analyst, and something along the same lines could surely be organised jointly by the professional bodies involved in the disciplines of the forensic scientist, such as chemistry, physics and biology, with forensic medicine probably as a separate course.

In my days classes of this kind were held in the evenings, and their success depended on the initiative and interest of the individual prepared to sacrifice his spare time for the purpose. Nowadays however, daytime release and sandwich courses make such further education much easier to acquire, and the system allows participants to follow a gainful career while training for the more specialised branch of science. Something of this nature could probably be operated within the present scheme of higher education, and the comparatively small classes involved should not involve a major financial burden. Thus, specialist lecturers would be drawn from the ranks of existing forensic scientists, who would lecture on their own particular subject and be paid accordingly, so that only a small full-time staff would be required to instruct on the general background aspects of the course.

However, lectures and laboratory work alone do not make a forensic scientist, and the course should include opportunities for seeing the law in action, and possibly also, of obtaining scene-of-crime and court experience.

The importance of all this needs no emphasis to members of the Society. Successful completion of such a course and passing an examination of appropriate stringency, would provide a hallmark for the forensic scientist; and if the scheme is conducted under official or other accepted auspices, then it could well become a qualification recognised in the Courts of Law for the description of a forensic scientist. One can even visualise international recognition of such a qualification, since few countries have anything equivalent to it already.

As one of the few non-official members of the CIBA Working Party, I felt constrained to emphasise continually that any such scheme of training and qualification, with the facilities for instruction that it provided, should be made available on an equal footing to the bona fide private forensic scientist, who, is usually called to give evidence by the Defence. I have already emphasised in these columns the possibility and danger of the extinction of this species, and here may be at least a partial solution to the problem. There is however, one very important aspect of the matter which cannot easily be solved in this way, and this is the case of the non-official expert who specialises in one comparatively restricted aspect of forensic science; for instance, handwriting, car accidents or photography. Such a person can justifiably be described as a scientific expert in his own subject in every sense of the term, but he often has little or no general scientific background of university degree standard, and the problem of bringing him into the suggested scheme of qualification could involve difficulties. Yet in fairness, he should not be excluded from acquiring a suitable qualification. The problem is likely to cure itself in the passage of time, when specialists in such fields will be drawn only from the ranks of graduates, who will acquire the general qualification and specialise afterwards.

This question of the training of the forensic scientist was discussed at some length by some sections of the recent Fifth International Meeting of Forensic Sciences at Toronto. The feeling common to all the discussions I heard was that basic scientific training to graduate standard is essential; that students should have a ground knowledge of the various aspects of forensic science, including extra-mural work; and that specialisation in any particular one of them should come afterwards possibly through the medium of working experience.

It is good to know the CIBA Foundation discussion is unlikely to be the last word on this subject. There is however, much to be done in establishing and working out the details for the training courses and in setting up the examining and qualifying body. Most of the persons best qualified to assist in the implementation of this work are members of the Forensic Science Society and/or The British Academy of Forensic Sciences. This pinpoints another common objective of the two bodies, and strengthens still further the case for amalgamation.

J.G.

11(1) - 1971: What is the Future for the Study and Practice of the Forensic Sciences in Britain?

It is a matter of simple observation that in the present state of the forensic sciences contradictory trends are at work. In recent years there has been in many quarters, but especially in Britain and in the United States, an increasing literature of forensic science. Yet this is occurring at a time when academic instruction in these fields is, at any rate in the United Kingdom, apparently in decline. Previous editorials have drawn attention to the deplorable fact that forensic medicine has ceased to be a subject of study at several Universities, and that great difficulties exist in the way of training the forensic pathologist of the future. A crisis situation is foreseen in a few years' time when most of the present forensic pathologists come to retire. In this situation only the London teaching hospitals, Sheffield and certain Scottish Universities have so far been able to retain their forensic medicine departments while facilities for laboratory training of forensic scientists is also fairly strictly limited. In Scotland forensic medicine is still traditionally taught to most medical and law students though even there it began to degenerate when the Regius Chair in Edinburgh remained unfilled. Only in Strathclyde University is there any formal course of instruction for forensic scientists as such. Where the materials are increasingly available on which teaching and research in forensic science might proceed it is a pity that fewer students are enabled to set themselves to the task.

To be honest, however, there are shortcomings also in the literature. Most lawyers, for whom the science is primarily conceived, are too busy to take it seriously. Too little interchange of ideas takes place between the English speaking areas where the publications circulate with which most of the members of this Society are familiar, and the French and German and Eastern European areas where much good work is done. Though Continental literature takes a fair cognisance of the published work of the English-speaking parts of the world it is too rarely that this situation is reciprocated. Even within the English speaking domain there is evidence of partisanship and preference which restricts in some degree the exchange of ideas and information and reduces the spread of a common pool of knowledge. And the continuing duplication of the major societies remains a byword.

It is interesting to speculate whether British entry into the Common Market, which would increase the mobility of labour and break down many of the barriers presently restricting communications with Continental countries, would also improve the exchange of personnel and of technical information and experience, and reduce the difficulties of evaluating and applying the work being undertaken elsewhere.

On the legal side there is no doubt that entry into the Common Market would profoundly affect some areas of the law such as commercial and industrial law, and would exert a more subtle influence on other aspects of law such as evidence and procedure. Whether the influence of Continental attitudes to the criminal process, the concept of expert evidence as a guiding force for the Court ratl.er than a partisan weapon, and the rationalising and drawing together of the British legal systems in face of the broadly similar Continental systems would occur is a matter of speculation, but such tendencies would surely exist.

It does seem that a wider knowledge of foreign languages and perhaps a greater degree of Continental study and exchange training will be required of the future forensic scientist whether or not formal entry to the Common Market is achieved. In such a situation it is interesting to learn that this Society is shortly to reconsider the terms of its Constitution under which the Council has guided its affairs since 1959. There can be few who would dispute that the Forensic Science Society has made a significant contribution to the practice and the literature of the forensic sciences in Britain throughout that period.

But what measure of achievement can the Society claim in obedience to the primary statement of the purposes of its existence as these stand in its Constitution which opens with the words: "The object of the Society shall be to advance the study and application of forensic science"? Is there not room here for a renewed initiative and a greater emphasis upon the fundamental duty which rests on every generation to pass on what it knows to those who follow?

A.R.B.

16(2) - 1976: The Greeks had a Word for it

And the Scots usually have a phrase which, in all probability, can be neither pronounced nor correctly interpreted by the majority of the English. There is a world of difference between "She's no awfy weel" (She is a little "off colour" – medically speaking) and "She's awfy no weel" (She is at death's door). But then the English, and even the Scots, cannot always agree on what they mean by the same word or phrase: take Education and/or Training for example. In Forensic Science circles, which is what we seem to have been going around in for years with regard to education and training, there has been considerable recent interest as shown by the several meetings and discussions, not to mention editorials, on the subject but there has been relatively little forward movement. However, let us be fair, there have been some encouraging signs of appraisal and action. Dr. Whitehead has reported on the findings of the Forensic Science Society Education Committee (this Journal, October 1975) and the Council of the Society has already implemented one of the proposals in donating an annual prize for the most meritorious student attending the M.Sc. course in Forensic Science at the University of Strathclyde. It must now seek to pursue with vigour other items of its declared policy and not allow the dust to settle on yet another document.

Also relatively new in some British Forensic Science Laboratories are "in house" training courses for graduate entrants – albeit short introductory courses but they are a start and it will be interesting to see how they develop. There is too, I believe, a growing acceptance of the value of appropriate University postgraduate instruction which is geared to motivate and orientate suitable graduates and not only train them in relevant analytical methodology and its forensic applications, but also to guide them as potential expert witnesses.

The ability to communicate in simple, unambiguous terms understandable by non-scientists is a pre-requisite of the successful forensic scientist and, although the development of this ability may come with practice, its initiation is an essential part of early training. So, with the proper utilization of the educational facilities already available in Britain, the prospects for the training of entrants at Scientific Officer level can quickly brighten, even though the vagaries of the recruiting system and the stop–go nature of recruitment to the Forensic Science Service still cast their clouds.

There are, of course, other levels of training in forensic science as such, whether for technicians on the one hand or graduates requiring refresher courses on the other: those areas also require the attention which they deserve and which they now get in relation to some other professions.

Quite apart from continuing to study during the practice of their particular sciences, forensic analysts should increasingly participate in educating others on the applications of their work-the extremely wide range of application of science to problems connected with both Civil and Criminal Law. Here again, action on the part of the Council of the Forensic Science Society in producing a Directory of Independent Consultants should help in the creation of new contacts between scientists and lawyers, and in the promotion of the use of forensic science. Of course the role of the scientist and the value of his work in providing information and opinion for the Courts is well recognised, if not always fully appreciated, by the police but with them, as with lawyers, there is often a communication gap to be bridged. I have read elsewhere and in another context that discussion requires of a participant two things – comprehension and the appropriate vocabulary: this is most certainly true in the producer – consumer dialogue so necessary if we are to achieve the full and effective use of forensic science in our Courts. It is for the scientific expert to appreciate that "on the day" it is the words, and the way in which they are used that count most: equally, it is for the lawyer to realise that the expert in the witness box may only answer the questions which are put to him – he cannot proffer unsolicited comment! Perhaps we each recognise the other's problems but a greater understanding of each other's language would surely reduce the bilateral unease so often associated with the interpretation of science for the law. It is all a matter of education. For too long we have merely looked at the problems without doing very much to solve them. We must improve the operation of the present system or, as suggested by the Society's immediate past President, and others, work to change the system – either should be possible. In the words of Robert F. Kennedy, "Some men see things as they are and say, why?: I dream things that never were and say, why not?".

Frank Fish
Glasgow,
Scotland.

44(4) - 2004: Wither Academic Forensic Science?

(Editorial)

Robert Forrest

Academic forensic science at British Universities appears to be flourishing; or is it? Currently some 53 British Universities invite applications from school leavers and others for courses with the word "forensic" somewhere in the title. If entrants to those courses hope to be forensic scientists or criminalists (Scene of Crime Officers) then some of them, perhaps most of them, will be severely disappointed. I would happily accept a paper for this journal describing surveys of the occupational history of recent alumni of such courses; despite putting out some feelers, so far no such paper has been received.

The truth is, of course, that the problem lies with the way British Universities are funded. It is, perhaps, unfair to suggest that the 19 members of the Russell group of universities, the British Ivy League, are not interested in teaching undergraduates as a group, but they are very interested indeed in getting in research grants from prestigious grant awarding organisations. My own two children, both at Russell group universities, have had no complaints about their teaching. They do not seem to have experienced the FO-FO* teaching technique so popular on some courses where academics are under extreme pressure to get grants and publications rather than to teach those who come to University to learn. Others, in particular some medical students, complain bitterly about such teaching methods. And some employers apparently do not like the products of such courses. Most students doing forensic science courses at undergraduate level have the benefit of experiencing classic face-to-face teaching in lecture theatres, laboratories and tutorials. The forensic component of such courses needs input from genuine forensic practitioners. Practical exercises such as counting the number of tablets in simulated stomach content may be budget friendly but they don't help develop the skills and knowledge that the students need to build on.

Very few of the Russell group of universities offer undergraduate courses in forensic science. It may be that they don't need to offer them to get students into their chemistry and other hard science courses from which future forensic scientists will develop. Hard Science is losing its popularity in many universities. An important factor in the strategic decision making process of many non-Russell universities is that if you can combine a course in a relatively unpopular subject such as chemistry with superficially attractive forensic modules, some of which might actually be taught by forensic scientists with real experience of practice, others of which might not be, then you have a bait that can be used to entice applicants to take the hook of an otherwise unpopular course. The glitter of CSI Miami might translate to increased recruitment for the Giggleswick University College's nice new course in forensic actuarial studies. (I apologise to any university

---

*"FO-FO; an acronym that can be politely translated as "depart rapidly from my presence and find out for yourself".

that actually offers a course in forensic actuarial studies; no insult is intended and I would be delighted to consider any research-based paper that the staff of that department might wish to submit to this journal). When a university starts offering combined degrees in Forensic Investigation and Religious Studies one might think that this trend has perhaps gone a little too far. The Holy Inquisition put away its investigative tools many years ago and Chesterton's Father Brown was only ever a fictional character. The problem with these combined study courses is, of course, that in real life the scientific knowledge comes first and forensic practice comes next. You can't be a forensic scientist without being a scientist. A three year combined studies course with a forensic component at an English university is going to be pushing it to turn out someone with the skills to be employable as much more than a laboratory aide or to benefit from a one year taught masters course in forensic science. Four year courses, such as the standard Scottish undergraduate courses or MChem courses, are much more appropriate.

There is some indication that the Russell group of universities may be voting with its feet; they are research and not teaching driven and some appear to perceive their Forensic Pathology departments, which are largely staffed by practitioners, as anachronisms. These departments might make major contributions to teaching and be largely self-funding by their practice, but they do not generate the research income so beloved by Russell group vice-chancellors. The cynics divide vice-chancellors into two classes; those who wish they had a medical school and those who wish they hadn't. The vice-chancellors who have medical schools can perhaps also be divided into two classes; those who haven't got departments of forensic pathology and those who wish they hadn't. Getting rid of the department of forensic pathology might enhance a medical school's performance at the next Research Assessment Exercise and hence its income from central funds, but it won't do a great deal for the ability of its graduates to fulfil such basic tasks as the accurate completion of certificates of the fact of death. It is probably mere coincidence that Dr Shipman graduated from a medical school with a department of forensic pathology (since closed) and killed a substantial proportion of his victims in the hinterland of a medical school without a department of forensic pathology. The point is that universities funded by grant income and not by student numbers may see forensic departments of any flavour as being a less than desirable asset.

If I could wave a magic wand and put things to rights what would I do? Well, apart from whatever it takes to get truly joined up government, which may not actually be compatible with the democratic process, what I would do is this: I would encourage the development of four year undergraduate courses in England and Wales in which students who wanted to become forensic scientists got a thorough grounding in the one science of their choice and an overview of the other important sciences that support forensic practice, followed by sufficient exposure to the realities of forensic science work to be capable of being taken on as competent trainees on graduation, or to proceed to taught or research higher degrees. I would ensure that all universities who offered undergraduate courses with "forensic" in their title had to publish in their prospectuses accurate details of the career destinations of their graduates. Finally, I would encourage the development of research-based academic departments of forensic science and forensic pathology in the Russell group of universities.

48(2) - 2008: Educating the Next Generation

In 2004 the Science, Engineering, Manufacturing and Technology Alliance (SEMTA) report on Forensic Science: Implications for Higher Education was published [1]. A year later, [March 2005], the House of Commons Select Committee on Science and Technology seventh report, "Forensic Science on Trial" [2] was unveiled. Within this document was a section on education in forensic science in which higher education providers were heavily criticised for their "seeming" exploitation of the interest amongst young people in forensic practice by engaging in the proliferation of forensic science courses. The report stated

> "A search of the Universities and Colleges Admission Service website for "forensic" undergraduate courses produces a list of 401 degree courses at 57 universities. These range from "Forensic Science" through to "Forensic Science and

Human Resource Management....." "Citizenship Studies and Forensic Science"...... and "Football Technology and Forensic Computing" ....the expansion in provision of forensic science degrees "does not reflect the limited employment prospects in forensic science nor is it in response to employers in the sector"....rather,... the growth was a result of student interest in forensic science, which was, at least in part, stimulated by television dramas featuring forensic scientists and high profile coverage of forensic science in books and by the media."

Evidence was also given that a large proportion of the forensic science courses

> "provided poor preparation for a career in forensic science and were 'a savage waste of young people's time and parents' money'...... degree courses and other higher education opportunities [were] of widely differing standards and content, often hybrid in order to attract a wide range of students, often unsuited to the needs of employers, and sometimes encouraging unrealistic employment expectations among students"

Forensic science providers stated that the educational requirement for prospective employees at reporting officer level remained a good science degree (chemistry, biochemistry, genetics etc.) and that any 'forensic science' qualification should be at masters level.

While the influence of popular fiction, television, film and the media in general is, probably, at this point undeniable, it has arguably also given rise to unrealistic expectations. The increase interest by young and old alike in forensic science and crime scene investigation has been well argued over the last number of years. Indeed an internet search for the so called 'CSI effect' results in over 250,000 web sites when searched on Google and even has its own Wikipedia page [3], so it must be true! The necessity to deliver complicated scientific evidence to a CSI loving audience of jurors with perhaps unrealistic expectations of what we can do, how fast we can do it and with what certainty we can link items together is a continuous challenge. Unfortunately there are also some police officers and legal practitioners who also fall under the CSI spell.

The report also emphasised the fact that, while the number of forensic science and related courses were increasing, the numbers of science courses (chemistry and physics in particular) were decreasing. Unfortunately this decline has to a certain extent continued in the three years since the select committee report was issues. Some have advocated that the continued success of "forensic" named courses should be capitalised upon and that it should be possible to 'teach science through forensic science'. On reflection, I have a number of problems with this statement. On the one hand, forensic science is perhaps a useful media by which to encourage students' interest in the fundamental sciences, but (in my view) one cannot become a competent forensic scientist without first becoming a competent scientist in the specific field of study. In its most fundamental form, forensic science is an application of scientific knowledge, skills, practice and evaluation, not a fundamental field of study in its own right.

The general consensus of the 2005 Select Committee report was that both forensic science and other science employers considered a degree in chemistry or some other pure science to be preferable to a degree in forensic science. While these were general comments and there were also a number of institutions praised for the quality of their 'forensic' degree programs and the resultant employment of their graduates within the sector. Also of interest was that at around the same time [2004/2005] similar discussions were taking place with the US and Australian higher education and forensic science sectors which were facing a similar, though not quite as dramatic, issue in relation to the growth of forensic science courses in their own countries.

All of this was four years ago, so where are we now?

The Select Committee reported 401 undergraduate degree courses at 57 institutions. When I checked the UCAS [4] web site in early March [2008] there were a staggering 482 undergraduate courses offered by 70 institutions. More than 20% of the 320 UK higher and further education providers now offer an undergraduate course with 'forensic' in the title. So much for the 'forensic education' bubble bursting! Forensic science and football technology (thankfully) is no longer offered but other courses such as, forensic science and music, American studies and forensic science, dance and movement and forensic studies and forensic science and tourism are still advertised. Probably a more concerning development is that since 2004/5, the number of UK postgraduate courses with 'forensic' in the title has grown from around 15 to 112 available for the next academic year offered by no less than 47 higher education institutions. The cynic within me wonders whether this has occurred as a direct response to the forensic science providers comments within the Select Committee report which made the point that the forensic science education for prospective employees should be at postgraduate level.

These statistics beg the question as to what is now being done to try to grapple with the interaction between the higher education providers and the forensic science service providers in order to develop sensible courses which provide the graduates with at least some hope of employment within the sector? In 2006, The United Kingdom forensic science education group (UKFSEG) was established with the aim (amongst others) to provide a link between higher education providers and forensic science providers and trainers. However the number of higher education providers who actually attend and potentially interact with this group are still few which is not to say that the potential for wider engagement is not there. The higher education academy has also established a forensic science special interest group (sig) to provide resources and information accessible to the wider higher education community. The recently established [2007] Forensic Science Advisory Council (FSAC) has also, as part of its terms of reference, highlighted the importance of interacting with the higher education sector. Indeed the UKFSEG has a seat at the table and provides an opportunity for direct communication and consultation between the higher education sector and the forensic science community where consultation will (one hopes) include and reflect the views of the higher education sector as widely as possible.

The 2005 Select Committee recommended that the Forensic Science Society (which was able to nominate a forensic scientist to the Forensic Science Advisory Council) establish a higher education accreditation scheme for the forensic science component of undergraduate courses. Very recently this has been expanded to cover postgraduate degree provision. The undergraduate accreditation scheme went live in 2006, and to date 11 UK Universities delivering between them 28 undergraduate and 4 postgraduate courses (provided by only 2 institutions) have been accredited. So far, only one undergraduate course in the UK has been fully accredited by the both the Royal Society of Chemistry and the Forensic Science Society giving an indication, perhaps, of the degree of underlying science available within the degree courses on offer. A number of other undergraduate courses have also been recognised by the RSC. Some higher education institutions are interacting with Skills for Justice as a preferred route to link their course work with professional practice which hopefully will ensure that a standard credible within the profession is reached. More recently, Skills for Justice and the Forensic Science Society are joining up their thinking and discussing the way forwards together in relation to the further development of accreditation schemes which may be applicable to education within the sector at the various levels.

It would be fair to say that between the FSAC, Skills for Justice and the Forensic Science Society initial steps are at least being taken in the UK to try to provide appropriate information for prospective students in relation to course choice in the forensic science area. Whether this information will help guide the future generation of forensic scientists to find an educational path that will ultimately benefit the profession remains to be seen.

References

1. House of Commons, Science and Technology Committee Forensic Science on Trial Seventh Report of Session 2004–05.
2. http://en.wikipedia.org/wiki/CSI_Effect [accessed 08/03/08].
3. Science, Engineering, Manufacturing and Technology Alliance (SEMTA) report 2004.
4. http://www.ucas.ac.uk/ [accessed 08/03/08].

Niamh Nic Daéid

48(4) - 2008: Letter to the Editor

Dear Madam,

Thank you for your editorial "Educating the next generation" summarizing the plight – if that is the right word – of forensic science education at British Universities. Would you permit me to offer a view from a Canadian perspective.

It seems it is at the postgraduate level where recent UK growth has been most startling, but not surprising – it is where enrolments most equate with income. In principle, there should be less likelihood of this trend emerging in Ontario. New postgraduate degree programs must be approved by the Ontario Council on Graduate Studies. Masters and Ph.D. students are guaranteed funding at Ontario Universities – if they can meet the admissibility standards. Are any places on the 112 postgraduate forensic programs in the UK supported by research council scholarships.

The horizon is not universally bright, however. "Professional" Masters are exempt from student funding guarantees and there is a possibility that deregulated programs could be introduced – again for reasons that are more fiscal than academic. In the Canadian context, this would result in forensic science students paying fees subsidizing infrastructure and staff resources for the shared benefit of other science students who do not pay fees, but receive funding. A Masters in Forensic Science hardly offers the financial prospects of an MBA and I sincerely hope Canada heeds the British experience and does not follow this route, but the possibility of it brings me to the crux of my letter, which is the situation of forensic science as a peer discipline in the academy.

It seems more than evident that the problems faced in the professional practice of forensic science and medicine relate to inadequacies in training and research. The social and economic costs of miscarriages of justice are huge, and even a consideration limited to English speaking jurisdictions shows these occurrences to be continual and widespread. Education and research are in the realm of the universities, but – despite the remit – academia is ill equipped to deliver.

Even when accreditation ensures scientific and professional criteria are met, I suggest that a fundamental piece of the academic jigsaw is still missing – that is, high quality academic research. Despite the plethora of degree programs, how many universities can be said to be conducting internationally prominent curiosity driven research in forensic science or medicine? How can graduate degree programs be of any substance without a forensic science graduate research training environment supported by real forensic science research faculty? How can there be research in forensic science and medicine without proper funding council support.

Accreditation may again help. The American Academy of Forensic Sciences requires that forensic science be treated equally to the other sciences and this criterion offers a route to academic development – although cynics may wonder where the other sciences are treated so badly.

Experience may indicate forensic science is used to prop up the moribund, but with advocacy a more collegial and symbiotic arrangement might prevail. Similarly, one anticipates the profession would like to see their science have a proper place in the academy – and all that goes with it. Perhaps it is an advocacy issue.

The alternative is likely to be more poor science, more miscarriages of justice and more adverse governmental commissions

Martin Evison
Forensic Science Program, University of Toronto, Canada

Editor's response,
The landscape of forensic science research is very complex. A common understanding between the stakeholders (including end users, practitioners and academic community) of exactly what we mean by 'forensic science research' has not been achieved. Neither do we collectively understand what we are trying to research and why, and/or how to conduct research that will have meaning and can be appropriately contextualized to the requirements of the criminal justice system. Academic institutions, the professional agencies and end users have to work together to achieve a successful outcome and to be in a position to influence the provision of, and

secure core funding for high level, high quality and high impact research. This means each of us understanding and respecting the landscape of the other and rising to the challenge

Science and Justice **48** (2008) 196

48(4) - 2008: Letter to the Editor

Forensic science on trial – still! Response to "Educating the next generation" [Science and Justice, 48 (2008)]

Dear Madam,

Forensic science education in the UK at undergraduate level has been around for over a decade, it is clearly expanding and will continue to do so for as long as there is an interest in science, the criminal law system and as long as they both continue to be portrayed and glamorised on the television, radio and in the written media. The continued public excoriation of the quality of pedagogic provision by its own industry appears not only unfair; it is now largely unfounded and incorrect. If the forensic science community cannot start to portray a more positive and accurate picture of itself in the 21st century then it will be guilty of a self-fulfilling prophecy of destroying its own well earned credibility. Clearly, 10 years ago now, when the public interest in forensic science directed failing science courses to adapt their content and create new courses, it was done with a degree of haste as nationally, we watched reports of student numbers falling-off from the traditional courses such as chemistry, biology and physics. However, universities are well versed in course construction and delivery and have strict guidelines for course structure and review of the quality assurance systems for provision, delivery and assessment. It was always going to be the case that in the 'early days' the content was developing, but this is true for any new degree course. We can all look back at our first crime scene assessment and smile with a nostalgic wince, but today, the crime scene scenarios are of such quality, that many academic facilities are shared with local constabularies or other organisations (e.g. H.M. Revenue and Customs)

As to "what is being done to try to grapple with the interaction between the higher education providers and the forensic science service providers in order to develop sensible course which provide the graduates with at least some hope of employment."

The Forensic Science Society accreditation was the first creditable step for HEIs towards demonstrating a good level of competence; not all universities offering forensic science have yet gone through this process or perhaps never will, depending on their goals. There are currently ongoing discussions between Skills for Justice and the Forensic Science Society. Forensic Science Society accreditation could focus on curriculum content while Skills for Justice 'Skillsmark' accreditation could be more focused on the provider institution. There may be therefore, an opportunity to use accreditation to drive continuous improvement and there are clear benefits in combining the Forensic Science Society and 'Skillsmark' standards.

The quality of all UK degree courses is University accredited which has an international quality mark; UK education is considered the best, so whatever degree people get it is accepted that it is good. It could be suggested therefore, that there is no need for a FS degree to gain a quality mark from organizations such as the FSSoc or SfJ if the end point isn't necessarily a career in forensic science. On this basis, the FSSoc and SfJ would assume a career in forensic science but this isn't necessarily the intention for most HEIs offering FS courses.

As Paul Chin from the Physical Sciences Centre of the Higher Education Academy says "HEIs have their own drivers and that is educating people on courses they want to attend. Science education has to adapt to currently decreasing numbers and if forensic science can attract new students to train as scientists then this means survival for many university departments. In the ever increasing business approach, HEIs need to market courses to attract students and the UK university identity is a good quality mark for attracting students. One example is UCLAN where the chemistry department diversified into forensic science provision to counter the national trend of falling student numbers, to the point where a single honours chemistry course was no longer viable. Having survived dwindling numbers, the department has now managed to start offering pure chemistry again. So one could argue that forensic science kept science provision alive and whether UCLAN were FSSoc accredited or not, this was good for science and for UCLAN. Needless to say, UCLAN offer good quality forensic science provision and engages actively with a range of professional organisations."

The Science and Justice article expresses concern that "whilst forensic science is...a useful media by which to encourage students' interest in the fundamental sciences...one cannot become a competent forensic scientist without first becoming a competent scientist in the specific field of study" one could disagree with this and the evidence lies in the good number of high quality degree classifications obtained at Staffordshire University and indeed at many other universities this summer. It is further confirmed by the fact that many of these graduates have found employment in the sector and are well on their way to a flourishing and successful career.

Forensic Science whilst multi-faceted in its areas of endeavour is indeed a fundamental field of study in its own right and worthy of training to BSc, MSc and PhD levels in HEIs. It is perhaps comparable to saying that whilst entomology or molecular biology (for example) are worthy in their own right, biology per se is not. Just as ballistics or blood spatter (for example) are worthy in their own right, Forensic Science is the corollary to biology in this example. Both are not mutually exclusive so it is possible to be educated as a scientist in conjunction with developing forensic science skills. The former does not preclude the latter.

There are now a number of organisations working together which 5 years ago either did not exist or would not have worked together even if they had. There has clearly been a steep learning curve for HEIs in the development of courses, teaching strategies and up-skilling of academic staff in order to deal with the new rigours of Forensic Science teaching. There has to be credit given to academia in the UK for achieving this to such a level now, that Forensic Science providers are engaging in innovative and collaborative ways with HEIs and indeed employing the graduates that come from these courses.

HEIs are now being seen as strong partners in research strategies for a number of providers and the growth of the Forensic Institute Research Network (FIRN) and the annual international FORREST conferences are demonstrations of the valuable input that HEIs can offer to the furtherance of new knowledge for use in a forensic context. The annual 'Regional Forensic Science Student conference' held as part of the FIRN agenda, is a testament to the success and quality of basic yet robust research that is now being conducted at undergraduate level within Forensic Science courses.

The opportunity for undergraduate and postgraduate students to present their research as a poster or as a talk to their peer group, is a unique transferable learning experience for them and shows the wider academic/practitioner community that new knowledge is being added to the forensics research arena.

Just as each summer the media driven stories of the "downgrading of GCSE and A-level qualifications have become dumbed-down from the golden-years" resurface, the Forensic Science teaching community periodically is beaten by the media-driven story of 'Forensic Science and football technology' combinations. It is true, that it is a requirement of many universities that modular courses are available in many varied combinations. This results in some of the more curious combinations being a possibility. The reality however, is that course leaders would counsel prospective students down a more appropriate pathway of combinations and so 'Forensic Science and macramé' would never materialise on a degree certificate.

It is not reasonable to state in the article that "one cannot become a competent forensic scientist without first becoming a competent scientist" why is one mutually exclusive from the other? – Clearly they are not; one can become a competent forensic scientist at the same time as one is becoming a competent scientist. Otherwise one might argue, for example, that one could not become a competent biomedical scientist before first becoming a competent scientist. This is clearly not how biomedical science is taught or how graduates in the biomedical sciences are trained.

Clearly, organisations such as the United Kingdom Forensic Science Education Group (UKFSEG) and the Forensic Institute Research Network have acted as conduits to facilitate dialogue and interaction between the higher education providers and the forensic science providers. It is incorrect in the article to say that the numbers of HE providers that actually attend and potentially interact with the UKFSEG are still few. The UKFSEG whilst still 'new kids on the block' is well thought of amongst academics and is keenly supported as I personally evidenced at a UKFSEG special interest group meeting that I presented and chaired a session at in Northumbria last year.

In fact, Staffordshire University is hosting a Special Interest Group meeting later in 2008. Equally, the Forensic Institute Research Network in collaboration with the Higher Education Academy – Physical Science Centre host very successful and internationally attended annual conferences called FORREST (FORensic RESearch and Teaching). All are most welcome to attend to present both scientific and pedagogic material; the next conference will be hosted at Liverpool John Moore's University around June 2009.

The interaction with the recently established Forensic Science Advisory Council with the Higher Education sector and the growing number of universities successfully gaining Forensic Science Society accreditation is a testament to the interaction with the industry and the further development and improvement of provision to put the graduates in the best possible position of obtaining appropriate employment upon graduation. The fact that 11 UK universities have now gained FSS accreditation is not evidence that the other university courses are of lesser quality. It is simply that this sort of process takes time. It is a very positive move that Skills for Justice and the Forensic Science Society are discussing joint ways forward for accreditation and this should be taken as a positive marker that both organizations have confidence in HE provision.

Undergraduate and Postgraduate students are not naive, they are bright, articulate, customer focused and fully cognisant of the UK and indeed global jobs market in forensic science. All forensic science courses that I have been involved with in terms of running them or validating the initial degree, have a component in which students are given instruction on how to prepare for work-interviewing techniques, Curriculum Vitae writing and job searching (which is a skill in itself). It could be argued perhaps that we should expect these to be the skills that students come to the university with, or perhaps even have as innate skills, but as it is clearly not the case, so they are taught how to develop these skills. As part of this process, they are selfaware or made aware of the current jobs market.

Once graduated, they hit-the-deck running in applying for work and many of them succeed. Some do not, but that is the nature of any job-market, from accounting to zoo-keeping. The article suggests that it has been due to the efforts of the Forensic Science Advisory Council, Skills for Justice and the Forensic Science Society to "try to provide appropriate information for prospective students in relation to course choice in the forensic science area".

This is unfair to the HE sector who invest a lot of time and money in Open Days and in making academic staff available to chat with prospective students to ensure that they and indeed 'mums and dads' are fully aware of what the education sector and industry expects and what the best choice is for the student.

Each UK University has a Careers Department who work closely with academic colleagues to ensure that information on offer is current and useful.

Paul Chin from the HEA observed that "With the development of forensic science courses our jointly funded SEMTA report: [http://www.heacademy.ac.uk/assets/ps/documents/forensic_science_implications_for_higher_education_2004.pdf] showed that forensic science courses were attracting students who would not otherwise have studied science at all. So this counters the argument that we are not producing more (good quality) scientists. Quite the contrary, and we need a society with more scientifically literate graduates, whether they become forensic scientists or not. Also, it is still relatively early for the statistics from Forensic Science course first destinations, but speaking to Forensic Science students informally, they are very employer aware and know what they want to get from their course. They also know what extra training/postgraduate education they may need if they wish to pursue a career in forensic science. They fully understand HEIs are not trying to dupe them into thinking a forensics course automatically qualifies them for a career in the industry."

Like it or not, many students wish to study for the interest and enjoyment of the subject and still gain good employment in their early careers. Forensic Science isn't the necessary conclusion of a Forensic Science degree, in exactly the same way as any other degree. For example, all engineering graduates don't necessarily want or expect to become engineers.

So, the future is very positive for students and the educational provision of forensic science in the UK. The HE sector is clearly interacting with the industry at a level not possible before. The HE sector has made great strides in upskilling its current academic staff and in integrating experience forensic practitioners into the academic world.

There is a good feeling at conferences and industry based meetings. The words Mickey-mouse are used much less today that they were 5–10 years ago and if anything is proliferating, it is the number of courses and conferences at which HE practitioners and forensic practitioners are sharing the stage and workshop environments.

Forensic Science is a maturing discipline where the research is beginning to blossom. Can the forensic science (practitioner) community claim the same rigour to its research as is undertaken and published by universities? One only has to look how many criminal cases have collapsed due to the 'unauthenticated' forensic science research? The forensic science community should be working in conjunction with HEIs to improve the quality of forensic science research instead of criticising it and in doing so preventing further development to the benefit of everyone.

If we as a joint industry cannot be positive and forward thinking, then the outdated naval-gazing attitude will be the biggest 'criminal' in forensic science provision in the UK.

John P. Cassella
Department of Forensic Science, Faculty of Science,
Staffordshire University, Mellor Building, College Road,
Stoke on Trent, ST4 2DE, United Kingdom

49(1) - 2009: Letter to the Editor

Dear Madam

Forensic science and Mickey Mouse.

I write in response to Professor Cassella's reply (Forensic Science on Trial – still!) to your editorial *Educating the next generation* (Science and Justice, 48 (2008) 59–60). Good forensic science, like good research, is based on (amongst other things) the discovery of reliable facts on which to test hypotheses and base logical arguments. Reliable facts are rare in Professor Cassella's letter which is characterized more by celebratory rhetoric, lack of rigorous argument and patronizing ignorance. There are so many assertions made that it is virtually impossible to deal with them all in a response of reasonable length, so I will limit myself to the most serious and least convincing. Amongst these are: 'research is beginning to blossom'; 'academic research in forensic science is of a higher standard than that done by practitioners'; and 'significant numbers of criminal trials have collapsed as a consequence of poor research done by practitioners'.

The last of these is a serious allegation. If Professor Cassella has evidence which suggests this to be the case he should publish it as it is a matter of public interest. If not, he should withdraw his comment.

In relation to research, the European Network of Forensic Science Institutes (ENFSI) is so concerned about the lack of research capability and capacity in forensic science that it has, for the first time, instituted a research committee to lead and develop this area. ENFSI represents around 60 forensic institutes in Europe including all of the major providers in the UK.[1] Lack of research[2] was also one of the subjects addressed at the recent Forensic Science Society AGM. In my presentation I produced data on research publication rates

---

[1] For more information on this see my recent editorial in Science & Justice Volume 48, Issue 4, December 2008, Page 163.
[2] Fraser, J. 'Why we need more research' Forensic Science Society AGM, Wyboston, 2008.

for various organizations (academic and operational). The average number of peer reviewed papers published in the past decade by universities in the UK that teach forensic science was around 2.6. This is based on papers published in Science & Justice and other (non medical) journals with the word 'forensic' in their title. Two universities account for almost two thirds of all publications and around half of the universities surveyed had not published a single peer reviewed paper in 10 years. The largest number of papers published by a single UK organization (the Forensic Science Service) was 127 in 10 years. By way of comparison, the Chemistry Department[3] of the University of Strathclyde published 122 papers in 2007. In other words the publication rate of the largest UK producer of peer reviewed papers in forensic science roughly equates to one year's publication output for a single department in one university. This data is imperfect since it does not take into account RCUK funding income, the Research Assessment Exercise (RAE) and various other indicators of research activity which I would welcome information on in this journal. Nonetheless it clearly illustrates the immense gulf between forensic research and other disciplines.

From these facts we can safely reject two of Professor Cassella's assertions. Firstly, that 'research is blossoming' since most universities are either not doing forensic research or cannot[4] get it published in peer reviewed journals, and that academics are better researchers than practitioners. We can also identify the latter assertion for what it is – wishful thinking – perhaps picked up at one of the (apparently now diminishing) 'Mickey Mouse' meetings.

This pattern of ignorance and assertion that peppers Professor Cassella's letter provides a general view of forensic science which is about as relevant to the real world as intelligent design is to evolution. He would do better to heed his own advice and try to 'portray a more accurate picture'.

Setting aside Professor Cassella's specific points for the moment to make some more general observations, one wonders where this distorted picture of forensic science which seems to be shared by many academic institutions has come from. At this point I have to speculate as (funnily enough) no research has been done in this area. But if we work from the premise that the vast majority of individuals who teach forensic science have never examined a crime scene, written a statement or given expert evidence in court, then it seems to me that we are off to a bad start. Couple this with the fact that secondary sources of knowledge, books, the web etc are often poor and misleading only exacerbates the situation. Finally, there are partnerships, traditionally a good source of knowledge exchange. But this depends on what knowledge you seek. Some partners are very well informed and good to work with, some are less good, and some are plain bad and ought to be avoided. Some academic institutions appear unable to make these distinctions. It is clear that forensic science teaching cannot be 'research led' and therefore the questions remains: what are the valid knowledge sources of current forensic science teaching? What is truly sad in all this is that the traditional roles and strengths of academia are being set aside in the rush to legitimize and market their apparent expertise, knowledge and experience in forensic science.

The role of academia in forensic science is to generate and communicate new knowledge and seek to improve the current state of affairs by critical reflection and examination. Academia should be addressing the big questions in forensic science of which there are many, including:

- How valuable in educational terms is a degree in forensic science?
- How good is the evidence base for forensic practices?
- Why is there virtually no available funding for forensic research?
- Why is it that police knowledge of forensic science generally remains poor?
- What contribution does science make to justice?

---

[3] The Centre for Forensic Science is one of a number of sections in the Chemistry Department.

[4] Since universities are assessed on research output and this attracts funding, I am assuming that it is unlikely that they carrying out research but do not publish it.

Hardly any of these questions are being researched in any way, for reasons which I explored in my recent presentation at the Society AGM. Academic institutions should be working hard to address these issues as they would provide primary sources of knowledge to enhance their understanding, teaching and experience of forensic science. Such knowledge would also enhance the development of forensic science.

There is an aggrieved tone to Professor Cassella's letter: he seems to feel he is being treated unfairly. If so he should perhaps take a longer view of matters. From my personal experience forensic science has always been on trial – it is something you have to get used to.

Jim Fraser
Centre for Forensic Science, University of Strathclyde, UK

SECTION V: FORENSIC SCIENCE AND THE LAW

The interaction between the legal and scientific professions is, of course, often the ultimate consequence of criminal (and many civil) investigations. Legal procedure has been in existence in one form or another for many years prior to the developments and application of forensic science. Indeed, it is fair to say that at it's highest level, legal practice dictates to forensic practitioners the constraints within which they must work and in particular defines a rigour and structure to which the scientists must adhere.

The interface between science and law, however, is not a comfortable one. The effective use of scientific evidence in court is difficult and often problematic for the lawyers. The legal rules that underpin the introduction and use of such evidence is often poorly understood by the scientists who sometimes struggle to make themselves understood when presenting oral evidence, particularly to the jury. The experience of presenting oral evidence is viewed by many forensic practitioners as challenging and one in which the benefit of experience becomes essential. The understanding of the presented evidence by the tryers of fact is critical. The onus is on the forensic practitioner to deliver their information in complex and sometimes apparently hostile circumstances and on the lawyer to ensure that the experts present the information in a means understandable by the jury.

The difficulties resulting from the presentation of DNA evidence have highlighted the importance of clarity of expression by the scientists and much development work has been undertaken to try to address this issue in particular. The introduction of gatekeeping mechanisms such as the Daubert criteria in the USA to keep so called 'junk science' out of the witness box has been one approach taken to develop structures for the use of scientific evidence. Something similar may ultimately occur in the UK.

A considerable number of editorials have been penned over the years which discuss both the legal process (and in some cases specific legislation) and the interaction between science and the law. The effectiveness of the interaction is difficult to assess and difficult to develop but whether we like it or not the interaction is a central part of our criminal justice systems. The issues highlighted are not new, rather there have been recurrent themes around the requirements of being an expert witness, the use of terminology and the abilities to deliver information with simplicity and clarity.

Fifty Years of Forensic Science: A commentary   Edited by Niamh Nic Daéid
© 2010, John Wiley & Sons, Ltd.

1(2) - 1960: An Expert Witness Looks at the Courts

W. Garner
Consultant Chemist, Richmond, Surrey, England

> *Various differences are described between the work of an expert witness in arbitration cases, in actions in the Civil Courts, and in cases in the Criminal Courts. Comments are made on the duties of the expert in various types of cases. Some of the difficulties experienced in both civil and criminal cases are discussed. An examination is made of some aspects of prosecution evidence in the Criminal Courts.*

Although the words "Forensic Science" are comprehensive and include commercial as well as criminal work, in practice they seem to be mainly associated with the work of the expert witness in the criminal Courts, and the first issue of this Journal would appear to support this interpretation.

The expert witness who works mainly in the commercial Courts finds that a considerable amount of adjustment of outlook is necessary in the criminal Courts, due not only to the different procedure, and even the different arrangement of the Court, but especially to the quite different atmosphere, and the presence of a Jury.

My own work (textiles and chemicals) has been mainly in the Queen's Bench and Chancery divisions, i.e., commercial disputes, patent actions, workmen's compensation cases, and one or two divorces. However, on the criminal side, my experience, though limited, has included quite a variety of cases, ranging from murder, manslaughter, and robbery with violence, down to such things as re-use of National Health Insurance Stamps, and fraudulent misrepresentation under the Merchandise Marks Acts.

Arbitration

In commercial work, there is often a choice between arbitration and a hearing in the Courts. Arbitration has the great advantage that the proceedings are not reported in the press, and indeed are not usually made public at all. A further advantage is that a hearing date can usually be arranged quite quickly, and is a fixed date known well ahead.

One of the most infuriating parts of the work of the expert witness is the inconvenience and waste of time caused by the extraordinary method, if method there be, by which the date of a hearing is arranged in the Courts. I have sometimes thought that it is perhaps a deliberate part of the English system of justice, to arrange for the parties to be kept hanging about in the corridors, until patience is exhausted, and they settle rather than wait any longer.

The fee which the expert witness receives for leaning against a wall for a few hours, does not compensate for the boredom. It is, however, better than the treatment which non expert witnesses have to put up with in the criminal Courts, where they may have to spend some days in a draughty entrance hall, waiting their turn to be called.

The decision whether to arbitrate or not, often depends quite a lot on the expert's opinion. In general, if a case involves difficult technical points, or commercial customs, or trade opinions, my feeling is that it is likely to be dealt with better by an arbitrator who is engaged in the trade himself, than by a Court of law. This is especially so because the Courts seem to me to be inclined to pay excessive attention to the wording of letters or documents, which were written without any thought that some day they would be scrutinised by trained legal minds seeking to find out the precise meaning of phrases. Many a case may have been lost because of some thoughtless letter, written in a hurry, which changed the legal position without altering the commercial position to the mind of a business man.

It is, moreover, extremely difficult to explain, in the witness box, and with the necessary simplicity and brevity, a highly technical matter which perhaps requires a considerable background of knowledge for proper understanding. In the Courts, I have more than once felt that my own attempt had been successful, only to find that on re-examination, Counsel (previously carefully educated in the subject) drew out further explanations, showing that the Judge had been quite misled by me on some important point. A lengthy re-examination is a sign of a poor performance as a witness. Some Judges, of course, do on occasion show real brilliance in getting hold of a complex technical case, but in general I feel that the Courts are rather afraid of science. This difficulty is much greater with a Jury, which can not ask questions. In arbitration, however, before an arbitrator who is himself an expert, the position is much easier for the expert witness, as there is at least a common language.

Sale of Goods Act Cases

When a dispute arises, the expert can come in at one of several stages. The most satisfactory is when he is called in at the first sign of trouble. In some cases, however, he is telephoned the day before the hearing, when the patient is either dead or dying.

The two main cases are (a) the buyer decides to reject the goods, but the seller will not have them back. In this case, the buyer refuses to pay, and the seller issues a writ. The buyer then becomes the defendant, though in some cases he may have to open the hearing. (b) the buyer takes the goods and pays for them, but subsequently finds they are faulty, often in circumstances where he has lost the right to reject. He then becomes the plaintiff in an action for damages. In either case, the main technical aspects centre round the Sale of Goods Act 1893, Sections 13, 14 and 15.

An important difference between commercial and criminal work, is that in the former, the Courts come to a decision on the balance of probabilities, whereas in the latter the prosecution has (theoretically) to prove the case beyond reasonable doubt.

Cases in which one party is one hundred per cent. in the right, rarely get into the Courts, for obvious reasons, except when a large sum of money is involved and a participant is inclined to take a gamble on the Court decision, for the sake of a relatively small increase in the amount at risk, or to gain time. In the ordinary case, both parties have some right on their side. Perhaps, taking the legal and technical points together, the average case shows 40% of right on each side, and the Courts are really asked to decide on the basis of the middle and disputed twenty per cent. Sometimes a case is strong technically and weak legally; sometimes it is the other way about.

Evidence in Chief

The expert witness should realise this position, and should not feel that he may lose the case for his client if he admits or volunteers any facts in favour of the other side. I personally consider that the evidence in chief should be a statement of all the facts, for and against the client, and should indicate clearly that the expert opinion has been reached as a balanced judgment, in the light of all the facts. Cynics, however, say that one should admit any facts the other side can prove.

Counsel do not always have the same idea: they like their client's geese to appear as pure white swans. Consequently it is sometimes difficult to achieve the desired impartial presentation of all the facts, as Counsel may seem to hasten over some parts of his brief.

I feel that this is a mistake. On the lowest level, if an expert has damaging facts dragged out of him during cross examination, it gives the impression that he is taking sides, or endeavouring to conceal something, and this diminishes the weight to be attached to his final opinion. Further, a full statement of facts leaves opposing Counsel with nothing much to get hold of, a rare but desirable state of affairs.

If a client's case will not stand this treatment, it is the duty of an expert to try to keep it out of Court. In a criminal case, where the expert may not have so much influence, he can at least try to ensure that an impartial and balanced statement of the facts is put forward in the witness box. Personally, if I give evidence in Court, this indicates that I believe my client is in the right, on balance, as regards the technical aspects. The expert witness has no right to form an opinion about the merits of the case otherwise. A person may appear to be unscrupulously trying to get out of a contract, but if there are technical facts in his favour, he has the right to expect some reliable person to present these facts to the Court. Further, when the whole of the evidence is heard, there are usually some surprises, on both sides of the case.

There is one special case, however. It sometimes happens that an expert has examined some material, and has formed an opinion adverse to his client, and will obviously not be called upon to give evidence. I think that nevertheless it is his duty to put in an appearance in Court during the hearing. If he does not, the opposition will without difficulty guess the reason. They may even issue a subpoena, and treat the expert as a hostile witness if he refuses to play the desired role. An expert witness is, in the first place, paid a fee to give advice to his client, and the opposition are not entitled to the expert's opinion in a situation of this kind. A friend of mine, in such circumstances, heard by accident that a subpoena had been issued, and thereupon packed a bag and departed for a holiday without leaving his address, until the case was over. The dangers of this possibility are obvious: in one criminal case where I was dealing with textile evidence, I refused to express an opinion upon some broken glass, as I am not an expert on glass, but the prosecuting Counsel told the jury that they might think it significant that I had not given evidence about the glass.

Cross Examination

Although the expert witness should be as impartial as possible in his evidence in chief, which in any case is given on oath, I think that his neutrality can cease at this point. In practice, it often has to cease, because, like the animal which is labelled dangerous, as when attacked it defended itself, he has to support his original facts and opinions against criticism. If he is wise, he will have kept a few things up his sleeve, and will have slightly understated his case in chief, so that cross examination enables him to strengthen his opinions and to show that he could have made his formal evidence stronger in the first place.

An expert usually does a good deal more work than appears from his evidence, and much of this work is merely preparation against possible questions in cross examination. It is certain that if Counsel finds some point has not been investigated, he will suggest to the Court: this is the really vital point in the case, it is very lax of Mr. Expert not to have considered it, and in the absence of such consideration Mr. Expert's opinion cannot be worth much. However, the Judge has been a barrister himself, and no doubt considers such tactics no more than amusing, but I feel that it is a different matter when a jury is involved.

Cross examination of an expert witness should be a discussion between two professional people. Often it is, but even then it can be difficult enough for the expert. It is extraordinary how a case which appears cast iron technically, can land an expert in great difficulties, whilst on the other hand, a case which is rather thin, may go through without the slightest trouble. It is remarkable how difficult Counsel can be, at times, to an expert who knows rather more about the subject than the barrister.

When Counsel treats the expert witness as though he were an interested commercial witness, with a stake in the case, and especially when Counsel attacks the credit of the witness, I think retaliation is justified. There are various ways in which an expert can make Counsel work very hard for his money, if Counsel becomes unpleasant, though I do not propose to discuss them here.

It is useful to watch what notes opposing Counsel is making. In one case, I rather extravagantly said that a certain detergent could be made in an ordinary kitchen. Counsel wrote this down, underlined it, and put a cross against it. Over lunch, therefore, I calculated a kitchen recipe, and when, as expected, Counsel asked in cross examination "Could I make it in my kitchen?" I was able to give him the recipe in terms of eggcupfuls and teaspoons, which was not quite what he expected.

At times the cross examination part of the proceedings is exciting, and perhaps then the witness may give replies or comments which are more emphatic or far reaching than would have been made in cold blood. I do not feel that the expert need lose any sleep about this, because the expert on the other side is no doubt liable to do the same thing in his turn, if he has not done so already.

Cross examination is an extremely powerful weapon, and renders the English system of justice much more searching than the various continental systems in which the expert does not give verbal evidence, but puts his opinions on paper. Theoretically, a considered opinion of this kind appears to have obvious advantages over opinions which are sometimes expressed without opportunity for consideration, and which may be somewhat different from what would have been said after due reflection. However, in practice, my continental colleagues appear to "get away" with paper opinions which would render them liable to be torn to pieces if they gave verbal evidence in the same terms in an English Court.

Counsel

In cross examination, it is very desirable to answer "Yes" or "No" and then stop, if possible. I remember one vital commercial witness who was asked, in a case involving the West Indies, if he was doing any business with Jamaica. He replied "No, not now." Counsel asked the meaning of "not now," and in a few minutes the witness was found to have been engaged in various transactions which had ended by a period in prison. His evidence thereafter did not seem to carry much weight. Counsel told me afterwards, that his question was quite at random.

We do not expect that loquacity on the part of an expert witness will have similar consequences, but the general rule is to give Counsel as little to get hold of as possible. When an expert's evidence has been strong, it is a favourite trick of Counsel to trail as many red herrings as possible, and to confuse the issue with irrelevancies.

Some Counsel, however, frame their questions in such a way that it is not possible to reply "Yes" or "No". The famous example is "Have you stopped beating your wife?" Frequently, after a series of such questions, Counsel accuses the witness of prevaricating, and asks why he cannot reply yes or no to a simple question. On one occasion a particularly irritating Counsel particularly irritated me in this way, and I had to ask him: Do you want the bare truth, or the whole truth?

Occasionally a witness asks a question, and Counsel may snub him by saying "You are not entitled to ask me questions." The position is, however, that the witness can ask what he likes, but Counsel can refuse to reply to a question if a reply is inconvenient. If Counsel thinks of a good reply, he will reply without protest.

The expert should feel under no necessity to be impartial or neutral in the "behind the scenes" part of his work. Here he is paid to be part of a legal team. It is, in fact, his duty: (a) to brief Counsel and solicitors on how to present the technical aspects in the strongest way (b) to state the case which the other side will probably put forward, and to explain what counter measures and counter witnesses should be used (c) to educate Counsel on the general technical background so that he can deal with experts in cross examination.

The expert should also sit behind Counsel in Court, and it is his duty to seize on any mistakes or exaggerations made by any of the opposition witnesses, and especially the opposition expert. There may be a bit of fun to be got out of twisting the tail of the latter, bearing in mind that one's own tail may be within reach also.

Some experts make thoughtless mistakes which can get them into difficulties. In one case, the weight per square yard of some fabrics had been calculated, obviously by logarithms, and had been stated to the second decimal place. This witness was asked the size of the patterns examined, and these proved to be the size of a large postage stamp, which could not be measured to better than half a millimetre. In these circumstances the witness abandoned the second decimal place, then the first decimal place, and was finally in doubt about the unit figure. He was asked what was the accuracy of his weights, and in a moment of aberration said "I don't know what you mean by accuracy." The Judge then said, "Well, Mr. Expert, if you don't, you are the only person in Court who doesn't." This does not help the expert very much in impressing the Court.

Pleadings

I would like to say a word about the Pleadings. In one case where a solicitor was sued for negligence, it was suggested, as one ground, that the Pleadings had not been shown to the expert. The Judge in this case seemed greatly surprised that this ever happens, but solicitors vary a great deal in their practice. Some show the expert nothing, whilst others show him the bundle of correspondence, the full set of Pleadings, Advice on Evidence, and so on. I myself think that it is a very important duty of an expert witness to see the Pleadings very early, in certain types of case, and to make sure that they are a true interpretation in legal terms, of the technical facts.

In one case, some rolls of cloth were alleged to be faulty by reason of some creases which were present in the central part of the width of the cloth. The cloth was also, as is common, folded to half width along the full length, so that, of course, there was a single straight line crease down the centre. The Pleadings alleged that there was "a crease" down the central part of the piece. In the Court, the supplier's Counsel, at a suitable moment, said that he was surprised to find the defect alleged in the evidence was a different defect from that alleged in the Pleadings. He had come prepared to meet the pleaded defect, but in order to meet the evidential defect he would have to call new witnesses from Manchester. If Counsel was not aware of the facts, certainly the suppliers of the cloth were, because they had seen the defective cloth. However, the Court accepted the objection, and the buyer found the case adjourned, the lost costs being to his account. I seem to remember that the parties tossed a penny outside in the corridor, to settle the matter. If it was not in this case, it happened in another.

The expert has, of course, no responsibility at all for the Pleadings, even if he does read them and comment upon them, but it is wise to ask to see them, if the solicitors do not supply them, in many types of case.

The Other Expert

When the expert is acting for the defendant in a case, the evidence of the Plaintiff is usually, though not always, heard first. Here is a position where the expert can not be in the least neutral. He must listen to the evidence, and provide every possible bullet for Counsel to fire in cross examination. A properly carried out combination of forces, may even result in all the desired evidence being elicited from Plaintiff's own witnesses, so that the only reason for the defence expert going into the witness box is to help to qualify for his fee for attendance, on taxation, if his client is successful.

The legal world is a very small one, and an expert who is regularly giving evidence in his own field of work, quickly gets to know the group of Counsel who are popular with solicitors having clients in his field. It sometimes happens, in a case, that the expert knows all the Counsel, and both the solicitors, and maybe both parties to the dispute, whilst the Judge may have heard him give evidence before. The witness who only occasionally gives evidence may "do his best for his client" by stretching the elastic as far as it will go, but an expert who is really interested in litigation should remember that a case is only a case. A Counsel has to be an advocate, but an expert witness should not be.

In the interests of his clients in general and for his own sake also, it is important to try to obtain a reputation for being fair. He should not mind people saying that he is wrong (occasionally, that is), but he should not like anyone to say that he has been biased.

Further, an expert who confines himself to his own field, and does not give evidence about textiles today, and tricycles tomorrow, quickly finds that the expert witnesses who he frequently meets in the Courts, are not numerous. He will probably know all the likely ones by name and reputation, and possibly most of them personally, whilst some may be old friends. Generally speaking, it is unlikely that there will be serious differences about the facts; the differences will be in the relative weight to be given to the facts: that is, in the opinions. In most cases I have been prepared to accept the facts put forward by the opposition witnesses.

In Fleet Street they have a saying: Dog does not eat dog. I personally think that it is a mistake from all points of view, to criticise the expert on the other side, as Counsel sometimes invite one to do. Of course, if he has made a mistake, full use can be made of it, but in my own field the opposition experts have made regrettably few mistakes. Only in the case of one of them, has it struck me as curious how remarkably and invariably coincidental are the opinions of Mr. X and his client. Mostly they are an independent lot, who, if not standing quite vertical in the Courts, are not unreasonably tilted.

Before leaving this aspect of the work, I would like to stress the importance of making a note of any conversations relating to the case. The expert witness does not often have to give evidence about conversations but it does happen. Without these notes, I often can scarcely remember having the conversation at all. In such cases, when in the witness box myself, I have often been impressed by the recollection of the phenomenal memories of business men, who are able to relate, verbatim, conversations of a casual nature which took place some years ago. I would like to know how they do it.

These few notes will have indicated that I have no criticisms of importance about the High Courts and the County Courts. I frankly find such legal work fascinating and satisfying. It has to be admitted that although the aim of the proceedings is justice, the technique is something in the nature of a game of chess, perhaps, before the hearing, and a cricket match during the hearing. As in a cricket match, during the case often nothing much happens for a long time, but when it does happen, it is sometimes very sudden and dramatic, even in an ordinary commercial case, especially when some Counsel are bowling. As in a cricket match, the spectators sit about for a long time on very hard seats, and think how much better they could do the batting, or bowling, themselves. The expert witnesses are usually fairly evenly balanced, and both sides can usually afford to pay for the man they want. In particular, the expert witness usually *is* an expert, with the appropriate qualifications and experience.

Criminal Cases

In the criminal Courts, my limited experience has shown some important differences, not the least of which is that a case can not be "settled". The police never withdraw, and the accused cannot. Usually the accused is at risk regarding his liberty, and occasionally regarding his life: this makes the atmosphere more tense. After any case the expert usually has an attack of *esprit d'escalier* and thinks of all the things he could have done better, or differently, even when his client has been successful. In a criminal case, he may add to his professional doubts the worry that perhaps if he had done so and so, his client might have fared better. The thought of a man in gaol because of a mistake, could be troublesome.

The really great disparity between civil and criminal work is, however, with regard to resources. The police, having decided to investigate, can set in motion their vast machine, and in particular, they can call on the services of several score of specialist scientists in the various Home Office laboratories and at Scotland Yard.

The accused, however, very often has little or no money and has to apply for legal aid. If he cannot qualify for this, then he often is required to put his solicitor in funds to cover a reasonable part of the estimated costs of defence. In some cases he may have to raise money at great inconvenience to himself: in one cases my client had to sell his house. If the accused wins the case, it is very rarely that he can recover any costs from the prosecution: he has to pay heavily and perhaps cripplingly for the privilege of showing that the police had made a mistake in bringing the case.

The Defence Expert

The defence can not usually afford more than one expert; sometimes they can not afford even one, and some haggling may have to go on about fees. There is frequently doubt as to whether the expert will get paid, at least in full, if the client loses. In some cases he does not get paid anything at all, except for the odd guineas disbursed by the Court to witnesses called under subpoena. It is a matter of luck as to whether the solicitor manages to find the right expert for the case. The Forensic Science Society may be able to alter this part of the position, but I am doubtful, as solicitors do not seem to have any kind of central source of information on such matters.

When the expert has been found, he wishes to examine the exhibits. These have usually been in police possession for weeks or months, and much of the time they have been in police laboratories, where as many people as are necessary have spent as much time as they think necessary, with their own equipment, and with colleagues available for consultation.

The expert witness is not allowed these same privileges. Usually the police will not let the exhibits leave their possession. In one case I had to pack a suitcase with a microscope and various sundries, and travel to an Assize Court, where I carried out my examination on a windowsill in a corridor, whilst the case was being heard. The Home Office experts watched every move, and various police were about to ensure that I did no conjuring tricks with the exhibits.

In London the expert has to visit Scotland Yard. My very limited experience of this is that the Scotland Yard scientists personally could not possibly have been more helpful and considerate, and indeed friendly.

There is also a reasonable amount of good general equipment there, but obviously they can not have the special equipment which a specialist expert has collected in his own laboratory for his own purposes. In a particular case, my opinion was that the Scotland Yard apparatus was not adequate for a proper examination of the textile material which constituted the exhibits. I therefore asked if the police could not bring the exhibits to my own laboratory. The Scotland Yard scientists appeared to be sympathetic to this, and in fact half suggested it, but permission was refused. I therefore had again to pack a suitcase with some of my own apparatus, including my own microscope, and take it to Scotland Yard, but I was not able to take one item which I particularly wanted, because it was too bulky and heavy.

Qualifications of Prosecution Experts

I have now to deal with a rather delicate subject, namely the qualifications of some police experts, and the way they give their evidence, but I wish to make it clear that I have no reason whatever to criticise the character or honesty of anyone at all.

When an expert says from the witness box that he is representing a Home Office Laboratory, or uses the words, magic to a jury (who all read detective stories) "Scotland Yard laboratory" it is pretty certain that the average jury will be inclined to think that the expert can not possibly be wrong. The defence expert is someone they have never heard of, and if he disagrees with the Home Office, they think: "Poor fellow, he has not the same facilities or experience." In these circumstances, I feel strongly that when an accused person's life or liberty is at stake, the scientific evidence should be given by an expert who is clearly neutral and not part of the man hunting team, and who is irreproachably well qualified to give the technical evidence.

In my own field of textiles, a little learning can be a dangerous thing and can lead to wrong conclusions. In one case, facts which admittedly, at first sight, seemed to me to point strongly to a connection between an accused person and the scene of a crime, had quite a different appearance on closer examination, and led me to the discovery of a woman's coat, which I think provided a very much better explanation of the facts, and which at least provided more than "reasonable doubts" about the correctness of the prosecution theory. I will therefore consider the position regarding textile experts.

The Textile Institute has about 8,000 members, who need only pay a small annual subscription to receive the Journal, and who need have no textile qualifications at all. Firms or laboratories can subscribe to the Journal, which is of international repute and is regarded as indispensable in all textile laboratories. The Institute has an examination scheme which has awarded the associateship to some 2,000 people, whilst there is also a Fellowship which has been awarded to perhaps 300 Associates. Associates and Fellows are entitled by Royal Charter, to describe themselves as "chartered textile technologists".

Now, members of the Scotland Yard staff fairly frequently give evidence involving textile fibres, and this evidence may be of a nature which at least purports to connect the accused with the scene of the crime. According to my latest information, Scotland Yard do not subscribe to the Textile Institute Journal, and no member of the laboratory staff, I am informed, is even a member of the Institute, much less an Associate or a Fellow, or a chartered textile technologist. Indeed my impression is that there is not a single chartered textile technologist in the Home Office Laboratories. In one case the prosecution scientist who had given evidence on a textile subject, very honestly told the Court, in cross examination, that he was not a textile expert.

I have had a fair amount of business experience, and can read a balance sheet, and have to keep an eye on the books of my own firm. Nevertheless, if I were to give evidence in Court on a matter of accountancy, no doubt there are those who would be surprised that a chartered accountant had not been selected in my place, especially if a person's liberty might depend upon the evidence.

"Consistent with..."

There is also a certain kind of evidence which we do not find in the High Courts, namely evidence where the expert says that such and such facts are "consistent with" the police theories. This is a very useful expression. In one case, a man was accused of manslaughter in a running down case. The police found one...ONE...wool fibre, of a very common type and colour, on the windscreen of his car. The victim was wearing a cloth cap of a tweedy character, in which were woven several yarns of various colours. The evidence given was that the presence of this wool fibre was "consistent with" it having arrived on the windscreen by contact with the cap. I could not dispute this statement, but it was quite easy to show that if a wool fibre of this kind were required from the cap, it would be necessary to pull out one fibre per second, with a pair of tweezers, for several hours, in order to be sure of getting a fibre matching the one on the windscreen.

I heard one witness go further than this, by missing out the "consistent with" entirely. The case concerned robbery with violence, and the accused had been wearing a particular jacket at the hour of the assault, but claimed an alibi. The accused from time to time assisted a waste metal dealer, who collected old metal, including copper and lead, and pipes or articles painted with white lead paint, and wore the jacket during such work. The police expert applied the notorious benzidine test to the jacket, and obtained a faint reaction. I have no transcript of the evidence, but my recollection is that he stated quite baldly, that he found blood on the jacket. He certainly did not explain to the court that the benzidine test gave a reaction with a large number of substances, including lead paint and blood, and that the reaction could have been due to either cause. He did not say that the test was merely presumptive for blood, and that blood could not be said to be there unless specific confirmatory tests could be applied. It does not alter this position, that the expert told me afterwards, and I am sure that it was his honest belief, that he was satisfied the reaction was due to traces of blood.

The expert who finds himself in the position of having to explain all this to a jury, realises that the damage is done: the Home Office expert found blood on the jacket. Moreover, he may later hear prosecuting Counsel warn the jury not to be blinded by science.

Cross Examination

There are also some peculiar conceptions in the criminal Courts about the role of cross examination. It appears that Counsel may be more prone to attack the credit of an expert witness than they are in the commercial Courts. In the Rouse case, a motor engineer had given evidence, and the first question in cross examination, which I have seen mentioned several times as an example of brilliant cross examination, was: "What is the coefficient of expansion of brass?" The question was no doubt carefully chosen because it was highly unlikely that the particular kind of witness involved, would know the answer. So far as I have been able to see from the accounts of the case which I have read, knowledge of the coefficient would have made no difference at all to the opinion of any expert on the point at issue, and scarcely any expert would have had it in his head, in any case.

I am told that Counsel consider the choice of the first question in cross examination, as by far the most important part of their preparation for attacking the witness, their hope being, no doubt, to get the witness on the defensive from the word "go". I suppose this is legitimate gamesmanship, and an occupational risk for an expert witness, but the case quoted was only successful because the expert merely knew his own subject, and was not an expert on the art of meeting cross examination. Perhaps some day someone may lose his life, not because an expert's opinion is incorrect, but because the expert is inexperienced in the Courts. A person who has given evidence some scores of times, knows full well how difficult cross examination can be, and perhaps an expert unused to the Courts is at an unfair disadvantage unless protected by the Judge.

The Jury

Finally, there is the question of the jury. I think it is remarkable how wooden and impassive a jury can look. Those of us who have served on a jury know that there is always the feeling of business neglected, and work piling up, and on top of this much of the procedure is formal and tedious. Moreover, it is impossible for an expert witness to go into more than the most elementary technical detail, without feeling that he is likely to be above the heads of some non scientific members of the jury. Perhaps the best approach is to give evidence to the Judge and to ignore the jury, as the Judge can ask questions, and will in the end sum up the case.

If the witness box is adjacent to the jury box, as it is in some Courts, occasionally the witness can overhear disconcerting remarks made by jurors to each other. In one case, after an hour or so of my own evidence about textile fibres, a woman juror remarked to her neighbour, within my hearing: "If this case goes on much longer I shall get fibercitis".

For these and other reasons, I confess I do not like criminal work. I am bound to say, that so far as expert evidence is concerned, the persons responsible for the various conditions and matters to which I have referred, cannot be accused of weighting the scales of justice in favour of the defence.

I feel, however, that although one can refuse a commercial case because the fees are not high enough, or because there is something about it which one does not like, it is not ethically correct for a scientist to refuse to give evidence in a criminal case, in which his evidence may assist the accused, for almost any reason whatever. In my only murder case, the accused was brought from serving a sentence for another crime, to attend his trial, and the surrounding circumstances of the case seemed very unpleasant indeed to me, but my evidence pointed to manslaughter, and so it had to be given.

Probably in most criminal cases the expert can make a fair guess as to "who dun it", and the police are perhaps not often seriously wrong, but there is always the exceptional case, and the expert for the defence must be available. It is, after all, for the Courts to decide.

3(2) - 1962: The Design of Law Courts

Most men and women who spend a large proportion of their working life in courts of law will welcome the more frequent erection of new court houses in Great Britain to replace the gloomy old museums, some of which have given service which can be counted in centuries rather than in years. These old buildings are characterised by a supreme indifference to the comforts of all concerned (with the possible exception of the judge) and by the maximum amount of inconvenience to advocate, witness, jury and public alike.

Few specialist witnesses will have escaped the indignity of trying to manipulate a large exhibit with one hand and an equally large sheaf of notes with the other, in the absence of any surface other than a two-inch wide ledge designed to take nothing larger than a testament or a glass of water.

Many of the students from newly independent countries, who crowd the public galleries at our Assizes, may agree that justice can be seen to be done but will not as readily agree that it can be heard, such is the poor acoustic quality of most of our courts. In some of the poorer ones even a sight of the participants in a case is denied to the public by the judicious (?) placing of the dock which effectively blocks all view of the proceedings with the exception of the comings and goings of the witnesses.

The view that since such court designs have served for hundreds of years then this is in itself proof of their adequacy, is no argument in a society which, until less than a lifetime ago, denied an accused person the right to give evidence on his own behalf.

In the design of new courts due regard must be given to the increasing reliance upon physical evidence, and the provision of facilities to manipulate exhibits on adequate surfaces in adequate lighting and in a court of good acoustic quality. The visual evidence shown in photographs, maps and diagrams should not be considered the monopoly of the judge, jury and advocates but should also be exhibited in positions where it can also be seen by those members of the public who wish to see how justice is administered in their society. It should also be exhibited in a way that all participants can see the point being illustrated simultaneously.

The erection of a law court is, for any local authority, an infrequent event. An architect to such an authority may have adequate experience in the design of schools and offices but his extrapolation of his experience to law courts may be less than sufficient. The opportunity given by rebuilding programmes must not be wasted and an investigation should be immediately started on a national or (even international) basis, by lawyers, police officers, psychologists and architects into the optimum environmental conditions for that judicial decision making which is the function of our courts.

6(4) - 1965: Bowlers, Brollies and Bi-Focals

This is a questioning age. There has never been a time in history so given to enquiries. The Vassall Case, the Lynskey Tribunal, the Profumo affair to name but three. And the enquiry into the enquiry – the recent re-examination of the Timothy Evans trial. It might therefore hardly seem surprising that lawyers themselves have begun to question and examine their own profession. Yet this is indeed a revolutionary development. Not for generations have answers been sought, far less obtained, to such questions as "What do lawyers do?" "What do they earn?" "What are their skills?" "How are these acquired?" "What function do they serve?" For the first time the legal profession is now beginning to show some desire to improve its image, some will to understand its constitution and nature, its potentiality and purpose.

In a fascinating book which will surely take its place as a classic of pioneer social studies, a sociologist and a lawyer have provided the first documented insights into such aspects of the legal profession in England[1]. The book is designed to accentuate the importance of the task of enquiry and to spur on empirical investigation. Its theme is already the concern of many thinking members of both branches of the legal profession. Even the Government seem to be taking a hand in the process by referring the question of the profession's restrictive practices to the Monopolies Commission. This should produce interesting material. On quite a mundane level the legal profession has much to learn. Scientists will immediately think of the physical business of so arranging the work of the Courts that the time and energies of witnesses are not expended in endless waiting, and many will ask why when the medical profession have been able to adopt an appointments system for hospitals the legal profession seem unable to devise some such system of general application for the hearing of Court cases.

The fundamental criticism of the legal profession is that they have chosen to isolate themselves from the life of the community which the law exists to serve, to avoid the self-censure which would have followed a proper examination of how they have discharged their functions, and to concentrate in their ivory towers upon the "easy money available for the staple work of conveyancing and probate". These are sweeping criticisms and much can and will be said against them. But they contain sufficient truth to cause the legal profession some unease.

In the process of reappraisal which must follow the pressures of criticism, of social change and of Government action, the legal profession will have a new opportunity to re-orientate itself. In this it must confront the facts of modern living. The impact of science has been at a minimum in its contact with law and lawyers, and a new informed encounter could benefit both participants. A recent editorial in this Journal[2] demanded a concerted effort by all whose interests lie in these fields to sink their differences and unite to examine in detail the relation of science to the service of justice in the modern community.

From the scientific side recent thoughtful papers[3,4] have stressed the need for consideration of the future of forensic science. From the legal side it is clear that changes are in view which will prepare the way for the kind of deep and searching examination this Journal has proposed. If that preparation is effective the way is open for great improvements in the application of forensic science in Great Britain and for consequential effects upon the many countries which look to Britain for a lead in such matters. And lawyers may be on the point of discarding their Dickensian image so that at last they emerge, blinking, into the light of the twentieth century.

A.R.B.

---

[1] *Lawyers and the Courts* – Brian Abel-Smith and Robert Stevens; Heinemann, 504 pp., 63 1.
[2] The Vacant Headquarters – *Journal of the Forensic Science Society* 1965; **6** (2): 65.
[3] Whither Forensic Science: Dr. Hamish Walls – 1966 *Medicine Science and the Law*, **6**, 183.
[4] The Future of the Forensic Sciences: Dr. Julius Grant – 1966 *Medicine Science and the Law*, **6**, 206.

8(1) - 1967: The Expert Witness

This editorial is written from the point of view of what may be described as the professional expert witness, as distinct from the expert on a particular subject who may occasionally be called upon to give evidence. The difference is, of course, that the gainful occupation (or one might say, profession) of the former is giving evidence, whilst that of the latter is pursuing his particular expertise; giving evidence in his case is incidental. In the realm of criminal forensic science, with which this editorial is chiefly concerned, the biggest class of expert witness is of course the staffs of the forensic science laboratories, with their specialised fringe colleagues such as fingerprint experts, photographers, etc. As a class their laboratory resources, qualifications and training are impressive, and their integrity high, but they are called by the Prosecution and there are many times when it is their evidence which (usually quite rightly) carries the day in its favour.

British law, however, requires more than this; justice must be seen to be done, and the Defence has the right to call its own scientific expert. It then has to fall back on the relatively small band of independent professional forensic scientists, often late in the day, and often also without any clear idea of who is best able to help in the case in question. This almost invariably happens after the case has been through the lower Court, so that the expert who accepts the case must usually work against time, and with such exhibits or other clues as the police have collected from the scene of the crime. This means that he has no first-hand information of his own; he does not have the opportunity of investigating the crime first-hand in the sense that the police have; or of collecting his own specimens. Such experimental work as he feels necessary must be carried out in a police forensic science laboratory with unfamiliar equipment; or in his own laboratory with a police officer in attendance mounting guard over the exhibits. Since this all requires organisation through official channels he is reticent about asking for opportunities to put second thoughts to the test.

Let me make it clear that I have always experienced the utmost co-operation in these circumstances, but they cannot do other than place the expert called by the Defence at some disadvantage. Nor does it end here. The police forensic science laboratory is a hive of specialists, each a member of a team which can concentrate on one particular type of problem, such as stains, traces, blood groups, fibres, etc. The independent expert may know quite a lot about all of these, probably as much as and possibly more than his official opposite number in some instances. However, since he only deals with a proportion of the defended cases, he can seldom claim to have examined as many samples of one kind in a given period of time, and this exposes a flaw in the armour of the Defence which prosecuting Counsel is often quick to exploit. One can hear the question coming – "How many alcohol in blood tests did you carry out last year?"

The situation outlined above has developed in recent years; and it must inevitably develop further in the future as science becomes more and more specialised, and apparatus becomes more and more costly and, therefore, to an increasing degree outside the resources of a private practice dependent on Legal Aid fees. It is not difficult to foresee the time when the independent forensic scientist, as understood in the past, will become extinct, for the simple reason that he cannot compete with the resources, financial and otherwise, of the State.

The solution to this problem is difficult to suggest, and indeed at present nobody seems particularly concerned about it. From time to time it has been urged that there should be a greater measure of co-operation between the forensic science experts on both sides so as to avoid clashes on purely experimental facts (such as the identity of a poison or a fibre, or the specific gravity of a glass fragment), where there is only one correct answer. Thrashing out differences of this kind in Court can do no good to the cause of justice or to the profession of forensic science. The answer would possibly be some form of joint laboratory work on the exhibits involved in the first instance, so that the Defence expert could have some say in deciding what experiments should be done where the supply of material is limited. The interpretation of the results obtained is, of course, an entirely different matter, and here each expert would advise his own side independently.

A scheme of this kind might well mean in many cases that the two scientists find themselves in agreement both on results and on interpretation. The Defence might then be abandoned or based on other grounds; or alternatively, the Prosecution might be dropped. In such cases the duration of the hearing could be shortened, and a good deal of valuable time on the part of experts would be saved, especially if unchallenged, purely experimental evidence could be given in writing. This approach has never found great favour with the legal profession; the idea of two scientific experts getting together and "settling the case" is one which could hardly be expected to appeal. Often there is full justification for this, because legal and other considerations have to be taken into account, as well as purely scientific facts.

Another possible alternative is that adopted in some countries, where one forensic science expert who is not associated specially with either side, advises Counsel or the Judge, giving evidence so to speak, for both sides. With the present system of our law, where each side calls its own witnesses who are subjected to examination and cross-examination, such a procedure presents obvious difficulties, especially since the resources at the disposal of the scientist would have to be such that only the State could provide them. This would immediately associate him with the Prosecution, however fair he might be as an individual. Moreover, he might be even wrong in his work or in his interpretation of it, and there would be nobody to check him or to demonstrate the fact.

So the problem remains, and it may well do so until the extinction of the independent professional expert compels public attention. In the meantime the independent expert must continue to try to know more and more about less and less; and endeavour to finance laboratory equipment to enable him to do so out of his more rewarding civil forensic work and general consulting activities.

J.G.

8(2) - 1967: Two Encouraging Cases

In the recent murder trial of *H.M. Advocate v. Hay*[1] the High Court of Justiciary in Scotland accepted the most detailed scientific evidence linking bitemarks on the victim's body with the unusual dental characteristics of the accused youth, and on that indispensable evidence the jury returned a verdict of guilty. It is hoped shortly to publish a full account of this case which marks an important and decisive stage in the acceptance of forensic odontology in the United Kingdom. The case was also important in that the Court approved an unprecedented police warrant applied for *before arrest* to compel submission to dental examination, measurements and photographs[2]. In so doing the Court displayed an appreciation of the urgency of securing and preserving evidence vital to the all-important question of identity.

Not to be outdone the Court of Appeal in England have confirmed in an important judgment[3], which may well encourage many similar applications, that where issues of paternity are concerned the judges of the High Court of Justice have power, stemming from the ancient *parens patriae* jurisdiction, to compel the child and the putative parents to submit to blood tests provided that it is in the child's interests that the question of paternity should be so settled. Although the consent of parties will still be required in all other cases (such as divorces in the County Courts, or bastardy or matrimonial proceedings in Magistrates' Courts) the High Court have given implied approval to the use of blood tests in suitable instances.

These two cases denote a significant improvement in the outlook of the highest Courts in the United Kingdom towards scientific evidence and suggest that where it can be of value the Courts are prepared to adopt the forwardlooking modern approach which this Society has advocated in recent Editorials[4].

A.R.B.

---

[1] The *Scotsman*, 2nd March 1968.
[2] *Hay v. H.M. Advocate 1968 S.L.T. (Notes) 05.*
[3] *B.R.B. v. J.B. 1968 2 All E.R. 1023* – Lord Denning M.R., Diplock and Sachs L.J J.
[4] *Journal of the Forensic Science Society*; Bowlers, Brollies and Bi-focals **6**, 163; Demanding Scientific Evidence **7**, 175.

10(1) - 1970: Law and Order

At the time of writing, a General Election is impending in the United Kingdom and many important issues are being publicly debated. Of these the question of law and order has taken a prominent place in the speeches of certain politicians. While it is arguable that law and order should not become a party issue, it is beyond question that a new Government of whatever complexion must place the problems of attrition of public respect for law, the rising crime rate, the need for improvement in policing and in crime detection, and in the enforcement of law and the improvement of punishments high on their list of priorities. The mischief caused by increasing offences of violence, for example, is not confined to those who suffer actual harm, but spreads throughout the community creating suspicion and mistrust which multiply fears and even engender violence in others. The relaxing of moral standards reflected in more liberal attitudes to sexual conduct, in the abolition of censorship and in the legalising of abortion may have their admirable side but must not be allowed to permit conditions in which those who value their integrity are at risk. The new freedoms, like the old, must be freedoms within the law. Wherever the boundaries are drawn there must be effective and efficient detection procedures for those who transgress acceptable limits. No one concerned with the detection of serious crime is in any doubt about the reality of the truly evil elements which have still to be contained. Clearly then the police have a vital role to play, at least as vital as they ever had in more settled times. This Society has a close interest in the police and especially in those functions of the police which can benefit from the specialist help of the scientist and the laboratory technician. Whichever party succeeds to office, therefore, can count upon the support of the Forensic Science Society for any improvements in the means available to the police for carrying out these tasks.

It is well, however, to recall that there are tensions at work within society, and within its various agencies. There are the tensions within the police forces themselves: the tendency of the uniformed branch to find themselves in opposition to or at least in competition with the criminal investigation branch. There are the tensions within the law: the movements of reform which would radically redefine the scope of the criminal law, as, for example, in the field of drug control and of sexual behaviour. There are the tensions between those who prosecute crime and those who provide at public expense the legal services for the citizen accused of crime. There are the tensions within the field of forensic science: the pressures to concentrate resources on existing centres and current needs with a certain disregard of the training of the forensic scientists of the future.

What is clear is that in a time of rapid social change when so much is challenged the police have a particularly difficult task. They must sympathetically enforce even the more trivial of the laws, exercising their limited discretions wisely and in accordance with the temper of the times. They must absorb a good deal of the dissatisfaction forcibly expressed by the young who find themselves in constant protest against the apparent rigidity of society, and they must still maintain the fight against the really stark evils of the cruel and brutal minority who seek always to enslave and destroy.

If the Forensic Science Society can do something to improve communications in those areas of tension within the United Kingdom and perhaps even to extend and back up the confidence of those working in similar situations at home or abroad it will have contributed in some measure to a better future, a stabler community and a more neighbourly world.

A.R.B

12(2) - 1972: There is a Time to Speak

In 1968 under the title "The Biggar Murder"[1] this Journal published a fairly full account of the Scottish murder trial of *H.M. Advocate v. Hay*[2] in which the principal evidence incriminating the accused Gordon Hay, in the

---

[1] The Biggar Murder: Dental, Medical, Police and Legal Aspects: Harvey W., Butler, O., Furness, J., and Laird, R.: (1968) *J. Forens. Sci. Soc*. **8**, 153–219.
[2] *1968 S.L.T. 334; [1969] Crim.12.R. 39.*

murder of a girl named Linda Karen Peacock, was the testimony of expert witnesses who claimed that marks on the body of the victim were bite marks which could be linked to the teeth of the accused youth. Moreover, these witnesses claimed that unique ring marks on the girl's bruised tissues also matched similar characteristics in the youth's teeth. At the trial the Crown produced, in addition to the evidence of pathologists and police who had seen the body, the detailed evidence of Professor Keith Simpson, Dr. Warren Harvey and Mr John Furness. The defence evidence, which in substance merely questioned whether the jury could be satisfied beyond reasonable doubt that the marks on the victim's body were caused by the teeth of the accused, was given by Professor George Beagrie and Mr Torquil McPhee. These two witnesses having given evidence to the best of their ability agreed that in some respects they did not have the experience to be regarded as experts in forensic odontology. The jury by a substantial majority returned a verdict in favour of conviction and the youth, on account of his age, was ordered to be detained during Her Majesty's pleasure. The case was recognized on several counts to be an unusual and unique one and not unnaturally it has found a place in the annals of forensic odontology[3] as well as in the law reports[3]. It is therefore not surprising that discussion of the case has continued and that the dental evidence has been re-appraised beyond the shores of Scotland. This is entirely legitimate and an exercise to which no exception could be taken, least of all by those concerned for the good name of forensic science.

The principal critic of the case has been Dr Soren Keiser-Nielsen, the international authority on the literature of forensic odontology. His criticisms have fallen into two categories. Of the first category dealing with the scientific conduct of the investigation Dr Keiser-Nielsen wrote in a letter to the Editor of this Journal[4] that the mark on the victim's body was *assumed* to be a bite mark whereas the first point to determine should have been whether it was a bite mark or some other kind of mark; and secondly that the starting point of the investigation was merely a single photograph of the mark. In a subsequent paper[5] Dr Keiser-Nielsen wrote at greater length expanding these strictures and launching into a criticism of the presentation of triangulation evidence at the trial. While these matters are for forensic odontologists to debate it seems to the writer to be clear from the report of the case printed in this Journal, and it certainly was the case, that the assessment of the mark as being either a bite mark or a mark caused by some other object is not a question reserved for dentists and that it was adequately canvassed at the trial. The evidence of the two pathologists and of Inspector Butler and Detective Sergeant Paton who saw the body concurred with the evidence of Professor Keith Simpson, Dr Warren Harvey and Mr John Furness who studied the photographs (and was really unchallenged by the defence witnesses) that the marks on the victim's body formed one bite mark; and this conclusion was reached before anyone in the case even looked at Hay's teeth[6]. Indeed it is strange to observe that in his own considerations of the material in the case at the time Dr Keiser-Nielsen himself came close to thinking that the marks in question were due to the teeth represented by four models specified in Table 8 against the initials A.N.O.[7] These were the initials used to designate his incipient contribution to the case since he was to withdraw at an early stage.

As regards the criticism that the trial was based upon a single photograph, many more photographs were of course taken by Detective Sergeant Paton and only the clearest of these was eventually referred to and produced at the trial. The others would doubtless have been available to the defence had they wished to examine them, as indeed they may well have done.

The criticisms of evidence about triangulation seem to have sprung from an unguarded use of that term by the Lord Justice-Clerk in his charge to the jury[8] which led to the erroneous supposition that Inspector Butler had endeavoured to identify the transparencies of the models of Hay's teeth with the photograph of the marks on the body by reference only to three points. In fact although three particular teeth were emphasized sixteen points at least in the upper and lower jaws corresponded with characteristics recorded in Hay's teeth by

---

[3] See relevant dental literature. and for instance Muncie, W. The Murder of Linda Peacock (1968) *Police J.*, **41**, 319–340: (1969) *Aust. Police J.*. **3** (4), 285–311.
[4] (1969) *J. Forens. Sci. Soc*. **9**, 222–223.
[5] A Bite-Mark Case: Some forensic dental reflections: (1970) *Tandlaegebladet*, **74**, 6, 651–661.
[6] Muncie, W. (1968) *Police J.*, **41**, 319–340. at p. 336.
[7] Harvey, W., *et al*., cited supra at p. 208.
[8] Harvey, W., *et al*., cited supra, at p. 202, line 33.

methods checked by different persons and independently recorded through four separate laboratories. While the error is one which a casual reader might be forgiven for making, the jury had the benefit of hearing the whole of the evidence. But these are matters for forensic odontologists to pursue: and the models, notes and photographs still exist to enable them to do so.

The second category of Dr Keiser-Nielsen's criticism is of an entirely different character and prompts this editorial. The first point is raised in his Letter to the Editor[9] in which he explains that he was invited to travel to Scotland to examine the dental evidence on behalf of the prosecution and having told the Procurator Fiscal that the bruise mark in question need not be a bite mark, and even if it were, could not be definitely identified as the product of the accused's teeth, his views were "discreetly overlooked",[10] the prosecution "found no further use for his services",[11] and from a potential ally he "turned suddenly into an opponent".[12] The second complaint that his request that his views about the supposed bite mark should be brought to the notice of the defence was forgotten[13] or disregarded[14] seems to be based on the fact that he was not invited to participate further in the case; and his final complaint is that he was subsequently escorted out of the country.[14]

These allegations together form such an indictment of Scottish justice that some elaboration in reply is necessary.

In the first place the information which this Journal received holds good. The Crown authorities naturally regard as private the unsigned statements which a potential witness makes to them, but as the Editor's Note[15] following Dr Keiser-Nielsen's letter made clear they did indicate that in this case the views of Dr Keiser-Nielsen as expressed to the Procurator Fiscal do not match with the views which he has since expressed; and undoubtedly he withdrew and declined to give evidence in the case. Counsel for the defence was so informed at the time. That this was the true state of affairs seems to be corroborated also by the accounts of his views which Dr Keiser-Nielsen gave to others involved in the case, by the contents of Table 8 against the initials which were generously accorded to cover any embarrassment to him, and by such documents as still survive in the hands of the other investigators.

In the United Kingdom, where the adversary system of criminal law operates, each side in a case must make its own arrangements to provide what evidence it requires. Naturally the expert witness is sought whose evidence most nearly supports the view which the party seeks to set forth, and this is done without in any way putting pressure upon the witness to conform. It is true that the defence are sometimes at a disadvantage because they frequently have less time, less information, even less prestige and less resources at their disposal than the Crown. Since the introduction of criminal legal aid, however, the facilities have greatly improved and it is certainly improper to draw the conclusion which Dr Keiser-Nielsen has drawn that "the stronger side wins".[12]

The position of the expert consulted but not engaged is a delicate one. It is the practice of the Crown in any serious case in which their investigations disclose a witness whose evidence supports the defence to make at least the existence of that witness known to the defence legal advisers. Indeed in cases involving evidence of insanity or diminished responsibility – the area in which the problem is most frequently encountered – it is not uncommon for the psychiatrist originally engaged by the prosecution to be allowed instead to give evidence for the defence. From what has been said it is clear that this tradition of openness and fairness was observed in the Hay case as in any other. What is not and cannot be known, of course, is why the defence did not choose to call Dr Keiser-Nielsen, and why they appear to have disregarded his existence.

---

[9] Cited supra.
[10] Author's Abstract of his paper A Bite-Mark Case cited supra in (1971) Scand. Soc. forens. Odont. Newsletter, **5**, 93. The abstract goes well beyond what is contained in the paper.
[11] A Bite-Mark Case, cited supra.
[12] In correspondence with Dr Warren Harvey reproduced in (1972) Scand. Soc. forens. Odont. Newsletter, **6**, 21.
[13] Letter to the Editor cited supra.
[14] Author's Abstract of his paper cited supra.
[15] Editor's Note: (1969) J. Forens. Sci. Soc. **9**, 223.

One would have thought that Dr Keiser-Nielsen should have been the last person to raise the question. That they took no action at all may well have been due to the fact that they saw no likelihood of being able to challenge the formidable Crown evidence, that they respected Dr Keiser-Nielsen's reported desire to withdraw from the case, that their field of action was limited by the instructions of their client, or even that they did not fully appreciate the issues which were then at stake. All of this is speculation, but what is certain is that nothing which transpired entitled Dr Keiser-Nielsen to infer that his evidence was hushed up or that he was hurriedly got out of the way. On the contrary, the police officers who went to the trouble of driving him to the airport were merely exercising the customary courtesies for which it seems they have been ill rewarded. And it is significant that the only voice of complaint is, not that of the accused or of his advisers, but that of the expert who was not engaged.

Alistair R. Brownlie

12(3) - 1972: Not Pygmalion Likely

(Rushton v. Higgins)

With the problems of road safety being as pressing as they are and the annual total of death and disablement on Britain's roads running at such a terrifyingly high rate it would be irresponsible to make light of any aspect of the efforts to curb the drinking driver. There has however always been a ludicrous side to the procedures which the drinking driver must undergo. The official description of the driver's police-aided exit from his car usually follows a standard stumbling pattern. His eyes as seen by sodium vapour lighting are usually said to be glazed. His breath smells strongly of alcohol and invariably he fumbles from pocket to pocket when asked to produce his driving licence.

The report of the clinical examination carried out by the police doctor usually contains its humorous passages. As often as not the driver is able to walk in a straight line (if he can walk at all) though when required to execute the important manoeuvre of touching his nose with his forefinger or balancing on one leg he may be found wanting. His failure to give a coherent history of his activities and of the meals and refreshments he has consumed since breakfast may be seen as rather sinister, and of course he must be prepared to recollect all the diseases from which he has suffered in his entire life, the name, address and telephone number of his solicitor, the capital city of his native land or the nine times table if he desires to survive the memory test.

But in the realm of the prescribed level offence drinking drivers' antics may be seen as even more remarkable and the requirements of the law must sometimes startle and occasionally amuse the unfortunate subject. To say that the Road Safety Act 1967 has been repealed, though true, might be to engender false hopes particularly among this section of the motoring public. In fact the provisions of that Act relating to drink and driving have been wholly re-enacted in sections 6 to 11 of the Road Traffic Act 1972. But the Court decisions which followed from the original Act, despite the statutory changes, remain still in point. From press and other comment it seems that these decisions appear to some people to reflect little credit on the law and to others to call in question the sanity of lawyers in general. They include such decisions as that you may be driving whilst stationary[1]; that you may avoid the consequences of drinking and driving by drinking a bit more[2]; that a policeman is in uniform although he has taken his helmet off[3]; that a police warning given to a driver may be effective although the driver is comatose and unable to hear it;[4] and that the consent given by a driver to laboratory tests may not be consent.[5]

---

[1] *Pinner v. Everett [1969] 3 All E.R. 257.*
[2] *Rowlands v. Hamilton [1971] R. T.R. 153: [1971] Crim.L.R. 366.*
[3] *Wallwork v. Giles [1970] Crim.L.R. 109.*
[4] *R. v. Nicholls [1972] R. T.R. 308.*
[5] *Rushton v. Higgins [1972] Crim.L.R. 440; 116 Sol.J. 469; 122 New L.J. 449*

The latter of these decisions concerned one Rushton who had the misfortune, while driving, to be stopped, breath tested, found positive and arrested. At the police station Rushton was required in the usual way to provide a laboratory specimen of blood or urine. He elected to give blood, but when the doctor proposed to take an intravenous specimen from his arm he refused saying that he had previously suffered ill effects from venepuncture and instead offered a capillary blood specimen from a finger. The doctor was not prepared to take this and Rushton was treated as failing without reasonable excuse to provide a specimen for a laboratory test. On appeal by case stated to the Divisional Court of Queen's Bench from the Todmorden Justices it was held that the offer of capillary blood had been a conditional offer and for all practical purposes a refusal to give blood. The Divisional Court followed an earlier case[6] in which a motorist who offered blood from his big toe was held to be refusing to provide a specimen. A doctor acting in accordance with proper medical practice was, they said, entitled to nominate the manner in which the specimen should be taken and the point from which it should be extracted.

This may sound reasonable enough but the unpopular Road Safety Act 1967 was originally sold to the country on the basis that capillary blood would be taken from finger or ear lobe. Such was the proposal set forth in the White Paper[7] in 1965 with the comment "This should remove the objections felt by some people to giving a specimen of blood." The kits issued by the authorities through the Forensic Science Laboratories to police for use in connection with such offences included two sterile lancets for the purpose of drawing blood.[8] Government-issued publicity material[9] stressed that blood tests would be taken quite painlessly by pricking a finger or ear lobe: and even the posters drawing attention to the new tests depicted a finger dripping dramatically with blood.[10] What has happened apparently is that over the last five years the motoring public have preferred the less painful insertion of the syringe to capillary puncture, and some authorities now supply police surgeons with sterile syringes to meet this demand.[11]

The result of the decision of the Divisional Court is therefore that the motorist who decides to offer a blood specimen in the manner contemplated when the legislation came into force will now in effect be punished by conviction and loss of his licence (since refusal to provide a laboratory specimen attracts the same punishment as conviction for the prescribed level offence itself), a radical change which has been brought about with the support of the Courts by the decision of medical men who are neither answerable to nor perhaps conscious of the wishes of the legislators. Surely it is quixotic and wrong that those who wish to follow the original procedure should be punished for doing so.

Alistair R. Browlie

12(4) - 1972: Where have all the Lawyers gone?

(A verbatim report of a lecture prepared for the Society's Annual Meeting, November 1972. – Ed.)

The papers presented at society meetings normally deal with one or two of the branches of forensic science with an eye to describing something of the present status and present achievement of each subject.

When you think of it the depth of study, scholarship, research and practical application in each of these fields – in general forensic science – in pathology, in serology – in toxicology, all lead up to a practical issue. That issue is the whole purpose and essence and the reason for the existence of forensic science – the resolution of a problem or a series of problems, the settlement of a dispute, the ascertainment of fact. To most

---

[6] *Solesbury v. Pugh [1969] 1 W.L.R. 1114; [1969] Crim.L.R. 381.*
[7] *Road Safety Legislation 1965–6 (Cmnd. 2859) at p. 13.*
[8] *The Practical Police Surgeon (1969) p. 91.*
[9] *The New Law on Drinking & Driving – The Facts you should know.*
[10] *Letter from Dr. Anne E. Robinson to The Law Society's Gazette Vol. 69 p. 789.*
[11] *Drink Drugs & Driving: Walls & Brownlie (1970) P. 64.*

of my audience today the earlier part of the forensic science equation is the more familiar – that part which treats of science itself. Rut it is not pure or even applied science with which we are concerned it is *forensic* science. The term "forensic" is derived of course from the Forum at Rome, that portion of the Eternal city which extended from the foot of the Capitoline Hill to north east of the Palatine, the Roman place of assembly for judicial and other public business; hence the Courts of Justice. In modern times these Courts form the social instrument for the resolution of problems between citizen and citizen, to some extent between citizen and the State, and in respect of matters of law and order between the State and the citizen.

In passing it is a constant source of irritation to me and I hope to others to read so often in newspapers the expression "forensic evidence" for what is intended to be "forensic science evidence". *All* evidence given in Court is forensic evidence.

Well then it is with the "forensic" or legal side of the forensic science equation that I am concerned today for although it represents the consumer, the customer and the *raison d'être* of forensic science, it has been neglected or misunderstood or ignored for too long. I would like in short to raise the question "where have all the lawyers gone?"; "why are the consumers apparently so uninterested in the product?"; "why has the contact of the sciences with law so often produced a confrontation rather than an eager linking of hands across professional frontiers?"

The Unequal Partnership

I suppose it is obvious to us all that the partnership *is* unequal. Take for instance the membership of this Society. For some years we have published a list of our members possessing legal qualifications in the Scottish Legal Directory. (The English Law List, though it publishes a list of legal members of the British Academy of Forensic Sciences, declines to publish our list.) At the time of publication of our last list[1] the membership of this Society including affiliations abroad stood at about 950. Of these only 29 were legally qualified. It is true that we have acquired a few more lawyers since then, but the proportion is still much about the same.

The British Academy of course has a special legal section and a degree of association with the English Law Society. Still, its legal membership stands according to the best information I have been able to receive at only a fraction of its total membership.

Take the contents of our Journal. For every hundred papers published on a specifically scientific theme I doubt if there are three on a specifically legal theme. The Journal *Medicine Science and the Law* despite its title, the fact that it was until last year sponsored by a legal publisher, and the rather greater preponderance of legal members in the British Academy, over the last three complete years published the following principal papers:

Vol. 9 for 1969, 23 scientific, 6 legal
Vol. 10 for 1970, 33 scientific, 2 legal
Vol. 11 for 1971, 27 scientific, 6 legal

Now that the Journal is to be published by a scientific publishing house is it likely that the legal content will increase? Of course you will say, and rightly say, but science is the same throughout the world-law varies from State to State and sometimes with idiosyncratic judges and juries you may think, from Court to Court. Would you not then expect to find much more written upon the perplexing legal problems, the patchwork of legal rules and practices? Would you not expect to find lawyers pressing anxiously upon the forensic scientists to supply new methods for resolving old problems, new means of throwing light upon those matters which the law has always found difficult to analyse, and new techniques for improving the efficiency of the Courts themselves?

But what is our experience? Is it not that law and the lawyers have proved resistant to change. That they have been slow, not to say obdurate, in their approach to new scientific ideas or discoveries. Have you

---

[1] *The Scottish Legal Directory (1972)* p. C88.

noticed that lawyers have been in the forefront of those seeking to establish the indisputable facts in any given situation: that they have flocked to learn of the scientific theories which support this conclusion or that? How many lawyers have the slightest appreciation of the tentatives of science, the tools with which the scientist works to understand the world about him; the process of hypothesis covering all the observed facts but discarded as soon as the facts refuse to fit it – the mathematics of probability – the constantly up-dated exchange of knowledge between disciplines and between workers throughout the world – the single-mindedness with which the scientist (working at his best) pursues his quest, and the judicious integrity which he constantly strives to maintain so that his work shall be reproducible at the hands of any competent worker in any similar situation elsewhere in the world. Surely the truth is that scientists have had to nudge lawyers into reluctant acceptance of the knowledge and experience that they offer: that they have often been rewarded with suspicion and hostility, and that lawyers have in general exhibited an inbuilt and sometime arrogant resistance to forensic science? It is to examine this resistance and some of the reasons for it that this paper has been written.

The Early Days

There has been an association of law and the sciences from earliest times, but an association that was temporary, intermittent and tolerated only so long as it could not be avoided. From the early days of both Roman and Jewish law surgeons seem to have been called upon to testify in Court employing their medical knowledge to assist the fact-finders. The judges of the Sanhedrin for example were themselves required to possess knowledge of the general sciences.[2] From Greek sources the well-known dash of Archimedes through the streets of Syracuse crying "Eureka" had its origin in an early experiment in forensic science. For at the moment of his immersion Archimedes is said to have been seeking a method of assaying the proportion of gold in Hieron's crown thought to have been fraudulently adulterated with silver alloy and to have struck on the idea of immersing it in water to see how much liquid it displaced by comparison with a genuine one. Time does not permit to trace the fragmented history of the beginnings of forensic science through the Dark Ages and the Renaissance to more modern times. But it is hardly possible to avoid the impression that wherever there was a marriage of scientist and lawyer it was a union of necessity rather than a love match. In general the demand for science in support of the law has come from police, from government agencies, from a few medical or scientifically trained experts who have followed a private interest. From the work of these stalwarts (and few if any of them had formal legal training) the legal profession have benefited inestimably. The foresight of Lord Trenchard (another non-lawyer) in the 1930's provided England with what have now become her present series of Forensic Science Laboratories which I suppose stand high if not highest in the world league. As Dr. Hamish Walls[3] has put it "The pedigree of forensic science, as it is practised today, is by forensic medicine out of police work". But even the stipulation that these forensic science laboratories are to be equally at the service of the defence as they are of the prosecution[4] is not, so I am informed, attributable to the request of lawyers. Indeed I doubt if even today more than a small proportion of lawyers actually realize that these facilities lie to their hands.

Some Reasons

When you look for some of the reasons to account for this division between law and science both of which are forms of man's culture attempting to explain, understand and universalize human experience, you are struck by the differences of purpose between science and the law. The law's purpose is not advancement of

---

[2] *Jewish Encyclopaedia*: Funk & Wagnalls, New York, Vol. 8, p. 409.
[3] Walls, H. J. (1968) *Forensic Science* p. 1.
[4] Curry A. S. "Forensic Science in Great Britain": *Law Medicine Science and Justice* (ed. Larry Alan Bear) p. 432.

knowledge: it is the maintenance of the fabric of society, the peaceful settlement of disputes and increasingly the engineering of social change. Science on the other hand seems to me to be concerned with description and examination of natural forces and phenomena and the search for new knowledge. No wonder the confrontation of lawyer and scientist in the Court setting is often so unsatisfactory. Do you remember the litigant in Henry Cecil's novel *Friends at Court* who exclaims at the end of a case "what a lot of time and money it has cost to arrive at the truth." "The truth?" said Roger "No one in Court said anything about arriving at the truth."

The adversary system of trial in which, as Sir Roger Ormrod has observed, there are practically speaking no parameters[5] is also often blamed for fostering the division which we have observed between scientists and lawyers. The former tend to want to range through all knowledge to find an answer to the problem at issue: the latter know themselves to be restrained by the requirements of legal relevance to consider only the matters which the parties have chosen to bring before the Court for consideration. It is this concept which in the field of criminal law enables lawyers to live with their consciences and to sleep quietly in their beds at night. The question before the criminal Court is not whether the accused is a rogue and a blackguard. The question is whether *on the evidence* it has been proved beyond all reasonable doubt that the accused has committed a specific offence. You may think that this distinction is one invented by lawyers for their self-perpetuation but of course this is far from so. The restriction of the Court's enquiry to specific relevant evidence is essential to keep the enquiry within bounds, to enable the accused to know what it is he is alleged to have done; and to prevent random prosecution of the citizen with no clearly recognizable offence in view.

It is often said that the lawyer and the scientist have different mental attitudes. Where the issue demands that the scientist should give expert evidence in Court it is vital that the solicitor or counsel should have an early consultation with his expert. Failure to clear the ground and to be assured that each is on the other's wavelength is one of the commonest causes of interdisciplinary misunderstanding. Our President in a paper delivered some years ago to the British Academy,[6] with his customary attention to practical detail, stressed the need for this prior consultation and the desirability that lawyers likely to be involved in litigation should learn to understand at least the methods of approach and lines of thought of the scientist. Professor Keith Simpson has also stressed the need for prosecution Counsel more often to discuss their difficult cases with their expert witness, a thing which Counsel are often reluctant to do[7].

If unfamiliarity with the modes and methods of forensic scientists is in part responsible for the coolness of lawyers I suspect that the sheer bulk and the rapidly proliferating spread of scientific materials also plays its daunting part as a disincentive to the lawyer to become involved. Those legal members of our society who have after a time decided to resign membership have in my experience been those who have been unable to attend meetings of the society and whose only experience of it has been perusal of the Journal. Excellent as the Journal papers have been for the scientific reader, there is no doubt that they have presented a very formidable obstacle indeed to the comprehension of the legally trained observer. For that reason I have myself always advocated the interspersing here and there of occasional more general, and to the nonscientist, more palatable material. And I also hold the view, unpopular perhaps in certain circles, that however technical a paper may be there is no excuse for it to be presented in anything less than clear, precise and meaningful language. There have been those who took leave to doubt that sentence on the inner cover of every issue of our Journal which says, as though it needed to be underlined, "The language of the Journal is English".

Another reason which may go some way to account for the absence of interest among lawyers is their fear of the scientist. Perhaps because of differences of background and of education the lawyer seems determined to feel that in meeting the scientist he is about to be confronted with something difficult to comprehend. Dr. Walls has written of this instinctive reaction[8] in a recent entertaining book. I think too that there is also

---

[5] Ormrod, Sir Roger: "Evidence and Proof: Scientific and Legal" (1972) *Med. Sci. Law* **12**, 9 p. 12.
[6] Grant, J. "The Future of the Forensic Sciences", 6 *Medicine Science and the Law* (1966) 206 p. 208.
[7] Simpson K. "The Art of Forensic Pathology" (1969) *J. Forens. Sci. Soc.* **9**, 199 p. 202.
[8] Walls, H. J. *Expert Witness* p. 177.

a fear in criminal cases at least that the resources of scientific investigation are fully available only to the forces of authority and that they are weighted against the citizen. The use of more and more sophisticated instrumentation in forensic science laboratories again makes it more than ever necessary for the expert to prepare carefully and explain fully to the lawyer the significance of the complex techniques.[9] There is also a fear more pronounced in America than in this country that law and science must achieve a proper balance and that current scientific techniques which are imperfectly understood may be the precursors of radar, personnel surveillance, computer memory banks, electronic eavesdropping, narconalysis and the Quatermass dominance of the mind-benders. Against all of this the law has a duty to stand in defence of the civil liberties of the citizen.

To be honest of course the diffidence of the lawyer in facing up to the scientist is as nothing compared with the antipathy felt by the scientist for his treatment at the hands of the law. The strict question and answer method of eliciting the evidence of the scientist in Court is generally extremely unsatisfactory not least when the questioner imperfectly understands the matter on which he is posing questions. Scientists also have to get used to the idea that the only laboratory which the law has for testing its theories is the courtroom in which the conditions under which decisions affecting people's lives and property have to be made are sub-optimal[10] and so the law is forced to demand a higher degree of certainty and predictability as a necessary expedient to avoid experimentation in the application of legal sanctions. The Aristotelian approach which underlies the adversary process is expressed in the view that "a man shall more easily and discreetly judge of things if he have heard the reasons on both sides contending like adversaries".[11]

This is all very well but to the participant it often seems that to set the parties fighting is a curious way to administer justice. Sometimes this atmosphere of contest antagonizes medical and scientific witnesses setting them at variance with colleagues in the legal profession. The law has not always looked kindly upon the expert witness. As recently as 1931 one of the classic textbooks on evidence contained the criticism that the testimony of the expert deserved least credit with the jury: "They do not indeed wilfully misrepresent what they think but their judgments become so warped by regarding the subject in one point of view, that even when conscientiously disposed, they are incapable of forming an independent opinion. Being zealous partisans their Belief becomes synonymous with Faith as defined by the Apostle, and it too often is but the substance of things hoped for, the evidence of things not seen".[12]

I would hasten to add that in my experience of the Courts I have never encountered anything remotely resembling the creatures just described and I would much prefer the opinion of Lord Macmillan expressed in these words "I am prepared to pay tribute to the fairness which they in general exhibit... Of one thing I am certain, and that is that no scientific man ought ever to become the partisan of a side: he may be the partisan of an opinion in his own science if he honestly entertains it, but he ought never to accept a retainer to advocate in evidence a particular view merely because it is the view which it is in the interests of the party who has retained him to maintain. To do so is to prostitute science and to practise a fraud on the administration of justice... The true role of the expert is to afford the Court the best assistance he can in arriving at the truth and if he bears this duty in mind he will never go far wrong."[13]

There is not time to explain in detail how greatly this role of the expert differs from the role of the advocate whose duty it is to articulate his client's case to the best of his ability however much he may personally dislike it and even doubt its validity. But it is one of the points of friction between science and the law where tensions tend to develop.

---

[9] Curry, A. S. "The Use of Large Instrumentation in Forensic Science" [1968] *Crim. L.R.* **555**; Curry, A. S. "Instrumentation in Forensic Science": *Law Medicine & Science* (ed. Larry Alan Bear), p. 476.
[10] Ormrod, Sir Roger: "Evidence & Proof: Scientific & Legal", (1972) *Med. Sci. Law* **12**, 9 p. 11.
[11] Aristotle: Metaphysics: Sicor 2 ch. 1.
[12] Taylor: *Treatise on the Law of Evidence* (12th edn.) 1931.
[13] Lord Macmillan: *Law and Other Things* p. *251*.

The processes of witness examination and cross-examination are also fruitful fields for misunderstanding between the professions. Cross-examination particularly tends to become a contest in forensic expertise between the witness and the cross examiner, and a controlled, moderate technique has to be developed before an expert can begin to feel able to give his evidence in a relaxed fashion. One of the most interesting experiments I have recently observed is the use of closed circuit television at Strathclyde University in teaching aspiring forensic scientists Courtroom technique and the playback on Videotape recordings of their efforts which later make very telling teaching material. I think the Society might very profitably at some future date arrange a joint meeting with experienced court practitioners for a discussion and demonstration of these forensic techniques.

Finally what can be done to bring about a greater communication of ideas between the scientist and the lawyer? I think that reform would have to begin at the beginning with education. It is a sad comment that at a time when we are witnessing a degree of expansion of forensic science work we are also having to watch the concurrent reduction in the teaching of forensic medicine and an almost total absence of facilities for the teaching of forensic science. I doubt if either of the two principal societies has yet really faced its responsibilities in this connection but the Academy has at least prepared observations.[14]

A second consideration is in regard to the literature of forensic science.

The subject is now well served particularly by this Society's Journal, but I have the feeling that more should be done to encourage the fruitful co-operation of scientists and lawyers in writing about the subjects to be found at the interface of law, medicine and science.

When it comes to Court procedure I think that the Society should encourage scientific witnesses to follow the suggestion of Sir Roger Ormrod[15] and to adopt some of the conventions of the Bar. Counsel customarily disclose in advance to their opponents the list of cases to which they will refer in argument and are also under a duty to draw the attention of the Court both to the authorities on which they found and also to those which are against them. If expert witnesses were to adopt the habit of exchanging reports before trial and consulting with one another to establish the real extent of agreement or disagreement this would avoid some of the more unedifying disputes which tend to bring professional men into disrepute and cause even lawyers to lose their tempers. In a case some years ago the judge Mr. Justice Glyn Jones observed on hearing that medical reports had not been exchanged that "if agreement could not be reached the doctors should be locked up together until they did agree".[16] One wonders if they have yet been released.

More intelligent attention is now being paid by both lawyers and scientists to the problems of expert evidence thanks to societies such as this[17] and something is being done (though insufficient from the legal side) to bridge the interprofessional gap. I should like to adopt the view of Sir Roger Ormrod that it would be a splendid thing if scientific witnesses were to regard themselves as under a rigorous duty to disclose to the Court the limits of accuracy of the evidence they give[18] and whether other contrary opinion exists elsewhere within their profession. In this way the scope of dispute would be narrowed, the cogency of their expert evidence sharpened and their standing considerably enhanced, both in the eyes of one another and of the Court. It seems to me not inconceivable that the Forensic Science Society might some day assist in establishing standards of professional conduct for expert witnesses so improving the practice of the Court and drawing the professions of medicine and the forensic sciences more closely into accord with the ancient profession of the law.

Alistair R. Brownlie

---

[14] Memorandum: "Forensic Medicine & Forensic Science and Legal Education" (1971) *Med. Sci. Law* **11**, 3.
[15] Ormrod, Sir Roger: "Scientific Evidence in Court", [1968] *Crim. L.R.* **240** p. 246.
[16] *Dalton v. Clark & Fenn* [1963] 107S.J. 595.
[17] Cf. Garner, W. "An Expert Witness looks at the Courts" (1960) *J. Forens. Sci. Soc.* **69**; "The Expert Witness", (1961) *J. Forens. Sci. Soc.* **2**, 19.
[18] Ormrod, Sir Roger: "Evidence & Proof: Scientific & Legal", (1972) *Med. Sci. Law* **12**, 9 p. 19.

13(2) - 1973: An Honest Opinion

The opinion of an expert witness on a particular question should not be materially affected by his appearance in court, either for the prosecution or for the defence. His opinion will be based on the evidence available to him and, therefore, in theory at least, the view that he takes will be quite unbiased. Such a witness, however, will often feel morally bound to do his best for his side, an attitude not in any way discouraged by the respective lawyers, and there is no doubt this may affect his overall attitude and approach to the case. As a direct consequence of this the scope and direction of any search of the literature may be influenced and references may be taken out of context and ultimately may result in a limitation of the witness's ability to give a truly honest opinion. These problems are much more obvious when the expert is engaged to help the defence with their case, and perhaps lend scientific support to some alternative explanation put forward by the defendant's lawyers. A prosecution witness is under much less pressure. His opinions may have been formulated relatively slowly as the whole case is constructed and may even have the advantage of being the most obvious explanation.

A basic part of any medical training is the recognition that nothing is certain or inevitable and, therefore, the expert called upon to give an opinion on medical matters for the prosecution will often afford himself an escape route by stating that, while he has little doubt that the circumstances of the case are as indicated, it is not possible completely to exclude some other explanation. All medical and scientific witnesses appearing for the crown must bear in mind that they are generally witnesses to both fact and opinion, and that their views will go some way towards proving the case beyond reasonable doubt; views they must be prepared to explain to the court, and defend against expert cross examination.

Witnesses for the defence on the other hand should never forget that it is not their duty to prove the defendant innocent. All that may be required to obtain the release of the prisoner, is to introduce an element of reasonable doubt into the Crown case. To embark upon some complicated theory or defence argument may do the witness little credit and will probably not influence the jury.

In 1947 Mr. Justice Denning[1], as he then was, said "If the evidence is so strong against a man as to leave only a remote possibility in his favour which can be dismissed with a sentence 'of course it is possible but not in the least probable' a case is proved beyond reasonable doubt; but nothing short of that will suffice". It is the first duty of the defence expert to advise on the shortcomings of the medical or scientific aspects of the prosecution case and his credibility is often increased by conceding the prosecution claims and simply questioning the standard of their proof. Adherence to these principles will go a long way to prevent the taking of sides and the resulting attempts to discredit one expert in favour of another.

This editorial was stimulated by a tribute to the late Professor Francis Camps by H.B.M. in the *Lancet*[2]. It was stated "In court he was a good witness, but tended to take sides in some of his cases, and to the purist not the perfect expert witness". There is no doubt that most forensic scientists would consider such a tribute little short of damning but there must be few forensic experts about whom such a comment could not equally be applied. Such an attitude, reflects not so much upon the integrity of the witness but rather implies a total commitment to the adversary system of our criminal courts.

Much criticism has been made of the attitude adopted by Sir Bernard Spilsbury towards the end of his distinguished career and yet it may be suspect that many of his critics secretly admired his supreme confidence and panache and involuntarily strove to mimic him. It often appeared that an opinion held by Spilsbury must be correct because it was unquestionably the best in Europe. It seems likely that it would be no longer possible for such a cult to surround any present-day expert and so distort the reasoning of the courts. All witnesses giving

---

[1] *Miller v. Minister of Pensions (1947), 2 All E.R. 372*.

[2] "Obituary", (1972), *Lancet* **2**, 139. 75.

scientific evidence would be well advised to limit opinions based solely on personal experience especially if they are contrary to the accepted authoritative literature.

An expert may be under considerable pressure by the lawyers in a case to stretch his opinion further than he really wishes. He may even be asked to lend support to the opinions of a colleague and friend with whom, on the particular matter in hand, he cannot entirely agree. He must resist these pressures for few cases depend on scientific or medical evidence alone and the jury can be expected to adopt a common sense and therefore not necessarily scientific attitude to the case. Everyone knows the problem of countering the view that a single stab wound could have been accidental. How many stab wounds must there be before the defence will concede an intended assault? Professor Keith Simpson recounts[3] a case in which a pathologist produced by the defence, apparently ignoring the prosecution evidence that a considerable amount of phosphorus had been found in the bodies of the accused's two former husbands, said that he would suggest one had died from heart failure and the other from cerebral thrombosis. He further stated that he was merely putting these forward as suggestions. "If I was asked to put a cause of death" he said finally, "I would put the cause of death as unascertainable". Professor Simpson comments that "To utter such illogical nonsense publicly is not only to damage one's reputation for fair mindedness but to do one's profession a disservice".

There is little satisfaction in discrediting a colleague and in so doing demonstrating to the court that his opinion lacks sincerity and may even fall little short of professional perjury. In the oath a witness swears to tell the truth, the whole truth and nothing but the truth. This must include an honest opinion.

J.A.J. Ferris

15(3) - 1975: Modern Times

"Battledore and shuttlecock's a very good game, when you aren't the shuttlecock and two lawyers the battledores, in which case it gets too excitin' to be pleasant" Pickwick Papers (Samuel Weller).

"The first thing we do, let's kill all the lawyers" Henry VI Part 2 Act 4 (Jack Cade).

Because I believe that the first quotation above constitutes in the minds of the vast majority of lay witnesses a considerable understatement and because I suspect that most professional witnesses have at one time or another heartily endorsed the second, I felt considerable trepidation in accepting the Editor's invitation to contribute to this issue of a journal which I have always admired if not always (in its more esoteric aspects) been able fully to understand. Indeed, it has always been one of the advocate's problems that in the modern world he has to fit the changing conditions of a technical society into a framework of procedure originally designed for a far simpler social structure. Not unnaturally I take the view that the original design has stood the test of time in an admirable manner and I am not here to advocate its abolition or drastic amendment. I believe that the system of criminal justice in Great Britain is certainly as good as any other and far better than most. Indeed, I go further and take the view that the English jury, imprecise and aggravating though it may be on many occasions, is an extremely effective instrument for firstly bringing to bear on the administration of the criminal law those lay standards of "right and wrong" which should be an important part of its base and, secondly, preserving the police, judiciary and lawyers from "political" involvement: to see what I mean one has only to consider what would have happened if the guilt as well as the sentences of such people as the pickets charged in the Shrewsbury building site case had been decided by lawyers.

---

[3] Simpson, K., (1967), *A Doctor's Guide to Court*, (2nd edn), London: Butterworths.

Whether or not the views which I hold and have sought to express above will in the end prevail is for future decision, but what I do feel is that much could be done to improve in many small ways the nature and quality of the way in which evidence is presented in court so as to give juries (let alone judges and advocates) or magistrates a clear, memorable picture of the evidence and of the rival contentions of both prosecution and defence.

Such improvement seems to me to demand two things: First, a recognition by all concerned that there are two sides to every case and that the contentions of the Defence may be just as valid, let alone worthy of consideration, as those of the Prosecution. May I make it clear that I do not subscribe to the view that the rate of acquittals by juries show either that the system itself is bad and ought to be changed so as to reduce that number or that defence lawyers are dishonest and/or crooked and/or bent (whatever your favourite word is) or both. The rules which govern my profession are very strict indeed whilst the profession itself is small: any slippery or dishonest barrister would very soon be discovered and suppressed.

Amongst the things which I would like to see follow from this recognition is something in the nature of a formal acknowledgement of the fact that certain persons such as members of staff of the forensic science laboratories and pathologists normally instructed by police authorities are in a sense officers of the court and freely available for consultation by both sides so that, e.g. a defence solicitor can telephone the laboratory and ask to see the member of staff concerned, interview and take a statement from him, ask his assistance upon the issues and upon the strength of his conclusions and not feel in any way that the course he is taking is wrong. In my area (North Eastern England) this sort of thing is already done to a considerable extent on an informal basis usually on the day of the trial but what can be done in those circumstances tends to be limited in the more complicated cases. I also take the view that it would do no harm if police officers, like other lay witnesses, were also freely available for interview and consultation by the Defence without the suggestion of "tampering" sometimes made when this sort of action is attempted.

Such suggestions, to be effective, demand a considerable degree of collaboration amongst a number of people, but if they could be made to work their adoption would in my opinion lead to considerable saving of both time and temper during actual Court proceedings.

Second, I would like to see a reconsideration by those primarily concerned with the presentation of evidence (and in particular expert evidence) of the methods used in such presentation with a view to making the whole thing simpler. Every solicitor or barrister who has ever watched a pathologist giving evidence in (say) a murder trial involving multiple injuries and trying to demonstrate by reference to his own body the nature, whereabouts and extent of the injuries has surely wondered whether that is the best way in which to place such evidence before the jury. The same applies, I suspect, to those who have watched a forensic scientist holding in his hand a bundle of clothing which has been weeks in polythene and trying to explain to the jury where the blood stains are, the way in which they were distributed and/or the path the knife did or did not take through various articles of clothing. To take it a stage further, the sight of a policeman who actually attended at the scene of the crime, trying to explain to the jury the relationship which various photographs bear one to the other and to the general picture is not one which is calculated to bring any pleasure to his superiors. This aspect of the matter was brought home to me very sharply when I attended the recent symposium on sexual offences held by the Society at the University of Leeds and listened to various speakers talking in a matter of fact way about aids to investigation such as videotape recordings and using detailed and sophisticated slides to illustrate the point they wish to make.

No one, I trust, either wishes or hopes to turn a courtroom into a combination of television studio and lecture theatre but it does occur to me that this Society, containing as it does members of many different investigating agencies, might find it worthwhile to turn its attention to possible ways in which to improve the presentation of scenes of crime, pathological and forensic evidence to the Courts. In some cases, this has already been done and we have learned that there is no insuperable obstacle to the playing in Court of tape recordings, e.g. in blackmail cases or the screening of films in e.g. obscenity cases. I therefore propose to exercise the advocate's prerogative and make a series of suggestions, leaving other people to try and work out the answers.

For instance:

1. Where the scene of crime itself is important, as for example in a rape case where consent is an issue, would it be possible to work out a method of presenting to the Court a short film or series of slides designed to illustrate that no woman in her right mind would have consented to sexual intercourse in such a place as that. Experience has taught me that photographs just don't do this.
2. Still on scenes of crime, is there any reason why, in cases where physical signs are found *in situ* e.g. footprints, cigarette ends, bloodstains, weapons, clothing, used contraceptives etc., there should not be a universal use of scale diagrams to show the relevance and relationship of such pieces of evidence. A close-up photograph of a mass of vegetation with a cigarette end in the centre of it may not be all that assistance.
3. Turning to the pathologist, it would be of enormous assistance in many cases if there could be uniformly used, in conjunction with the usual photographs, simple outline drawings of the human body showing the whereabouts and relationship of the various injuries sustained. May I also suggest that consideration be given to the development of a model of the human body which could be used to demonstrate the particular aspects of any particular case e.g. the position in which it is suggested the victim was sitting, standing, lying or leaning at the time of the attack, the angle at which the knife entered, the shot was fired or the axe descended, the way in which the victim was gripped or held in order to cause particular injuries and so on. On the basis that an ounce of demonstration is worth a pound of talk, such a figure would be invaluable.
4. Why should not the forensic scientists join with the pathologists in using the model which I have suggested? Such a figure would surely be of great assistance where significance is sort to be attached to the position of marks on clothing, the significance of tears in a particular place on a particular garment, the distribution and/or nature of blood stains etc.
5. Again with the forensic scientist, why should not the techniques of presentation used by the handwriting and finger print experts be extended to paint similarity cases, tyre mark similarity cases and so on. If necessary, the use of slides should be considered and in this connection is there any reason why the Society should not consider the design of a suitable set of equipment which could be standardised for use in Courts. This would mean that an usher could be trained in its use and the equipment together with the model of the human body which I have suggested and any other device for the presentation of evidence could come to be regarded as just as much part of the court furniture as pencils and notebooks.

May I finally add a reference to my belief that although there are two sides to every criminal trial (and it is with crime that I have been concerned) the system as we know it in this country can only continue to function if all those involved in the administration of justice as we know it collaborate to a marked extent. In other words, if we do not hang together we shall all hang separately.

Arthur M Yerson
Leeds, England

16(3a) - 1976: A Camel is a Horse...

Tradition has it that in a certain institution the director required that all newly appointed staff showed a facility to play the old English game of Cricket. As the years passed the director's questions at interview tended more and more to probe the applicant's ability to play the game rather than his professional ability. Finally, the story goes, the interview process was streamlined so much that each new candidate, as he entered the interview room, was presented with a cricket ball at high speed and the shouted word "catch!" Those who did, passed. Those who didn't, failed.

The reduction of the information gathering process to such bare essentials is self-defeating in that the sparse information collected may have no value to any but the most prejudiced of minds but the opposite danger is that of surrounding an essential point with a mass of peripheral, if not irrelevant, detail. The common-law countries have long recognised this in their legal processes. Thus, we are not presented with the impossible task of finding the entire *truth* of a situation but only with the practical problem of determining if the evidence adduced is sufficient, or insufficient, to satisfy the jury that the allegations are adequately supported.

Scientists have much to learn from lawyers in the posing of questions, and the need to learn grows more acute each day as the scientist becomes more removed, in his laboratory work, from those commonsense processes which make up the fabric of everyday life. Modern scientific instruments have a beauty all their own, a beauty which stems from the extension of the operator's senses far beyond those of the common man and which opens up vistas showing that LSD has nothing on NMR, and Heroin comes a poor second to Scanning Electron Microscopy. Thus the method becomes the problem and the mission gives way to the discipline.

We scientists need re-educating in the asking of practicable and profitable questions. Unfortunately one source of this re-education now only exists in vestigial form. How many among us have undergone the apprenticeship of long hours in the witness waiting room talking with detectives about the mechanics of crime detection? How many of us have listened, fascinated, as a practised advocate strips away the surface barriers from the evidence as a housewife strips an onion or a bridegroom strips his bride, to reveal in all its nakedness the simplicity of truth?

Let us consider the process of information-passing and question-posing by reading the following statement:

A sentence, then, may be viewed as a series of words chosen to successively modify each other in such a way as to eliminate more and more unintended concepts from the listener's choice as the sentence progresses. At the end of the sentence the listener's freedom of choice is then as restricted as may be necessary to the purpose of the communication

(Cartier, 1963).

From this we have clear pattern of construction for our statements and questions. This pattern, moreover, is not necessarily bound by formal grammatical rules. It can also provide a justification when the Laboratory Director, not at his best early in the morning, snarls at you "well?" for you to reply "well what?"

And the title of this editorial? "A Camel is a Horse......"? Ah yes! Didn't Alex Issigonis once say "A Camel is a Horse Designed by a Committee"? But that, as the actress said to the bishop, is another problem.

T.H.

Reference

Cartier F.A., 1963, *ETC*, **20**, 141.

17(2&3) - 1977: The Four Letter Swear Word

All vows, oaths, and pledges, we publicly renounce. Let them all be relinquished and abandoned, null and void, neither firm nor established.

(ancient prayer)

From time to time the Journal publishes papers concerning the presentation of evidence in Court, but very little space has been devoted to taking the oath. Many years have passed since I first performed this operation. It seemed to me then an unnecessary procedure and now I am more convinced than ever of its futility

I would classify witnesses into three types:-

1. those who will tell the truth whether bound by the oath or not,
2. those who may not tell the truth anyway,
3. those who are overawed by the legal process and who may be terrified into telling the truth.

I would like to think that most people belong to the first group, but in any case I feel that very few fall into group 3.

Is the "swearing-in" procedure intended to assure the Court that the witness will tell the truth, or is it designed to reinforce his efforts to be truthful. When a witness is recalled after an interval, Counsel has often been heard to say, "remember you are still on oath" as if to indicate to the Court that the witness has once again transcended human frailty and returned to a sublime state. Let us consider the method of taking the oath. It may be taken using the Testament or Koran, or by breaking plates, or with a covered head, and no doubt in many other ways. These methods possess a religious connotation and must be highly subjective. Evidently, fear of the wrath and retribution of the deity concerned is the overriding factor. Often, however, a witness, when taking the Testament, does not think of it as a "holy book" and is encouraged in this deficiency when the usher says to him, "take the book in your right hand...". On the other hand, to avoid the impression that I am speaking as an agnostic, I must equally question the value of "affirming" – often used by the professional witness (does he choose this method of taking the oath in order to satisfy his philosophical needs?)

The manner in which the oath is taken varies enormously. Some (fortunately very few) are semi-literate, stumbling over the words and hardly understanding their meaning; some stand stiffly as if to emphasize their righteousness and look towards the heavens (usually barred by a dust-laden ceiling) pronouncing the words like the prophets of old. Others present a casual, almost contemptuous manner, which is common among members of the police force. Does an inexperienced jury take all this into consideration when assessing the reliability of the witnesses' evidence? Should it be considered at all? A Crown Court Judge recently said to the jury "Some people proclaim the truth in their demeanour and this is obvious to everyone. Others fail to do so". A defendant has the right to make a statement in his defence "from where he stands" without taking the oath. My impression is that this rarely meets with the Judge's approval and it may be thought by the jury to indicate some diversion from the truth. I see it merely as a method of avoiding cross-examination so that it is the "box" and not the "book" which is relevant.

Without wishing to broaden this article into a discussion on semantics, I cannot resist questioning the meaning of certain phrases used in the oath. I think I can see the difference between "the truth" and "the whole truth", although often I find that I am not given the opportunity of telling the whole truth and I suspect that many Forensic Scientists will agree. However, I have tried very hard to recognize the difference between "the truth" and "nothing but the truth", without success.

The futility of the expert witness taking the oath seems obvious to me. Nevertheless, I would like to refer to something said by Lord Jessel and I hope that Mr. Leonard Caplin, Q.C. will forgive me for stealing his quotation (Caplin, 1961).

"In matters of opinion I very much distrust expert evidence, for several reasons. In the first place, although the evidence is given upon oath, in point of fact the person knows he cannot be indicted for perjury, because it is only evidence as to a matter of opinion.... But that is not all. Expert evidence of this kind is evidence of persons who sometimes live by their business, but in all cases are remunerated for their evidence.... Now it is natural that his mind, however honest he may be, should be biased in favour of the person employing him, and accordingly we do find such bias".

In fairness I must say that these words were uttered nearly 100 years ago and one would hope that both the minds of expert witnesses and judges have changed considerably since that time.

It is no revelation to state that taking the oath before giving evidence bears a similarity to taking the marriage vow. However, there are two obvious differences. Firstly, it is the meaning of the words of the former, but the implication of the words of the latter, which often are not understood. Secondly, the marriage vow is very rarely taken by anyone who at the time has no intention of abiding by its conditions. Paradoxically, the oath taken in Anglo Saxon courts appeared to serve a far more useful purpose than nowadays and was even capable in itself of proving guilt.

"The method of testing whether the oaths were good was to see whether any of the oath-swearers faltered after the oath, or forgot the formula, or even dropped the book upon which they were swearing, in which case the oath was said to burst and the accused was guilty". (Hargrove, 1966).

Some time ago an elderly man was trying in vain to provide an alibi for his accused daughter in a murder trial. It was quite obvious to everyone in the court that the poor fellow was not telling the truth. Needless to say the lady was eventually convicted.

I use this narrative to illustrate an obvious incongruity, and one which I believe supports my argument most forcibly. It is well known that perjury is often committed (by witnesses called for the prosecution as well as for the defence) and this offence against the Perjury Act will occasionally form the subject of a subsequent trial. The accused may well be again required to swear on oath before a new jury!

I must accept that the witness box is a suitable place from which to give evidence, but taking the oath seems to me as archaic as the existence of the docks.

Tennyson Harris

References

Caplin L, 1961, *J. Forens. Sci. Soc.*, **2**, 23.
Hargrove B 1966, *J. Forens. Sci. Soc.*, **6**, 172.

18(3&4) - 1978: Not for the Faint Hearted

The forensic scientist has two distinct functions. He is firstly a part of the hunt for the criminal and later, usually after a charge has been made, he becomes a provider of witness-statements which may be used in court as tending to incriminate or exonerate the accused. Few would dispute that, in the United Kingdom at least, most of his time is taken up in the latter function and that, in the main, his evidence is of a corroborative nature. In those cases where the scientist's findings strongly support exoneration the case is seldom brought to court.

The average forensic scientist approaches report writing with caution. He attempts to set out clearly those findings which he feels are relevant in relation to the charges and to the alleged circumstances of the case. To this extent he must be involved in the investigative process to the minimum degree of knowing (only by hearsay) what the charges and/or alleged circumstances are.

Thereafter he will set down, with care, a series of statements which his experience and due reflection cause him to believe will be supportable in the witness box in the lace of testing cross examination. In many cases these statements will represent a conservative expression of the views he holds. Useful though they indisputably are, such statements are usually only corroborative to a charge which has already been made on other evidence and which will go ahead even in the absence of scientific evidence.

Consider now the forensic scientist's job as a hunter. Here he must produce evidence to support or negate the hypotheses of the investigating officer. What he must do here is to provide, and provide quickly, advice to the investigating officer which will allow optimum pathways in the investigation process to be chosen so that limited police time and manpower can be applied in the optimum way. Often a scientist's intuitive views (yes, even scientists use intuition!) may lead him to advise the investigator to adopt a particularly fruitful path of enquiry on the basis of evidence that would be difficult to present, much less scientifically defend, in court. Thereafter the charge and trial may proceed in the absence of the scientist but based on evidence and statements which were gained by following the path advised by the scientist.

Which of the two functions is the more important? Should the scientist be predominantly an investigator or an arbitrator? Endless and fruitless discussion could take place and few would wish to become involved in it. However, if we ask the related question 'which of these two functions is the more common?' the question is easily answered. Not only is the scientist's function as a producer of' statements more common than his job as a hunter but it is becoming increasingly so. This leads to the question 'should it be so?' The facile answer is 'yes'. The scientist is a lofty judicial creature only one rung down the ladder from the judge himself. Not for him the involvement in a fascinating, exciting and socially desirable chase. He must stay apart, unbiased and pronounce on phenomena supplied to him by third parties. Facile answers are often the correct ones but more and more detectives and scientists are questioning this one.

Is not the scientist's major contribution to the crime detection process not so much a series of techniques but an attitude of mind? Is not the laboratory function, invaluable though it is, overshadowing a more valuable overall contribution? Where this contribution lies within the particular legal and social systems of free nations, must become a matter for wider and freer discussion. The role and influence of the scientist, in or out of court, will undoubtedly increase as a result of the enhanced precision with which he can define the circumstances of a crime. His success in utilising his own technology will demand in turn that he, whether he likes it or not, will have to face up to questioning his true role in society.

The future offers no shelter for the faint-hearted amongst us!

W.I.

19(2) - 1979: Preliminary Hearings – Just or Unjust – Justified or Unjustified

As a result of historical origins of great difference, there are two quite distinct systems of criminal prosecution in Great Britain, the system in England and Wales and the system in Scotland. However different the structure of these two procedures is, there is one central assumption o both, namely that a defendant or accused is innocent until he is proved guilty. The recent committal proceedings at Minehead have reminded the country of the characteristic of the procedure in England, which is largely historic and presently, in my belief, archaic, superfluous and unfair, and certainly prima facie contradictory of the presumption of innocence. Few people will not have read or heard on television precis of parts of the evidence of the Thorpe case, and most of those will have already come to some conclusion about some of the charges or the facts from which they arise, and it is from those people that the 12 members of the Jury who eventually try the case will be drawn. The committal proceedings in England were introduced 500 or more years ago as a safeguard against the habit of the Barons to try people whom they wished to dispose of on trumped-up charges on no evidence. Accordingly it was decided that the people should have an opportunity to scrutinise the case before the defendant could be tried and thus to block bogus disposals. Those of course were in the days when there was no Press and no instant communication and people could disappear rather easily and rather permanently without appeal. In Scotland by contrast committal proceedings have long since been purely symbolic and at their zenith merely represented an opportunity for an accused person to protest his innocence or state his defence at the earliest possible opportunity. Thus in Scotland the first word of evidence that a juror hears is from the mouth of the first witness, whereas the jurors in England will not only have read bits of the evidence in the Press, heard bits of the evidence on television, and discussed bits of the evidence at home and at work, but they will also, once empanelled, have the doubtful benefit of an account of what the evidence is supposed to be going to be from Crown Counsel. It is quite beyond the comprehension of the Scottish practitioner to understand how the juror could sustain the presumption of innocence to the point where he first hears a word of evidence. The English system doubles the cost to the defendant or the State and therefore also the benefit to the legal fraternity who are the first to leap to its defence. Firstly they claim that a few cases are thrown out at committal proceedings and therefore those people are saved the cost of a trial and the torment of waiting for one, which may be years. The answer to that argument is quite simple. It is absurd to double the expense of the majority in order to halve the expense of a handful. It is equally absurd to protract the waiting period for the majority in order to curtail it for a few. In Scotland everyone only has to pay for and sit through one hearing and all trials on indictment must conclude in 110 days if the person is in custody and 12 months if he is not. The Tucker Committee recommended the abolition of publicity at committal proceedings. This was rejected by the House of Commons 25 years ago but I have introduced a Bill to achieve that reform which has the overwhelming support of the majority of the House of Commons and will shortly become law. That will be a useful point from which to abolish the whole anachronistic procedure of committal proceedings in England which have long since ceased to serve justice and now manifestly frustrate it.

Nicholas Fairbairn
House of Commons
February 1979

[The passage through the Commons of Fairbairn's bill was interrupted by the dissolution of Parliament in April 1979 – Ed.].

20(2) - 1980: The Canons of Expertise

Recent events in British courts have highlighted the perennial question of when an expert is qualified to give evidence. In general, the court requires two assurances: firstly, an assurance of the level of the practical and theoretical competence of the witness and, secondly, an assurance that he did the work himself.

Simple though these two aspects appear, they are rather more complicated and inter-connected than one would think at first view. Isaac Newton, arguably the greatest scientist the world has ever produced, is reputed to have said: "If I have seen further than most men it is because I have stood upon the shoulders of giants". What Newton was saying was that his own work, matchless though it was, was based upon an enormous amount of previous work by his predecessors. This indebtedness to others for the theoretical framework of knowledge is general throughout science and, whilst the student may be asked to confirm the major aspects of a theory, all would agree that it is quite beyond anyone's capacity to confirm every single theoretical point upon which one's practice is based.

Essentially, the attitude that the scientist adopts is an inductive one. Here a comparatively small sample of experimentation, consistent with the inductive framework of his training, is taken as confirmation of that framework. As his professional life goes on, he will, of course, be able to be more confident about the soundness of this theoretical framework, although inconsistencies may be found, and it is based upon such inconsistencies that advances in science are made.

On a more practical basis, one must also, in the real world, accept the practical work of many contemporaries. How many forensic scientists, each time they use a bottle of reagent, confirm that the bottle contains what appears on the label? How many pathologists, at autopsy, will reject the practical experience of their colleagues regarding cause of death, whether this experience be passed by the published word, the lecture process, or even casual mention? Does the chemist have to make every reagent and every single instrument setting himself? Must a biologist personally dispense every aliquot of antiserum? Can a scientist depend to any degree upon an assistant and, if so, must that assistant be in the same room, the next room, in the same building, or can the work be done, by the assistant, in the absence of the expert himself.

Is the modern scientist justified in using electronic instruments, the detailed workings of which he is usually unable to comprehend, and the mechanism of which he is nearly always incompetent to reproduce? Is he justified in using the instrument as a "black box" into which he puts his analytical samples and out of which he extracts his analytical results? Can he take one step backward even further from the analytical process and allow an assistant to use the "black box"?

The time has come to make some attempt to define reasonable criteria upon which a court may, with some confidence, accept a witness as competent to give the evidence he proposes to give. Three criteria which are necessary, and possibly sufficient, are as follows

1. the witness should be qualified to give the evidence,
2. the witness should have had effective control over the person who did the examinations which are subject of the evidence, and
3. the witness should ensure that the results which he produces in court are, as far as he is able to ascertain, the correct ones.

Let us take these three criteria in turn:

The witness should be qualified to give the evidence. This implies that both (a) the witness's professional supervisors should be satisfied that he is qualified and (b) the court should be satisfied that he is qualified. Although formal qualification is, and must remain, a function of the court, in practice courts usually accept membership of the staff of certain organisations (e.g., the Home Office Forensic Science Service in England and Wales), together with, where relevant, certain university degrees and professional qualifications. This places a heavy burden on laboratory directors to see that their court-going staff are qualified to give the evidence they purport to give. It also places a similar burden upon universities and professional institutions to ensure that such degrees and certificates as they award are valuable and meaningful in their reputed context.

Effective control over the person who has done the examination. This criterion is presumably satisfied if a witness has done the examination himself. Where the examination is done by an assistant, it is the duty of all expert witnesses to see that they have control, and of their managers to see that an environment is provided in which the control is real and effective. There is no place, in the Common Law countries at least, for the conveyor belt mentality where the expert degenerates into a mere report writer who does little laboratory work and whose authority, in court, is largely based upon the fact that he writes a lot of reports.

He should ensure that the results produced are correct. This criterion probably contains the nub of the problem which faces the modern scientific expert witness. The wide range of specialities in which, individually, he cannot hope to become an expert are at his finger tips and he uses them every day. The only possible way that he can judge that the results obtained are correct is by regularly putting test samples through the system when he knows, in advance, what the answers are. Thereafter the production of a correct answer by his assistants and by his machines will allow him to build confidence in that massive inductive framework upon which all modern expertise is based. This procedure goes under various names such as "quality control", "quality assurance" or "performance monitoring". In many modern forensic science organisations, these procedures are already an established fact, both for the monitoring of individuals and of laboratories.

Should we then not expect the court itself to take the final logical step of monitoring the performance of its own expert witnesses? A new and radical proposal, one might think, It is, however, not new and, surprisingly, the proposal has come from that most conservative of professions, the Law itself. Glanville Williams, [1963], in his book "The Proof of Guilt", made just such a suggestion relating to handwriting experts. Williams says "... give him twenty or fifty specimens of handwriting by as many different people (including the accused) and ask him whose writing most nearly resembles the disputed one."

The age when the value of expert evidence was assessed largely by the degree of authority exuded by the professional witness in court is past. Forensic scientists must now define, carefully, their new criteria of expertise.

AT

Reference
Williams G., 1963, *The Proof of Guilt*. Stevens and Sons, London.

24(2) - 1984: Have You Heard The One About...

(Editorial)

One of the features which would distinguish today's forensic scientist from his forebears is his place of work. Almost all forensic scientists who are active in the criminal investigation side of the subject operate from laboratories which are large, at least by the standards of the past. Now a large laboratory brings with it certain advantages. It pleases the politicians in local government, who are often the paymasters, and it is convenient to fit the catchment area of a laboratory to suit some other geographical catchment such as a county. The larger laboratories, with their greater workload, can justify the provision of higher capital cost apparatus on the grounds of a sufficient number of cases requiring it, and in some instances on the grounds of increasing cost effectiveness with regard to labour charges. The larger laboratory and its large workload means that, on the whole, the forensic scientists in the laboratory are exposed to a greater range of cases, and this collectively enhanced expertise, together with the opportunity of sharing "Case Intelligence", should make them more effective. The larger laboratory, perhaps operating in conjunction with its similar neighbours, can operate in-service training schemes and can evolve systems for the introduction of new techniques. It is also easier for the large laboratory to operate effective quality assurance schemes. The greater workload and staffing may enhance cross-fertilisation and thereby encourage new developments to the benefit of forensic science as a whole.

A large laboratory therefore brings with it a certain operational structure, of accountable management. There is a downflow of delegation of duties and authority and an up-flow of responsibility. All of this should make for an efficient, effective and enjoyable working environment for the forensic scientist and there are many industrial models to suggest this could be so. Forensic science has something special about it, however, and the models from the outside world do not necessarily transfer exactly. Problems can and do arise as a consequence of increased laboratory size and these should be a major concern for forensic scientists.

Most are due to the natural tendency to make the laboratory structure one in which a certain group of individuals, classified by experience or by grading, perform a particular task. To begin at the beginning, searching of exhibits will be carried out by a group who have no other interest; they will perform no assays on trace material which they remove; they will not produce any written report other than that for use within the laboratory; they will not be court-going officers. Very often they will be amongst the more junior staff in the laboratory. Now, searching of the exhibits must be just about the most important task in a forensic science laboratory. It is by looking at material that one best gets a flavour for the case, a taste of what has happened. It is also of utmost importance in that only evidence observed at searching can be analysed and, of course, the purpose of the whole exercise of the forensic science laboratory is to produce evidence. If the significance of something is overlooked by the searcher, then that evidence is lost to the court. It is an awesome task to place on the shoulders of junior staff and the sense of delegating that particular role could be questioned.

The same structure gives rise to another problem, the question of continuity of evidence when the case comes to be presented in court. The reporting officer may be asked who did the work and indeed what was his or her personal contribution to the report. This is a universal problem at present, but fortunately it appears to be being resolved in a sensible manner. Some relatively recent examples of it are to be found in the excellent Scientific Sleuthing Newsletter [1, 2, 3]. Thus, in *Commonwealth -v- Manning*, in a Pennsylvania murder case, the defendant argued that the trial court erred in allowing the prosecution's expert to testify to the presence of a drug in the defendant's body fluids, because the expert did not himself actually conduct any of the tests on the sample. The High Court rejected the argument by concluding that the prosecution had laid an adequate foundation since the record established that the expert had absolute control over the testing procedures and was actually involved in the tests, this being verified by his testimony that he directed how and what was to be done with the specimens.

The Pennsylvania Supreme Court has reinforced this by upholding a medical examiner's testimony and the results of toxicological examinations not personally conducted by him, on the grounds that he was an acknowledged expert and the standardised procedure was performed at his direction. Still in toxicology, but moving state, in *United States-v- Bastanipour* it was held that identification of heroin using a computerised data programme in an instrument (GCIMS) to identify the questioned substance was acceptable; an appeal on the basis that the expel t did not personally recall the spectra on which the analysis was based and did not have any information on the wherewithal or operation of the computer programme was not upheld.

These decisions were reflected in the United Kingdom, during the course of *Preece-v- Her Majesty's Advocate*, when the question of whether a forensic scientist had performed all of the tests himself was raised. In the course of the debate it was proposed that it was quite normal practice in scientific laboratories – and forensic science laboratories were no different in this regard – for tests to be carried out by a number of individuals and the report be based on their amalgamated findings. The appeal judges found this was acceptable, provided that the tests were carried out under the supervision of the expert witness and that his report made clear the parts that he had performed personally [4].

Chain of evidence questions also generate another problem, namely who of all those involved could reasonably be regarded as an *expert* witness. The duties of an expert witness were also discussed during *Preece -v- Her Majesty's Advocate*, and there it was made quite clear the court regarded an expert as someone who had not only the right but *duty* to express an opinion, in other words not simply to carry out tests and report the findings but to tell the court what the findings mean [4]. That approach reinforces the commonsense of the hearsay decisions cited above, since it is likely that only the forensic scientist at the reporting end of the chain would be regarded by the court as an expert rather than as a lay witness.

References

1. *Scientific Sleuthing Newsletter*, Volume 7, Item 2021, Box 196, McLean, Virginia.
2. *Scientific Sleuthing Newsletter*, Volume 7, Item 2056, Box 196, McLean, Virginia.
3. *Scientific Sleuthing Newsletter*, Volume 7, Item 2117, Box 196, McLean, Virginia.
4. *John Preece v. Her Majesty's Advocate. High Court of Justiciary, Edinburgh: Lord Justice-General (Ernslie), Lords Cameron and Scott. June 19, 1981*. The record of the hearing is unreported, but the instances cited here are taken from the notes of WJ Tilstone and JW Thorpe who were present on the public benches throughout the appeal.

24(5) - 1984: Master or Servant?

(Editorial)

"Believe in those who seek the truth. Distrust those who claim to have found it"

(Edisbury)

The forensic scientist is a special person in court, since the expressing of an opinion is something not given to many witnesses, and may indicate the regard in which the expert is held by the court, or so we would like to believe. Of course, the real reason is that the court requires an interpretation of our findings to assist it in its deliberations, and the opinion is a duty, not a privilege [1]

The idea of helping the court is commendable in theory; the practice is less satisfactory. Take the case of an individual with glass fragments found on his shoes and accused of breaking the window of a jeweller's shop.

Laboratory analysis matches the glass on the shoes to that of the shop window. The scientist, acting on the instructions of the prosecuting authorities, may be presented with a question something along the lines "Are your findings consistent with the accused breaking the window and entering the shop?" The answer, with or without qualifications, could be "Yes". The same factual evidence could also be the subject of the question "Are these findings consistent with the accused walking past the broken window on his way to work?" That likewise may demand an answer in the affirmative.

Now sometimes these two questions would be put to the same forensic scientist by lawyers representing the two sides in an adversarial system of justice. The scientist may well feel aggrieved and feel his authority and ability are being questioned. Even worse, the second question might be put to a different expert witness called by the defence to illustrate "Newton's Law" of forensic science – "to every expert there is an equal and opposite expert". In this instance the first scientist, who performed the tests after all, will again feel aggrieved, and his status unreasonably challenged. He should not feel so. He is there as the servant of the court. His duty is plain. It is to play his part in the court procedure and abide by the rules which apply.

The question of whose servant is not always so simple. The scientist's first contact with the case will have been when he was instructed by the prosecuting authorities to investigate the scene or exhibits, and to prepare a report. He might reasonably object to being called "servant" in these circumstances, but he is certainly engaged in an instructor–client relationship at that stage. His work is done at the instigation of the prosecution, his liaison is with police officers or officers of law, with whom he has probably built up a good professional, and indeed personal, relationship over a number of years. Clearly, his position is one of assisting them. That assistance is rendered by his expert and proficient analysis and interpretation, even if his findings eliminate the suspect and stop what had until then seemed a profitable line of enquiry.

When he comes to court, his master changes and the circumstances of his role likewise change. In giving his opinion he must consider his findings and all reasonable interpretations of them. This is not the same as considering in advance every possible alternative – that would require the writing of a book on each and every case – but is simply a matter of considering likely alternative explanations [2]. It may be that the alternatives which occur to him are limited or many. They could be individually detailed, or a phrase such as "other explanations are possible" might be used.

At all costs, the scientist must seek the truth and be seen to seek the truth. He must endeavour to produce results of the highest possible standard and his opinion must be a true and fair reflection of the meanings or meaning of these. He must never feel that he has to choose one of a possible set of alternatives and disregard the others. Only by explicit demonstration of his abilities and his fairness will he indeed be a master of his art in serving the course of justice.

References

1. Editorial. Have you heard the one about. *Journal of the Forensic Science Society* 1984; **24**: 77–79.
2. Editorial. Patience. *Journal of the Forensic Science Society* 1983; **23**: 1–2.

25(4) - 1985: Don't Panic

(Editorial)

My introduction to matters forensic came during my training for a different profession, that of hospital biochemist. I had been called out one night for an emergency drug overdose, had just finished the blood gas analysis, and was about to begin the drug screen, when the telephone rang. The patient had died and no more emergency work was required. Next morning it seemed like a good idea to complete the drug screen, but not so – I was firmly instructed not to analyze the blood, which was to be passed on to "the forensic scientists". That took some swallowing; there I was, deemed capable of analyzing the sample in the pressure circumstances of attempting to keep the patient alive, but not to be allowed to do the same work now he was dead! However, my supervisor gently straightened me out – it was nothing to do with relative ability or importance, but I had to understand it was now a legal matter and the unfortunate analyst would have to go to court, and we all know what dreadful places they are, don't we.

The clinical chemist can readily be forgiven for that attitude, brought about by ignorance and inexperience. Sadly, some forensic scientists share their view, and many of the remainder have only become comfortable in the court setting by experience rather than instruction. In this issue of the Journal we hope a start will be made to replace ignorance by knowledge, through the publication of the first of a series of three papers written by Ann Priston, a forensic scientist. The papers attempt to give an introduction to English Law and Courts.

The articles are of necessity restricted in scope. They only apply to one legal system, and even in Britain they are not universally applicable. They are written from the perspective of a forensic scientist, not a lawyer, and thus have an orientation in some parts which will not suit the lawyer. Finally, some might think it strange that they do not say more of the legal history and standing of the Expert Witness. However, these comments miss the essential point of the papers – they are an introduction to the English system, and aimed at forensic scientists. All forensic scientists should have some interest, and young, English forensic scientists should find much welcome information which will help make them at ease in the legal setting. The papers may not constitute a Hitchhiker's Guide to the Legal Galaxy, but younger forensic scientists in other jurisdictions could well take them as a starting point for informed discussion.

27(4) - 1987: Philosophy and Obligations of a State-Funded Forensic Science Laboratory

(Editorial)

The philosophy and obligations of a state-funded forensic science laboratory will depend to a large extent on the manner in which the state chooses to administer it. Within the limitations of these variations, the obligations are the same, namely to provide a scientific service to clients, with integrity and quality, and within the setting of the appropriate legal framework. The philosophy is not necessarily common, however, and this Editorial will propose four principles encompassing an operational philosophy for forensic science laboratories.

The first philosophical issue is that scientific method demands knowledge of relevant information. Scientists do not work in the dark, but rather they operate in an environment illuminated by prior observation and theory. It follows from this that good scientific practice is incompatible with "editing". The first principle of operation is, therefore, that cases are undertaken only on the understanding that there is full provision of relevant information and materials before work commences, that the scientist has a free hand in deciding the appropriate scientific tests which are to be applied, and that the report issued must be complete and not edited in any way.

The word "forensic" in forensic science is an adjective describing the milieu in which the science is applied. We may not agree entirely with the way in which the law operates, but we, in turn, must be prepared to operate within the confines of the accepted modus operandi of that system. This means, for example, accepting the concept of presumption of innocence within an adversarial system, whereby the Prosecution is required to prove the case beyond reasonable doubt and the Defence is obliged to represent the client's interests. This system, and the obligations consequent on a provider–client relationship, place constraints on our freedom to divulge information. The second principle of operation is, therefore, that no information on a case will be divulged to anyone other than the instructing party except in the course of the due and proper operation of the legal system, for example, when giving evidence or with the permission of the instructing party.

This does not conflict with our obligations as scientists not to edit, but rather controls the circumstances in which information may be exchanged. The third principle of operation is, therefore, that when circumstances permit disclosure of the results of scientific investigation, and of their significance, such disclosure shall be honest and complete.

An essential element of the adversarial system of justice is the right, indeed, requirement, of the Defence to test the evidence to be laid before it by the Prosecution. It is a common complaint of forensic scientists that their evidence has not been understood, or that Defence appraisal has been by those who do not possess the experience, apparatus, or even, on occasion, the intellect and integrity, to evaluate correctly the scientific evidence produced by the state laboratory. It is axiomatic to this approach that the resources – intellectual and technological – are concentrated almost entirely in the hands of the state laboratories. Fairness within the justice system, and even-handedness as scientists, demand that there is equality of provision of resources, quantitatively and qualitatively, to the Defence as well as to the Prosecution. The fourth principle of operation is, therefore, that the resources of the laboratory should be available to the Defence on the same footing as to the Prosecution.

Many scientists and investigators object to this. Scientists feel threatened by the apparent lack of confidence. It is not a lack of confidence; it is the requirement for justice to be seen to be done, and, indeed, competent scientists should be pleased and proud to have their work evaluated and declared to be of the highest order. There is but one objection which requires consideration, and that is the rare occasion when work commissioned by the Defence would result in convincing evidence of guilt, but would not be disclosed. There are ways around this, but even if there were not, it is so uncommon as to be an acceptable price to pay for the greater benefit of the even-handed approach.

27(5) - 1987: Answers Are Easy

(Editorial)

Farmer Brown suffered severe and permanent injuries in a collision between a horse he was riding and a vehicle. At the trial of the driver, Brown was asked in cross examination "Didn't you tell the police at the scene that you never felt better in your life?" "Yes, I did" was the reply, whereupon counsel sat down with a satisfied look.

In re-examination, only one question was asked: "Will you tell the court the circumstances in which you made that response?"

"Yes" Farmer Brown replied. "After the accident, my horse, which had broken a leg, was thrashing around. A policeman from the accident squad went up to it, put his revolver to its head and shot it dead. He then went to my dog, which had broken its back and was howling in pain, put his gun to its ear and also shot that dead. He next came over to me and asked how I felt. I replied I never felt better in my life!"

Answers are indeed easy, but, as this tale shows, they won't necessarily take the court in the right direction. Farmer Brown could easily be Scientist White, except that counsel for Brown knew the question to ask in order to elicit the correct information. Too few lawyers seem to know the questions to ask us.

That is partly their fault. Science is too difficult to bother. Indeed some of them may have chosen an arts education, and thence the Law, because they found matters scientific too incomprehensible. Having read several reports from a variety of laboratories, however, I am far from convinced we are blameless. Jargon abounds, and combines with a reluctance to discuss the meaning and limitations of the work, to render reports of little value.

Why can't we write reports that allow the non-scientist reader – lawyer, judge, juror – to understand what we did, what we found, and what it means? Maybe courses in language would be more appropriate for forensic scientists than courses in statistics.

29(2) - 1989: Science and Law, A Marriage of Opposites

(Editorial)

Forensic science is the progeny from a marriage of divergent philosophies. Many distinguished members of this profession have avoided the influence of law, lawyers, courts, and even crime scenes, by isolating themselves in laboratories. This is not unlike other science fields. Medical breakthroughs may come from individuals who, themselves, never see patients. Industrial chemists provide a multitude of formulae, compounds, and solutions which enhance the quality of, and sometimes disintegrate, the lives of humans. The discovery of better or worse solutions, medications, or techniques do not invalidate the earlier history of science fields from which they come; improvements normally continue the scientific progress. Herein lies the impediment to progress in forensic science provided by the criminal justice system. Science continues to change or it ceases to be science, but the law rarely changes or it ceases to be law. Because the courts and large doses of law are the final stage in the application of forensic science, demands are continually placed on laboratorians to adapt to a legal philosophy. It is impossible to acquiesce completely.

The scientist testifying in a court of law does so as a scientist, not as a member of the legal profession. Yet what makes a good witness? Being "unshakeable" and avoiding having any statement discredited is required of the science "expert". No scientist should agree to absolutes, unless talking about temperature or adiabatic systems. Yet lawyers demand absolutes, not only in a given testimony but throughout a span of years. If new discoveries alter the original conclusions, the scientist must refrain from disclosures or be branded as inconsistent. Earlier stages of a growing and changing field are thus invalidated in court as having been "too new to have been accepted by the scientific community". What law demands is the establishment of precedents in science as in law. This in essence requires that science no longer be science. Knowledge once acquired is not permitted to change or to modify or to grow, thus denying an active role of science in forensic evidence.

What science experts fail to note is that lawyers are as awkward with the union as the scientists. Consider demanding a solid, unshakeable answer, and receiving variations, limited theories, probabilities, and percentages instead. The solicitor is faced with prospects that the physical evidence in a case may be judged unacceptable in a year, or two, or twenty. For individuals whose years of training are conditioned by an absolute requirement of precedent, the changing field of scientific research is daunting and to be avoided at all costs. The trend, thus, is to favour those scientists most willing to be inflexible, unshakeable, and continually adhering to basic premises long since refuted by newer, more open-minded researchers. Because independent experts may find a good portion of their income derived from court appearances, these individuals may be the most intimidated by the system. The result is to impede change, to discourage active research and evaluation of new concepts which could prevent the embarrassments occasionally experienced with reversals of highly publicised cases.

The answer is not for scientists to become lawyers nor is it for lawyers to become scientists. The answer to the union of science and law is a compromise on both roles and philosophies in cases where forensic evidence is introduced. An adversary form of justice should provide an arrangement in which science and law can meet. It will, however, only succeed if there is true freedom to disagree among scientists. To deny a concept, supported by conscientious research, which may be new to some members of a scientific community, permits injustice to occur and impedes the development of new and useful information. Like the offspring of any marriage, the future and success of forensic science depends upon a mutual and workable relationship between the parents, law and science.

Anita KY Wonder

34(3) - 1994: The Image of the Scientist and the Lawyer

(Editorial)

(This editorial is based on the paper presented to the Spring Meeting of the Forensic Science Society at Heriot–Watt University, Edinburgh, 25–26 March 1994)

If you visit the town of St Andrews in Fife with its ancient University, as did the late Sir Cedric Keith Simpson, the forensic pathologist – so he told me – every year, you will see in South Street the wrought iron railings and gateway of St Mary's College, and displayed in the metalwork the inscription IN PRINCIPIO ERAT VERBUM (In the beginning was the Word). St Mary's is a theological college and no doubt you recognize the quotation as being the splendid opening words of St John's Gospel. Like the Society's own motto, these words were taken from the Vulgate and to me they have always suggested a suitable maxim for the legal profession, because, for lawyers, words are everything [1]. Without them there is no law. They are the beginning, the stock-in-trade and the end of the law. When words fall silent so too does the lawyer and so does the law.

No doubt scientists also use words, but not exclusively. Mathematics, graphs, calculations, statistics, weights and measures, atomic shorthand, even the ball-and-stick 3-dimensional simulations like the double helix can convey scientific truth, and much reliance is placed upon them, and nowadays even by the manipulation of them by computers. Not for nothing is the projectionist given a holiday when a lawyer addresses this Society. In all the 35 years of The Forensic Science Society, a number of distinguished lawyers (and some others — I place myself in the latter category) have given addresses — never once, I believe, with the use of visual aids. You see the lawyer puts his trust not in pictures but in words, — or to be more specific, the pictures he draws are drawn in words. And so it is a pleasure for me — during the projectionist's break — to consider briefly with you in this predominantly scientific audience, the fundamental interaction, both reflection and reality, which lies at the root of the Forensic Science Society's purpose — that is the interface between science and law, the "chemistry" which ought to enable information to be transmitted from the scientist to the lawyer and back again, a process of transmission which is sometimes faulty, sometimes more apparent than real, and rarely as effective as it should be. As in the case of an imperfect, dirty or corroded electrical connection, the current's flow can be intermittent or less than satisfactory. Not only that, but since none of us is perfect, the lawyer and the scientist may not be, or appear to be, what they profess to be and the public's perception of either as well as the one's perception of the other may be at fault.

The image of the scientist and of the lawyer in the eyes of the public has, of course, always been suspect. Let me take the lawyer first because he is more familiar to me. The public's perception of lawyers has always been a little jaded. From the 16th century, we lawyers are always reminded of Shakespeare's Cade, who fantasized "If I were king — as king I will be — there shall be no money, all shall eat and drink on my score and I will apparel them all in one livery that they may agree like brothers, and worship me their lord"; and Dick's caustic response: "The first thing we do, let's kill all the lawyers" (Shakespeare, Henry VI, Pt 2, Act 4, Sc 7, 1). But lawyers weren't killed. They have flourished. Their task is to consider and nurture the legal framework of freedom in which we live, to support the ends of justice, to guide the perplexed and speak up for the feeble and the wronged, to help the inarticulate to say what they would say if they had the ability; to avoid litigation if disputes can be settled, and to fight them if fight there must be; to enable ordinary citizens to transact business safely in life and to secure their affairs in death; to see fairness applied even to the weakling, the underdog and the person accused of crime, and all this without the use of a suit of shining armour or a double-edged sword. All has to be achieved by words.

Of course the public's perception of the lawyer may be that he is a fixer. That for a sufficient sum of money paid him, probably in advance, he can produce any desired result. It is certainly the case that sometimes a lawyer's knowledge of law, or even of fact, gives him an edge in this respect. I was able to win an acquittal recently in a road traffic prosecution in which my client was charged with ignoring a halt sign at a particular junction. He was minded to plead guilty, but having passed that junction twice a day for years, I knew that there had never been such a sign there — only a broken white line. His trial was a success — it foundered utterly: but then he should never have been charged in these terms. The words were wrong. The common perception that a lawyer's task is to "make the worse appear the better reason" (Milton: Paradise Lost, Bk 2,1,109) is unfair. Nor is it his task in criminal cases to get his client off, but rather to ensure that his client is convicted of no more than the evidence properly laid against him justifies. Frequently ethics come in to play, though the public may not believe it. To take a small illustration of a questionable defence in a recent drink-driving case, the rather inexperienced police witnesses were asked by me to read out the terms of the Camic printout.

They did so from the witness box confidently enough until they came to the date – "31 February". The expression on their faces as the realization dawned for the first time that there was something far wrong, was a joy to behold. Fortunately my question "If the date is so wrong how can you be sure of the correctness of the breath analysis?" was never answered because the prosecutor hurriedly dropped his case. I knew that the dating function of the machine was independent of the analytical function – but was I wrong to ask?

One can see how George Bernard Shaw, that arch cynic, was able to write that "the theory of the adversary system is that if you set two liars to exposing each other, eventually the truth will come out" [2].

The image of the lawyer has in Scotland taken a terrible beating in recent years, not so much because of what the majority have done well enough, but because of what a tiny minority have done. One solicitor ran off to Uruguay with several million pounds of clients' money and another more recently was put upon by fraudsters who persuaded him to invest all of his clients' substantial funds in a fictitious international venture which proved to be a mirage. We Scottish solicitors operate a guarantee fund, set up under the Solicitors (Scotland) Act 1980 section 43, whereby the honest professionals make good the losses caused to clients by the dishonesty of our weaker brothers (so far I think our sisters have not seriously offended) and we hope thereby to regain some of the trust lost in the eyes of the public.

Like our colleagues in England, we Scots solicitors have in recent years become sensitive to the way we are perceived by the public, and by means of market research and advertising campaigns we have tried to make the man in the street aware that the solicitor is a professional, that he has a place in a just society and that he is to be readily approached and always trusted. The slogan "It's never too early to consult your solicitor" has met with public approval although interestingly enough the profession themselves hated the campaign [3].

A somewhat similar situation has obtained in England, and a similar problem. How can the public's image of the lawyer be made to conform to the professional reality which lawyers wish to promote and believe to be the truth?

And what of the scientist? Here I speak subject to correction by those whose knowledge is much greater than mine. But it is obvious even to an outsider that the scientist – or at least the forensic scientist – has in the past five or six years had a rough ride. First there was a series of complaints about scientists whose performance was alleged to be substandard. Whatever the reality – and in the case at least of Dr Alan Clift, I for one entertained doubts as to whether his performance was so bad – the public perception fanned by sensational reporting was disastrous. Alan Clift was rather unfairly placarded in the press as "Dr Blunder" [4] and in the most scandalous of court proceedings – Scottish, I regret to say – his professional integrity was dismantled in circumstances where, after a lapse of 8 years, he was forced to repeat the serological evidence he had given and which evidence was compared to that of a battery of leaders of his profession, without Dr Clift being afforded the right to be represented in court as even a shop-lifter would have been entitled to be. The judgement in that case of Preece v Her Majesty's Advocate [5] threw light on the law of the expert witness; it marked a milestone in the court's expectations of forensic scientists, and it dealt a serious blow to the public acceptance of forensic science.

But of course, more was to come. A series of serious criminal convictions obtained years before in English criminal trials was exposed to re-examination, as a result of which the forensic science evidence was criticized and held to be unsatisfactory. Probably the most publicized were the cases of the alleged bomb-makers known as the Maguire Seven, convicted on 4 March 1976, in regard to which the First May Report presented in July 1990 [6] recommended to the Secretary of State that the whole scientific basis upon which the prosecution was founded (and it was founded on little else) was in truth so vitiated that on this basis alone the Court of Appeal should be invited to set aside the convictions. Various members of our Society were closely involved. This was accepted and the convictions were quashed by the Court of Appeal on 26 June 1991. Further consideration of the thin layer chromatography analysis of traces on the hands and under the fingernails of the accused, and of the possibilities of contamination thereof, were rehearsed in the Second May Report in November 1992 [7], but this did nothing to rehabilitate the image of the forensic scientist or to reassure the public of the integrity of forensic science.

Superimposed on all this challenging of scientific evidence was the fact that the morale of the scientists working in the English Forensic Science Laboratories in the eighties had reached rock bottom. To quote the reply given to the Home Affairs Committee of the House of Commons on 30 November 1988 in response to a query about the morale within the service, the General Secretary of the Institution of Professional Civil Servants replied "I think to be honest it is bloody awful" [8] – a comment which many members of this Society echoed with feeling from their own experience. Now following the reorganization of the Forensic Science Service as a freestanding agency the outlook is better, according to "The Forensic Science Service", a publication issued by the Service when, in April 1991, it became an Executive Agency of the Home Office. The image of the forensic scientist is being re-established and the procedures of quality assurance and quality control are coming into play.

But it is undeniable that in the eyes of the public (who understand little or nothing of the background to these changes), the forensic scientist has been portrayed as an incompetent idiot or a pawn of the police whose own (i.e. police) reputation has unhappily been subjected to the severest criticism, especially in respect of procuring so-called confessions by highly doubtful means. It is perhaps ironic that more recently it has been the evidence of forensic scientists applying the electrostatic deposition analysis test to the material in police notebooks which has been instrumental in showing up the cases in which the statements in police records have been concocted from different sources or at different times (for some account of the technique, see [9]).

I think there is no doubt that it can be said that lawyers, police and forensic scientists have all come under severe public condemnation in recent years. Yet we know that only a tiny minority of solicitors has been dishonest, only a very few forensic scientists have suffered really damaging criticism and only a small section of the police force has given way to improper practices. Obviously this is a time for working to reinstate the image of the solicitor, the forensic scientist and the policeman as professionals whose integrity can be relied upon, and to match the reality to that new image. But the further point I wish to make is that the central business of forensic science also has to be addressed. This is the intercommunication of all those professionals whose duties meet at the doors of the court when investigation and forensic science come to provide the fruits of their work to judge or jury. At that point we simply have to improve the interchange of information, the mutual understanding of what is said or not said – the place of the word. I have trawled through the entire 34 volumes of this Society's Journal and the comparable volumes of Medicine, Science and the Law and (apart from the writings of Sir Roger Ormrod [10]) found next to nothing on this vital theme.

Time does not permit me today to elaborate on this but at least may I record my suggestions for consideration by this Society.

First, the Society must make it a priority at symposia, in whatever department of forensic science, to try to engage a lawyer to speak and not just to speak and depart, but to remain and listen. Yes, I like that comment by Bill Rodger that law and forensic science are closely related [11] – but so were Cain and Abel. Certainly every aspect of forensic science eventually has to be laid before the court and the sooner the legal input is received and assimilated the better.

Secondly, in whatever aspect of the forensic sciences, let us pay special attention to words – to the expressing of the scientific content in language which the layman can understand and the expressing of the legal content in equally clear speech. This will eventually pay dividends in court and in interprofessional understanding.

And thirdly, and perhaps most important, let this Society take the initiative and keep taking the initiative in offering training courses to solicitors in the various aspects of forensic science. I have often asked "Where have all the lawyers gone?" [12, 13]. It is not enough to say that they are too busy, too innocent of scientific knowledge to be involved. The Society must be pro-active in offering this kind of training (what Jim Thorpe has called "re-education in an alien discipline" [14]).

I take my final quotation from a former President of this Society – Arthur Chapman, a policeman who in his Presidential Address as long ago as 1979 said;

"The lawyer, because of his isolation, too often self-inflicted, from the forensic scientist, loses the opportunity to see, absorb and present important criteria which may be concealed in written scientific jargon or revealed by discussion."[15]

What wise words these were, and how we have failed to follow them up and attack that self-inflicted isolation. Let us now make it a priority to refurbish and renew the image of the scientist and the lawyer and to match the new image to a new reality of co-operation, understanding and respect.

References

1. Brownlie AR. *Precognition and the technique of the interview*. Presented at the Law Society of Scotland Advocacy Training Course, University of Stirling, 24–27 July 1980.
2. Quoted in Barrett D. Scientific evidence in an adversarial system with a lay audience: a problem for justice? *Journal of the Forensic Science Society* 1991; **31**: 271.
3. Marketing Working Party Report in Annual Report of the Law Society of Scotland, 1993.
4. See, for example, The damage done by Dr Blunder. *Daily Mail*, 7 September 1981.
5. *Preece v HM Advocate [1981] Criminal Law Review, 783*.
6. Rt Hon Sir John May. Interim Report on the Maguire Case. London: HMSO, 12 July 1990.
7. Rt Hon Sir John May. Second Report on the Maguire Case. London: HMSO, 3 December 1992.
8. The Forensic Science Service: Home Affairs Committee First Report, Volume 2. London: HMSO, 1989: 129.
9. Radley RW. Determination of sequence of writing impressions and ball pen inkstrokes using the ESDA technique. *Journal of the Forensic Science Society* 1993; **33**: 69.
10. Ormrod Sir R. Evidence and proof – scientific and legal. *Medicine, Science and the Law* 1972; **12**: 9.
11. Rodger WJ. Forensic science – policy option. *Journal of the Forensic Science Society* 1986; **26**: 69.
12. Brownlie AR. Where have all the lawyers gone? *Journal of the Forensic Science Society* 1972; **12**: 547–552.
13. Brownlie AR. The Solicitor and Forensic Science. In: Caddy (ed) *The Uses of Forensic Science*. Edinburgh: Scottish Academic Press, 1987.
14. Thorpe JW. DNA or Abracadabra? *Journal of the Forensic Science Society* 1993; **33**: 202.
15. Chapman A. Terra firma. *Journal of the Forensic Science Society* 1979; **19**: 3.

AR Brownlie
SSC, Edinburgh

38(2) - 1998: The Role of the Forensic Scientist in an Inquisitorial System of Justice

(Editorial)

In the same way that there is great variety within the adversarial system of justice, both between countries and sometimes within countries, the same applies to those parts of the world that live by the inquisitorial legal systems. The criminal legal system which operates in French speaking European countries is based on a unified code, the Criminal Code, derived from Roman Law, the French Revolution and the Napoleonic Code. It is divided into two parts. A general part describes the principles of the law and a special part defines crimes and their punishment. The limited space available here does not allow a fundamental discussion of the system, but it is hoped to explain how forensic science can be used in a different legal system and how that system affects the way science is implemented.

The continental system as described below has two distinct phases: the investigatory/inquisitorial phase, and the trial phase. During the investigation and further, during the trial, there are three guiding principles which judges employ and each plays an essential role in the way forensic science is used.

The first one, the *liberté des preuves* (literally 'freedom of proof') means that there is no codification of the evidence. Any type of evidence can be accepted by a judge (save illegal proof, and even this may be accepted in evidence under certain circumstances [1]). This, in essence, means that a judge may accept a certain type of evidence in one case and reject it in another (obviously arguments and justifications must be given) and as a consequence there is no such thing as a 'Law of Evidence'.

This leads to a second principle – *la liberté d'appréciation* – which gives to the judge ample freedom and scope to assess, appreciate and evaluate the weight of the evidence brought to him within the context of the case (there is no such thing as the 'Frye standard' and guidelines to help the judge). Although a judge can accept what may be considered unsafe evidence, he will usually not do so because of precedents and the risk of appeal. On those few occasions when he wishes to accept such evidence he will do so only after ample discussion and argued justification. For example, commonly accepted evidence (such as fingerprints as a means of identification) could be rejected by a judge who must then justify his decision, e.g., circumstantial data, or the way the evidence was collected by the witness – expert, technician, policeman, etc.

Finally, recognising the essentially psychological nature of judgment, a third guiding principle must be adhered to by judge(s) an/or jury before they arrive at a final decision – *l'intime conviction* – the ability to judge according to one's 'soul and conscience'. The judge does not have to weigh each type of evidence proposed, he may combine evidence types in a way which is very much based on experience and intuition in a fairly subjective way. But then, in the judgment he must make clear what arguments led him to his final decision. The courts do not propound arguments as to the measure of doubt to qualify it as 'reasonable', but the way *in dubio pro reo* applies is similar practice in the adversarial system.

This highlights the preeminence of the judges in the justice system. There is hardly any mention of 'expertise' or 'forensic science' delimiting the use of science in criminal law and specifically in the Criminal Code itself. The only specific mention of science is concerned with the mental state of the defendant (psychiatric expertise). Otherwise, the only reference to 'experts' concerns failure to deliver what was requested of the scientist through corrupt practice, false expertise, etc., and the potential punishments for the expert!

Other rules are necessary to make the Criminal Code work. Criminal procedure codes detail powers and roles of judicial officers, how courts operate and how an investigation is conducted and directed, etc. Such codes vary widely from country to country or even within one country: in Switzerland there are 26 different cantonal (state) codes and one federal code for crimes under the federal jurisdiction (international traffic of humans, terrorism, currency counterfeiting, etc).

All these procedure codes vary especially in the relative importance of the inquisitorial versus the adversarial phases of the process. In the inquisitorial phase, or 'instruction' phase as it is sometimes called, the work is generally undertaken in secret under the responsibility of an investigating magistrate or judge (*le juge d'instruction*). It is for the investigating magistrate to direct the police to acquire evidence, to employ forensic experts and to generally administer the investigation. His powers are similar to those of the Procurator Fiscal in Scotland.

During the initial stages of the investigation, there may be limited use of scientific expertise. Scientific support for crime investigation given by police identification departments may be all that is used (SOCO, fingerprint specialists, routine and basic forensic science). In some instances a scientist, doctor of legal medicine or another appropriate expert, may be called in the initial stages of the investigation (suspect death cases, fires, plane crashes, etc.) but it is necessary for the investigating magistrate to intimate his request in writing. Obviously this may only be a written confirmation *a posteriori*. This is done through an *ordonnance d'expertise* (ordinance) which contains detailed instructions and questions to be answered by the expert.

This is one advantage of the inquisitorial system for the forensic scientist. The investigating magistrate delegates some of his powers and the scientist can investigate a scientific question in the way he sees fit. There is no pressure to take either the prosecutor's view or the defendant's view. The independence is usually total (within the law) and guarantees impartiality.

A difficulty can arise from the way the written ordinance is formulated depending on the level of competence and experience of the investigating magistrate. He might not give due consideration to whether the questions are possible to answer or even relevant, and also forbid answers to questions that were not asked, despite the expert's opinion that they are pertinent and should be brought to the attention of the magistrate (this is rare, but has happened). He might select incompetent experts and refuse to act on external requests (this can infuriate parties to the case, as demonstrated in well publicised international cases). All this is subject to appeal. On the request of the forensic expert some magistrates write a complementary ordinance to cover potentially pertinent outcomes (or requests based on information submitted by parties to the case). In an ideal situation, before writing the ordinance and questionnaire, the magistrate contacts the forensic scientist and asks what kind of help the scientific investigation might bring to the case. The resulting scientific reports are sent to the investigating magistrate.

Depending upon the local procedure, there will be a variation in the information surrounding the arrest of a suspect which will be supplied to the defendant and his counsel. Questions may arise as to the expertise of the experts, the pertinence of questions, and also questions that have not been asked to take into account a new version of the events. The defendant can request deeper investigation of allegations to take into account facts favourable to the defence, and to ask new questions of the forensic scientists and to have them carry out more scientific investigations. The investigating magistrate can chose to act and accede to these demands with a new ordinance or an extension of the original commission to the forensic expert, with questions added by the defence. Or, if the personality of the expert is contested, the ordinance may be given to a second expert agreed to by the defence. This process should guarantee the rights of the defence and avoid the problem of disclosure, because the report is given to the magistrate. The investigating magistrate can also decide that there is no reasonable grounds for the defence claims, e.g., requests made purely to prolong the procedure.

Only when he is satisfied with all the evidence does the investigating magistrate charge a suspect and make a referral order to the appropriate court for trial.

When the defendant is charged and a referral order has been made an appeal may be introduced. An appeal may be lodged to a special court (*chambre d'accusation* in Switzerland, usually assembled from judges of a supreme court) to have a case reinvestigated on the basis of specific questions. It is possible, at this stage, to reject expert opinion and to submit questions to which the investigating magistrate must seek answers before referral to trial. Since the defence has full access to the file and information, they can use this information to question the reports of any experts. This usually helps to clarify scientific issues prior to the adversarial phase of the system. If the appeal is accepted the case is sent back to the investigating magistrate to complete investigations according to the decision of this court. It may be decided that some or all of the expenses of further investigation are born by the party(ies) requesting the reopening of the investigation (pending the outcome of the case). When the investigating magistrate has fulfilled all his responsibilities the proceedings move into the second and adversarial phase.

The public prosecutor (*procureur*) and the defence both use the file produced by the investigating magistrate to support 'accusation' or 'defence', and it is their role to try to influence the judge in his or her perception of the evidence. Usually scientific questions have been dealt with during the instruction/investigation phase. It is for this reason that the expert is rarely called to the court during the adversarial phase except to explain certain scientific or technical points. Even before the trial begins, if the defence lawyer is unsatisfied by the answers to his or her questions, he may then elect to contest the expert's report in court. The judge can decide to stop the trial and request a supplemental scientific investigation and report or, alternatively, summon the scientist to explain/interpret any scientific findings. Unless the circumstances are exceptional there will not be any private experts 'for' the defence introduced or accepted into the legal process because there was ample time to contest scientific evidence in the inquisitorial phase.

During the trial the court can pause and, by agreement with the public prosecutor (who is not the investigating magistrate) and the defence, interrogate an expert or appoint a new expert to answer particular scientific questions. The expert then has an obligation to answer all questions which the court has agreed in advance and which can be put to the expert by either side. There is nothing to prevent the defendant and his lawyer from seeking the advice of outside expertise on what questions to ask the court's scientific expert. But, this 'private' advisor cannot be called to testify without the approval of the court because of the risk of an unacceptable bias.

This process of justice offers great advantages for forensic science since the scientist is not exposed to the cross fire of judicial theatrics. Some critics argue that the lack of challenge in court means that scientific evidence is of a lesser quality, that the competence of experts is not verified, etc. But verbal scrutiny may just show up the better actors, not necessarily better scientists.

If it is, nevertheless, the case that the scientific evidence is of a lesser quality, then the system is not the cause. The cause has been, until now, a less than desirable awareness of the scope and limitations of scientific evidence by the legal profession on the continent. This will perpetuate until defence counsels become more aggressive and contest dubious science. There has been a recent trend for many inquisitorial courts to place scientific arguments before the court and let judges make decisions. It must be noted too that until relatively recently the development of forensic science in a number of continental countries has been hampered by the effects of World War II causing science to fall behind on the continent, in contrast to the flourishing of forensic science in English speaking countries since the early fifties.

Another benefit of the inquisitorial system is that the full details of the investigation are given to the judges before the commencement of the trial so that the judges have a complete understanding of what is being placed before the court.

It is suggested that the system briefly (imperfectly) described here is much better suited for scientific discovery and debate. It is favourably disposed towards scientific evidence rather than the theatrical hyperbole often perceived from 'adversarial' systems. Scientific evidence has its place in the forum, not scientific debate.

Professor Pierre Margot,
University of Lausanne,
Switzerland

Reference

1. Bénédict, J. 1994, Le sort des preuves illégales dans le procès pénal, doctoral thesis, Law Faculty, Lausanne University, Ed. Pro Schola, Lausanne.

40(2) - 2000: And What of the Evidence!

(Editorial)

"It is a capital mistake to theorize before you have all the evidence. It biases the judgement."

Sherlock Holmes 'A Study in Scarlet'

In the forty years of the Society's existence, the nature of expert evidence and its perceived role in the criminal justice system has changed, even if the basic purpose has not. Any person, who has the experience to give an informed opinion on a matter outside the experience of the court, may give 'expert' evidence. It is for the Judge to decide whether someone who is put forward as an 'expert' is properly qualified to assist the court. Normally paper qualifications will be taken as sufficient proof of expertise, however, where there is a challenge to the competence of an individual to give an opinion on the fact at issue, then the Judge must determine whether those qualifications, and/or the individual's practical experience, justify his giving expert opinion. The Judge must also decide whether the individual concerned has a special or particular knowledge which the court overall does not possess, and that this knowledge has been acquired by detailed and studious examination of materials and information, thus enabling an expression of opinion to be given on the basis of observation, examination and research by the witness or others similarly qualified. The role of the expert witness is to assist the court with the benefit of his experience and to provide possible/probable (scientific) reasoning which then allow the court to form opinions and to make judgements.

Yes, that is where it was, forty years ago.

There are anomalies in the role of the expert in our trial process, whether criminal or civil.

Unlike other witnesses, the expert is entitled to express opinions. If the expert gives a sincere opinion squarely within his field of expertise, he can make a valuable contribution to the discovery of truth. The danger is if the expert is lured, or tempted, into expressing opinions on matters not within his professional expertise.

Unlike other witnesses, the expert witness is paid. The great American authority Judge Learned Hand, a century ago stated the point briefly when he wrote: "The expert becomes a hired champion for one side". It is perfectly proper for a professional person, giving both his time and his expertise to assisting the court, to receive appropriate remuneration. He should, however, maintain standards and resist the temptation to become partisan.

Although it is true to say that no expert ought to be asked the 'question at issue' which the court has to decide, if an expert 'point of issue' lies at the heart of a case, and the evidence of the expert witness is accepted, then this may unbalance the function of the court. In practise this occurs. If experts qualified in a particular discipline disagree, how can a judge or how can a jury choose between them? Fortunately this anomaly is usually mitigated by other evidence.

There is also no clear cut definition which analyses the characteristics which a body of knowledge must possess to be the proper subject of expertise. Fortunately, in the principal fields of medicine, natural science, engineering, handwriting and so on, this is self evident.

But what of the 'soothsayers'?

Does the existence of these anomalies mean that we should dispense with expert evidence? Obviously NO: for in the course of legal proceedings, issues frequently arise which can only be resolved with the guidance of those with specialist knowledge of a particular discipline, outside the ordinary understanding of the court in general. The need is to do everything we can to ensure that expert evidence is deployed to support the ends of justice and not the reverse.

This is one objective of the professional Institutes and Societies; it is also the objective of the new Council for the Registration of Forensic Practitioners. Let us hope it becomes a regulatory body with teeth. One which will not only register people in such a way that you can readily identify their area of expertise, but also one which will eject those who fall below the standard: that may be more difficult to achieve.

It is also the objective of the Woolf proposals which, although built around the Civil court procedures, will rapidly seek to influence work in the Criminal court. The proposals embodied in Part 35 of the Civil Procedure rules, "The Expert's Declaration", and the shortly to be published "Code of Guidance for Experts", clearly set out the expectations which will apply to all experts by emphasising the overriding duty of the expert to the court.

The Civil Procedure rules give responsibility to the Judge to have a management influence on the case. One Crown Court Judge (in the Criminal Court) is already commenting about what he sees as a growing menace, i.e. the calling of multiple experts in criminal trials with the consequences of delay, additional cost, and introducing undue complexity. It seems likely that he would welcome active management leading to efficient time-tabling, stringent criteria for the selection (and number) of appropriate experts and pre-trial conferences to identify areas of agreement/disagreement – these to be disclosed in writing 28 days before the trial.

How far are we away from solutions to some of these problems? Perhaps not as far as we might think.

Our pre-trial system, although described as 'adversarial' is, in fact, very much 'inquisitorial'. The conduct of the case until charge is almost exclusively in the hands of the police, and largely remains so until the trial, receiving only minimal direction from the prosecuting authorities. Under a current project in some areas, only indictable offences are proceeding straight to the Crown Court after arrest. This enables the Crown Courts to carry out more case management than ever before which may lead to them exercising persuasive control over the use of experts. Judges would expect membership of recognised professional bodies with disciplinary functions to be the norm. A code of practice would make clear the expert's duty to the court, as well as governing the way in which experts report and give evidence, including a duty to disclose what material/information they have considered, any alternative conclusions and the relative merit of those conclusions.

Experts, who do not acknowledge compliance with the code, would be at risk of their evidence being ruled inadmissible, or, of the jury being warned that they may wish to attach less weight to that evidence.

Now that would be different from forty years ago.

Dr Norman T Weston

41(3) - 2001: The Boundaries of Expert Evidence

(Editorial)

A case heard in the Court of Appeal in 2001 epitomises the problems faced by the Expert who gives opinion evidence in Criminal Cases [1, 2]. The case, one of a conspiracy to rape, involved issues related to the capacity, and apparent capacity, to give real consent of a woman who was estimated to have had a blood alcohol concentration of the order of 200 milligrams of alcohol per 100 millilitres of blood at the time of the incident. Part of the grounds for the appeal centred round the evidence of an expert witness for the prosecution who, when asked whether the complainant could have been able to communicate and appear rational replied to the effect that she would probably have been seen to be "someone who was not in control of her behaviour or judgement". At the Trial, the Defence objected to the expert's evidence of the grounds that it went to an "ultimate issue" in the case. That is to say that the expert was expressing a view on one of the central issues to be determined by the Court. However, the Court of Appeal reiterated the opinion that the old common law rule that an expert could not express opinions on the ultimate issue is not longer extant. The Judgment in Stockwell, a case cited by the Court, expressed the view that the rule was now only a matter of form, not of substance [3]. The Expert can, in effect, express a view as to an ultimate issue, but it is then up to the Judge to make it clear to the jury that they are not bound by the expert's opinion. The problem in the present case was not primarily the expert's opinions, but, in particular, the fact that the trial Judge had not given the jury a direction to the effect that they were not bound by the expert's opinions but that the matter was for them to decide. The Court of Appeal noted, not with approval, that the trial Judge had not made use of the Judicial Study Board's specimen directions on the way in which juries should approach expert evidence [4].

It may well be thought that these cases do not sit well with the somewhat convoluted conventions that the English courts impose upon those giving evidence in DNA cases [5]. Arguably the reason given for the Court of Appeal in setting out those conventions, including the rubric that the DNA expert should not express an opinion as to the likelihood that the defendant donated the crime scene stain, are just as applicable in other cases where expert evidence is given. DNA experts are effectively banned from giving opinion evidence on this important ultimate issue because it "requires consideration of factors other than those within his area of expertise". This same argument could be applied equally well in virtually all other cases where expert opinion evidence is given in the criminal courts. If it were applied uniformly, how much psychiatric evidence, for example, would be put before the jury?

The boundaries of expert evidence may soon assume new importance in the English Criminal Justice System. A White Paper on the future of Criminal Justice (2001) implies that there is likely to be a reduction in the proportion of cases heard in the Crown Court [6]. That is to say, a reduction in the number of cases heard by juries. This will inevitably lead to an increase in the number of cases heard by magistrates, as well as an increase in the number of occasions experts will be asked to give evidence in the Magistrates' Courts. Those of us who have done both know only too well that giving evidence before a bench of Lay Magistrates can be a very different experience to giving expert evidence in the Crown Court. The temptation to assume an advocacy role when giving evidence in the magistrate's court is something one is sometimes tacitly, or even not so tacitly, invited to succumb to and is something that has to be resisted. At the other end of the spectrum, giving expert evidence to Courts where a Panel of Experts assists the Judge, perhaps in lieu of a jury, will be a challenging, if not a chastening, experience.

The future looks interesting; if the old aphorism that "experts don't try cases, juries do" is to retain something of its validity, then we will need to rely more than ever on the good sense, bolstered by the Human Rights Act, of the Judges in the Higher Courts. I hope they will not let us down.

Robert Forrest

References

1. *R v Ugoh & others. [2001] EWCA Crim 1381*.
2. Trio jailed for student rape plot are freed. *The Times*, Friday June 15th 2001.
3. *R v Stockwell (1993) 97 Cr App R 260*.
4. http:llwww.cix.co.uW-jsb/specdir/evid.htm#part33
5. *R v Doheny. [1997] Cr App R 369*
6. Criminal Justice: The Way Ahead. CM 5704. HMSO, London 2001. (http://www.official-documents.co.uk/document/5074/5074.pdf)

41(4) - 2001: Reform of the Criminal Justice System in England and Wales

(Editorial)

Lord Justice Auld's mammoth report into the English Criminal Justice system, a clear labour of love which was 22 months in the gestation, was published on 8 October 2001. Normally, the publication of such a document with its many proposals for reform, some merely fine-tuning and some nothing but radical (for England) would have attracted widespread publicity. However, other events in the world outside have overshadowed it. Nonetheless, if readers of this journal can drag themselves away from the television coverage of the latest Afghan war, they will find a visit to the Criminal Courts Review home page well worth while [1]. This is particularly so as the Government has announced that a White Paper and then legislation, 'when parliamentary time allows', will follow a period of consultation ending on 31 January 2001.

Only ten of the 687 pages specifically deal with expert evidence. The topics covered include:

- The competence and objectivity of expert witnesses;
- The suitability of expert evidence;
- The way in which expert evidence is presented;
- Inequality of arms between prosecution and defence experts;
- Delays in obtaining expert evidence;
- The effects of Court listing practices on forensic practitioners;
- Poor pay for publicly funded defence experts.

Most of what is said makes nothing but good sense. The recommendations include:

- The concatenation of expert witness registers into one organisation to oversee the accreditation and regulation of forensic scientists of all disciplines. As the report says, there is only one strong candidate – the CRFP;
- The introduction of a declaration that the witness understands that his duty is to the court and not those instructing him at the start of a statement as is currently a requirement in the post Woolf Civil Procedure Rules [2];

- The imposition of a duty, and a reaffirmation of the power, of the criminal courts to restrict expert evidence to that which is reasonably required to resolve issues of importance. One could see possible appeal grounds here if this duty is applied too vigorously to exclude expert evidence.
- The criminal courts should not have the power to impose, appoint or select an expert, but prosecution and defence should be encouraged to use a single expert where that can be agreed. Pretrial meeting of experts for the parties should become the norm and indeed the court should have the power to direct such a meeting with identification of issues agreed and not agreed and the preparation of a joint statement for use in evidence. One wonders if in some cases the court will have to provide a sponge to mop up the blood!
- Review of the law relating to hearsay evidence in the context of laboratory practice.
- Use of video conferencing techniques both for pretrial conference and in the giving of expert evidence.

Lord Auld recognised that the practice of shopping around by the defence for expert evidence does take place. He has resisted making any recommendation that there should be a requirement for the defence to disclose all their experts' reports, commenting that this is inappropriate in an adversarial system where the burden of proof is with the prosecution.

What is music to all our ears is his recognition that publicly funded expert fees are 'meagre for professional men in any discipline' and his hope that the Legal Services Commission will raise the fees for this work appropriately. I hope the equivalent body in Scotland, where such fees often hardly cover costs, also takes note. Most of Lord Auld's recommendations do not have significant net cost implications, for example; the cost of video conferencing technology should be self-financing. However, any increase in fees will be expensive. I can see that being one recommendation that will not be implemented.

Lord Auld's final comment on experts creates a window of opportunity for the Society. He points out that the courts need to increase their familiarity with and understanding of forensic science. We already have a significant number of coroners amongst our members; now is the time for us to go out and recruit members amongst the judiciary and magistracy.

Robert Forrest

References

1. http://www.criminal-courts-review.org.uk
2. Civil Procedure Rules, Part 35.3.

42(3) - 2002: Justice in a Goldfish Bowl

(Editorial)

ARW Forrest
Editor, Science & Justice

A few days ago I emerged from giving evidence at a high profile inquest to find myself facing a massed phalanx of reporters and cameras from both the print and electronic media. It was none the less unpleasant for being expected. A day or so later, I was taken by surprise in Blackpool; at the end of the lunch break, as I turned the corner in front of the Town Hall, where I was giving evidence at another interest, I found myself staring into yet another TV camera. I was caught for posterity with a mouthful of chicken and mayonnaise on wholemeal. That was both unpleasant and unexpected.

It is inevitably the case that some investigations and the court proceedings that follow will lead to an unusual amount of attention from the media. In general terms, in a free society, no one can object to the right of the press to report facts, subject to the protection of the vulnerable, the interests of justice and a reasonable degree of respect for the privacy for the individual not in public life. That is not to imply that there is any real law of privacy in England and Wales. Breaching the legal limits set for confidentiality and the regulators' limits for invasion of privacy is something that editors and their publishers do at their peril. The public interest is not always, or even often, congruent with the interest of the public as perceived or even set by those managing the media. This, of course raises the question of who decides what the public interest is. The academic answer is that the courts, informed by legislation and common law set those limits. Many apparatchiks make the day to day decisions affecting a person's privacy whilst acting in the course of their duty or what they perceive their duty to be. One does not have to be a cynic to think that sometimes those with the power to do so spread the blanket of confidentiality more in the interests of their masters than in the wider public interest.

Jurisdictions vary significantly in the way in which confidentiality in the investigative and judicial process is handled. In Scotland, for example, there are much greater controls on the reporting of trial and pre-trial proceedings than there are in England and Wales. (Of course, the Internet makes a nonsense of this. A high profile Scottish case may have only the most limited real time coverage in the Scottish media; anyone with Internet access can read the English editions of newspapers covering the case). Yet in Scotland, unlike England and Wales, court proceedings can be filmed with the permission of the Judge, for later use, most notably in documentary programmes. In the United States there is the morbidly fascinating Court TV with live transmissions of high profile and sometimes other trials and the ready availability of depositions and other materials on the Internet. This can lead to the interesting phenomenon of jury sequestration, where jurors may be confined for weeks or months in a hotel with court officials controlling their television viewing and censoring their newspapers so that the pristine purity of their deliberations is not sullied. In short, the constitutional right of the press to print whatever they will is preserved at the expense of the jurors. The utility of sequestration is somewhat questionable. As Dominic Dunne pointed out during the OJ Simpson trial – a one hour conjugal visit gives you 45 minutes to discuss the case with your partner...

In any case, are jurors really more susceptible to publicity than judges? The law in England implies that they are, because proceedings before and during appeals heard by judges alone can be much more freely reported than trials in the Crown Court. It will be interesting to see if there is a change in the perception that English juries need such protection from the risk that they might read about the case in the media if the proposals that it become much more difficult to avoid jury service by statutory exemption is enacted into law. Whilst one might speculate that defence advocates may not welcome an increase in the numbers of people in the typical jury pool reading broadsheets rather than tabloids whilst waiting to be called, prosecutors and judges are likely to welcome such a change. This may not be because of any expectation that a conviction is more likely, but rather in the hope that it will be easier to ensure that at least some members of the jury will achieve a good understanding of the difficult concepts of law and the complex evidence they may be asked to deal with. On the occasions when I sit as a deputy coroner in a jury inquest touching the death of some poor soul who has died in a complex industrial accident I feel a great sense of relief if I find that one or two people on the jury have clearly got a post sixth form education. I sometimes feel guilty over this, but the plain fact is that it does make the presentation of evidence and law to the jury so much easier.

The expert faced with the attention of a mass of cameras and reporters for the first time will not find the experience pleasant.

In the UK it is rarely, if ever, appropriate to allow oneself to be interviewed immediately after giving evidence. Simply confirming the facts of how one's name is spelt and who one's employer is seems reasonable. If one has prepared a list of technical words that one might be using in evidence for the court writer, to help with her spelling, a print reporter will appreciate a copy and there is no reason why he should not be given it off camera. Journalists, despite opinions to the contrary, uniformly want to report factual matters accurately and promptly and it is appropriate to help them achieve this within the parameters set by the requirements of the court and one's employer. What the tabloid sub-editor then does with the journalist's report is outwith their control. When tracked by a television camera, it is helpful to remember one or two rules; don't look at the camera and don't look at your feet. Being filmed walking into a lamppost with downcast eyes is going to do nothing for your professional reputation.

Inevitably, high profile trials and investigations will attract the attention of the press. Everyone involved in the investigative process must be prepared to find himself or herself suddenly, and perhaps unexpectedly, the focus of media attention. Anticipation of the possibility and some preparation, even if only discussion shorthand with more experienced colleagues may make the experience easier to handle.

© The Forensic Science Society 2002

Keywords Forensic science, editorial, inquest, media, reporting, jury.

42(4) - 2002: Gristle in the Sausage...

(Editorial)

ARW Forrest
Editor, Science & Justice

Bismarck is famously said to have remarked that making law and making sausages are both activities best carried out outwith the view of the consumer. The sensation of nausea that one sometimes encounters when reading Hansard attests to the truth of that aphorism; it is entirely comparable with the feelings produced by watching a graphic documentary on black pudding production in the hinterland of Barnsley. It isn't only that process of production that can distressing effects on the spirits or the viscera; the nasty bit of gristle that sometimes sticks in ones teeth when eating a canteen sausage is comparable with the sinking feeling that a bad clause in otherwise good legislation can produce.

The Police Reform Act 2002 is a generally unexceptional piece of legislation. It does introduce one major change. Up to now the collection of non-consensual blood samples from detained persons has been something that requires the authorisation of a senior police officer. The legal fiction of implied consent extant in many US states where the assumption is that if you are driving, with or without a licence, you have by implication consented to supply blood, urine or breath samples at the lawful request of a police officer has never been applicable in the UK. Rather, in the UK, the driver has had a choice: provide the sample(s) requested or commit a "failure to provide" offence. It was, and in the vast majority of cases still is, down to the driver. If he chose not to provide the samples, he has to take the consequences. Now, if a police officer, any police officer, no rank being specified, considers a driver, or a person who might have been a driver, from whom he would be entitled to require to provide a blood sample is incapable of consenting to the provision of the blood sample for a medical reason (my emphasis) he can ask a medical practitioner to collect the sample without the consent of the donor. There is a let out for the doctor asked to collect the sample. He need only do it if he considers it is fit for him to do so. "Fit" in this context is not defined in the act and the doctor requested is under no obligation to tell the police officer his reasons why he does not consider it fitting to collect the sample.

Later, the donor of the sample can be approached to allow the sample to be subject to what the Act describes as "a laboratory test". Failure to give permission without reasonable cause is an offence. Presumably, the sample donor would only be approached when he has recovered the capacity to give proper consent; in fact, the Act is silent on that point.

The Act is confusing enough to provide fertile ground for defence and civil rights lawyers; issues such as the capacity of a police officer to make medical judgements and whether or not a person with post head injury memory loss can be expected to reasonably make a judgement over whether or not to allow a sample collected from him earlier immediately spring to mind to be subject to a (single?) laboratory test are obvious ones. No doubt the finely honed intellects to be found between High Holborn and the Thames will think of many others.

How did this bit of indigestible gristle get into the Act? Could it have been made more digestible? It very much seems to have been a prime example of hard cases making bad law. One of the seminal documents was "Blood, Sweat and Beers", a report prepared under the aegis of the Police Research Award Scheme. It includes several examples of cases where police time was wasted and/or where a less than just outcome may have been achieved in particular cases. Some of those cases can be interpreted as showing deficiencies in hospital police liaison procedures or in reflecting the under funded provision of accident and emergency services in the UK. When the Police Reform Bill was going through Parliament Candy Atherton MP contributed to the debates, particularly in respect of the provisions relating to the non-consensual collection of blood samples. She described the tragic death of a young woman in her constituency. She died in a crash having come into collision with a vehicle driven by a person who had been seen by witnesses to have been drinking earlier in a public house. The surviving driver was taken unconscious from the scene to hospital from whence he discharged himself as soon as he recovered consciousness. He was not arrested when he took his discharge and he was subsequently successfully prosecuted for reckless driving. Ms Atherton considered that the law, as it then was, in not allowing the non-consensual collection of blood from an unconscious patient for forensic purposes introduced a degree of inconsistency into the law; the unconscious patient after a crash could not have blood collected from him for forensic purposes to either exclude or confirm the presence of intoxicants.

Doctors are rightly very reluctant to collect blood samples other than in the interests of their patients and with their consent. Nonconsensual diagnostic and therapeutic procedures are tightly regulated by law. In general, if the patient cannot give proper consent then diagnosis and treatment has to be confined to doing only that which is necessary for the patient's immediate welfare. In short the Kantian view of treating the patient as an autonomous end in himself dominates. The utilitarian view that the needs of the many predominate over the right to autonomy of the individual in some situations can be set at different thresholds. Few would argue with setting the threshold at a level where a person may be subject to the forcible collection of intimate samples in terrorism cases for example. Setting the threshold at the point established in the Police reform Act is arguably inappropriate in cases of simple drink driving although it may not be when the incident under investigation involves death or serious injury to parties other than the driver.

How could this bad law have been made better? Firstly, it is unfair to expect police officers to make complex medical judgements about the capacity of a person to give or withhold consent. Many forensic medical examiners who hold the Diploma in Medical Jurisprudence are approved for the purposes of s.12 of the Mental Health Act 1983. These cases are relatively infrequent and it may well be practical to have such a practitioner make the decision as to whether or not the subject is in fact medically capable or incapable of properly consenting. In the alternative, the decision to ask a doctor to take the samples without consent could be taken by a more senior officer, the duty traffic inspector, for example. Logically, it would be appropriate for person from whom blood has been taken without consent to be examined to determine that he is able to give proper consent for the testing of the sample before he is asked to give that consent.

The law on the nonconsensual collection of blood samples from possibly intoxicated drivers is, as it stands, a meal ticket for lawyers rather than the clear and straightforward guidance for the police, medical profession and courts that it ought to be.

43(3) - 2003: Coroners – What Next for Death Investigation in England and Wales?

(Editorial)

ARW Forrest
Editor, Science & Justice

'I have taken great care not to laugh at human actions, nor to weep at them, nor to hate them, but to understand them.'

Baruch Spinoza

The fundamental review into death certification and the investigation of death, commissioned by the government, finally reported its findings in June 2003 after two years of deliberation [1]. The final reports of other ongoing inquiries by the retained organ commission and the Shipman enquiry are yet to come. Their findings and recommendations may or may not be in agreement with the fundamental review and who knows what scandals about the activities of miscreant and murderous doctors and nurses whose activities have not been detected by the current system for death investigation and certification may emerge in the meantime? Will the report fare any better than the two main reports into the practice of coroners of the last century, both of which sank without trace? [2, 3] One thing is quite clear; doing nothing is not an option. Simple consideration of the ongoing effect of the European Convention of Human Rights on English Coronial Law makes that perfectly clear.

At present, as the report points out, coroners are a law unto themselves. They have a very wide discretion in the way they practise. Whilst this may enable a coroner to deal humanely with particular difficult cases, bending the law to meet human need and angst, this flexibility produces such unpredictable variations in practice that a death that might be the subject of a two day inquest in one jurisdiction may, in a jurisdiction a few miles away, be dealt with only the minimum of investigation. The bereaved deserve more certainty in the investigation of the death of their loved ones. Similarly, the local authorities that currently appoint coroners have used widely varying practices for recruitment. These range from advertisement only on the local authority's web site, a technique for restricting the field to only those candidates the local authority might wish, for its own reasons, to appoint, through advertisements in the depths of *The Guardian's* Wednesday "Society" recruitment advertising supplement amongst the 30,000 boondoggles a year like "Five-a-Day Coordinators" and "Tobacco Control Managers" [4] to those authorities which advertise coroner's posts in all three of the *Law Society Gazette*, *British Medical Journal* and *The Times*. The recommendation that coroners be removed from their present archaic combination of local authority recruitment and employment, the generally benign oversight of the Home Office when in office, with the Lord Chancellor having the final power of dismissal for gross misconduct, and be transplanted into the Lord Chancellor's Department, like other judicial officers, was a reform so obviously desirable that it came as no surprise when it appeared in the report. Unfortunately, shortly after the report was published, the Prime Minister announced the abolition of the office of the Lord Chancellor in his summer reshuffle. Whether or not this is constitutionally possible remains a moot point.

Another recommendation that is hardly controversial is that the numbers of coroner's districts be reduced to 60 or so, with the appointment of a Chief Coroner for England and Wales. The suggestion that a statutory Coronial Council be set up to develop evidence based standards for the selection of those deaths that require special investigation and also to promulgate standards for post mortem examinations and other methods of investigating deaths, including, one hopes, standards for toxicology, is to be welcomed. Whilst the Royal College of Pathologists has done much good work in developing autopsy and other standards, it remains a college for pathologists, not coroners, even though a coroner does sit on its forensic pathology sub-committee.

The suggestion that the certification of the fact of death be separated from the certification of cause of death only reflects what now happens in most parts of the country; in many hospitals a nurse may certify the fact of death rather than disturb the sleeping junior doctor, whilst in the community, many districts have now developed protocols which allow a paramedic to certify the fact of death. The report recommends that the cause of death be certified by two medical practitioners, this to apply to all "routine" deaths, not just those where the body is to be disposed of by cremation. The payment of "ash cash" to doctors completing the forms of application for cremation would, as a by-product, be abolished. Whilst it is, of course, the case that no responsible professional could ever be diverted from his or her duty by the thought of the possible loss of a payment of £45 for a cremation certificate, I personally applaud the removal of this source of temptation. I suspect many medical practitioners with a practice largely devoted to the care of the elderly will have their incomes adversely affected by this reform.

Possibly the most interesting proposal is the establishment of a post of Statutory Medical Assessor, for each of the new coroner's districts, to work alongside the judicial coroner and to provide medical input, with a consequent coordinated medical and judicial approach to the investigation of non routine deaths. The report also sees this person as having a role in the statistical analysis of patterns of death as well as other duties such as appointing and overseeing the second certifiers of the cause of death and liaison with bereaved families. This will be an interesting post for those who fill it, but it will require a range of knowledge, expertise and personal qualities that are difficult to find in one person.

The present government has shown that its appetite for constitutional reform is undiminished despite, or possibly even because of, its various other problems. We can expect legislative reform of the coronial system of death investigation in the next parliament, if not in this one. The reforms are unlikely to follow exactly the recommendations of the fundamental review, in that the Shipman Enquiry report into, inter alia, how Harold Shipman got away with it for so long, also ought to inform reform of the present system when it is published. The higher courts too will have their say. There is an interesting little spate of coronial cases currently going through the High Court, Court of Appeal, and House of Lords. Middleton, the most interesting of these, is due to have been heard by the House of Lords by the time this editorial is published [5].

One thing is for sure, I do not envy the parliamentary draughtsmen who will have to put together the legislation reforming the coronial system; pruning and grafting everything that has grown up since coroners were established in about 1194 will be no mean task. They will surely envy their predecessors in 19th Century Massachusetts who established medical examiners with a short bill, the first clause of which was: "The office of coroner is hereby abolished".

References

1. Death Certification and Investigation in England, Wales and Northern Ireland. The Report of a Fundamental Review 2003. Cmd 5831. The Stationery Office, Norwich 2003.
2. The Broderick Report. Report of the Committee on Death Certification and Coroners. Cmd 4810. 1971.
3. The Wright Report. Report of the Departmental Committee on Coroners, Cmd 5070. 1936.
4. Costing Jobs. Jonathan Woolharn. Adam Smith Institute Briefing. www.adamsmith.org/policy/publications/industry-and-employment-pub.htm#jump7. Accessed 29 June 2003.
5. *R (Amin) v Secretary of State for the Home Department, R (Middleton) v Coroner for West Somerset. [2002] 4 All ER 336, CA.*

44(3) - 2004: The Human Tissue Bill – An Opportunity About to be Missed?

(Editorial)

The Human Tissue Bill currently before the UK Parliament might be thought to bring much needed clarification of the current law. Unfortunately, the drafting of the Bill is anything but clear in many important respects [1]. The various scandals and enquiries leading up to the publication of the Bill will be well known to UK readers. The, at best arrogant, certainly morally repugnant and at worst unlawful, retention and sometimes disposal of organs and tissues with emotive connotations such as the brain or the heart, after post mortem examination and without the consent of the relatives of the deceased, has been a matter of concern to some members of the public and the politicians who represent them for several years.

Yet there is a paradox; there appears to be considerable public support for the proposal that after death, in the absence of evidence that the deceased has made a positive declaration in life that he does not want his organs to be harvested after death, the deceased's organs should be removed for therapeutic purposes. This may be something that is for the public good. Organ transplantation is accepted as desirable and legitimate by all of the major religions in the UK. Organs for transplantation are not the only material that can be harvested from the body after death and used for the public good. Material can be obtained for research both for medical purposes and to advance other areas of knowledge in the interests of the public.

At present in the UK the vast majority of post mortem examinations are done without the consent of the deceased's relatives, on the authority of the coroner or procurator fiscal who is directing the investigation into the death. The coroner can only authorise the collection of material from a particular deceased if it is to assist in establishing who the deceased was and where, when and in what broad circumstances he came by his death. Nonetheless, there have been cases where samples have been collected from other deceased person's bodies to investigate particular points in an investigation. For example, in an investigation of a murder with insulin where issues arose as to the interpretation of the concentrations of C-peptide and insulin in urine, samples were collected from other bodies taken into a public mortuary to address the point. Arguably, such action was in the public interest, may not have been unlawful and would not have been problematical to most, but certainly not all, people living in the UK. After all, the fate of a substantial amount of the urine and blood in a body subject to post mortem is to be simply flushed into the public drainage system. Less controversially, the research into the incidence of drugs in the bodies of victims of road traffic crashes, arguably went well beyond what a coroner might have thought he needed to establish the circumstances of the death in an individual case and yet has attracted no criticism [2].

The effect of the present Human Tissue Bill, if enacted into law, would prohibit the collection of such samples without "appropriate consent". The penalty for carrying out such activity without "appropriate consent", and I warn you, you will have to read the Bill several times before you will be able to work out what is meant by "appropriate consent", could be a maximum of three years in prison.

In practical terms getting consent for the collection of samples for such research at a coroner's post mortem will be impractical. It is a difficult enough task to tell the relatives that there has to be a post mortem examination, let alone ask for consent for the collection of samples for research or any other of the purposes that the Bill specifies as requiring consent.

There is more; if a sample is submitted to a laboratory for forensic examination for the purposes of the coroner and for the investigation of a crime, if any remains after the examination it would not be possible to use it for other purposes. For example if a toxicologist wished to make up standards for an assay using samples of vitreous humour, this would probably be unlawful.

The Medical Research Council has expressed a number of concerns about this Bill that should be broadly shared by the forensic science community in the UK [3]. These concerns include the lack of clarity in the drafting of the Bill generally, the definition of "appropriate consent" and who can give it, the issue of qualified consent, that is to say consent to the use of material for one purpose but not another, and a variety of other matters.

Tinkering with this Bill may not be enough. A thorough redrafting is necessary to ensure that there is clarity in the law and that there is provision, perhaps on the direction of the Human Tissue Authority, that the Bill proposes be set up, to allow the collection and retention at post mortem of small amounts of body fluids and non emotive tissues, such as muscle, for research as it is normally understood and for other purposes in clinical, forensic and research laboratories. If we are all to be carrying identity cards in a few years time perhaps one field on that card should be to allow us to give advanced consent to the use of parts of our bodies for research (in the broadest sense of the term) purposes after our death. I'll put my money where my mouth is; when I die my colleagues are welcome to whatever bits of my body they might find useful. I'd rather they had it than the worms eat it.

Robert Forrest

References

1. http://www.publications.parliament.uk/pa/cm200304/cmbills/049/2004049.pdf (accessed 26 May 2004).
2. Tunbridge R J, Keigan M, James F J (2001) The Incidence of drugs and alcohol In road accident fatalities Report No. TRL495. Wokingham Berkshire: TRL Ltd
3. http://www.mrc.ac.uk/pdf-postioning-paper-htb.pd (accessed 26 May 2004)

46(2) - 2006: All's Fair in Love and War

(Editorial)

Dr N Nic Daéid

I recently found myself on the witness stand in a case in the Sheriff court in Ayr. As the cross examination progressed it became clear to me that I had been 'Googled' by my learned colleague, the results of which were forming the basis for a number of his questions. This made me think (later on the train home) about the nature and amount of information available about any of us which may become 'fair game' in these situations and what, if anything, we can do to prepare ourselves.

A statement made in the House of Lords by the Attorney General, Lord Goldsmith, (14 Feb 2006) referred to new guidance for the expert witness which essentially focuses on the requirements made of such witnesses in the area of disclosure. It makes very interesting reading particularly in relation to disclosure of unused materials etc. The document also makes reference to the expertise, competence and credibility of experts and how one might go about ensuring this. The guidance, (available from the Crown Prosecution Service [1]) will affect all experts in England and Wales who are not police employees, and is in response to public and professional concerns arising to recent issues surrounding expert evidence following the Sally Clark and related cases. (Experts who are employees of the police will continue to work under the requirements of the CPIA 1996 [2] which has similar requirements.

The requirement for experts to produce a 'self-certificate' is mentioned – a form which, in essence, relates to the provision of information which may adversely affect an individual's credibility or competence in their role as an expert. While we all know and understand that experts may differ in opinion (and recent cases such as the McKie case in fingerprint identification have particularly illustrated this), this in itself is not necessarily an issue. So long as the expert has fulfilled his/her role correctly, and provided that an opinion has been arrived at objectively, derived from careful research and examination of all materials presented and is honestly held in light of the circumstances, then the expert has done his/her duty to the court. Their duty "to furnish the judge and jury with the necessary scientific criteria for testing the accuracy of their conclusions" (Davie v Edinburgh Magistrates, 1953), and thereby clarify the minds of the jury and judge in matters of which they may be ignorant or confused is paramount. If the expert's opinion is not ultimately persuasive to the jury, then that does not mean that the expert is wrong or incompetent, so long as they have performed within their area of expertise and/or competence. Indeed, (to paraphrase Roberts [3]), such results may be due to the limitations of criminal proceedings or unrealistic institutional demands and expectations, rather than inadequacies of scientific method or a failure on the part of the experts.

Where things can come unstuck is often in the delivery of evidence, demeanour in court and how the difficult questions are handled. A legitimate (though arguably questionable) tactic, is to seek to equate an expert's experience with their competence (particularly with less experienced experts), with a view to undermining their credibility with the jury. Some of us will have memories of experiences which we found uncomfortable and difficult during rigorous cross examination which focused on such issues and it is in this very area that the self-certificate may come to our aid.

Guidance on the preparation of the self-certificate is given in Annex K of the Disclosure Manual. The questions asked include a declaration of previous convictions, cautions or penalty notices, civil court proceedings, adverse findings relating to professional competence and credibility, or proceedings brought by a professional or regulatory body and any other adverse information which may exist. This provides an opportunity for the expert to declare any of these at the outset, bearing in mind that Google may do it for you, particularly if any matters received media attention. Barristers are also advised through their own specialist publications to be keenly aware of the necessity to establish the strength of the expert opinion on which they wish to rely. They are counselled to ensure that their experts have remained unbiased and fair in the expression of their results so that accusations of impropriety and overstepping the mark will not arise in the court room arena.

In Scotland, of course, these rules (as yet) do not apply. For those of you who work as expert witnesses North of the border, may I suggest that you 'Google' yourself to see what the opposition may come up with!

References

1. http://www.cps.gov.uk/legal/section20/ (last accessed 05 June 2006)
2. Criminal Procedures and Investigations Act 1996
3. Roberts P, Zuckerman A *Criminal Evidence*, Oxford University Press, Oxford, 2004

SECTION VI: FORENSIC MEDICINE

The study of human anatomy has long fascinated men of science and medicine and as far back as the Ebers papyrus (circa 1550BC), one of the earliest medical documents known, the features of the human heart were detailed and described. Some of the greatest pillars upon which we build our modern ideas of philosophy and intellectual achievements (Hippocrates, Aristotle and Galen) were fascinated and inspired by their studies of early medical science. This fascination and desire to understand how the body works has driven many to minutely document the intricacies of the human body and indeed great artists such as Michelangelo, Da Vinci, Caravaggio and Rembrandt are renowned for their precise detail in representing the human form.

In forensic science, we also have a significant linkage with medicine and many of our early pioneers were medically trained. Forensic pathologists, charged with determining the cause, manner and (if appropriate) circumstances of unexplained or sudden death remain highly trained and work closely with the relevant medico-legal authority (Coroner, procurator fiscal, medical examiner) as an essential part of the forensic process where death has occurred. The desire to strive to understand what has occurred to cause a death has been a driving force in medico legal matters and early development of the forensic sciences is peppered with the notable inclusion of forensic pathologists. The role of the forensic pathologist has always been one of vital importance in suspicious death investigations. In the UK, the Brodick report produced in the early 1970s debated and reported, in considerable detail, the issues relating to the medical certification of death and the certainty that the cause of death should be established as accurately as possible. This report changed the manner in which deaths in England and Wales were investigated by Coroners and subsequently certified and was commented upon in the early editorials relating to forensic pathology.

The developments in forensic pathology over the past five decades have perhaps not been as dramatic as in other fields of forensic science even though it has arguably been one of the aspects of forensic work most exposed and glamorised by television programs. That is not to say of course that there hasn't been progress. Many forensic pathologists working in the UK continue to work out of University Medical departments or faculties and it is interesting to note that many of the medically focused editorials and comments discuss and lament the plight of such positions as practitioners become increasingly aligned to more commercial rather than collegiate drivers.

The topic of regulation has also been discussed and a parting shot from the outgoing Chief Executive of the Council for Registration of Forensic Practitioners (CRFP) now itself defunct ("Eight years on" volume 47 issue 2 – see section 1) provoked an irritated response from the Association of Forensic Physicians (volume 48 issue 2 – section 1) who discussed how the Faculty of Forensic and Legal Medicine of the Royal College of Physicians was working to develop and maintain standards of competence and ethical integrity across the profession. Indeed the Royal College of Physicians and other related and interested parties are now engaged with the Forensic Science Regulator as part of the forensic pathology specialist group with the remit to explore the setting of standards and maintenance of competency.

Fifty Years of Forensic Science: A commentary   Edited by Niamh Nic Daéid
© 2010, John Wiley & Sons, Ltd.

The interaction between the forensic pathologist, forensic scientist and police investigating officers has perhaps not always been comfortable as often occurs within expert teams. The presentation of complex medical evidence in court can also be problematic given the complex nature of the evidence and there are perhaps very few medical degrees that directly address this communication issue and perhaps an area of future educational development that could be addressed.

N. Nic Daéid

5(4a) - 1964: The Smallest Room But One

The recent emigration of a senior English forensic pathologist to Australia, primarily because of working conditions said to be 'dreary, dismal and even Dickensian'[1], has once again momentarily focussed attention on the sad plight of those pathologists regularly condemned to perform Coroners' autopsies in the mortuaries of the English rural, and smaller urban, districts.

Small, poorly lit, wretchedly ventilated, freezingly cold in winter, malodourously warm in summer, often without refrigeration or proper working surfaces and with their woefully inadequate Victorian plumbing in a permanent state of semi-occlusion from the anatomical debris of decades, these buildings still stand in council yards, by sewage works and rubbish tips all over the land, the subject of the prying curiosity of agile children and awkward silences at local council meetings. Next to public conveniences, to which many of them bear a curious and revealing architectural resemblance, they are usually the smallest buildings erected and maintained by the local authority and one cannot help but feel that their size accurately reflects the interest taken in them. The architectural and pathological deficiencies of these rural mortuaries have been widely publicised, particularly in the *Lancet*[2, 3, 4], and the general state of mortuary accommodation in the country was the subject of an A.C.P. special committee investigation in 1960[5]. The associated problems of staffing and cleaning these small premises on a part-time basis and of providing for the proper viewing of bodies by relatives are well known. Even the transport of bodies to and from the mortuary often creates difficulties, inasmuch as the police, who in some areas traditionally perform this task, and the local ambulance service both contend, and with some justification, that this work falls outside their proper line of duty. The use of local undertaking firms to provide this transport can give rise to resentment if the work is not shared equally between the interested parties. The time wasted by a pathologist travelling between these village mortuaries is relatively enormous and since almost none of them are on the telephone he is incommunicado from the instant he sets out until his return to base. All these and many other disadvantages have been pointed out on many occasions and yet these places still survive. Worse, it is still the practice for even major medico-legal autopsies, including cases of murder involving the whole paraphernalia of the C.I.D., finger print, photography and forensic science people, to be carried out in these tiny local mortuaries, a custom fraught with inconvenience and danger to all concerned.

There are, however, recent signs that some local authorities are at last beginning to realise the inadequacy of the facilities they have provided. Mortuaries are slowly being upgraded by the piecemeal installation of such things as refrigerators, benching, new sinks and better lighting. Though the intention may be good, the immediate effects of these changes are not always so. Refrigeration usually markedly reduces the already tiny working area still further, whilst in two mortuaries known to the writer the new 'fridge' is so sited that the freshly autopsied cadavers have to be manoeuvred outside in view of the street before they can be placed in it! Further, is this bit by bit tinkering really what we want? The more money which is now spent by local councils in patching up these places, the more difficult it becomes ultimately to recommend their closure. Is this then not the time, when the wind of change is blowing or preparing to blow through our entire Coroners' system, for a great reassessment of our public mortuary service and its re-shaping to meet future needs?

Surely basic to all such planning should be the removal of the responsibility for providing post mortem facilities, at any rate, from the smaller local authorities and the vesting of it in the County Council or some other central regional authority. The financial burden of building, maintaining and staffing a mortuary is a large one to a small council and the money is at present largely recovered from the County Council anyway, through fees paid by the Coroners for the use of the premises. Handing over to a central authority would relieve

---

[1] (1965) *Daily Telegraph*, 14th August.
[2] (1942) "In England Now." *Lancet*, **1**, 237.
[3] (1946) Editorial. *Lancet*, **1**, 388.
[4] (1959) Widdicombe File. *Lancet* **11**, 1081.
[5] (1961) Mortuary Design and Hazards. *J. Clin. Path*. **14**, 103. 175.

the local council of this burden and would not substantially increase the County's financial commitments. It would further enable the central authority to assess the autopsy facilities available in the region and to make the best use of these taking into account geographical, technical, transport and population factors.

One envisages at least one main public mortuary, in each region, preferably sited close to a Home Office Forensic Science Laboratory or a University Department of Forensic Medicine, or both, and forming with these places a central medico-legal institute – fully equipped to deal with all major forensic problems.

The transfer of a body from one Coroner's area to another is a simple matter of informal agreement and no loss of jurisdiction over the case is involved so that this would prove no problem in practice.

At the periphery, almost all of the small village morgues now in use could be closed entirely or perhaps modified so that their sole function was the storage and identification of bodies. No mortuary at present dealing with less than 200 cases per year would be likely to survive except for unusual geographical reasons. Their place could be taken by the establishment at suitable sites in the region of three or four large modern mortuaries, preferably near to premises suitable for use as a Coroner's Court which could, in conjunction with the central medico-legal institute, deal with all of the Coroner's work for the whole area.

Such places would, of course, be staffed by full-time mortuary personnel and indeed could serve as accredited training centres for mortuary technicians in the same way as the central institutes could for aspiring forensic pathologists.

Some of them might well be Regional Hospital Board/County Council joint user establishments based on large newly-erected hospitals and indeed this seems a sensible way of avoiding duplication in the provision of mortuary facilities, providing that the administrative balance of power could be maintained.

In some remote areas the need might be met, as it is at present in many places, by the responsible authority coming to some financial agreement with the local hospital over the use of the mortuary when necessary. This is in the writer's view perhaps the least desirable arrangement, since many of the local hospital mortuaries are themselves in a parlous, poorly equipped state and also some National Health Service pathologists, understandably, come to regard hospital mortuaries as very much their own so that difficulties can, though with the exercise of tact rarely do, arise, when they require to be suddenly requisitioned for an outside expert performing what may well be a long autopsy.

Financially, part of the cost of a comprehensive mortuary scheme could be met by the various local authorities using the service in any one region either by block grant or on a 'per capita' basis. The increased cost of transporting bodies over the longer distances would be partially offset by the saving in travelling allowances paid to pathologists. The amount of transport required would surely justify the creation of a special body-carrying service – infinitely preferable to the indiscriminate use of ambulances which is the rule in most places to-day. Each mortuary would clearly require one or two vans and appropriately trained operating staff to be used for body collection within its own area.

Perhaps the greatest saving which would accrue from the introduction of such a scheme, however, would be that of the pathologists' time. As the investigation of sudden and unexpected death in the community steadily becomes more rigorous and thorough, it seems likely that the number of medico-legal autopsies 176 required will, quite properly, rise substantially and there is at present certainly no indication of a future plethora of either hospital or forensic pathologists to deal adequately with this situation. Indeed, for various reasons, of which poor working conditions is only one, recruitment into forensic pathology gives cause for the gravest anxiety as to the future of the speciality. It is, therefore, surely sensible that conditions be provided for our forensic pathologists, which enable them to make the fullest and most economical use of their time, skill and experience. When fifteen years of a man's liberty can still turn on a pathological opinion, surely only the highest standards of professional judgement, exercised in the most favourable conditions, can be acceptable.

A series of talented individual pathologists have in the past gained for Britain an enviable reputation in the field of forensic pathology, despite the inadequacy of the facilities available to them. We have muddled through to the top in the best British tradition, in dingy mortuaries and cramped inconvenient laboratories while on the Continent centralisation and the establishment of modern medico-legal institutes has proceeded apace. We surely still have the individual talent – let us provide such facilities here as will encourage its full development and use in the fight against crime.

A.U.

7(3) - 1966: Decline and Fall

It is a depressing paradox that in spite of the recent resurgence of interest in the wider scene of the forensic sciences, the long-established interest of the universities in forensic medicine seems to be rapidly on the wane.

In less than a decade, two energetic professional associations have been founded, two excellent journals launched and many enthusiastic meetings held.

The Establishment themselves have been stirred to action – perhaps inevitably is the face of increasing crime and more clamorous public opinion. They have set up a Research Laboratory, advisory committees and an Interdepartmental committee as well as generally encouraging the increased use of scientific aids in law enforcement. Mass communication – television, newspapers and other means of popular exposition of forensic matters – has brought an awareness of the discipline to every man-in-the-street.

Yet, in the face of all this, academic forensic medicine has gone steadily downhill until there is now a danger of its complete extinction. With one or two notable exceptions in London, the universities appear to look upon the specialty with complete apathy, or even open antagonism. The Chair of Forensic Medicine in Birmingham was one of the first to go, the department being fragmented.

The Chair at Edinburgh has remained empty for some years. The Readership at Sheffield has been demoted to a lectureship and the department converted into a sub-department under the Professor of Pathology. All but one medical school in England and Wales has abandoned the degree examination, so that the great majority of new doctors now have little incentive to learn any legal medicine.

Now, and perhaps the most serious threat of recent years, is the fate of the only professorial department outside London (excluding Scotland). Professor Polson is soon to retire and the future of the well-known Leeds department hangs precariously in the balance – a balance, one might guess, that might be tipped one way or the other by the long-awaited report of the Home Office Brodrick Committee.

If Leeds is demoted, as have other departments, then the already makeshift career structure of the full-time forensic pathologist will crumble so badly that not only will there be no new recruits, as is the situation at present, but the existing younger men will be tempted to desert the sinking ship for more progressive disciplines.

What are the causes of this academic blight – and might it not be justified? Primarily, forensic medicine has fallen between not two, but three stools.

At the inception of the National Health Service in 1948, it was excluded as a speciality, which was unfortunate, both from the point of view of its development, its contribution to the community and, not least, the remuneration of its practitioners.

There remained the Home Office and the universities and a somewhat unhappy compromise has grown up between them. On the one hand, the Home Office wants the services of a forensic expert, but does not want to pay for them, whilst on the other hand, the universities – with few exceptions – seem neither to want the man nor want to pay him, suffering him to remain mainly because his appointment already existed. One only has to look around the country and try to find a department that has actually expanded – with one notable exception, the trend is in the reverse direction. In most universities forensic medicine is virtually self-supporting, this forming the only basis for its toleration. Either all fees are paid in and a fixed salary given, or a small part-time salary is offered, the pathologist making up the rest by his individual efforts. One can hardly visualise a department of mathematics, anatomy or languages functioning on this basis. The university argues that police and coroner's work is a service to the community, on a par with sanitary inspectors and refuse-collecting, and should be similarly provided by the public authorities.

The work load of a forensic pathologist is so great that he has little opportunity for research, this not endearing him to the academicians. Further, by their own edicts, teaching has been pruned to a travesty of what is necessary and this again reduces the attractiveness of forensic medicine to the university fathers.

The alternatives would be either to abandon academic forensic medicine altogether or to take it under the wing of the Home Office. Of the two, the first seems the most likely to occur unless a halt is called to the present process of attrition. The hospital pathologists already perform about eighty per cent. of all coroner's autopsies, mainly the non-criminal sudden deaths. Without them, British legal medicine would grind to a rapid halt. It has been advocated that all forensic pathology should be handed over to the clinical pathologist, in spite of the fact that it already encroaches appreciably into the clinical duties of many of them. Apart from a few very experienced and enthusiastic men, the majority would not want this added burden and responsibility. The prospect of standing with policemen in muddy fields at three in the morning, of subsequent days wasted in court and the prospect of a verbal lashing by Counsel, does not attract most hospital pathologists. More important, in spite of what many may say to the contrary, the expertise of forensic medicine – both technical considerations and mental orientation – can only be learned by much experience; to spread the available experience of criminal cases so thinly over the country so that each clinical pathologist saw but a few cases a year would be a most undesirable and retrograde step.

The other alternative – direct employment by the Home Office – seems out of the question for practical reasons. If every Forensic Science laboratory had a full-time pathologist, all the histological facilities available in universities would have to be re-duplicated and valuable liaisons such as those with anatomy and dental departments would be lost. If his only function was to deal with criminal cases, he would be underemployed, as the Home Office would have little interest in him doing routine sudden-death work. It would require a major administrative upheaval and a great increase in man-power to set up what would virtually be a National Forensic Service on the continental pattern, though inevitably this must come at some time in the distant future.

The only immediate solution is the continuance and improvement of the traditional association with the universities. This could be attained by the added stimulus of a direct Treasury grant to sweeten the present academic attitude. Outside London and Scotland, there is at present a forensic foothold in Bristol, Cardiff, Sheffield, Leeds, Manchester, Liverpool and Newcastle. If a direct subsidy was given to each of these universities, on the condition that the money was spent on establishing or maintaining a separate department of forensic medicine, then the university would have someone to teach and research without having to grudgingly count their own pennies – and the Home Office would have a first-class service available, even if it cost them a little more than the ridiculous pittance that they hand out as an honorarium at present.

And, just as important, there might then be a few recruits attracted into forensic medicine – if not, the police are one night soon, going to find themselves standing alone in that muddy field.

B.K.

10(3) - 1970: How Much Specialisation in Pathology Can We Afford?

Last year 110,000 post-mortem examinations were carried out in England and Wales on the authority of the Coroner, to establish the cause of death where that was unknown or uncertain, or where it was thought to be unnatural, as by accident, suicide or murder.

Over 80% of these autopsies were performed by pathologists whose training and experience lies in clinical or academic pathology rather than in forensic pathology.

The remainder were done by pathologists specialising in forensic pathology, usually in a university department.

Where serious crime is known to have occurred or is suspected the Police ask for the services of a pathologist who has specialised, or who has taken a special interest in, the investigation of such cases. The pathologist called in may be from the university department, or may be one who, though practising in general pathology, is nominated by the Home Office to carry out this work and who agrees to be on call at all times.

In 1963, at the Third International Meeting in Forensic Immunology, Medicine, Pathology and Toxicology, Professor Cyril Polson outlined proposals for a National Pathology Service along the lines of the Home Office Laboratories, with Regional teams of whole-time forensic pathologists, trained or in training, carrying out all the autopsies required by the Coroner or by the Police.

He argued persuasively that the clinical pathologists who at present time handle the bulk of these cases are conditioned to the medical rather than the legal aspects of disease, that their reports too often omit details of injuries and their interpretation, or are frankly too brief to be of any value in the event of suspicion subsequently being aroused.

Accepting that the censures on clinical pathologists are often justified, accepting that they have been responsible for many a small sin of omission and commission, as well as for some major errors, should such a large band of able pathologists be dismissed in this way, in favour of whole-time Government employed pathologists living solely in an atmosphere of forensic medicine, divorced from clinical medicine and pathology.

The bulk of deaths are deaths from natural disease, or where natural disease has played a large part. This is not disputed. The greater experience of the hospital pathologist over the forensic pathologist in this field is self evident.

It is true that too often the hospital pathologist may treat a post-mortem as routine when it deserves at least very special care, and perhaps an expert opinion.

If the Police feel that their investigations are being hampered because his simple examinations lack ordinary, as opposed to expert, care, or that the evidence is presented inadequately in Court, then let them tell the Coroner so, or failing satisfaction, the Home Office. A very great deal of money is paid out annually for these post-mortem examinations and the Home Office has a right to know that it is being spent wisely.

But if the manpower to staff Polson's service were available, and if the even greater funds necessary were forthcoming from the universities, Home Office or Coroners Society, is the alternative, a team of whole-time forensic pathologists, likely to do much better? Is it likely to detect more crime, or to investigate more fully the natural deaths? A series of large teams would be bound to 127 include many a very ordinary pathologist in addition to those of quality whom we know today. Is their index of suspicion likely to be sustained in face of the 10, 15 or even 20 post-mortem examinations a day which they may be expected to perform any day, and every day? Dr. H. R. M. Johnson in an interesting review of 28,000 autopsies carried out by a small team of well-trained but perhaps overworked forensic pathologists in London was able to report finding only one single case of hitherto unsuspected murder in a ten-year period. Perhaps the area served was so efficiently policed that all but one were detected before autopsy, but perhaps the explanation for this low yield of unsuspected crime should be sought in the massive turnover, with an unavoidable fall in suspicion index, inattention to or unavailability of good clinical and social records, or lack of close liaison with the Police officers most closely concerned with the circumstances.

The hospital pathologist has the great advantage over his whole-time forensic colleague that he has far fewer autopsies to perform, has access to hospital records, has easy informal exchanges with the hospital clinicians and very often knows the general practitioner well and learns to value his judgment.

Because he has time to think about the one or two autopsies, which is as many as most hospital pathologists carry out in one day, and to investigate many of them histologically, the importance of an unusual set of clinical or social aspects of a case may be appreciated when they might have been passed unnoticed in face of a heavy post-mortem load. The successful detection and investigation of a recent case of murder by repeated arsenic poisoning was possible largely because of the close association of the pathologist with the hospital physician and general practitioner. A tentative diagnosis made from such consultations and a study of the hospital records may alone make possible the proper investigation, and subsequent presentation of the case in Court.

The hospital pathologist has the further advantage of repeatedly measuring his 'forensic findings' against a solid background of 'normal' pathology, and by feeding the forensic material back to the general practitioners and hospital consultants both sides benefit.

Should we not turn to better use the many advantages the clinical pathologist has, rather than replace him by whole-time forensic experts, conditioned always to appear for the Crown? Can we not develop his suspicion index, heighten his powers of forensic deduction?

Here perhaps might lie the justification for the development of a few active urban and regional centres of forensic medicine, through which all pathologists contemplating Coroners' post-mortems might be obliged to pass. These centres have already shown that they can raise the standards of some clinical pathologists to the level that is acceptable by the Police, and this Editorial is a plea, not for the dissolution of such centres but for their expansion, although not in the way that Professor Polson envisaged.

D.F. Barrowcliff

12(1) - 1972: "The Six-and-a-half-year Itch"

The Brodrick Report,* as might well be expected of any document which took almost seven years to produce, is massively thorough and shows evidence of minute attention to detail, though one possible sin of omission is the failure to do more than mention the role of the forensic sciences, Pathology apart, in the investigation of sudden and unexpected deaths in the community.

Its recommendations which, for the most part, will be welcomed as tending to streamline and modernize the present system, mainly concern the future of coroners and their proceedings, the pathology and ancillary services available to them and the future form of certification before disposal of the dead.

In this last context, the simplification of the procedure required for disposal by cremation will be widely applauded, provided only that the higher standards of accuracy required of doctors signing the new form of death certificate are accepted by the profession and enforced by the authorities.

It is pleasing to find, particularly in view of the many attacks made upon it over the years, that the coroners system of England and Wales has stood comparison with systems in operation elsewhere and that the Committee recommends its continuance, albeit in a more flexible form better suited to the style of contemporary society.

It should not detract from the value of the Committee's recommendations on coroners and their procedure that many of these were predictable and indeed have been advocated by informed opinion for many years. Thus there are to be fewer coroners; most will be full-time salaried officials with the approximate status of a Stipendiary Magistrate and have larger jurisdictions tied into the new County Authorities System. The power of committal for trial from inquest is, as most coroners will be delighted to know, to vanish and, indeed, the decision to hold an inquest at all is now to be, with only three exceptions, entirely a matter for the coroner's discretion. Three further welcome proposals are that legal aid should be available for representation at an inquest, that a simplified procedure for appeals from coroners' decisions should be introduced, and that riders to verdicts should be abolished. In general, the coroner's role is seen as mainly a medico-social one concerned primarily with the accurate determination of the medical and circumstantial causes of death for statistical purposes rather than with the investigation of crime, which latter aspect of his duties is very much played (some would say overplayed) down in the Report. The considered view of the Committee that the opportunity for secret homicide is now insignificant may sound, to some readers of this Journal, a shade too complacent. Against this background of decreasing engagement with court procedures and legal formalities,

---

*Report of the Committee on Death Certification and Coroners. (London, 1971, Her Majesty's Stationery Office)

and increasing concern with what are often mainly medical matters, it is difficult to agree with the view expressed in the report that a legal rather than a medical training provides the better qualification for a coroner, though the arguments on both sides are succinctly set out. Certainly the proposal to exclude doctors who have no formal legal training from the coronership seems rather a harsh one which will rob the office of many alert and enquiring minds.

The civilianization of coroners' officers is also a recommendation with which many experienced in the working of the present system will profoundly disagree.

Even in these iconoclastic days the uniform still has some effect in persuading witnesses making statements during coroners' investigations that the matter is one of some importance and that an approximation of the truth, however awkward or embarrassing had better be proffered. When more sympathetic methods are required then "civilianization" need take no more time than it takes to remove a tunic and slip on a sports jacket – an exercise at which most coroners' officers are singularly adept – and the access which these officers afford to a system of rapid communication and investigation is, in practice, invaluable. Perhaps a compromise solution with the new jurisdictions having available both civilian officers and those seconded from police ranks would have been ideal.

The only branch of the forensic sciences considered in the Report is Pathology and, on the whole, the proposals for providing pathological services to coroners and the police in the future reflecting, as they seem to, the political and personal opinions of the Committee, are the most disappointing part of the entire Report, and certainly the least in contact with present-day reality.

In effect, coroners' pathology, always a field in which the individualist and pathological entrepreneur has excelled, is to be nationalized and engulfed within the National Health Service as "the Coroners' Component" of that Service. The coroner using such a service will no longer be free to select for himself a pathologist on whose skill, accuracy and lucidity in any particular type of case his experience has taught him to rely. This delicate task will be performed for him by the inevitable "designated officer" who may be a pathologist or, possibly (horror of horrors), a senior medical administrator with, as the Committee blithely admits, no personal responsibility for the reports of the investigations instigated by him. The lucky hospital pathologist thus selected will, presumably, immediately leave his surgical biopsies, hospital autopsies and routine laboratory administration work to be completed later, and fall to at once upon the coroner's case, eager to earn a fee for the National Health Service which may be used to purchase a new microscope for his laboratory – at least that seems to be the theory of it. Actually the Report is (perhaps understandably) somewhat coy on the question of finance but the implication seems clear enough. National Health Service pathologists are to be asked to perform at least the same volume of coroners' work as formerly and probably very much more if the other recommendations of the Report are implemented, either without any financial reward at all or for only a proportion of their present fees, the rest passing to the Health Service.

It would indeed be surprising if this aspect of the Report were greeted other than coolly by pathologists who have in the past regarded fees from coroners' cases as legitimate "perks"; one of the few forms of private practice open to them in their speciality. Indeed this work is presently authorized as Category 2 employment and any attempt to change these arrangements would presumably require re-negotiation of the consultants' National Health Service contracts.

In addition, the Committee seems to have failed to take into account that much of the coroners' work is done in extra-sessional time – or that pathologists doing it habitually exceed their essential sessional commitments to the hospital.

To provide a complete coroners' service within the National Health Service on a formal sessional basis would require the appointment of from 200 to 300 new consultants in morbid anatomy plus ancillary staff and equipment – an expensive method of tackling this problem even were such large numbers of highly trained men available. They are, of course, not available and it would be many years before they could be. Meanwhile, recruitment to the speciality of Morbid Anatomy is not likely to be encouraged by the Committee's attitude to fees.

The proposal to base the future pathological service for the police as well as that for the coroners – a dubious distinction this, as the Report itself admits – in the Health Service has at least the merit of providing a long-needed career structure for the aspiring forensic pathologist and may eventually do something to swell the sadly depleted ranks of this speciality. However, it would appear that University Departments of Forensic Medicine, whose very existence for the most part nowadays depends upon their ability to pay their own way, are to be largely deprived of virtually their only source of income, i.e. the fees from routine coroners' work, to say nothing of the experience that such work affords. If this is done without other moneys being made available to them the Report speaks hopefully of a subvention from the Home Office – then the end is in sight for many departments.

This would be, even in the Committee's view, a pity, for they are envisaged as being responsible for teaching and research in the subject as well as for providing some or all of the pathological cover for the police in their respective areas.

Perhaps the most useful practical suggestion contained in this section (Chapter 24) of the Report, is that there should be local consultations initiated by the Home Office and involving Police Authorities, Regional Hospital Boards and, where applicable, University Departments of Forensic Medicine, to review the present arrangements for forensic cover, to decide if these need alteration or reinforcement and if so how best, from the facilities and manpower available, this may be effected. Unlike the remainder of the Report's recommendations on Pathology, this one could be implemented immediately without undue expense or great upheaval and it might result in rapid improvement in some areas which presently constitute a problem.

Alan Usher

13(4) - 1973: For Action This Day

(*A Personal View*)

Those who are interested in the investigation of unexpected and unnatural deaths, or even indeed in the certification of expected deaths, can be forgiven if they exhibit a little impatience from time to time towards those who govern England and Wales.

For 9 years now the present system with all its anomalies, irritations and even contradictions has struggled on under a question mark; for the first seven we were asking "What changes will be recommended?" and for the last two "When will they be introduced?"

The impending changes in local government seemed initially to offer an ideal opportunity for the introduction of many of the useful innovations recommended by the "Committee for the Investigation of Death certification and Coroners", but it has been thrown away. Furthermore the reorganization of the National Health Service offers an ideal opportunity to introduce such changes into the administration of pathology as may be desirable for the more efficient servicing of the medicolegal investigative system – not, one may add, all of these advocated by the Brodrick Committee.

Why, one asks, are those who make decisions in these matters so blind to the difficulties which they impose on others by their inactivity and failure to communicate their intentions? Or are they too cynical to care whether they create difficulties or not? One could argue that those who do not like working under these conditions can find other ways of earning a living, but this is not really an answer to the problem. We are told that there is a shortage of Parliamentary time and that there are other things of greater moment to be dealt with. This must of course bring a wry smile to the faces of those who from time to time have had to supply material to answer some Parliamentary questions. The truth of the matter is that there will always be matters of greater political importance than death certification, coroners, pathologists and a host of other minority interests. Are we to assume that they can never be dealt with? Is it too much to ask that some Parliamentary time be set aside solely for the purpose of dealing in due course with matters of minor importance? Until this happens the anomalies persist, the frustrations multiply and as far as Coroner's work is concerned, the public are inconvenienced at a time when they are least able emotionally to cope with such inconvenience.

One would like to know how many thousands of people each year have to attend inquests which do not serve any useful purpose and which are held solely to comply with the Coroners Acts. How much money do these inquests cost? How many harmless and innocent people each year have their private affairs (and sometimes secret shames) exhibited before the public to no good purpose? How many grief-stricken parents have their loss compounded by an obligation to observe the requirements of an obsolete statute? Are these indeed matters of minor importance for which there is no Parliamentary time? A nation which professes to care for the quality of men's lives should be able to find time to deal with matters which so deeply affect people's feelings.

Nor are these the only considerations involved. How many totally inaccurate but legally valid death certificates are issued annually? A glimpse of the answer to this question comes from time to time to coroners and pathologists when an application is made to remove a body out of England after a normal death certificate has been issued but there is sufficient uncertainty to justify an autopsy.

In about half of such cases the recorded cause of death is completely erroneous, and in the remainder it is often incomplete. It is a sobering thought that in spite of the vast changes in pathological thinking, resources and efficiency in the last hundred years, in spite of the development of a complex statistical department to deal with mortality data, and in spite of the current upsurge of interest in community medicine, Parliament cannot find time to introduce the legislation which is necessary to enable these three agencies to do their work efficiently. Daily in dozens of medical publications, mortality rates are quoted which are based in part upon inspired guesswork.

With the public interest suffering at so many points it is almost frivolous to mention again the frustrations of those who work under the system, but in the long run even their disenchantment can operate against the public good.

Unless there are reasonable conditions of work in any profession there will be disaffection and difficulties in recruitment. How can the continuity of either the pathology or coroner sections of the medicolegal investigative system be maintained with men of the right calibre if their futures are so persistently cloaked in an aura of mystery and non-communication? First-class forensic pathologists are now so few that they could all meet comfortably in one of Alan Usher's celebrated "Smallest Rooms" (1965) and their up and coming successors could assemble in anyone's smallest room. Coroners, on the other hand (except for those in Greater London), are all going to lose their appointments on 31 March 1974, and some reasonably expect to be reappointed by the new counties.

Do they know upon what terms? They do not. Have they a realistic salary scale or in the case of whole-time coroners any scale at all? They have not.

They have always put up with about half the County Clerk's salary – and some of them have a pension from previous employment or have some other source of income – so why bother? The need to bother is just this, that unless more consideration is given to the career prospects and working conditions of both forensic pathologists and coroners, the choice for those who have to fill the vacancies in these fields in the future in England and Wales will be limited to the failures, the alcoholics and the drug addicts. No-one undertakes this work in any capacity with a view to making a fortune but enthusiasm has its limits. If this dire state of affairs is allowed to develop, another inter-departmental committee will have to sit for another 7 years to reach the same conclusion as the last, namely that we do really need a medicolegal investigative system staffed by the right kind of people.

H. H. Pilling

Reference

Usher A., 1965, *J. Forens. Sci. Soc.*, **5**, 175.

14(4) - 1974: Chair Legs Wanted

It is with a sense of relief that one can at long last note a slight thaw in the Ice Age which has been afflicting United Kingdom Forensic Medicine for so long.

After the subject had come to the verge of academic extinction, the past 18 months has seen a sudden, and welcome, restatement by the universities of their recognition of its role in the medical schools, expressed in the creation or refilling of no less than six chairs of forensic medicine and two readerships.

The first, in chronological order, was in Leeds, where the only established chair in England had been occupied with distinction for 23 years by Professor Polson until his retirement in 1970. For some time it had seemed likely that after his retirement the chair would be abolished and the department closed. However, in 1972, soon after the publication of the report of the Brodrick committee, the decision was taken to fill the chair which he had vacated and to maintain the department; and the new professor was duly appointed in July 1972.

Next came Edinburgh. The Regius Chair, which had been the first to be created in the United Kingdom in 1807, had been empty for 13 years since the death of Professor Douglas Kerr in 1960. The department had been kept alive by the exertions of Dr. Fiddes, the senior lecturer, and after his death in 1972 the future for the department seemed gloomy. However, in 1973 Dr. Mason was appointed to the chair, after his distinguished career as pathologist to the Royal Air Force, Institute of Pathology, during which he had developed the medical side of the investigation of aircraft disasters to a fine art. Then came appointments in London and Northern Ireland. After the deeply regretted death of Professor Francis Camps it was pleasant to find the value of his two erstwhile assistants recognized, and to see that the tradition at the London Hospital was maintained by the appointment to a personal chair of Dr. Cameron, previously senior lecturer at London, while Dr. Johnson, now at St. Thomas's, was appointed to a readership. Meantime the very senior forensic pathologist in Northern Ireland, Dr. Marshall, was appointed to a richly deserved personal chair in Belfast.

To return to London University, two further important and long deserved appointments were Dr. Keith Mant to a personal chair at Guy's in succession to Professor Keith Simpson, and Dr. Bowen to a readership at Charing Cross Hospital.

And last but by no means least, once more north of the border, the culmination of the series was the filling of the other Regius Chair, at Glasgow, by the appointment of Dr. Harland to succeed Professor Gilbert Forbes.

So, six chairs and two readerships in the last couple of years must surely be considered to be an indication of academic support for the subject. This is particularly important at a time when there has been a progressive reduction in the amount of teaching of forensic medicine in the under-graduate medical curriculum, to the point of complete extinction in some areas. Concern about the results of the paucity of instruction in this subject has been expressed by the medical defence organizations, and although their anxieties must be presumed to be mainly actuated by financial considerations, yet the same concern could well be expressed for the effects of lack of teaching on the conduct of future doctors in the witness box, and in their relationships with the legal authorities, their conduct of the examination of the victims, or those accused of violent crime, and so forth. Moreover an equally important field is in postgraduate teaching, both for doctors, and for persons in other aspects of forensic work, such as police officers, the standards of whose training in other aspects of criminology is achieving ever greater levels of expertise in their own training schools.

Facilities for full-time postgraduate students are important both from overseas and from our own country. There have been a number of comments recently about the place of forensic science, or of police science, within the universities, and the move towards the rejuvenation of academic departments of forensic medicine would provide convenient initial loci for such endeavours, or at least points of liaison. Thus within them, postgraduate students might be able to work for higher degrees in some subject within the broad spectrum of the forensic sciences, as a preliminary to the development of fully organized courses of study, or even separate academic departments of such allied subjects as forensic science or criminology.

Such opportunities as these for further development of the forensic sciences in an academic environment have now been put firmly within the realms of possibility by the actions of the universities. Now if the academics have made their contribution towards the welfare of the subject, then it is time that others made theirs.

The timing of the developments suggests that a major factor in forming the decision of the universities was the report of the Brodrick committee or at least that part of it which dealt with a pathology service for the police. The report stated that there was definitely a place for academic departments of forensic medicine, to carry out teaching and research, and a limited service commitment in their area, in a proportion of the medical schools. Such departments would carry out some, but certainly not all of the pathology service in their area, and they should be supported in part by a subvention from the state.

The importance of this last recommendation will bear stressing. Some time ago Bernard Knight, in an article in this Journal, drawing attention to the deplorable state of forensic medicine, outlined very succinctly the reasons for the decline of academic support for it (Knight, 1967). A particularly strong reason, and one which all those working in such academic departments are well aware of, was the reluctance of university authorities to foot almost the entire bill for providing a department whose predominant function was to provide a service for organizations outside the university. If that was the case, and we know very well that it was, a couple of years ago, there is an even more significant financial embarrassment to universities now, when their resources are considerably more circumscribed, and when they are having to count every penny.

If then, in their time of monetary distress, they have been willing to continue to provide support for the forensic departments, then it is doubly a duty of those agencies of the state who derive a service, either directly or indirectly from the work of such departments, to contribute to their support.

It can of course be said that the members of such departments do derive financial support, in that they are paid the statutory fees which their service work attracts, i.e. the fees paid by the coroners for autopsies and inquests, and by the Crown Courts for attendance to give evidence. In fact the finances earned in this way only approach the cost of running such a department if the members undertake a service commitment which is so great as to leave them no time for performing the other traditional activities of academic departments, teaching and research. And these are the activities which, apart from being quite obviously the most important aspects of their work, are also those aspects which are specifically referred to by the Brodrick committee.

For instance in the report of the Royal College of Pathologists on staffing and work-load, the number of autopsies considered appropriate for each member of a teaching department of pathology was 150 per annum, and 200–300 for a nonteaching department, in addition to surgical specimens. Now at current rates of Coroner's fees of £12 for an autopsy with inquest and £7.50 for an autopsy alone, 150 autopsies would bring in about £1500 per annum. Thus each member of staff would earn for the university not more than one-third of his annual salary, leaving the other two-thirds, and the total cost of technician and secretarial staff wages, running costs, equipment etc., to be borne by the university.

Few forensic departments can attempt to limit their workload to that outlined by the College of Pathologists, but if the department attempts to make a greater contribution towards its cost to the university by doing more and more autopsies, this has the obvious self defeating effect of leaving less and less time available for teaching and research. Moreover it is self evidence that there is a critical number of autopsies which can be performed consistent with maximum efficiency. This number must vary from person to person, but since there is no reason why coroner's autopsies should deserve to be done with less thoroughness and skill than non-medicolegal ones, then it would seem that the figures given by the College of Pathologists can be taken to apply, in general terms.

It is, perhaps, particularly important that the state, presumably personified by the Home Office in this case, should contribute financially in order to prevent this state of affairs continuing. The contribution which each academic department makes to the overall pathology service for the police is obviously very significant in its own area, but viewed against the requirements of the country as a whole is not over-riding, since many areas are serviced by non-academic National Health Service pathologists, and the suggestions of the Brodrick committee would tend to reduce even the present service commitment of the academic departments. What is, or should be of paramount importance in the activities of the departments is active and wide-ranging research into the numerous problems in all aspects of forensic medicine, to which there are at the present time no answers.

If one considers the field of forensic pathology alone, anyone in active practice in this field knows how much better his investigations of any particular case would be if only there were more accurate and reliable methods of, for instance, determining the time of death, the age of an injury, the mode of death and the time taken to die from any particular cause, the separate existence or otherwise of a dead baby, the age of an unidentified middle aged or elderly person, the amount of force necessary to cause an injury, the order in which injuries were sustained and so on. Such a list merely hints at the problems. And to investigate them a great deal of fundamental research into such things as biochemical and other changes in the body after death, histochemistry and physicochemistry of tissues and wounds, bacteriology of the surface and interior of living and dead bodies, the inherent radiation of tissues and in many other fields, is required.

And this doesn't begin to touch on all the problems involved in the morbid anatomy of poisoning. Indeed, as everyone in this field of forensic pathology is aware, the things we know about with reasonable certainty form a pitiful molehill beside the vast, dark and misty mountain of our uncertainties.

Thus it is now vitally important that the academic departments should be given the means to start on the vast amount of work waiting to be done. Relief from the financial strain of attempting to be self-supporting is one form of aid required. The other is the provision of adequate staff to carry out the work. All departments are grossly understaffed. The common situation of a professor and one member of staff is ridiculous. But new recruits will not be forthcoming while the uncertainty of the prospects of a decent career in forensic medicine persist.

The Brodrick report outlined a form of career structure, embracing both academic departments and the National Health Service. Many of its suggestions have been found objectionable by various official medical bodies. However, whether this, or some other plan is considered appropriate, a form of career structure with official blessing is vital if recruits of suitable calibre are to be available.

The universities have made a valuable and generous contribution towards the development of the academic status and the overall progress of forensic medicine, and, through it, all the forensic sciences. Now it is time for the other people, who should be interested, to do something beyond paying lip-service. We now have plenty of Chairs. Let's have some support for them; the legs badly need strengthening.

D.J. Gee

Reference

Knight B., 1967, *J. Forens. Sci. Soc.*, **7**, 121.

15(2) - 1975: That Muddy Field

Forensic pathology is dying. Some might even say that it is already dead and only awaits lawful burial. Certainly if the dramatic flight from the full-time practice of legal medicine in Britain by some of its younger specialists is any indication, then the crisis prophesied by so many during the last twenty years has now arrived.

Before 1971 the lengthy gestation of the Brodrick report accounted for an apparent stagnation in forensic medicine circles, but that has been published and now gathers dust on some shelf in Whitehall. Many of its recommendations may have been unpopular but the one aspect of the Brodrick report which was not disputed was a recommendation that the University departments of Forensic Pathology in England and Wales should receive financial support from the Home Office in the form of a direct subvention.

The Universities have always taken the view that they are prepared to pay for the academic and research activities of a Forensic Pathologist but that they should not be expected to pay for a service commitment, to the Coroners and to the Police, which has no direct link with the function of the University department. This eminently reasonable attitude has recently been underlined by the recognition in some medical schools of the contributions made by their medico-legists and the awarding of several personal chairs (Gee, 1974). Such good faith however, has not been complemented by any response from the Home Office; rather the reverse. It is difficult to conceive how the Home Office imagines that a retainer in the order of £200 per year is in any way a realistic price for the services of a forensic pathologist on twenty four-hour call, with the resources and goodwill of his department thrown in.

If Forensic Pathology is dead then surely it has been slain by central government. It may be that before 1971 they did not know what they were doing or if they did know, did not know it was wrong. However, since the publication of the Brodrick report, pleading the McNaughten Rules has no relevance and perhaps a plea of "diminished responsibility" may now be more appropriate.

What can be done? Certainly it is too late to prevent the death but perhaps there is an opportunity to draw from the funeral pyre some bright new phoenix.

Could it be that the whole concept of the Home Office Pathologist should be reconsidered? After all, the only part of the country in which full-time Forensic Pathology exists in any strength is in London, an area where the Home Office is unable to exert any direct control. Perhaps if the police were to retain their own pathologists some of the problems could be overcome. The concept of a police pathologist retained by police authorities and not directly by the Home Office is not a new one. Such are the bases of the Scottish and London systems.

In the past one of the arguments in favour of Home Office control was that such experts could be seen to be independent of the police. This is a view supported by few and, in the non-medical field, contradicted by the existence of the Metropolitan Police Forensic Science Laboratory with its impeccable international reputation.

Has the time now also come for non-medical forensic science experts to be attached to police forces on a permanent basis as well? Could it be that such a team, a forensic scientist together with the pathologist, could provide the type of practical consultative advice which the growing number of police scenes-of-crime examiners now require? If the Home Office continue with their programme of amalgamation and rationalisation then large areas of the country will be left with no on-the-spot experts to help them. Surely the only hope for the future is for the police to establish their own cadre of expert advisers.

At present the whole of the North East of England is without a Home Office Pathologist. In two years time the Forensic Science Laboratory at Newcastle-upon-Tyne will be moved 90 miles south to Wetherby in Yorkshire. In 1967 Dr Bernard Knight envisaged the time when the police would find themselves standing alone in a muddy field with a murdered body and no expert advice to hand (Knight, 1967). Today the Police Forces of Northumbria and Durham may be lonely with no pathologist; tomorrow they may be standing in total isolation. If Central Government and the Home Office cannot take heed of the warnings and advice of the experts then surely the time has now come for the police to take action themselves.

J.A.J. Ferris

References

Gee, D. J., 1974, Chair Legs Wanted, *J. Forens. Sci. Soc.*, **14**, 271.
Knight B. H., 1967, Decline and Fall, *J. Forens. Sci. Soc.*, **7**, 121.
Report of the Committee on Death Certification and Coroners, 1971, London, Her Majesty's Stationery Office.

(Opinions expressed in Guest Editorials do not necessarily reject those of the Editor or the Council of the Society — Ed.)

16(1) - 1976: A National Medico-Legal Service for Scotland

Despite her traditions Scotland has not escaped the impoverishment of forensic service and personnel affecting the United Kingdom. With exciting prospects of an Elected Assembly the time is opportune for the introduction of a redesigned service offering a new medical specialty and career structure.

In its agonal state prophesied over the years (Camps, 1970; Gee, 1970) and now graphically depicted by Ferris (1975), English forensic pathology has its epitaph, "died of deprivation and neglect" pre-empted by a northern neighbour.

Incredibly within twenty miles of Edinburgh, seat of the first British chair of forensic medicine (Guthrie, 1958), "Natural Causes" without qualification is an accepted term of death certification. Standards of this order in 1975 cannot be remodelled. Replacement is urgent if this drift to the provocative nihilism of John Hume in his "Essay on Suicide" that "man's life is of no more importance to the universe than that of an oyster" is to be halted.

Objectives and emphasis in all legislation on death will relate to the times and reflect the attitudes of both the law makers and those responsible for its enforcement. How accurately are environmental influences and needs of society mirrored and served? Perhaps the very diversity of aims militates against a fundamental purpose in death certification. Can a single provision really encompass such objectives as: the legal proof of the fact of death; identification; determination of the cause of death; provision of mortality and vital statistics; disclosure of research opportunities; detection of preventable disease and other hazards; exposure of industrial dangers; exclusion of criminality and finally disposal of the dead?

Dr. William Farr, described as "a master of the methods by which arithmetic is made argumentative" and first Compiler of Abstracts in the Registrar General's office following the 1836 Act, charted the way for either a declaration of intent, change of emphasis or extended objective viz., the accurate determination of the cause of death in death certification. Sadly the resources and stage of development of pathology and forensic medicine in particular were alike unable to exploit this challenging prospect.

Indeed the succession and repeal of the Registration of Births, Deaths and Marriages (Scotland) Acts, 1854, 1855 and 1860, the Amending Acts of 1910 and 1934 with that of the Registration of Still Births (Scotland) Act of 1938 and now the current 1965 Registration of Births, Deaths and Marriages (Scotland) Act highlights this search for conceptual identity in the principal objectives of the law in death certification. Paul (1973) illustrates the effect of varying emphasis and purpose which required the 1926 Birth and Deaths Registration Act to make registration of the death compulsory before disposal and this despite the 1836 and 1874 Acts. The need for the 1971 Brodrick Report indicates continuing deficiencies and imbalance in what the law seeks to achieve by death certification. The Report stresses the axial role of the accurate determination of the cause of death and refers to the considerable contribution this makes towards the investigation of sudden and unexpected death. Current practice is somewhat removed from this pivotal goal.

Section 24(1) of Part III of the Registration of Births, Deaths and Marriages (Scotland) Act 1965 imposes the duty of certification on the registered medical practitioner in attendance during the last illness without stipulation of temporal proximity nor provision as in England for either declaring this or informing the Procurator Fiscal. Reporting of cases remains voluntary. The signed box for appraisal of the Coroner on the English form is not adopted. Except for cremation there is no obligation to view the body. It is the implementation of Section 24(2) allowing some practitioner other than the attendant doctor to sign the certificate if so able which provides the majority of routine forensic cases and characterises the Scottish system by insistence on the exclusion of criminality as the major consideration. The confidence level in granting these death certificates without recourse to autopsy, "guesswork" Spilsbury called it, is not necessarily evidence of superior clinical acumen nor a guarantee of more accurate diagnosis. A full external examination assisted by experienced mortician officers fortified by police enquiry into the circumstances generates assurance within the dictated broad limits of decision between natural and unnatural death but cannot imply constant correctness of medical diagnosis.

Evaluation of the autopsy as an aid has to be realistic for, if not conducted properly by forensic men of experience, its value is illusory. The legal safeguard of the two doctor system operated in Scotland, Spain and elsewhere is theoretical and in danger of being honoured more in the breach than the observance faced with the limited numbers and availability of trained forensic specialists. With a current Turkel autopsy index of roughly 10 compared with London at 26, present practice, standards and attainment does less than credit to the Scots pioneers Duncan and Christison and their modernising successors Kerr and Imrie.

Ferris (1975) sternly castigates the Home Office for the English dilemma and helpfully suggests a remedy in the development of a specialist police pathologist function. Whatever the culpability of the Home Office it is difficult to escape the logic of police passivity as in Scotland in the decline of a service so manifestly beneficial to them. Can police committees of local politicians and councillors, so effectively controlling policy, have the financial resources or untrammelled vision for perspective in these areas?

Insistence on the exclusion of criminality as the predominant aim with comparative indifference to other claims in tandem with this proscribes the Scottish objectives in death certification. Unfettered by any responsibility to determine the precise medical cause of death and with complete freedom to nominate the prosecutor any parallel aims of death certification must expect perfunctory treatment at official Fiscal level. Such compulsorily singular concentration with an exclusive confidentiality acknowledges minimal further obligation to the society which invests it. These medico-legal investigations proceed as the unco-ordinated function of university departments of forensic medicine, local authority police surgeons, hospital pathologists and general practitioner police doctors linked solely in respect of their Fiscal authorisation and instruction. Balance is not, as is claimed, a feature of such haphazard endeavour. A more preferable national service would still encounter the restrictive Fiscal remit and although promising a career structure its basic forensic pathology character would minimise its attraction. An emancipated system of wider potential and opportunity is required. Perhaps the concept of Medico-Legalism (Nagle, 1970) is the key.

A new specialty, the Medico-Legal Officer could provide the comprehensive integrated service with career prospects and recruitment appeal. The post would be that of a medical executive funded by central government and responsible to the Secretary of State for Scotland. Medico-legal duties would be both civil and criminal with national co-ordination effected through the central administration of the Principal Medico-Legal Officer.

Investigation enquiry and report to Crown Office into all sudden unexpected and unnatural deaths, including autopsy and laboratory examinations would become the responsibility of the new office. Examinations with or without postmortem would be available to legal representatives in civil cases of liability as in compensation or negligence. Autopsy on purely scientific grounds would be performed at the discretion of the Medico-Legal Officer if accompanied by authorised request on behalf of either clinicians or relatives.

The Medico-Legal Officer would be in lawful possession of all bodies within his jurisdiction with immediate power to autopsy so dispensing with the Sheriff petition and warrant.

Ethical and legal problems attached to securing organs for transplantation could be mitigated by direct participation and co-operation of the Medico Legal Officer.

Crematorium referees should henceforth be nominated from the Medico Legal Office. Joint participation by all concerned together with the Medico Legal Officer in "anaesthetic deaths" would realise a more purposeful form of investigation with direct scientific feed-back to those most directly concerned and interested.

On request advice on all briefs, civil or criminal, would be provided to both Crown and Defence, to plaintiff and defendant's solicitors.

Influences or trends evident from the manner of death or other investigations and having potential prophylactic value as in suicides would be transmitted to the appropriate responsible or lawful authorities for example the University department of forensic psychiatry, the police or social welfare services.

Efforts at relating this new system to the needs of society make it incumbent upon the Secretary of State to respond to observations and recommendations embodied in the annual report from the Principal Medico-Legal Officer. Overprescribing would be an early candidate for such action.

In addition to the more accurate vital statistics provided, the Principal Medico-Legal Officer would be responsible for the creation of a medico-legal Reference Bureau, a principle acceptable to the Crown Office, of indexed annotated information on case material with due regard to confidentiality and accessible to interested professional practitioners thereby affording a vicarious share to all in the total pool of national medico-legal experience.

Besides the examination of accused and victim of assault or sex crime the Medico-Legal Office could become the centre for examination of prospective vehicle drivers in any projected compulsory fitness tests. Insurance companies might favour this facility for their particular purposes. To secure the invaluable clinical balance and expertise within the service and incidentally extend its appeal the feasibility of acting as medical officers to Her Majesty's Prisons with part-time secondment on a general practice panel could be examined.

Back-up laboratory services for the Medico-Legal Office are in no less need of integration. Probably this will be best achieved by a central reference laboratory dealing with sophisticated investigations and directing research while maintaining certain extant peripheral units for routine examinations of lesser complexity such as blood alcohol estimations.

A wealth of unexplored, certainly unproclaimed talent, within the forensic specialities ensures functional capability for this expansive service. Forensic pathology excellence alone for example grafts medico-legal expertise on to a competence in general medicine pathology and bacteriology, in neuro- and paediatric pathology, the principles of surgery and anaesthesia, gynaecology and obstetrics with applied embryology, anatomy, physiology and dentistry.

Indeed it is the continued self-devaluation with exaggerated emphasis on the pathology of trauma with due respect to learned treatises (Havard, 1960; Williams, 1958) which leads the uninformed to equate the part with the whole.

Terms like criminal pathology are meaningless obfuscations. While it may be speculative that accommodation of forensic pathology within the framework of the Royal College of Pathologists unconsciously perpetuates this relegation membership undoubtedly seduces forensic novices into other branches of pathology with clearer promotional prospects.

Academic qualification for the Medico-Legal Officer specialty must recognise the peculiar requirements of the practice. Their exemplary acute awareness of public need suggests the University of Strathclyde might view this aspect constructively and with sympathy. A selective but intensive law component in the course would suffice. An insignificant number of Fiscals have undertaken organised medico-legal studies and in routine enquiries employ increasingly unqualified lay precognition officers.

The implicit teaching and research role of the Medico-Legal Office will have regard to local facilities. Joint enterprises and mutual exchanges with the various University departments, police colleges and others stimulates forensic enquiry and enhances the status of the subject.

These proposals for a new medical specialty are submitted for detailed analysis, discussion and feasibility studies. They are founded on the philosophy of Medico-Legalism which offers more scope as medico-legal practice and could be a promising means of responding to the needs of a complex modern society given the inadequate fabric and desperation of current practice.

Implementation and rescue will demand vision and courage in the face of embattled traditionalism. The degree of statutory dismantling or provision would not appear contradictory and might hopefully earn an historic medicolegal first among the bills of a newly Elected Scottish Assembly. Excitement, challenge, opportunity – shades of the world of Tidy Christison and Littlejohn but what will be the verdict of the forensic practitioners of 2075 on our actions and decisions? May we expect resolution with the devolution?

R. Nagle
Edinburgh
Scotland

References

Camps, F. E., 1970, *The Times*, 1 March.
Ferris, J. A. J., 1975, That Muddy Field, *J. Forens. Sci. Soc.*, **15**, 91.
Gee, D. J., 1970, *The Times*, 8 March.
Guthrie, D., 1958, *A History of Medicine*, Thomas Nelson and Sons Ltd., Edinburgh.
Havard, J. D. J., 1960, *The Detection of Secret Homicide*, Macmillan & Co. Ltd., London.
Nagle, R., 1970, Medico-Legalism, *Med. Sci. Law*, **10**, 3, 158.
Paul, D. M., 1973, Recommended Changes in Death Certification, Cremation Regulations, and Coroner's Procedure, Modern Trends in Forensic Medicine – 3, Butterworths, London.
Williams G., 1958, *The Sanctity of Life and the Criminal Law*, Faber and Faber Ltd., London.
Report of the Committee on Death Certification and Coroners, 1971, London, Her Majesty's Stationery Office.

19(1) - 1979: Sudden Death of British Nationals Abroad – Problem for Pathologists, Coroners and Relatives

The coroner's system which obtains in England and Wales ensures that cases of sudden and unexpected death are usually fully investigated. Havard (1960) expressed some reservations as to the efficiency of the system but the Brodrick Report (1971) did not support his views. The systems employed in different parts of the United States vary widely. Many cities and States now have a Medical Examiner, but in others, the appointment of coroner is an elective office, and is frequently political. Coroners in Wisconsin a few years ago included undertakers, grocers, a furniture dealer, and a bowling alley operator (Camps, 1968). Many States are now improving their coroner's systems. Ohio and Louisiana both insist that their coroners be legally qualified.

The system used in most other countries, including those in Europe, is that described by Havard (1960) as the "continental system". No executive officer is exclusively responsible for the investigation of sudden and unexpected death.

The death is usually reported, in the first instance, to the local police. If crime is suspected, the local examining magistrate and/or public prosecutor are informed. Investigation of death is only a small part of these officers' duties, and the methods, standards, and degrees of enthusiasm with which their investigations are pursued vary widely. The deceased's relatives, in a strange country and confronted with the added handicaps of a police investigation and a strange language, often suffer as a result. Indeed, many complain vociferously upon their return to the United Kingdom that they were treated with little sympathy, and often, with frank suspicion.

The costs of bringing a body home are very high. International air transport regulations and local laws usually require that the body be embalmed, and that a suitable sealed coffin be used. These expenses are often in the region of £500.

In addition, the local sanitary department may require that the coffin be sealed in the presence of their officers and a fee of up to £60 may be charged for this service. The cost of any autopsy frequently devolves upon the relatives – fees of up to £250 may be charged – and the Death Certificate provided is all too often couched in terms which are not only unacceptable to the Registrar General, but also fail to satisfy insurance companies in cases where doubt exists as to whether the death was due to accident or to natural causes.

Several cases have given rise to national concern in recent months. In late 1978, a baby died of asphyxia when it slipped through its cot rails, whilst on holiday in Spain. The father alleged that he was threatened with arrest by the Spanish authorities until he withdrew his complaints about the safety of the cot.

He was also assured that an autopsy had been performed, and this was stated on the death certificate, which gave "external asphyxia" as the cause of death.

An examination when the body was brought back to the United Kingdom revealed that no autopsy had been carried out – the skin of the chest had been incised, but the rib cage was intact. Attempts by the Coroner and the parents' legal advisers to obtain copies of the police file were met with flat refusals from the Spanish authorities, as were requests for photographs and measurements of the cot.

In February of this year the body of a middle aged male was flown back from Malta. The coroner ordered an autopsy, but the pathologist found that all the internal organs had been removed, so that no further examination was possible.

Bodies in a similar state have arrived from Rumania, Poland and Israel. The author was recently asked to examine the body of a man aged 37 years who had died, in suspicious circumstances, in a Middle Eastern country. The accompanying documents disagreed as to whether he had died after 48 hours intensive care, or had died in the ambulance on the way to hospital. The cause of death was given as "extreme weakness of the nervous and muscular systems due to alcohol misuse, with pre-existing disease of the heart, liver and kidneys".

Unfortunately only the head and neck had been embalmed. Cavity fluid had been poured over the partially dissected internal organs. The heart and neck structures were missing. Repeated requests for a copy of the post mortem report have been ignored.

The author has personal experience of bodies where no autopsy has been performed (although the relatives have paid for one) and of unembalmed putrefying bodies enclosed in distended coffins (although a certificate of embalming has been produced).

In one case, the death of a young adult male who died whilst swimming was certified, after autopsy, as due to "coronary thrombosis". The coronary arteries had not been opened. They were free of atheroma and no thrombus was found.

It seemed more likely that the death was accidental, although it was impossible to prove that death was due to drowning. Unfortunately for the relatives, the deceased had taken out insurance against accidental death only. The insurance company involved refused to honour the claim, and the relatives sustained financial loss thereby.

Coroners' practice in dealing with these deaths varies. Some coroners request a re-examination of all bodies returned to their area. Others simply examine the accompanying certificates, and authorise disposal provided the relatives express no disquiet. All the coroners who have been consulted have expressed dissatisfaction with the existing system for the examination and disposal arrangements. Their criticisms of practice in certain Mediterranean countries are particularly harsh.

The time has now come for some form of international agreement upon procedures for the investigation of deaths of foreign nationals whilst on holiday or business outside their native country. The Ninth Meeting of the International Association of Forensic Sciences will be held in Bergen in 1981. Perhaps some discussion should take place, with a view to the production of a recommended international autopsy protocol and embalming procedure which will not jeopardise subsequent re-examination. The co-operation of international Travel Agents Associations should also be sought, to ensure that tour operators and couriers are fully au fait with legal and funeral practices. Such action would not only spare relatives' feelings; it would protect their legal rights.

M.A. Green
Leeds

References

Brodrick, J. L., 1971, Report of the Committee on Death Certification and Coroners Cmnd 4810, London: H.M.S.O.
Camps, E., 1968, *Gradwohl's Legal Medicine*, 2nd Edition, Bristol: Wright.
Havard, D. J., 1960, *The Detection of Secret Homicide in Cambridge Studies in Criminology*, Vol. 11. London: Macmillan.

41(2) - 2001: "Best value" in forensic pathology

(Editorial)

"Government and co-operation are in all things the law of life; anarchy and competition the laws of death".

John Ruskin *1819–1900*.

It has been interesting being a fly on the wall for the last few months watching a group of forensic pathologists and police forces circle around each other like hungry coyotes eyeing a juicy dead sheep as they try to negotiate a new contract for pathology services. The "T" word has been bandied about, despite the simple fact that it is difficult to run a competitive tender when there is effectively a monopoly supplier. The whole saga, which is still not settled as I write this on 23 March although the current contract expires at the end of the month, would make a suitable case study for either a particularly masochistic MBA or politics student writing a thesis on counterforce strategies during the Cold War. Or possibly both.

The plain and simple fact is that there are not enough forensic pathologists in the UK, in particular in England, at present. (The Scots, as usual, do things better.) Attempts at competitive tendering simply result in, at best, angst and dysfunctional relationships between people who should be working together in the interests of justice and, at worst, disruptive churning of the very small pool of persons who are on the Home Office List of Consultant Forensic Pathologists.

What can be done to remedy the situation? Increasing the size of the pool has a very long lead time; a bright school leaver who decides she wants to be a forensic pathologist is going to have a long haul ahead of her. Taking a very linear and, in my view, a rather sub optimal approach to the training, she would spend five years getting her basic medical qualification, one year as a pre-registration medical practitioner, four years at the shortest training as a histopathologist and then an additional one year training in forensic pathology. Assuming that she passes all her examinations and interviews first time that is a lead time of eleven years. Add in an extra year for an intercalated BSc to supplement the rather sparse technical education now on offer at many English medical schools, one or two years of post graduate clinical training in areas useful to a potential forensic pathologist, such as paediatrics, accident and emergency medicine or psychiatry, an extra year or two of consultant practice as a pathologist before starting training again as a forensic pathologist and a year of full time research for an MD and the school leaver is into her mid thirties before she starts independent practice as a forensic pathologist.

How can the problem be addressed? Well, one can always lower the standard. The ACPO murder manual recommendation that only pathologists on the Home Office list should carry out post-mortem examinations in murder cases isn't written in stone. Perhaps the Coroners could be persuaded to allow pathologists not on the Home Office list to do, for example, simple domestic stabbings... Yes, well, one could try that option. It might be rather an expensive one in the long run, but it could be attractive to some seagull managers in the short term. One could threaten the monopoly – taking a leaf from the old industrial robber barons' book and import cheap labour. There must be plenty of well-trained pathologists in the less developed world who would jump at the chance to come and practice in the UK. Hmm, apart from the dubious morality of recruiting the most valuable resource of any developing country, its professionals, to a developed country like the UK, there could be some problems there. For example, it will take them at least a year of additional training for an overseas recruit to pass the necessary examinations unless a dual approach is taken; i.e. recruit from overseas and lower the standard.

A rather better approach might be to reduce the number of cases that each pathologist on the Home Office list does each year by training a cadre of pathologists who do mostly hospital practice in advanced autopsy technique. A Diploma examination for pathologists who have completed their basic training in histopathology in Coronial Autopsy Technique could improve the somewhat uneven quality of coronial autopsies in non-suspicious sudden deaths and, by increasing the overall standard of coronial autopsies would reduce the possibility of a prosecution failing when it becomes apparent after the post-mortem examination that the death may, in fact, have been homicidal. The training and examination might provide a useful additional revenue stream for the Royal College of Pathologists. Hopefully, even those who generate information from the specimens collected by our pathology colleagues would be allowed to have some input into their training. By taking over some of the workload on the investigation of apparently non-suspicious sudden deaths from the forensic pathologists, better use could be made of their time. Regional consortia of full time forensic pathologists, perhaps employed on salary through a special health authority, could allow the development of special interests and expertise by forensic pathologists giving adequate cross cover and an improvement in the quality of the service offered to investigators and to the courts.

The enquiries arising out of the current brouhaha over the retention of organs and other material by pathologists and the Shipman enquiry will provide the information necessary to revise the Human Tissue Act and Coroner's Act. This will give the new parliament an opportunity to create a legislative environment in which forensic pathologists' unique contribution to the criminal justice system can be restructured much more constructively than by simply attempting to apply competitive tendering in what is a very distorted marketplace. It's an opportunity not to be missed.

Robert Forrest

42(1) - 2002: Herding Cats

(Editorial)

ARW Forrest
Editor, Science & Justice

Management is a concept which, by and large, is an anathema to forensic pathologists. The practice of forensic pathology has provided at least some rugged individualists with the opportunity to pursue a career in medicine untrammelled by what many pathologists perceive to be the over intrusive and counter productive micro-management that is the bane of the life of the vast majority of medical practitioners in the UK; those who practice exclusively within the National Health Service. Nonetheless, it is abundantly clear that the current way in which forensic pathologists are managed, or fail to be managed, in England & Wales cannot be continued. A system needs to be established that will ensure that medico-legal autopsies are carried out in a timely manner by competent forensic pathologists to agreed quality standards, in properly equipped mortuaries with appropriate performance audit. The pathologists should participate in structured professional development, be subject to peer appraisal, with teeth, annually and should receive remuneration that is competitive being at least comparable with the total earnings of consultants employed by the NHS. Training issues, for the next generation of forensic pathologists, have to be addressed. An additional factor is that the need for timely post mortems as the first golden hours of the investigation slip by and the PACE clock ticks away means that there must be adequate cover arrangements available. Those commissioning the post mortem should not have to spend time tearing their hair out looking for a pathologist, nor, particularly after the hard lesson of the Selby (Great Heck) rail crash, should exhausted pathologists be expected to drive many miles to a scene or to a remote mortuary.

These considerations, together with the library and IT resources needed for a forensic pathologist to do her job properly, means that the single handed forensic pathologist working in professional isolation has to become a thing of the past.

All of this needs to be addressed with "Joined Up Government" in mind. The future management of forensic pathologists cannot be dealt with in isolation from the fundamental review of the coroner's system now in progress. Nor can it be considered in isolation from the future of that other group of medical practitioners who sometimes contribute to criminal investigation, the forensic medical examiners.

One solution to this problem may be to encourage forensic pathologists to organise themselves in a chambers type of system, analogous to that used by barristers. Four or five together covering a population of around two million souls would appear to be a not unreasonable grouping. It would facilitate the development of specialisation, for example, one of the group might have an interest in drug abuse deaths, another in deaths under medical treatment and another in infant deaths. Unfortunately, there aren't enough of forensic pathologists to go round at present. Hence the need to train more of them. But it takes two to three years to train an experienced hospital pathologist to the point where she is capable of independent practice as a forensic pathologist. There is also the important point of whether or not enough trainees will come forward.

Pathology and pathologists are hardly the flavour of the month after the kicking the profession has had from press and politicians following Bristol and Alderhay. Hospital medical practice, with improved techniques for obtaining biopsy material from the living increasingly relies on the histopathologist; as their numbers decrease and the demand for their skills in hospital practice increase, so they are able to command salary supplements and working conditions that make the lifestyle of forensic pathologists somewhat less attractive by comparison with their colleagues working in the NHS than would otherwise be the case.

Another source of forensic pathologists at present is the part timers; those who combine the role of consultant pathologist to the Home Office with their day job of consultant in histopathology to an NHS Trust. When coupled with the increasing emphasis within the NHS on meeting centrally set targets, hospital pathology managers are unlikely to look with favour at the prospect of hosting a part time forensic pathologist who may disappear unpredictably to scenes, mortuaries and courts, perhaps leaving colleagues to cover politically sensitive clinics and thus compromising the Trust's ability to meet those crucial centrally set targets on which a manager's job may depend. (Whether those targets actually save lives is an entirely separate issue).

Let us suppose forensic pathologists could be persuaded to organise themselves into chambers, perhaps in association with allied professionals such as anthropologists or forensic archaeologists. How should they be funded and monitored? For most forensic pathologists, being incorporated into a tightly managed structure such as the Forensic Science Service would be unacceptable, particularly if there was any suggestion of them being professionally accountable to anyone other than a medical practitioner. Their answer to the implied threat of he who pays the piper also calls the tune, apart from a spirited expression of their need to be independent and to appear to be independent may well be that there is plenty of money to be earned by assisting the Courts as an expert at the request of the defence, and probably even more to be made as an expert pathologist in civil cases. The current shortage of pathologists in the NHS means that those forensic pathologists who are not yet terminally differentiated would have no problem in leaving forensic pathology and returning to full time practice as histopathologists.

Voting with their feet if they were to be faced with being managed to the extent that most forensic scientists are is a very real option for forensic pathologists. So who hold the ring? Who gets the unenviable job of trying to herd the unherdable? The NHS wouldn't want them; already the problem of clinical academics with posts in forensic pathology having to hold honorary contracts with NHS trusts causes problems when they have to investigate hospital deaths where there are suggestions of negligence or malfeasance in their host trusts. So some central body, analogous to a combination of the Bar Council, to set, audit and enforce compliance with professional standards, and a body dealing with funding, including funding for training, would need to be established. It would have to represent major stakeholders including the Council for the Registration of Forensic Practitioners, the Association of Chief Police Officers, the Home Office, the Judiciary, the Crown Prosecution Service and those who employ the majority of the poor souls who have to examine the samples collected by forensic pathologists, the Forensic Science Service How it might be constituted must be a three pipe problem at the very least. All options would need to be considered with one exception; the status quo. Change is needed and needed sooner rather than later if investigators and courts are to get the help they need from the next generation of forensic pathologists.

SECTION VII: AN INTERNATIONAL COMMUNITY OF FORENSIC SCIENCE

International Aspects of Forensic Science

"Competition has been shown to be useful up to a certain point and no further, but cooperation, which is the thing we must strive for today, begins where competition leaves off" (Franklin D. Roosevelt).

It is interesting that an American would be asked to comment on international matters. Being a young nation, however, may provide us with a clearer perspective on things than is seen from deeply within. Four themes emerged from a review of the editorials regarding international forensic science activities and I would like to briefly touch on each in turn. Those themes are vision, politics, philosophy, and what I call the business of forensics.

Vision

One nearly universal theme throughout these editorials is that historically, like clean air, recycling, and polite behavior, everyone is in favor of international cooperation but have done very little about it. Other than the obvious agency of the International Association of Forensic Science (and see "Politics" below), few professional entities have taken a strong lead on the issue. The European Network of Forensic Science Institutes (ENFSI) has recently made huge strides with its Working Groups on the various disciplines in the forensic sciences, promoting a modicum of standardization – at least as much as can be tolerated across the loose federation that is the European Union – and publishing open and transparent documents for all to use as they see fit. Despite the stalwart and persistent efforts of ASTM, International's Committee E30 on Forensic Science in the US, standardization has been largely ignored by many laboratories. The work of the Technical and Scientific Working Groups in the US has also been extremely valuable in creating a consensus of views but has been variably adopted in actual practice. As one commentator in *Science and Justice* said,

> "All this leads me to venture to suggest that the problems encountered and solved by the Forensic Science Society are in the true sense of the word a microcosm of those which will be encountered in forming an International body in Forensic Science, something which, as I indicated at the beginning of my address, is an object of which I am sure we all approve. This could be done by setting up a federal structure of national scientific societies, and this new structure should make no attempt of any kind at supervising the activities of its national constituent groups."

Thus, in the modern context, we see the emergence of The International Forensic Summit (TIFS) which is intended to promote information sharing on a global scale, identify forensic science issues and promote solutions to those issues, and to serve as subject matter experts on global forensic science issues (www.theforensicsummit.org). It has taken, regrettably, mass disasters and terrorism to promote cooperation between forensic agencies but if these horrific events become focal points for collaboration and communication, then perhaps they have served some useful, rather than senseless, purpose.

Politics

There are a few truisms about forensic science that bear repeating under this heading:

- it has never been funded to a level that reflects its societal importance,
- the market is too small to support the diversity the profession and science truly represent,
- the political and legal demands often get in the way of scientific demands, and
- its practitioners are not the masters of their own professional destiny

Having said this, however, does not absolve us of these political realities:

- our sibling sciences and professionals (barristers and police) have to swim in the same water as the rest of us,
- scientists typically make lousy managers, and
- rational decisions derived from data are neither neither necessary nor sufficient requirements for political action.

I often joke that forensic scientists have been treated so sadistically over the years that we no longer need our critics – we've become masochists and can mistreat ourselves to their standards better than anyone. As one commentator pointed out, health care will always win out over forensic science for funding. That may be but that reality ignores the fact that we have let ourselves become politically flabby and complacent. Our agencies may restrict what political actions we can take – and I'm not advocating revolution, here, so stay with me – but that does not mean we should be without recourse. Politics is in its barest sense social relations about governance or power. We cannot abdicate our responsibilities in those issues that affect forensic science; otherwise, politics becomes what Paul Valery called it, "... the art of preventing people from taking part in affairs which properly concern them." Note, for example, the political need for a fast turn-around-time in a serious case which may ignore, despite the actual need for a speedy response, the realities of the sciences involved: It may not be possible given the evidence, facilities, personnel, or desired timeframe. *How*, not *that*, forensic scientists handle this type of politics defines how other agencies perceive us and we may have taken enough science courses but not enough communication courses to properly deal with political issues.

The commentary over the years reflects these ideas, even to the regret that too many new journals dilute the distribution of the current ones (and particularly *Science and Justice*) around the globe. Smacking of hegemony, this kind of regret limits the natural expansion and (re)definition of the forensic professions. The regret of expansion is also seen in the growing pains of the international meetings, what they mean as a reflection of what we perceive the discipline as being. As a market, a group, forensic science is dwarfed by many of its professional sibling's associations. A new conference or a new journal necessarily is seen as cutting the cake into that much smaller of pieces. The trend in the commentaries, though, indicates growth, expansion, and development of forensic science internationally and we should not give up on ourselves just yet.

Philosophy

A persistent question throughout the editorials is "What is forensic science?". Good question. I have always thought that the rote answer, "Science applied to the law", was weak and self-defeating. Yes, forensic science does address scientific questions in the service of the justice system but not exclusively the police, the courts, or other legal entities. Most of all, forensic science serves the public good by providing inclusive or exclusive evidence that promotes a demonstratively more accurate resolution to a legal issue than would occur without it. In one editorial, a sage scientist notes, "All scientific tests have defined limits of sensitivity, accuracy, and reproducibility but this does not mean that a particular test is invalid or wrong because of these limitations. Similarly, experiments performed to test a particular hypothesis must be relevant to the theory being tested and any departures from this theory must be compensated for or explained." One has only to skim the recent National Research Council's report, *Strengthening Forensic Science in the United States: A Path Forward*, to see this as a core concept that has been ignored by both forensic scientists and, I might add, by some on that august group. The limits of *scientific* sensitivity, accuracy, and reproducibility goes to the heart of many of the problems that have historically hectored forensic science, including the concept of individualization. Yet we daily struggle with the question of what we are as a profession and a science; we do this, in my opinion, because we have adopted the malice of our critics and are applying it to ourselves (masochism from institutionalized sadism) with no conceivable means of recourse. We cannot see the answers because we have accepted the criticism uncritically, just as we have often accepted our foundational precepts uncritically without an eye to testing them in the light of modern science.

Another question that has bedeviled forensic science, particularly in the global context, is the purpose of professional associations. The IAFS has changed its demographics to include all of the forensic sciences (it was originally oriented towards pathologists) and now the triennial meetings offers more than an opportunity for practitioners in the range of forensic science to meet each other and exchange news and views on what is new. The more-inclusive conferences now provide a venue to develop common ground between specialties, generally enhancing the awareness of what forensic science is and can be. A better-defined international forensic science profession is good for all.

The Business of Forensic Science

The final theme is what I have called the business of forensic science, that is, how do forensic laboratories work as business units. Forensic laboratories occupy an interesting niche. As a production facility, they receive raw materials (evidence) of uncertain quality yet are expected to create products (reports) at a better-than six sigma level of quality (3.4 defects per million products). Money is only an input for a forensic laboratory, not an output; therefore, profit, as a measure of any sort of productivity, is out the window. Personnel are organized in silos that are defined by what material or product they analyze (DNA, firearms, fibers, etc.). Most forensic managers are scientists first and managers second, if at all. Scientists as managers tend to devalue what they see as the softer aspects of management (human resources, communication, conflict resolution), figuring that, if they were smart enough to get a science degree, surely they can be successful at supervising ("I'm an organic chemist; arguing over parking spaces is simple"). Ironically, these are the very skills they need to be successful as a manager and a leader. The corollary is imagine giving an ambassador a gas chromatograph, 100 drug samples, and saying, "Well, you've mastered international diplomacy, so you certainly can work out this contraption." Different skill sets, different education, different outcomes.

The rising expectations for forensic science (and we'll leave out any mention of "The CSI Effect" as a stalking horse) have placed it in a tough spot: The management of scarce resources demands better managers *and* better scientists. Typically, we only educate and train for one of those skill sets. The editorials indicate that the identification, recruitment, retention, and succession of employees from graduates to retirees is the single greatest challenge facing forensic science. Absent adequate pay, absent a scientific purpose, absent a scientific mindset, those eager young graduates who majored in forensic science *precisely because they love science and want to earn a decent wage* will go to another industry. This dire state was made clear in one editorial: "The immediate consequence of this will be a reduction in the standards of scientific evidence and a rapid realization that forensic science has become no more than a second-class laboratory support system presenting barely credible evidence in court. I would suggest that the general morale in the forensic community is already suffering as a direct consequence of budget cut-backs on training and recruitment." Sound familiar?

"It is perhaps not wrong to relate cost-benefit analysis to demands for capital equipment in a system that is not a revenue generator." To this day, this kind of statement raises the hackles of many a forensic manager. "You can't put a price on justice," they'll say. No, not the concept of justice; we may not want to say that the investigation of a child's death cost some specific sum of money, but it did and we may be called to account for those expenditures. Forensic science worldwide needs to shed the haughty avoidance of talking about money and get down to the real brass of costs. And not costs for the sake of pinching pennies but simply because *managers need to know what their costs are to control them, to justify them, and to enhance them*. The editorials reflect this – at least the more recent ones do – noting that flexibility and creativity are called for to solve pernicious problems:

- "Efficient forensic laboratory services in the next few years must implement technological changes by cost-effective means. This may involve some reorientation of laboratory services"
- "... are we doing things as well as we could? Do we, for example, need more structure or less, and are there barriers or thresholds that need to be broken down before progress can be made?"
- "In these days of budget constraints, [managers] need to make sure that the activities we specifically support are worthwhile, whilst still subscribing to the general belief that international forensic science is beneficial."
- "[Do] the end results (knowledge, information, contacts, etc.) merit our time, energy, and the cost involved in the participation?"

The theme of this next decade will be the management of forensic sciences, mark my words. The research and science will, perforce, take care of itself to a large extent. Reorienting ourselves to a new perspective and skill-set will take effort, dedication, and a willingness like we have rarely seen before.

Concluding on a hopeful note, one editorial states,

> "[T]here is a constancy in forensic science today which is rewarding. That constancy is shown by increasing self-imposed demands for reliability of evidence and a thirst for knowledge. Forensic scientists are keen to experiment, to refine and develop, and probably most important of all, to communicate their findings to their peers and in turn to seek avidly results of work from other laboratories. The truly international nature of this professional concern is reflected by the membership of the Forensic Science Society and the circulation of [Science and Justice]."

I could not agree more.

Max M. Houck

9(3) - 1968: Another Academy

Recently there has come into our hands a new Journal in the field of forensic science. This is The Australian Journal of Forensic Sciences which commenced publication with its first number in September, 1968. The editorial offices are at 175 Macquarie Street, Sydney, New South Wales, 2000. The Journal is the Official organ of the Australian Academy of Forensic Sciences. The Academy which appears to owe not a little to the inspiration of the British Academy of Forensic Sciences was set up following three years of personal approaches made to eminent members of the medical and legal professions in particular. The moving spirit seems to have been a distinguished psychiatrist, Dr. Oscar R. Schmalzbach, who is now the first Secretary-General. The Foundation Meeting was held on 20th April, 1967, following which an elaborate organisation similar in most respects to that of the British Academy emerged. Of the 89 foundation members, judging by their degrees, roughly half represented the medical profession, while rather less were lawyers and the remainder divided equally between police and scientists. The inaugural number of the Journal contains the Presidential Address by The Honourable Mr. Justice Le Gay Brereton, on Evidence in Medicine, Science and the Law, and there are also papers on Identification of Handwriting, Determination of Sex, Industrial Poisoning Hazards and a case note on a triple homicide.

While one is pleased to have this evidence of increasing activity in the forensic science field in Australia it is possible to regret the duplication of the rather top heavy apparatus enjoyed by the British Academy, and presumably the similar emphasis on the aim of establishing a criterion of acceptance by which members may be recognised in Courts – a feature which has seemed to some members of this Society to savour of self-recommendation. At a time when the Forensic Science Society has also established contact with Australian scientists, police and lawyers it is also a trifle disappointing if the creation of the Australian Academy should make for any division of the efforts of workers in the forensic sciences in that Continent. It is commonly said that in the United Kingdom the interests of forensic science could more economically be served by a single society, and a single though enhanced journal, but for the present such an ideal remains unattainable.

These things having been said, however, it is a pleasure to welcome the newcomer to the field of publishing in medicine, science and the law. Much good can come from an exchange of views and experience across the professional and academic boundaries, and the congratulations of this Journal are extended to the new arrival. The Forensic Science Society hopes for an active and free-ranging examination of the role of the forensic scientist and for much new thinking on the education of the police and the lawyer in matters touching the forensic sciences. Australians doubtless have useful contributions to make in this important dialogue, and we look forward with anticipation to reports of new work, valuable experience, fresh approaches and constructive thinking from the Australian Journal.

We can also offer our new contemporary an early commendation, for our researches have revealed that, so far at least, the new Journal is priceless.

A.R.B.

15(4) - 1975: International Co-operation in Forensic Science

An edited version of an address read to the Seventh International Meeting of Forensic Sciences in Zurich on Monday September 8th, 1975, at the opening of the Scientific Programme.

There is a story about the child who went to church and heard a very long sermon on the subject of "Sin" and was afterwards questioned about it by his parents. He remembered the title well enough, but when asked for more detail about the sermon could remember nothing other than that the preacher "was against it".

Just as it is a fair assumption that all preachers are against sin, so it seems to me that when speaking to the participants of an international meeting on Forensic Science, it is safe to assume that all those present are in favour of International Co-operation in Forensic Science, and it would be pointless to present arguments in favour of it.

If all are in favour, why have we so far no formal organization established? While I do not intend to detract in any way from the large amount of work that has been put into organizing the seven meetings in this series, or to question their success and value, do they really meet the full needs of International Co-operation? In his address of welcome, the President of the I.A.F.S., Professor H. Hartmann said that one of the aims of the Association was to prevent the domination of Forensic Science by any one group of its practicioners. This is, I believe, a most important principle and is one which has always been adopted by the Forensic Science Society as will be apparent later.

Our Society was founded in England in 1959 not because it was ever visualised as an exclusively British Society, but it had to start somewhere. Since then it has successfully overcome many of the problems which will be encountered in any attempt to form a permanent international body in Forensic Science, and I want therefore briefly to describe its activities and hope that those of you who are already familiar with its history will forgive me for taking your time.

The Forensic Science Society regards Forensic Science as based on team efforts, and has consequently enrolled Lawyers, Doctors, Scientists and specialist Police Officers on an equal basis, and its Past Presidents have come from each of these callings. It has not sought to be a qualifying professional body, neither has it been associated especially with the prosecution side in criminal proceedings and indeed amongst its members are many eminent independent experts who carry out investigations on behalf of defendants, and who in some cases confine their activities almost exclusively to civil cases. It might thus be better described as a Learned Society, than a Professional Organization.

Since 1959 the Society has grown to a membership of almost 1500, of whom 400 reside outside the United Kingdom, and one member of its elected Council, the governing body, currently lives in Canada. It organizes two multidisciplinary symposia each year, as well as a number of regional meetings. Two years ago it held its first meeting outside the United Kingdom (in France), and it is hoped that this venture will be frequently repeated in the future. The main link with our non-United Kingdom members is at present through the quarterly issues of the Society's Journal and through three associated societies, one in the United States and two in Australia.

As a non profit-making body, the Society has used some of its funds to publish two editions of the World List of Forensic Science Laboratories, as a contribution towards facilitating international communications at the most basic level, and has been greatly assisted in preparing these publications by its world-wide membership and contacts.

Whilst it does not grant any kind of qualification to members, it is currently seeking to expand its educational activities by providing short residential courses, studentships and prizes, as well as by publishing educational monographs on Forensic Science. Recently it has established a permanent office with an Administrative Assistant where some 5000 items of mail per year are handled.

All this leads me to venture to suggest that the problems encountered and solved by the Forensic Science Society are in the true sense of the word a microcosm of those which will be encountered in forming an International body in Forensic Science, something which, as I indicated at the beginning of my address, is an object of which I am sure we all approve.

This could be done by setting up a federal structure of national scientific societies, and this new structure should make no attempt of any kind at supervising the activities of its national constituent groups. It is on this basis that the Forensic Science Society conducts its relations with its associated societies, as I have already mentioned. International federations of this type are represented by, for example, The International Union of Pure and Applied Chemistry and the International Standards Organization. Such bodies could be those on which an International Union of Forensic Science Societies, which I propose should be formed, might model itself. It is clearly not appropriate to go into details of the actual organization at this stage. I would merely like to say that an adaptation of the object of the Forensic Science Society to meet the international situation, in the following terms, viz "To advance the study and application of Forensic Science and to facilitate cooperation between national organizations interested in Forensic Science" would provide a sound starting point for such an International Union. This object would be carried out both by promoting the dissemination of information in the field of Forensic Science and by organizing international meetings not only to pass on information, but additionally to provide for personal contact between workers in this field, something which the most cunningly interfaced computers can never provide.

This is now the seventh International Meeting of Forensic Sciences. Six previous ones have passed without it proving possible to harness the need for permanent international cooperation, which we all feel, into tangible form. I wish to offer the resources of the Forensic Science Society, already with some experience in these matters, as the nucleus of an attempt to form an International Union of Forensic Science Societies, and invite any of you who can in any way help towards its formation to write as soon as possible to the Forensic Science Society, PO Box 41, Harrogate, England. To allow the Seventh International meeting to pass without some constructive steps would be to miss one opportunity too many.

David Patterson
President

17(1) - 1977: Crime in the Cornfields*

If one had to choose the major event in the forensic scientists' calendar the vote would doubtless go (national and disciplinary interests notwithstanding) to the triennial conferences of the International Association of Forensic Sciences. This body dies after each conference then rises immediately with the appointment of a new president, like a Phoenix from the ashes, to begin a three year programme of preparation. A working committee is appointed by the new president from colleagues in or near the new location and together they labour for three years arranging accommodation, lecture programmes and all the things necessary when a thousand participants descend upon them eager to find out what's new in forensic science.

The system has worked remarkably well although, inevitably, with some variation. Few people would match Zurich with Toronto or Edinburgh. Equally few people would wish to replace the present simple, but largely effective, system by one which contains the large politicking element inevitably associated with the full democratic method applied on an international scale with modest funds.

But the system has its less attractive aspects. The method of appointing the new President and choosing the new location is by a committee consisting of past presidents, or at least those of them who attend the particular meeting, selecting from a list of individuals (at least some of whom apply) who offer accommodation and all the other necessary facilities. This restricts the field of choice of President and, though none would dispute the eminence of some past presidents of the I.A.F.S., one sees parallel features in the situation to that which some years ago caused one church editor to complain that the authority of some newly appointed Anglican bishops stemmed only from the appointments themselves.

Another unhappy feature of the system is that, despite the large and multidisciplinary range of membership of the Association, all presidents save one have belonged to the same discipline. Isn't the Presidency of the I.A.F.S. too important to be awarded exclusively to those capable of providing accommodation for a meeting? How can we, without setting up a surfeit of managerial functions, ensure that the appointment of President in some measure reflects both his eminence as a forensic scientist and the disciplinary makeup of the Association?

The question of location of meetings was solved early in the history of the Association by a decision to restrict the Association's proceedings to the English language. This has effectively meant the restriction of the meetings to Anglo-Saxon countries or to small countries where the English-speaking tradition is strong.

---

*The next meeting of the International Association of Forensic Sciences will be held in Wichita, Kansas in the Cornbelt of the U.S.A.

This step, admirably effective at the beginning, now seems to be unnecessarily restrictive. Would it really be too difficult to go to the major non-English speaking countries and run a meeting where papers may be given in the host language or in English? Little practical difference would be noted in the published proceedings since the great majority of papers would still be in English. The specialist sessions in English would have the substantial attendance we have come to expect at these meetings whereas the specialist sessions in the host language would have the advantage of a local audience. The plenary sessions should be of a restricted length and in either English or in the host language.

To solve the twin problems of appointing a suitable president and gaining a suitable venue one solution would be to appoint a President solely on the basis of eminence and service to the Forensic Sciences and also to appoint a Chairman of the organizing committee from among those with adequate facilities and suitable abilities. Thus the host country would still have an appointment of high status although the President himself may not be a national of that country. The President should be elected by popular vote and he and the committee (consisting as it now does of the past presidents) should then make their first task the appointment of a new Chairman. Thus we maintain the flexibility and stability of the present arrangement combined with the democratic process.

Where shall we go under the new arrangements?

Let's go to Italy, the country of beautiful people where Syracusa thought up absorption–elution bloodstain grouping forty years before anyone else, or to the other side of the Mediterranean, to Spain. Let's go even further, to Latin America, say to Argentina where man first solved murders by fingerprints and where we can learn that fingerprint classification systems other than Galton–Henry are both possible and effective and where the name Vucetitch is honoured. We could go to France, the country of Bertillon, inventor of the first classified personal identification system, or to Austria the country of Landsteiner the greatest ever serologist, or to Germany, country of major progress in forensic science, of Einstein and of Hockheimer the best wine in the world!

Whatever the scientific revelations to be made in the cornfields of Kansas the forensic calendar must thereafter be marked 'B.W.' (Before Wichita) or 'A.W.' (After Wichita). We can't go on as we are.

It won't be the first time something useful has been done in a cornfield besides growing corn.

A.N.

23(2) - 1983: Reaching Out

It sometimes seems that there is an almost infinite variety in systems of Law throughout the world. There are inquisitorial systems and accusatorial systems; some countries employ public prosecutors who not only lead the proceedings in Court but are responsible for the direction of activities at the investigative stage. Within these variations there is a further layer of variety with some offences in some countries heard before juries, others dealt with summarily, and still others dealt with by a panel of judges. The variety is repeated in the manner in which courts deal with forensic science evidence. In some instances the norm is to deal with a written report which is read aloud by a non-scientist to the Court, others make more frequent and indeed regular use of oral presentation of evidence by a scientist, and still others try to find areas of common ground between defence and prosecution which are accepted by written consent. Different varieties can be embodied in a single legal system, for example the pre-trial assessment of scientific evidence by a panel of experts resulting in an agreed written report being presented to the Court, as happens in Denmark.

Despite all these varieties, there is a constancy in forensic science today which is rewarding. That constancy is shown by increasing self-imposed demands for reliability of evidence and a thirst for knowledge. Forensic scientists are keen to experiment, to refine and develop, and probably most important of all, to communicate their findings to their peers and in turn to seek avidly results of work from other laboratories. The truly international nature of this professional concern is reflected by the membership of the Forensic Science Society and the circulation of the Journal.

Although the Society was founded by a handful of enthusiastic Englishmen and maintains its administrative and policy-making structure within the United Kingdom, approximately half of the members reside in other parts of the world and half or more of the subscribers to the Journal also are located outwith the United Kingdom.

In welcoming this internationalism and its repercussions, we accept that not only do legal systems vary in broad and fine detail, but there are substantial cultural differences in different parts of the world, including those which share a common language. Even that language may not be as common as we think. There is no doubt that American English, both written and spoken (even disregarding the accent) is quite different from English English as indeed are Irish, Welsh and Scottish English.

It is a particular pleasure for me therefore to welcome with this issue of the Journal three Associate Editors, Bryan Finkle from Salt Lake City, Doug Lucas from Toronto and George Sensabaugh from San Francisco. Each is eminent in his own area of Forensic Science, and taken together they not only add breadth and depth to the Editorial side of the Journal but also represent our recognition of the need for a broader cultural base in our peer review system. It is a first step, but we feel a very significant one, and we would now ask contributors of papers from the North Americas to send their manuscripts to the appropriate Associate Editor.

24(1) - 1984: 1984 and All That

(Editorial)

September 1984 sees the 10th Triennial Meeting of the International Association of Forensic Sciences (IAFS). The venue is the ancient University city of Oxford, the occasion auspicious, the history regrettably obscure.

It all began in Belgium in 1957 with a two-centre meeting (Brussels and Ghent) and titled the International Meeting of Forensic Pathology. The intention was to provide a venue for pathologists interested in forensic pathology and the pathology of trauma to meet and discuss problems of interest, but the programme included firearms identification and forensic chemistry. The next was held in New York in 1960 and called the Second International Meeting on Forensic Pathology and Medicine, but again the programme was more generally based than might be expected from the title, and included criminalistics, serology and toxicology. This may be why the third meeting in London in 1963 was called the Third International Meeting in Forensic Immunology, Medicine, Pathology and Toxicology, although the 1966 meeting in Copenhagen reverted to a simpler title – the Fourth International Meeting in Forensic Medicine.

Despite the apparent restriction in scope, such non-medical topics as gas chromatography and infrared spectrophotometry were dealt with, and it was in Copenhagen that the International Association of Forensic Sciences was born, with a constitution and the triple objectives of developing the forensic sciences, assisting the exchange of scientific and technical information, and organising a triennial meeting. History was not forgotten, and the first meeting of the new body, in Toronto in 1969, was named the Fifth International Meeting of Forensic Sciences. This form has been maintained through the Sixth (originally Belfast but transferred to Edinburgh), Seventh (Zurich), Eighth (Wichita) and Ninth (Bergen) International Meetings of Forensic Sciences.

Cheerfully embracing all the forensic sciences, the International Meetings offer more than an opportunity for practitioners in specialties of forensic science to meet each other and exchange news and views on what is new. They provide them with a venue to meet their peers in other specialties, to develop common ground, and to enhance their general awareness of forensic science. This has not been achieved entirely without pain. One of the features broadening the basis of early, medically-orientated meetings was the holding of the London conference in conjunction with the First International Meeting in Questioned Documents. The multi-interest approach was even more obvious in 1966, when the Second International Meeting in Questioned Documents, the Second Triennial Congress of the International Association of Forensic Toxicologists, and a meeting of the American Medical Correctional Association (in Copenhagen!) were all held in conjunction with the main meeting.

Although historically this mélange helped to broaden the basis of the international meetings, the relationship between IAFS and specialist groups in the forensic sciences, who would hope to make an international meeting of their own the vehicle for presentation of the speciality at the IAFS triennial meetings, is delicate. Guidance was given by the organisers of the Sixth Meeting who made it clear that Questioned Documents, for example, had to be integrated into the programme in the best way as seen by the IAFS Meeting Committee, who would take an over-view of the entire programme, and this approach has prevailed to date. Interdependence and flourishing of international co-operation with the forensic sciences is to be encouraged, but those who wish an independent platform at about the time of the triennial meetings can also gain guidance from the IAFS history. In 1966, when so many groups held meetings in conjunction with the main programme, the second European Congress on Poison Control Centres was timetabled to follow on from the International Meeting, thereby enhancing participation in the Poison Control Centre Congress and affording an opportunity to those who would otherwise only have been interested in that congress to meet more of their colleagues and friends and to learn something of forensic science in general. This pattern is being maintained in 1984.

Although the objectives of IAFS are clear and predictable, the workings of the constitution with regard to organisation are somewhat less obvious. The past-presidents meet to consider applications from individuals for Presidency in the succeeding triennium. In theory therefore, the presidential line is one of distinguished forensic scientist passing office to distinguished forensic scientist. Since the prime duty of the president is organising the International Meeting it is quite clear that the resources for organising a successful meeting should also weigh heavily on the minds of the Committee. The Forensic Science Society lent its support to the candidacy of Stuart Kind for the current presidency by agreeing to allow its administrative facilities to form the backbone of the organisation of the Oxford meeting, with already visible benefits. The officers of IAFS, and the Section Secretaries and Chairmen, have been actively promoting the meeting throughout the world for the past year or so. The response has been overwhelming and Oxford 1984 is clearly a date which no self-respecting forensic scientist in any of the sub-disciplines will wish to miss. We look forward to it with confidence and enthusiasm.

27(3) - 1987: Forensic Science and the Justice System in the Late Twentieth Century

(Guest Editorial © Forensic Science Society 1987)

JAJ Ferris

Department of Pathology, University of British Columbia, Vancouver, BC, Canada

The historical evolution of the forensic sciences, with the formation of multiple sub-specialities including almost every subject known to man capable of supporting the designation science, has in large part been dictated by the evolution of science itself. At the turn of the century, it became apparent that contemporary scientific techniques could be used to support the police in their criminal investigative roles. Until that time the principal scientific input into crime investigation had been from university departments of forensic medicine and pathology, but it soon became apparent. that almost all branches of the newly developing scientific revolution could be applied to the field of crime investigation. The general philosophy that appeared to develop, and is still with us today, is that any scientific technique which can be applied to such work can be absorbed into this new, ever-expanding community of forensic sciences.

As we approach the end of the twentieth century, the increasing rate of discovery in basic biology, bio-engineering and computer science, has inundated the forensic community with a wide array of technical innovations. Because of the improved systems of communication and public education provided by all forms of media, the general public and the courts are aware of these technical advances and consequently the public and the judicial system demand a second to none forensic science service that takes full advantage of every new expensive technology. How is it going to be possible to fulfil these expectations in the face of continuing limitations on funds and resources?

It is apparent that the only way to reconcile these rising expectations for forensic science services within the limited resources available is by collaboration between laboratory professionals in all fields of forensic science in the cost-effective use of laboratory facilities.

It is difficult at present to persuade new graduates from universities to accept standards of pay and promotion no longer comparable with industry. If we are unable to offer such new recruits an opportunity to take part in innovative research and development, they will be rapidly disillusioned and flee the system. The immediate consequence of this will be a reduction in standards of scientific evidence and a rapid realization that forensic science has become no more than a second-class laboratory support system presenting barely credible evidence in court. I would suggest that the general morale in the forensic community is already suffering as a direct consequence of budget cut-backs on training and recruitment.

How to maintain a high quality of forensic laboratory service in the face of constraints on funding will continue to be a critical issue until the end of this century. One obvious approach is to pool professional and technological resources into larger laboratory communities. It is apparent, however, if we look at the funding support available to the various branches of forensic science and forensic pathology, that the direct budgets available to the traditional forensic science laboratories far exceed those available to areas such as my own, namely forensic pathology. However, if we look beyond these traditional budgets and barriers, and see that the forensic pathology community invariably operates as part of large university-based clinical laboratories, and if we consider forensic pathology as simply representing a division of the whole field of laboratory medicine, a comparison of the relative financial resources available to the forensic pathologist and nonmedical forensic scientists shows a significantly altered fiscal picture.

For example, in the city of Vancouver in British Columbia there are four principal hospitals associated with the University of British Columbia. The hospital at which I am based, Vancouver General Hospital, used to be the largest hospital in Canada and is one of the largest hospitals in the Commonwealth. Today, as a result of specialization in some areas of clinical medicine and decentralization in others, this hospital, in terms of its overall size, has lost some of its past glory but not its reputation.

Our University Department of Pathology Chairman oversees not only the operation of this huge department but also all of the academic and research activities involving the whole of laboratory medicine in this hospital group. The laboratory budget for Vancouver General Hospital is approximately $15 million CAD but the laboratory budget for the entire group is approximately $40 million. In addition to this direct funding, over $6 million of research grant money is placed on an annual basis at the disposal of the laboratory staff. Since most of the pathologists in the group have university appointments and since these hospitals have a long traditional association with the university, there is a general understanding that up to 25% of the time of all members of the University Department of Pathology may be devoted to academic pursuits. This means that not only is there a $6 million research budget directly funded, but there is an additional "hidden component" of $4 million applied directly to research and development funded through the health care budget.

Working within this large department of pathology with its own specialty laboratories whose location is dictated only by logistical convenience, I can draw upon almost any resource component of this network to support the activities of my forensic pathology service. Comparing this with the problems associated with funding of forensic laboratory services, which are administered and directed by government, who invariably find themselves working in isolation from the rest of the scientific community, one can rapidly see that not only is there a technical resource advantage to a university-based forensic science service, but the financial resource potential is very considerable indeed.

It is misleading, however, to suggest that such apparent disparities in budgets for research and development between medical laboratories and forensic science laboratories occur only in Canada. I would suggest to you that such differences in funding are typical throughout the Western world. Consider, however, the very great shortfall in funding not only for research and development but for routine forensic sciences in the Third World where governments everywhere are attempting to divert what funds they have available to them to health care. It is a political fact of life that health care will always take priority over the forensic sciences for funds. If we can accept this and learn to live with it, the solution to some of our budgetary problems for the human, biological and toxicological aspects of forensic sciences may become more apparent.

At present the forensic science laboratory services can be divided into several distinct groups. Much of forensic biology is human biology; toxicology is really a form of laboratory-based applied pharmacology; forensic serology and immunology, which in many laboratories are now distinct from forensic biology, are unashamedly direct developments from laboratory medicine.

No one would suggest that the nature of the samples submitted to forensic science laboratories is in any way directly comparable to the type of material routinely investigated in a medical laboratory. Nevertheless, the problems in the area of body fluid and body fluid stain examination are relatively constant, namely, sample deterioration with age, sample size, drying, distortion and decomposition. There is no real reason, however, why the particular problems associated with forensic science field work cannot be applied at an early stage during the research and development of a new clinical technique. There is no reason why medical research laboratories could not be developing forensic procedures in parallel with the procedures required for patient care and diagnosis.

The ELISA technique as it develops in forensic immunology offers an opportunity to add an invaluable parameter to the area of body fluid identification. The major disadvantage, however, seems to be the cost of purchasing fully-automated equipment such as dispensers and spectrophotometers. Although some success has been demonstrated with manual techniques, such automated procedures, if available, are going to allow for the more cost-effective use of immunoglobulin allo-typing. Such automated equipment is available in many clinical hospital laboratories.

In the area of forensic toxicology, the pattern of work of the forensic toxicologist is often dictated by the pressures of the judicial system. Most forensic toxicology laboratories are concerned primarily with the detection of crime by the identification of restricted drugs or by the identification of toxic or fatal levels of drugs. Coroners, however, involved in the investigation of death and, in particular, in the investigation of human factors associated with unnatural deaths, may not be directly concerned with the identification either of restricted drugs or toxic levels of drugs. It may become important to identify drugs at therapeutic or below therapeutic levels. Many forensic toxicology laboratories are unwilling, or unwilling to take the time, to analyze for drugs in concentrations that may have no criminal significance.

In my own area in British Columbia, the segregation of forensic toxicology services into criminal and non-criminal is now almost complete. The Royal Canadian Mounted Police (RCMP) Crime Laboratory is concerned almost exclusively with toxicology tests as part of an investigation of criminal activity. The British Columbia Coroners Service, however, requires an extensive and speedy toxicology service. As a result, a separate provincial forensic science laboratory has been established, funded directly by the Coroners' Office, with the resulting duplication in equipment and staffing, and the attendant problems of quality control associated with any division of responsibilities.

The Department of Clinical Toxicology at Vancouver General Hospital is one of the largest and best-equipped toxicology laboratories in the country and yet its responsibility is almost exclusively in the area of clinical toxicology, research and development. Each of the laboratories considers itself expert and of course, the quality of results produced by the laboratories is comparable.

Unfortunately, quality of service is often assessed by the consumer, usually the police and courts, not on the basis of accuracy or reproducibility of results, but on the rapidity with which results are produced. For example, the average turnaround time for toxicological screening in the RCMP Crime Laboratory is 6 weeks. The average turnaround time in the Coroners' toxicology laboratory is 10–14 days. The average turnaround time for toxicological screening in the hospital toxicology laboratory is 6 hours for a preliminary result with a full final follow-up report within 12–24 hours of the sample being received.

The reasons for the significant disparity in turnaround time between these three laboratory services is a reflection, not of the quality of staff or equipment, but of a combination of the pressures and expectations of their role, and therefore directly reflects the overall budgeting. No forensic toxicologist will deny that with adequate financing he would be unable to compete in terms of turnaround time and quality with any clinical laboratory anywhere in the world. However, realistically, this funding is not available and will not be available.

Disparity in funding for research and development is becoming such a critical issue that important techniques are not being developed with the vigor that our courts and criminal investigative systems could reasonably expect. I would like to illustrate this point by giving the particular example of the application of DNA fingerprinting to forensic sciences.

The use of DNA analysis will revolutionize identification procedures in forensic immunology resulting in certainty as to the origin of tissue, provided material from a suspected source is available for comparison purposes. In the past twelve months, a series of papers have appeared in which a simple Southern blot technique has allowed for the positive identification of blood samples using a variety of human DNA probes. Jeffreys and colleagues have calculated that the probability of DNA fragments from any two unrelated individuals being identical when a two enzyme and probe system is used is considerably less than 5×10^{-19}. These techniques have recently withstood the rigors of the British legal system and were upheld as valid in a case of disputed paternity.

Clearly, the next step is to apply these procedures to the identification of body fluid stains. We in Vancouver have outlined a simple DNA dot blot technique to differentiate human males and females, as well as humans from other animals, by the examination of dried bloodstains of varying ages. This work was performed in the Molecular Probe Laboratory in the University Department of Pathology in Vancouver where a wide variety of probes are routinely being used to assist with the identification of genetic abnormalities in children.

In order to develop independently a single DNA laboratory, the forensic science community would be required to invest approximately $250,000 US in equipment and facilities alone. Such a laboratory would require minimum staffing by two technologists specially trained in these procedures, since once an analysis has been initiated, it cannot be stopped halfway to allow for holidays or sick leave. In Vancouver, we have identified the cost of sharing this laboratory with a research and development program for forensic science. We have decided to develop a forensic science DNA fingerprint laboratory in conjunction with our existing hospital molecular probe laboratory and have recently received a research grant of $64,000 from the Attorney General in British Columbia and from the British Columbia Law Foundation to establish such a joint laboratory. Clearly, the satisfactory development of a DNA fingerprint laboratory in forensic science can most effectively and efficiently be done in conjunction with existing medical laboratories on the basis of sharing of facilities, training and existing knowledge.

I believe that the re-integration of laboratory services within forensic science and, in particular, the re-integration of medical laboratory services can be only to the long term advantage of the science of crime investigation. The technical and administrative problems associated with such a reorientation of thinking are not insurmountable. The basic problems are the biases that have developed between the medical and non-medical branches of forensic science.

The traditional view is that forensic science conducted within a medical laboratory setting must be under the control of the forensic pathologist. This is not true. Forensic pathologists, in their efforts to find kudos and status, have insisted on financial and administrative independence from other branches of laboratory medicine and, as a result, they have found themselves isolated and deprived of funding. The forensic pathologist must also integrate himself with his clinical laboratory colleagues. Status is not achieved by independence. Reputation is based on quality of work.

The problems of the reintegration of forensic sciences have to be measured against the super-specialization that is occurring within all branches of forensic science. The current conflict within forensic sciences is that the technical expertise required to give evidence in court is such that it is almost impossible for the expert witness to have an overall comprehension of the relevance of his own particular area of expertise.

Opinion evidence, because of its special status within an adversarial judicial system, must be accepted with caution. The areas of expertise of the witness must be clearly defined. For example, forensic pathologists are expert in the interpretation of injuries, injury mechanisms and causes of death, both natural and unnatural. Bloodstain pattern analysis is an area of expertise in which most pathologists, and many forensic pathologists, have no training and have made no particular study. The opinions that they may express in this area may be on the basis of individual case experience rather than careful objective study. Such opinions are likely to be determined by what the expert may expect to happen, based on his understanding of basic principles, and not upon what he knows to happen, based on knowledge and experience. Any super-specialization must result in a narrowed area of expertise for the witness in court. This means that the scope of the opinion evidence witness has to be very clearly defined and limited to his own area of knowledge.

It is important, therefore, that the opinions expressed in court under the qualification of expert should be confined to the area of proven expertise, and that other opinions should be subjected to limited or very specific qualification. Without such witness control, the special privileges of the expert opinion witness may be abused and the court may be misled by opinions which fall short of the usual judicial standards associated with the qualified expert. It must always be remembered that titles, status or degrees should not allow an opinion witness to stray beyond his area of proven expertise.

Opinion evidence is dependent upon the reliability of observations and the accuracy, validity and relevance of evidence tested. Often the quality of evidence submitted to the expert for analysis is questionable. It is important that the expert should not be held responsible for the quality or integrity of evidence that he or she has not been responsible for collecting and selecting. Opinions are based on evidence available and such a basis should be clearly defined. The expert must be allowed the right to modify and change opinions if further evidence becomes available or if the reliability of certain evidence is subsequently questioned.

Tests performed by any particular expert are subject to certain standards of proof, and even in the most exact areas of forensic science, no conclusions can be considered absolute. Forensic experts, experienced in the requirements and expectations of a particular judicial system, accept that standards of proof are measured in degrees of probability based on personal knowledge, training and experience. Numerical or statistical evaluations of such standards of proof may be either inappropriate or misleading when applied to expert opinions. Within the context of forensic science, qualitative tests performed by experienced scientists may have greater probative relevance than quantitative tests with their apparent, rather than real, reliability.

Reasonable doubt should not be measured in terms of statistical probabilities. Such numerical values may be inappropriate in determining reasonable doubt. If a particular standard of proof is required, it is for the court to advise the expert of this standard and ask him if his opinions and conclusions fall within, these, the court's, standards. The inexperienced expert must be made aware of these standards of proof, otherwise reasonable doubt may be equated with any standards short of absolute proof or conversely may be measured in terms of balance of probabilities. Clearly, this is exactly the sort of problem that may occur when the super-specialist with his relatively limited court experience may be unfamiliar with the requirements of opinion evidence in civil or judicial proceedings and unless the terms of his evidence are clearly defined for him, significant confusion may arise.

I have heard it stated on a number of occasions in court that one can never draw a positive conclusion from a negative result. This statement, which is an apparent scientific truism, in the context of a criminal trial is fundamentally incorrect. It all depends upon the expectations of the results of a test. For example, a negative test for blood may mean either that no blood was present or that the procedure was incorrect. If it can be shown by parallel control tests that the procedure was correct, then a negative result can be reasonably considered to mean that blood was not present within the limits of that particular examination.

All scientific tests have defined limits of sensitivity, accuracy and reproducibility but this does not mean that a particular test is invalid or wrong because of these limitations. Similarly, experiments performed to test a particular hypothesis must be relevant to the theory being tested and any departures from this theory must be compensated for or explained. Any particular part of scientific evidence can be contested. However, it is the competence and experience of the scientist as an expert forensic witness that is the best measure of the real value of the opinion.

Clearly, then, one of the greatest problems confronting forensic science and the presentation of expert evidence in court is the training of the judicial system to understand the limitations and relevance of scientific evidence and the training of the forensic scientist to understand the requirements of the judicial system. If super-specialization within the forensic sciences is a fact of life, and I believe it is, the best, way to overcome the problems and to improve the education and knowledge base of these super-experts is to have large integrated laboratories where individuals are aware of the areas of expertise of their colleagues and have frequent forums where they have an opportunity to hear and discuss the problems encountered by other forensic scientists in areas which they themselves may have no special experience.

Earlier I highlighted the importance of the reintegration of medical and non-medical forensic sciences. However, it may be that all of us, within the field of forensic science and medicine, because of our inherent biases, can no longer be completely objective and are perhaps not the best people to determine our own future. When it comes to a question of introducing a new technology in forensic science, perhaps such projects should be studied by a multi-disciplinary group including representatives of the judicial system, the police, forensic science, universities and the private sector. Decisions should be made with the full awareness of resource implications, department goals and the complex needs that the technologocial advances must serve.

It is perhaps not wrong to relate cost benefit analysis to demands for capital equipment in a system that is not a revenue generator, but is subject to global budgeting. Efficient forensic laboratory services in the next few years must implement technologocial changes by cost effective means. This may involve some reorientation of laboratory services, some decentralization of research and development and a sharing of expertise that cross traditional scientific boundaries.

Acknowledgement

This paper has been abbreviated from the presentation made at the 56th meeting of the Australian and New Zealand Association for the Advancement of Science, Palmerston North, New Zealand, in January 1987.

29(4) - 1989: Echoes of Empire

(Editorial)

The Society rightly prides itself on being an international society with members in 64 countries. Yet there is a very obvious bias in that perhaps, not surprisingly, 87.4% of members live in English-speaking countries and only 12.4% live in Europe and Asia. Of the English-speaking countries our colleagues in the USA make up a substantial 15%. Echoes indeed of an empire which still resound even after 200 years following that famous 'tea-party' in Boston leading to the Declaration of Independence by the USA in 1776.

Nevertheless should we not now prepare ourselves for the great changes that will come about in Europe in 1992? Trade barriers will come down and new employment opportunities will present themselves. In this latter respect, of particular interest to the Society are the directives issued by the Community for the mutual recognition of diplomas, certificates and other evidence of formal qualifications. For workers in a number of health care fields, medical practitioners, nurses, pharmacists and midwives for example, directives have already been issued.

There are a number of steps the Society should consider:

- Asking all members, via a short questionnaire, if they speak a language other than their own. Applications forms of membership should include the same question.
- Having the abstract at the top of the papers published in the Journal in two or three additional languages, e.g., French and German and perhaps Spanish.
- Arranging a meeting on the Continent on a topic of wide interest, e.g., "the role of DNA profiling in the Forensic Sciences", or maybe "Accident investigation in transport by road, rail, sea and air". Brussels would be the obvious place being easily accessible from all parts of Europe including the UK and of course would also be symbolic. Holland too is conveniently located and in The Hague we have the Headquarters of the International Court of Justice – again this would be symbolic for a Society dedicated to the pursuit of Justice through the application of Science and Technology.
- Council should appoint a member to follow any changes in legislation within the EEC and ensure we are kept up to date with new legislation which may affect our Society. We should ensure that we take a significant role in influencing the framing of any legislation which may directly affect us.

The Channel Tunnel may provide a physical link with the Continent but it is also necessary to ensure that we are psychologically prepared as well, otherwise we may indeed find ourselves isolated as "little Englanders".

PH Whitehead

30(2) - 1990: A Matter of Choice

(Editorial)

The twelfth meeting (24–30 October 1990) of that remarkable organisation, the International Association of Forensic Sciences, is approaching fast. The beautiful Australian city of Adelaide, named after the queen consort of William IV, will host the meeting under the distinguished presidency of ex-JFSS Editor, Dr William J Tilstone. Already the preliminary programme lists thirty-six "thematic symposia", and if one adds the plenary lectures, poster sessions and pre-conference workshops, it is evident that the meeting will be every bit as varied and interesting as any of its eleven predecessors.

It is against this kaleidoscopic background that the Council of Past Presidents (elected for life) meets and decides upon a new president for the succeeding three years. This august council, of undisputed eminence, will have the difficult task of choosing amongst a variety of possibilities.

Already there are two formal proposals before, Council (for Linkoping in Sweden and Düsseldorf in Germany), each with its individually proffered attractions. In addition, it is known that an offer (perhaps two) will most likely come from California and there are also moves afoot to attract the meeting to the Basque country of northern Spain. But that is not all. Planning meetings have already been held in Lyons with a view to drawing the 1993 conference to that centre of French forensic excellence. Home of Locard, headquarters of Interpol, location of the inter-regional forensic science laboratory and the university department of forensic medicine, Lyons also boasts the French National Police College.

All the above alternatives add up to a surfeit of choice for Council which takes no account of the possibility of even further offers. But at least one thing is clear. The Council of Past Presidents must now take into account the opinions of forensic scientists world-wide if it is justifiably to retain the description of "international". A discussion of how this is to be done might be the most interesting item on offer at Adelaide.

30(4) - 1990: They Threatened its Life with a Railway Share

Every three years the international forensic science community stirs. The stimulus is the triennial international meeting run by the International Association of Forensic Sciences. From a participant's perspective, it's great fun, a chance to meet old, and make new, friends in toxicology, in serology, in pathology, in questioned documents. For each of us, the area boundaries tend to be quite discrete, and all those other strange people are just adding to the general 'buzz' of the gathering.

From the organizer's perspective, it's a bit different. We speak of the 'forensic sciences' in the plural, but what are they – where, objectively, are their individual boundaries? The last three meetings have each had some twenty subject areas, often making multiple sessions mandatory. The result can be clashes of interest, rooms with an audience but no speaker, and a generally inflexible time-table. Some participants like this, regarding it as our version of the Olympics as they dash hither and thither. Others find it frustrating.

Whatever the perspective, it is a clear illustration of the variety and complexity of the forensic sciences. Our customers are varied and complex too. Take the simplest example of a laboratory located in a police department and staffed by serving police officers. There should be no problems of identity – they are part of the police department to serve its needs. If all they do is to provide assistance to investigators, that may be true. But it isn't. They also provide evidence at trial. That evidence will be tested by the defence. That testing may include examination by some of the best people in the world in the specialist area dealt with in the report. The testing will be quite partisan, but will be made against a backdrop of community expectation that science is absolute. Ultimately, the evidence will be judged by yet another party – the court.

The police officer may be a member of a forensic science association which has a code of ethic – another customer. If we move from the police laboratory, for example to pathology, the expert will be a registered medical practitioner. This introduces still another set of customer requirements for the forensic scientist to meet. The pathologist may be investigating a matter on the instructions of a coroner. That matter may end up as a murder trial. The requirements of the final court are quite different from those at the start.

If we are to do our job properly, we have to know what it is and to whom it is being addressed. The idea of identifying our customers and their needs conflicts with much tradition in the forensic sciences. In the past we have concentrated on ourselves – the personalities, the technology. This concentration on product is not the best environment for development. A narrow preoccupation with so-called concrete matters usually results in a declining industry – just look at the fate of the railroads in the last 75 years.

I hope that we succeed in attracting more of our customers to our meetings. Today's issues are their issues – the laboratory accreditation, discovery of evidence, speeding up the time to process cases in the laboratory. Who knows what tomorrow's issues will be? One thing is sure, they will still be our customers' issues, and we had better develop the ability to listen or we'll go the way of the railroads.

WJ Tilstone
President, IAFS 1990

Title reference
(Lewis Carroll: *Hunting of the Snark, the Beaver's Lesson*)

38(3) - 1998: International Forensic Science

(Editorial)

Forensic science is international – there is no doubt about that.

There are many good reasons to back up this statement. Let me offer two. Firstly, all of us involved in science per se see ourselves as part of an international community. How else would we share the research, the training and education, new ways of doing things, good practice? Good ideas and innovation are not the prerogative of any one country or organisation. As in all walks of life, discussion and debate generally improve the quality of the outcome – the whole is greater than the sum of the parts.

Taking that as a given, should we not ask ourselves whether we are doing things as well as we could? Do we, for example, need more structure or less, and are there barriers or thresholds that need to be broken down before progress can be made? In these days of budget constraints, managers in my position need to make sure that the activities we specifically support are worthwhile, whilst still subscribing to the general belief that 'international forensic science' is beneficial.

This brings me to my second reason. Forensic science is more than just a science. It is, amongst other things, the application of science to support the criminal justice process. If this process, or part of this process, is international, then forensic science itself has to be conducted on that basis. Increasingly this is so, particularly in the areas of terrorism, drugs and what is known in the UK as 'organised crime', and more recently in the investigation of paedophile rings and of course DNA analysis itself. In all these areas we need the ability to exchange information on a common basis. But do we have that common basis and are we doing enough? If not, what more should we be doing and how should we be doing it?

Journal editorials over the past two years indicate a great interest in these issues. However, discussion in any forum quickly shows that there is a wide range of views on what is important not least because of different justice systems, different relationships with investigating authorities and different budgets and national structures. Arguably the last is often the most important in influencing attitudes.

Most would agree on the core issues – the need to share research; pursuit of a common approach towards quality through accreditation of our systems and procedures to international standards; sharing of best practice in laboratory design and use of equipment; and, perhaps most importantly, effective training and assessment of our scientists to ensure their competence – with all these in place we will have a solid foundation and common basis for developing databases and exchanging information.

At a parochial level (personal and organisational) I would add the importance of coming together on how to take a holistic view of the whole forensic process in order to maximise the contribution of forensic science to fair and impartial justice. By that, I mean from scenes of crime to giving evidence in court – how and what evidence is collected; how this is used to support investigation; and how cases are assessed, analysed and interpreted to provide information to the court.

Over recent years I have become much more involved in these issues because getting the international context right seems to me crucial to the future of forensic science.

Modern communications are shrinking the world. Differences in standards and good practice become more obvious and can lead to challenging questions in court. Loss of credibility in one country affects us all. Technology is changing rapidly and the opportunities arising from the prospect of miniaturisation including the routine presentation of results in real time needs to be thought about now. Such new methodologies will be our tools to provide added value. However, ultimately the value of forensic science lies in the people who practice it. It is their professionalism and commitment that needs to be nourished and developed now to support the changes ahead.

These are all issues that are best tackled collectively. I am not one of those who believe in mandatory standards of uniformity. But I do believe there is space for a collective view on how forensic science can contribute in terms of outcomes and benefits throughout the whole forensic process. How that is achieved will inevitably depend on national differences, although who would argue against the need for quality in terms of accuracy and reliability and a sound assessment of the strength of the evidence as the benchmark to be adopted by all?

I come back to my earlier questions in terms of whether we have got the international framework right. My short answer is that there is more to do, but it is undoubtedly heading in the right direction. Many of us in Europe are committed to ENFSI – the European Network of Forensic Science Institutes which formally came into being in 1995, through membership of Directors of Forensic Science Institutes. Its aim is to promote co-operation between its members and their laboratories. Much progress has been made especially after the agreements of the first strategic plan for the organisation. ENFSI has established framework documents to guide the work of the organisation – notably through its annual meeting, the work of its Board, and the work of its Working Groups and Committees. These have strengthened and consolidated ENFSI as an organisation. It has begun to position itself as a source of advice to international organisations – it has been adopted by the European Union Police Co-operation Working Group as its advisory body on forensic science issues. The European Commission is sponsoring the work of the DNA Working Group in support of the Sexual Trafficking of Persons programme (STOP). This is specifically aimed at the exchange of DNA data across country boundaries in the fight against serious and series crime.

At our April 1998 meeting in Lisbon we extended our membership to 36 members covering most of the major public sector laboratories in both Western and Eastern Europe. The success of the ENFSI European Academy meeting in Lausanne 1997 was widely acclaimed and it was decided that this should be a regular event. In 2000 it will be held in Cracow. The importance of the work of the specialised working groups which come under ENFSI is now fully recognised in the work of ENFSI. We decided to hold a meeting in Autumn 1998 between ENFSI members and Working Group Chairmen to take forward the whole question of sharing developments and good practice guidelines. More generally, discussion and debate helped us to understand each other's cultures better, an important feature of any international meeting.

Contacts are now being established with other similar organisations around the world. ENFSI is forging a relationship with the American Society of Crime Laboratory Directors (ASCLD) and Senior Managers of Australian and New Zealand Forensic Laboratories (SMANZFL). Joint aims and a strategy have been agreed. There are, of course, many other international meetings which develop the international context including the International Association of Forensic Sciences next meeting in Los Angeles in 1999 and Interpol in Lyons 1998, both of which are held triennially.

I hope you, like me, will be thinking about the issues I have raised, especially if you attend any of these meetings. Are we clear about the purpose, aims and benefits? Are we doing enough or too much? Are we doing it in the best way? I will not be coming up with prescriptive answers but I would like to contribute to the discussion and debate. I will be supporting the development of international forensic science and will be keen to see that it is patently to the benefit of fair and impartial justice.

Janet Thompson

Science & Justice 1998; **38**(3): 141–142

40(4) - 2000: Courts, Politicians and Constitutions

(Editorial)

More than a few members of the Society have contributed to the investigation of war crimes in former Yugoslavia. A few have had experience in either giving or leading evidence in the trials that followed those investigations. As a learning experience, it must be unparalleled. One of the lessons that has come out of the Balkan inferno is that a Court staffed by Judges and Advocates with backgrounds from many different jurisdictions can be made to work. The Civil and Common law traditions, inter alia, can come together to produce a court that works in specific circumstances with a limited remit to produce a just result, although there is certainly no any sort of equality of arms between the resources available to the prosecution and defence.

After Nuremberg, Yugoslavia and Ruanda, the wheels are now in motion to set up an International Criminal Court. On 17 June 1998 a United Nations Conference in Rome approved a treaty, the 'Rome Statute', which, when implemented, will establish an International Criminal Court (ICC). 120 countries voted for the treaty,

21 abstained and seven, including the United States, voted against it. The ICC will be constituted, under the aegis of the United Nations, when a total of 60 countries have ratified the treaty. So far, only 10 countries have ratified the treaty but 96 have signed it and are processing the ratification, at varying speeds, through their own legislatures. The ICC will have the power to try individuals for war crimes, crimes against humanity and genocide, as defined in the Rome Statute and in the documents being drawn up by the UN to implement it.

There is considerable opposition to the ICC, in its presently proposed form, in the United States. Their concerns, as set out in a bill submitted to the US Senate by Senator Jesse Helms, the Chair of the Senate Foreign Relations Committee, are that the ICC will have the power to prosecute and to, in the event of a finding of guilt, order the punishment of US military personnel, government officials and even politicians, even though the US is not a signatory to the treaty. In addition, the drafters of the bill express concern that the procedures of the ICC offer less protection to the accused than US citizens are entitled to under the Bill of Rights. The Bill of Rights includes the right to a trial by jury, the right not to be forced to provide self incriminatory evidence and the right to confront and cross examine all witnesses for the prosecution. Not only would the bill prohibit US and state governments from co-operating with the ICC, but it authorises the US President to use 'all means necessary and appropriate', bribery being specifically excluded, to the secure the release of US military personnel and government officials detained against their will by the ICC. Indeed, the bill goes further; the government of any NATO country or other major allies of the US could request US help to get their military personnel or citizens released from the custody of the ICC. The potential for international friction, let alone the material it provides for Hollywood blockbusting scripts and the next Jack Ryan novel, are obvious.

Of course, this bill may never become law. It is currently grinding its way through the US legislative process, having been referred to the House of Representatives Foreign relations committee on 14th June 2000. It does seem to have some powerful support, particularly from some of the black letter constitutionalists in the Republican Party. If, or when, it does become law, should we worry?

The short answer is yes, of course we should. Quite apart from the political overtones, the prospect of the most powerful nation in the would not only standing aloof, but being, by law, positively antipathetic to any involvement in the ICC does not bode well for its future. We only have to remember the fate of the League of Nations. Without US participation the ICC will be a rather bereft organisation. It may be that the way forward lies not the establishment of a permanently constituted International Criminal Court, but rather to continue to set up ad hoc Criminal Courts to deal with Ruandas and Yugoslavias as they arise. This might be a workable solution that would be acceptable to the US, at least until the next 'Wag the Dog' scenario goes wrong.

Has the US got a point? Arguably, they have. Whilst it would be difficult for an international criminal court to operate effectively in every case if it had no jurisdiction in countries that were not signatories, it could operate reasonably well if it were to be granted jurisdiction by UN resolution on a conflict by conflict basis. Veto in the Security Council could then protect the legitimate interests of particular countries. However, that is not what the signatories of the Rome Treaty agreed to. Essentially, they agreed to an abrogation of a small part of their national sovereignty to the ICC. More to the point, from the point of view of court going forensic scientists, are the concerns raised about the processes of the ICC legitimate ones? In England we have seen a number of changes in the criminal justice system which would be unconstitutional in the US, including the loss of the right to question witnesses in person in certain cases, the ability of a court to draw an adverse inference from silence and the proposed alteration to the right to a jury trial in some cases. These changes do not, so far, seem to be associated with increases in the numbers of inappropriate convictions. The drift towards a more inquisitorial criminal justice system, as perceived by some commentators on the English legal system, would be totally contrary to the adversarial traditions of US trial lawyers, and would be fought tooth and nail to and through the Supreme Court if it happened in the US. Even if the US did ratify the Rome Treaty, vigorous political and legal opposition to any attempt by the Federal Government to hand over any US citizen to the jurisdiction of the ICC could be expected.

So, where does that leave us? When the dust of a US election year has settled, things might be a little clearer, but will any members of the Society be giving evidence in a permanently established International Criminal Court in the next few years? I hope so, but I'm not holding my breath.

Robert Forrest

46(3) - 2006: It's a Big World Out There

(Editorial)

Dr N Nic Daéid

In recent years there seems to be an ever increasing number of conferences, seminars and working group meetings all bidding for our attendance. Not only do we need to decide which of these events are of value to us both personally and professionally, but we need to be persuasive of our managers/funders to let us attend. This can in itself be a challenge as we try to justify the costs and juggle what is probably our most valuable commodity, time, while still attempting to actually have a life outside of work. One of the questions we face is does the end result (knowledge, information, contacts etc) merit our time, energy, and the cost involved in the participation?

Over the last decade and a half there have been some significant developments in forensic science at a European level with the establishment of the European Network of Forensic Science Institutes (ENFSI) and the 16 ENFSI working groups as well as the European Academy of Forensic Science. I expect that all of us who have participated in the working groups and meetings have seen the benefits and challenges of a greater European dimension to our work and the development of forensic science across the continent. Many of the UK forensic science providers are represented on the various ENFSI working groups and some UK forensic scientists are also invited to attend or participate in some of the SWG (scientific working groups) or TWG (technical working groups) in the USA, also striving (broadly speaking) for the same objectives as the ENFSI groups and in some cases there are formal links between the two. Our antipodean colleagues also have similar organisations such as the Senior Managers Australian and New Zealand Forensic Laboratories (SMANZFL) which again has a number of similar scientific advisory groups carrying out development in various areas. Then there are more specialised organisations aiming at particular disciplines within forensic science such as TIAFT (for toxicologists), the IAAI (for fire investigators) and the fingerprint society to name but a few, all of which have a valuable contribution to play. The tri-annual Interpol Forensic Science Symposium for laboratory directors presents three year literature reviews covering various evidence types. If you don't know about this look at their website where the reviews are available as downloadable documents.

There is a huge amount of information out there, available to all through the various websites, but it's also good to be able to meet people face to face. There are annual international meetings which provide either a multidisciplinary focus such as the American Academy of Forensic Science Meeting (next meeting in Texas in February 2007) or more discipline focused such as the TIAFT and SOFT meetings. More locally in the UK, the Forensic Science Society meetings provide both single issue one day conferences and broader topic based weekend conferences. Every three years is the European Academy of Forensic Science (next meeting to be held in Glasgow in 2009) and the International Association of Forensic Science meeting (next meeting to be held in New Orleans in 2008). Add to these the myriad of other organisations offering specialist group meetings and the various Universities now jumping on the forensic band wagon to offer conferences for weary practitioners and your head can start to spin! It is not difficult to see a situation where one could easily attend a conference a month, if not more frequently than that.

There are many changes going on at National and International level within Forensic Science. It's so easy to get caught up in the "day-to-day" and perhaps become a little parochial in our attitude and thinking and it's good to take a step away from the bench, court or crime scene to look at the broader view. We can gain a lot from communication with our colleagues at home and overseas and the dissemination of this information through seminars and verifiable media is very important to the modem forensic scientist and criminal justice professional. Networks and conferences are extremely useful and for the most part progressive in moving the various disciplines on but also, I would suggest, present some challenges in the management of the vast amounts of information and collective knowledge that they produce. As a consequence we face some challenging questions. Do we as a community actually have any efficient mechanisms to manage and disseminate this knowledge? Is there any mechanism whereby we can efficiently avoid duplication and reinvention of the wheel? Is this the role of scientific journals, other publications or websites? Is there anything more efficient we could use? What are the resource implications and drawbacks?

These days I try to keep up with research and development through the scientific literature where I can at least be assured the material has some credibility. Websites are useful but many can lack peer review (though there are those that argue that this is an old fashioned system of academic elitism) which may lessen the value of their content. If I go to a conference it's generally only if I think the content is going to be sufficiently interesting or the speakers sufficiently well known through practice or research that I'm fairly confident I'll learn something new. Otherwise my time is too precious to waste. The question of how to keep up to date and manage our way through the increasing amounts of information and knowledge in a way that is progressive, achievable and above all useful to our professional practice is clearly a tricky one. Answers on a postcard please.

Some Useful Websites: (all accessed Sept 2006)

http://www.nifs.com.au/SMANZFL/SMANZFL.html?index.asp&1
http://www.enfsi.org/
http://www.tiaft.org/
http://www.interpol.int/Public/forensic/lFSS/Default.asp

Index

Note: Names in italics refer to authors

accreditation 34, 43, 45–6, 55, 56, 58
Adams, Denis case 156
admissibility of evidence *see* standards of evidence
advertising of services 10
Aitken, C.G.G. 126–7, 151–2
alcohol breath tests 85–6, 106
alcohol concentration *see* body alcohol concentration
Allen, M.J. 65–7
arbitration 192, 221
Association of Forensic Physicians (AFP) 73–4
associative evidence 145–6, 148–50
    see also evaluation and interpretation of evidence
Auld report 113, 240–1
Australia
    Chamberlain case 22–4
    Edward Charles Splatt case 22–4
Australian Academy of Forensic Sciences 277
autopsies *see* post mortem examinations

Barrowcliff, D.F. 254–6
Bastanipour case 226
Bayesian approaches 126, 151–2, 156–7
bitemarks 203–7
Blakey, D.C. 48–52
blood alcohol concentration 86, 106, 239
blood grouping 88
    admissibility 98–9
    population frequencies 96–7
blood sampling, consent 208, 243–4
bloodstaining 82, 285
body alcohol concentration
    alcohol breath tests 106
    back calculation 111
    and driving 83–7, 207–8, 243–4
breath alcohol 85–7, 105
British Academy of Forensic Sciences 6, 9, 168, 209
Brodrick Report 256–8, 262, 264
Brown, Albert Greenwood case 22, 98–9
Brownlie, Alistair R. 4–7, 9–10, 85–7, 155–7, 177–8, 201, 203–13, 230–34, 277

Caddy, Brian 32–4, 64–5
Caddy Report 38, 72
Canada
    forensic science services 282–7
    professional certification 25
    training 183
case assessment and interpretation (CAI) *see* evaluation and interpretation of evidence
Cassella, John P. 184–7
Chamberlain case 22–4
CIBA Foundation 175, 176
circumstantial information 41–2
Civil Procedure rules 238, 240–1
Clark, Sally case 158, 162, 248
Clift, Dr Alan 231
clinical pathology 254–6
clothing analysis 48–52
    see also bloodstaining
commercial courts 192–200
committal proceedings 221–2
Committee on Death Certification and Coroners *see* Brodrick Report
communication
    inter-professional 75, 208–13
    skills 75
    unrestricted 107
    see also publishing
competence criteria 222–4, 248–9
computer control 89–90
confidentiality 241–3, 265
consent 207, 243–4
context-free examination 160–1
continual professional development (CPD) 74–6
Cooke, Stephen case 156
coroners' procedures 244–6, 256–8
Council for the Registration of Forensic Practitioners (CRFP) 71–3, 238
court design 200
court privileges 67–8
court procedure
    commercial cases 192–200

Fifty Years of Forensic Science: A commentary   Edited by Niamh Nic Daéid
© 2010, John Wiley & Sons, Ltd.

court procedure (*continued*)
   criminal cases 192–200
   cross examination 192–200, 229
   preliminary hearings 221–2
   question-posting 217–8
   security procedures 68
   taking the oath 218–20
courtroom technique *see* presentation of evidence
crime scene investigation 56–8, 147, 148
criminal courts 192–200
criminal investigation 16, 220–1
criminal procedure 235, 240–1
cross examination 192–200, 229

Daéid, N. Nic 74–6, 116–19, 161–3, 180–2, 248–9, 294–5
data processing 89–90
Daubert criteria 161
Davis, Roger J. 43
death certification 245, 256–8
Deen case 156
De Forest, Peter R. 56–8
defence expert 192–200, 202, 214, 240
definition of forensic scientist 7–9
dental evidence 203–7
Diploma in Document Examination 38
DNA database 113–16
DNA profiling 100–2, 116–17
   automation 47
   boundaries of evidence 239–40
   international perspectives 60
   presentation of evidence 161–2
   retention of samples 113–14
   statistical evaluation of evidence 156
   techniques 285
Docherty case 156
document examination 38
Doyle, Sean 119–20
drug facilitated sexual assault 160
Drug Recognition Expert (DRE) 106
drugs and driving 105–7

education of forensic scientists *see* training
ethical considerations 19
   alcohol technical defense 111–13
   post mortem material 108–9, 246–7
European Academy of Forensic Science 117, 294
European Network of Forensic Science Institutes (ENFSI) 187, 289–91, 294
evaluation and interpretation of evidence
   associative evidence 148–50
   circumstantial evidence 147
   context-free 160–1
   cooperative approaches 75, 202–3, 213, 216
   DNA profiling 157
   standards of evidence 18–20, 22–3, 24, 97–8, 115, 161–2, 286
   Sudden Infant Death Syndrome (SIDS) 158
   unconscious bias 41
   see also presentation of evidence; statistical evaluation of evidence
'evidence in chief' 192–200
evidence value *see* standards of evidence
Evison, Martin 183
expert witness 18–20, 24, 34
   alcohol technical defense 111–13
   boundaries of evidence 239–40, 287
   certification 248–9
   code of practice 237–9
   commercial cases 192–200
   competence 222–4, 248–9
   confidentiality 241–3
   criminal cases 192–200, 239–40
   defence expert 192–200, 202, 214, 240
   objectivity 154
   see also presentation of evidence

Fairbairn, Nicholas 221–2
Ferris, J.A.J. 214–15, 262–3, 282–7
fingerprint analysis 168
FIRMS (Forensic Isotope Ratio Mass Spectrometry) Network 119–20
Fish, Frank 178–80
footwear marks 105
Forensic Institute Research Network (FIRN) 185
forensic medicine 251–4
forensic odontology 203–7
forensic pathology *see* pathology services
forensic science
   historical perspectives 118–19
   is it 'science' 22–4
   predicting future developments 53–4
Forensic Science Advisory Council (FSAC) 182
forensic science profession
   accountability 61
   accreditation 34, 43, 45–6, 55
   certification 25, 248–9
   communication skills 75
   competence assessment 59–63, 66
   court privileges 68–9

criminal investigation role 220–21
definition of forensic scientist 7
historical perspectives 1–3, 16–17, 32–4
independence 45
mechanical skills 93
objectivity 154
professionalism 9
public image 4, 33, 230–4
qualifications 8, 25, 38–9, 61,
    65–7, 198
registration 61, 71–3
scope of profession 13–14
specialisation 2, 4, 15,
    286
status 22–4
training *see* training
see also expert witness
Forensic Science Regulator 77–9
forensic science services
    accreditation 43, 56, 58
    advertising of services 10
    for civil cases 265
    competence criteria 222–4
    at the crime scene 56–8
    funding 39
    international perspectives 282–7
    in the market place 53, 69–70
    pathology *see* pathology services
    philosophy and obligations 228–9
    private 30, 55–6, 69–70, 202
    quality assurance *see* quality assurance
    regulation 70, 77–9
    relationship with the police 19
    Scotland 7
    value for money 48–52
Forensic Science Society 6, 8
    accreditation of courses 182, 184
    activities 277–9
    international perspectives 287–8
    occupational coverage 14
    professional conduct and standards 10
    professional qualifications 38–9
    scope of activities 32–4
FORREST (FORensic RESearch and Teaching) 185,
    186
Forrest, A.R.W. (Robert) 67–8, 70–1, 105–13,
    158–61, 239–47, 269–72, 291–3
Fraser, Jim 69–70, 117–18,
    187–9
Frye standard 22, 98

Garner, W. 192–200
Gaudette, B.D. 148–50, 151–2
Gee, D.J. 260–2
Gordon, Michael case 156
Grant, Julius 7–9
Green, M.A. 267–9

hair analysis 83, 95, 172
Harris, Tennyson 16–21, 217–20
Hay, Gordon case 203–7
Health and Safety at Work Act 17
Hensel, Elliott B. 5, 92–3
historical perspectives 1–3, 16–17, 32–4,
    118–9
Home Office Forensic Science Service
    (HOFSS) 26–32
    agency status 48–52
    funding 39–40
    and Met Lab 52
hospital pathologists 254–6, 283
Human Tissue Bill 246–7
human tissue retention 108–9

information transfer 177
    keeping up to date 109–11
    research findings 117–18
    see also communication; publishing
inquisitorial system 234–7
Institute of Forensic Science 9
instrumentation 89–90
International Association of Forensic Sciences
    (IAFS) 104, 278–9, 281–2, 289
International Criminal Court (ICC) 291–3
international perspectives 273–94
    Australia 22–4
    Canadian education of forensic scientists 183
    death overseas 267–8
    developing countries 60
    DNA profiles 60
    information exchange 177
    inquisitorial system of justice 234–7
isotope ratio mass spectrometry (IRMS) 119–20

Jamieson, Allan 58–63
Journal of Forensic Science 70–1
juries 199–200

Keiser-Nielsen, Dr Soren 204–7
Kelly–Frye case 38
    see also Frye standard

Kershaw, Alan 71–3
Kind, S.S. (Stuart) 26–32, 53–4, 63–4, 83, 104
knowledge exchange *see* information transfer

laboratory services *see* forensic science services
law and order 204
legal profession
    appreciation of forensic science 208–13
    communication with 178–9
    public image 230–4
legislation
    Health and Safety at Work Act 17
    Human Tissue Bill 246–7
    legal reforms 6
    Police and Criminal Evidence Bill 19
    Police Reform Act 2002 243
    professional involvement in 16–17
    likelihood ratio approaches 120

Maguire Seven 232
Manning case 225–6
Margot, Pierre 234–7
McKie case 248
Meadow, Professor Roy 158–9
Metropolitan Police Forensic Science Laboratory (Met Lab) 52
mortuaries 251–3
Muir, A.A. 10–13
Multi Enzyme System 98

Nagle, R. 264–7
New Zealand 91
Norfolk, Guy A. 73–4

oath, taking the 218–20
objectivity 154

paternity, proof of 88, 203
pathologists
    specialisation 254–6,
    training 269
    working conditions 251–3, 258–9
pathology services 253–4, 262–3
    'best value' 269–70
    international perspectives 282–7
    overseas 267–8
    reorganisation 256–8
    universities 179
Patterson, David 4, 277–9

Peacock, Linda case 205
performance monitoring 26–32
    see also quality assurance
Pilling, H.H. 258–9
pleadings 192–200
police
    management practices 35–7
    priorities 48–52
    relationship with forensic science services 48–52
    reoganisation 10–11
    training 7
Police and Criminal Evidence Bill 19
Police Reform Act 2002, 243
post mortem examinations 244–6, 254–6, 260–2
post mortem material 108–9, 246–7
Preece, John case 226, 232
preliminary hearings 221–2
presentation of evidence 78
    commercial cases 192–200
    criminal cases 192–200
    methods 215–7
    standards of proof 286
    statistical evaluation 125–6, 155–7
    see also evaluation and interpretation of evidence
private forensic science services 30, 55–6, 69–70, 202
professional conduct 10
professional ethics 19
professional organization 5–6, 9–10, 68, 77
professional qualifications 7–8, 25, 38–9, 61, 66–7, 198
property offences 84–5
prosecution experts 198
public image 4, 33, 230–4
publishing 94, 97, 177
    journal 109–11
    of legal aspects 209, 255
    of research 99, 187–9
    without restriction 107

qualifications 8, 25, 38–9, 61, 65–7, 198
quality assurance 26–32, 43, 55
    advisory body 291
    competence criteria 222–4
    total quality management (TQM) 58

Ramsay Report 51
Rankin, Brian W.J. 76–7
Rayner Report 49
regulation 70, 77–9

see also accreditation; standards
Rennison, Andrew 77–9
research 117–18
   forensic medicine 253–4
   laboratories 87
   laboratory experiments 91
   priorities 150
   publishing 99, 100, 187–8
   survey of activities 169–75
   targetting 102–3
   universities 87, 187–9
road accidents 84
Rodger, W.J. 16–21
Rouse case 199
Royal College of Physicians 73
rules of evidence *see* standards of evidence
Rushton case 208

Sale of Goods Act cases 192–200
saliva analysis 93
Science and Justice 70, 109–11
Scotland
   forensic medicine 264–7
   forensic science services 6–7
   presentation of evidence 18
   trial reporting 242
secretions grouping 93
'security' paints 85
Sedley, Stephen 113–16
Selinger, B. 25
semen analysis 93
serology methods 98
   admissibility 98–9
Shipman, Dr Harold 180, 246
Simpson, O.J. trial 54
Skills for Justice 182, 184
Skillsmark 184
specialisation 2, 4, 15, 286
Splatt, Edward Charles case 22
standard operational procedures (SOPs) 56
standards 77–9
standards of evidence 18–20, 22–4, 97–8, 115, 161–2
   see also presentation of evidence
statistical evaluation of evidence 125–6
   associative evidence 148–50
   Bayesian approaches 151–2

population frequencies 96–7
standards of proof 286
Sudden Infant Death Syndrome (SIDS) 158

Taylor, Damilola case 72
textile experts 198
Thompson, Janet 289–91
Thorpe, J.W. 96–7, 102
Tilstone, W.J. 22–4, 41–2, 289
Totty. R.N. 25–6
training 175–6
   courses 8, 74, 179–80
   forensic medicine 73
   mechanical skills 93
transferred materials 85, 145–6
   see also associative evidence
trial reporting 241–3

United Kingdom Forensic Science Education Group (UKFSEG) 182, 184–7
United States
   coroners 267–9
   drug impaired drivers 106
   expert witness 225–6
   Kelly–Frye case 38
   professional certification 25
   qualification of forensic scientists 8
universities
   courses 74, 179–80
   forensic medicine 251–4
   pathology services 180
   research 87 187–9
   services to the police 260–2
Usher, Alan 256–8

Wall, Ian F. 73–4
Welsh case 157
Weston, Norman T. 237–9
Whitehead, P.H. 39–40, 287–8
Williams, Paul 111–13
Williams, R.L. 38–9
Willott, G.M. 102
Wonder, Anita K.Y. 229–30

Yallop, H.J. 13–14
Yerson, Arthur M. 215–17
Young case 98